BESTSELLING

MW01089891

Standard LESSON COMMENTARY

KJV SEPTEMBER–AUGUST 2024–2025
KING JAMES VERSION

Editorial Team

Jason Hitchcock
Jane Ann Kenney
Ronald L. Nickelson
Taylor Z. Stamps

Volume 72

Standard®
PUBLISHING
part of the David C Cook family

In This Volume

Index of Printed Texts

The printed texts for 2024–2025 are arranged here in the order in which they appear in the Bible.

Don't forget the visuals!

The thumbnail visuals in the lessons are small reproductions of 18" x 24" full-color posters that are included in the *Adult Resources* packet for each quarter. Order numbers 978-0-784739-13-6 (Fall 2024), 978-0-784739-63-1 (Winter 2024–2025), 978-0-784740-13-2 (Spring 2025), and 978-0-784740-63-7 (Summer 2025) from either your supplier, by calling 1.800.323.7543, or at www.standardlesson.com.

Cumulative Index

A cumulative index for Scripture passages used in the STANDARD LESSON COMMENTARY *for September 2022–August 2026 is provided below.*

✝

Notes

_____
_____
_____
_____
_____
_____
_____
_____
_____
_____
_____
_____
_____
_____
_____
_____
_____
_____
_____
_____
_____
_____
_____
_____
_____
_____
_____

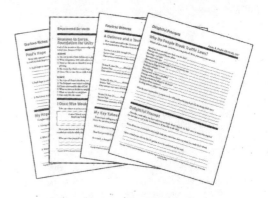

Get the Most from Every Lesson!

Worship in the
Covenant Community

Special Features

Lessons
Unit 1: Leaders Set Worship Example

Unit 2: Songs of the Old Testament

Unit 3: Psalms of Thanksgiving and Praise

Quarterly Quiz

Use these questions as a pretest or as a review. The answers are on page iv of This Quarter in the Word.

Lesson 1

1. Abram chose to live in the land of Canaan. T/F. *Genesis 13:12*
2. God promised to make Abram's descendants as numerous as _____. *Genesis 13:16*

Lesson 2

1. God had kept His promise with whom? (Abraham, Jacob, David) *1 Kings 8:24*
2. One consequence of the people's sin was that they would be taken captive by enemies. T/F. *1 Kings 8:46*

Lesson 3

1. Hezekiah asked the Lord to hear the words of _____. *2 Kings 19:16*
2. God promised that a remnant would come out of Jerusalem. T/F. *2 Kings 19:31*

Lesson 4

1. Josiah instructed the Levites to carry the ark on their shoulders. T/F. *2 Chronicles 35:3*
2. How many days was the observance of the feast of unleavened bread? (three, five, seven) *2 Chronicles 35:17*

Lesson 5

1. The Lord is "my strength and _____." *Exodus 15:2*
2. Who was Aaron's prophetess sister? (Miriam, Joanna, Hannah) *Exodus 15:20*

Lesson 6

1. David asked God, "create in me a _____ heart." *Psalm 51:10*
2. David asked God to restore the "joy" of what? (repentance, forgiveness, salvation) *Psalm 51:12*

Lesson 7

1. "My God, my God, why hast thou _____ me?" *Psalm 22:1*

2. David compared himself to what animal? (worm, ant, grasshopper) *Psalm 22:6*

Lesson 8

1. The psalmist proclaimed that ultimately the weakest people would "glorify" the Lord. T/F. *Isaiah 25:3*
2. The Lord will "swallow up death" and wipe away people's tears. T/F. *Isaiah 25:8*

Lesson 9

1. The psalmist proclaimed that God is what? (choose two: redemption, salvation, anchor, rock) *Psalm 62:2*
2. The psalmist states that people would pour out their hearts to God. T/F. *Psalm 62:8*

Lesson 10

1. The Lord's rod and staff will _____ David. *Psalm 23:4*
2. What two things will follow David "all the days of [his] life"? (choose two: grace, mercy, goodness, love) *Psalm 23:6*

Lesson 11

1. The Lord loves the _____. *Psalm 146:8*
2. The psalmist directs people to "praise God in his _____." *Psalm 150:1*

Lesson 12

1. The people of God are called "the sheep of his pasture." T/F. *Psalm 100:3*
2. The psalmist directs people to enter the courts of the Lord with thanksgiving. T/F. *Psalm 100:4*

Lesson 13

1. The Lord had searched and known the psalmist. T/F. *Psalm 139:1*
2. The psalmist asked, "Whither shall I go from thy _____?" *Psalm 139:7*

Quarter at a Glance

by Collin Schlotfeldt

"And ye shall be my people, and I will be your God" (Jeremiah 30:22). God's covenant—His enduring promise of relationship and presence—is central to the worship of His people. Worship is the act of ascribing worth to and celebrating the glory of something or someone. The truth is, *all people worship*. For the people of God, the question is, *who* will receive our worship? Is the triune God—Father, Son, and Holy Spirit—the only one we will choose to direct our worship toward?

Scripture reveals a pattern to the worship of God's people: God reveals himself, and His people respond through their worship. In the stories of Scripture, we read how they responded: they sang songs, raised their hands, played instruments, danced to music, and did good works of service.

The lessons of this quarter examine the worship that God's people have offered. Although the ways His people worship may have changed throughout history, the reason for their worship remains the same: a faithful response to God.

Worship as Response

This quarter's first unit gives examples from the Old Testament of God's people responding to God's revelation through worship. Abram (Abraham) built altars to mark an occasion when the Lord called him to greater faithfulness (Genesis 13:8-18, lesson 1). Solomon offered worship upon the awareness of the people's tendency to sin (1 Kings 8:22-24, 48-50a, lesson 2). Hezekiah worshipped the Lord after being reminded that the Lord alone is God (2 Kings 19:14-20, lesson 3). Josiah demonstrated spiritual leadership by calling the people back to proper worship by adhering to the requirements of the covenant (2 Chronicles 35:1-6, 16-19, lesson 4).

These examples demonstrate how the people's worship of God is a response to the Lord and His work. Through worship, God's people proclaim that the Lord truly is the worthy Lamb of God!

Worship as Song

The songs of the Old Testament were one way for the people of God to respond to the Lord's work. While we may not know the melody of these songs, their lyrics reveal what the Old Testament people of God may have felt as they experienced His power and goodness.

These songs of worship are found throughout the Old Testament. Moses and Miriam celebrated God's power to bring the deliverance of the Israelites (Exodus 15:1-21, lesson 5). The prophet Isaiah praised God for His deliverance (Isaiah 25:1-10, lesson 8).

> The truth is, all people worship. *For the people of God, the question is,* who will *receive our worship?*

In the Old Testament book of Psalms, we see examples of confession (Psalm 51, lesson 6), petitions for deliverance (Psalm 22, lesson 7), and proclamations of trust in God (Psalm 62, lesson 9). Thanksgiving and praise were among the main themes of the songs of the Hebrew Psalter.

Worship as Thanksgiving and Praise

The final unit of the quarter focuses on the Hebrew psalter. The psalmists invite us to "praise the Lord" (Psalm 146:1, lesson 11) by making "a joyful noise unto the Lord" (100:1, lesson 12). The worship of the people of God should be filled with thanksgiving and praise to the Lord, for He is our good shepherd who sustains us (Psalm 23, lesson 10). The Lord is not distant and far off from us. Instead, the Lord is near us and has invited us to have a close relationship with Him (139:1-12, lesson 13). As you study the worship practices of the people of God, consider how your worship is a response to the truth that the Lord is the one who is worthy of praise.

Get the Setting

For the ancient Jewish person, music and song had a great deal to do with worship. But worship was not expressed solely through those things. It was more important for the worship of the one true God to include encounters between the spiritual and physical realms. We see the importance of this in various psalms. One example is Psalm 119:105: "Thy word is a lamp unto my feet, and a light unto my path." The impact of the Scriptures did not merely result in increased knowledge for the psalmist. The stress on the origin of the Scriptures had real and vital implications too.

Reminders Through Places

From the altars used in the days of Abraham to the tabernacle carried by the Israelites to the temple built by King Solomon, God's story was told through physical components. The altar was where sacrifices were offered as acts of worship. The tabernacle and temple that followed—the figurative dwelling places of God himself (1 Kings 8:27; Acts 17:24)—were far more elaborate than the simple altars of earlier days. Rich in symbolism, the tabernacle and the temple were feasts for the senses. As their symbolism brought the story of God to life (or, rather, back to life), worshippers were reminded of the covenant between them and God. The two proper responses to this reminder were worship and obedience.

Reminders Through Feasts

The most valuable reminders are those that influence behavior. And one of the best kinds of reminder in this regard is *reenactment*. A primary vehicle for these were the various feasts of ancient Israel, the Feast of Passover undoubtedly being the most important. We see this feast's importance in 2 Chronicles 35, where Josiah reinstituted this celebration, which had been established more than 800 years earlier!

Passover was one of three annual pilgrimage feasts, the other two being Pentecost and Tabernacles (they go by various other names as well; compare Exodus 23:14-16; Numbers 28:16-31; 29:12-34). By involving a meal, the reenactment was enhanced by taste and smell. Unleavened bread, bitter herbs, lamb bones, etc., all played their part in bringing the story of God's provisioning back to life.

Worship Through Actions

Under the old covenant, the psalms often connected worship of the spiritual God with the physical actions of the earthly worshipper. Just two examples are Psalm 47:1 ("O clap your hands, all ye people; shout unto God with the voice of triumph") and Psalm 149:3 ("Let them praise his name in the dance: let them sing praises unto him with the timbrel and harp"). How many such actions still apply under the new covenant yet have been bones of contention throughout the centuries? But as the revelation of God's words, God's works, and even God himself prompted acts of worship, so must it be with us.

Worship in Truth

We take care, however, not to worship God as we imagine Him to be (Isaiah 44:13-20; Romans 1:25; etc.). Instead, we worship as Scripture reveals Him to be (1 Samuel 3:21; Acts 17:26-31). Our worship "in truth" (John 4:23-24) will be revealed not only in our verbal confession (Romans 10:9-10) but also in and through our actions (1 John 3:17; 5:2; etc.).

True worship, whether in word or deed, focuses on the true God. "I [John] fell at his feet to worship him [an angel]. And he said unto me, See thou do it not: I am thy fellowservant, and of thy brethren that have the testimony of Jesus: worship God: for the testimony of Jesus is the spirit of prophecy" (Revelation 19:10).

This Quarter in the Word

Answers to the Quarterly Quiz on page 2

Lesson 1—1. Lot. 2. True. **Lesson 2**—1. David. 2. True. **Lesson 3**—1. Sennacherib. 2. True. **Lesson 4**—1. False. 2. seven. **Lesson 5**—1. song. 2. Miriam. **Lesson 6**—1. clean. 2. salvation. **Lesson 7**—1. forsaken. 2. worm. **Lesson 8**—1. False. 2. True. **Lesson 9**—1. rock, salvation. 2. True. **Lesson 10**—1. comfort. 2. goodness, mercy. **Lesson 11**—1. righteous. 2. sanctuary. **Lesson 12**—1. True. 2. False. **Lesson 13**—1. True. 2. spirit.

Lesson Cycle Chart

International Sunday School Lesson Cycle, September 2022–August 2026

Year	Fall Quarter (Sep, Oct, Nov)	Winter Quarter (Dec, Jan, Feb)	Spring Quarter (Mar, Apr, May)	Summer Quarter (Jun, Jul, Aug)
2022–2023	**God's Exceptional Choice** Genesis, Exodus, Deuteronomy, Judges, 1 Samuel, Ephesians	**From Darkness to Light** 2 Chronicles, Isaiah, Joel, Luke, 1 Corinthians, 2 Timothy, James, 1 Peter	**Jesus Calls Us** Matthew, Mark, Luke, John, Acts	**The Righteous Reign of God** Prophets, Matthew, Romans, 1 Corinthians, Galatians
2023–2024	**God's Law Is Love** Luke, John, Acts, Romans, 1 Corinthians, Galatians, Colossians	**Faith That Pleases God** Ruth, 1 Samuel, 2 Chronicles, Proverbs, Prophets, Matthew, Luke, Romans, Hebrews	**Examining Our Faith** Matthew, Mark, Luke, Acts, Romans, 2 Corinthians, 1 Peter, Jude	**Hope in the Lord** Psalms, Lamentations, Acts, Epistles
2024–2025	**Worship in the Covenant Community** Genesis, Exodus, 2 Samuel, 1 & 2 Kings, 2 Chronicles, Psalms, Isaiah, John	**A King Forever and Ever** Ruth, 2 Samuel, Psalms, Matthew, Luke	**Costly Sacrifices** Exodus, Leviticus, Numbers, Deuteronomy, 1 & 2 Chronicles, Ezra, Matthew, Hebrews, 1 John, Revelation	**Sacred Altars and Holy Offerings** Genesis, Gospels, Romans, 1 Corinthians, Ephesians, Hebrews, 1 Peter
2025–2026	**Judah, From Isaiah to Exile** 2 Kings, 2 Chronicles, Isaiah, Jeremiah, Ezekiel	**Enduring Beliefs of the Church** Exodus, Psalms, Gospels, Acts, Epistles, Revelation	**Social Teachings of the Church** Genesis, Exodus, Deuteronomy, Nehemiah, Psalms, Prophets, Gospels, Acts, Epistles	**Faithful Witnesses** Judges, 1 Samuel, Amos, Gospels, Acts, 2 Timothy, Philemon

Handling Doctrinal Differences

Teacher Tips by Ronald L. Nickelson

The teacher of the Bible class I attended asked me if I would take the teaching duty for a few Sundays in his absence. I agreed to do so.

The long-standing practice of the class was to study through books of the Bible, and I thought a temporary change of pace would be beneficial. So I announced that we were going to consider what the Bible said regarding a particular doctrine.

The announcement immediately drew a cry of protest. One participant, obviously in distress, stated that doctrine was divisive—every church she had ever been involved with had had fights and splits over doctrine. So before I encountered any disagreements over the truth of any particular doctrine, I was confronted with an objection to studying doctrine at all! And what the person didn't realize was that even a through-the-books approach involves the study of doctrine.

Why Study Doctrine?

As used in the Bible, the word *doctrine* simply means "what is taught," referring to the content of teaching. There is such a thing as sound doctrine (1 Timothy 1:10; 2 Timothy 4:3; Titus 1:9; 2:1); its opposite is false doctrine (1 Timothy 1:3; 6:3). To distinguish between the two is to separate what is true (that is, conforms to reality) from what is false. Therefore, one reason that we study doctrine is to discern the existence of false doctrine.

The Bible is God's communication with us. And, as one writer has noted, "He intends for everything He says to have one specific true and right meaning." Therefore, whenever two Christians disagree about the meaning of a statement in the Bible, one (or both!) of them must be wrong. Think about it: one person believes that tithing still applies in the New Testament era, and another person does not. They can't both be right! And a false doctrine that spreads can be a cancer within the church (Titus 1:11). How should we as teachers approach this kind of problem when it presents itself?

A Starting Point

One popular starting point for handling doctrinal differences is to distinguish between "essential" doctrines and "nonessential" ones. This distinction has been sloganized in various ways. One example is "In matters of faith, unity; in matters of opinion, liberty; in all things, love."

This slogan is appealing. And it can be useful if its terms are carefully defined. We shouldn't have much problem with the phrase "matters of faith" meaning "doctrinal beliefs that are essential for salvation" (example: Hebrews 11:6). The main challenge concerns the second phrase since the word *opinion* can be understood in more than one way (check online dictionaries). We are also cautious about using the word *nonessential*. If it's addressed in the Bible, then it is, in some sense, "essential."

A Preventative Approach

The best way to handle doctrinal disagreements during your teaching is to address them before they arise. The Standard Lesson Commentary will often alert you to "hot-button issues" in this regard. That way, you can disarm a doctrinal bomb before it has a chance to be dropped by a class member.

You may have noticed that this commentary doesn't stake out doctrinal positions on such issues. The approach, instead, is (1) to acknowledge and describe the issue, then (2) to give one or two of the strongest arguments for each side in an even-handed way and (3) let you, the reader, decide. This can be the model for approaching doctrinal disagreements in your class. As you do so, let 1 Corinthians 1:10 undergird your effort: "I [Paul] beseech you, brethren, by the name of our Lord Jesus Christ, that ye all speak the same thing, and that there be no divisions among you; but that ye be perfectly joined together in the same mind and in the same judgment."

Abram Builds an Altar

Devotional Reading: Philippians 4:10-19
Background Scripture: Genesis 12–13

Genesis 13:8-18

8 And Abram said unto Lot, Let there be no strife, I pray thee, between me and thee, and between my herdmen and thy herdmen; for we be brethren.

9 Is not the whole land before thee? separate thyself, I pray thee, from me: if thou wilt take the left hand, then I will go to the right; or if thou depart to the right hand, then I will go to the left.

10 And Lot lifted up his eyes, and beheld all the plain of Jordan, that it was well watered every where, before the Lord destroyed Sodom and Gomorrah, even as the garden of the Lord, like the land of Egypt, as thou comest unto Zoar.

11 Then Lot chose him all the plain of Jordan; and Lot journeyed east: and they separated themselves the one from the other.

12 Abram dwelled in the land of Canaan, and Lot dwelled in the cities of the plain, and pitched his tent toward Sodom.

13 But the men of Sodom were wicked and sinners before the Lord exceedingly.

14 And the Lord said unto Abram, after that Lot was separated from him, Lift up now thine eyes, and look from the place where thou art northward, and southward, and eastward, and westward:

15 For all the land which thou seest, to thee will I give it, and to thy seed for ever.

16 And I will make thy seed as the dust of the earth: so that if a man can number the dust of the earth, then shall thy seed also be numbered.

17 Arise, walk through the land in the length of it and in the breadth of it; for I will give it unto thee.

18 Then Abram removed his tent, and came and dwelt in the plain of Mamre, which is in Hebron, and built there an altar unto the Lord.

Key Text

Abram removed his tent, and came and dwelt in the plain of Mamre, which is in Hebron, and built there an altar unto the Lord. —**Genesis 13:18**

Worship in the
Covenant Community

Unit 1: Leaders Set Worship Example
Lessons 1–5

Lesson Aims

After participating in this lesson, each learner will be able to:

1. Outline the events that led to Abram's building an altar.

2. Explain the significance of Abram's actions.

3. Create a physical reminder of a time when God worked in his or her life.

Lesson Outline

Introduction

A. Sacred Spaces

With our signatures on the contract and an offer accepted, the deal was done. We had sold our house. It was only a small condo on a quiet cul-de-sac, but we had been there for over ten years. While saying goodbye, we realized how the space had become more than four walls and a roof to our family; it had become our home.

Sure, the place had its problems when we arrived. My spouse and I had primed and painted over the worn trim; we had fixed the ceiling crack in the kitchen, and—the proudest project of all—we spent a summer tiling a bathroom. That was one of those projects we would never have started had we known the time and effort required.

But when we stepped back and looked around the place, every corner held some special significance and a memory to replay. We thought of our kids who learned to crawl across the carpet. We thought of the family dance parties that woke the neighbors. We thought of our friends who shared griefs and joys around our table. If the walls could talk, they had a decade of stories to tell.

In the narrative of Genesis 13, Abram begins to call a new land his home. He probably had projects on his mind and things he wanted to improve. But he took the time to thank God and claim a space as sacred, meaning set apart for God's purpose. For generation after generation, the descendants of Abram (renamed Abraham in Genesis 17:5) would tell his stories and would refer to this place.

B. Lesson Context

Since the day Adam and Eve were expelled from Eden, the fact of humanity's sinfulness has been nothing new in any era. It was and is a persistent problem. Thus, it was left up to God to restore creation.

The divine restoration plan started in Genesis through a series of covenants and promises made to 75-year-old Abram and his wife (Genesis 12). Their descendants—the nation of Israel—would be the instrument through which God would send the Messiah into the world to inaugurate the new creation. Jesus fulfilled God's cosmic design. Through

Jesus, a person can become a child of Abraham, joining the family of God by faith rather than physical birth (Galatians 3:7; compare Romans 4:16).

Abraham—known as Abram in today's lesson—is a hero of faith (Hebrews 11:8-12). He is described that way not because he was perfect or sinless, but because by faith, he left his home when called to do so by God (Genesis 12:1). God's covenant with Abram included promises of land, progeny, and blessing. It took centuries for all this to become a reality. The conversations between God and Abram that begin in Genesis 12 are instrumental in revealing the development of a personal relationship between the two.

But the text under consideration for today deals with a distraction detailed in Genesis 13:1-7. Abram had decided to take his nephew Lot on the journey to Canaan (Genesis 12:5), a decision that resulted in problem after problem. One such problem is the immediate context of today's lesson:

> Lot also, which went with Abram, had flocks, and herds, and tents. And the land was not able to bear them, that they might dwell together: for their substance was great. . . . And there was a strife between the herdmen of Abram's cattle and the herdmen of Lot's cattle.
> —Genesis 13:5-7.

I. Abram's Offer
(Genesis 13:8-9)
A. To Avoid Arguing (v. 8)

8. And Abram said unto Lot, Let there be no strife, I pray thee, between me and thee, and between my herdmen and thy herdmen; for we be brethren.

To be a nomadic *herdmen* was a common occupation in the ancient Near East. The success of this lifestyle depended upon the land's ability to provide. The territory of Canaan and the Jordan River valley was quite suitable for such an occupation; the Old Testament describes this land about 20 times as flowing "with milk and honey" (examples: Exodus 3:8; Numbers 13:23-27).

The problem here was what might be called "too much of a good thing." Despite the land's abundance, Abram and Lot had too much livestock for the area to support (see Lesson Context;

compare Genesis 26:19-22). Thus their respective herds came into competition for a fixed set of resources. To prevent any *strife* that could have endangered their herds, Abram suggested a resolution predicated on their shared kinship.

This instance is not the first time in Genesis that competition between close relatives presents itself (consider Cain and Abel in Genesis 4). Nor is it the last (consider Esau and Jacob in Genesis 26–28, Laban and Jacob in Genesis 29–31, etc.).

What Do You Think?

How should believers deal with conflict and quarrels that arise with family members?

Digging Deeper

How might Matthew 18:15-17; Ephesians 4:25-32; and Colossians 3:12-15 inform how you deal with conflict?

B. To Avoid Crowding (v. 9)

9. Is not the whole land before thee? separate thyself, I pray thee, from me: if thou wilt take the left hand, then I will go to the right; or if thou depart to the right hand, then I will go to the left.

The location where Abram made this offer was "between Bethel and Hai" (Genesis 13:3). At an elevation of 2,900 feet, Bethel is one of the highest places in the region. Taking the square root of that number and multiplying the result by 1.22459 yields approximately 66—that is the distance in miles that Abram and Lot can see before the horizon makes things no longer visible. Therefore, it's easy for us to imagine the two men standing on a high vista as Abram makes this offer to Lot.

How to Say It

Canaan	*Kay*-nun.
Esau	*Ee*-saw.
Gomorrah	Guh-*more*-uh.
Laban	*Lay*-bun.
Mamre	*Mam*-reh.
Sodom	*Sod*-um.
Zoar	*Zo*-er.

See God's promises ahead of you and believe.
Hebrews 11:8

Visual for Lesson 1. *Show this visual as you discuss the lesson conclusion regarding the faith of Abraham as described in Hebrews 11.*

The offer assures that they will separate, but Abram risks a great deal by allowing Lot his choice. The text says nothing of God's direction in the affair, but Lot's self-interest will lead to his unraveling after his departure from the land of Canaan.

We may wonder if Lot is counted as part of Abram's "father's house" (Genesis 12:1) and thus shares the promise of Genesis 12:2-3. The text merely says, "Lot went with him" as Abram departed for Canaan (12:4). Thus, we do not know whether Lot accompanied Abram by invitation to do so or if he merely was a tag-along party crasher.

Wisdom or Experience?

The animal kingdom is often harsh and unforgiving to its younger generations. For example, spotted hyenas are highly aggressive to their cubs, often killing all but the strongest soon after their birth. Cubs continue to compete with one another and adult members of the pack so that only the strongest survive to adulthood. Then, the clan runs off any young males, who must find a new pack or create one of their own when they reach maturity.

You would expect emperor penguins to be a gentler species, right? They're so cute on TV! The parents cooperate as they swap tending and hunting roles while their expected offspring develops inside its single egg in the winter. But once the chick is old enough to survive without help, the parents abandon it to fend for itself along with other young penguins.

Hyenas and penguins are just two examples from nature. Humans don't have to act like animals, though. Abraham is an example of how the older generation can teach someone of a younger generation by offering choices that result in the older person's making sacrifices. It's been said that there are two ways to learn things: through wisdom and through experience. *Wisdom* is when you learn from the mistakes of others; *experience* is when you learn from your own mistakes. Lot's choice eventually resulted in the latter. What can you do to switch from learning by experience to learning by wisdom?   —A. W.

II. Lot's Choice
(Genesis 13:10-13)
A. His Inspection (v. 10)

10. And Lot lifted up his eyes, and beheld all the plain of Jordan, that it was well watered every where, before the LORD destroyed Sodom and Gomorrah, even as the garden of the LORD, like the land of Egypt, as thou comest unto Zoar.

Much like the present day, access to water was a requirement for survival in ancient times. No water means no livestock. Moreover, in ancient times, all wells had to be dug by hand (compare Genesis 26:12-22, 32-33). An abundance of watering springs was part of God's original creation (2:6), which is what the verse means by the phrase *the garden of the Lord*. The Jordan River valley is compared to *the land of Egypt*, where annual flooding of the Nile River makes the land fertile.

The town of *Zoar* is about 64 miles from where Lot and Abram were standing. The town played an important role for Lot and his family when *the Lord* destroyed *Sodom and Gomorrah* (see Genesis 19:18-30). Furthermore, the reference to the destruction of these cities suggests that this event was widely known among the original audience of Genesis. The placement of this reminder in the text likely prompted the original audience to recall that, although Lot initially seemed to have chosen the most favorable land for selfish reasons, it did not ultimately lead to a positive outcome for him.

B. His Selection (v. 11)

11. Then Lot chose him all the plain of Jordan; and Lot journeyed east: and they separated themselves the one from the other.

As Lot stood next to his uncle, he undoubtedly thought he had the better deal regarding the choice of land. But as events of Genesis 18–19 unfold, he may have come to realize how poor his choice was! Lot's selected territory means that he will be moving *east,* given the reference point in 13:3. In the Genesis narrative, traveling to the east has been associated with moves away from God. First, Adam and Eve were driven eastward from the garden (Genesis 3:24). Next, Cain moved east to the land of Nod, "out from the presence of the Lord" (4:16). Finally, the builders of the city of Babel are reported to have an eastward orientation or destination (11:2).

C. His Destination (v. 12)

12. Abram dwelled in the land of Canaan, and Lot dwelled in the cities of the plain, and pitched his tent toward Sodom.

Lot's departure to *the cities of the plain* identifies his new home as being just barely inside *the land of Canaan,* according to the boundary designations in Genesis 10:19. The phrase *pitched his tent* points to a nomadic lifestyle (Isaiah 13:20). The Hebrew preposition of the verse at hand describes this action as being *toward Sodom.* Soon enough, however, the preposition changes: in Genesis 14:12, he is described as living "in Sodom." In 19:1, he is described as sitting at the city gates, a place of importance. These verses depict Lot's transition from being a nomad to becoming a permanent foreign resident, as evidenced by his living in a house (19:2).

D. His Environment (v. 13)

13. But the men of Sodom were wicked and sinners before the LORD exceedingly.

In selecting where to live, Lot had apparently not considered the moral climate, only the availability of water (Genesis 13:10, above). Specific information regarding the nature and depravity of *the men of Sodom* is found in Genesis 19:4-5 and Ezekiel 16:49-50.

> **What Do You Think?**
> How can believers safeguard themselves from sinful behavior while living or working in an environment hostile to God and righteousness?
> **Digging Deeper**
> How can believers be a humble and godly influence in such an environment? How might Matthew 5:3-16 and 1 Peter 3:15-16 inform your response?

A Cautionary Tale

The talent of Whitney Houston (1963–2012) was evident from when she was a small child. From an early age, she was an energetic choir member and soloist who raised the roof of her church with a powerful voice and confident stage presence.

She was discovered by a music executive and signed her first record deal in 1983 at 20 years old. She went on to become one of the most popular stars of the 1980s and 1990s. She sold over 200 million records, won numerous awards, and starred in various films.

Unfortunately, superstardom also had its dark side, and it eventually engulfed Whitney. She struggled with addiction and a troubled marriage that brought negative publicity and kept her in a downward spiral. Tragically, she passed away at age 48 when she drowned in a bathtub; heart disease and cocaine were determined to be contributing factors.

The experience of stardom for a young person can lead to overwhelming pressure as various voices attempt to speak into his or her life. We can't know whether or not Whitney's downward spiral came about because of questionable influences. Regardless, it is true that poor choices can lead to disastrous outcomes.

Lot's decision to live near Sodom was one such poor choice; it opened the door to destructive people and influences. The apostle Paul, quoting the Greek poet Menander (342–292 BC), reminds us to "be not deceived: evil communications corrupt good manners" (1 Corinthians 15:33). What kind of company do you keep? Do Paul's directives in 1 Corinthians 5:9-10 offer clarity?   —A. W.

III. God's Promises
(Genesis 13:14-16)

A. Of Land (vv. 14-15)

14-15. And the LORD said unto Abram, after that Lot was separated from him, Lift up now thine eyes, and look from the place where thou art northward, and southward, and eastward, and westward. For all the land which thou seest, to thee will I give it, and to thy seed for ever.

With Abram alone, God makes a more expansive promise of territory in the land of Canaan (compare Genesis 12:7). If we assume the same location as in Genesis 13:3, then the visibility computations of 13:9 above still apply. Thus, when God invites Abram to look *northward, and southward, and eastward, and westward,* that man can see as far as 66 miles in any direction. If we imagine Abram standing in the middle of a circle with a visibility radius of 66 miles, the result is Abram's potentially being able to view about 13,700 square miles. That's about one-third the size of the state of Tennessee.

We also note the second mention of Abram's *seed* (compare Genesis 12:7). The word *seed* is often used as a collective singular noun to refer to a line of descendants, but it can also be used of an individual; Isaac will become this "seed" to Abram, the child of promise from God (21:12). Centuries later, the apostle Paul will note the difference between the singular and plural uses of this word regarding Abraham's descendants (see Galatians 3:16).

B. Of Progeny (v. 16)

16. And I will make thy seed as the dust of the earth: so that if a man can number the dust of the earth, then shall thy seed also be numbered.

Here the word *seed* is used as a collective noun, standing for the enormous number of Abram's future family. The verse contains a complex hyperbole: if *the dust of the earth* could be counted (and it can't), then Abram's future descendants could be counted as well (and they can't either; compare Genesis 15:5). We should keep in mind that at this point childless Abram is 75 years old (12:4).

IV. Abram's Tour
(Genesis 13:17-18)

A. Receives the Directive (v. 17)

17. Arise, walk through the land in the length of it and in the breadth of it; for I will give it unto thee.

In the ancient world, walking the length and breadth of a land was equivalent to claiming ownership of it. Therefore, in accordance with legal tradition, God instructed Abram to survey the land by walking through it. We note that the boundaries with which Abram was familiar in Genesis 10:19 have mismatches with the borders described in Numbers 34:1-12. We keep two things in mind as we compare and contrast those differences. First, God promised in Genesis 17:8 to give "all" the land of Canaan to Abram and his descendants. What God gave to the Israelites in Numbers 34 probably reflected the Israelites' track record of rebellion at the time (compare and contrast Ezekiel 47:13-23). They could have had "all" the land of Canaan had they obeyed fully. But they didn't (Judges 1:27-35).

Second, several centuries elapse between the time of Genesis 13 and Numbers 34. Boundaries can change in location and name, given the rise and fall of cities and various other currents of history.

> **What Do You Think?**
> What steps can you take to ensure that the material blessings God gives you will be used to serve Him and love others?
>
> **Digging Deeper**
> How might you use non-material blessings (such as wisdom, time, or expertise) to serve God and others?

B. Responds by Building (v. 18)

18. Then Abram removed his tent, and came and dwelt in the plain of Mamre, which is in Hebron, and built there an altar unto the LORD.

Abram responded to the directive and chose to live about 30 miles south-southwest of his location of Bethel stated in Genesis 13:3. The elevation of *Hebron* allows viewing of Sodom, Gomorrah, and Zoar. Perhaps Abram chose this location to keep an eye on Lot (see Genesis 14). The importance of

Hebron is reflected in its being mentioned by name more than 60 times in the Old Testament.

An additional reference is the nearby *plain of Mamre*. The word translated as "plain" can also refer to trees, as it does in Genesis 35:8 and Hosea 4:13. In gratitude for God's provision and attention, Abram constructed *an altar* to offer sacrifices in worship. Stone altars were common to ancient Near Eastern religions, and Abram would have been familiar with their use. They also serve as monuments and places of memory (compare and contrast Joshua 22:26-28). They remind the observer of commitment and significance. Abraham and his wife, Sarah, were buried in a cave near their home in Mamre (Genesis 23:17-20; 25:7-10).

> **What Do You Think?**
> How can you create a "monument" or another reminder to help you remember God's provision and attention?
> **Digging Deeper**
> Who will you recruit to help you plan and establish such a "monument"?

Conclusion

A. That Was Then

God's first words to Abraham (as Abram) were a directive to leave home (Genesis 12:1). He left his extended family behind as he journeyed toward and within the land God had designated. God deliberately separated him from his past to create a new nation from him—a nation to usher in the Messiah. We may wonder how homesick Abraham became from time to time. We may also wonder if Abraham ever wished he hadn't taken Lot along!

The importance of Abraham (lived about 2000 BC) in salvation-history should not be overlooked. His names "Abram" and "Abraham" appear on the pages of the Old and New Testament nearly 300 times, with about 28 percent of those occurring in the New Testament. In Hebrews 11, Abraham is enshrined in "Faith's Hall of Fame." His example has much to teach us yet today.

B. This Is Now

In a sense, Abraham's story is ours as well. God wants us to know the Messiah He has sent. But for that to happen, sometimes God has to separate us from relationships, events, jobs, etc., that stand in the way (Mark 10:28-31; Luke 5:27-28). Those separations may come either *in order that* we may know Jesus or *as a result of* knowing Him.

Those who have experienced such severances may have an inkling of Abraham's faith. His willingness to place faith in God before all else makes him stand apart, a hero of faith (Hebrews 11:8-10; compare Galatians 3:9). God expects similar faith even today. When we believe we are called to a different situation, God may not reveal all the details of how to do so and why. If He did, then there would be no room for faith!

We should not be surprised if our journey involves taking a "Lot" along. In the Genesis narrative, that man was nothing but trouble for his uncle. More importantly, it's vital that we not *be* a "Lot"!

> **What Do You Think?**
> How will today's Scripture text inform your response when you experience a difficult situation on your faith journey?
> **Digging Deeper**
> Who is a "Lot" that God might be asking you to take along on your faith journey?

C. Prayer

Father God, send us into the troubled world as Your ambassadors so that we may make disciples as we remind others of what You have done for us. Give us eyes like Abraham to perceive the nature of faith. May we not be a short-sighted "Lot"! We ask this in the name of Jesus. Amen.

D. Thought to Remember

Be ready to exercise a faith like Abraham's.

Visuals FOR THESE LESSONS

The visual pictured in each lesson (example: page 12) is a small reproduction of a large, full-color poster included in the *Adult Resources* packet for the Fall Quarter. Order No. 9780784739136 from your supplier.

Involvement Learning

Enhance your lesson with KJV Bible Student *(from your curriculum supplier) and the reproducible activity page (at www.standardlesson.com or in the back of the* KJV Standard Lesson Commentary Deluxe Edition*).*

Into the Lesson

Announce a "Pictionary"-style game wherein one or more volunteers sketch examples of "major sources of conflict" on the board. Class members are invited to discern that topic.

Alternative. Distribute copies of the "Conflict Resolution" exercise from the activity page, which you can download. Have learners work in pairs to complete the exercise as indicated. After sufficient time to do so, reconvene for a whole-class discussion.

After either activity and discussion, say, "Conflict is as old as humanity. Let's see how one conflict recorded in the Bible was settled unselfishly."

Into the Word

Ask two learners to take turns reading aloud the verses of Genesis 13:8-18. Then break into pairs or small groups to evaluate the reason(s) for the dispute between Abram and Lot. Distribute handouts (you prepare) with one or more of the following questions printed on them. (Expected responses are in italics—do not put them on the handouts):

1. When, if ever, did God instruct Abram to take his nephew Lot with him to the promised land? *(God never did.)*
2. Since Lot and Abram were close relatives, why did they keep their livestock property separate? *(This is a matter of speculation, but see Genesis 30:25-43 for cultural clues.)*
3. What factors are not recorded as playing a part in Lot's choice to settle near Sodom and Gomorrah? *(There is no mention of Lot's having considered the moral climate of the area he chose.)*

After discussion, transition by saying, "It would not be right for us today to build altars to make sacrifices, now that Jesus has provided the full and final sacrifice for our sins. However,

in Old Testament times, an altar or other structure was erected to commemorate something important." Refer to one or more of these texts as examples: Genesis 28:18-22; 35:1, 14; Joshua 4:1-7; 1 Samuel 7:12.

Into Life

Ask the class to share some of the great things God has done for them. Follow that discussion by asking how those blessings could be memorialized in some way that honors God—a way of informing others of those blessings. (*Teacher tip*: don't ask more than one question at a time; allow responses to the first question before asking the second.)

If participants seem to have a hard time getting started here, follow by saying, "Imagine if you were to place a few items on a shelf or in a scrapbook as a reminder of God's aid in a victory. What might some of those items be?" Expect learners to mention things such as an expired driver's license to recall how God has kept you safe in your travels or a photo of your family to recall an event when family members worked together to overcome a financial challenge.

Option. Form participants into study triads. Then distribute copies of the "Creative Problem-Solving" activity from the activity page, which you can download, to discuss and complete as indicated. (Feel free to delete, add, or modify the questions and options in advance.)

After discussions in triads, reconvene for whole-class sharing. Encourage participants to share examples of issues they are still trying to resolve. *Cautions*: (1) don't put anyone on the spot to share information that is too personal, and (2) stress that the sharing is a time for encouragement, not a time for "giving advice." Ask learners for commitments to pray for those who request it. Conclude with a minute of silent prayer in that regard.

Solomon Dedicates the Temple

Devotional Reading: Psalm 34:11-22
Background Scripture: 1 Kings 8:22-53

1 Kings 8:22-24, 37-39, 46, 48-50a

22 And Solomon stood before the altar of the LORD in the presence of all the congregation of Israel, and spread forth his hands toward heaven:

23 And he said, LORD God of Israel, There is no God like thee, in heaven above, or on earth beneath, who keepest covenant and mercy with thy servants that walk before thee with all their heart:

24 Who hast kept with thy servant David my father that thou promisedst him: thou spakest also with thy mouth, and hast fulfilled it with thine hand, as it is this day.

37 If there be in the land famine, if there be pestilence, blasting, mildew, locust, or if there be caterpiller; if their enemy besiege them in the land of their cities; whatsoever plague, whatsoever sickness there be;

38 What prayer and supplication soever be made by any man, or by all thy people Israel, which shall know every man the plague of his own heart, and spread forth his hands toward this house:

39 Then hear thou in heaven thy dwelling place, and forgive, and do, and give to every man according to his ways, whose heart thou knowest; (for thou, even thou only, knowest the hearts of all the children of men;)

46 If they sin against thee, (for there is no man that sinneth not,) and thou be angry with them, and deliver them to the enemy, so that they carry them away captives unto the land of the enemy, far or near;

48 And so return unto thee with all their heart, and with all their soul, in the land of their enemies, which led them away captive, and pray unto thee toward their land, which thou gavest unto their fathers, the city which thou hast chosen, and the house which I have built for thy name:

49 Then hear thou their prayer and their supplication in heaven thy dwelling place, and maintain their cause,

50a And forgive thy people that have sinned against thee.

Key Text

What prayer and supplication soever be made by any man, or by all thy people Israel, which shall know every man the plague of his own heart, and spread forth his hands toward this house: Then hear thou in heaven thy dwelling place. —1 Kings 8:38-39a

• 17

Worship in the Covenant Community

Lesson Aims

After participating in this lesson, each learner will be able to:

1. Summarize Solomon's prayer.

2. Analyze the structure and movement of Solomon's prayer at the temple dedication.

3. Write a prayer to dedicate the congregation's meeting place(s) to the Lord.

Lesson Outline

Introduction
  A. Consecration? Dedication?
  B. Lesson Context
I. Impassioned Prayer (1 Kings 8:22-24)
  A. Solomon's Postures (v. 22)
  B. God's Uniqueness (vv. 23-24)
II. Oppressive Circumstances (1 Kings 8:37-39)
  A. Sword, Famine, Plague (vv. 37-38)
    Turn First?
  B. Hear, Forgive, Act (v. 39)
III. Inevitable Sin (1 Kings 8:46, 48-50a)
  A. Anger, Captivity, Exile (v. 46)
  B. Hear, Sustain, Forgive (vv. 48-50a)
    Forgiveness and Reconciliation
Conclusion
  A. People as Sinners
  B. God as Defender
  C. Prayer
  D. Thought to Remember

Introduction

A. Consecration? Dedication?

Years ago, a young preacher just out of seminary was setting up for an evening audio-visual presentation in the church sanctuary. He needed a place to put the equipment, and he eventually spotted the ideal place: the communion table. But as he began moving it into place, his wife warned him, "That's the communion table."

The self-confident preacher knew that, of course. But he also knew that, ultimately, the table was just an ornate piece of wood. So what if its normal use was to hold the trays of the communion elements? Couldn't it serve other functions as well?

But his wife stepped up her caution by stressing again that *"That's the communion table!"* In so doing, she recognized something that her husband hadn't: the existence of a disposition of many in the congregation who considered some things to be consecrated (or set apart) for certain tasks only.

Various words describing the concept of consecration occur over 250 times in the Old Testament. It is an act by which a person or thing is set apart for service to God (examples: Exodus 29:44; Leviticus 8:10). In the New Testament era, however, the idea of consecration applies to just people, not to things. Even so, there exist issues of conscience in this regard. So the preacher wisely heeded his wife's warning.

B. Lesson Context

The ceremony in 1 Kings 8 consecrated the newly built temple in Jerusalem. Temple construction had begun in 966 BC and required seven years for completion (1 Kings 6:1, 38). That completion in 959 BC marked an important transition in Israelite history, as the location of encounter with the holy God became immovable, with the temple replacing the portable tabernacle. The first half of Solomon's 40-year reign was focused on building the temple and palace (9:10). Today's lesson from 1 Kings 8 considers a portion of the dedication prayer at the ceremony for the finished temple, over which King Solomon presided.

Several preparatory elements led up to this prayer: the temple had been completely furnished

(1 Kings 7:13-51), the ark of the covenant had been brought into the temple (8:1-9), and the king had "blessed all the congregation of Israel" (8:14). The prayer of dedication that followed (8:23-53) is the second longest prayer in the Bible—in the neighborhood of 1,000 words! (The parallel in 2 Chronicles 6:14-42 is of similar length.) Only the prayer in Nehemiah 9:5-38 is longer.

But the prayer's outsized length doesn't mean that King Solomon merely rambled on and on (compare Matthew 6:7). Quite the opposite: the prayer is clearly organized. We see that organization in 9 of the prayer's 31 verses selected for today's study.

Pray to the Lord who keeps promises.

Visual for Lesson 2. *Allow one minute for individuals to follow the visual's prompting to pray to the Lord who keeps promises.*

I. Impassioned Prayer
(1 Kings 8:22-24)
A. Solomon's Postures (v. 22)

22. And Solomon stood before the altar of the LORD in the presence of all the congregation of Israel, and spread forth his hands toward heaven.

The standing posture of prayer Solomon adopts is the most commonly seen in ancient Near Eastern art. Other postures, especially kneeling or prostration, were legitimate, of course (examples: 1 Chronicles 29:20; 2 Chronicles 29:29). And by the time Solomon concludes the prayer, he will have switched from standing to kneeling (1 Kings 8:54; the changeover is explained more fully in 2 Chronicles 6:12-13).

In both postures, the fact that Solomon extended *his hands toward heaven* adds an aura of solemnity and earnestness (compare Exodus 9:29; Deuteronomy 32:40-41; Lamentations 3:41; Daniel 12:7). It reflects the idea of God as being far "above" creation, not just spatially but also figuratively. Humans look "up" to God, seeking help during their hour of need (Deuteronomy 4:39; John 8:23).

Solomon voiced his prayer not just for his own benefit but on behalf *of all the congregation of Israel.* These were especially those Israelites who were in attendance personally for the temple dedication (1 Kings 8:1-2). Their presence is important partly because they must overhear the exhortations to avoid sin and partly because God wishes to empha-

size the relationship with the people of Israel. They were united with each other and God by their history, present life, and hope for a blessed future. In a sense, they are being dedicated as much as the temple when we note the blessing mentioned in 1 Kings 8:14 (compare 2 Samuel 6:18).

B. God's Uniqueness (vv. 23-24)

23. And he said, LORD God of Israel, there is no God like thee, in heaven above, or on earth beneath, who keepest covenant and mercy with thy servants that walk before thee with all their heart.

The following two verses are worded almost identically with 2 Chronicles 6:14-15. The confession emphasizes the uniqueness of God, an idea that appears in many biblical texts (examples: Psalms 115:3-8; 135:15-18). *The Lord God of Israel* brooks no rivals (Deuteronomy 4:15-20; 5:7; etc.).

One area of His uniqueness appears in keeping a *covenant* in His merciful love. This language comes from Deuteronomy 7:9, 12, and it reflects the direction of that book. While Israelites were responsible for obeying God's commandments, their relationship with God rested primarily upon His covenant promise. It was not earned by human merit.

Even so, the verse at hand emphasizes the attitude of the people. As indicated by "the Shema" (which means "hear") in Deuteronomy 6:4-5, the people should hear and receive the Law of Moses with enthusiasm, commitment, and even rejoicing, as emphasized throughout Deuteronomy. Mindless, routine obedience cannot be the goal of the relationship because it is not sustainable. Those who follow God without enthusiasm will stop following at a slight provocation (Matthew 13:1-9).

24. Who hast kept with thy servant David my father that thou promisedst him: thou spakest also with thy mouth, and hast fulfilled it with thine hand, as it is this day.

The promise to *David* that his offspring would build the temple (2 Samuel 7:13), now fulfilled, is evidence of God's faithfulness. The eventual destruction of kingship and even that of the temple did not cancel God's plan for Israel; rather, God used those events to symbolize His presence as they pointed to greater, eternal realities regarding spiritual and heavenly kingship and temple. God may carry out His promises in various ways, but the promises always remain just that.

> **What Do You Think?**
> Which of God's scriptural promises has He already fulfilled?
>
> **Digging Deeper**
> How does recalling His fulfilled promises encourage your faithfulness in waiting for the fulfillment of the rest?

II. Oppressive Circumstances
(1 Kings 8:37-39)
A. Sword, Famine, Plague (vv. 37-38)

37. If there be in the land famine, if there be pestilence, blasting, mildew, locust, or if there be caterpiller; if their enemy besiege them in the land of their cities; whatsoever plague, whatsoever sickness there be.

The Old Testament often summarizes the calamities that may befall God's people in terms of "sword," "famine," and "pestilence" (examples: 1 Chronicles 21:11-12; Jeremiah 14:12). These three general categories speak to oppression and/or fatalities caused by human adversaries, meager harvests, and disease, respectively. *Blasting* (blight), *mildew, locust,* and *caterpiller* result in famine as crops are destroyed (compare Psalm

78:46; Amos 4:9; Joel 1:4). These predictions of calamities come from the greatly expanded listing in Deuteronomy 28:15-68.

> **What Do You Think?**
> What are some examples of disasters or crises modern people fear and need God's help to withstand?
>
> **Digging Deeper**
> When we pray to God for help with these kinds of issues, what is our responsibility to act? Consider James 2:16.

38a. What prayer and supplication soever be made by any man, or by all the people Israel.

Solomon asks God to reply to any prayer offered by those either in the temple or mindful of it. You may notice that the word *or* is italicized in your edition of the *King James Version*. That's how the *KJV* indicates that there is no word in the text of the Hebrew language being translated. Thus the word *or* is the translators' best judgment for smooth reading.

On the other hand, the ancient Greek translation (the Septuagint) omits the phrase *by all the people Israel*. The prayer does envision Gentiles praying, beginning in 1 Kings 8:41. But here the focus remains on Israelites as those especially subject to the curses following a violation of the covenant (again, see Deuteronomy 28).

38b. Which shall know every man the plague of his own heart, and spread forth the hands toward this house.

The phrase *the plague of his own heart* speaks to pangs of conscience (compare 1 Samuel 24:5; Romans 2:15; etc.). Each person knows his or her own troubles and can express them in prayer as *hands* are lifted *toward this house* (compare and contrast Exodus 9:29; Job 11:13; Psalm 88:9; Isaiah 1:15). This may work on two levels: (1) the suffering of the people as a whole may be expressed in different ways by different individuals, and (2) each person should be aware of his or her details and ably communicate about them to God. In other words, prayer can take many forms. On the one hand, it depends partly on forms shared by the community as a whole over time. On the other hand, it depends partly on individual experience and perception.

Turn First?

One of the many tragedies of World War II was the Bengal Famine of 1943. India at the time was still part of the British Empire and engaged in the global struggle against the Axis powers. The Japanese Empire had already conquered neighboring Burma (present-day Myanmar) and was poised to invade India. Much of the local harvest was diverted to the needs of the global military effort, leading to the starvation of at least two million people in the Bengal province.

Mahatma Gandhi, a leader in India's growing independence movement, refused to accept aid from the British government or foreign aid agencies because he believed that would compromise India's self-sufficiency. He didn't want to perpetuate a cycle of dependence on foreign powers. Instead, he urged India's population to use their own resources to help one another through the crisis. This effort was very controversial and only partially successful.

Where do you turn first for help during a crisis? Is your first impulse to cry out to governmental agencies? Is it to rely on your own resources in the pride of "rugged individualism"? Or is your first turn toward God? —A. W.

B. Hear, Forgive, Act (v. 39)

39. Then hear thou in heaven thy dwelling place, and forgive, and do, and give to every man according to his ways, whose heart thou knowest (for thou, even thou only, knowest the hearts of all the children of men).

Humans do well to know their own hearts and minds as God knows them (compare Hebrews 4:12-13). That's an ideal to strive for, although it is impossible to attain since God knows us better than we know ourselves (1 Corinthians 11:28-32; 2 Corinthians 10:12). Indeed, we humans have a tendency toward self-deception (1 John 1:8). If God responds to prayer based on an assessment of need (and He does; see Matthew 6:8, 32), how much more are His responses in reaction to the direction of one's heart (13:58)!

The divine response follows a sequence that begins with an appeal for God to "hear"; this is a feature in ancient Israelite prayers (examples: Psalms 5:1; 27:7; 28:2; 54:2; 64:1; contrast 22:2; Lamentations 3:8, 44). Then God forgives, since a request for help usually accompanies self-assessment and turning away from sin. Then God acts appropriately. This sequence is relevant because the moral and spiritual ground must be cleared before action occurs.

At the same time, God does assess the *ways* of the person praying. Wicked people who defy God's call cannot utter legitimate prayers. That's because their intention is not to change their ways but to escape some immediate trial (see Proverbs 15:29; Isaiah 58:1-9; Hosea 6:1–7:16; 1 Timothy 2:8).

The verse also insists that God knows the thoughts of all people, not just Israelites. This insight leads to the expectation that Gentiles may also pray toward the temple and ask for God's help.

III. Inevitable Sin
(1 Kings 8:46, 48-50a)
A. Anger, Captivity, Exile (v. 46)

46. If they sin against thee, (for there is no man that sinneth not,) and thou be angry with them, and deliver them to the enemy, so that they carry them away captives unto the land of the enemy, far or near.

The prayer takes an important turn, assuming that the people may sin so grievously that the covenant might fail as the Israelites are removed from their promised land. This event did occur. However, the prediction goes beyond the curses for disobedience in Deuteronomy 28:15-68 to promises

How to Say It

apartheid	uh-*par*-tate.
Babylon	*Bab*-uh-lun.
Corinthians	Ko-*rin*-thee-unz (*th* as in *thin*).
Deuteronomy	Due-ter-*ahn*-uh-me.
Gentiles	*Jen*-tiles.
Mahatma Gandhi	Muh-*hot*-muh *Gone*-dee.
Septuagint	Sep-*too*-ih-jent.

of prosperity in Deuteronomy 30:1-10. These envision the loss of the land as a punishment, and the return to it as an effect of God's mercy, respectively. The relationship between Israel and God was not based on human achievement but on God's love and kindness.

So the prayer ends with a request that God will renew the people even after their communal sins have resulted in the curses of Deuteronomy 28:15-68. Even the collapse of their culture ought not to be the last word. God remains just and punishes sin, but He also shows mercy.

This verse should not be read as an excuse for sin. "God knows I'm human and will forgive me," a sentence often heard in Christian circles, is a statement of extreme arrogance and careless indifference to the moral and spiritual demands of faith. It is not a statement honoring God or taking human duties or capacities seriously. It distorts Solomon's point here. The prayer does not ask for cheap grace because it accepts the reality of punishment for sin.

> **What Do You Think?**
> Is it possible to know that a hardship is God's judgment in your life? Explain your answer with biblical evidence.
>
> **Digging Deeper**
> What danger does assuming another person's hardship is God's judgment pose to presenting the gospel?

B. Hear, Sustain, Forgive (vv. 48-50a)

48. And so return unto thee with all their heart and with all their soul, in the land of their enemies, which led them away captive, and pray unto thee toward their land, which thou gavest unto their fathers, the city which thou hast chosen, and the house which I have built for thy name.

This part of Solomon's prayer assumes that suffering will cause people to reflect on their lives and amend them. It also assumes that God will hear their prayers of repentance when uttered in a land of exile. This means, in turn, that God's presence is universal and that He is interested in the prayers of people seeking change and redemption.

The verse also reveals the idea of praying toward the temple in Jerusalem. It may be the earliest evidence for that practice. Much later, Daniel prayed, facing Jerusalem while in Babylon (Daniel 6:10). This practice shows how posture indicates the direction of the heart. A good (and bad) example of this is Ezekiel 8:16, which describes "about five and twenty men, with their backs toward the temple of the Lord, and their faces toward the east; and they worshipped the sun toward the east."

> **What Do You Think?**
> What does it look like to turn back to God with all your heart and soul?
>
> **Digging Deeper**
> Who do you trust to help you identify when you need to repent and return to the Lord?

49. Then hear thou their prayer and their supplication in heaven thy dwelling place, and maintain their cause.

It's one thing to *hear,* but another thing to *heed* (see the distinction in Ezekiel 33:4-5). We see both elements in this prayer, with the request to *maintain their cause* as the heeding part. The "cause" has been given to the Israelites by God; it is the very reason for the existence of their nation (Deuteronomy 7:6). Thus, the prayer ultimately is that God's will be done as the nation of Israel fulfills its divine purpose. And God is certainly interested in having His will done!

50a. And forgive thy people that have sinned against thee, and all their transgressions wherein they have transgressed against thee.

God takes no pleasure in our suffering, even when we have earned it (Ezekiel 18:32; 33:11). Spiritual reform sometimes results in suffering, since we need to eliminate certain attitudes and behaviors. But even the suffering draws the compassion of God and of righteous people. We hasten to add that neither this verse nor any other Bible text implies that all suffering is deserved. Much is not (compare Luke 13:1-5; John 9:1-3).

Forgiveness and Reconciliation

The collapse of the apartheid regime in South

Africa in the early 1990s could easily have resulted in revenge-filled ethnic warfare. We need to look no further than the Rwandan genocide of 1994 to see a brutal outcome to such a war. Yet this did not happen, in large part due to the work of South Africa's Truth and Reconciliation Commission in 1996.

Chaired by Desmond Tutu, the commission made a point to listen to the stories of victims and perpetrators alike. Both groups were encouraged to work through a process of forgiveness and reconciliation.

We should want both of those two things not only from others but also from God. Forgiveness and reconciliation involving one will often be inseparable from forgiveness and reconciliation involving the other. Which of these five passages convict you the most in that regard: Matthew 5:23-24; 6:14-15; 25:45; 1 Corinthians 8:12; and Colossians 3:13? Why?   —A. W.

What Do You Think?

What gives you confidence that God has forgiven your sins?

Digging Deeper

How do you offer the gift of forgiveness to others?

Conclusion

A. People as Sinners

One of the most puzzling features of prayer in the Bible occurs in this prayer at the dedication of the temple. Here, Solomon voiced the nation's prayer for forgiveness as part of its ongoing life together. In this case, Solomon prayed for forgiveness of sins that had not yet been committed!

In that regard, the prayer serves as a reflection on the entire history of Israel, from the time of the exodus of 1447 BC (481 years in the past as Solomon uttered this prayer) to Nebuchadnezzar's forced removal of the citizens of Judah in 586 BC (380 years after the prayer). For us to understand the prayer, we must place it within this larger context, the story of Israel in the promised land, covering the entire books of Joshua through 2 Kings. Both that history and Solomon's prayer reflect a realistic assessment of the human condition and the tendency of human beings to fail. The Bible does not try to pretend that a perfect, sinless time existed at some point after the Garden of Eden. Idolatry and oppression occurred regularly; they still do. Solomon's prayer foreshadowed the outcome found in 2 Kings 25. Even so, Israel's story, as recorded in the books of Joshua through 2 Kings, is not an obituary but a warning and an invitation to a better life.

B. God as Defender

Solomon's prayer rests on the assumption that God seeks to heal and forgive, even when (or especially when) sins threaten to overcome the sinners. God defends penitent people from those who would oppress them—and even from themselves. The worship by Old Testament Israel and the New Testament church celebrates the expansive nature of God's mercy. We are thereby reminded to beware of the traps that require it.

The prayer in 1 Kings 8 is, therefore, realistic but also hopeful. The dedication of the holiest spot on earth (at the time) was connected to the reality of unholiness. Solomon cast the nation of Israel as a whole on the mercy of God. In so doing, Solomon sought God's commitment to continue working with the people continuously as part of their centuries-long process of learning and obeying.

Today, the church would do well to recover the biblical practice of confession of sins, both of individuals and of the church as a whole. Part of that recovery would involve acknowledgment that the temptations to harm others or dishonor God do not go away. We will need forgiveness in the future, and we need humility in the present. Solomon's prayer shows us a way forward.

C. Prayer

God of mercy, Lord of love, hear the cries of all who need You. Even when our sins have trapped us in suffering, show us mercy. Do not let us be overwhelmed by our bad decisions or those of others. As Jesus called even those who betrayed Him to feed His sheep, call us into Your eternal kingdom. In Jesus' name, we pray. Amen.

D. Thought to Remember

Sin is real, but so is God's mercy.

Involvement Learning

Enhance your lesson with KJV Bible Student *(from your curriculum supplier) and the reproducible activity page (at www.standardlesson.com or in the back of the* KJV Standard Lesson Commentary Deluxe Edition*).*

Into the Lesson

Brainstorming. Ask learners to name things (not people) that are important to them. The responses can include physical items, good causes, intangible things that affect them, etc. Create a list on the board as responses are voiced. (You may wish to limit responses to one or two per person, depending on class size.)

Wrap up the brainstorming by saying, "Things that are important to us are usually dedicated to a specific purpose—one purpose and one purpose only." Then work through the list as a class to determine which entries are considered "dedicated" in this sense.

After a few minutes of discussion, say, "In our lesson, we are going to look at Solomon's dedication of the Jewish temple and think about what parallels there may be to 'dedications' today."

Into the Word

Ask three volunteers to read aloud the three segments of today's lesson text, one segment each. Then divide the class into three groups, designating them as the **Confession Group**, the **Disaster Group**, and the **Repentance Group**. Distribute handouts (you create) of the following questions.

Confession Group. Read 1 Kings 8:22-24. 1– In what posture was Solomon praying? 2–What did Solomon confess about God? 3–What was Solomon emphasizing about the Israelite's relationship with God?

Disaster Group. Read 1 Kings 8:37-39. 1– What did Solomon ask God to do in various circumstances? 2–What do these verses say about God's power? 3–What do these verses say about the people's relationship with God?

Repentance Group. Read 1 Kings 8:46, 48-50. 1–Under what circumstances was God requested to act mercifully? 2–What do these verses say about God? 3–What do these verses say about the people's relationship with God?

After allowing for eight minutes of discussion, reconvene for whole-class interaction. The answers to the questions should be obvious from the texts at hand. Talk through the different things that are in Solomon's prayer, including praise and submission to God, along with requests for the practical and spiritual needs of the people. Have on hand a dozen or so blank pieces of letter-size paper. Use them to list responses as participants voice them, one response per sheet of paper. Tape them to the board, arranging them in a way that results in an outline or structure of how Solomon prayed.

Into Life

Gesturing toward the outline just created, ask, "What elements in Solomon's prayer should we adopt into our own personal prayer lives?" Dig deeper by challenging every answer with a response that begins with "But what about . . . ?" Here are some *examples*: For a response regarding conclusions about Solomon's prayer posture, you could ask, "But what about his change in posture in 1 Kings 8:54?" For a response regarding conclusions about God's hearing of prayers, you could ask, "But what about times when God refuses to listen, as in Lamentations 3:8, 44?"

Stress at some point that although our meeting places for worship are not parallel to the temple as the ancient Israelites' meeting place for worship, we can still dedicate our church buildings for holy purposes. Allow learners one minute to write a simple prayer in that regard; allow an opportunity to share. *Option:* Dig deeper by distributing copies of the "Dedicating Your Temple" exercise from the activity page, which you can download. Allow work in triads to complete as indicated, followed by whole-class interaction.

Option. Distribute copies of the "Inspirational Places" exercise from the activity page. Have learners complete it individually in a minute or less. This can be a take-home if time is short.

Hezekiah's Prayer

Devotional Reading: Romans 8:29-39
Background Scripture: 2 Kings 19:1-34

2 Kings 19:14-20, 29-31

14 And Hezekiah received the letter of the hand of the messengers, and read it: and Hezekiah went up into the house of the LORD, and spread it before the LORD.

15 And Hezekiah prayed before the LORD, and said, O LORD God of Israel, which dwellest between the cherubims, thou art the God, even thou alone, of all the kingdoms of the earth; thou hast made heaven and earth.

16 LORD, bow down thine ear, and hear: open, LORD, thine eyes, and see: and hear the words of Sennacherib, which hath sent him to reproach the living God.

17 Of a truth, LORD, the kings of Assyria have destroyed the nations and their lands,

18 And have cast their gods into the fire: for they were no gods, but the work of men's hands, wood and stone: therefore they have destroyed them.

19 Now therefore, O LORD our God, I beseech thee, save thou us out of his hand, that all the kingdoms of the earth may know that thou art the LORD God, even thou only.

20 Then Isaiah the son of Amoz sent to Hezekiah, saying, Thus saith the LORD God of Israel, That which thou hast prayed to me against Sennacherib king of Assyria I have heard.

29 And this shall be a sign unto thee, Ye shall eat this year such things as grow of themselves, And in the second year that which springeth of the same; And in the third year sow ye, and reap, And plant vineyards, and eat the fruits thereof.

30 And the remnant that is escaped of the house of Judah Shall yet again take root downward, and bear fruit upward.

31 For out of Jerusalem shall go forth a remnant, And they that escape out of mount Zion: The zeal of the LORD of hosts shall do this.

Key Text

O LORD our God, I beseech thee, save thou us out of his hand, that all the kingdoms of the earth may know that thou art the LORD God, even thou only. —2 Kings 19:19

Worship in the
Covenant Community

Unit 1: Leaders Set Worship Example
Lessons 1–5

Lesson Aims

After participating in this lesson, each learner will be able to:

1. Explain the historical circumstance behind Hezekiah's prayer.

2. Distinguish Hezekiah's response to God from the responses of other Old Testament kings.

3. Create a plan to respond to any crisis with immediate prayer to the Lord.

Lesson Outline

Introduction

A. "Spare Tire" Prayer Life?

Have you ever heard of a "spare tire" prayer life? A person with such a prayer life uses prayer just as people use spare tires—only in emergencies.

The *how*, *when*, and *why* of a Christian's prayers constitute a major indicator of his or her spiritual maturity. A spiritually healthy individual has a regular (daily) practice of prayer that draws heavily on Scripture. Such a prayer life begins by listening to God through His written Word. The spiritually mature Christian realizes that prayer is less about talking and more about listening to what God has already said. There's no sense in seeking God's approval on, say, an adulterous relationship since God has already said, "Thou shalt not commit adultery" (Exodus 20:14; compare Matthew 5:27-30).

God will not answer certain types of prayers in a positive way—or even at all (examples: Psalm 18:41; James 4:3). We must ask according to His will (1 John 5:14-15). These facts apply to times of crisis as well—today's lesson.

B. Lesson Context

The reign of godly King Hezekiah (716–687 BC) over the southern kingdom of Judah was a time of trouble. Previously, in 722 BC, the Assyrian Empire had annexed the northern kingdom of Israel along with areas to the north and east of it. In 702 BC, the Assyrian ruler Sennacherib invaded Judah, destroyed the major city of Lachish, and besieged Jerusalem itself (the two cities being about 30 miles apart). Jerusalem survived only after Hezekiah agreed to pay tribute to the Assyrian king (2 Kings 18:13–19:13; 2 Chronicles 32:1-19; Isaiah 36:1–37:13).

The account in today's printed text also appears in Isaiah 37, almost word for word. This double placement reflects the close relationship between the king and the prophet, which appears in the story itself.

The text under consideration reports a conversation between Hezekiah and God, with the prophet Isaiah as the go-between. In 2 Kings 19:1-5, the king sent messengers to the prophet asking for his help communicating with God. Isaiah's answer promised that God would create a distraction to the Assyrians (19:6-7). The blasphemous and arrogant statements by the Assyrians did not help their cause (19:8-13)!

Texts that are parallel to those in today's lesson are Isaiah 37:14-20, 30-32, and 2 Chronicles 32:20. On the godly character of King Hezekiah, see 2 Kings 18:1-8.

I. Hezekiah's Prayer
(2 Kings 19:14-19)
A. Preparation (v. 14)

14a. And Hezekiah received the letter of the hand of the messengers, and read it.

The contents of *the letter* that *Hezekiah received* are found in 2 Kings 19:10-13. The letter is only about 100 words long in English and 60 in Hebrew; its contents are threatening. The hostile sender was Sennacherib of Assyria. Being able to read and write was unusual at the time, although Israel's leaders apparently were all literate (Deuteronomy 17:18-19; compare and contrast 2 Samuel 11:14; 2 Kings 5:4-7; 10:2-7; Jeremiah 36:11-15).

14b. And Hezekiah went up into the house of the LORD, and spread it before the LORD.

The house of the Lord is the temple in Jerusalem. The point of departure for King *Hezekiah* regarding the task we see here was likely his nearby palace. The phrase *went up* when referring to travel to the temple was generally accurate, as the temple sat at a higher elevation than most other landmarks (compare Isaiah 37:14; Jeremiah 26:10).

The fact that Hezekiah *spread* the letter *before*

How to Say It

Adonai (Hebrew)	Ad-owe-*nye*.
Amoz	*Ay*-mahz.
anthropomorphic	*an*-thruh-puh-**more**-fik.
cherubims	*chair*-uh-bimz.
Elohim (Hebrew)	El-o-*heem*.
Hezekiah	Hez-ih-*kye*-uh.
Sennacherib	Sen-*nack*-er-ib.
Shearjashub	*She*-are-*jah*-shub.
Yahweh (Hebrew)	*Yah*-weh.

the Lord implies that the king asked God to read it and respond in a way that reflected Israel's place as God's people of the covenant. While 2 Chronicles 23:6 confirms that only the priests were to enter the temple, it's hard to believe that the phrasing here means that Hezekiah stood outside that building. Emergency situations call for unusual measures (compare Luke 6:3-4)!

> **What Do You Think?**
> What prevents you from going to God in prayer when you receive disturbing communications?
> **Digging Deeper**
> What first step could you take to make this a habit?

B. Adoration (v. 15)

15a. And Hezekiah prayed before the LORD, and said, O LORD God of Israel, which dwellest between the cherubims.

Hezekiah's prayer invites us to reflect on God's names. At the most foundational level, you may find it surprising that God is known by three single-word names. When they are transliterated —that's where you swap letters of the Hebrew alphabet for similar-sounding letters in English —those three names are *Yahweh*, *Elohim*, and *Adonai*. But what about all those lists on the internet that claim "16 names of God," "God's 20 names," etc.? Most entries in such lists consist of one of the three names mentioned above combined with a descriptor (examples: "the living God" in Joshua 3:10; "a jealous God" in Deuteronomy 4:24; 5:9; 6:15). In the text at hand, the phrase *O Lord God* translates both the names *Yahweh* and *Elohim*. The longer phrase *Lord God of Israel* adds a descriptor; that exact phrase is not rare—it occurs in more than a hundred places in the Old Testament.

Another descriptor is added with God's dwelling between the cherubims (compare 1 Samuel 4:4). The creatures known by that designation are mentioned dozens of times in the Old Testament. The most familiar discussion of cherubims is in conjunction with the ark of the covenant and

Lord, show that
You are King!

Visual for Lesson 3. *Discuss with learners what it might look like for the Lord to demonstrate His kingship in your community.*

the place to meet with God (Exodus 25:17-22; 37:6-9). The word translated "dwellest" can refer to a place where someone in authority sits, such as a throne or judgment seat (examples: Exodus 18:13-14; Deuteronomy 1:4; Judges 4:5; 1 Kings 1:46-48; 2:12, 19). The idea that God figuratively dwells in a place on earth is reflected in Exodus 15:17; 1 Kings 8:13; Psalms 132:13-14; 135:21; and Matthew 23:21. Affirming that this concept is not intended to be interpreted in a literal sense are 1 Kings 8:27, 30, 39, 43, 49; and Acts 17:24.

15b. Thou art the God, even thou alone, of all the kingdoms of the earth; thou hast made heaven and earth.

King Sennacherib of Assyria had claimed that other nations and their gods were powerless to stop his army (2 Kings 18:19-35). However, Hezekiah knew that the only true God was indeed God *of all the kingdoms of the earth.* This status necessarily derives from His role as Creator. The phrase *thou hast made heaven and earth* is reminiscent of Genesis 1:1. But Hezekiah was not quoting that passage. Rather, the text shows the idea that all things are part of the Lord's creation and, therefore, all things are subject to the Lord. Creation implies ownership. That idea lay at the heart of Israel's confession.

C. Supplication, Part 1 (v. 16)

16. LORD, bow down thine ear, and hear; open, LORD, thine eyes, and see; and hear the words of Sennacherib, which hath sent him to reproach the living God.

The language here is anthropomorphic, which means attributing human characteristics (having *ear, eyes,* etc.) to God. He knows all things, of course (Psalms 139:2; 147:5; Hebrews 4:13; 1 John 3:20). Psalms of lament frequently ask God to hear the petitioner's cry (examples: Psalms 4:1; 64:1) or to look at a situation (examples: 35:17, 22; 53:2). Sometimes He chooses to react positively on that awareness (Exodus 3:7), sometimes in a negative way (Jeremiah 7:16-20).

To reproach the living God is to mock, taunt, or ridicule Him. Sennacherib did this through his officer (2 Kings 18:35; 2 Chronicles 32:16-17; compare 1 Samuel 17). Could there be a greater blasphemy?

D. Agreement (vv. 17-18)

17-18. Of a truth, LORD, the kings of Assyria have destroyed the nations and their lands, and have cast their gods into the fire: for they were no gods, but the work of men's hands, wood and stone: therefore they have destroyed them.

Sennacherib was at least partly right: *the kings of Assyria* had indeed *destroyed the nations and their lands* (2 Kings 17–18). Since the Assyrians had been able to do this, it logically follows that the *gods* of the conquered nations were powerless, therefore, fit only for *the fire* (compare Deuteronomy 4:28; Isaiah 44:9; Acts 17:29). The fact that an invader could destroy the idols proved their impotence. On this point, Hezekiah agrees with Sennacherib! But then the question was whether Sennacherib could defeat the Lord.

> **What Do You Think?**
> What are the modern "gods" of your society?
> **Digging Deeper**
> How does your church guard against being seduced by these gods?

The Non-Gods of Kiev

Have you ever heard of Perun? What about Dazhbog, Stribog, or Veles? Unless you have studied pre-Christian Ukrainian history, it's unlikely that you have. These were the main deities worshipped in Kievan Rus, the precursor state to both Ukraine and Russia, until AD 988. For millennia, such fictitious gods were believed to control the weather, agriculture, fertility, and wealth. But all those prayers and sacrifices fell on deaf ears and eyes of idols of wood, stone, and metal (compare Isaiah 44:9-20).

Things changed when Prince Vladimir I rose to the throne of Kiev. Wanting to unite his kingdom under a single religion, he attempted to convert his people to Orthodox Christianity. But old ways were hard to break. When the population resisted, he ordered that idols of the old gods be thrown into the river—and their die-hard supporters after them. Despite such a wrong-headed conversion method, Christianity eventually became deeply rooted in Ukraine. The gods of wood, stone, and metal were forgotten.

Everyone worships something. Those who think that statement to be untrue are worshipping themselves; they have placed themselves on the thrones of their own hearts. Today, we may not see many people bowing to idols of wood and stone, but that doesn't mean that the problem of idolatry is nonexistent. The main problem is idols of the heart (compare Ezekiel 14:1-11). Where are you most in danger of slipping into such idolatry?
—A. W.

E. Supplication, Part 2 (v. 19)

19. Now therefore, O LORD our God, I beseech thee, save thou us out of his hand, that all the kingdoms of the earth may know that thou art the LORD God, even thou only.

Hezekiah closed his prayer with the desire that *God* would triumph over the invaders. Sennacherib had rightly claimed to be superior in his encounters with foreign powers. Nevertheless, the survival of Jerusalem would prove the superiority of Judah's God to all others.

Hezekiah wished all the nations to know about that superiority. This theme appears at many points in the Old Testament when Israel sought (or should have sought) to extol God before the Gentiles (1 Kings 8:41-43; 1 Chronicles 16:23-29;

Isaiah 49:6). But Israel would not succeed in that task unless the nation stopped profaning the name of *the Lord* in the sight of *the kingdoms of the earth* (Ezekiel 20:9, 14, 22; 36:20-23; 39:7).

What Do You Think?
Is God's glory diminished if He does not choose to deliver you from difficult situations? Explain your answer.

Digging Deeper
How can you give God glory in situations from which you have not experienced the relief of deliverance?

Leave It on God's Desk

Lena set to work with her usual diligence when her boss asked her to compile a report of recent sales data. As she looked at the figures, she began to realize the serious financial condition of the company. So she went beyond what her boss asked her to do and compiled a second report. It featured recommendations for fixing the problem.

As she placed both reports on her boss's desk, doubts entered Lena's mind. She had a nagging feeling her second report would anger her boss, resulting in it being ignored or—worse—misapplied. So she spent the next couple of weeks fretting and losing sleep.

Noticing this change in demeanor, Lena's boss correctly guessed the cause. So he called her in and said, "Thank you, Lena. I knew I could count on you to go above and beyond. And I know how much you care about the company and your coworkers. But keep in mind that once you put something on my desk, you must trust me to react appropriately. Your job is just to bring it to me."

Lena's problem was that she had tried—perhaps subconsciously—to take the boss's responsibility onto herself, being unsure that he would do the right things. How often do we spread out our problems before God but then don't quite believe that a right outcome will result? After we have done our part (compare Isaiah 6:8), let us, like Jesus, become comfortable praying, "Not my will, but thine, be done" (Luke 22:42).
—A. W.

II. God's Response
(2 Kings 19:20, 29-31)
A. Prayer Heard (v. 20)

20. Then Isaiah the son of Amoz sent to Hezekiah, saying, Thus saith the LORD God of Israel, That which thou hast prayed to me against Sennacherib king of Assyria I have heard.

The material in the eight verses following this one gives God's full response to Hezekiah's request. The verse at hand is the preface to those eight; it notifies Hezekiah that God has *heard*. For God to "hear" also implies a willingness to "heed" (compare and contrast Matthew 13:13-15, quoting Isaiah 6:9-10).

> **What Do You Think?**
>
> How do you usually pray for leaders in your nation? allied countries? hostile regions?
>
> **Digging Deeper**
>
> What would change if you shifted the focus of your prayers regarding help for or judgment of these leaders?

B. Sign Promised (vv. 29-31)

29. And this shall be a sign unto thee, ye shall eat this year such things as grow of themselves, and in the second year that which springeth of the same, and in the third year sow ye, and reap, and plant vineyards, and eat the fruits thereof.

This part of Hezekiah's prayer is the other bookend to 2 Kings 19:21-28. Those verses taunt the Assyrian king, throwing his boasts of conquest back in his face.

The eventual defeat of the Assyrian army would mean a return to normal agriculture over time. The Assyrians were adept at siege warfare (2 Kings 17:5), and this time-consuming tactic led to the destruction of vineyards, orchards, etc., as the invaders foraged and otherwise lived off the land during the siege. A liberated land therefore required time to restore agriculture.

The first two years depicted here echo Leviticus 25:5. These two years would require faith as

survivors of the war scrambled for food. Faith requires long-term thinking. Surely this points to God's profound care for the people of Jerusalem and Judah! Their nation would survive one of the most desperate moments in their long history, despite all earthly odds.

30. And the remnant that is escaped of the house of Judah shall yet again take root downward, and bear fruit upward.

By referring to *the remnant*, God's response acknowledged that not all Judeans would escape what was to come. Yet a kernel of the nation would survive and flourish (Zephaniah 2:6-7). The verse before us, therefore, moves from an earthly sense of the text just before it to one of projecting imagery that includes spiritual robustness (compare Isaiah 11). The prophet Isaiah even named his son Shearjashub, which means "a remnant will return" (Isaiah 7:3; compare 10:21-22). This concept is so important that it has given rise to a subfield of study today known as the "doctrine of the remnant."

31a. For out of Jerusalem shall go forth a remnant.

Here we see an instance of parallelism that characterizes Hebrew poetry. The use of parallelism is evident in the repetition of similar ideas using different yet connected words. Thus "the house of Judah" from the previous verse parallels *Jerusalem* here. The identical English words *remnant* in these two verses hides the fact that the words are different in Hebrew—one being a verb, the other being a noun.

31b. And they that escape out of mount Zion.

The parallelism continues, with *they that escape* reflecting the previous two instances of "remnant." *Mount Zion,* for its part, is parallel to the previous "house of Judah" and "Jerusalem."

31c. The zeal of the LORD of hosts shall do this.

In addition to the parallel text of Isaiah 37:32, this phrase is reflected in Isaiah 9:7. The *Lord of hosts* designation is one of the combination name-and-descriptors discussed earlier. Interestingly, the word *zealous* is virtually synonymous with the word *jealous*. We usually think of jealousy as a negative thing. But it can be positive when the fervency (zeal) is appropriately motivated and informed. We see the positive side in John 2:17 (quoting Psalm 69:9) and the opposite in Philippians 3:6 (compare and contrast Zechariah 8:2).

Conclusion

A. ACTS in Action

This account reveals a faithful leader seeking God's help on behalf of an entire nation during a time of great crisis. This aspect of spiritual leadership remains relevant. Asking for God's help is still an important part of such leadership. The threat may come from many directions, but it often comes from those who aspire to control others involuntarily. The leader must be alert to such a danger and align the people's hopes with God's desires, as Hezekiah did.

One way to do this is via the ACTS method of prayer. This acronym speaks to a four-stage prayer pattern:

Adoration: Recognizing God for who He is;
Confession: Admitting one's sins;
Thanksgiving: Expressing gratitude for God's blessings already received;
Supplication: Requesting God's intervention or blessings.

This pattern, with various emphases, is seen in Hezekiah's prayer. Such prayers often come naturally to people who believe God can help them in crisis, assuming that God has no reason to dismiss such prayers (contrast Lamentations 3:8, 44; Ezekiel 8:18; 1 Peter 3:7). Indeed, in today's text, God answered promptly and positively.

But supplication in and of itself isn't the whole of the ACTS-pattern prayer battle; it's only one-fourth. A vital part of the ACTS prayer pattern is ensuring some balance among its four aspects. The prayer lives of many Christians lack such a balance. That deficiency is seen when we spend most of our prayer time asking for things (supplication), with little time spent in adoration, confession, and thanksgiving.

Consider Hezekiah's prayer again: he didn't start with his plea for help; he started with adoration. Then he moved to recognition of sin—

Assyria's sin of blasphemy. We may think that "confession" involves only one's personal sin, but the Bible witnesses to corporate confession as well (Leviticus 16:21; 26:40; Ezra 10:1; etc.).

Moving to the aspect of thanksgiving, this is difficult to detect in this singular prayer of Hezekiah. But thanking God was a big part of Israelite prayer practices (1 Chronicles 16:34, 41); a prayer of King David witnesses to all four ACTS elements (29:10). Returning to the aspect of supplication, another challenge in this area is to pray with right motives. Such motives align with God's stated will (Matthew 6:10; James 4:3, 15).

A further challenge is not to use prayer as a spare tire—"only in emergencies"! Today many Christians face crises of persecution, famine, political unrest, injustice, etc. It's important to pray for issues that affect the body (James 5:14-15), but this is where the "emergency, spare tire" practice seems to reveal itself the most.

A Christian once counted the prayers and their nature as he sat through 10 weeks of an adult Bible class. When the 10 weeks were up, he analyzed the resulting 133 prayers to see patterns. He discovered that every prayer could be categorized in one of three ways: prayers for bodily healing or preservation of life (97 prayer requests); prayers for "situations" such as grief, marriage, and job loss (33 requests); and prayers for spiritual issues (3 requests). Contrast that with what Jesus had to say about prayer in Matthew 6:5-15.

> **What Do You Think?**
> Can you identify disparities concerning the 10-week examination and your personal prayer experience?
> **Digging Deeper**
> What change could you make to be more in line with Jesus' teaching?

B. Prayer

Father, may we pray with right motives and right priorities! In Jesus' name we pray. Amen.

C. Thought to Remember

Pray with one desire: that God's will be done.

Involvement Learning

Enhance your lesson with KJV Bible Student *(from your curriculum supplier) and the reproducible activity page (at www.standardlesson.com or in the back of the* KJV Standard Lesson Commentary Deluxe Edition*).*

Into the Lesson

Brainstorming. Announce that you desire the learners' advice for the "crisis response kit" you are creating for your household. Ask what should go into such a kit. Jot responses on the board.

After a few minutes, direct attention one of two ways, depending on whether or not anyone mentioned *prayer* as a necessity for a household's crisis response kit.

- If prayer was *not* mentioned, say, "It's natural to think in terms of [name some items listed on the board] and other items of a physical nature. But why isn't prayer included?"
- If prayer *was* mentioned, say, "It's a good thing to have prayer in our crisis response kit. But if we pray only or primarily in a crisis, what does that say about our spiritual maturity?"

Allow a few minutes for responses and reactions to your question. Use this as a transition point to introduce the crisis-prayer of Hezekiah.

Into the Word

Ask a learner to read 2 Kings 19:14-19. Then invite someone else to read 19:20, 29-31. Set the historical stage for these passages by explaining the setting as set forth in the Lesson Context.

Introduce the in-depth study by asking a participant to be a "scribe"; ask your scribe to stand at the board as elements of Hezekiah's prayer will be compared and contrasted with God's responses.

Begin the compare/contrast by reading again 2 Kings 19:14-19 slowly. As those six verses are read, encourage class members to voice salient points. If participants are slow in starting, suggest they think in terms of what Hezekiah *thought, said,* and/or *did.* (Don't be too hasty in offering this suggestion; allow 15 seconds of silence for learners to wrestle with the task.) Do the same with 19:20, 29-31.

With salient points listed on the board for both sections of the text, move to compare/contrast by saying, "Next, we will examine which aspects of Hezekiah's prayer ended up being addressed specifically by God, which aspects of God's response went above and beyond what Hezekiah requested, and which aspects, if any, of the king's prayer did not draw a response from God."

Logistical notes: If you are using a whiteboard, have your scribe use erasable markers of differing colors for the cross-connections between elements of the two sections of text. If using a chalkboard, use connecting lines of different types (dotted, dashed, etc.). This exercise can also be accomplished in small groups, depending on the size of your class. In that case, create handouts appropriate for the task. *Recommended:* Best learning will occur if you, the teacher, have studied the entirety of 2 Kings 19 thoroughly beforehand.

Option. For deeper study on how God does and does not respond to prayers, distribute copies of the "Four Outcomes of Prayer" exercise from the activity page, which you can download. Form learners into study pairs to complete as indicated. For faster completion, one person in the pair can look up the Old Testament texts while the other looks up the New Testament ones. Reconvene for a whole-class discussion of results.

Into Life

Draw participants' attention back to the "crisis response kit" with which you opened the lesson. Then form study pairs or triads to propose a plan to respond to any crisis with immediate prayer to the Lord. Challenge them to state their plan in terms of what a prayer in a time of crisis *must* include, what it *should* include, and what it *could* include. (*Option.* Using small groups for this task is ideal, time permitting; during ensuing whole-class discussion, groups can "debate" one another regarding the must, should, and could elements.)

Option. As learners depart, distribute copies of "Hezekiah's Prayer Scramble" as a take-home.

Josiah Celebrates Passover

Devotional Reading: 2 Chronicles 34:8, 14-27
Background Scripture: 2 Kings 22–23; 2 Chronicles 34:1–35:19

2 Chronicles 35:1-6, 16-19

1 Moreover Josiah kept a passover unto the LORD in Jerusalem: and they killed the passover on the fourteenth day of the first month.

2 And he set the priests in their charges, and encouraged them to the service of the house of the LORD,

3 And said unto the Levites that taught all Israel, which were holy unto the LORD, Put the holy ark in the house which Solomon the son of David king of Israel did build; it shall not be a burden upon your shoulders: serve now the LORD your God, and his people Israel,

4 And prepare yourselves by the houses of your fathers, after your courses, according to the writing of David king of Israel, and according to the writing of Solomon his son.

5 And stand in the holy place according to the divisions of the families of the fathers of your brethren the people, and after the division of the families of the Levites.

6 So kill the passover, and sanctify yourselves, and prepare your brethren, that they may do according to the word of the LORD by the hand of Moses.

16 So all the service of the LORD was prepared the same day, to keep the passover, and to offer burnt offerings upon the altar of the LORD, according to the commandment of king Josiah.

17 And the children of Israel that were present kept the passover at that time, and the feast of unleavened bread seven days.

18 And there was no passover like to that kept in Israel from the days of Samuel the prophet; neither did all the kings of Israel keep such a passover as Josiah kept, and the priests, and the Levites, and all Judah and Israel that were present, and the inhabitants of Jerusalem.

19 In the eighteenth year of the reign of Josiah was this passover kept.

Key Text

Josiah kept a passover unto the LORD in Jerusalem: and they killed the passover on the fourteenth day of the first month. —**2 Chronicles 35:1**

Worship in the
Covenant Community

Unit 1: Leaders Set Worship Example
Lessons 1–5

Lesson Aims

After participating in this lesson, each learner will be able to:

1. Explain the setting and guidelines for the first Passover celebration mentioned in Exodus 12.

2. Evaluate the significance of Josiah's renewal of the Passover observance for Israel's ongoing relationship with God.

3. Create a plan to revitalize one neglected spiritual practice.

Lesson Outline

Introduction
    A. Rituals or Ritualism?
    B. Lesson Context
 I. **Preparation (2 Chronicles 35:1-6)**
    A. Decision Made (v. 1a)
    B. Date Designated (v. 1b)
    C. Priests Assigned (v. 2)
      The Power of Encouragement
    D. Levites Instructed (vv. 3-6)
 II. **Celebration (2 Chronicles 35:16-19)**
    A. By an Order (v. 16)
    B. With a Feast (v. 17)
    C. In Comparison (vv. 18-19)
      Regarding Influencers
Conclusion
    A. Embracing Rituals
    B. Prayer
    C. Thought to Remember

Introduction
A. Rituals or Ritualism?

When you hear or read the word *ritual,* is your immediate reaction positive or negative? Chances are your first reaction is negative, as the word *ritual* conjures up mental images of tedious formal ceremonies that bear little relevance to reality. We may also think rituals are just "going through the motions" of a periodic observance, where one's thoughts and attitude don't match one's actions while the ritual is underway (examples: Isaiah 29:13; Mark 7:6-8).

But aren't celebrations of birthdays, anniversaries, graduations, etc., rituals in a good sense? Perhaps we can move toward clarity by distinguishing between *ritual* as a good thing and *ritualism* as a bad thing. We humans need ritual, in its best sense, for the formation and flourishing of our relationships. Rightly practiced, rituals help us remember the past as it explains the present and helps us plan wisely for the future (example: 1 Corinthians 11:23-26). Regarding our worship of God, rituals only have meaning if they are followed with obedience to God (examples: Isaiah 1:11-17; 1 Corinthians 7:19). Further, ritualism without discernment risks placing a person under divine judgment (example: 11:27-30)

God knows our need for ritual. That's why He established annual feasts (Exodus 23:17; etc.) for the Old Testament covenant people. Today's study examines the renewed practice of one such ritual.

B. Lesson Context

Today's lesson takes us to the year 623 BC, "the eighteenth year of the reign of Josiah," king of Judah (2 Chronicles 35:19). That moves us forward some 336 years after King Solomon's dedication of the temple in 959 BC (lesson 2) and 79 years after King Hezekiah's prayer in 702 BC (lesson 3). The year 623 BC positions the events of today's lesson right at 100 years since the Assyrian Empire cast Israel's 10 northern tribes into exile in 722 BC (2 Kings 17). Unbeknownst to the Judeans of the time, their removal from the land lay only 37 years in the future (that is, 586 BC).

The 31-year reign of Josiah (641–609 BC) over the southern kingdom of Judah was a time of respite from the consequences of sin. This was a direct result of Josiah's godly leadership (2 Chronicles 34:2-7). In the process of purifying the land and renovating the temple, a certain priest found "a book of the law of the Lord given by Moses" (34:14). Some today believe this to have been a copy of Deuteronomy (see terminology in Deuteronomy 29:21; 30:10; 31:26).

King Josiah was shaken to his core when he heard the book read (2 Chronicles 34:19). He acted immediately, receiving both bad and good news in return (34:20-28). Even so, he continued to exercise godly leadership in both word and deed (34:29-33). His leadership included reinstituting the celebration of the Passover. This neglected feast had been instituted more than 800 years previously to mark the divine liberation from Egyptian slavery (Exodus 12; Deuteronomy 16:1-2). The feast's revival is a focus of today's lesson.

I. Preparation
(2 Chronicles 35:1-6)
A. Decision Made (v. 1a)

1a. Moreover Josiah kept a passover unto the LORD in Jerusalem.

The beginning of this verse and the beginning of 2 Chronicles 35:19 form the bookends of this account. The celebration of *passover* in this text was not only an act of obedience to the Law of Moses, but it was also an act of covenant renewal (see Lesson Context). Passover had not been celebrated for some time—or at least not in the manner that King *Josiah* intended to celebrate it (2 Chronicles 35:18; compare 30:5b). Hezekiah, who reigned over Judah from 716 to 687 BC, celebrated an extended Passover after he had renovated and reopened the temple (29:3–30:27).

Both observances, one by Hezekiah and the other by Josiah, are detailed for the readers of Chronicles (compare the much more condensed version in 2 Kings 23:22-23). And both were held *in Jerusalem*, the place where God put his name (Deuteronomy 16:5-7).

Celebrate God's work.

Visual for Lesson 4. *At the beginning of class, point to this visual and ask learners to provide examples of ways to celebrate God's work.*

B. Date Designated (v. 1b)

1b. And they killed the passover on the fourteenth day of the first month.

The statement *they killed the passover* becomes clearer when we realize that the writer is talking about the Passover lamb (Exodus 12:21). With the phrase *on the fourteenth day of the first month* (that is, sometime in late March or early April), the writer presents this Passover celebration as firmly rooted in the Law of Moses (Exodus 12:6; Numbers 28:16; Deuteronomy 16:1-2). Decades earlier, King Hezekiah deviated from the stipulation regarding *the first month,* but he had good reasons for doing so (2 Chronicles 30:1-20).

The record of Hezekiah's Passover observances in 2 Chronicles 30 and Josiah's Passover in 2 Chronicles 35 invited the postexilic readers of Chronicles (536 BC and later) to renew the observance of Passover and reaffirm their covenant with God. The Passover celebrations of Hezekiah and Josiah were rooted in the state of the two men's hearts (2 Chronicles 29:2; 34:1-2).

C. Priests Assigned (v. 2)

2. And he set the priests in their charges, and encouraged them to the service of the house of the LORD.

King Josiah established the agenda. We may look with great skepticism at church-and-state combinations today, but not so in ancient Israel. Here we see a king (a civic ruler) authorizing and directing *priests* (religious leaders) in their forthcoming role. Josiah placed the total weight of the monarchy behind the priestly *service,* as King Hezekiah had done (2 Chronicles 31:19-21).

The word *charges* reflects the idea of "tasks" or "responsibilities." Regarding those responsibilities and the arrangement of the priesthood, see 1 Chronicles 24:1-19; 2 Chronicles 13:11; 23:6. The word translated *encouraged* occurs dozens of times in Chronicles, revealing its importance to the author. It speaks of "strengthening" (examples: 2 Chronicles 32:5, 7).

What Do You Think?

How can you encourage those who have devoted themselves to full-time ministry in the church?

Digging Deeper

How will you also encourage those who volunteer in the church but are not full-time ministers or staff members?

The Power of Encouragement

The year was 1991. The Buffalo Bills and the New York Giants were down to the last eight seconds of Super Bowl XXV. The Giants were ahead 20–19 when the Bills' kicker Scott Norwood lined up to attempt a 47-yard field goal. Norwood was no amateur. In 1985, he beat out nine other kickers in training camp to win his spot playing for Buffalo.

The next day's headline said it all: "Wide and to the right: The kick that will forever haunt Scott Norwood." The Giants celebrated, the Bills groaned, and Scott walked off the field with a sagging spirit.

Friends rallied with letters of cheer. They offered sage advice about one kick not being the measure of his life. They reminded him of his achievements. But Norwood was tormented by mental replays of the kick. When the Bills returned to Buffalo, he wanted to melt into the background at a reception at city hall. He had let down his fans. To his surprise, however, people in the crowd of more than 25,000 held signs of support as they chanted, "We want Scott!"

Disappointments are part of the human experience. But encouragement from other people can reverse the sting of disappointment and regret. Perhaps this is where Josiah took a page from Hezekiah's playbook (compare 2 Chronicles 30:22 with 35:2). Will you?   —A. W.

D. Levites Instructed (vv. 3-6)

3a. And said unto the Levites that taught all Israel, which were holy unto the LORD.

It's helpful to recall at this point that all priests are *Levites,* but not all Levites are priests (compare Deuteronomy 17:9, 18; 18:1; 21:5; 1 Kings 12:31). Since the Levites had a teaching role in Israel, the priests had that role as well (Nehemiah 8:9). These teachers were responsible for guiding *Israel* in the lawful conduct of the nation's rituals. For that role and others, the Levites were expected to lead the way in being personally *holy unto the Lord.* To be holy is to be "consecrated" or "set apart" (1 Chronicles 15:11-14).

3b. Put the holy ark in the house which Solomon the son of David king of Israel did build.

This text begins with the first of a series of directives to the Levites. The reference to the need to *put the holy ark in the* temple recalls the initial placement of the ark there, some 336 years earlier (see Lesson Context and 2 Chronicles 5:2-10). *David* reigned from 1010 to 970 BC, with his son *Solomon* reigning from 970 to 931 BC after him.

We do not know why the ark was no longer in the temple, but the culprit was probably evil King Amon, who reigned over Judah from 643 to 641 BC. The ark of the covenant was necessary for a complete reformation of the temple service. The temple was the resting place for the ark because God dwelt in it and was enthroned on the ark's cherubim (1 Chronicles 13:6; 28:2; 2 Chronicles 6:41). The ark represented the presence of God, and it also symbolized God's commitment to Israel.

3c. It shall not be a burden upon your shoulders.

The Levites were the only ones authorized to carry the ark (Deuteronomy 10:8; 31:9; 1 Chronicles 15:2). The original instructions were that they were indeed to carry the ark on their *shoulders* via poles (15:15). Thus, Josiah's directive here seems curious. Perhaps he was aware of the first disastrous attempt to transport the ark to Jerusalem (2 Samuel 6:1-7) and misunderstood what had caused the disaster.

3d. Serve now the LORD your God, and his people Israel.

The Levites served *God* by carrying out their duties per those listed in 1 Chronicles 23:28-31. These duties changed when the immovable temple replaced the portable tabernacle (1 Chronicles 23:25-26).

4-5. And prepare yourselves by the houses of your fathers, after your courses, according to the writing of David king of Israel, and according to the writing of Solomon his son. And stand in the holy place according to the divisions of the families of the fathers of your brethren the people, and after the division of the families of the Levites.

The Levites were to prepare themselves for service by organizing themselves by their respective clans based on *the houses of* their ancestors. *David king of Israel* provided a list of these clans in 1 Chronicles 23:6-23, and *Solomon his son* followed the same pattern as documented in 2 Chronicles 8:14. Levites, like priests, rotated their service according to the *divisions* of their ancestral *families* per 1 Chronicles 24 (compare Luke 1:8).

What Do You Think?
How do you prepare yourself and your family to be attentive to God's direction during worship services?

Digging Deeper
How do you deal with distractions that might prevent you from serving God?

6a. So kill the passover.

The verse outlines three instructions along with the rationale for their implementation. Regarding the phrase *kill the passover*, see commentary on 2 Chronicles 35:1, above. More explicit guidelines regarding the Passover lamb are found in Exodus 12:1-28.

6b. And sanctify yourselves.

Priests and Levites had been expected to *sanctify* themselves for their tasks for Hezekiah's Passover several decades earlier (2 Chronicles 30:3, 15).

Since this was only one of several tasks assigned to them, they were required to purify themselves following the sacrifice. This was an issue of setting a person or thing apart for a sacred task, rooted in the original sanctification of Aaron, his sons, and their priestly line (Exodus 29; Leviticus 8:1-6).

6c. And prepare your brethren, that they may do according to the word of the LORD by the hand of Moses.

The first four words in this partial verse translate an uncertainty in the original Hebrew text. This kind of uncertainty is known as a textual variant. Some manuscripts have wording that translates as what the Levites were to do to prepare their *brethren;* others have wording that translates the text as directives for preparing the sacrificial Passover lamb for those fellow Judeans.

Turning to the ancient Greek translation of the Old Testament (the Septuagint) doesn't help. The English translation of this partial verse contains the phrase, "Prepare *it* for your brethren, to do according to the word of the Lord, by the hand of Moses." The italicized nature of the word *it* indicates that that word is not present in the text being translated from the Septuagint. Instead, the translators have added the word *it* for smooth reading. Both ideas—of preparing fellow Judeans and preparing Passover lambs for those Judeans—are present elsewhere in the text, so there's no new information added either way.

In Exodus 12:1-11, 21 and Deuteronomy 16:1-

How to Say It

Assyrian	Uh-*sear*-e-un.
Corinthians	Ko-*rin*-thee-unz (*th* as in *thin*).
Deuteronomy	Due-ter-*ahn*-uh-me.
Ezra	*Ez*-ruh.
Hezekiah	Hez-ih-*kye*-uh.
Hilkiah	Hill-*kye*-uh.
Jerusalem	Juh-*roo*-suh-lem.
Josiah	Jo-*sigh*-uh.
Judeans	Joo-*dee*-unz.
Levites	*Lee*-vites.
Septuagint	Sep-*too*-ih-jent.
Solomon	*Sol*-o-mun.

8, the people sacrificed their own lambs. In Hezekiah's Passover, however, it seems that Levites and lay people killed Passover lambs (2 Chronicles 30:13-17). However, in Josiah's Passover, there is no indication of anyone other than priests and Levites as having slain the Passover lambs.

II. Celebration
(2 Chronicles 35:16-19)
A. By an Order (v. 16)

16a. So all the service of the LORD was prepared the same day, to keep the passover.

This verse sums up the various preparatory details of 2 Chronicles 35:7-15. All told, at least 41,400 animals were available for sacrifice in Josiah's Passover (2 Chronicles 35:7-9). This was more than twice the number for Hezekiah's Passover earlier (30:24). A considerable number of animals were needed to feed all the people since the celebration involved meals (Exodus 12:11; Matthew 26:17; etc.).

16b. And to offer burnt offerings upon the altar of the LORD, according to the commandment of king Josiah.

The Old Testament lists four types of blood sacrifices: the burnt, peace, sin, and guilt offerings. These are discussed throughout the book of Leviticus. Two of those four types are present here. The Passover animal sacrifice was a peace offering. One thing that distinguished this type from *burnt offerings* was that meat was available to eat from peace offerings, but not from burnt offerings (Leviticus 1:9; 7:15, 34-36; 9:3, 7). Bulls were often used for burnt offerings, and the whole animal was burned up to God. It was a dedicatory offering where the worshipper gave God everything and expressed total commitment.

B. With a Feast (v. 17)

17. And the children of Israel that were present kept the passover at that time, and the feast of unleavened bread seven days.

The meals continued throughout the week that followed as part of *the feast of unleavened bread* (Exodus 12:15-20; 2 Chronicles 30:21; 35:17). Technically, this feast is distinct from Passover. But

since the two occur right next to each other on the Jewish calendar, they are treated as a single celebration, practically speaking (compare Luke 22:1).

During the first Passover celebration (Exodus 12:1-30, 43-51), the Israelites were prepared to flee from Egypt. Hence, they consumed the Passover meal hastily. As a result, they ate unleavened bread—bread without yeast—because there was no time to allow the bread to rise.

> **What Do You Think?**
> How might you develop a plan to set aside seven consecutive days to take up a spiritual practice that would strengthen your faith in God?
> **Digging Deeper**
> How could you invite others from your class or congregation to participate in the practices over these seven days?

C. In Comparison (vv. 18-19)

18a. And there was no passover like to that kept in Israel from the days of Samuel the prophet; neither did all the kings of Israel keep such a passover as Josiah kept.

Samuel, considered the last of the judges and the first of the prophets, served as a judge from 1067 to 1043 BC (1 Samuel 7–9). Thus, there had not been *such a passover as Josiah kept* for over 400 years! It dwarfed Hezekiah's Passover (see commentary on 2 Chronicles 345:16a, above). It probably did so as well regarding the first Passover after return from exile, some 106 years later (Ezra 6:19-22). No figures for the number of animals sacrificed are given for the latter, but comparing numbers at two dedications of the temple may be insightful: Solomon's dedication of the first temple involved some 142,000 animals (2 Chronicles 7:5), while the dedication of the second (rebuilt) temple involved a little over 700 (Ezra 6:17)—a magnitude comparison of about 200-to-1!

18b. And the priests, and the Levites, and all Judah and Israel that were present, and the inhabitants of Jerusalem.

When we read that the attendees included *all Judah and Israel*, we remember that those two designations identify the southern kingdom of two tribes and the northern kingdom of 10 tribes. Many members of the latter had been exiled 100 years earlier (see Lesson Context). Thus *all . . . Israel* would refer to the few who had not been taken.

What Do You Think?

How can your class commemorate and celebrate God's work and faithfulness?

Digging Deeper

Who will your class select to spearhead the planning of such a celebration?

Regarding Influencers

A rare celebration attracted the world's attention in 2022. It was the Platinum Jubilee of Queen Elizabeth II (lived 1926–2022), marking 70 years of her reign. Four months of celebrations all over Britain and the Commonwealth honored the queen. Parades, speeches, and banquets were televised as local communities conducted their own recognitions. Accolades included recognition for her service during World War II, when she, as Princess Elizabeth, trained as a driver and mechanic at age 19.

No king of ancient Israel or Judah even came close to reigning for 70 years! Josiah himself reigned less than half that long. But what an influence that young king had, beginning at age 16 (2 Chronicles 35:1-3)! His godly initiatives are evident in every episode of his attempts to bring Judah back into compliance with God's expectations. His reinstitution of the Passover celebration at age 26 surely was a high-water mark for this youthful influencer.

But you're not a king or a queen? Ah, but you are—in whatever area of expertise you're best at. How can you be an influencer for Christ in that area?   —A. W.

19. In the eighteenth year of the reign of Josiah was this passover kept.

This note serves as a bookend to 2 Chronicles 35:1. The abbreviated account in 2 Kings 23:24 adds this assessment:

Moreover the workers with familiar spirits, and the wizards, and the images, and the idols, and all the abominations that were spied in the land of Judah and in Jerusalem, did Josiah put away, that he might perform the words of the law which were written in the book that Hilkiah the priest found in the house of the Lord.

Conclusion
A. Embracing Rituals

When Josiah kept the Passover ritual, he became a model of ritual faithfulness that originated in his heart. God has instituted certain rituals in the new covenant. At least two come immediately to mind: baptism and the Lord's Supper. Baptism is a ritual reenactment of Christ's burial and resurrection (Romans 6:3-4; Colossians 2:12). The Lord's Supper reenacts the Passover meal that Jesus shared with His followers the night He was betrayed (Matthew 26:17-29; Mark 14:12-26; Luke 22:7-23). The meal remembers Christ's sacrifice and death and focuses our attention and hope on His future return (1 Corinthians 5:7-8; 11:23-26).

These rituals invite us to participate in God's mission and God's story of redemptive history. They are touchstones of continuity and stability. They teach and remind, and God delights in our obedience as we seek Him through what He has commanded.

What Do You Think?

In what ways is the lesson's Scripture text applicable to modern audiences?

Digging Deeper

What takeaways from this lesson are most challenging to you?

B. Prayer

Heavenly Father, rekindle our appreciation for Your rituals! Focus our hearts and minds when we observe these rituals so that we might remember Your salvation and recommit our lives to You. Show us how we can observe these rituals of worship without becoming ritualistic. We pray in the name of Jesus. Amen.

C. Thought to Remember

Embrace God's rituals.

Involvement Learning

Enhance your lesson with KJV Bible Student *(from your curriculum supplier) and the reproducible activity* page *(at www.standardlesson.com or in the back of the* KJV Standard Lesson Commentary Deluxe Edition*).*

Into the Lesson

Ask volunteers to share their favorite memories of a childhood holiday tradition and why that memory is special. Then, ask other volunteers to think of a family holiday tradition that began when they were adults. What made that memory special? Talk as a group about how traditions and rituals change as we get older. How do age and tradition change the importance of those celebrations?

Alternative. Distribute copies of the "Celebrations Big and Small" exercise from the activity page, which you can download. After learners take no more than one minute to fill in the three blanks, form participants into triads to answer the two questions below their entries.

Transition to the next part of the lesson by saying, "Let's look at a Passover celebration that took place under King Josiah and think about how to apply lessons from it to life today."

Into the Word

Have a volunteer read 2 Chronicles 35:1-6 aloud. Then have another volunteer do the same with 35:16-19. Then form class members into two groups, no more than four per group (large classes can create duplicate groups). Distribute handouts (you create) with the information that follows:

Preparation Group. Compare and contrast Josiah's preparations for Passover in 2 Chronicles 35:1-6, 16-21 with the original instructions in Exodus 12:1-30 and Numbers 9:1-14; 28:16-24. What steps, if any, did King Josiah miss in his Passover preparations? Which steps, if any, do we simply lack information about either way?

Consecration Group. Determine what is being "consecrated" as you compare and contrast 2 Chronicles 35:1-6, 16-21 with Leviticus 11:44; 20:7; 2 Chronicles 29:34; 30:2-3, 15; Ezekiel 44:19; 46:20.

After allowing time to formulate answers, reconvene for a whole-class discussion. Evaluate those answers and discuss how Josiah's renewal of the Passover observance was (or was not) significant for Israel's ongoing relationship with God at that point. (*Option.* Conduct a role-play debate with one side proposing that King Josiah's Passover was significant in that regard, and the other side denying that it was; plan this in advance, giving both sides a copy of the Lesson Context.)

Into Life

Write on the board as headers of two columns each of these two phrases:

Preparation Today | Consecration Today

Then, to the left, write the words *Physical / Spiritual* as identifiers of two rows, one each. The overall result will be four intersections of the two columns and two rows. These four intersections naturally suggest four questions:

1–What physical preparation can I initiate for worship and kingdom service?

2–What spiritual preparation can I initiate for worship and kingdom service?

3–What physical consecration can I initiate for worship and kingdom service?

4–What spiritual consecration can I initiate for worship and kingdom service?

Have the grid and the four questions ready on handouts (you prepare) to distribute to small groups. Depending on the time available, you can have all groups work on all four questions; each group can work on just one question or some other combination. Reconvene the class and ask volunteers to share results. Conclude class time by distributing blank index cards and allowing one minute of silence for learners to pick one idea from each intersection for revitalizing his or her own devotional practices.

Option. Distribute copies of the "Word Search" exercise from the activity page as a take-home.

Moses and Miriam Lead in Praise

Devotional Reading: Psalm 104:1-9
Background Scripture: Exodus 14:21-31; 15:1-21

Exodus 15:1-3, 11-13, 17-18, 20-21

1 Then sang Moses and the children of Israel this song unto the Lord, and spake, saying, I will sing unto the Lord, for he hath triumphed gloriously: The horse and his rider hath he thrown into the sea.

2 The Lord is my strength and song, And he is become my salvation: He is my God, and I will prepare him an habitation; My father's God, and I will exalt him.

3 The Lord is a man of war: the Lord is his name.

11 Who is like unto thee, O Lord, among the gods? Who is like thee, glorious in holiness, Fearful in praises, doing wonders?

12 Thou stretchedst out thy right hand, The earth swallowed them.

13 Thou in thy mercy hast led forth the people which thou hast redeemed: Thou hast guided them in thy strength unto thy holy habitation.

17 Thou shalt bring them in, and plant them in the mountain of thine inheritance, In the place, O Lord, which thou hast made for thee to dwell in, In the Sanctuary, O Lord, which thy hands have established.

18 The Lord shall reign for ever and ever.

20 And Miriam the prophetess, the sister of Aaron, took a timbrel in her hand; and all the women went out after her with timbrels and with dances.

21 And Miriam answered them, Sing ye to the Lord, for he hath triumphed gloriously; The horse and his rider hath he thrown into the sea.

Key Text

Miriam the prophetess, the sister of Aaron, took a timbrel in her hand; and all the women went out after her with timbrels and with dances. —**Exodus 15:20**

Worship in the Covenant Community

Unit 1: Leaders Set Worship Example
Lessons 1–5

Lesson Aims

After participating in this lesson, each learner will be able to:

1. List God's attributes as sung by Moses and Miriam.

2. Trace the historical elements within Moses' and Miriam's celebratory songs of praise.

3. Write and sing a song of praise to God for His character and deliverance of His people.

Lesson Outline

Introduction
    A. The Power of Song
    B. Lesson Context
  I. The Song Introduced (Exodus 15:1-3)
    A. Recipient (v. 1)
    B. Reason (vv. 2-3)
  II. The Song Continued
             (Exodus 15:11-13, 17-18, 20-21)
    A. The Lord's Guidance (vv. 11-13)
    B. The People's Inheritance (vv. 17-18)
      Six Seedlings
    C. The Women's Response (vv. 20-21)
      Joyful Dance
Conclusion
    A. Sing to the Lord
    B. Prayer
    C. Thought to Remember

Introduction

A. The Power of Song

The power of song can transcend ethnic and national boundaries. In every country and every people group, songs are significant. According to many experts, music and singing can improve a person's sleep, mood, and cognitive performance while decreasing the effects of stress. Not only is it fun to sing along to your favorite song, but it might also contribute to a healthy lifestyle!

Songs can also improve a person's *spiritual* health. Through songs of worship, we learn the truths about God and strengthen our faith in Him. Further, such praises have the power to unite the people. Today's lesson consists of an ancient song that united the Old Testament people of God by remembering His work.

B. Lesson Context

The song in today's lesson comes from the book of Exodus, which is part of the Pentateuch, another name for the first five books of the Old Testament. These books have been traditionally attributed to Moses because he was well-educated (Acts 7:22) and skilled at detailed record-keeping (examples: Exodus 17:14; 24:4; Numbers 33:2).

The events of the exodus are traditionally dated to 1447 BC. Long before then, God had promised the land of Canaan to Abraham, Isaac, and Jacob (Genesis 13:14-15; 26:3; 28:13). The fulfillment of the promise seemed to be in jeopardy when Jacob and his family moved to Egypt because of a famine. Still, God worked through Joseph, a son of Jacob, so that the family could have all it needed during the years of famine (41:53-54).

Over the centuries, the Israelites witnessed significant leadership changes in Egypt. Eventually, there came a new king to whom Joseph's reputation meant nothing (Exodus 1:8). The original favor Jacob (Israel) and his sons experienced changed into servitude and oppression. After the Israelites spent 430 years in Egypt (12:40-41), God was ready to act to fulfill the promises (2:23-25).

It was during this time that Moses was born. It is well-known that a princess of Egypt adopted him, but he had to flee Egypt at age 40 after killing an Egyptian (Exodus 2; see Acts 7:23). Forty years later, Moses encountered the Lord at Sinai. God repeated the promise given to Moses' ancestors and called him to lead the enslaved Israelites away from Egypt (Exodus 3:8). God worked through Moses and Aaron (Moses' brother) to bring about ten plagues that devastated Egypt.

At that point, Pharaoh expelled the Israelites from Egypt (Exodus 12:31-33). It had been 430 years to the day since Jacob and his family entered Egypt (12:40-41). As God's people left Egypt, they were reminded again that their destination was Canaan (13:5, 11).

Pharaoh, however, changed his mind and decided to bring his labor force back (Exodus 14:5-8). The Egyptians pursued Israel to the edge of the Red Sea. It seemed that the Israelites were blocked by the sea, and victory for the Egyptians was assured, but God had other plans.

The Israelites crossed the Red Sea safely after the waters parted, but the Egyptians drowned when they tried to follow. The God of Israel was superior to any of the fictitious gods of Pharaoh! The crossing of the Red Sea was pivotal in the history of ancient Israel. The enslaved Israelites were free, beyond the reach of Pharaoh. Moses and the people responded with joyous singing (Exodus 15:1-21).

The first song in the history of this new nation is a song of rejoicing because of the victory that the Lord has obtained for the people. We note a minor difficulty in finding an appropriate designation for this song. Some students of the song have created designations for this song. These designations include "A Song of the Sea" (compare Exodus 15:1, 4-5, 8, 10), "A Song of Moses and Miriam" (compare 15:20-21), or "A Song of Moses and Israel" (compare 15:1). Another song designated as "A Song of Moses" can be found in Deuteronomy 32 (see the introduction in Deuteronomy 31:30).

I. The Song Introduced
(Exodus 15:1-3)
A. Recipient (v. 1)

1. Then sang Moses and the children of Israel this song unto the LORD, and spake, saying, I will sing unto the LORD, for he hath tri- umphed gloriously. The horse and his rider hath he thrown into the sea.

The use of the English word *Lord* with small caps indicates that the underlying Hebrew term reflects God's self-designation as revealed to Moses (Exodus 3:14). Its use in this verse highlights that the song is directed to none other than the only true and great God who had previously revealed himself to Moses.

The song praises the Lord for the ways He *triumphed* over Pharaoh and his army and thereby received honor (see Exodus 14:17-18). The *horse* and *rider* refer to parts of Pharaoh's army. Although his forces were considered all-powerful in their day, they paled in comparison to the power of the Lord (Isaiah 43:16-17).

The Lord's power was on display by casting the Egyptian armies *into* the waters of *the sea*. Through this powerful act, the Lord eliminated the most powerful military force of that era and showcased His unparalleled greatness (see Exodus 18:9-11). As a result, the enemy was incapable of a return attack on the Israelites.

> **What Do You Think?**
> How would you respond to the claim that this verse reveals God's lack of care for the suffering of animals?
>
> **Digging Deeper**
> How might Nehemiah 9:6; Psalm 36:6; Isaiah 11:6-9; and Matthew 6:25-26; 10:29 inform your response?

B. Reason (vv. 2-3)

2a. The LORD is my strength and song, and he is become my salvation.

This half-verse reflects the Israelites' response to the powerful work of *the Lord*. The people were pursued by the armies of Pharaoh (Exodus 14:23); the strength of the Israelites was inadequate to save themselves. Liberation came not through their own power but by the *strength* of the Lord (compare Psalm 28:8). Before crossing the Red Sea, Moses commanded the people to "stand still" and "see the *salvation* of the Lord" (Exodus 14:13-14). Psalm 118:14 and Isaiah 12:2

quote this half-verse as the writers look back to the miraculous strength of the Lord in bringing salvation to the people.

2b. He is my God, and I will prepare him an habitation; my father's God, and I will exalt him.

The song removed any possibility of misidentifying the *God* of Moses' ancestors; He is the single objective of the Israelites' worship. For centuries, the people would *exalt* God for what He had done for them in the exodus (see Psalm 22:3-5, lesson 7).

3. The LORD is a man of war: the LORD is his name.

The Israelites lived in a hostile world. They had been pursued by the nation that had enslaved them. Then, just weeks after the events of this song, the Israelites faced their first actual military conflict, against the Amalekites (Exodus 17:8-16).

The Old Testament describes the Lord as a divine *man of war* who would fight for His people (example: Isaiah 42:13; compare: Deuteronomy 3:22; Nehemiah 4:20; Zechariah 14:3). On some occasions, the Lord joined in battle with the Israelites (example: Deuteronomy 20:1-4). But at other times, the Lord went to war alone (example: Exodus 14:14). The Lord's *name* as a divine warrior is expressed later in the Old Testament by the phrase "Lord of hosts," with *hosts* referring to angelic armies (examples: 1 Samuel 17:45; Isaiah 13:4). It would have been easy for the Israelites to depend on their power or the power of other nations. Instead, the people of Israel were to trust that just as the Lord protected them and brought them out of Egypt, the Lord would continue to do so.

How to Say It

Amalekites	Am-uh-leh-kites or Uh-*mal*-ih-kites.
Korah	Ko-rah.
Miriam	Meer-ee-um.
Moriah	Mo-rye-uh.
Pentateuch	Pen-ta-teuk.
Pharaoh	Fair-o or Fay-roe.
Zion	Zi-un.

The New Testament contains similar imagery regarding conflict and the power of the Lord. God has not called His people to fight battles against flesh and blood, but against "principalities, against powers, against the rulers of the darkness of this world, [and] against spiritual wickedness" (Ephesians 6:12). Ultimately, God's people have been promised that the enemies of God, and even death itself, will someday be destroyed (1 Corinthians 15:23-28; Revelation 20:6-10, 14-15; 21:4).

What Do You Think?

In what situations is it comforting for you to think of God as a "man of war" (Exodus 15:3)?

Digging Deeper

In what situations is it a comfort to think of the Messiah as the "prince of Peace" (Isaiah 9:6)? Are these two designations contradictory? Why or why not?

II. The Song Continued
(Exodus 15:11-13, 17-18, 20-21)
A. The Lord's Guidance (vv. 11-13)

11. Who is like unto thee, O LORD, among the gods? Who is like thee, glorious in holiness, fearful in praises, doing wonders?

This verse contains two rhetorical questions that highlight the uniqueness of God. The Egyptians worshipped hundreds of gods and goddesses. However, those "gods" were fictitious and could not provide protection. By asking *who is like unto thee, O Lord, among the gods?* Moses emphasized the Lord's superiority over these pagan gods. This was a question for which Moses knew the answer: there is none like the Lord God (compare 1 Samuel 2:2; Isaiah 45:5; Jeremiah 10:6).

The second question builds on the first by distinguishing the ways that the Lord is incomparable to all other "gods." The *holiness* of the Lord describes His moral purity. The Lord God is *glorious* and perfect in every way (Deuteronomy 32:4; 2 Samuel 22:31; Matthew 5:48). The Lord is unique regarding His holiness (1 Samuel 2:2; Psalm 77:13).

Because the Lord is holy, His people are commanded to have lives of holiness (Leviticus 11:44-45; 1 Peter 1:15-16). For humans to be *fearful in praises* implies utmost respect and honor for the Lord and a willingness to follow His commands (example: Deuteronomy 10:12, 20-21).

The *wonders* of the Lord's work were displayed in His power to lead the Israelites safely across the sea on dry ground (compare Psalm 66:5-6). Even in Heaven is the Lord worshipped for His holy and mighty acts (see Revelation 15:4-5).

> **What Do You Think?**
> What are some "gods" worshipped by our culture, and in what ways is God more wondrous than those "gods"?
>
> **Digging Deeper**
> How will you celebrate the wonderful and wondrous ways God has worked?

12. Thou stretchedst out thy right hand, the earth swallowed them.

In biblical times, the right hand or being located at a person's right hand conveyed blessing (example: Genesis 48:17-20), demonstrated prestige (examples: 1 Kings 2:19; Matthew 22:44 [quoting Psalm 110:1]), or revealed power (example: Psalms 20:6; 98:1).

This verse uses a literary device called *anthropomorphism*, the practice of assigning human attributes to God (examples: Leviticus 20:6; Numbers 6:25-26; Deuteronomy 11:12). God does not have a physical body (John 4:24). The song uses this literary device to describe how the Lord conveys His power through His outstretched *right hand* (compare: Psalms 17:7; 138:7). The expression is used twice in this song, once here and in Exodus 15:6 (not in this week's lesson text). In this case, it celebrates God's victory over the Egyptians on Israel's behalf (Exodus 14:21-30).

Given that the song celebrates that *the earth swallowed them*, this verse also seems to point to future events. The Egyptian army was swallowed up by the sea, after all. Not long after the events of this song, Israel would see Korah and 250 rebels swallowed up when "the earth opened her mouth" (Numbers 16:32). In that instance, as when the sea swallowed the Egyptians, it was a sign of God's judgment on wickedness and delivering His people.

13. Thou in thy mercy hast led forth the people which thou hast redeemed. Thou hast guided them in thy strength unto thy holy habitation.

When we think about provision, we might consider material things like food and shelter. While it is true that God provided these things for the Israelites, their greatest need was by no means material. The Israelites had experienced enslavement, and their greatest need was redemption. The Lord demonstrated *mercy* by noticing their suffering and promising deliverance (Exodus 3:7-8). The concept of redemption consists of God's taking back or buying back what is rightfully His. God redeemed the people and took them back as people of His own (6:6-7). No longer were the people the possession of Pharaoh; instead, they would be the unique people of God.

After redeeming the people, the Lord led them to a *holy habitation*. The underlying Hebrew word translated *habitation* elsewhere refers to the tabernacle (2 Samuel 15:25), the city of Jerusalem (example: Isaiah 33:20), or a more general descriptor for the place of the Lord (example: Jeremiah 25:30). God was leading the people to the promised land of Canaan, the land where He would dwell with them (Genesis 17:8). The New Testament presents Christ as our redeemer, paying the price to purchase us from the slavery of sin (1 Corinthians 6:20; Galatians 3:13; 1 Timothy 2:5-6). God continues to lead His people to the ultimate holy dwelling beyond the physical realm (John 14:1-3; Hebrews 11:10). Thus, the saints in Heaven "sing the song of Moses . . . and the song of the Lamb" at their final destination (Revelation 15:3).

> **What Do You Think?**
> In what ways would (or should) your life change if you spent more time reflecting on and emulating God's holiness?
>
> **Digging Deeper**
> Which of these three texts spurs you most to start doing so today: Ephesians 1:4; Hebrews 12:14; 1 Peter 1:15-16?

The Lord is our salvation.

Visual for Lesson 5. *Point to this visual and ask for examples of other ways that the Lord has been the source of salvation for His people.*

B. The People's Inheritance (vv. 17-18)

17. Thou shalt bring them in, and plant them in the mountain of thine inheritance, in the place, O LORD, which thou hast made for thee to dwell in, in the Sanctuary, O Lord, which thy hands have established.

The Lord's leading to *bring* the Israelites into the promised land demonstrates His provision and the permanence of His care. The song acknowledges that the people's establishment in the land would come from the Lord's work to *plant them* and not because they made a name for themselves (compare 1 Chronicles 17:9-10; Psalms 44:2; 78:54-55; 80:8-11; contrast Isaiah 37:24-25). The land was an *inheritance* given to them by the Lord. It had been promised to Abram (Genesis 12:6-7) and confirmed to Moses (Exodus 6:2-4, 8). It would be the place of God's blessing to the people (Leviticus 20:24; Deuteronomy 8:7-8).

The land of Canaan is mountainous, unlike the flat, coastal region of Egypt where the Israelites had likely been enslaved. There are many mountains in Canaan, but the song probably refers to *the mountain* Zion (Psalm 2:6; etc.). Centuries after Moses, Solomon would build *the sanctuary* that is the temple on this mountain, also called Mount Moriah (2 Chronicles 3).

Six Seedlings

Two cottonwood trees grew in the backyard of my childhood home. The trees released thou-

sands of cotton-like seeds that floated through the air like little white puffs each spring. Some seeds would take root when they came to rest in the yard. The seedlings did not remain in the ground for long because my dad usually mowed them down as they sprouted. My sister and I always pleaded with him to let the seedlings grow. He eventually succumbed to our request, guiding us to plant six seedlings in evenly spaced rows in the front yard.

The seedlings eventually took root and matured. My sister and I were photographed standing next to the trees each year. By the time we moved out, the trees were taller than the house. When I drive past that old house, I marvel at the size of those trees, deeply rooted and mature.

After leading the Israelites out of Egypt, the Lord planted them in a new land. He wanted them to take root in that land and flourish as His people. Are you following the Lord, becoming deeply rooted in God's plan for you? Are you "like a tree planted by the rivers of water, that bringeth forth his fruit in his season" (Psalm 1:3)?

—L. M. W.

18. The LORD shall reign for ever and ever.

This verse repeats the song's central theme: *the Lord* is all-powerful and eternal in His *reign*. Unlike earthly rulers, the Lord's reign over His people will be forever (Psalms 45:6; 146:10; Revelation 11:15).

D. The Women's Response (vv. 20-21)

20-21. And Miriam the prophetess, the sister of Aaron, took a timbrel in her hand; and all the women went out after her with timbrels and with dances. And Miriam answered them, Sing ye to the LORD, for he hath triumphed gloriously; the horse and his rider hath he thrown into the sea.

This is the first explicit reference to *Miriam* in the Old Testament. It is possible that she was the sister who watched the "ark of bulrushes" that contained the baby Moses (Exodus 2:3-4). Miriam is also one of several women in Scripture who are designated as a prophet or *prophetess* (Judges 4:4; 2 Kings 22:14; Nehemiah 6:14; Isaiah 8:3; Luke 2:36; compare Micah 6:4). The book of Numbers records an event that shows how her service in this role was somewhat of a mixed experience. In a misdirected way, she believed (accurately) that God had spoken through her (Numbers 12:2). This statement, however, came in a bout of rebellion against her brothers. As a result of her rebellion, she experienced leprosy as a punishment from God (12:10). However, she was restored following her brother's petition (12:11-15).

A *timbrel* is the equivalent of a modern-day tambourine or hand drum. It was customary in the ancient world for women to celebrate various occasions *with dances* and *timbrels* (example: Judges 11:34; compare Psalms 149:3; 150:4; Jeremiah 31:4).

The refrain of the women's song celebrated how the Lord cast Israel's foes *into the sea*. It is very similar to the beginning of Moses' song, which also focused on the mighty acts of the Lord to save the Israelites (see Exodus 15:1, above).

The implication may be that Miriam is the one who leads the other women in a type of antiphonal rendition. (That's when one group answers another.) In any case, their words are a final reminder of how the most powerful nation in the world at that time was no match for the God of Israel.

> **What Do You Think?**
> What are some occasions that would be appropriate to label as "a time to dance" (Ecclesiastes 3:4)?
> **Digging Deeper**
> Why did you, or did you not, include "a church worship service" as one of your responses?

Joyful Dance

As a religion professor, my husband often took his students on field trips to observe various congregations and their worship services. Our young daughter and I often accompanied them to these services. One enthusiastic service stands out: the worship music was energetic, and the congregation moved and swayed to the music more than I had ever seen. During the service, a group of women with tambourines gathered in a semicircle before the sanctuary and began dancing to the music. As they did so, I saw my two-year-old daughter joyfully dancing. I smiled at how she could confidently dance as an act of worship, just as the women at the front of the room did.

My mind flashed back to the story of Miriam and the Israelite women as I watched a modern-day version of that example play out. How will you honor and worship God for His great blessings? Can you incorporate worship practices that you typically have not utilized?   —L. M. W.

Conclusion
A. Sing to the Lord

Singing helps diminish feelings of stress and anxiety by releasing "feel good" brain chemicals that alleviate pain. Singing also activates the portion of the brain associated with memorization—you can probably still sing the alphabet song!

Our songs of worship do these things and so much more. We sing in worship to the Lord because He is the source of our strength and salvation. Our worship also celebrates and remembers the Lord's goodness and faithfulness. The apostle Paul sang to the Lord in worship, even in imprisonment (Acts 16:25). "Psalms and hymns and spiritual songs" along with "singing and making melody in your heart" are marks of a life filled with God's Spirit (Ephesians 5:19; see Colossians 3:16). While there are specific situations when singing is not always appropriate (examples: Proverbs 25:20; Amos 5:23; 8:10; Ezekiel 26:13), the righteous people of God are called to sing praises to Him (Psalm 33:1-3). Sing to the Lord without hesitation!

B. Prayer

Lord God, we thank You for the example of worship and song presented in Scripture. Help us be further attentive to Your Spirit so that we might sing to You in all situations—good or bad. In the name of Your Son, Jesus, we pray. Amen.

C. Thought to Remember
The Lord has given us a reason to sing!

Involvement Learning

Enhance your lesson with KJV Bible Student *(from your curriculum supplier) and the reproducible activity page (at www.standardlesson.com or in the back of the* KJV Standard Lesson Commentary Deluxe Edition*).*

Into the Lesson

Divide the class into three groups, no more than four per group (large classes can create duplicate groups). Distribute a pen and a handout (you create) to each group with one of the following three song titles at the top: *Just As I Am, It Is Well with My Soul, Blessed Assurance*. Have groups write down the lyrics of the assigned song from memory as possible. After three minutes, have each group share what they wrote and compare their results to the lyrics.

Lead into Bible study by saying, "Songs can be a powerful tool for teaching because they can help reinforce important messages. Today's lesson will study a song that taught the Israelites of God's power and provision."

Into the Word

Ask a volunteer to read aloud Exodus 15:1-3, 11-13, 17-18, 20-21. Divide the class into three equal groups. Distribute handouts (you create) with the following questions for in-group discussion based on the lesson's Scripture text.

Actions of God Group. 1–What are some examples from the song of God's powerful actions? 2–What were the results of these displays of power? 3–How has God's power been on display in our congregation? 4–What are some results of His displays of power?

Provision of God Group. 1–What are some examples from the song of God's provision for the people? 2–What were the results of these displays of provision? 3–What instances of provision from God can you celebrate? 4–How has God's provision been on display in our congregation?

Attributes of God Group. 1–What are some examples from the song that highlight God's attributes? 2–How were these attributes on display to the Israelites? 3–What other attributes of God can you name? 4–How have you seen these on display in our congregation?

After five minutes, ask a volunteer from each group to share responses and ask them what the song reveals about God's character. Write responses on the board. (Keep responses on the board until class concludes.)

Alternative. Distribute copies of the "Song of Moses and Miriam" exercise from the activity page, which you can download. Have learners work in pairs to complete as indicated.

Option. Divide learners into triads and ask a volunteer to read aloud Revelation 15:1-4. Say, "This song taught by Moses and Miriam will also be sung by the victorious saints in Heaven. What significant themes in the song can also be celebrated by these saints?" Allow three minutes for triads to discuss before asking for responses. (Possible responses: the exodus led by Moses formed a pattern for the deliverance brought by the Lamb; the enemies of the people of God will ultimately be destroyed; the people of God can celebrate their inheritance).

Into Life

Point to the responses from the Into the Word activity written on the board, and say, "The song celebrated God's character and deliverance. Today, we have the opportunity to celebrate the same."

Form learners into groups of three. Give each group a large poster board along with markers and colored pencils. Instruct groups to write on their poster board some reasons for praising God for His character and deliverance. Then, ask groups to flip over the poster board and write a song of praise based on the reasons listed on the other side. (*Option.* Have groups use a sheet of printer paper instead of poster board.) After 10 minutes, have each group read or sing their song of praise.

Alternative. Distribute copies of the "My Song of Praise" activity from the activity page. Have learners complete the activity as a take-home. Tell learners that you will give volunteers time at the start of the next class to share their work.

Prayers of Repentance and Confession

Devotional Reading: 2 Corinthians 7:5-11
Background Scripture: Psalm 51; 2 Samuel 11

Psalm 51:1-4, 10-12, 15-17

1 Have mercy upon me, O God, according to thy lovingkindness: according unto the multitude of thy tender mercies blot out my transgressions.

2 Wash me throughly from mine iniquity, and cleanse me from my sin.

3 For I acknowledge my transgressions: and my sin is ever before me.

4 Against thee, thee only, have I sinned, and done this evil in thy sight: that thou mightest be justified when thou speakest, and be clear when thou judgest.

10 Create in me a clean heart, O God; and renew a right spirit within me.

11 Cast me not away from thy presence; and take not thy holy spirit from me.

12 Restore unto me the joy of thy salvation; and uphold me with thy free spirit.

15 O Lord, open thou my lips; and my mouth shall shew forth thy praise.

16 For thou desirest not sacrifice; else would I give it: thou delightest not in burnt offering.

17 The sacrifices of God are a broken spirit: a broken and a contrite heart, O God, thou wilt not despise.

Key Text

Create in me a clean heart, O God; and renew a right spirit within me. —Psalm 51:10

Worship in the
Covenant Community

Unit 2: Songs of the
Old Testament

Lessons 6–9

Lesson Aims

After participating in this lesson, each learner will be able to:

1. Summarize the circumstances that led King David to write Psalm 51.

2. Interpret Psalm 51 through the lens of King David's experience of repentance and forgiveness.

3. Confess and repent of personal and corporate sins.

Lesson Outline

Introduction

A. The Need for Confession

In second grade, my class held an end-of-the-year pizza party. Our teachers told us that there was just enough pizza for every student to have one—and only one—slice. As the party ended, I snuck the last slice and ate it without telling anyone. What I didn't know was that another student hadn't yet eaten. So, when that boy came to get his slice of pizza, there was none left for him.

When our teacher asked who had taken an extra slice, I kept my mouth shut. As the silence grew, I saw the sadness on the other boy's face. Overcome with guilt, I raised my hand and confessed what I had done. I apologized to the other student, the teacher, and the whole class. I was worried that they all would be upset with me. Instead, the boy hugged me and told me that he forgave me. My teacher encouraged me by telling me she was proud of my honesty. My relationship with my teacher and classmates was restored when I confessed my wrongdoing.

Although that experience was trivial, it taught me an important lesson about the need for confession and repentance. Before we can have forgiveness and healing, we need an awareness of our sins and an admission of our wrongdoing. Today's psalm gives us an example of such.

B. Lesson Context

Today's lesson comes from Psalm 51, a lament psalm. This type of psalm focuses on the psalmist's remorse, confession of sin, and request for forgiveness (compare Psalms 6, 32, 38, etc.). The psalm's superscription attributes authorship to King David.

Psalm 51 was composed after a particularly heinous and tragic series of events in his life, as the superscription notes. The psalm endures as a model for confession, restoration, and praise.

These events are recounted in 2 Samuel 11–12 and occurred while David was king (1010–970 BC). While David stood on the roof of his palace, he saw a woman bathing (2 Samuel 11:2-3). This woman was Bathsheba, the wife of Uriah, one of David's fighting men. David sent for her, slept with her, and made her pregnant (11:4-5). To conceal his actions, David tried to convince Uriah to sleep with her so that Uriah would think he caused his wife's pregnancy (11:6-13). However, David's schemes failed, and Uriah refused to sleep with his wife. As a result, the king resorted to having Uriah killed in battle (11:7) and marrying the now-widowed woman (11:27a). David's sinful actions "displeased the Lord" (11:27b).

Therefore, the Lord sent the prophet Nathan to convict David of his sin. Rather than blatantly expose the king's sin, Nathan used a parable—a short story—to uncover it. This parable presented two characters: a poor man who owned a beloved lamb and a rich man who owned many flocks of sheep. The parable described how the rich man took the poor man's precious lamb, killed it, and prepared it as a meal for the traveler (2 Samuel 12:1-4). The rich man's unjust treatment of the poor man infuriated David (12:5-6).

Nathan then revealed the parable's point: King David was like that rich man (2 Samuel 12:7). Although the king was exceedingly wealthy and powerful, he took that which was not his to take; he "killed Uriah the Hittite with the sword, and hast taken his wife" (12:9). Upon hearing Nathan's words and being convicted of his sin, David confessed of his wrongdoing and proclaimed, "I have sinned against the Lord" (12:13).

I. Confession
(Psalm 51:1-4)
A. Needing Mercy (vv. 1-2)

1. Have mercy upon me, O God, according to thy lovingkindness: according unto the multitude of thy tender mercies blot out my transgressions.

The Hebrew word translated in this verse as *lovingkindness* occurs over 200 times in the Old Testament, with varying English translations. It is sometimes translated as "mercy" (examples: Psalm 33:18, 22), "merciful kindness" (examples: Psalms 117:2; 119:76), or "goodness" (examples: Exodus 34:6; Psalm 107:8). The word generally describes God's faithfulness to His people. An aspect of God's mercy is demonstrated in His response to

sin (see Numbers 14:18-19; Daniel 9:9; Ephesians 2:4-5).

The word picture used by David is that of a ledger used by the Lord to record sins. To *blot out* something from that ledger would be to remove it entirely (compare Psalm 69:28). Centuries after David, God identified himself to the prophet Isaiah as the one who would blot out and no longer remember the sins of His people (Isaiah 43:25).

Transgressions are actions that willfully break God's law. The underlying Hebrew word translated *transgressions* is elsewhere translated as "sins" (examples: Proverbs 10:19; 28:13). David acknowledged that he had broken God's law by his actions with Bathsheba and against Uriah. David also knew that God is full of *mercy* (2 Samuel 24:14) and never-failing compassion (compare Lamentations 3:22). In his sorrow and remorse, David requested that God show mercy and demonstrate forgiveness by removing all records of his sins (compare Exodus 34:6; Micah 7:18-20).

> **What Do You Think?**
> How would you explain God's lovingkindness and tender mercies to someone who thinks God is harsh and unloving?
>
> **Digging Deeper**
> What Scripture texts come to mind to help your explanation (example: Psalm 103)?

2. Wash me throughly from mine iniquity, and cleanse me from my sin.

This verse demonstrates *parallelism*, a rhetorical device frequently found in Hebrew poetry. It occurs when a line of poetry uses words or phrases that are different but synonymous. The repetition emphasizes the writer's point. In Psalm 51:1-2, parallelism is seen in the use of the words *blot out*, *wash*, and *cleanse*.

David's transgressions were like a stain on a garment that needed washing. His request, *wash me thoroughly*, reveals his knowledge of the depth of his sinfulness and understanding that only God could remove the stain of sin.

God promised to cleanse His people from their sins (Ezekiel 36:25). In response, God's people should confess their iniquities (Jeremiah 33:8) and commit to lives free from wrongdoing (Isaiah 1:16).

Of the dozens of uses of the underlying Hebrew word for *cleanse*, most refer to the ceremonial cleansing required by the Law of Moses (examples: Leviticus 14; Numbers 8:7). God requires that His people live pure and holy lives, free from *sin*. By asking to be cleansed from *sin*, David sought to be made clean before God (also Psalm 51:7, not in our printed text).

B. Acknowledging Sin (vv. 3-4)

3. For I acknowledge my transgressions: and my sin is ever before me.

David could ask to be cleansed from sin because he knew the sins he had committed. For a person to *acknowledge* sin can be painful, but it must happen (compare Isaiah 59:12; Psalms 38:18; 40:12; contrast 1 Samuel 15:20-25). Awareness of sin must occur prior to personal conviction, which is required for true repentance and mercy (Proverbs 28:13; 1 John 1:9). David knew the extent of his *sin* (2 Samuel 12:13; compare Psalm 32:3-5). His admission of that fact to himself was his first step to confessing to God and receiving forgiveness.

More parallelism is displayed in this verse between the words *transgressions* and *sin*. We see this identical pair of terms stated in Psalm 32:5, another psalm by David.

> **What Do You Think?**
> What steps can a believer take to be attentive to the Spirit's conviction regarding his or her sin?
>
> **Digging Deeper**
> What things prevent us from hearing the Spirit's leading in this regard?

Stains Removed

The house we lived in when my children were little had white carpets. I did not prefer this flooring, especially in a home with young children and a dog. Replacing it would have cost too much for us, so it stayed. Almost daily, something spilled on that beautiful white carpet. Dirt, grass, and mulberry juice from the mulberry tree in our yard were frequent culprits. Every day was a constant battle to keep the carpet clean—a struggle I repeatedly lost.

Eventually, I hired a carpet-cleaning service. After seeing the filthy carpet, the technician frowned with discouragement. "It's okay if you can't get the stains out," I told him. "I know it's bad. Just get it clean." He agreed he would do his best. After some hours, he revealed the results of his labor: pristine, stainless carpets that looked new!

Sin has left its mark on us; our sins are like stains we can't remove. Before God can cleanse us from our sins, we need to acknowledge the presence of sin and repent. David realized that he had sinned and came before God to request cleansing. God has promised to make us clean, but we must go before Him with a repentant heart. What prevents you from coming to God today with a heart of repentance?   —L. M. W.

4a. Against thee, thee only, have I sinned, and done this evil in thy sight.

Our sins can harm others. And yet, sin is ultimately a failure to follow the commands of a holy and righteous God. Therefore, sin is ultimately directed against God (see Genesis 39:9). This half-verse echoes David's statement of confession after he had been convicted of his sin: "I have sinned *against* the Lord" (2 Samuel 12:13).

The phrase *done this evil in thy sight* reflects the statement made by Nathan to highlight David's sin (2 Samuel 12:9). Because of God's holiness, He cannot tolerate the sight of evil (Deuteronomy 4:25; Habakkuk 1:13). God sees the actions of all people (Psalm 11:4-5), even those done in private (Hebrews 4:13). David acknowledged the severity of his sin. Not only was he aware of his wrongdoing, but he was also aware of God's knowledge of that sin.

4b. That thou mightest be justified when thou speakest, and be clear when thou judgest.

Some psalms describe God as an all-powerful and all-knowing judge who, in His righteousness, will judge the behavior of His people (examples: Psalms 96:13; 98:9). Because all sin is ultimately directed against God, His judgment against it is *justified*. David knew this and was prepared to accept the consequences of his actions. The apostle Paul quoted this half-verse in Romans 3:4 to make the point that God is always righteous and correct in His judgment of sin.

II. Restoration
(Psalm 51:10-12)
A. Clean My Heart (v. 10)

10. Create in me a clean heart, O God; and renew a right spirit within me.

This verse continues a turn for David that began in Psalm 51:7 (not in today's print passage). The turn is from his confession of sin to his request for a renewed relationship. David acknowledged that only *God* could clean his heart from sin. As such, David's prayer suggests an important insight regarding the state of humanity: we are incapable of having pure hearts and living completely righteous on our own (compare Proverbs 20:9; Romans 3:10-12 [quoting Psalms 14:1-3; 53:1-3 and Ecclesiastes 7:20]; 1 John 1:10). Only God, through His mercy, can give people a *clean heart* and a *right spirit* when they turn to Him (Ezekiel 18:31-32; 36:25-27; 1 Timothy 1:5; Titus 3:5). Only after God has provided this spiritual renewal can people then follow Him with obedience and love (Ephesians 4:20-23).

B. Grant Your Presence (vv. 11-12)

11. Cast me not away from thy presence; and take not thy holy spirit from me.

Under the covenant of Sinai, obedience to God's commands was a condition for Him to continue to dwell with the people (Exodus 29:42-46; contrast Ezekiel 10:18). Those who did not keep those commandments would be removed from the community and, thereby, the presence of God (examples: Genesis 17:14; Deuteronomy 17:1-5). David had previously admitted that he had disobeyed God. In this verse are his requests that result from that wrongdoing. He was fearful that he might suffer the loss of God's *presence* as a result (compare Isaiah 59:2).

This verse is only one of three verses in the Old Testament that use the title *holy spirit,* the others being Isaiah 63:10-11; compare "his [God's] spirit" in Psalm 106:33. During the Old Testa-

Visual for Lesson 6. *Allow one minute for silent prayer on this request after discussing the commentary associated with verse 10.*

ment era, the presence of God's Spirit came upon certain people to empower them for a particular purpose (examples: Numbers 11:16-17; 1 Samuel 10:6; Micah 3:8). These rare instances prefigure the indwelling of the Holy Spirit that blesses all Christians today (Romans 8:9-11; 2 Timothy 1:14). However, through our sin, we risk deadening our attentiveness to the Spirit's influence. The apostle Paul warns strongly about the ways we might "grieve" (Ephesians 4:30) or "quench" (1 Thessalonians 5:19) the Spirit.

David had received "the Spirit of the Lord" after being anointed by Samuel (1 Samuel 16:13). The request that God *take not thy holy spirit from* David reflects that past experience. After David's predecessor, Saul, had sinned, "the Spirit of the Lord departed from Saul" (16:14; compare 18:10; 19:9). It's not stretching our sanctified imaginations too much to think that David was fearful that he would suffer likewise.

David's fears in this regard are understandable.

How to Say It

Bathsheba	Bath-*she*-buh.
Ecclesiastes	Ik-*leez*-ee-**as**-teez.
Habakkuk	Huh-*back*-kuk.
Hittite	*Hit*-ite or *Hit*-tite.
Hosea	Ho-*zay*-uh.
Lamentations	Lam-en-*tay*-shunz.
Uriah	Yu-*rye*-uh.

Since the introduction of sin into the world, humans have experienced guilt and shame when caught in sin. As a result, people often feel unworthy before the presence of God (examples: Judges 13:22; Isaiah 6:5). When we draw near to God with repentance, we can experience His presence and love (Psalm 23 [lesson 10]; James 4:8).

12. Restore unto me the joy of thy salvation; and uphold me with thy free spirit.

David's sin caused a sense of separation between him and God. At one time, God's *salvation* had led David to rejoice (Psalm 13:5). However, his feelings of *joy* had been replaced with grief because of the presence of David's sin.

David recognized that he could not experience transformation through his power; he needed God to provide support to *uphold* him. David had already acknowledged God's role in transforming David and strengthening the bond of their relationship.

> **What Do You Think?**
> How will you celebrate the joy of salvation in the upcoming week?
>
> **Digging Deeper**
> How will you go about such a celebration even if external circumstances seem less-than-ideal?

Sustained With Joy

A popular comedian once pointed out that joy and laughter should be communal experiences; humor is best when shared with others. To prove this point, the comedian described what he sees from the stage during a comedy set. The audience would typically respond to his routine by turning to one another, nudging each other, and laughing. These mutual experiences of joy and humor invite connections between people and build relationships among the audience members.

These experiences aren't limited to the audience of a comedy show. On several occasions, my coworkers and I have experienced the need for joy and humor. Once, during a difficult week at work, one coworker said something humorous. I then chimed in with a witty retort. We both laughed so hard that tears ran down our cheeks. Laughter, humor, and joy were the needed responses to relieve the stress of that challenging week.

David wanted to experience the joy that could come only from God's salvation. Such a joyous state came from David's right relationship with the God of salvation. What things have prevented you from experiencing the joy of God's salvation? What will you do to correct that?   —L. M. W.

III. Praise
(Psalm 51:15-17)
A. From My Lips (v. 15)

15. O Lord, open thou my lips; and my mouth shall shew forth thy praise.

With this verse, David's prayer of confession and repentance transitions to praise. He had confessed to God, requested forgiveness, and asked to experience a renewed relationship with God. As a result, David promised that he would use the experience of forgiveness as an opportunity to "teach transgressors [God's] ways" so that "sinners shall be converted unto [God]" (Psalm 51:13, not in our printed text). David's acknowledgment of his sin led him to seek repentance and use his life as an example to others for their correction.

This verse also demonstrates another use of poetic parallelism. *My mouth shall shew forth thy praise* parallels the statement "my tongue shall sing aloud of thy righteousness" (Psalm 51:14, not in our printed text). Praise is the proper response to God's love and mercy (63:3-5; Hebrews 13:11-15). David would respond to God's mercy with public displays of praise and worship. His goal was not to manipulate God into granting forgiveness. Instead, he expressed his commitment to worship God in response to receiving God's promised mercy.

B. From a Broken Heart (vv. 16-17)

16-17. For thou desirest not sacrifice; else would I give it: thou delightest not in burnt offering. The sacrifices of God are a broken spirit: a broken and a contrite heart, O God, thou wilt not despise.

David states the basis for his confession of sin and prayer for forgiveness. Through the Law of Moses, God established a system of sacrifices and offerings for the people of Israel (Leviticus 1–7). Therefore, at an initial glance, this verse appears to negate the role of this sacrificial system.

We can find an explanation by looking again at the context that prompted David to write this psalm (see Lesson Context). Under the Law of Moses, adultery and murder required capital punishment (Exodus 21:12; Leviticus 20:10). David knew that God desired a change of heart rather than sacrifices without any change (compare 1 Samuel 15:22).

Instead, God desires "internal" *sacrifices* from the contrite and repentant. These sacrifices include the attitude and stance of a person's *spirit* and *heart*. When people become aware of their sin, they will experience grief for what they have done—a "godly sorrow" that leads to repentance (2 Corinthians 7:10; compare Psalm 34:18). This sorrow results from having *a broken spirit* filled with sadness for not having loved and obeyed God as intended. However, experiencing sorrow for the sake of itself is not the intended goal. God desires that His people have a *contrite heart* that shows remorse for sinful behavior.

This verse also teaches us that religious observances and practices are ultimately meaningless if they are not followed by a change of heart that results in following and obeying God's commands (compare Isaiah 1:11-15; 29:13). God will *despise* such behaviors (see Amos 5:21-23). Rather than sacrifices and offerings for their own sake, God desires a changed heart that results in worship and obedience (see 1 Samuel 15:22; Hosea 6:6).

What Do You Think?
In what ways can a believer cultivate a broken spirit and a broken and contrite heart?

Digging Deeper
How can a person overcome desensitization to sin so that he or she can cultivate these things?

Conclusion
A. The Power of Confession

Regardless of the sins we may commit, David's words in Psalm 51 provide us with a model of acknowledgment, confession, repentance, and praise. We first acknowledge our sins and take ownership of our actions. Second, we confess our wrongdoing and repent. Repentance is a crucial and necessary aspect of the Christian life (Luke 5:32), and it pleases God (see Ezekiel 18:23; Romans 2:4; etc.). Through our confession, we are "healed" from the power of sin (James 5:16) and receive forgiveness from God: "If we confess our sins, he is faithful and just to forgive us our sins, and to cleanse us from all unrighteousness" (1 John 1:9).

Finally, because of our confidence in God's promises, we praise Him for His mercy toward us, demonstrated through forgiveness. When wayward Christians follow this model, they can experience the joy of living in relationship with God—a joy to be shared with others.

What Do You Think?
How has Psalm 51 changed how you approach your acts of confession and repentance?

Digging Deeper
Who can be an accountability partner to encourage you in a life of confession and repentance?

B. Prayer
Merciful God, Your love and mercy are great. As Your people, we want to be in a right relationship with You. We confess that we have not loved You or others as we ought. We repent of our sinful actions and humbly ask for Your forgiveness. We praise You because You have promised to cleanse us from our sins and give us a life of joy in a right relationship with You. In the name of Jesus, we pray. Amen.

C. Thought to Remember
Acknowledge. Confess. Repent. Praise.

Involvement Learning

Enhance your lesson with KJV Bible Student *(from your curriculum supplier) and the reproducible activity page (at www.standardlesson.com or in the back of the* KJV Standard Lesson Commentary Deluxe Edition*).*

Into the Lesson

Begin class time by asking learners to brainstorm a list of words that are synonymous with *sin*. Allow 90 seconds for them to shout out as many as they can. Write their responses on the board. Do the same with the following words: *acknowledge, confession*, and *praise*. Using the listed terms and their synonyms, determine the relationship between *sin* and *acknowledge, confession*, and *praise*.

Lead into Bible study by saying, "The psalm in today's lesson reveals to us the significance of these words: *acknowledge, confession*, and *praise*. How can this psalm inform your response to sin?"

Into the Word

Using the commentary and other resources, give a background summary of Psalm 51 and the events that led to its composition (see 2 Samuel 11–12). *Option*. Recruit a class member ahead of time to present a three-minute summary of this material to set the stage for today's Bible study.

Invite a volunteer to read today's text. Distribute handouts (you create) of the sentences below *without* the verse citations. Ask learners to mark them as *True* or *False*. Include space for additional written responses between sentences.

1–David requested grace according to God's lovingkindness. (Psalm 51:1)
2–David failed to recognize his sin. (51:3)
3–David proclaimed that he did evil in the sight of other people. (51:4)
4–David requested that God give him a clean heart and a new outlook. (51:10)
5–Despite his sin, David still felt the joy of God's salvation. (51:12)
6–David's sacrifices consisted of burnt offerings. (51:17)

Share that each sentence is false. In pairs, challenge learners to write verse references that show the falsehood of each statement and write out true sentences based on the verse(s) referenced. After calling time, bring the class back together. Let pairs share their corrected sentences.

Alternative 1. Distribute copies of the "All My Transgressions" exercise from the activity page, which you can download. Have learners complete it in a minute or less before discussing conclusions with a partner.

Alternative 2. Distribute copies of the "Cause and Effect" activity from the activity page. Have learners work in small groups to complete it as indicated. After calling time, have one member of each group share their group's responses.

Into Life

Distribute an index card and pen to each learner. In a minute or less, have learners write down a personal or corporate sin they wish to confess. Ask learners to reread Psalm 51:1-4, 10-12, 15-17 silently as a prayer of confession and repentance of individual sins. Then have learners join with a partner to reread the lesson Scripture, but this time as a prayer of confession and repentance of corporate sins.

Option. Print the following prayer on a sheet of paper and distribute a copy to each learner:

> Most merciful God, I confess that I have sinned against You in thought, word, and deed, by what I have done, and by what I have left undone. I have not loved You with my whole heart; I have not loved my neighbors as myself. I am truly sorry and I humbly repent. For the sake of Your Son Jesus Christ, have mercy on me and forgive me; that I may delight in Your will, and walk in Your ways, to the glory of Your name. Amen.

Encourage learners to place the copy in a location where they will see it each day. Ask learners to make time each day to pray this prayer of confession aloud. Begin the next class by asking learners to share their experiences as they made the prayer of confession a part of their daily routine.

A Plea for Deliverance

Devotional Reading: Psalm 107:23-32
Background Scripture: Psalm 22; Daniel 3

Psalm 22:1-11

To the chief Musician upon Aijeleth Shahar, A Psalm of David.

1 My God, my God, why hast thou forsaken me? Why art thou so far from helping me, and from the words of my roaring?

2 O my God, I cry in the daytime, but thou hearest not; And in the night season, and am not silent.

3 But thou art holy, O thou that inhabitest the praises of Israel.

4 Our fathers trusted in thee: They trusted, and thou didst deliver them.

5 They cried unto thee, and were delivered: They trusted in thee, and were not confounded.

6 But I am a worm, and no man; A reproach of men, and despised of the people.

7 All they that see me laugh me to scorn: They shoot out the lip, they shake the head, saying,

8 He trusted on the Lord that he would deliver him: Let him deliver him, seeing he delighted in him.

9 But thou art he that took me out of the womb: Thou didst make me hope when I was upon my mother's breasts.

10 I was cast upon thee from the womb: Thou art my God from my mother's belly.

11 Be not far from me; for trouble is near; For there is none to help.

Key Text

My God, my God, why hast thou forsaken me? Why art thou so far from helping me, and from the words of my roaring? —**Psalm 22:1**

Worship in the
Covenant Community

Unit 2: Songs of the Old Testament
Lessons 6–9

Lesson Aims

After participating in this lesson, each learner will be able to:

1. Identify the New Testament significance of Psalm 22.

2. Compare and contrast David's experiences with his trust in God.

3. Identify an area of personal trial and offer a prayer for God's help or rescue.

Lesson Outline

Introduction

A. Hymns of Lament

Most modern-day hymnals include indices that list hymns according to their themes and emphases. Such lists allow users to find hymns based on specific doctrinal topics. Possible motifs include *praise* (example: "Come, Thou Fount"), *thanksgiving* (example: "All Creatures of Our God and King"), *personal testimony* (example: "Blessed Assurance"), and *hope* (example: "In Christ Alone").

The book of Psalms served as the hymnbook for the Old Testament people of God. In that book, we find psalms of praise, thanksgiving, and hope, but we also see another side to worship: psalms of lament, grief, guilt, doubt, and anger.

Most often, it seems that our congregations' songs of worship focus on thanksgiving and praise, and rightly so: "For the Lord is great, and greatly to be praised" (Psalm 96:4). Rarely, however, does it seem that we are eager to sing songs and hymns that reflect the lament and sadness that we might feel. Perhaps it would do our congregations good to follow the book of Psalms and recover hymns and songs of lament for corporate and personal worship.

B. Lesson Context

By one estimate, there are six types of psalms in the Old Testament book of Psalms: lament, thanksgiving, wisdom, praise, psalms of Zion, and imprecatory. Most students categorize Psalm 22 as a lament psalm. Such psalms are characterized by the psalmist's attitude of personal anguish and the psalmist's petitions to God in response to some felt suffering.

Lament psalms typically contain a threefold structure, demonstrated by Psalm 13. First, lament psalms begin with a complaint or question, such as "How long wilt thou forget me, O Lord?" (Psalm 13:1). Second, the psalmist petitions or cries for help from the Lord, such as "Consider and hear me, O Lord my God" (13:3). Finally, the psalmist concludes with praise and worship to God: "I will sing unto the Lord, because he hath dealt bountifully with me" (13:6).

Psalm 22 contains these same elements. It begins with the psalmist's question (Psalm 22:1), transitions into a set of his petitions and cries for help (22:2, 11, 19-21), and concludes with his worship of God (22:22-23). Some students see aspects of both lament psalms and praise psalms in Psalm 22. As a result, these students divide the psalm into two parts: a lament psalm (22:1-21) and a praise psalm (22:22-31). Regardless of how we categorize and divide this psalm, it depicts the sadness and worship of someone suffering.

The psalm's superscription provides some information regarding context. First, it directs "the chief Musician" to sing this psalm to a tune apparently known to the psalm's original audience. Second, the superscription also tells us that Psalm 22 was "A Psalm of David." Like most psalms, this psalm does not indicate the situation that led David to compose the psalm (contrast Psalms 18, 51). One possibility is that David wrote this psalm while hiding from Saul (see 1 Samuel 23:7-29). Whatever the situation, we know from the verses after today's lesson text that David felt abandoned, isolated, and in danger. His body was failing and on the verge of death (Psalm 22:14-15, 17). His enemies had surrounded him like wild animals (22:12, 16), eager to attack (22:13, 21) and strip him of his clothing (22:18).

The writers of the New Testament connected the suffering of the psalmist and his prayer for help with the suffering of Jesus and His prayers during the crucifixion. Of New Testament quotations of and allusions to Psalm 22, most occur in the passion narratives of the Gospels:

- Psalm 22:1, quoted in Matthew 27:46; Mark 15:34
- Psalm 22:7-8, alluded to in Matthew 27:39; Mark 15:29; Luke 23:35-36
- Psalm 22:8, alluded to in Matthew 27:43
- Psalm 22:18, quoted in John 19:24
- Psalm 22:22, quoted in Hebrews 2:12

Some students have called this psalm "The Psalm of the Cross" because of its connections to Jesus' suffering and the lament He expressed to His heavenly Father while on the cross.

We may be drawn to interpret Psalm 22 only in light of Christ's suffering—and understandably so! But if we do, we will miss how it, in its original context, can inform our spiritual growth.

I. Petition by David
(Psalm 22:1-5)
A. God's Distance (vv. 1-2)
1a. My God, my God, why hast thou forsaken me?

David was surrounded by enemies who mocked him and were eager to see him destroyed (Psalm 22:12, 16). In light of this seemingly hopeless situation, David cried out to God. His cries were notably not directed to any random pagan god. Instead, he called on the God with whom he had a relationship: *my God* (compare 31:14).

By using this term of intimacy, David demonstrated confidence that the God who had entered into a covenant relationship with Israel would also be faithful and present to him. But David's situation was so dire that he felt compelled to ask *why* God seemed distant. Throughout the history of Israel, God had promised His presence with His people (example: Deuteronomy 31:6-8). The promise of God's presence anchored the hope of the psalmists (examples: Psalms 9:10; 37:28; 94:14).

While suffering on the cross, Jesus quoted this half-verse in Aramaic: "Eloi, Eloi, lama sabachthani? which is, being interpreted, My God, my God, why hast thou forsaken me?" (Mark 15:34). In the lead-up to and during His crucifixion, Jesus was mocked, attacked, and forsaken as He was handed over to death (examples: Matthew 27:27-31; Mark 15:29-32). The suffering led Jesus to feel abandoned by His heavenly Father. By quoting this psalm as a prayer, Jesus expressed anguish regarding the rejection that He experienced on the cross.

1b. Why art thou so far from helping me, and from the words of my roaring?

Any hope of rescue seemed *far* away (compare Psalm 22:19, not in our printed text). The kind of *helping* that David desired was deliverance from his enemies. All other avenues of deliverance had been exhausted; only the strength of the almighty Lord could save David (compare 10:1; 28:8).

The phrase *the words of my roaring* reflects the depths of David's despair. He was left to groan and cry out for any means of rescue. The sense of being abandoned by God led David to cry out as a last resort. His cries were like the roar of a wild animal in anguish (compare Psalm 32:3; Isaiah 5:29).

> ### What Do You Think?
> How would you respond to the claim that believers should not question God?
> ### Digging Deeper
> What Scripture texts support your answer?

2. O my God, I cry in the daytime, but thou hearest not; and in the night season, and am not silent.

David's cries for rescue were not a one-time occurrence; he petitioned God *in the daytime* and *the night season* for deliverance. It is understandable for God's people to cry out to God and question whether or not He hears those petitions (examples: Psalm 42:3; Lamentations 3:8, 44). However, unlike the experience of other psalmists, it seemed to David that God *hearest not* the man's cries (compare Psalm 88:1).

Sleepless Nights

The experiences of parenthood will inevitably include many sleepless nights! After my children were born, I awoke most nights for midnight feedings. As they grew older, my sleepless nights differed. Sometimes, I was awakened by a crying child, fearful of a nightmare. Other times, a child crawling into my bed would startle me awake.

As my children became teenagers, my sleepless nights took a different flavor. I stayed awake to welcome them home from competitions, dates, or jobs. Once they moved to college and would come back to visit, I kept vigilant watch through the early hours of the morning to confirm their safe arrival.

People experience sleepless nights for various reasons, including mental turmoil and spiritual anguish. The next time you face a sleepless night, will you consider praying to God about your fears? We can sleep with the promise that God will be with us—even in our slumber (Psalm 4:8). We can trust Him because He is the one who "neither slumber[s] nor sleep[s]" (121:4).   —L. M. W.

B. God's Deliverance (vv. 3-5)

3. But thou art holy, O thou that inhabitest the praises of Israel.

Although David had questioned why God seemed distant (Psalm 22:1, above), he still affirmed the unique characteristics of God. Notably, he proclaimed that God is *holy*, meaning He is totally perfect and free of any blemish of sin (1 Samuel 2:2; Isaiah 40:25; Habakkuk 1:13; Revelation 15:4; etc.). There would be none other who could save God's people. God's holiness is often the foundation of worship in the psalms (examples: Psalms 29:2; 99:3, 5, 9; 145:21).

For ancient Israel, God's presence was represented by the ark of testimony. He would reveal His presence "from above the mercy seat, from between the two cherubims which are upon the ark of the testimony" (Exodus 25:22; compare Psalms 80:1; 99:1). However, in the verse before us, God's presence is in the midst of His people as He *inhabitest the praises of Israel*. Even in distress, David could worship God—the only one who is holy, faithful, and present in the midst of suffering.

> ### What Do You Think?
> In what ways can you emphasize God's holiness in your personal and corporate worship?
> ### Digging Deeper
> How will your worship address other attributes of God, such as His love, mercy, faithfulness, or righteousness?

4-5. Our fathers trusted in thee: they trusted, and thou didst deliver them. They cried unto thee, and were delivered: they trusted in thee, and were not confounded.

The history of God's work with His people gave David confidence in God's faithfulness. Such reflection anchored David's worship and provided encouragement regarding God's active and all-powerful presence (compare Psalm 44:1-8). Other psalmists shared this view (examples: 78:53; 107:6).

Perhaps David was reflecting on the exodus from Egypt. While enslaved in Egypt, the people *trusted* God's promises to their ancestors—promises of blessing, descendants, and land (Genesis 15:14-18; 17:4-8; 26:2-6, 24; 28:13-15; 46:2-4). Trusting these promises and God's faithfulness, the people cried out that God would bring freedom from their enslavement (Exodus 2:23-24). God saw the people in their suffering, took pity on them (2:25), and *delivered* them from their oppression (12:31-42).

The word *confounded* typically means to be confused or perplexed. However, that is not its meaning in this verse. The underlying Hebrew word is translated elsewhere as "ashamed" (Psalms 25:2; 31:1; etc.), and that is the sense here. Those who hope in the Lord and trust His promises have hope that He will someday remove shame once and for all (Isaiah 28:16; Romans 9:33; 1 Peter 2:6).

The three uses in these verses of a form of the word *trust* reveal the tension between trust and suffering. Feelings of sadness, anger, and fear are often associated with grief—such are normal human emotions. However, in those moments, we can also trust that God is present and with us and will be faithful to us. Such tension reveals a "both-and" situation: we can *both* cry out in our suffering *and* trust that God will provide comfort (see 2 Corinthians 1:3-4).

What Do You Think?
Who is an ancestor of yours who demonstrated trust in God during a season of suffering?

Digging Deeper
How will you demonstrate trust in God so that you can be an example to future generations?

The Example of Ancestors

Sensing sadness from my teenage daughter, I went to her room to check on her. I lay in her bed beside her, hearing her sadness pour from her heart. When she finished, and we lay there in the quiet, I began telling her stories of her great-grandmother, a woman my daughter had never met. I told my daughter about her ancestor's passion, tenacity, and faith. I concluded by saying, "Your great-grandmother was a strong woman,

and you remind me a lot of her." I hoped that the example of her great-grandmother would strengthen my daughter's faith and character.

In the midst of the psalmist's trials, he reflected on the examples of his ancestors, specifically their faith and trust in God. Who is a "spiritual ancestor" for you—someone whose faith example you can follow? How can their legacy of faith strengthen your faith today? —L. M. W.

II. Insult from Enemies
(Psalm 22:6-8)
A. Despised (v. 6)

6. But I am a worm, and no man; a reproach of men, and despised of the people.

Worms are associated with destruction, death, and decay (examples: Deuteronomy 28:39; Job 21:26; Isaiah 51:8). David's self-identification as *a worm* and not a *man* reveals the extent of his negative self-assessment (compare Job 25:6). His enemies had treated him as though he was worthless and on the verge of death. He began to believe that their threats and vile hopes would come true.

The Lord had delivered David's ancestors (see Psalm 22:5, above), thus freeing them from feelings of shame. However, as David waited for rescue, he became *despised* by others and the object of their *reproach*. The Lord would need to intervene for David to experience freedom from his dishonor and shame.

B. Mocked (vv. 7-8)

7. All they that see me laugh me to scorn: they shoot out the lip, they shake the head, saying.

How to Say It

Aramaic	*Air*-uh-**may**-ik.
cherubims	*chair*-uh-bimz.
Corinthians	Ko-*rin*-thee-unz (*th* as in *thin*).
Eloi (*Aramaic*)	Ee-*lo*-eye.
lama (*Aramaic*)	*lah*-mah.
lament	luh-*ment*.
sabachthani (*Aramaic*)	suh-*back*-thuh-nee.

Although God seemed silent, David's enemies were not. They took advantage of David's situation to make a spectacle of his suffering. They ridiculed David and heaped *scorn* and insult on him because he trusted God. Mockery and insult led them to *shake* their heads out of disdain and disgust (compare Psalm 109:25).

8. He trusted on the LORD that he would deliver him: let him deliver him, seeing he delighted in him.

This verse reveals that David's enemies quoted his prayers back to him. However, they did so with a harsh and sarcastic tone (compare Psalm 42:10). The confidence of David's enemies is displayed as they sarcastically invited God to *deliver* David. They refused to believe that God would miraculously intervene for the good of David (compare 3:2; 71:11). To the suffering psalmist, their mocking words seemed to have a kernel of truth; their sarcastic invitation likely reinforced the psalmist's doubts and lament.

God's people often face scorn and ridicule from the unrighteous (examples: Psalms 31:11-18; 35:15-16; 69:7-20). Even Jesus faced ridicule (Matthew 27:39) and sarcastic incitements (27:43) while suffering, adopting Psalm 22:1 as His own in the process (Matthew 27:46; see above). In those moments of testing, we can trust that God will be faithful to us, even amid ridicule and mockery. This trust is our hope as believers (Hebrews 10:23).

III. Presence of God
(Psalm 22:9-11)
A. Since Birth (vv. 9-10)
9-10. But thou art he that took me out of

the womb: thou didst make me hope when I was upon my mother's breasts. I was cast upon thee from the womb: Thou art my God from my mother's belly.

David's delight in the Lord came from the ways that God had provided for him—a provision that began while David was still in his mother's *womb*. While "covered" in his mother's womb, he was "fearfully and wonderfully made" by a caring God (Psalm 139:13-14). God's care continued after David was born and received his mother's love, care and provision. God's care for His servant was on display from that man's conception to his birth and childhood. In another psalm, the psalmist proclaimed, "By thee have I been holden up from the womb: Thou art he that took me out of my mother's bowels: My praise shall be continually of thee" (71:6).

By reflecting on God's provision during his conception, birth, and upbringing, David demonstrated the reason for his *hope*. A form of the underlying Hebrew word translated *hope* is also translated as "trusted" elsewhere in this passage (Psalm 22:4-5), and that is the sense in the verse before us. David's trust in God was not based simply on any good feelings that David felt. Instead, David's confidence came from the certainty he had because of God's previous demonstrations of provision (see Isaiah 46:3-4). Although David experienced suffering and felt doubt, he demonstrated trust that God would provide, leading the psalmist to proclaim in worship: *thou art my God.*

B. Always Near (v. 11)
11. Be not far from me; for trouble is near; for there is none to help.

David's petition *be not far from me* is repeated later in the psalm (Psalm 22:19, not in our printed text). The petition to God reflects David's deep need for urgent deliverance from his enemies and his situation. The psalmists frequently petitioned for the nearness of God's presence when they faced trials and suffering (examples: 35:22; 38:21; 71:12). They knew that God is always-present (omnipresent; example: 139:7-12). Surrounded by trouble, the psalmists desired to experience God's presence through their deliverance from suffering.

The sort of presence that David desired was an act of deliverance from the *trouble* brought on by his enemies (compare 69:18). David sought the *help* that *none* other could provide, a deliverance that only God could give (see 142:4-6).

Conclusion

A. Space for Lament

Psalm 22 consists of David's lament and petition balanced with his praise and adoration. His questioning "Why?" (Psalm 22:1) resulted in his praise to God. David's cries of suffering turned to worship because of the belief that God would ultimately be faithful and bring deliverance. And David hoped that he would praise God and that all nations and people would someday praise God (22:27-31).

The lament songs of the Psalter give us an example of how we might express our fears, frustrations, sadness, and petitions to the Lord. These psalms model how believers can enter the presence of God and proclaim their concerns and frustrations. Even though God already knows our wants, needs, and fears, He invites us to express those things to Him through our prayers and songs.

Jesus modeled lament for us when, on the cross, He quoted this psalm. The Son of God asked His heavenly Father, "Why?" (Matthew 27:46). We, too, can ask "Why?" to our heavenly Father when we experience suffering and hardship. Therefore, our personal and corporate times of worship can include prayer, lament, and petitions to the Lord. But there are two cautions here. First, we should not let our *why* lead to questioning God's justice. Second, we cannot flourish by remaining in an endless loop of *why, why, why*. An answer to that

Be not far from me!

Visual for Lesson 7. *Show this visual as you discuss the commentary and discussion questions associated with Psalm 22:11.*

may never come. Eventually, we have to move from *why* to *what's next?*

Further, our congregations should be communities that encourage expressions of lament. Perhaps we can sing hymns of lament and hope, like "O God, Our Help in Ages Past." Another way to do so is through listening and supporting those suffering and grieving.

The psalms invite us to consider the role of lament in our worship. When we open our hearts to God and acknowledge our sadness and suffering, we depend entirely on Him. The psalms also model how we might praise God for His power and deliverance, even if our situations seem hopeless. How will the psalms be your hymnbook the next time you are in a season of suffering?

B. Prayer

Holy God, You are all-powerful and always present. You know us when we are experiencing joy and gladness and when we are experiencing sadness and grief. In seasons of lament, remind us to call out to You, even if all we can proclaim is our grief. We trust in Your unfailing love and Your faithfulness to us. Hear the cries of our hearts and come quickly to our aid so that we might experience the comfort and deliverance only You provide. In Jesus' name we pray. Amen.

C. Thought to Remember

Cry out to God!

Involvement Learning

Enhance your lesson with KJV Bible Student *(from your curriculum supplier) and the reproducible activity page (at www.standardlesson.com or in the back of the* KJV Standard Lesson Commentary Deluxe Edition*).*

Into the Lesson

Divide learners into triads. Lead into the activity by saying, "At some point, each of us will experience a crisis. At that time, we will need the support and care of others." Have learners answer the following question in their groups: 1–Who do you call on when you experience a crisis? 2–What about that person makes him or her the best first call in a dire situation? 3–How do you want that person to respond when you call on him or her?

After five minutes of in-group discussion, ask volunteers to share their responses. Lead into Bible study by saying, "When we are in dire straits, we w∴nt to know who we can depend on. As believers, ve know that we can depend on God. But what a᠊out when He seems to be ignoring our situation? The psalm in today's lesson can help us reframe our thinking without negating the negative feelings we may be feeling in such a situation."

Into the Word

Using the Lesson Context, give a background summary of Psalm 22. Be sure to include information about its genre and how the psalm is quoted or alluded to in the New Testament. (*Option.* Ask a volunteer to prepare this ahead of time.) After the presentation, ask the following for whole-class discussion: "What possible situation might have prompted David to pen this psalm?"

Write the following headers on the board:

How David Felt | What David Knew | What Is Revealed?

Divide learners into the same triads. Have them silently read Psalm 22:1-11 and answer the following questions for in-group discussion: 1–What feelings of David does this psalm communicate? 2–What true things did his feelings reveal? 3–What thoughts of David does this psalm communicate? 4–What true things did his knowledge reveal?

Have a volunteer from each triad offer their

group's answers. Write the responses on the board under the appropriate header.

Direct learners to return to their triads and answer the following questions, using the responses on the board to inform their answers: 1–What possible tensions could arise between how David felt and what he knew? 2–How could those tensions exist simultaneously?

Option. Divide the class into groups of four and have them research Scripture for examples of when people would have used the language of the psalm to affirm God's character and deeds as David did here. (*Possible examples could include Genesis 37:12-36; Exodus 1; 2 Samuel 15:13-30; Esther 4:15–5:1; Daniel 3:8-23; Job 19:1-13.*)

Into Life

Write the following questions on the board:

1. *Do you connect with this psalm or struggle to empathize with David? Why and how?*
2. *What is a struggle in your life or a personal trial that feels hopeless?*
3. *What evidence can you recall of God's faithfulness to you?*

Distribute an index card and pen to each learner. Ask a volunteer to read aloud Psalm 22 for the whole class. Then, instruct learners to write their answers to the questions on the index cards. After one minute, ask learners to flip over their index cards and write a prayer for God's help or rescue. After one minute, ask them to join a partner for prayer, asking for God's help.

Option 1. Distribute copies of the "A Psalm for Today" exercise from the activity page, which you can download. Have learners complete the activity in one minute or less before sharing their findings with a partner.

Option 2. Distribute copies of the "Personal Response" activity from the activity page. Have learners work in small groups to complete as indicated.

Praise for Deliverance

Devotional Reading: Ephesians 1:3-14
Background Scripture: Isaiah 25; Daniel 6:10-28

Isaiah 25:1-10a

1 O Lord, thou art my God; I will exalt thee, I will praise thy name; For thou hast done wonderful things; Thy counsels of old are faithfulness and truth.

2 For thou hast made of a city an heap; Of a defenced city a ruin: A palace of strangers to be no city; It shall never be built.

3 Therefore shall the strong people glorify thee, The city of the terrible nations shall fear thee.

4 For thou hast been a strength to the poor, A strength to the needy in his distress, A refuge from the storm, a shadow from the heat, When the blast of the terrible one is as a storm against the wall.

5 Thou shalt bring down the noise of strangers, As the heat in a dry place, Even the heat with the shadow of a cloud: the branch of the terrible ones shall be brought low.

6 And in this mountain shall the Lord of hosts make unto all people A feast of fat things, a feast of wines on the lees, Of fat things full of marrow, of wines on the lees well refined.

7 And he will destroy in this mountain The face of the covering cast over all people, And the vail that is spread over all nations.

8 He will swallow up death in victory; And the Lord God will wipe away tears from off all faces; And the rebuke of his people shall he take away from off all the earth: For the Lord hath spoken it.

9 And it shall be said in that day, Lo, this is our God; We have waited for him, and he will save us: This is the Lord; we have waited for him, We will be glad and rejoice in his salvation.

10 For in this mountain shall the hand of the Lord rest.

Key Text

In this mountain shall the Lord of hosts make unto all people a feast of fat things, a feast of wines on the lees, of fat things full of marrow, of wines on the lees well refined. —**Isaiah 25:6**

Worship in the
Covenant Community

Unit 2: Songs of the Old Testament
Lessons 6–9

Lesson Aims

After participating in this lesson, each learner will be able to:

1. Summarize the historical context of Isaiah the man.

2. Connect Isaiah's historical context to his specific assurances of God's faithfulness.

3. Write a personal testimony to God's faithfulness.

Lesson Outline

Introduction

A. When the Darkness Lifts

At times, darkness overwhelms. It happens to all; no one is exempt. Whether that darkness comes in the form of grief, poverty, sickness, or national tragedy, believers cry out to God for deliverance.

When we experience God's rescue, we naturally . . . do what? That's a crucial question because it will reveal the level of our spiritual maturity and devotion. There are affirmations of this in various places in the Bible. One New Testament example is Luke 17:17. One Old Testament example is found in today's text.

B. Lesson Context

Today's text comes from a section of Isaiah that is often called "The Isaiah Apocalypse" (chap. 24–27). This is because the scenes pictured are similar to the apocalyptic language (which is imagery describing the end of the world) found in the book of Revelation (compare Zechariah 9–14; Mark 13:24-27).

Isaiah became a prophet in the year King Uzziah of Judah died around 740 BC (Isaiah 6:1-10). By the time Isaiah appeared on the scene, the Israelites had been divided into two countries for almost 200 years: the northern kingdom of Israel and the southern kingdom of Judah. The prophet had a long ministry of several decades in Judah during the reigns of Jotham, Ahaz, and Hezekiah.

Isaiah's ministry began during a time of economic and military prosperity (Isaiah 2:7). But spiritual rot had set in (2:8), and it was only a matter of time before God intervened (2:9–4:1).

God's interventions took the form of oppression by foreign powers (Isaiah 7:20). One such oppression occurred during the reign of Ahaz of Judah (735–716 BC) when Aram (Syria) and the northern kingdom of Israel joined forces against Judah (2 Kings 16:1-10). Ahaz "saved" Judah by means of an unholy alliance with Assyria (16:7-9). That country eventually conquered northern Israel and exiled its inhabitants in 722 BC (17:6). The city of Jerusalem (in Judah) barely escaped the same fate in 701 BC (18:13–19:27). But that was only temporary. Jerusalem's reaction to that time of forthcoming darkness would reveal where the inhabitants' hearts actually lay (Jeremiah 7:1-8; compare Isaiah 42:20-25).

Isaiah not only served during difficult times, but he also foresaw them—not only for Judah, but for the idolatrous nations around her, such as Egypt, Edom, and Tyre (Isaiah 14:28–23:18). But while confrontation about sin was a critical part of the task of the prophets, that was not their only function; the prophets also provided hope. The situation looks utterly hopeless by the time the reader gets to Isaiah 24. That chapter's 23 verses are dire in their prediction of the devastation of the whole earth. The reason is given in Isaiah 24:5: "The earth also is defiled under the inhabitants thereof; because they have transgressed the laws, changed the ordinance, broken the everlasting covenant." The utter holiness of God that is unmistakable in Isaiah 24 is followed by a message of God's love in Isaiah 25. It bears a message of hope—today's lesson.

I. Praise the Lord
(Isaiah 25:1-5)

A. For His Judgments (vv. 1-3)

1. O LORD, thou art my God; I will exalt thee, I will praise thy name; for thou hast done wonderful things; thy counsels of old are faithfulness and truth.

Isaiah's response to the vision of devastation in chapter 24 was a prayer of *praise*. The prayer involves the prophet's use of two names for the same recipient: *Lord* and *God*. By adding the word *my*, the prophet leaves no doubt where his loyalties lie (compare Isaiah 40:27; 49:5; 61:10). The people of Judah were to have a personal relationship with and loyalty to the only true God. He is not a fictitious regional god (1 Kings 20:28) but the God who reigns over the whole earth.

Isaiah's reflection on God's *wonderful things* echoes a key element of some psalms: pondering God's accomplished works as indicators of His identity and character (example: Psalm 77; contrast 78:9-20). But in this regard, there's a difference between the psalmist's recall of God's

wonders and Isaiah's recall: the psalmist speaks of God's wonders that were tied to positive elements of His works and provisions, while Isaiah's praise was for the destruction God had wrought on sinful people and places. See the next verse.

2a. For thou hast made of a city an heap; of a defenced city a ruin: a palace of strangers to be no city.

History witnesses to the arrogance of those who trust in earthly protections. It's not wrong to take steps to protect oneself or others from harm (example: Nehemiah 3). But reliance on such human efforts to the exclusion of God leads to arrogance and disaster (examples: 2 Samuel 5:6-8; Proverbs 18:10-11; Daniel 4:19-33).

As we read the verse before us, we may wonder which *city* Isaiah refers to. Jerusalem could be the reference, given its destruction in 586 BC (Isaiah 64:10-11), but mentioning a palace of strangers (foreigners) works against this. Similar language of destruction is used for Damascus (Isaiah 17:1; compare Amos 1:3-5; compare 2 Kings 25:8-10). Another candidate is Tyre (Isaiah 23; compare Ezekiel 26:4). Given the grammatical construction of the phrasings, the best answer is "none of the above, specifically." Instead, the prophet acknowledges God's power over every city anywhere. No matter how *defenced* (fortified) a city or location may be, it is not, nor ever will

How to Say It

Ahaz	Ay-haz.
apocalypse	uh-*pock*-uh-lips.
Aram	Air-um.
Jotham	Jo-thum.
Tyre	Tire.
Uzziah	Uh-zye-uh.

Visual for
Lessons 8 & 12

With verse 6, ask learners to consider how hospitality can be a foretaste of God's own feast.

be, able to resist God's plans (Deuteronomy 3:4-6; 28:49-52). As the previous chapter of Isaiah 24 speaks of the entirety of the earth, so also does Isaiah 25 by considering God's sovereignty over all the earth's cities. In effect, the prophet uses the metaphor of a city for the whole earth.

2b. It shall never be built.

Destroyed cities and towns were often rebuilt. Ideal places for cities in the ancient world involved three criteria: (1) access to water, (2) access to one or more trade routes, and (3) defensibility. So a city that had been destroyed was subject to being rebuilt if those three criteria still held for a given location. For God to forbid a city ever being rebuilt indicates His extreme displeasure of what went on there (examples: Deuteronomy 13:12-18; Jeremiah 49:13). To ignore this prohibition was to invite the wrath of God anew (Joshua 6:26; 1 Kings 16:34).

Flipping the Script

See if you can identify what these four structures have in common: the Tower of Babel, the Reich Chancellery, Solomon's Temple, and the statue of Saddam Hussein that stood in Firdos Square. *Answer:* They are all no more—destroyed!

The Tower of Babel and its city were abandoned and left incomplete when the motive of the builders invited God's judgment (Genesis 11:1-9). The stunning Reich Chancellery, the seat of power of Hitler's Nazi regime in Berlin, was destroyed

when the city fell to the Soviets in 1945. Solomon's Temple, built with holy motives, was destroyed because of eventual idolatry (Ezekiel 8). Hussein's statue was pulled down as his oppressive dictatorship was terminated by force.

Although those four destructions have one or more common themes, we take care not to equate them with one another too readily or glibly. There are differences and unknowns to acknowledge. One thread of commonality among scriptural destructions is that such acts of divine judgment are usually connected with the deliverance of God's people from harm or oppression. But sometimes, the script is flipped, as judgment comes upon God's people by the hands of God-sent oppressors (Isaiah 7:18-20).

As we live in this fallen world, we know that relief from ungodly oppression does not always happen on our preferred timetable. Even so, God is still looking for those who would speak His Word to unholy power structures (compare Isaiah 6:8; Ezekiel 22:30-31). How will you recognize God's call if or when it comes to you?

—C. S.

3. Therefore shall the strong people glorify thee, the city of the terrible nations shall fear thee.

In the older language of the King James Version, the word *terrible* refers to "something that strikes terror." The concept speaks of those who live by the principle of "might makes right" (compare Isaiah 13:11). Such people have no regard for God (Psalms 54:3; 86:14).

The parallel between the first and second lines in verse 3 indicates *the strong people* and *the terrible nations* refer to the same group. That may make us wonder if repentance is the way they will *glorify* God. That's a possibility (compare Jonah 3). Another possibility is that any respect they have for God is forced and grudgingly given (compare Revelation 6:15-17).

B. For His Mercy (vv. 4-5)

4-5. For thou hast been a strength to the poor, a strength to the needy in his distress, a refuge from the storm, a shadow from the heat,

when the blast of the terrible ones is as a storm against the wall. Thou shalt bring down the noise of strangers, as the heat in a dry place; even the heat with the shadow of a cloud: the branch of the terrible ones shall be brought low.

The opening word *for* ties the previous discussion of the oppressive nations to a recognition of God's concern for *the poor* and *the needy*. When people groups neglect or abuse the most vulnerable, God comes to their defense. In that regard, Isaiah compares God to a *refuge from the storm* or a shade *from the heat* (compare Isaiah 14:30; contrast 30:2-3). A military image can be detected here because the word translated *strength* is also translated "fortress" elsewhere (Jeremiah 16:19; Daniel 11:7, 10).

A pithy description of how God acts is that He "comforts the disturbed" and "disturbs the comfortable." What we just considered describes the former; what Isaiah prophesies next describes the latter. The phrase *Thou shalt bring down the noise of strangers* is reflected more specifically in Jeremiah 51:55, where God is predicted to have "destroyed out of [Babylon] the great voice." Loud noise is a characteristic of war and other conflicts (Psalms 46:6; 74:23; Isaiah 13:4). But no matter how much noise the enemies of God and His people make, the God of Israel can silence it with His voice (66:6).

What Do You Think?

In what ways does the church demonstrate God's concern for the poor?

Digging Deeper

What roadblocks prevent your community from recognizing God's concern for the poor?

God's Levee

Have you ever filled thousands of sandbags in a single day? I did—or at least it seemed as if I did. The Mississippi River was overflowing its banks, and the dikes that held the river at bay needed to be raised and strengthened. Living nearby, I volunteered to help. As the day ended, I was as tired as I had ever been! But our team may have saved dozens of homes.

Dikes and levees are used everywhere to protect areas from flooding. But human instruments are subject to failure, whereas God's protection is not. Neither is His wrath. We decide whether we shall avail ourselves of His protection from the floodwaters of sin or be objects of the oncoming flood of His wrath.

See the outcome of option 1 in Psalm 124:1-5 and Isaiah 66:12; for the danger of option 2, see Job 27:20 and Isaiah 28:2.

How do you know which side of God's levee you are on?   —C. S.

II. The Lord Hosts a Banquet
(Isaiah 25:6-8)
A. Invitation to Dine (v. 6)

6a. And in this mountain shall the LORD of hosts make unto all people a feast of fat things.

This mountain refers to God's holy mountain in Jerusalem (Isaiah 27:13). The prophet locates a future banquet here as he uses that phrase a total of three times in 25:6, 7, 10). Beyond the devastation of the earth in Isaiah 24 and the judgment of the nations in Isaiah 25:1-5, Isaiah offers a hopeful vision because of what will happen on the mountain where Jerusalem is located. It is important to note that the forthcoming feast will be available *unto all people* (the word *people* is plural in the Hebrew text—people groups). The guest list for this feast is limitless (compare Luke 14:15-24; Revelation 19:19). No one is meant to be excluded, "on the outside looking in."

What Do You Think?

How could or does your congregation benefit from interaction with Christians from different nationalities?

Digging Deeper

What challenges prevent deeper relationships in this area, and how can your congregation address those?

6b. A feast of wines on the lees, of fat things full of marrow, of wines on the lees well refined.

This half-verse indicates the celebratory nature of the festival to come. The nature of the food and beverage indicates that this was not the regular diet of people who lived in Judah. Meat, which has bones *full of marrow*, was a rare delicacy, and *wine* was expensive and reserved for special occasions. These two are depicted together in a positive sense here and in Proverbs 9:1-2; they are depicted together in a negative sense in Proverbs 23:20 and Isaiah 22:12-13.

The phrase *wines on the lees* may sound strange to us. "The lees" refers to what is left over from the grapes after the initial stage of their pressing. Leaving wine on the lees strengthens its taste. Then when the wine is strained before consumption, what remains is wine of the highest quality. Clearly, God will serve only the best to those who attend this special feast (compare John 2:10). No shortcuts here!

This feast looks back to Exodus 24:1-11 where Israel ate and drank in the presence of God. They enjoyed a banquet where they saw God and experienced God's saving presence on God's holy mountain. This vision also looks forward to the messianic banquet in the age to come, where people will come from all over the earth to eat and drink in the kingdom of God with Abraham, Isaac, and Jacob (Matthew 8:11; Luke 13:29).

B. Deliverance from Death (vv. 7-8)

7-8. And he will destroy in this mountain the face of the covering cast over all people, and the vail that is spread over all nations. He will swallow up death in victory; and the Lord God will wipe away tears from off all faces; and the rebuke of his people shall he take away from off all the earth: for the Lord hath spoken it.

The *mountain* on which God will host a feast is the same mountain on which He will destroy something. There is salvation, and there is destruction. This salvation is deliverance from death itself. Death covers *the face of* all people. Everyone wears this veil as a shroud. Everyone is appointed to die (Hebrews 9:27). No one escapes death.

The banquet, therefore, celebrates the death of death. God will destroy death, and His people will celebrate life; see Paul's quotation of Isa-

iah 25:8 in 1 Corinthians 15:54. The apostle John, for his part, quotes Isaiah 25:8 twice: Revelation 7:17; 21:4. In the new heaven and new earth, there will be no more death or pain, no more mourning, and no more tears. The foundation of the Christian's assurance in this regard is the resurrection of Jesus (1 Corinthians 15:12-28).

> **What Do You Think?**
> When considering death, do you tend to dwell on the certainty of God's work or the uncertainty of exactly what life after death will be like?
>
> **Digging Deeper**
> How does either approach allow you to share your hope in the Lord with others who may not know Him?

III. Testify About Him
(Isaiah 25:9-10a)
A. What Will Be Said (v. 9)

9. And it shall be said in that day, Lo, this is our God; we have waited for him, and he will save us: this is the Lord; we have waited for him, we will be glad and rejoice in his salvation.

Isaiah 25 begins with the prophet's tribute of praise. Now the praise is on the lips of all who will come to the mountain of the Lord to share in the "wonderful things" to be provided there (Isaiah 25:1). Note the use of the pronouns *our*, *we* (thrice), and *us*. The language is similar to the often-sung words of Psalm 118:24: "This is the day which the Lord hath made; we will rejoice and be glad in it."

We should note that the Hebrew name Isaiah means "the Lord saves" or "the Lord is salvation." Given that the words *save* and *salvation* appear in this verse, also consider that the name *Jesus* means the same thing (Matthew 1:21). He is the one who has and will accomplish the wonders Isaiah described.

When banquet day arrives, no better words can be uttered than *This is our God!* The creator and ruler of life became its redeemer at the cross. Death held humanity in its grip until Christ accomplished His work; now Jesus holds "the keys to hell and death" (Revelation 1:18).

B. What Will Be Done (v. 10a)

10a. For in this mountain shall the hand of the Lord rest.

The hand of the Lord is active throughout the Bible. Sometimes it is associated with blessing (Joshua 4:23, 24; Ezra 7:6; Luke 1:66; Acts 11:21); at other times, it is extended for discipline or punishment (Exodus 9:3; Judges 2:15; Ruth 1:13; 1 Samuel 5:6). Here, however, the focus is on the hand's being at *rest* (contrast Isaiah 5:25; 9:21; 11:15; 19:16; 23:11). When God's hand rests upon the land, it gives the land rest and protects it from all enemies, including death. God will rest after He ushers in His new creation—the new heaven and the new earth (65:17-25; Revelation 21–22). Before that rest occurs, "The last enemy that shall be destroyed is death" (1 Corinthians 15:26). When death is defeated for good at the return of Jesus, it will be cast into the lake of fire (Revelation 20:14), never again to cause pain and tears.

What Do You Think?

Why is God's rest good news for people?

Digging Deeper

Can your own rest also be good for others? Explain.

Conclusion

A. Living Gratefully in Hope

Isaiah 25 provided a message of hope for God's covenant people. In response, a song of praise and victory was predicted to be sung by Judah in Isaiah 26. The message of today's lesson text was what assured that song. We mentioned in the Lesson Context that the section of Isaiah 24–27 has been called "The Isaiah Apocalypse"; the final and concluding work of this section is this: there will come a day when God gathers His people to worship Him in a place He has made holy.

People experience oppression in different ways and degrees. But everyone experiences death. We certainly should use godly methods and motivations to overcome oppression and injustice, as well as work for the sanctity of life. But as we do, we should remind ourselves that the complete presence of justice and absence of death in the life to come is what to focus on. It's coming! As we so focus, we experience and expect God's continuing faithfulness for our assured hope in ultimate deliverance.

One way to express this hope is to practice gratitude. We can do so in many ways. Some do so through music as they write and sing songs. Others do so via personal contact. Still others _____ [you fill in the blank]. One of the simplest ways to express gratitude and become thankful, even during trials, is to create a gratitude list daily, perhaps first thing in the morning or the last thing before bed. A daily gratitude list will remind you of God's many gifts. To name them is to offer thanks. Built into this naming is also an expectation of more good things from God, including the death of death. A gratitude list reorients our experience of the trial, recenters our faith, and expresses hope in the future.

As believers in Jesus, we anticipate and yearn for the messianic banquet hosted by Jesus in the presence of God (Matthew 26:29). As Israel shared in the blessings of God through the altar when they ate the sacrifices, so we share in the fellowship of body and blood of Jesus at the table when we eat and drink (1 Corinthians 10:14-17). It is a foretaste of the messianic banquet. When we eat and drink at the table of the Lord, we give thanks for the body and blood of the Lord. We also remember God's faithfulness and yearn for the death of death. We eat and drink, and we go out into the world to serve, comforted by hope (Acts 20:7-12).

B. Prayer

Father, we thank You for the promise of a banquet to celebrate Your faithfulness. Give us the desire and capacity to faithfully serve You in the present. In the name of Jesus. Amen.

C. Thought to Remember

Gratefully wait for the fulfillment of the promised death of death.

Involvement Learning

Enhance your lesson with KJV Bible Student *(from your curriculum supplier) and the reproducible activity page (at www.standardlesson.com or in the back of the* KJV Standard Lesson Commentary Deluxe Edition*).*

Into the Lesson

Ask the class to define the phrase "mountaintop experience." Expect an answer that references some spiritual high point, especially of knowing and loving God. In small groups, have learners find biblical examples of mountaintop experiences that fit or challenge their definition. Encourage volunteers in those groups to share their own experiences and what they have in common with the biblical examples. After a few minutes, ask volunteers to share with the class what they've found.

Lead into Bible study time by saying, "Today's lesson describes God's character and past actions as well as a future mountaintop experience and what God will do for His people. Let's take a look at how Isaiah describes both."

Into the Word

Option. Distribute handouts (you create) of the printed text of Isaiah 25:1-10a.

As a volunteer reads aloud, have learners close their eyes and listen to Isaiah 25:1-10a. Encourage learners to make note of phrases that stand out to them as you read the lesson text aloud. In pairs, have the learners discuss what struck them and why. Allow a few minutes for pairs to find and jot down other places in the Bible that share images or concepts with one or two of their marked concepts. (The commentary can help guide learners through the cross-references provided.)

Alternative. Distribute the "Right Words, Wrong Lines" exercise from the activity page, which you can download. Have learners work in small groups to complete as directed. After several minutes, bring the class back together to go over answers (found on the answer page at the end of the activity pages) and discuss any interesting or surprising connections they discovered.

On the board, write two headers, leaving room for a third to be added: *What God Has Done*

and *What God Will Do.* Have learners list God's actions in Isaiah 25:10a under the appropriate columns.

Option. If you distributed a handout of Isaiah 25:1-10a before, learners can work in pairs to mark God's former and future actions on their own sheets.

Have learners discuss the relationship between remembering what God has already accomplished and having confidence in what He will do in the future. Ask, "What are the implications of remembering or forgetting God's works?"

Into Life

Expand on the previous exercise by having learners brainstorm New Testament works that are fundamental for Christians to remember, as well as any additional insights as to what God plans to do in the future. Ask for the Bible references to these actions or promises. Allow time for discussion.

Add a third column to the board with the header *Our Response.* Have learners identify how Isaiah and the people did or would respond to God's work. Then in pairs, have learners discuss how they can respond to God in these same ways throughout the week to come. For instance, they might discuss what it might look like to praise God's name while grocery shopping or to rejoice in His salvation at family dinner.

After several minutes, ask learners to work alone for one minute on a personal testimony to God's faithfulness, based on what has been studied today.

Option. Distribute the "Personal Testimony" exercise from the activity page for learners to complete this task.

Close class with a prayer thanking God for what He has done and what He will do and asking for reminders of both throughout the week to come.

Trust in God Alone

Devotional Reading: Jeremiah 17:5-11
Background Scripture: Psalm 62

Psalm 62

1 Truly my soul waiteth upon God: from him cometh my salvation.

2 He only is my rock and my salvation; he is my defence; I shall not be greatly moved.

3 How long will ye imagine mischief against a man? Ye shall be slain all of you: as a bowing wall shall ye be, and as a tottering fence.

4 They only consult to cast him down from his excellency: they delight in lies: they bless with their mouth, but they curse inwardly. Selah.

5 My soul, wait thou only upon God; for my expectation is from him.

6 He only is my rock and my salvation: he is my defence; I shall not be moved.

7 In God is my salvation and my glory: the rock of my strength, and my refuge, is in God.

8 Trust in him at all times; ye people, pour out your heart before him: God is a refuge for us. Selah.

9 Surely men of low degree are vanity, and men of high degree are a lie: to be laid in the balance, they are altogether lighter than vanity.

10 Trust not in oppression, and become not vain in robbery: if riches increase, set not your heart upon them.

11 God hath spoken once; twice have I heard this; that power belongeth unto God.

12 Also unto thee, O Lord, belongeth mercy: for thou renderest to every man according to his work.

Key Text

My soul, wait thou only upon God; for my expectation is from him. —**Psalm 62:5**

Worship in the
Covenant Community

Unit 2: Songs of the Old Testament
Lessons 6–9

Lesson Aims

After participating in this lesson, each learner will be able to:

1. List the many ways God is a source of strength in times of trouble.

2. Identify the barriers to peace found in Psalm 62.

3. Create a plan for intentional time to wait quietly on the Lord.

Lesson Outline

Introduction

A. Song of Your Life

If you were asked to describe your life as it is now with a song, what song would you choose? Consider what characteristics make it the right song for this time. Is it the tone (major or minor key) or the instruments (a violin that sounds forlorn)? Is it the lyrics, expressing contentment or love or betrayal? Is it a song you sing with others or all by yourself? If you've been honest with yourself, you might feel an emotional *click* when you name the song of your life at this time.

Songs have long been part of worship, in part because of their power to express our deepest hopes and fears while drawing us back to God. Perhaps the importance of songs in our relationship with God is best understood when we find ourselves in trouble, not knowing where to turn. At such times, songs like Psalm 62 affirm God's power and love even as they help us express what we need to tell God.

B. Lesson Context

As prayers and songs, the Psalms give worshippers a voice. Sometimes it is the voice of lament (see Psalms 10, 13, 44, 77), and sometimes it is a voice of thanksgiving and praise (see Psalms 66, 107, 148). Lament prayers grieve suffering, and thanksgivings express gratitude. Psalm 62 is neither a lament nor a thanksgiving hymn, though it contains elements of both. Instead, this psalm can appropriately be called *a confidence psalm*. It expresses trust and hope in God in the middle of distress. Confidence psalms arise from an assured relationship with God. The psalmists are confident that God is their help and refuge. They trust in God's power and goodness, and they hope in God's faithfulness (compare Psalms 11; 23).

The superscript of Psalm 62 identifies Jeduthun as the leader of the choir (1 Chronicles 16:41, 42; 25:1-3; see Psalms 39, 77). He might have been someone like a songwriting partner to David (ruled about 1010–970 BC), who is identified as the writer of Psalm 62. Specific hardships are alluded to in the superscripts of David's psalms (see commentary on 62:3-4, below).

The power of poetry, especially set to song, is to allow not only the writer or singer to express themselves—fears, pain, trust, love—but also to speak for an audience in attendance. Psalm 62 invited Israelites to join the song, and it still does for us today.

I. Calm Amidst Trouble
(Psalm 62:1-4)
A. Wait on God (vv. 1-2)

1. Truly my soul waiteth upon God. From him cometh my salvation.

Truly translates a key word in this psalm (translated "only" in Psalm 62:2, 4-6 and "surely" in 62:9). Its repetition throughout the psalm emphasizes the truth of each statement, lending a heightened sense of the sincerity for the psalmist.

My soul identifies the seat of a person's commitments and loyalties. It is the "I" of personhood. *Waiteth* translates a rare Hebrew word in the Bible, occurring only four times (Psalms 22:2; 39:2; 62:1; 65:1). This waiting is restful, sometimes even silent. David was not an autonomous self but a dependent one. David entrusted himself to *God* because *salvation* comes from God, though we do not yet know from what David required rescuing (see 62:3, below). In this instance, salvation should not be thought of as a distant spiritual reality but as a present, physical rescue (examples: Exodus 14:13; 1 Samuel 14:45; Psalm 35:1-3).

Like David, we are wise when we entrust ourselves to the Lord and do not trust ourselves (Proverbs 3:5-6). Completely trusting God is related to the covenant (see Psalm 62:11b-12a, below). If David trusted God completely based on covenants in Israel, how much more should we, given that we have received what Israel hoped for (Hebrews 11)?

What Do You Think?
How would you describe the experience of finding rest for your soul in God?
Digging Deeper
What habits make resting in God possible regardless of your circumstances?

2. He only is my rock and my salvation; he is my defence; I shall not be greatly moved.

Repeating the word *salvation* is another way David emphasized his confidence that he would find what he needed from the Lord (see Psalm 62:1, above). Only God, the *rock*, can serve as the source of stability and rest. When God was David's *defence*, he could confidently and boldly profess that he could never *be greatly moved*—and so can we. Grounded in God's gracious salvation and protected by God's power, we confess that nothing will shake us (see also Psalms 30:6; 46:5; 55:22; 66:9; 112:6; 121:3). Our feet will not slip or give way. The soul committed to God alone is stabilized by God's saving work and protective care.

Quake Proof

Building earthquake-resistant structures in California isn't just wise; it's the law. The engineering solutions required to mitigate the effects of a violent earthquake can be quite impressive. A simple but effective method is to use cross beams to reinforce the strength of a structure. Another method is to have pistons within the structure that absorb the energy of the shock waves. Flexible foundations will sway with the vibrations; a pendulum method utilizes a large counterweight attached to the building to absorb some shock. Using materials that will bend without breaking or crumbling is also key.

Given a big enough earthquake, though, even well-designed buildings will fall. The mitigation techniques used are primarily meant to preserve human life; the rebuilding process of physical structures after a quake can still be vast. But there is no earthquake of life that is so large that God cannot help you stand. Call on your rock and your salvation, and He will see you through.
—C. S.

B. Confronting Enemies (vv. 3-4)

3. How long will ye imagine mischief against a man? Ye shall be slain all of you. As a bowing wall shall ye be, and as a tottering fence.

This verse and the next feature several contrasts between what has come before to what will come after. *Ye shall be slain* and the images of an unstable *wall* and *fence* contrast the transient nature of David and his enemies with the unchanging, faithful God, who is David's "rock" and "defence" (Psalm 62:2, above). The contrast highlights God's power versus the ultimate powerlessness of any human as well as God's integrity in His dealings with David against the unreliability of his enemies. We do not know the specific nature of the *mischief* David's opponents imagined, but we know that David's life was full of situations that might fit the bill (see 62:4, below).

4. They only consult to cast him down from his excellency. They delight in lies. They bless with their mouth, but they curse inwardly. Selah.

The Hebrew adverb translated *only* appeared in Psalm 62:1-2 (see commentary above). In the opening of the psalm, God is the only ground of assurance. But David's opponents lacked reverence for God, as evidenced by their total disregard for David, God's chosen king (1 Samuel 16:7-12; 2 Samuel 7:8-9; contrast 1 Samuel 24:5-7).

Speaking of himself in the third person, David suggested these opponents conspired *to cast him down from his excellency*, referring either to his position in Saul's court or to the throne itself. Some examples come from before David became king while he was part of King Saul's court or exiled from it (1 Samuel 18:10-11; 23:7-29; etc.; compare Psalms 57, 63, 142). Another possibility occurs decades later when King David's own son Absalom revolted against his father and tried to depose him (2 Samuel 15:13-14; compare Psalm 3). These and other efforts revealed David's enemies to be liars and hypocrites, willing to *bless with their mouth* while they *curse inwardly* (compare Matthew 23). They sought to undermine God's chosen and unjustly attacked David.

No one is sure what *selah* means. Since the book of Psalms was used in Israel's corporate worship and the psalms were frequently set to music (see Lesson Context, above), we can postulate that selah is a musical note, perhaps for a silent pause. This guess works well if the song leader wanted to invite the congregation to consider their own concerns as they prayed and sang the psalmist's words.

What Do You Think?

How do you handle opposition from people who speak well but have evil intent?

Digging Deeper

What verses inform your answer?

II. Calm Discovered
(Psalm 62:5-8)
A. Refocusing on God (vv. 5-7)

5-6. My soul, wait thou only upon God; for my expectation is from him. He only is my rock and my salvation. He is my defence; I shall not be moved.

These two verses form a sort of refrain, largely repeating what was expressed in Psalm 62:1-2 (above). *Wait* is a form of "waiteth" that appeared in 62:1. In Psalm 131:2, the same word is used, describing a weaned child with his mother. There as here, the image is of security, peace, and silence.

7. In God is my salvation and my glory. The rock of my strength, and my refuge, is in God.

This verse expands what is said in Psalm 62:1-2 and 62:5-6, above. Here as there, God is the psalmist's *salvation*, *rock*, and *refuge*. The only new language here is of God as the psalmist's *glory*. The word can also be translated "honour" (Psalms 26:8; 66:2; etc.). The first example of God's giving people glory is found at creation (Genesis 1:26-27; Psalm 8:5). We also think of Jesus' honoring people by becoming fully human in order to minister among us and die for our sins (Philippians 2:6-11).

What Do You Think?

Why was David able to express this kind of confidence in the Lord before Jesus' atoning sacrifice?

Digging Deeper

How can Old Testament stories of God's faithfulness bolster your own faith in Christ?

B. Admonishing the People (v. 8)

8. Trust in him at all times; ye people, pour out your heart before him. God is a refuge for us. Selah.

Imagine a temple worship service where a singer offers a testimony and expresses his or her hope in God's loving care. Then the singer turns to the congregation and invites them to share in this testimony. The singer calls the people of God to *trust* God, just as the singer does. God is not only the singer's refuge but is a *refuge for us*. The people of God share the same story. They rehearse the story of God's powerful deliverance through the exodus and His loving election of Israel as the people of His Old Testament covenant.

Because we trust in God's deliverance, we embrace Him as our refuge. As such, the singer also invites us to *pour out* our hearts to God. Our restful waiting does not require silence (see Psalm 62:1, above), though it can imply it (examples: 131:2; Lamentations 3:28; etc.). Rather, as we rest in God's care, we tell God the truth of our hearts.

What Do You Think?
Would it be accurate to say that you pour out your heart to God? Why or why not?

Digging Deeper
What is the most difficult thing in your life for you to talk to God about? What would happen if you prayed deeply about that thing today?

III. Calm Grounded in God
(Psalm 62:9-12)

A. Rejecting Insubstantial Help (vv. 9-10)

9. Surely men of low degree are vanity, and men of high degree are a lie. To be laid in the balance, they are altogether lighter than vanity.

A stark contrast is drawn between God and *men,* whether *of low* or *high degree.* These contrasts are meant to be understood together, indicating all people (compare Psalm 49:2). When compared to God, each person from least to greatest is *vanity* and *a lie.* The concept of vanity is familiar from the book of Ecclesiastes, which frequently uses

this same Hebrew word to assert the meaninglessness observed in human life (examples: Ecclesiastes 1:2, 14; 2:11; 3:19). The word describes a mist that appears for a moment and then dissipates.

In this way, anyone can be (metaphorically) weighed (*laid in the balance*) and found to be *lighter than vanity.* For ancient people, balance scales were vital to commerce. Coinage wouldn't be invented until sometime in the 600s BC, so transactions in David's day (about 400 years earlier) and for centuries following his reign were done by weight (examples: Genesis 23:16; 1 Kings 7:47). An unbalanced or loaded scale could cheat people out of precious resources (example: Amos 8:5). The weight of goods was truly important. When weighed against God on a balance scale, there is no substance to us (compare Isaiah 40:15). And this is the root of our untrustworthiness; this is what allows us to sin in the first place. We can try with all our might, but we lack the power to do most of the good we would like. And we ultimately cannot trust ourselves or others who hold no power for deliverance.

Weighing Air

When I was a boy, my classmates and I enjoyed weighing objects on our science lab's balance scale. I found great satisfaction in the tactile process of adding or subtracting weight until the scales balanced. I especially appreciated the brass weights that were used to give accurate results. Sadly for my childhood self, this method of measuring weight has largely fallen by the wayside in favor of spring or electronic scales.

People, regardless of their station, weigh as nothing on the scale of trustworthiness. We are so light that if the right scale existed, we might all float away instead of weighing even one ounce as being worthy of trust. When faced with the question of where to place your trust, will it be your fellow weightless creatures or the creator God?
—C. S.

10. Trust not in oppression, and become not vain in robbery. If riches increase, set not your heart upon them.

For the powerful, their success at *oppression* can

feel like safety. The illusion of having control over not only one's own life but also the lives of others creates a false sense of self-determination and influence over the world. In truth, oppressors need fear God's wrath and judgment for their sins—a lesson Israel (and Judah) would learn long after David's reign ended (example: Amos 2:4-16).

In the Hebrew practice of poetic parallelism, *robbery* stands parallel to the oppression of the previous line in encompassing any number of financial or material crimes. It is an effective strategy for maintaining one's power. But even *riches* obtained without extortion or other wickedness are not to be trusted (compare 1 Timothy 6:10, 17-19).

In short, no human resource can serve as a refuge from trouble. Rather than relying on creatures, David invites us to "trust in [God] at all times" (Psalm 62:8, above).

What Do You Think?

How do you prevent prudent financial decisions from becoming idolatrous trusting in your wealth (savings, retirement funds, etc.)?

Digging Deeper

What biblical advice would you offer to younger adults who are learning wisdom in their financial decisions?

B. Embracing Substance (vv. 11-12)

11a. God hath spoken once; twice have I heard this.

These two phrases poetically emphasize the efficacy of God's speaking. We might think of creation, when *God* had only to say a word, and what He said was created (Genesis 1). For David to hear God's speech *twice* might mean He repeated a particular message, or it could simply emphasize that David took what he heard to heart. The latter is certainly in view, based on the confidence David has expressed in the Lord.

11b-12a. That power belongeth unto God. Also unto thee, O Lord, belongeth mercy.

God's *power* stands in contrast to the illusion of power that people might have (see Psalm 62:9,

above). It has been alluded to several times already (see 62:1-2, 6-8, above), but here power is called out. For many, God's power, in combination with His wrath, is the primary way of understanding Him as revealed in the Old Testament (examples: Genesis 19; Deuteronomy 5:9; 2 Kings 17:16-23; Jeremiah 20:4-5; Jonah 3:1-4).

But a closer reading suggests that God's power cannot be understood without also considering His *mercy*. The Hebrew word translated "mercy" is frequently used in the context of God's covenant love and loyalty toward Israel (examples: Exodus 20:4-6; Deuteronomy 7:9-12). His mercy both initiated and sustained the covenant.

One example of God's power and mercy at work for Israel was the story of the exodus. Out of His covenant loyalty, God promised to bring Israel out of Egypt (Genesis 46:3-4), and He then began that work (Exodus 2:24). Bringing the Israelites out from their slavery as conquerors and providing for them in the desert—even in the face of multiple rebellions—were actions motivated by love and accomplished with power (15:13). Even the examples of God's wrath reveal His desire for mercy (see Genesis 18:20-33; Jeremiah 23:3; Jonah 3:10–4:2). Perhaps most striking is, even after pronouncing judgment for three or four generations, God says He shows love and mercy to thousands (Deuteronomy 5:10). This is a difference of degree; God limits His wrath and lets His love and mercy overflow.

We do not know whether David wrote this psalm before or after receiving God's promise of a house for David's family (2 Samuel 7). God was powerful to keep that promise centuries later, and through it, we experience God's love in Christ (Matthew 1:1). Unsurprisingly, then, many called on Jesus to have mercy on them throughout His ministry (examples: 9:27; 15:22; 20:30).

12b. For thou renderest to every man according to his work.

Paul alluded to this phrase in Romans 2:6 (compare Proverbs 24:12) and expressed a similar sentiment in 2 Timothy 4:14. Some students propose that neither David nor Paul seems to have had the Last Judgment in mind when making this assertion. Instead, God's conduct is appropriately contrasted with human conduct. Whereas we might act with a lack of integrity or with only selfish ends in mind, God acts out of His power and mercy and intends to set the world to rights.

Conclusion

A. Singing with David

Just as a song on the radio can feel like it was written for *you* at this *exact moment* in your life and expresses what you need to say, so too can psalms. Psalm 62 invites us to sing along with David and join him in his expression of confidence in God alone. Without identifying a specific situation in David's life, the psalm becomes that much more accessible for any situation we might relate to the feelings expressed within. Whatever troubled David, we have our own troubles. David models for us how to face our own struggles even though our troubles are different from his. We surrender every circumstance to God because we not only know God's strength and love, but we also know He will deal with evil and hold human beings accountable for their actions. Those who trust in God have nothing to fear; we fear neither God's judgment nor the troubles that have swamped us. The God of power and mercy will do what is just and right.

Without any further details, we can say with confidence only that David found himself in a turbulent situation. In the midst of it, the king still expressed supreme confidence in God. Sometimes joining David in song will mean singing praise to God, alone or with fellow believers. But other practices also nurture confidence in God, especially when misplaced faith in people falls apart. One example of pouring our hearts out to God (Psalm 62:8, above) could be reading the psalm as our own prayer. While doing so, we reflect on what we need from God, whether that is a change of circumstance or to strength to endure.

We could also read the psalm as a way to listen for God (Psalm 62:11, above). Listening for Him in all of Scriptures allows us to learn who He is, grasp what He desires for and from us, and build the relationship that He desires and we so desperately need. We must constantly and consistently open ourselves

Visual for Lesson 9. *While discussing verse 6, allow learners one minute to contemplate how the Lord is currently acting as their refuge.*

to the Word of God through listening to the reading of Scripture in community, studying Scripture in family and private moments, and memorizing Scripture. We devote time to mulling over the language of Scripture in order to listen to the voice of the Spirit so that we might come to know God and become like God in our conduct.

In these ways and more, we must recenter ourselves on God to be reminded of His power and mercy. Only then will our confidence be found in God alone, and only then will we, too, have supreme confidence in who God is and what He is willing to accomplish because of His great love.

B. Prayer

Our Father, You know we are often surrounded by troubles. Help us trust You so that peace and love might reign in our hearts by Your power and because of Your mercy. In the name of Jesus. Amen.

C. Thought to Remember

We trust God because He is willing *and* able to save us.

How to Say It

Absalom	*Ab*-suh-lum.
Ecclesiastes	Ik-*leez*-ee-*as*-teez.
Israelites	Iz-ray-el-ites.
Jeduthun	Jeh-*doo*-thun.
Selah *(Hebrew)*	*See*-luh.

Involvement Learning

Enhance your lesson with KJV Bible Student *(from your curriculum supplier) and the reproducible activity page (at www.standardlesson.com or in the back of the* KJV Standard Lesson Commentary Deluxe Edition*).*

Into the Lesson

Draw two columns on the board, labeling one *Heavy* and the other *Light*. Then ask learners to offer examples of pairs of objects that (1) share something in common and (2) demonstrate extreme differences in weightiness. An example to get them started could be a tricycle and a cargo plane; both are forms of transportation, but one is far heavier than the other. Other possible categories to spark thought could be mammals (or animals in general), objects found in nature, tools, etc. Allow a few minutes for volunteers to share their ideas.

Alternative. Distribute copies of the "Weighty Matters" exercise from the activity page, which you can download. Have learners work individually for one minute to complete as indicated.

After either activity, say, "It's easy to compare objects at extreme ends of the scale and know which will be weightier. In the same way, when we compare God to anything or anyone else we might trust, it is easy to see that He is the only true option. As we study today's lesson, pay attention to the ways David describes God, and how these truths prompt him to respond to everything else."

Into the Word

Ask three volunteers to read Psalm 62 in these sections: verses 1-4; verses 5-8; verses 9-12. As learners listen, ask them to make a note of any words or phrases that catch their ear, especially any that are repeated. After a second reading, ask learners to share what they heard and the significance of those words or phrases in this psalm. Consult the commentary for any questions that arise.

Divide learners into two groups. The **Who God Is Group** will list descriptions of God found in the psalm along with verse references; the **Who We Are Group** will list descriptions of people, also with verse references. While the groups work, write their group names as the headers of two columns on the board. When the groups have finished, have them take turns giving their answers until both lists are full. Compare the lists, putting a star next to any attributes that are shared between God and people, as described in Psalm 62. (Note: do not expect any stars here; see commentary about the absolute contrasts that David set up between God and people.)

Then divide learners into three groups to survey David's life for circumstances that might have provoked the writing of Psalm 62: the **1 Samuel 16–19 Group**, the **2 Samuel 1–7 Group**, and the **2 Samuel 11–19 Group**. Before they start, note that Psalm 62 does not offer a specific answer to this question, so there are no right or wrong answers. Groups should summarize any circumstances they find and any specific verse(s) that suggest a connection. When they have finished, allow groups to present their answers. Then talk together about the variety of circumstances that can fit this psalm. Ask what this suggests for applying the confidence David expressed in the Lord in students' own lives.

Alternative. Distribute copies of the "Sing Psalm 62" exercise from the activity page. Have learners work in pairs or small groups to complete as indicated. Allow time for groups to share with the whole class one example they found.

Into Life

Give each learner an index card. In one minute, each person should name a day this week and a specific time when he or she will wait quietly on the Lord, as well as what that waiting will look like. After the minute is up, have learners pair up to share their plans. Encourage learners to commit to this time and come back to class next week prepared to share with their partners what they experienced. End class with prayer.

Confidence in God's Shepherding

Devotional Reading: John 10:1-10
Background Scripture: Psalm 23; John 10:11-14

Psalm 23

1 The LORD is my shepherd; I shall not want.

2 He maketh me to lie down in green pastures: He leadeth me beside the still waters.

3 He restoreth my soul: He leadeth me in the paths of righteousness for his name's sake.

4 Yea, though I walk through the valley of the shadow of death, I will fear no evil: for thou art with me; Thy rod and thy staff they comfort me.

5 Thou preparest a table before me in the presence of mine enemies: Thou anointest my head with oil; my cup runneth over.

6 Surely goodness and mercy shall follow me all the days of my life: And I will dwell in the house of the LORD for ever.

Key Text

Surely goodness and mercy shall follow me all the days of my life: And I will dwell in the house of the LORD for ever. —**Psalm 23:6**

Worship in the
Covenant Community

Unit III: Psalms of Thanksgiving
3 Praise
Lessons 10–13

Lesson Aims

After participating in this lesson, each learner will be able to:

1. Identify poetic repetition in Psalm 23 and its significance.

2. Compare the psalmist's description of the shepherd with the New Testament's descriptions of the ministry of Jesus.

3. Create a reminder of Psalm 23's most helpful encouragement for the upcoming holiday season.

Lesson Outline

Introduction

A. Needy Creatures

When my spouse and I became parents, I remember the trepidation we felt. It seemed as if I had never beheld such a helpless creature as our daughter. Nearly all she could do was eat or sleep. I would sit beside her sleeping form, watching breaths move her tiny chest up and down. And I marveled that we begin life in this manner. Our only means of communication is a whimper or a yell.

Humans have a long period of development compared to other living creatures. We enter the world entirely dependent on others and remain so for several years. As time passes, we envision ourselves becoming more proficient at addressing our needs.

The truth is that many parts of our lives are not easy to control: our circumstances, environment, and health, for instance. We also cannot control the people around us. When we do not get our way, it is easy to slip back into our childhood self—the one who cries out for attention when needs are not met. The psalmists found comfort in letting God meet their needs.

B. Lesson Context

We know less than we would like about where and when the Psalter was assembled. There is clearly a consideration given to an arrangement of its 150 psalms; it is frequently noted that they are arranged in five "books," the first four of which conclude with "Amen," meaning "we agree" or "true" (Psalms 41:13; 72:18-20; 89:52; 106:48).

A connection to David is apparent in half the psalms. His name appears in the superscriptions of 73 of them, with 2 more psalms attributed to him in Acts 4:25 and Hebrews 4:7. Superscriptions are instructions or attributions appearing at the beginning of many psalms. Superscriptions are part of the text, although modern Bibles give them no verse number, and Bible software gives them a verse number of zero.

Although many superscriptions list one or more names, the relationship of the named person to the psalm in view is often unclear. Today's text is an example. Its superscription reads "A Psalm of David." This may indicate that David was the author, but the Hebrew preposition behind the English word *of* can also express relation or direction. This means that Psalm 23 could be *about* David or *dedicated to* him.

David first appears in Scripture as a keeper of sheep (1 Samuel 16:11). During a war with the Philistines, he continued to be responsible for the care of his father's flock (17:15, 20). That might seem to have been a safe, behind-the-front-lines kind of job, but in that role as a shepherd, David had fought both lion and bear (17:34-37).

It is also relevant to note that "shepherding" is a common metaphor in the ancient Near East, used especially for kings who protect and provide for subjects. This goes a long way to help explain the depiction of David. His introduction as a shepherd in 1 Samuel guides readers to anticipate that he would make a good king. This was an important development, for when the Israelites first asked Samuel for a king, they contravened the wishes of God (1 Samuel 8). But God nonetheless redeemed the monarchy and made an everlasting covenant with David (2 Samuel 7). Anything either by or about David is, therefore, important to consider.

I. God's Shepherding
(Psalm 23:1-4)
A. Provides (v. 1)
1. The LORD is my shepherd; I shall not want.

The first verse introduces a reversal: whereas David had been a *shepherd* himself (Psalm 78:70-72), God is David's shepherd. The metaphor of God as a shepherd is frequently used by Old Testament writers (examples: Genesis 48:16; 49:24; Psalm 28:9; Isaiah 40:11). Thus, the psalm is spoken or sung by an individual sheep of the metaphor. It would be strange for a shepherd to care for only one sheep. The psalmist does not feel the need to tell of any others. He focuses on the relationship between one sheep (himself) and the shepherd.

David was familiar with the role of shepherd, and he understood the great responsibility of providing for the needs of a flock. As domesticated animals, sheep are less able to provide for their

own needs. However good David may have been as a shepherd in meeting those needs, the psalmist depicts God to be all the more mindful in that regard. This confidence is evident in the phrase *I shall not want.*

Whatever need may arise for the speaker, God is ready and able to meet this need (compare Deuteronomy 2:7; 8:9; Psalm 84:11). A good shepherd will do this, but a bad shepherd will be far away when needs arise (compare and contrast Ezekiel 34:1-16; Jude 12). God is not distant (John 10:7-16; 1 Peter 2:25).

> **What Do You Think?**
> How do you practice finding contentment in the Lord?
> **Digging Deeper**
> Write a brief prayer identifying situations in which you need the Lord to guide you to greater trust in Him.

B. Leads (v. 2)
2a. He maketh me to lie down in green pastures.

The phrase *green pastures* reflects an image of ideal summertime abundance in the land of Canaan. But such abundance can be hit and miss in its semiarid climate as it experiences little or no rainfall for five months of the year. Shepherds constantly had to scout the best locations for grazing sheep (Genesis 13:5-6; 37:12-17).

Maketh me to lie down reveals the causative force of the Hebrew verb. Sheep are at ease as they are provided rest alongside their food.

2b. He leadeth me beside the still waters.

While sheep have the ability to survive without water for up to seven days, they are likely to consume a significant amount when the opportunity arises. The imagery of *still waters* is unusual since the flowing water of a river or stream is the preferred image for needs that are met (Psalms 36:8; 46:4; Revelation 7:17). At least two interpretations of *still waters* have been proposed.

One reading holds that the shepherd brings the flock to a natural body of water free of fast-flowing rapids—hence "still." A difficulty for this interpretation is that shepherds tended to rely on wells to water flocks (Genesis 29:1-8). Moreover, fast-flowing water was not common in this land.

Another way of understanding the image is to take the word *still*—a noun in the original language—to refer to a place of rest. This is a frequent translation of this word elsewhere (examples: Psalm 95:11; Isaiah 32:18; 66:1). It reinforces the image of a place where sheep feel free to lie down, unthreatened.

Whichever interpretation most accurately conveys the psalmist's intended imagery, the central message remains that the shepherd leads the sheep instead of driving them. This presents a picture of tender direction, as depicted in Isaiah 40:11. Furthermore, this picture is deeply rooted in the theology of the exodus, when God guided the Israelites through the wilderness (Exodus 13:21-22).

My Experience as a Shepherd

I once owned sheep. My wife and I have a seven-acre field that we allowed a neighbor, who owned sheep and cattle, to cut for hay. He was not wealthy but wanted to give us something for the hay. Thus, he gave us two sheep.

While it seemed a blessing initially, it quickly became a burden. We put the sheep behind fences to keep them safe. But that required a fair amount of fencing. I didn't have money for fence posts, so I cut down some small trees, stripped the limbs, and made posts out of those. The cobbled-together result kept the sheep in for several days, but they eventually figured out how to squeeze underneath the fence. Once they did that, they were everywhere. After a couple of years of "shepherding," we gave up and returned the sheep to the neighbor.

The wonderful thing about God is that He is a much better shepherd than I ever was or would be. He always has the resources to lead the sheep to safe places and to provide for them (us). That fact is beyond question. The only question that emerges concerns the extent of our faith in this truth. How strong is your trust?   —C. S.

C. Restores (v. 3)

3a. He restoreth my soul.

The psalmist is calm and untroubled as God's provision for physical needs coincides with God's provision for non-physical needs. The same thought, using the exact two Hebrew words translated *restoreth* and *soul,* appears in Psalms 19:7; 116:7; Proverbs 25:13; and Lamentations 1:16. Many psalms plead for God's restoring favor (compare Psalms 6:4; 25:16; 31:2; 69:16; 71:2; 86:16; 88:2; 102:2; 119:132). This one, however, views that favor as an accomplished fact.

3b. He leadeth me in the paths of righteousness for his name's sake.

The imagery of shepherding continues. One way of thinking about God's leading *in the paths of righteousness* is to imagine forks on the road of life. When a fork is encountered, one must choose which way is the right one (compare Psalms 5:8; 85:13).

But we should not miss a distinction between the closely related words *right(eous)* and *righteousness.* We can do no better than listen to the apostle John on this point: "If ye know that he is righteous, ye know that every one that doeth righteousness is born of him. . . . Little children, let no man deceive you: he that doeth righteousness is righteous, even as he is righteous" (1 John 2:29; 3:7).

A faithful or righteous shepherd—as God is—leads the faithful of the flock into right paths. God proves to be faithful; it is not in His nature to be otherwise!

What Do You Think?

How is God's name and reputation enhanced by guiding you along the right paths?

Digging Deeper

What part do you play, if any, in enhancing God's name? Cite verses that support your answer.

D. Protects (v. 4)

4a. Yea, though I walk through the valley of the shadow of death, I will fear no evil. For thou art with me.

The psalmist continues by now emphasizing the protection side of God's shepherding. We would all prefer that there would be no more dark valleys of life. Nevertheless, there are, and there will be, until Jesus returns. There is no promise that the Christian will not have to endure such valleys—quite the opposite (Matthew 10:22; 24:9). But we do indeed have a promise of God's presence (Matthew 28:20; John 14:16-17; Hebrews 13:5).

The presence of God should signal the absence of *fear*. Fear is a God-given emotion that helps protect us. When our fear is justified because of real and imminent danger, it can save our life (assuming that fear doesn't turn into panic). Fear (and its lack) can be related to *evil* in several ways. First, a person might fear neither evil nor God because he or she has embraced evil (Psalm 36:1-4).

Second, a godly person can fear evil by deciding to avoid it because getting too close to it runs the danger of falling into its clutches (Proverbs 14:16; 16:6; 1 Corinthians 15:33; etc.). Third, a godly person doesn't fear evil because he or she knows that God's presence is stronger than any evil that may lie in the path (Psalm 49:5-6, 15). This third option is in view here.

> **What Do You Think?**
> Identify dark valleys you have encountered or currently face.
>
> **Digging Deeper**
> Does God lead you differently if you entered that valley because of your own choices? Explain your answer.

4b. Thy rod and thy staff they comfort me.

Rod and *staff* are tools of the shepherd. The Hebrew word that is translated "rod" also can take the sense of a "sceptre"—a sign of authority (example: Psalm 45:6) that might be used to inflict pain or punishment (2:9; 89:32). The word translated "staff" refers more to a walking stick or a cane (Exodus 21:19; Zechariah 8:4). The psalmist is comforted by the fact that God has these metaphorical tools at His disposal.

How to Say It

Philistines	Fuh-*liss*-teenz or *Fill*-us-teenz.
Psalter	*Sawl*-tur.

II. The Lord Supplies
(Psalm 23:5)
A. Safety (v. 5a)

5a. Thou preparest a table before me in the presence of mine enemies.

With a new verse comes a change in metaphor. Sheep do not dine at tables, so the shepherd imagery seems to have given way to something new. God is now depicted as a gracious host who has prepared a fine meal for the psalmist to enjoy. This could signify a role-reversal for King David since kings were known to have splendid tables to feed many people (compare 1 Kings 4:27). Preparation *in the presence of mine enemies* could be intended to make these enemies jealous or simply to show that God was not hiding the display of His favor. Because of God's protection and provision, they can do nothing to harm the psalmist.

The verse just prior to this one bridges the two images. In verse 4, the psalmist spoke of a death-defying journey through shadowy places. And now he imagines a feast for himself, the weary traveler. Roads and mountain paths were dangerous in ancient times. Much later, under Roman rule—when roads had greater security for travelers—Jesus still would speak of thieves on the road between Jerusalem and Jericho (Luke 10:30). Enemies on the road were a danger for all travelers.

It is impossible to say whether the psalmist has particular enemies in mind, perhaps the literal foes of David. His anointing as king made several enemies, not the least of which was his predecessor, King Saul (1 Samuel 16:13; 19:1; etc.). A related text refers to a time "when [David] was in the wilderness of Judah" (Psalm 63; see Lesson Context), and it speaks of enemies seeking his life (63:9-10).

> **What Do You Think?**
> What verses encourage you to wait for God's action against your enemies rather than taking revenge yourself?
>
> **Digging Deeper**
> What can you learn about God while you wait for His action?

B. Election (v. 5b)

5b. Thou anointest my head with oil.

The host honors the guest by anointing his *head* with oil (compare Psalms 45:7; 92:10). Given the fragrances that were available to add to olive oil (see 45:8; Proverbs 7:17), such anointing is a soothing and refreshing experience for a weary traveler. This anointing was not done for Jesus when Simon the Pharisee hosted Him for dinner, an intentional oversight noted by Jesus (Luke 7:46).

The psalmist possibly intends a double meaning: he may be recognizing David's physical anointing to be king over Israel (1 Samuel 16:3, 12-13; compare 2 Samuel 5:3) while acknowledging God's continual anointing in spirit. The latter projects an image of God as an hospitable host, with all the trappings of a grand meal involved. Since pouring oil happened in various contexts, the image fits both.

C. Abundance (v. 5c)

5c. My cup runneth over.

The psalmist continues to acknowledge God's benevolence as host. Presumably, the host has given the guest a large cup of wine (compare Jeremiah 35:1-5), and the guest is satisfied. The Hebrew word translated *runneth over* occurs elsewhere only in Psalm 66:12. There, it is translated "wealthy place" in the context of being rescued by God. This cup of satisfaction is equivalent to the waters of Psalm 23:2b, above.

When an Overflow Isn't Too Much

The abundance of an overflowing cup might seem silly or even wasteful to some. But an "overflow" of water is a truly happy thing for my family! We live more than half a mile from the nearest water line, and to extend it to our house would cost thousands of dollars. Digging a well is not financially feasible either. So we use a cistern: a 1,500-gallon polyethylene tank that holds our water supply.

We have run out of water on occasion. Filling the tank manually means 8 trips of 20 miles each to the nearest potable water filling station. That's a considerable use of gasoline! And don't even bring up the issue of winter weather!

So we rejoice when it rains so we can fill the tank to capacity. It means a couple of months of not worrying about running out.

We don't think about it much when we have enough to keep body and soul together. When that is not our situation, we might sink into worry (contrast Matthew 6:25-34). We often forget that our divine host has plenty of resources. While there will always be times of scarcity, our God occasionally gives us an overflowing cup. The prime example in which an overflowing cup was given was when God sent His Son into the world to save it. When times get tough, is that fact the first thing you shift your mind to?   —C. S.

III. The Psalmist's Future
(Psalm 23:6)

A. Accompanied by Blessings (v. 6a)

6a. Surely goodness and mercy shall follow me all the days of my life.

The text has twice mentioned hardship: danger in the dark valley (Psalm 23:4) and enemies in sight of the host's table (23:5). If the psalmist feels that he is being chased by death and evil, then he imagines that God's *goodness and mercy shall* pursue him all the more. It's insightful into God's character to see how the two Hebrew words translated as "goodness" and "mercy" are paired in other passages (see 69:16; 86:5; 100:5; etc.).

> **What Do You Think?**
> What gives you confidence that goodness and mercy follow you when circumstances suggest otherwise?
>
> **Digging Deeper**
> How would you counsel someone who has lost sight of God's mercies because of present hardships?

B. With God (v. 6b)

6b. And I will dwell in the house of the LORD for ever.

The final line provides a fitting conclusion for the psalm as it vividly depicts nearness to God. The psalmist shared a table with God and expected to remain *for ever*. He did not expect to be shown the door. A *house* for any god in the ancient Near East was a temple. But in David's lifetime, God had no temple, and He denied permission for David to build one for Him (2 Samuel 7:1-7). This fact of history points to *the house of the Lord* being the heavenly dwelling.

Conclusion

A. Needy for God

Psalm 23 is short, at only six verses. By contrast, the 150 psalms in total average about 16 verses each. But the influence of Psalm 23 is not limited by its length. The striking elegance of how the psalm begins results in many Christians memorizing its opening line easily and effortlessly: "The Lord is my shepherd; I shall not want."

However, if we limit ourselves only to that opening line, we miss the second important image of the psalm: that of God as host. Of course, it would be strange to imagine sheep dining at tables. This is a poetic text, and the juxtaposition of metaphors enhances the meaning. Two images—God as shepherd and God as host—collectively portray the Lord as caring and thoughtful toward His people.

What the psalmist proclaims is more radical than readers typically grant. He lived in a world where food and drink were not always easy to find. He saw enemies behind each corner of the road, not from a sense of paranoia. Nevertheless, he trusted that he was loved and remembered by God. He saw that God was with him, satisfying all needs.

The same can be said of us today as we place Psalm 23 in our hearts. By meditating on it, we can be encouraged to present our everyday needs to God, expecting trust to be honored. God is righteous and faithful.

However, this psalm would be misapplied if taken to endorse laziness or blind optimism. God provided for David's every need, but David remained in the wilderness for a long time! He was fleeing from men who wanted to murder him, and at every turn, he must have wondered whether he was on the path God provided. His faithful reliance was tested by desperate circumstance rather than by mere inconvenience. Thus, Psalm 23 can

Follow the way of the Good Shepherd.

John 10:11

Visual for Lesson 10. *Before closing in prayer, allow time for learners to offer their own silent thanks for Jesus' shepherding His flock.*

speak clearest to those who genuinely don't know where their next meal is coming from or are in real and present danger of being victimized. But whether that scenario or the looming challenge of a figurative wilderness to risk wealth, reputation, etc., Psalm 23 is ready to speak to us.

In this era of the new covenant, we remember that the shepherd who is God is also the shepherd who is Jesus. Like the image of the Psalm, Jesus declares, "I am the good shepherd, and know my sheep, and am known of mine. . . . I lay down my life for the sheep" (John 10:14-15). This profound act of God's provision in that last line goes beyond what any ordinary shepherd would think to offer; just the thought strains the credulity of the metaphor. No earthly shepherd would be expected to die for sheep! However, Jesus was no earthly shepherd—He was (and is) the Son of God. He is pursuing us with more goodness and mercy than we would know to anticipate. Yield to His offer!

B. Prayer

Heavenly Father, we thank You for Your presence! Your provisions astound us. Thank You for sending Your Son, Jesus, who set the example of trust as He paid sin's price. We pray in His name. Amen.

C. Thought to Remember

God has provided, is providing, and will provide.

Involvement Learning

Enhance your lesson with KJV Bible Student *(from your curriculum supplier) and the reproducible activity page (at www.standardlesson.com or in the back of the* KJV Standard Lesson Commentary Deluxe Edition*).*

Into the Lesson

Option. Display a peaceful nature scene and play sounds of gentle water flowing as students arrive for class. Encourage students to sit quietly as you wait for everyone to arrive.

Allow a few minutes for pairs from last week to discuss their experience waiting quietly on the Lord (see the Involvement Learning page for lesson 9).

Say to the class, "Sometimes we need to seek out the rest that God intends for us. Other times, we are aware that the ways He leads us are for our own good. Today we'll look at one of the most familiar Bible chapters to discover how God promises His loving care to those who follow Him."

Into the Word

Divide the class into groups of three to pursue one of two Bible studies. Make sure about half of the class does each one.

Sectional Study. Distribute a handout (you create) with three headings in a chart: *Shepherd (vv. 1-3)*; *Companion (v. 4)*; and *Host (vv. 5-6)*. To the left of these headings, write the following prompts: *What God Does*; *Main Thought*; *Encouragement for the "Sheep."* Learners should fill out the chart according to these prompts; encourage drawing in other verses that come to mind in the process.

He, You, and I. Distribute a handout (you create) with three prompts: *"He" Statements* (statements about who God is or what He does); *"You" Statements* (expressions directed to God); and *"I" Statements* (how "I" interact with the Lord). Learners should describe the relationship between the Lord and the psalmist.

Option. Distribute the "The Good Shepherd" exercise from the activity page, which you can download. Assign some students to work on this instead of the other two prompts or in addition to them.

After several minutes, call the class together for the groups to report. Encourage groups to jot down the main ideas they hear from others' presentations. After volunteers have presented, allow for discussion about the main points and any questions the class may have. Consult the commentary as necessary.

Into Life

Option. Extend the above discussion by reforming the class into groups of three. This time, assign one of the key ideas from Psalm 23 to each group: Shepherd, Companion, Host. Ask group members to brainstorm with each other ways God has functioned in their assigned role in their lives. Ask volunteers to share how they need God's presence in their lives in one of these three roles in the coming weeks. As they share, jot down their needs on your board.

Conclude your discussion by calling on class members to make a list answering the question, "So what?" Ask them to name what the promises of this psalm can mean to believers today. Encourage them to reference promises fulfilled in Christ.

Alternative. Distribute the "Personal Paraphrase" exercise from the activity page. Allow one minute for learners to complete, assuring them they will not be required to share their answers, though the opportunity will be extended. Allow learners either to pair up to share their responses *or* spend a few minutes in quiet individual prayer.

Distribute blank recipe cards to the class. In light of the approaching holiday season, ask each learner to write a short "recipe" that will help them remember important encouragement from Psalm 23. Allow volunteers to share their recipes. Suggest that learners slip their recipe cards into a cookbook or other spot where they will see it throughout this season. Then close by praying Psalm 23 together as a class.

Songs of Praise

Devotional Reading: Psalm 148
Background Scripture: Psalms 146–150

Psalm 146

1 Praise ye the LORD. Praise the LORD, O my soul.

2 While I live will I praise the LORD: I will sing praises unto my God while I have any being.

3 Put not your trust in princes, Nor in the son of man, in whom there is no help.

4 His breath goeth forth, he returneth to his earth; In that very day his thoughts perish.

5 Happy is he that hath the God of Jacob for his help, Whose hope is in the LORD his God:

6 Which made heaven, and earth, The sea, and all that therein is: Which keepeth truth for ever:

7 Which executeth judgment for the oppressed: Which giveth food to the hungry. The LORD looseth the prisoners:

8 The LORD openeth the eyes of the blind: The LORD raiseth them that are bowed down: The LORD loveth the righteous:

9 The LORD preserveth the strangers; He relieveth the fatherless and widow: But the way of the wicked he turneth upside down.

10 The LORD shall reign for ever, Even thy God, O Zion, unto all generations. Praise ye the LORD.

Psalm 150

1 Praise ye the LORD. Praise God in his sanctuary: Praise him in the firmament of his power.

2 Praise him for his mighty acts: Praise him according to his excellent greatness.

3 Praise him with the sound of the trumpet: Praise him with the psaltery and harp.

4 Praise him with the timbrel and dance: Praise him with stringed instruments and organs.

5 Praise him upon the loud cymbals: Praise him upon the high sounding cymbals.

6 Let every thing that hath breath praise the LORD. Praise ye the LORD.

Key Text

While I live will I praise the LORD: I will sing praises unto my God while I have any being. —**Psalm 146:2**

Worship in the
Covenant Community

Unit 3: Psalms of Thanksgiving and Praise
Lessons 10–13

Lesson Aims

After participating in this lesson, each learner will be able to:

1. Summarize why God is to be praised based on Psalms 146 and 150.

2. Provide examples from the Scriptures of God's care described in these psalms.

3. Identify an example of God's care in his or her life and write a short praise of thanks.

Lesson Outline

Introduction
  A. The Power of Praise
  B. Lesson Context
I. Praise (Psalm 146:1-2)
  A. The Lord (v. 1)
  B. Exhortation (v. 2)
II. Trust (Psalm 146:3-10)
  A. Misplaced in Princes (vv. 3-4)
  B. Perfectly Placed in God (vv. 5-10)
    Global Help
III. Exhortation (Psalm 150:1-6)
  A. Where (v. 1)
  B. Why (v. 2)
  C. How (vv. 3-5)
  D. Who (v. 6)
    What Sound?
Conclusion
  A. Praise Your Heavenly Father
  B. Prayer
  C. Thought to Remember

Introduction

A. The Power of Praise

When I was 10 years old, my mother threw a 40th birthday party for my father. My dad had been a highly successful high school athletic coach for 15 years. In that time, he had led over 100 young adults to Christ. But a string of difficult years had made my dad eager to retire from coaching. Former athletes had moved on with their lives and no longer called. He began to feel that he had nothing more to contribute. He wondered if his work had been in vain.

My mother knew that my dad needed encouragement. She called up every single one of his former athletes and asked them to come to our hometown for a party. She rented out a nice restaurant and told my dad it was just a normal birthday party with his family. We walked into the dining room to find it packed with nearly 200 of his former athletes. For the next several hours while we ate dinner, I watched person after person get up to a microphone and share some special memory in praise of my dad. And as he received the stream of praise and encouragement, my father's weariness fell away, and he became joyful again.

Finally, I read my dad the letter I had written to him. I felt overwhelming pride over my father as I lent my voice to the parade of other voices in praise of him. I felt connected to him and to all the other people whose lives he had changed. Praising someone else benefits not only them but also ourselves.

B. Lesson Context

The book of Psalms ends with five psalms of praise (Psalms 146–150). Each of these psalms begins with the admonition to praise the Lord, which suggests that there are common links between them (see Psalms 146:1; 150:1, below). Some have suggested that the initial declaration, "Praise ye the Lord" (Psalm 146:1, below), is actually a title of the work. Both the writer and date of composition are unknown.

Psalm 146 and Psalm 150 are the bookends of this final grouping. At the same time, these two psalms have distinctive elements. Psalm 146 exhorts the reader to rely on God alone and praises Him in part to illustrate how reliable and awesome God is. Psalm 150, on the other hand, is a relatively simple call to praise God. In both psalms, however, the psalmist reiterates the need to consider God's mighty deeds and show gratitude for them.

I. Praise

(Psalm 146:1-2)

A. The Lord (v. 1)

1. Praise ye the LORD. Praise the LORD, O my soul.

Praise ye the Lord is a translation of a Hebrew word most Christians know very well: *hallelujah* (see Psalm 150:1, below). The exhortation to praise is given first to the psalmist—to his *soul*, the seat of the mind and will. If Psalms 146–150 are linked by the common command to praise God (as posited in the Lesson Context), then the psalmist's choice to begin Psalm 146 with an exhortation to oneself is likely significant. Praise leaders, preachers, and other leaders in times of worship do well to adopt a habit of such encouragement for themselves.

B. Exhortation (v. 2)

2. While I live will I praise the LORD. I will sing praises unto my God while I have any being.

Here the psalmist responded to his own exhortation with a commitment to praising *the Lord* for the entirety of his life. The two sentences in this verse are parallel to one another, and their points are essentially the same. The repetition of two thoughts that are nearly equivalent in meaning creates emphasis. This technique is found frequently in Hebrew poetry.

The speaker has expressed a full and firm commitment to glorifying the name of *God* for as long as he lives (contrast Psalms 6:5; 30:9; etc.) This commitment will find fulfillment not only in discourse (146:2a) but also in song (146:2b). That distinction may imply praise both in conversation and in worship settings, encompassing all of life.

II. Trust

(Psalm 146:3-10)

A. Misplaced in Princes (vv. 3-4)

3. Put not your trust in princes, nor in the son of man, in whom there is no help.

The speaker shifts focus to warn against placing one's trust in human leaders. While this shift is initially unexpected, it makes considerably more sense when read in light of the psalmist's expression of commitment to praising God in the previous verse. Israel and Judah were tempted at various points to make alliances with pagan nations rather than trusting in God. This legacy of infidelity eventually led to the fall of both the northern kingdom of Israel and the southern kingdom of Judah (2 Kings 18:11-12; 24:20).

Human leaders ultimately cannot provide true and lasting *help*. Even though life's circumstances can make trusting God difficult, the psalmist urged his readers to commit to affirming God's goodness by praising Him alone through it all.

4. His breath goeth forth, he returneth to his earth; in that very day his thoughts perish.

The reason why one should not put trust in humans (Psalm 146:3, above) is because people are not only powerless but transitory (see also 118:8-9). Our earthly lives have an ultimate limit in death. And when we die, any outstanding goals we have die with us. We are no longer able to affect the land of the living directly; only the indirect effects of our legacies remain to influence others. Thus, any mortal is unworthy of the kind of trust that others often place in them. Death is the ultimate example of the frailty of human beings (Ecclesiastes 7:1-2). The rest of the psalm picks up this point of contrast between mortal, powerless human beings and the powerful, immortal, and merciful God.

What Do You Think?
What experience do you have of trusting a person instead of God?

Digging Deeper
Can this experience help you minister to someone who has been betrayed by someone they trusted? Explain.

B. Perfectly Placed in God (vv. 5-10)

5. Happy is he that hath the God of Jacob for his help, whose hope is in the LORD his God.

This verse returns to the one in whom trust should really be placed: *the Lord*. Jacob is singled out here among the patriarchs (see Exodus 3:15). The probable reason is that *Jacob* here refers to Israel, the collective name for God's people (Genesis 32:28; 35:10; Exodus 1:1, 7; etc.). The expression emphasizes God's special care for Jacob the individual in particular, then to his descendants by extension. Just as God cared for the man Jacob, so the person who calls on *the God of Jacob* for help is exceedingly *happy*. This trust stands in contrast to the misplaced faith in human beings (Psalm 146:3, above).

6a. Which made heaven, and earth, the sea, and all that therein is.

Here the psalm shifts to highlight some of God's acts and characteristics that make Him worthy of trust and praise. God's role as creator of the entire cosmos and all its occupants (Genesis 1) shows how infinitely powerful He is (compare Job 38–41). Similar appeals to God's creative might as justification for hope and trust can be found in Psalms 115:15; 121:2; 124:8; and 134:3. In fact, when the people of Judah returned from exile, they and their leaders likewise confessed their sins to God and referred to God's creation of the universe in their praises to Him (Nehemiah 9:1-6).

The sea sometimes serves as a metaphor for chaos in the Old Testament (examples: Psalms 74:13-15; 89:9; Jonah 2:2-6), and some ancient peoples believed that the chaotic sea predated the existence of the gods (compare Genesis 1:2). The psalmist asserts that God not only precedes the sea but created it, which speaks highly of God's great power over even the chaos it represented.

What Do You Think?
What aspects of creation give you confidence regarding God's faithfulness?

Digging Deeper
Beyond offering praise, how do you express your thankfulness for God's natural gifts?

6b. Which keepeth truth for ever.

Here the psalmist introduces the next major set of reasons to trust in and praise God: His faithfulness. The claim that God *keepeth truth for ever* refers to God's constant loyalty to His people. The speaker does not switch topics here; God's faithfulness is rooted in His role as the creator of the cosmos. The link between God's fidelity and His role as creator was established in Genesis. After the flood waters receded, God made a covenant with humanity and all other living creatures, promising that He would never again destroy the world as He had before (Genesis 8:21-22; 9:9-17).

7a. Which executeth judgment for the oppressed.

God's care for *the oppressed* would have surprised many in the ancient context, as financial prosperity was often seen as a sign of divine favor. While God has sometimes blessed His people materially (examples: Genesis 24:35; 1 Kings 3:10-14), a lack of means is not necessarily a sign of divine disfavor, although it could be (example: Haggai 1:1-11). Even so, the psalmist notes that God pays special attention to those who don't have enough (examples: Leviticus 19:10; 25:35; Deuteronomy 15:7-11; Isaiah 58:6-12; Ezekiel 18:5-17). We can also point to Jesus' identification with these groups (see Psalm 146:7b-8a, below) in His teaching on judgment (Matthew 25:37-45) and in His own summary of His earthly ministry (see Luke 4:16-20, as quoting Isaiah 61:1-2).

We do well to note that asserting a particular care for the oppressed does not suggest God's lack of concern toward non-oppressed people or even oppressors themselves. After all, His care falls on everyone regardless of one's standing (examples: Leviticus 19:15; Matthew 5:45).

7b-8a. Which giveth food to the hungry. The LORD looseth the prisoners. The LORD openeth the eyes of the blind. The LORD raiseth them that are bowed down.

One category of the oppressed are *the hungry*, pointing to a lack of necessities. The next three phrases should be read in parallel. The reference to opening *blind* eyes is most likely a metaphor for freeing *prisoners*, and the state of being *bowed down* is also associated with imprisonment (Isaiah 61:1-2).

8b-9a. The LORD loveth the righteous. The LORD preserveth the strangers; he relieveth the fatherless and widow.

These phrases highlight persons for whom God has a special concern. The first are *the righteous*, whom the text specifically identifies as those whom God loves. The second are *the strangers*, those who are foreign to the land. God's special concern for the plight of the alien is illustrated in the Pentateuch (also called the Torah, the first five books of the Bible), as multiple laws demand the fair and generous treatment of those who are not part of the people of Israel (Exodus 23:9; Leviticus 19:34; Deuteronomy 1:16; 24:14).

The third highlights God's special care for *the fatherless and widow*, also emphasized in the Torah (examples: Exodus 22:22-24; Deuteronomy 10:18; 27:19), wisdom literature (examples: Psalms 10:14, 18; 68:5; Proverbs 15:25), and the prophets (example: Isaiah 1:17; Jeremiah 22:3; Malachi 3:5). Indeed, James 1:27 affirms that God considers care for widows and orphans as a defining component of "pure" and "undefiled" religious faith.

> **What Do You Think?**
>
> What is our responsibility toward people like those named in verses 7-9?
>
> **Digging Deeper**
>
> How is your church working to address needs within your community?

Global Help

The International Rescue Committee (IRC) is a shining example of an organization that works tirelessly to champion the cause of the oppressed in times of conflict and disaster. With a global reach, it provides aid and assistance to those in need, especially in vulnerable communities. The organization offers essential services such as health care, education, and protection to those most in need. The IRC also provides people with the tools and resources to build better futures for themselves and their families. They empower individuals with vocational training, financial assistance, and other resources to create sustainable livelihoods.

The work of the IRC reminds us of the potential to make a positive difference in the world through helping those in need. But ultimately, this work is God's; His concern is global, and His help is available to all. How does your own work reflect God's heart for caring for "the least of these" (Matthew 25:40)? —O. P.

9b. But the way of the wicked he turneth upside down.

In looking after the righteous, the alien, the widows, and the orphans, God specifically acts against the designs and interests of *the wicked*. This is an example of what is called "antithetical parallelism." This feature of Hebrew poetry supports the point of the second thought (the half-verse before us) from the opposite perspective of the first thought (in the half-verse before this one).

10. The LORD shall reign for ever, even thy God, O Zion, unto all generations. Praise ye the LORD.

In contrast to human leaders, God will reign *for ever*. This eternality, coupled with His creative power, means that God is able to do anything He desires. And this God is the God of Zion, the name for the hill upon which Jerusalem was built (see 2 Samuel 5:6-7). By invoking the name *Zion*, the psalmist calls the readers' attention to the fact

How to Say It

Israel	*Iz*-ray-el.
Jerusalem	Juh-*roo*-suh-lem.
shofar *(Hebrew)*	*show*-far.
Torah *(Hebrew)*	*Tor*-uh.
Zion	*Zi*-un.

Visual for Lesson 11. *Briefly go over this chart while discussing the Lesson Context; it can be used to review psalms from previous lessons.*

that their God chose to place His glory in Jerusalem (1 Kings 8:1-11). With that reminder, the psalm concludes with a final exhortation to *praise ye the Lord.*

III. Exhortation
(Psalm 150:1-6)
A. Where (v. 1)

1. Praise ye the Lord. Praise God in his sanctuary. Praise him in the firmament of his power.

Psalm 150 also opens with the exhortation *praise ye the Lord* (see Lesson Context; Psalm 146:1 [above]). But right away, we are confronted with an interpretive difficulty: Do the next two exhortations speak of where God is or where the person doing the praising is to be? We need to look for clues.

The precise location of God's *sanctuary* and its proximity to *the firmament of his power* is debated (compare Psalm 11:4). The sanctuary could refer to the temple in Jerusalem (example: 1 Chronicles 9:28-29) or to God's heavenly home (example: "holy habitation" in Psalm 68:4-5). The parallelism of the verses and the reference to *the firmament of his power*—a heavenly location—may support the celestial sanctuary (examples: Isaiah 6:1-4; Revelation 5). It is also possible, however, that the verse calls for worship in both earthly and heavenly realms. In that case, the psalmist would

have envisioned the entire universe gathering to praise God (compare Psalms 96, 148).

B. Why (v. 2)

2. Praise him for his mighty acts. Praise him according to his excellent greatness.

Any discussion of God, whether concerning the Father, Son, or Holy Spirit, will essentially deal with (or presuppose conclusions to) two issues: *who God is* (in His nature and essence) and *what God has done* (in His acts of creating, ruling, and redeeming). To *praise him for his mighty acts* honors God in terms of what He has done; to *praise him according to his excellent greatness* is to honor Him in terms of His essential being and character. General references to God's "mighty acts" can also be found in Psalms 106:2; 145:4, 12; etc., with content expounded in texts such as Psalm 136.

C. How (vv. 3-5)

3. Praise him with the sound of the trumpet. Praise him with the psaltery and harp.

The next three verses identify the various instruments that the psalmist envisioned being used to praise God. These instruments are taken both from the religious rites of the priests and prophets and from the realm of the laity, which implies that every form of music should be mustered to glorify God.

The first instrument mentioned is the priestly ram's horn *trumpet*, called the *shofar*. These were used in worship (Leviticus 25:9), as a signal in war (Joshua 6:4-9, 20), to warn of danger (Joel 2:1), to express joyous celebration (2 Samuel 6:15), to herald news (1 Samuel 13:3), at the installation of a king (1 Kings 1:34), and to call to assembly (Jeremiah 4:5).

The psaltery and harp were stringed instruments mentioned together seven times in the psalms (here and in Psalms 33:2; 57:8; 71:22; 81:2; 92:3; and 108:2). They were also used by the prophets in their ministering (1 Samuel 10:5; 1 Chronicles 25:1, 6), and David famously played such an instrument for Saul to drive away the spirit that afflicted him (1 Samuel 16:23).

4. Praise him with the timbrel and dance. Praise him with stringed instruments and organs.

The timbrel is similar to a modern tambourine, being small enough to be held in the hand. Use of this rhythm percussion instrument is associated with dances of joy several times in the Old Testament (examples: Exodus 15:20; Psalm 149:3), even joy that has the wrong focus (Isaiah 5:11-12).

The term *stringed instruments* likely refers collectively to the various kinds of such instruments rather than a third type. The *organs* could refer to a pipe or collectively to various kinds of wind instruments but distinct from horns.

5. Praise him upon the loud cymbals. Praise him upon the high sounding cymbals.

The percussion section is mentioned in this verse. It is possible that two different instruments are in view here. Alternatively, the same instrument may have been used in different ways. Regardless of the exact items to which the text refers, the idea is that those present to praise God should make loud and joyful noises.

D. Who (v. 6)

6. Let every thing that hath breath praise the LORD. Praise ye the LORD.

The psalm concludes by identifying the persons who should praise God. *Every thing that hath breath* could refer to human beings, specifically, into whom God breathed the "breath of life" (Genesis 2:7). However, animals are also said to possess the "breath of life" (7:15). Consequently, it seems likely that the psalmist has invited all creation to participate in praising the Creator (compare Psalms 69:34; 103:22; 148:1-10).

What Sound?

When my niece was about three, a favorite pastime of mine was to ask her what sounds different animals make. Some of these were quite easy for her—a cat, a dog, a rooster. But when I asked, for instance, how a bunny or a fish sounds, she would grow quite serious. Sometimes she would remain silent in her contemplation, and sometimes she'd vocalize something off-the-wall just to make us both laugh.

Imagine all the animal sounds we can mimic—and all those we don't even know—joining in with our human worship. That is the call of Psalm 150:

to praise unabashedly. What a sound when *all* of creation joins in His praise!

—J. A. K.

> **What Do You Think?**
> How does it feel to assume that all of creation is praising God around you?
>
> **Digging Deeper**
> What opportunities outside of weekly worship services do you have to join in praising the Lord of creation?

Conclusion

A. Praise Your Heavenly Father

I was eager to praise my earthly father. I saw all that he did for me and how he cared for me, and I always looked up to him. Many of you likely can relate to that.

But we often fail to praise our Heavenly Father the same way. We take His blessings for granted, as though these were given to us by nature rather than a loving God. We brag about what someone has done for us, but we never share with others the ways that God shows His mercy toward us. In fact, we are prone to grumbling and complaining about how difficult the circumstances of life can be.

Psalms 146 and 150 exhort us to praise God for all the great deeds He has done and continues to do for us. When we gather together in praise of our heavenly Father, we not only align ourselves with the admonitions of Scripture, but we also grow in our intimacy with God and with other believers. Moreover, when we remind ourselves of and meditate on God's gracious acts on our behalf, we grow in our gratitude toward God and our resistance to grumbling. We can come to appreciate God's blessings more and find joy in our lives even in (or especially in) difficult circumstances.

B. Prayer

Heavenly Father, remind us daily of all Your mercies to us. Fill our hearts with gratitude and our mouths with Your praise. In Jesus' name we pray. Amen.

C. Thought to Remember

God deserves our praise.

Involvement Learning

Enhance your lesson with KJV Bible Student *(from your curriculum supplier) and the reproducible activity page (at www.standardlesson.com or in the back of the* KJV Standard Lesson Commentary Deluxe Edition*).*

Into the Lesson

Begin today's session by reading each of the following statements to your class. Poll the class after each statement to see how many agree with it and how many disagree. *Option.* You may want to display these or distribute them on a handout (you create).

1. Too much praise will keep a child from reaching his or her full potential.
2. The most praiseworthy person in my life has also been the most influential.
3. I can praise you without diminishing myself.
4. There aren't many situations or people in my life really deserving of praise.

Divide the class into groups of two or three. Ask class members to choose one of the statements and to explain to their partner(s) why they agree or disagree with it.

After a few minutes for discussion, tell the class, "Today's lesson is all about praise we can always feel good about: praise to God our Father. The psalmist was effusive with his praise. Let's open our Bibles to discover why."

Into the Word

Ask each group from the previous exercise to combine with one other group. In these new groups, class members should examine Psalms 146 and 150 to complete a handout of a chart (you create) with the following headings: *Chapter and Verse*, *Why Praise?*, and *How to Praise?*, noting for each section from the texts why and/or how the psalmist encourages praise.

Option. Ask some or all the groups to list the praiseworthy actions of God they find in Psalm 146. Besides each one, they should jot down ways they see God doing these things in our world today. If they have time, groups could do internet research to discover ministries or other agencies through whom God is working to accomplish each one.

Give the class six to eight minutes to work in groups before calling them together for an all-class discussion of the psalms, reviewing their group findings and conclusions.

Alternative. Distribute copies of the "Words About Praise" exercise from the activity page, which you can download. Allow learners to work in pairs to complete as instructed.

Into Life

Challenge class members to identify their own personal reasons to praise God from the list of reasons they compiled in their Bible study. Tell them to write or circle the encouragements to praise that mean the most to them. Then, in their groups, they can share what they've chosen and why.

Encourage individuals to write a brief praise prayer of a few words or one or two sentences and to share what they've written with the group. Then each group should choose one of the prayers for the whole class to hear. Close today's session with a prayer made up of these praises read aloud by those who wrote them.

Option. Point some or all of your groups specifically to Psalm 146:7-9 and challenge them to brainstorm ways God could use class members to do each praiseworthy work. Ask them to consider how God would be praised by each idea they mention.

Alternative. Distribute copies of "Chronicle of Praise" exercise from the activity page. Encourage learners to complete the chart in their personal times with God each day in the coming week. (You may want to make time in next week's session for members to share any insights or conclusions that came to them because they completed this activity.)

In your closing prayer time, include prayers for God's help in pursuing their ideas in the coming days.

A Song of Thanksgiving

Devotional Reading: Ephesians 5:1-2, 15-20
Background Scripture: Psalm 100

Psalm 100

1 Make a joyful noise unto the LORD, all ye lands.

2 Serve the LORD with gladness: Come before his presence with singing.

3 Know ye that the LORD he is God: It is he that hath made us, and not we ourselves; We are his people, and the sheep of his pasture.

4 Enter into his gates with thanksgiving, And into his courts with praise: Be thankful unto him, and bless his name.

5 For the LORD is good; his mercy is everlasting; And his truth endureth to all generations.

Key Text

Enter into his gates with thanksgiving, and into his courts with praise: be thankful unto him, and bless his name. —Psalm 100:4

Photo © Getty Images

Worship in the Covenant Community

Unit 3: Psalms of Thanksgiving and Praise

Lessons 10–13

Lesson Aims

After participating in this lesson, each learner will be able to:

1. Identify the psalmist's reasons for grateful praise.

2. Articulate why giving thanks is appropriate for all creation.

3. Make a plan to better recognize and seize opportunities for thanksgiving.

Lesson Outline

Introduction

A. An Invitation to Joy

The confession that God constantly cares for humans points us to the reality of mystery. Why should God care? Would it be appropriate for an eternal being to care about such short-lived creatures as human beings? Given the apparently unnecessary suffering in the world, and in Israel's history specifically, how can we know that God cares? Most of the Bible concerns these questions. Its answers should provoke a profound sense of wonder in all of us.

Psalm 100 makes a simpler point, however. It confesses that God shows profound care for a whole people, the Israelites, preserving them during times of political and social turmoil, teaching them how to live better lives through the Torah, and listening to their prayers whether the people were praising or lamenting. That view of God's work lies at the very heart of the faith of both the synagogue and the church. We are part of a great flock tended by the shepherd who drives away the wolves and leads us to good pastures, as Psalm 23 says (see lesson 10).

B. Lesson Context

Psalm 100 is familiar to many Christians through the hymn "All People That on Earth Do Dwell," whose tune is called "Old Hundredth." The superscription to Psalm 100 states the obvious. The psalm concerns praise, or better, thanksgiving. Anyone singing this psalm should come to God with deep gratitude.

The book of Psalms is actually a collection of five books or sections. Most Bibles note these book divisions (often with Roman numerals) at the beginnings of Psalms 1, 42, 73, 90, and 107. Altogether these five books feature 150 poems.

Psalm 100, today's text, is found in the fourth of these five books. Many scholars consider this section of Psalms (that is, Psalms 90–106) to be the answer to the problem presented in the first three books: the Davidic dynasty established (Psalm 2); the flourishing of that dynasty (Psalm 72); and the failure of that dynasty (Psalm 89). The emphasis in Book IV of Psalms is simply that God reigns!

The verbs throughout the psalm that are plural invite all who hear the psalm to join in praising God. The original singers were to express their appreciation for God's work among them in the central location, the temple in Jerusalem (compare 2 Chronicles 5:2, 12-13). The reason for the gratitude appears in Psalms 93–99, which should be read along with Psalm 100. Since it is so short, it seems unlikely that it should stand by itself. Rather, it concludes a sequence of psalms that concern Israel's joyous celebration of God's benevolent kingship. Much of the psalm has precise parallels in Psalms 95, 96, and 98.

I. An Invitation to Worship
(Psalm 100:1-2)
A. Open to All (v. 1)

1. Make a joyful noise unto the LORD, all ye lands.

The single Hebrew word here translated with the phrase *make a joyful noise* occurs 28 times in the book of Psalms. Four of those instances involve making such noise *unto the Lord* (see Psalms 95:1; 98:4, 6). The oldest English translation, that of the Wycliffe Bible of AD 1395, challenged the reader to "sing ye heartily to God." The same verb is used for the shout at the siege of Jericho (Joshua 6:5, 10, 16, 20). The call to shout with joy in worship speaks to the high enthusiasm and excitement that should surround the praises of the faithful community (compare Ezra 3:11).

All ye lands translates a Hebrew phrase that appears 17 times in the Psalter. In 15 of those instances, the translation is "all the earth" or "the whole earth," and that is the sense here (examples: Psalms 33:8; 96:9). Even so, some students think that the text calls the faithful of Israel, wherever they may be, to prayer and praise. This interpretation is supported by many texts that call Israel to faithful worship of the Lord (example: 95:6-10). And the focus might be on Israelites who were forced to migrate to many lands, and about whom the prophets were concerned (example: Hosea 11:10-11). This cannot be proven, however, as no date or author is given for the psalm.

Another interpretation is that the challenge to prayer and praise is for Jew and Gentile alike, anywhere in the world. Like Psalms 148–150, this understanding of the text expects that not just Israelites will join in praising God, but all human beings (compare Psalms 22:27; 96:7). How will this occur? The psalm does not spell out how Gentiles should know about God's mercy and kindness (although the gospel message will clarify this later).

The idea that Gentiles will come to know about Israel's God is a repeated theme of the Old Testament. For example, Abraham's family was to be a blessing to "all families of the earth" (Genesis 12:3; compare Galatians 3:8). The prophet Isaiah drew on this idea (Isaiah 2:1-4; 49:6; 60:3), as did other prophets (examples: Micah 4:1-4; Zechariah 9:10). A third possibility is that the writer might have embraced intentionally the ambiguity of whether he was speaking to Israel as dispersed in the world or to both Israelites and Gentiles everywhere. Certainly, the psalm eventually came to have the bigger vision. All human beings may join in the worship of God in the full knowledge that God welcomes all into a deep relationship (Acts 3:24-26).

> **What Do You Think?**
> When do you find yourself desiring to make a joyful noise to the Lord?
> **Digging Deeper**
> Do you ever stifle this urge? Might your answer change if you sensed "all the lands" joining in that celebration?

Praise the Lord

Every Sunday morning, believers from diverse backgrounds and walks of life gather as a congregation to worship and praise God. Despite their differences, they come together in love and devotion to God. They start their worship by singing hymns and offering prayers of thanksgiving, expressing their joy and gratitude for all the blessings in their lives. Their collective voices create a beautiful harmony that fills the sanctuary, and the spirit of unity and peace permeates throughout the congregation.

As they worship and praise, this congregation embodies the message of Psalm 100:1. They enter God's presence with joy and thanksgiving, recognizing and celebrating the goodness and faithfulness of God. Their worship is not merely ritualistic but is a genuine expression of their heartfelt devotion and gratitude toward Him. Their faith and hope in God's love and provision shines through their worship, and it serves as a powerful reminder that no matter how difficult the circumstances might be, the Maker's presence and goodness remain constant. Can the same be said of your own prayer, praise, and worship practices?　　　　　　　　—O. P.

B. With Gladness (v. 2)

2a. Serve the LORD with gladness.

The invitation comes with certain expectations. The first is that serving *the Lord* can't be separated from worshipping Him (Matthew 4:10). The deity served is the deity worshipped, and vice versa (1 Kings 9:6, 9; 16:31). Another expectation concerns the attitude or motivation that people bring to that privilege. We do not *serve* God primarily out of fear of violating His rules, nor do we serve as those who merely tick off boxes as a matter of ritual or for personal gain. Either approach assumes that our good works will justify us in God's eyes. Rather, we serve *with gladness,* a word translated "joy" elsewhere. This approach dispels worry and allows for simple trust in God's mercy. The word translated "gladness" occurs 14 times in the book of Psalms, where it is also translated "joy" (Psalms 16:11; 43:4; 137:6). This sense of joy occurs in individuals and in the community.

The life of worship and service should be filled with joy whenever possible and deeply honest when it is not (compare 2 Corinthians 1:3-11; Philippians 1:12-18). While not under consideration in this psalm, it is important to recognize that Israel used laments to help them express the disorientation and pain they experienced (see the book of Lamentations). Asserting that we are to serve and worship the Lord with gladness is not an exclusive call to speak *only* happily to God. He has made room for all our experiences, as we see most clearly in the incarnation of Jesus.

2b. Come before his presence with singing.

The invitation to *come,* here and in Psalm 100:4 (below), is similar to Psalm 95:2, 6. Singing is mentioned more than 130 times in the Psalter, and joy takes concrete form as the community assembles in doing so. The psalm invites those hearing it to take delight in both God's merciful work and their fellow human beings' celebration of that work.

Ancient *singing* normally was accompanied by musical instruments, including stringed lyres or harps, wind instruments such as pipes, flutes, or ocarinas, and percussion instruments such as drums or shakers (compare last week's lesson on Psalm 150). The talents of the people come together to express their pleasure in God's goodness. We see a similar embrace of creativity in service to God in His calling of Bezaleel and Aholiab "to devise cunning works, to work in gold, and in silver, and in brass" (Exodus 31:4). We do well to consider how we, too, are allowing our skilled artisans to lead us into the worship of our creative God.

II. An Invitation to Know
(Psalm 100:3-5)

A. Who God Is (v. 3a-b)

3a. Know ye that the LORD he is God.

We now come to the beating heart of Psalm 100. Here is the first key idea of the verse: *the Lord*—the God of Israel who rescued the people from Egyptian bondage, gave them the promised land, and sustained them repeatedly in times of crisis—is the one and only true *God.* Other "gods" do not merit the name.

Since the psalm probably addresses the whole world, and not just Israel alone, the confession that "the Lord he is God" is to be offered by all human beings. Or in other words, the evidence of God's deity, as revealed in the exodus and other miraculous events of Israel's history, also extends to non-Israelites (Gentiles). This idea also appears in, for example, Psalms 46:10 and 83:18.

The main idea of the psalm is the call to *know* God. Human knowledge of God is always limited and entirely dependent on God's self-revelation. We can know only what God has equipped us to know. And the main thing we know is God's mercy to human beings. By calling Abraham and his descendants to be a people, God was forming a people who could be an example of the possibilities of righteousness and mercy for all human beings. The psalm invites its Jewish singers and all who overhear them to experience confidence in God's willingness to be with the reader in a deep relationship. Peoplehood is worth celebrating.

Knowing God is an important way the New Testament talks about the experience of being a Christian. The Gospel of John, in particular, speaks of evidence as it relates to coming to the knowledge of the deity of Christ (John 4:39-42; 6:69; 8:28; 20:30-31). What we can know, we know through the revelation of the Son (1:18; compare 1 John 1:1; 2:13-14; 4:2). This idea does not appear in this form in the Old Testament, of course. Yet its core ingredients do.

3b. It is he that hath made us.

The second idea, or rather confession, is that the Lord's status as the unique God means that He is the Creator. Ancient religions sometimes thought of the creator as a retired deity, the ancestor of the current leader of the gods of their pantheons. For the Bible, there is only one God, and so God must be the Creator.

> **What Do You Think?**
> What reassurance can you take from God's forming His people, not our forming ourselves into His people?
> **Digging Deeper**
> How do you experience freedom in light of God's work forming us?

B. Who We Are (v. 3c)

3c. And not we ourselves. We are his people, and the sheep of his pasture.

We did not make *ourselves*, having no godly power to do so. Saying so implies God's continued power over us and our relative powerlessness in the face of the Lord who formed us. The phrase *we are his people* implies a shared history and hope for the future, a deep relationship marked by prayer and service.

The last part of the verse restates and deepens that idea (compare Psalm 95:6-7). "Shepherd" was a royal title (example: 2 Samuel 24:17), with God being the heavenly king who cares for human beings (compare Psalm 23; John 10:11-18). While the image of Israel as a flock can have negative connotations—the sheep for the slaughter, etc. (Psalms 44:11, 22; 49:14)—it more ordinarily has a positive meaning. The image may be one of mutual love and desire for relationship (examples: 77:20; 78:52; 79:13; 107:41). Even the negative uses are such because they hope for a positive relationship that does not seem available at the moment (examples: 74:1; 80:1-7).

Why the Servant Smiled

At the funeral of Kevin, a dear friend who dedicated his life to serving others, the officiant fittingly referred to him as a "smiling servant." Kevin recognized that God's people are in His safekeeping, just like sheep in a meadow under the care of a good shepherd. By embracing God's authority, Kevin knew he would be protected and find joy. He believed in God's protection and care, so he gave back to others with a warm, comforting smile that brought joy to those around him.

How to Say It

Aholiab	Uh-*ho*-lih-ab.
Bezaleel	Bih-*zal*-ih-el.
Gentiles	*Jen*-tiles.
Jerusalem	Juh-*roo*-suh-lem.
Mishnah	*Mish*-nuh.
pantheons	*pan*-thee-ahnz.
tabernacles	**tah**-burr-*nah*-kulz.
Torah (Hebrew)	*Tor*-uh.
Wycliffe	*Wye*-clif.
Yom Kippur	Yohm Ki-*poor*
	or Yahm Ki-*poor*.

Visual for
Lessons 8 & 12

Ask learners to consider who they are inviting to the Lord's feast and how they are doing so.

The faith and trust behind his smiles were not just a knowledge of facts but also an understanding of the relationship between the Creator and the created. Until his last breath, Kevin completely understood this, so he smiled.

Kevin's life exemplified the peace and joy found, even in life's troubles, when we recognize God's love and care. Who reminds you to trust in God's care? And who are you reminding, by word and deed, to do the same?   —O. P.

C. Why We Should Praise (vv. 4-5)

4a. Enter into his gates with thanksgiving, and into his courts with praise.

This psalm was to be sung in the temple as part of congregational worship (see Psalm 100:2b, above). *Gates* and *courts* together form the part of the temple precinct to which the congregation had access. The temple centered on the holy of holies, which only the high priest could enter once a year in order to offer a sacrifice for atonement (Hebrews 9:7). A court outside of this was open to priests, another outside that to men of Israel, and the courts on the outside perimeter were available to women and Gentiles.

Because a large group was being called to praise, this psalm probably was sung at a major holiday when Israelites made a pilgrimage from the countryside and gathered at the temple in Jerusalem. Some scholars have connected this song to the feast of tabernacles (see Levit-

icus 23:33-43) but without great certainty. In the third century AD, the collection of Jewish law called the Mishnah reported the tradition that the priests in the temple sang Psalm 94 on Wednesdays and Psalm 93 on Fridays. So it is possible that Psalm 100 also figured in daily rituals, but this is also very uncertain. There are not enough specific clues in Psalms 93–100 to answer the question confidently.

What is more certain is that the psalm envisions a congregation singing it inside the temple courtyards, as do Psalms 24:7-10; 120–134; 149–150. These speak of processions, dancing, and crowds preparing themselves for worship together. Psalm 100 also excludes usage during a day of fasting or remorse (like Yom Kippur—the Day of Atonement; see Leviticus 16; 23:26-32). Such an observance would require a different sort of psalm.

> **What Do You Think?**
> What physical places remind you of entering God's temple?
> **Digging Deeper**
> How does praise shift if you are doing it all the time, no matter where you are, since you are part of the temple of the Lord (1 Corinthians 3:16)?

4b. Be thankful unto him, and bless his name.

To *bless* God means to praise Him and give thanks to Him, or to give Him all proper due (compare Psalm 96:2). The congregation should praise God and elevate His *name* above all others. The congregation should revere God and treasure the opportunity to be in His presence. Worship, then, is not primarily a moment for inspiring people, but a time for connecting people to God as it brings to memory our deep dependence on God's love.

5. For the LORD is good. His mercy is everlasting, and his truth endureth to all generations.

The psalm ends with closely connected reasons for human praise. The statement that *the Lord is good* is no mere cliché, for many ancient deities were far from good. The notice of God's goodness appears frequently in the book of Psalms, often as a reason for praise and confidence in the possibilities of a good life (examples: Psalms 25:8; 34:8; 86:5; 119:68; 145:9).

But how can God's goodness be proven? *His mercy* is seen in example after example of repeated acts of healing, forgiving, and rescuing Israel from oppressors. That merciful goodness has appeared again and again in Israel's history, as psalms reciting God's deeds show (examples: Psalms 105–106). God's goodness appears in the permanent nature of His trustworthiness (compare 98:3).

The word translated *truth* means "faithfulness," and it is translated that way in numerous passages (examples: Psalms 36:5; 89:8; 119:90). Thus, the idea is more than "factual accuracy." God's promises and actions are reliable, providing an unfailing guide to human happiness.

Because God's faithfulness endures *to all generations,* Psalm 100 points to the future. The countless experiences of the people with God illustrate divine faithfulness. The people's worship should recall those experiences. It should also express their confidence that such faithfulness awaits their descendants. Hope is "baked into" the worshiping congregations, understanding of reality and its behaviors.

Conclusion
A. Looking to the Future

The center of Psalm 100 invites those singing it to know God's goodness. That goodness shows up in God's unfailing loyalty to Israel and repeated acts to help and heal them and other human beings.

Psalm 100 concludes a group of psalms by inviting all human beings, and especially the people of Israel, to worship God in the joyful knowledge that He loves them and will care for them. By ending a group of psalms this way, Psalm 100 creates a sort of infinite loop. It invites us to begin with Psalm 93 and sing the rest of the hymns of praise, and when we reach Psalm 100, we can start over again.

Throughout these hymns, God the king brings salvation and joy to a needy and expectant people. They acknowledge that blessing with the only resource they can: their collective singing.

Psalm 100 ends with a look toward the future. Far from regarding the fate of the succeeding generations as bleak or hopeless, this psalm assumes that an eternal God will always care for those who come after. The invitation to praise extends to all people. It is not a distraction from the nitty-gritty details of life but a way of helping us understand what those details can mean when we submit them to our Creator.

This perspective is worth recovering today because it frees us to find ways to bless our descendants rather than leaving them with problems and burdens. The hopefulness and joy of the psalm invites us to live in ways that future generations will remember us with approval. In reading or singing this psalm today, we can be confident that the God whom Israel trusted is still trustworthy. The hope to which they aspired, we also can embrace.

B. Prayer

Our God and King, You are enthroned in the highest heaven and in the heart of the humblest person. You alone are God, and You have made us in wonderful ways. Help us to celebrate what You have done, are doing, and will do for all Your creation as You sustain and bless all the things You have made. Help us to recall who we are, Your treasured people, so that we may invite others into that same sense of belonging. In Jesus' name we pray. Amen.

C. Thought to Remember
Know that the Lord is God and praise accordingly!

Involvement Learning

Enhance your lesson with KJV Bible Student *(from your curriculum supplier) and the reproducible activity* page *(at www.standardlesson.com or in the back of the* KJV Standard Lesson Commentary Deluxe Edition*).*

Into the Lesson

Group the class into pairs or triads and distribute or post these questions: 1–What is the last thank-you card or expression you received? 2–What is the last thank-you card or expression you sent? 3–How did you feel when you received thanks? when you did not?

Give the groups five minutes and ask each individual to choose one of the questions and answer it in their group. Tell the class, "Today's psalm gives us words to express our thanks to the One who deserves it most. As we study, you can evaluate how well and how often you tell Him thanks."

Into the Word

Combine each group of two or three with another for Bible study. Assign all of your groups *one* of the following activities. Or use *two* or all *three* of these activities among the groups.

Option 1. Ask learners to brainstorm or research hymns and worship songs based on Psalm 100. Compare the lyrics of the songs with the Bible text to find those you feel most faithfully share its meaning. Consider singing together or listening to a public domain version of one of these songs, either now or toward the end of class.

Option 2. Distribute a handout (you create) with the following prompts for group members to answer as they consider Psalm 100:

Verses 1-2: Describe the emotions here. Write one sentence to summarize the main idea of these verses.

Verse 3: What does praise affirm about our relationship with God?

Verse 4: Where are we supposed to praise and thank God? What does this say about the kind of relationship He wants to have with us?

Verse 5: How do these statements about God qualify Him for praise like no one else?

Option 3. Distribute the "Why Worship?" exercise from the activity page, which you can download. Groups should complete the activity as indicated before coming together as a whole group to discuss answers based on Psalm 100. Record answers on the board as learners speak.

Give your groups at least 10 minutes to work on any of these activities, and then allow several minutes for them to report and discuss as a class.

Into Life

Divide the class into their prior groups. Choose one or two of the following activities, asking groups to complete them simultaneously.

Option 1. Distribute blank paper and pencils. In three subgroups, learners should jot down reasons to be thankful according to the category assigned to them: **The Personal Group, The Home and Family Group**, and **The Church Group**. Encourage them to be specific, even if trivial. After the minute has passed, ask volunteers to share one item from their list with their entire group. Ask volunteers, "How do you feel about thanking God for blessings like those you've listed?"

Option 2. Distribute card stock, markers, stickers, and other art supplies. Ask members in groups to make place cards for a family dinner, maybe even Thanksgiving dinner. Each card should contain a quote or paraphrase from a verse or section of Psalm 100, along with the name of one person at the table. As they're working, volunteers should tell each other about the people who are coming to dinner. *Note.* Be sensitive that class members may be mourning the absence of family or friends from holiday gatherings this year.

Option 3. Distribute the "Responsive Reading" exercise from the activity page to be completed as indicated.

After calling time on the chosen activities, ask learners how they can better recognize and seize opportunities for thanksgiving in the coming week. Encourage them to write these plans down and act on them. Close class with prayer.

God's Promised Presence

Devotional Reading: Exodus 33:12-23
Background Scripture: Psalm 139

Psalm 139:1-12

1 O Lord, thou hast searched me, and known me.

2 Thou knowest my downsitting and mine uprising, thou understandest my thought afar off.

3 Thou compassest my path and my lying down, and art acquainted with all my ways.

4 For there is not a word in my tongue, but, lo, O Lord, thou knowest it altogether.

5 Thou hast beset me behind and before, and laid thine hand upon me.

6 Such knowledge is too wonderful for me; it is high, I cannot attain unto it.

7 Whither shall I go from thy spirit? Or whither shall I flee from thy presence?

8 If I ascend up into heaven, thou art there: if I make my bed in hell, behold, thou art there.

9 If I take the wings of the morning, and dwell in the uttermost parts of the sea;

10 Even there shall thy hand lead me, and thy right hand shall hold me.

11 If I say, Surely the darkness shall cover me; even the night shall be light about me.

12 Yea, the darkness hideth not from thee; but the night shineth as the day: the darkness and the light are both alike to thee.

Key Text

O Lord, thou hast searched me, and known me. —**Psalm 139:1**

Worship in the
Covenant Community

Unit 3: Psalms of Thanksgiving and Praise

Lessons 10–13

Lesson Aims

After participating in this lesson, each learner will be able to:

1. List the things that God knows based on Psalm 139:1-12.

2. Explain the imagery of light/dark and God's sight in this psalm.

3. Create a nightly reminder of God's loving care.

Lesson Outline

Introduction
 A. Human Limitation
 B. Lesson Context
 I. Unsearchable Knowledge (Psalm 139:1-6)
  A. Complete Awareness (v. 1)
  B. Complete Insight (vv. 2-3)
  C. Complete Understanding (vv. 4-6)
   Talk to Someone
 II. Unavoidable Presence (Psalm 139:7-12)
  A. In Space (vv. 7-10)
   To Be Known by God
  B. In Darkness (vv. 11-12)
Conclusion
 A. God's Presence and Knowledge
 B. Prayer
 C. Thought to Remember

Introduction

A. Human Limitation

The progress of technology has facilitated an interconnected world. The sheer volume of information that is available thanks to the internet is staggering. But the wealth of knowledge also serves as a reminder of humanity's limitations in experiencing every corner of the globe within a single lifetime. Visiting every country might seem possible. But with approximately 4 million cities and towns across the globe, we realize that just seeing a country will not give us the experience of all those varied places—let alone lightly or uninhabited regions.

Moreover, humanity has only begun to explore the vast expanse of space and the depths of the oceans. In this regard, when we consider the smallness of our plot of land on earth compared to the vastness of space and the oceans, we are reminded of humanity's limited ability to explore. In today's lesson, the psalmist offers insight into this.

B. Lesson Context

Although one ancient manuscript ascribes Psalm 139 to a man named Zechariah (not the prophet) sometime in the 700s–600s BC, most scholars accept the traditional attribution to David. According to Scripture, David was a man who sought after the very heart of God (1 Samuel 13:14), exemplified by his demonstration of faith when he faced Goliath (17:47). He was a man of integrity who chose to trust in God when presented with an opportunity to kill Saul in a cave (24:8-10). Even after conquering his enemies and receiving the promise that his kingdom would be established forever, David remained humble (2 Samuel 7:18; see commentary on Psalm 139:5b, below).

Several difficulties confront us when reading this psalm. First, there is no reference to a particular historical circumstance. This means that a specific historical context, even in David's life, cannot be determined. Context is a great help in interpretation, so the questions presented below reflect to some degree the question of the context of this psalm's being written. Second, a thorough examination of Psalm 139 reveals complexities in its structure that complicate a straightforward interpretation of David's intent.

To analyze the psalm's content, some scholars have proposed dividing it into sections of praise (vv. 1-18) and lamentation (vv. 19-24) based on the initial expressions of gratitude followed by anguish. These can further be broken into four stanzas of verses 1-6, 7-12, 13-18, and 19-24. These issues also prevent this psalm from fitting neatly into conventional categories of psalms, which, when clear, can also aid in understanding ancient texts.

And finally, the text assumes that David was beset by wicked adversaries opposed to him and to God. These individuals harbored animosity toward God, profaned His name, and spoke maliciously against Him (Psalm 139:19-22, not in our printed text). Furthermore, David implored God to probe his innermost being and guide him toward eternal life (139:23-24, not in our printed text). But the connection between the verses we will study today (139:1-12) and these opponents is unclear, and how early lament or protest begins is also hazy.

I. Unsearchable Knowledge
(Psalm 139:1-6)
A. Complete Awareness (v. 1)

1. O LORD, thou hast searched me, and known me.

This verse introduces a central theme of the chapter, which is further emphasized by its near repetition in the conclusion of this psalm (Psalm 139:23, not in our printed text). God's complete knowledge, often referred to as His omniscience, is the attribute that encompasses His infinite awareness and understanding of everything that has ever happened, is happening, or will happen. He is entirely aware of all things. But David did not set out to write a doctrine of God's knowledge. David assumed God's omniscience as fact and did not make an argument to convince others. David's intention was not to teach about God's infallible, complete knowledge, but instead to marvel at it in awe and perhaps even in fear (see 139:7-12, below).

We might think of this verse as beginning a courtroom drama, with the *Lord* trying the evidence of David's character (*thou hast searched me, and known me*). The Hebrew word translated *searched* is the same expression employed to describe a cross-examination in a judicial context (Proverbs 18:17). God is the judge who has meticulously scrutinized and comprehensively understood all the evidence required to judge the heart's motivations.

B. Complete Insight (vv. 2-3)

2. Thou knowest my downsitting and mine uprising, thou understandest my thought afar off.

The psalmist employs the terms *downsitting* and *uprising* to convey God's knowledge of an individual's entire day (see 2 Kings 19:27; Psalm 44:21; Ecclesiastes 12:14; Hebrews 4:13; 1 John 3:20). The two extremes point to God's total knowledge; nothing is left out. (The literary device of naming opposite ends of a spectrum to indicate everything in between is called *merism*.) Jesus' knowledge of people's inner lives is one marker of His divinity recorded in the Gospels (examples: Matthew 12:25; Luke 5:22; John 4:16-19).

3. Thou compassest my path and my lying down, and art acquainted with all my ways.

The psalmist emphasizes that God possesses knowledge of both public and private aspects of one's life, from their travels (*my path*) to their rest (*lying down*). The Hebrew term translated *compassest* in context is an image of sifting grains to separate the grain from the chaff (compare Ruth 3:2; Isaiah 41:16). This suggests God's metaphorically sifting David's life to separate chaff from wheat. A helpful analogy to clarify this notion involves likening the process to a gemologist who scatters an array of gemstones across a table, enabling the individual examination of each specimen for quality (compare Jeremiah 17:10; see Psalm 139:23-24, not in our printed text).

C. Complete Understanding (vv. 4-6)

4. For there is not a word in my tongue, but, lo, O LORD, thou knowest it altogether.

In human communication, the potential for misinterpretation looms large. This is perhaps especially apparent in text-based media when we realize how much of comprehension comes down to non-verbal cues, such as tone and body language. Even when face-to-face, myriad factors can create misunderstandings no matter how carefully words are selected—not least the words *themselves*, which can have wide variations in meaning and are highly context-dependent. Given the perils of communicating even when both parties are acting truthfully, the risk of being deceived by a bad actor is always high (consider Romans 16:18; 1 John 4:1). In stark contrast, God possesses an unparalleled ability to comprehend every *word* even when it is mere thought or intention. No context or body language confuses His understanding.

> **What Do You Think?**
> What other verses point to prayer as a gift to us rather than a need of God's?
>
> **Digging Deeper**
> What value can you discern in intentionally allowing prayers in the Bible to shape your prayer life?

Talk to Someone

As clients express themselves, counselors carefully listen to their words, observe their body language, and assess their emotions. Therapists' training and experience allow them to pick up on subtle cues and anticipate the direction of the conversation. By utilizing their well-honed intuition, insight, and expertise, counselors can help their clients make sense of their experiences, uncover underlying issues, and start on a road to healing and growth.

Therapists and counselors exemplify how we can strive to know and understand those around us more deeply. But even a well-trained therapist or counselor could be fooled; after all, they're still human! In contrast, Psalm 139:4 emphasizes the all-knowing nature of God, who is aware of our every thought and word before we even speak to them. God knows us intimately, including our deepest thoughts and emotions. What comfort can you find this week in speaking to the Lord who knows you and loves you?   —O. P.

5a. Thou hast beset me behind and before.

Here David's focus shifts from the pure fact of God's knowledge to the action He takes with this knowledge. *Beset* is multifaceted, indicating an act of confinement, binding, or encircling. This can have positive or negative implications, depending on context. Most frequently, it denotes the plight of a city besieged by hostile forces (Deuteronomy 20:12, 19; 1 Samuel 23:8; Daniel 1:1; etc.). In one instance, however, the word is used by the beloved's friends: "If she be a door, we will inclose her with boards of cedar" (Song of Solomon 8:9). A similar concept, though with a different word entirely, is used to describe God's protection of Job: "Hast not thou made an hedge about him, and about his house, and about all that he hath on every side?" (Job 1:10). The evidence suggests David was experiencing God's presence *behind and before* as a hindrance of some kind.

5b. And laid thine hand upon me.

The metaphor of God's *hand* might shed some light on the context of "beset." Although God is an immaterial being and does not possess physical appendages such as hands or feet, the writers of Scripture were constrained by the limitations of human language in their attempts to depict God in a way that would resonate with their audience. There is precedent for desiring God to turn His attention to someone else, as communicated here with the metaphor of His hand. For instance, after eating the forbidden fruit in the Garden of Eden, the *last* thing Adam and Eve desired was an audience with the Lord (Genesis 3:8)! Job asked God to withdraw His hand (Job 13:20-21). And Ezekiel described God as striking His hands together to punish Judah (Ezekiel 22:13). Later, John the Baptist uses a winnowing metaphor to describe Jesus' hand at work in judgment (Matthew 3:12; see Psalm 139:3, above).

We should not discount that David could have experienced God's attention as being too intense for the man to bear (compare Psalms 25:7; 32:4). This psalm has no confession of sin—and, in fact, it asserts David's blamelessness. But one wonders if God's nearness was bringing to light what David would have preferred to leave in darkness. We might think of the time between his transgressions with Bathsheba and her husband and Nathan's confrontation; David seemed to be living in denial of his sin (2 Samuel 11:1–12:13; contrast Psalm 51 [lesson 6]). This or a similar incident could account for wanting some space from God's knowledge and presence. Far from experiencing God's presence as an unmitigated blessing, David seems at least to struggle with the experience, if not to outright struggle *against* it.

6. Such knowledge is too wonderful for me; it is high, I cannot attain unto it.

This verse effectively conveys the profound distance between the positions of God and humanity (compare Job 42:2-3; Isaiah 55:9-11). After contemplating the inscrutable nature of God's mind, David concludes that God's *knowledge* is far beyond the grasp of human comprehension. Rather than succumbing to despair, the psalmist portrays this phenomenon positively, evoking a sense of awe and amazement toward God. Furthermore, this reality leads the psalmist to acknowledge that he is "fearfully and wonderfully made" (Psalm 139:14, not in our printed text).

II. Unavoidable Presence
(Psalm 139:7-12)
A. In Space (vv. 7-10)

7. Whither shall I go from thy spirit? Or whither shall I flee from thy presence?

This verse marks the beginning of Psalm 139's second stanza. This pair of questions can be read as an escape attempt (compare Genesis 3:10; Jonah 1:3) or as an oblique acknowledgment of sin (compare Isaiah's cry in Isaiah 6:5), praise, and adora-

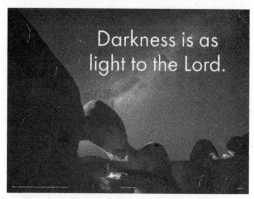

Visual for Lesson 13. *Point to this visual as you pose the questions associated with verse 12 for class discussion.*

tion for God's constant *presence* (compare Psalms 16:11; 21:6; 51:11 [see lesson 6]; etc.), or some mixture of these. If the above reading of David's having found God's presence to be heavy is correct, then the first sense is most likely in view. David might have found God answering the king's questions with some questions of His own: "Can any hide himself in secret places that I shall not see him? saith the Lord. Do not I fill heaven and earth?" (Jeremiah 23:24).

But even after fleeing from God, Jonah found relief in God's ability to save even from "the deep," considered to be the furthest place from God's heaven (see Jonah 2:2-6). So we might assume that, though David felt God's scrutiny too much, in the end, this would be a relief compared to a reality in which God was absent.

The portrayal of God's omnipresence (presence everywhere) within this psalm is unique in the context of the ancient Near East. Most, if not all, other deities in the region were considered to have a limited, geographic sphere of influence (example: 1 Kings 20:28). They were not expected to be present other than in the place where they reigned. This highlights a key difference between those so-called gods and the Lord: He reigns over and is present in all places, not to mention the fact that the regional gods are entirely fictional, to begin with! This understanding substantiates that David's writing stemmed from a deeply personal and intimate understanding of God rather than a mere appropriation of general religious concepts from nearby cultures.

8. If I ascend up into heaven, thou art there. If I make my bed in hell, behold, thou art there.

The word *if*, found four times in the English translation of Psalm 139:8-11, indicates the hypothetical nature of the declarations that follow. The first two of those verses give examples of places where David could not physically go to flee from God's presence (see Psalm 139:9, below). *Heaven* is obviously a no-go, as it is God's home (1 Kings 8:30, 39, 43; etc.), and David couldn't get there on foot in any case. In ancient Israel's understanding of the world, multiple levels of heavens existed above the earth (see Deuteronomy 10:14; 2 Corinthians 12:2). This suggests that the contrast of heaven with *hell* is another merism, where a combination of two contrasting parts refer to the whole. In this case, considering that the place of the dead was believed to be under the earth (example: Numbers 16:30), these two places are as far from one another as can be (compare Job 11:8; Isaiah 7:11; Amos 9:2; etc.). David's presence in either would not hide him from God.

What Do You Think?
How would you counsel someone who wants to trust God but struggles with the fact that He does not always intervene to prevent evil from occurring?

Digging Deeper
What assumptions about God and the world need to be confronted to face that question honestly?

9. If I take the wings of the morning, and dwell in the uttermost parts of the sea.

In contrast to the vertical imagery of the previous verse, David shifts to horizontal imagery. *Wings of the morning* is a poetic reference to sunrise, which happens in the direction east. *The sea* refers to the Mediterranean Sea, which lay to the west of Israel. Taken together, we see another merism as David describes going as far east as possible and as far west as was known. Hence, the depicted imagery expresses God's abundant pres-

ence, extending as far as the distance between the east and the west (compare Psalm 103:12). What David knew instinctively the prophet Jonah would find out the hard way when he was told to go east to Nineveh but tried to flee by going west to Tarshish (Jonah 1:1-3).

10. Even there shall thy hand lead me, and thy right hand shall hold me.

Having established the hypothetical situations of the previous two verses, David identified two comforting actions linked to God's omnipresence. First, David could be guided by the *hand* of God regardless of David's location. This assurance was grounded in the understanding that one is never in a place where God cannot provide guidance (example: Psalm 23:4 [lesson 10]).

Second, David asserted that one cannot be beyond the reach of God's protection and salvation, as exemplified by the phrase *right hand shall hold me* (compare Psalms 18:35; 21:8; 63:8). This assurance brought comfort to David, who had in mind his adversaries who sought to do him harm (139:19).

What Do You Think?
In which current situations do you find God's presence in your life comforting?

Digging Deeper
Do you find His presence alarming in others? Does this suggest that a new course of action would be wise for you?

To Be Known by God

Ignatius of Loyola (1491–1556) was the prominent founder of The Society of Jesus (the Jesuits). He authored a book titled *The Spiritual Exercises*, which focused on spiritual development. The book emphasized the importance of respecting and serving God as the sole Creator and supreme Lord of the universe.

Ignatius's teachings on the omnipresence of God were encapsulated in a section of his book called "Principle and Foundation," which serves as the fundamental basis for the spiritual exercises. Ignatius drew insight from Psalm 139 regarding this. His interpretation of this passage is that our purpose in life is to be known by God, who is present in every situation.

We relate to God in (at least) three ways: as our Creator, Ruler, and Redeemer. God is omniscient (all-knowing) and omnipresent (present everywhere) in these aspects of His nature. What behavior or thought process do you need to change personally to better acknowledge this fact?

—O. P.

B. In Darkness (vv. 11-12)

11a. If I say, Surely the darkness shall cover me.

David introduces another conditional statement; the *darkness* here is figurative (metaphorical). Darkness characterizes the time when thieves are prone to operate (Job 24:16). Thus, this "if" statement fits David's previous questions about attempted concealment.

11b-12. Even the night shall be light about me. Yea, the darkness hideth not from thee, but the night shineth as the day. The darkness and the light are both alike to thee.

These conclusions all speak to the futility of trying to hide anything from God. Even opposites such as *darkness* and *light* make no difference to God's knowledge of David's physical and spiritual locations and status. The metaphor of God's illuminating presence is continued in the New Testament and is ascribed to Jesus Christ (see John 1:4-5; 3:19-21; etc.).

What Do You Think?
What darkness would you like reassurance that God sees through?

Digging Deeper
What difference does it make that Jesus has been revealed as the light of the world, which the world cannot understand (John 1:5, 9-10)?

Conclusion

A. God's Presence and Knowledge

The vastness of the world's information and the multitude of places yet to be explored can be exciting and terrifying; God's boundless wisdom and presence provide solace to believers in either and all cases. Even if humanity were to one day journey to the surface of Mars, God's omnipresence ensures that He is already there. For those who trust in Him, the omniscience and omnipresence of God offer a sense of security and salvation. It is essential to recognize that God did not create the universe only to abandon it to its own devices. Rather, He is actively involved and present in every aspect of creation. There can never be too much to know for the infinite God.

David acknowledged his inability to comprehend all knowledge, which underscores the incomprehensibility of God's omniscience. And it's uncertain whether, in the writing of this poem, David was reassured or troubled by God's full knowledge and relentless presence. But these characteristics certainly did comfort David in other cases.

Like David, we might find ourselves in a situation when God's knowledge and presence make us uneasy. Or we might unreservedly embrace these attributes as comforts in our present circumstances. In either case, we can strive to know God better and to praise Him, offer Him our confusion and anxieties, and ask Him for help against all the evil we confront.

B. Prayer

All-knowing and all-present God, we lift our hearts to You. May we take comfort in knowing that You are always with us and will never be surprised by anything we think, say, or do. Help us glorify You in all things so that Your presence and knowledge are a comfort and not a warning to us. We pray in Jesus' name. Amen.

C. Thought to Remember
Take comfort in God's unsurpassed knowledge and presence.

How to Say It

Ignatius	Ig-*nay*-shus.
merism	*mare*-izm.
omnipresence	*ahm*-nih-**prez**-ence.
omniscience	ahm-*nish*-untz.

Involvement Learning

Enhance your lesson with KJV Bible Student *(from your curriculum supplier) and the reproducible activity page (at www.standardlesson.com or in the back of the* KJV Standard Lesson Commentary Deluxe Edition).

Into the Lesson

Divide the class in half for a debate. The **Out Loud Team** will argue for the benefits of having no personal secrets; the **Hush Team** will argue for the benefits of keeping one's secrets. Allow a few minutes for the debate teams to jot down their ideas before asking for opening statements, rebuttals, and final statements.

Instead of declaring a winner, ask the two halves to discuss in their own group what they thought were the ideas with the most merit from the other side. Then bring the class back together to discuss what ideas they found most compelling from both teams.

Lead to Bible study by saying, "We know we don't have any secrets with God. Is that always reassuring? Today's psalm leaves room for us to be both comforted and frightened by God's knowledge and presence."

Into the Word

Ask a volunteer to read Psalm 139:1-12 out loud. As learners listen, have them jot down reasons this is a *comforting* psalm. Ask a second volunteer to read the lesson text one more time so learners can list reasons it is a *frightening* psalm. In pairs (or small groups), ask learners to discuss the reasons they heard for comfort and fright in this psalm.

Next, have the pairs consider whether the psalm is *either* comforting *or* frightening or if it can be *both* comforting *and* frightening. Encourage learners to cite verses in Psalm 139 that support their answers, as well as other evidence from the Bible. After a few minutes, bring the class back together to discuss their thoughts. *Note:* the class need not reach a consensus about this psalm in order to have a fruitful conversation.

Alternative 1. Distribute the "Known by God" exercise from the activity page, which you can download, to be completed as indicated in small groups. After calling time, ask volunteers to share their work. Allow time for class discussion.

Alternative 2. If your class has artistically inclined learners, ask them to work in small groups to create visual representations of the scenes in which the psalmist cannot escape God's presence. These can be individual scenes (if they want to be more detailed) or longer comic-strip-type images if they work alone. As they work, have them discuss how such pictorial interpretations can be used to teach children and adults alike about God's presence. Encourage these learners to share their work with someone outside of class and come to class next week prepared to share about that experience. Allow time for volunteers to share their work with the whole class.

Into Life

In learners' original pairs, have them brainstorm the implications of God's presence in a world that we see contains much evil. Ask them to consider what barriers to and opportunities for evangelism God's presence poses.

Distribute slips of paper and pencils. Display the following phrase: "Something most people don't realize about me, but I'm glad God does . . ." Ask students *anonymously* to jot down a response to this prompt. Collect the slips of paper and then redistribute them among the class members. Ask volunteers to read what's written on the slip they receive.

Alternative. Point students to the second exercise "Read and Reflect" on the activity page, to be completed as indicated.

After either activity, give learners one minute to silently reflect on what would be a meaningful nightly reminder of God's loving care. Ask volunteers to share their ideas. Encourage learners to create this reminder and place it somewhere it will be visible before learners go to sleep. Close class with a prayer.

A King
Forever and Ever

Special Features

Lessons
Unit 1: Jesus, the Heir of David

Unit 2: Our God Reigns

Unit 3: Life in God's Kingdom

Quarterly Quiz

Use these questions as a pretest or as a review. The answers are on page iv of This Quarter in the Word.

Lesson 1
1. The women praised the Lord because Naomi was not without a _____. *Ruth 4:14*
2. Luke states that Jesus was about 30 years old when He began His public ministry. T/F. *Luke 3:23*

Lesson 2
1. The word of the Lord came to whom? (David, Nathan, Samuel) *2 Samuel 7:4*
2. The Lord declared that David's house, kingdom, and _____ would be forever. *2 Samuel 7:16*

Lesson 3
1. "Zacharias was filled with the Holy Ghost, and _____." (prayed, prophesied, worshipped) *Luke 1:67*
2. The child would be called "the prophet of the Highest." T/F. *Luke 1:76*

Lesson 4
1. Where did Joseph begin the journey to Bethlehem? (Capernaum, Jerusalem, Nazareth) *Luke 2:4*
2. The heavenly host proclaimed "_____ to God." (Honor, Praise, Glory) *Luke 2:14*

Lesson 5
1. The blind man said, "Jesus, thou Son of David, heal me." T/F. *Luke 18:38*
2. Jesus restored the man's sight by placing mud on the man's eyes. T/F. *Luke 18:42-43*

Lesson 6
1. The psalmist asked God, "lift up thine _____. *Psalm 10:12*
2. The psalmist describes God as being a "helper of the _____." *Psalm 10:14*

Lesson 7
1. "The Lord reigneth, he is clothed with _____." *Psalm 93:1*

2. What body of water lifts its "voice" to the Lord? (rivers, lakes, floods) *Psalm 93:3*

Lesson 8
1. The Lord will renew youth like doves. T/F. *Psalm 103:5*
2. The Lord remembers that "we are _____." *Psalm 103:14*

Lesson 9
1. The Lord's dominion endures through all _____. *Psalm 145:13*
2. The psalmist states that the Lord is righteous in all what? (thoughts, actions, ways) *Psalm 145:17*

Lesson 10
1. Jesus taught that people should pray in a way that others will notice. T/F. *Matthew 6:5*
2. Jesus taught that people should pray for what kind of bread? (daily bread, bread of life, bread of heaven) *Matthew 6:11*

Lesson 11
1. Jesus described John the Baptist as "Elias," who was to come. T/F. *Matthew 11:14*
2. Jesus pronounced "woe" to what two cities? (choose two: Bethsaida, Capernaum, Chorazin, Tyre) *Matthew 11:21*

Lesson 12
1. Jesus told the young man to sell his possessions and give to the poor to have _____ in heaven. *Matthew 19:21*
2. The young man obeyed Jesus' directives regarding wealth. T/F. *Matthew 19:22*

Lesson 13
1. The Son of man will gather all _____ before His throne. *Matthew 25:32*
2. The Son of man will put sheep at His left hand and goats at His right hand. T/F. *Matthew 25:33*

Quarter at a Glance

by Jon Miller

This quarter explores the broad sweep of Scripture's teaching regarding God's reign—teaching that culminates in the proclamation of Jesus as the earthly exhibition of that kingdom. Beginning with key moments in the history of Jesus' ancestors, this quarter highlights Jesus' birth as the Son of David. The quarter then moves to a four-week study of psalms that extol the reign of God. The conclusion of the quarter provides a look at Jesus' teachings on life in God's kingdom.

Jesus, the Heir of David

The first unit of lessons prepares us for the Christmas season by introducing us to members of Jesus' lineage. Each individual in that lineage is a testament to God's faithfulness and His glorious plan for His kingdom. This royal lineage would culminate with the rule and reign of Jesus Christ.

The example of Ruth demonstrates the ways that God's plan for His kingdom defies human expectations. Even though Ruth was a Gentile (non-Jewish person), she was welcomed and loved (Ruth 4:9-17, lesson 1). Through this Gentile woman, God continued His plan for an eternal kingdom and eternal King. Her descendants were included in the genealogy of Jesus (Luke 3:31-32).

Other members of Jesus' lineage demonstrate the surprising ways that God works. King David's behavior was a mixed bag, but his "house and . . . kingdom" (2 Samuel 7:16, lesson 2) would be forever. His royal line would eventually lead to the promised Messiah, Jesus of Nazareth. Zacharias, a relative of Jesus who lived at the time of Jesus' birth, considered how his own son would prepare the way for Jesus. Zacharias's son, John, would become "the prophet of the Highest" and one who would "give knowledge of salvation" (Luke 1:76-77, lesson 3).

The Scripture text of lesson 4 reveals the culmination of the long-awaited hope. Luke's Gospel highlights how Jesus' birth, as the heir of David, brings good news to the world—even to lowly shepherds (Luke 2:1-16). The first unit of lessons concludes with a glimpse of Jesus, the "Son of David" (18:38, lesson 5), who bestows mercy on those in need.

Our God Reigns

The songbook of the ancient people of God, the Psalms, praises the reign of God. Through these songs, God's people find comfort in the assurance of God's reign (Psalm 10:12-18, lesson 6). He is the eternal and all-powerful King (Psalms 47, 93, lesson 7), who is "merciful and gracious, slow to anger, and plenteous in mercy" (103:8, lesson 8). As such, God's people praise His righteous name for His powerful acts as ruler of an everlasting kingdom (145:10-21, lesson 9).

> Citizens of this heavenly kingdom are called to faithful obedience to the King.

Life in the Kingdom

The quarter concludes with four lessons from the Gospel of Matthew in which Jesus explains the nature and obligations of life in His kingdom. This manner of living consists of prayer marked with praise, petitions, and forgiveness (Matthew 6:5-15, lesson 10). Life in this kingdom will not be marked with ease. In fact, citizens of this heavenly kingdom will inevitably face resistance in this world, for "the kingdom of heaven suffereth violence" (11:12, lesson 11).

Life in the kingdom will often involve reorienting expectations. When a rich young ruler sought eternal life through his good deeds, Jesus pointed him toward a more profound understanding of kingdom living (Matthew 19:16-30, lesson 12). More than anything, citizens of this heavenly kingdom are called to faithful obedience to the King, even in unexpected contexts (25:31-46, lesson 13).

Get the Setting

by Ronald L. Nickelson

Why bother reading this page? Of what practical importance is it to "get the setting"? Why "waste time" studying a setting or context that won't change a statement's meaning?

To answer these questions, we first need to understand that the words *context* and *setting* mean the same thing in terms of our discussion here. Another thing to realize is that *context* can be addressed in terms of two subcategories: *historical context* and *literary context*.

The Historical Context

This kind of context considers what else was going on at the time that the event or thought of the text occurred. Words are not spoken, nor do events occur, in a vacuum! The first lesson of this quarter invites special attention in this regard. Taken in isolation, the book of Ruth may seem to be little more than a quaint love story that revolves around curious cultural practices. But the text takes on a certain sharpness when considering its historical context is the dreary period of the judges.

Spanning roughly the years 1380–1050 BC, the era of the judges was a time when "there was no king in Israel: every man did that which was right in his own eyes" (Judges 21:25). The book of Ruth, then, is a countercultural story in that the characters in the story go to appropriate lengths to make sure to do the right thing in *everyone's* eyes. The book self-testifies to its place in history, being an account of the great-grandparents of David, whose descendant Jesus would reign as King forever.

The historical settings in the lesson texts of this quarter are both continuous and discontinuous with that of the book of Ruth. Elements of continuity are the facts of sin, foreign oppression, and a persistent emphasis on King David. Elements of discontinuity across our 13 lessons include a shift in perspective from the old covenant to the new covenant, a change from an expected Messiah

to the advent of the Messiah, and the presence of clearly delineated power structures within Israel.

The Literary Context

This subcategory of context investigates the kind of literature in which the text appears. Is it parable? sarcasm? apocalyptic? history? poetry? There are other categories, but you get the picture.

Each type of literature has its own distinctive recurring characteristics and, therefore, distinctive guidelines for interpretation as the original author intended for the text. Parables use fictional elements to stress important real-life points (examples: Jesus' parables). In sarcasm, the writer means the opposite of what he or she is saying (example: Isaiah 47:12). Apocalyptic literature includes content on ultimate realities (example: Mark 13).

History is the type of literature for lessons of units 1 and 3 for this quarter. The authors intended these texts to be understood as having really happened to real people at a real time in history. (Note: this use of the word *history* is an issue of "what happened," while the issue of historical context, previously discussed, is an issue of "when it happened.")

Poetry is the type of literature in the four lessons of unit 2. This literature draws out emotion from its audience, but that doesn't mean the poetry is fictional. An example is Psalm 93:2 from lesson 7: "Thy throne is established of old: thou art from everlasting." The poetry elicits the emotion of wonder from the reader. One way that poetry achieves this is through the use of synonymous parallelism, the practice of stating a singular thought—not two thoughts—expressed by two synonymous lines.

Bible Reality

Without any awareness of historical or literary context, even children can pick up a Bible and learn eternal truths. We can do so as well. But if we are ignorant of historical and literary contexts, we won't reach the level of spiritual maturity that we should.

This Quarter in the Word

Answers to the Quarterly Quiz on page 114

Lesson 1—1. kinsman. 2. True. **Lesson 2**—1. Nathan. 2. throne. **Lesson 3**—1. prophesied. 2. True. **Lesson 4**—1. Nazareth. 2. Glory. **Lesson 5**—1. False. 2. False. **Lesson 6**—1. hand. 2. fatherless. **Lesson 7**—1. majesty. 2. floods. **Lesson 8**—1. False. 2. dust. **Lesson 9**—1. generations. 2. ways. **Lesson 10**—1. False. 2. daily bread. **Lesson 11**—1. True. 2. Chorazin, Bethsaida. **Lesson 12**—1. treasure. 2. False. **Lesson 13**—1. nations. 2. False.

Map Feature

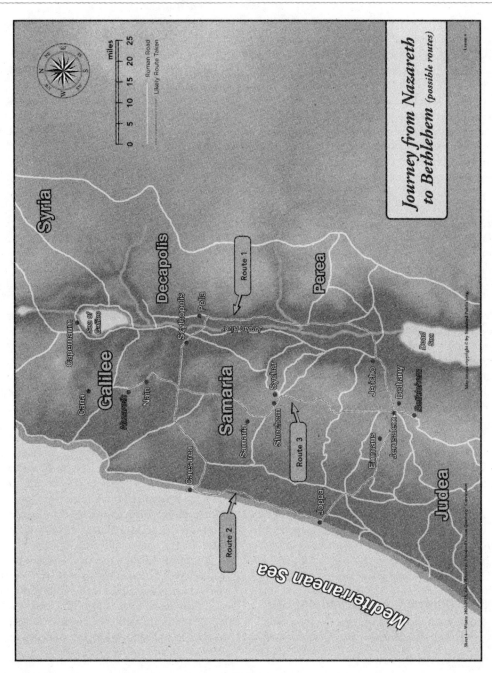

"Here's a Question . . ."

Teacher Tips by Brent L. Amato

After decades studying teachers, I have observed that the most popular teaching method is lecture. Yet, often, it is the least effective method. I've heard it said that "It's not what's taught, but what is caught." Therefore, how do you determine if your students are connecting with you and learning from your teaching? Questions are part of the answer!

Before we dig into the *what*, *which*, and *how* of questions, remember that every lesson must answer two overarching questions. The first is "So what?" Nothing may be "caught" unless learners see relevancy! The second question is "Now what?" Your ability to demonstrate the significance of the lesson material will help the students move toward a response. Without it, nothing might change!

What Is Communicated

What can questions communicate to your students about you? First, questions show that your focus is on the students. Learners understand that you came to class prepared and with them on your mind. How often do we teachers get consumed by our teaching and our lessons? You might find yourself so enthused about a Lesson Context that you forget to tailor your lesson to your students' needs. By taking time to prepare questions, you communicate to your students that they're important and they count for more than attendance. Good questions show you're sincerely glad the students attended and maybe even that they are appreciated.

During a particular class, a student may want nothing more than for someone to pay positive attention to him or her. Asking good questions is an effective tool to draw out the less vocal, energize the disinterested, direct the disruptive, and affirm all the students you teach.

Which Questions to Use and Not Use

Some questions are more effective than others. Less effective questions are closed (requiring only a yes/no or brief answer), overly complex, vague,

"leading" (based on a hidden or not-so-hidden agenda of the teacher), confusing, or insignificant (detracting from the main idea of the lesson). Such questions may stifle the learning process.

Well-designed questions, with no "pat" answers, stimulate thought. Better questions are often application-oriented; that is the direction taken by the five discussion questions you see in each lesson of this commentary. Good questions take time to develop, so they should be prepared in advance.

How They Help

Questions were a large part of Jesus' teaching style. What can we learn from Him? Jesus, the master teacher, used questions to determine desires (John 5:6), stimulate thinking (Luke 9:25), restore a relationship (John 21:15-17), challenge customs (Matthew 15:3), and encourage faith (Mark 4:40). Are you doing this in your classroom with the questions you use?

Jesus also used sequential questions to clarify attitudes. Consider these: "Whom do men say that I the Son of man am? . . . But whom say ye that I am?" (Matthew 16:13, 15). These simple yet profound questions helped the disciples move beyond public opinion to personal confession.

Further Questions

But I'm sure you still have questions about questions. How do "declarations of truth" fit with questions? You need both. How long should you wait in silence for an answer to your question? For adults, 60 seconds (maintaining eye contact and restating the question, if necessary). If no answer is given, should you answer it? Try not to. Can you answer a question with a question? Why not? Should you always allow time for questions? Yes.

If there are no further questions, start preparing to ask some good ones. Then watch what happens to your relationships with your students, to class interaction, and to "what is caught"!

Jesus' Ancestry

Devotional Reading: Galatians 4:1-7
Background Scripture: Ruth 1–4; Luke 3:23-38

Ruth 4:9-17

9 And Boaz said unto the elders, and unto all the people, Ye are witnesses this day, that I have bought all that was Elimelech's, and all that was Chilion's and Mahlon's, of the hand of Naomi.

10 Moreover Ruth the Moabitess, the wife of Mahlon, have I purchased to be my wife, to raise up the name of the dead upon his inheritance, that the name of the dead be not cut off from among his brethren, and from the gate of his place. Ye are witnesses this day.

11 And all the people that were in the gate, and the elders, said, We are witnesses. The LORD make the woman that is come into thine house like Rachel and like Leah, which two did build the house of Israel, and do thou worthily in Ephratah, and be famous in Bethlehem.

12 And let thy house be like the house of Pharez, whom Tamar bare unto Judah, of the seed which the LORD shall give thee of this young woman.

13 So Boaz took Ruth, and she was his wife. And when he went in unto her, the LORD gave her conception, and she bare a son.

14 And the women said unto Naomi, Blessed be the LORD, which hath not left thee this day without a kinsman, that his name may be famous in Israel.

15 And he shall be unto thee a restorer of thy life, and a nourisher of thine old age. For thy daughter in law, which loveth thee, which is better to thee than seven sons, hath born him.

16 And Naomi took the child, and laid it in her bosom, and became nurse unto it.

17 And the women her neighbours gave it a name, saying, There is a son born to Naomi, and they called his name Obed. He is the father of Jesse, the father of David.

Luke 3:23, 31b-32

23 And Jesus himself began to be about thirty years of age, being (as was supposed) the son of Joseph, which was the son of Heli.

31b Which was the son of Nathan, which was the son of David,

32 Which was the son of Jesse, which was the son of Obed, which was the son of Booz, which was the son of Salmon, which was the son of Naasson.

Key Text

The women her neighbours gave it a name, saying, There is a son born to Naomi, and they called his name Obed. He is the father of Jesse, the father of David. —**Ruth 4:17**

A King
Forever and Ever

Unit 1: Jesus, the Heir of David

Lessons 1–5

Lesson Aims

After participating in this lesson, each learner will be able to:
1. Name individuals in the ancestry of Jesus.
2. Explain the importance of that ancestry.
3. Sketch a spiritual "family tree."

Lesson Outline

Introduction

A. Grafted In

Some years ago, my wife and I researched various ways to use our 12 acres of land to make supplemental income. We considered growing chestnuts, partly because they grow well in our climate. As part of the process of learning about this possibility, we went to a seminar about grafting. Grafting is a process in which a branch of one tree adheres to a rootstock of another tree of the same general type. The process is intended to benefit both the grafted branch and the rootstock tree.

In today's account, we focus on a particular point in the genealogy of Jesus, a "grafting in" of sorts. This addition to the family tree yielded abundant blessings, and it continues to bless.

B. Lesson Context

Almost nothing can definitively be said about the date or author of the book of Ruth. But the lack of attribution need not hinder our understanding of the book or our text today (Ruth 4:9-17). The events recounted in the book of Ruth took place in the period of the judges in Israel (1389–1050 BC; Ruth 1:1). This time in Israel's history was marked by the people's recurring failure to keep their covenant with the Lord (Judges 2:10-13; 3:7, 12; 4:1; etc.). In contrast to the disheartening accounts in Judges, Ruth tells the story of a handful of people living in faithful obedience to God.

The book of Ruth culminates in a genealogy of David (Ruth 4:18-22). Genealogies are found in literature from around the ancient Near East. Many of these examples recount a ruler's lineage and were intended to legitimize a monarch's reign. This function of genealogy hints at one reason the book of Ruth was written: to show God's providence at work in King David's ancestors, whether during or shortly after his kingship, or even after Israel was divided in two. Tracing Jesus' lineage to David in Luke's genealogy, covered in part below (see Luke 3:23-38), answered an important question: What right had Jesus to claim to be the king in Israel who fulfilled God's promise to David? How could Jesus be the Messiah? For more context on the book of Luke, see lessons 3–5 of this quarter.

I. Naomi's Family
(Ruth 4:9-17)

Having come to Bethlehem as widows, Naomi and her foreign-born daughter-in-law Ruth faced an uncertain future. But Ruth's character and hard work won her favor with Boaz, a relative of Naomi's. Events came to a quick climax: Naomi had a plan to enlist Boaz's help (Ruth 3:9-13), and Boaz wasted no time putting his own plan into action (4:1-8). (For more context, read the entirety of Ruth 1–4.)

A. Boaz Acts (vv. 9-10)

9. And Boaz said unto the elders, and unto all the people, Ye are witnesses this day, that I have bought all that was Elimelech's, and all that was Chilion's and Mahlon's, of the hand of Naomi.

Boaz's desire was to redeem Naomi's land holdings and to marry Ruth. The laws regarding selling a family property are found in Leviticus 25:25-34 (compare Jeremiah 32:7). The gist of the regulation was that a sale of Israelite land was more of a lease since the land would return to the sellers' family when they could afford to redeem it or, at the latest, in the Year of Jubilee (Leviticus 27:16-25). Because of the importance of land in Israel, the bias was to sell the property within a tribe to keep it in the extended family. For this reason, the family member who purchased the

How to Say It

Boaz	Bo-az.
Chilion	Kil-ee-on.
Elimelech	Ee-lim-eh-leck.
Ephratah	Ef-rah-tah.
Heli	Hee-lie.
levirate	leh-vuh-rut.
Mahlon	Mah-lon.
Naasson	Nah-sahn.
Pharez	Fair-ezz.
Zarah	Zair-uh.

God, please work through our families.

Visual for Lesson 1. *Allow learners one minute to pray for their families, both physical and spiritual, that God's will be done for and through them.*

land was called a kinsman or kinsman-redeemer. And though property was generally inherited from father to son, there was precedent for a woman's holding land (see Numbers 27:1-11; 36:1-12).

When a nearer kinsman abdicated his right to buy the land (and marry Ruth), *Boaz* stepped in (Ruth 4:1-6). In doing so, he took on the role of a kinsman for *Naomi* by buying the land that had belonged to her husband, Elimelech, and her sons, Mahlon and Chilion. At least ten *elders* were present (4:2), along with many *people. Witnesses* at this time served much like an oral form of a notary public for such transactions.

10. Moreover Ruth the Moabitess, the wife of Mahlon, have I purchased to be my wife, to raise up the name of the dead upon his inheritance, that the name of the dead be not cut off from among his brethren, and from the gate of his place. Ye are witnesses this day.

This is the first time we learn that *Ruth* had been *the wife of Mahlon* (not Chilion); this identification was likely due to the legal nature of the proceedings. Boaz repeated the phrase, "Ye are witnesses this day," identically worded as in Ruth 4:9 (above), creating bookends that open and close his formal, legal argument. There would be no doubt in the future that Boaz acted with integrity in redeeming the land or marrying Ruth.

The language around marrying Ruth is like that of levirate marriage (Deuteronomy 25:5-10; see commentary on Ruth 4:10, below). But a few details prevent its exact characterization as such. First, *Ruth* was a *Moabitess*, not an Israelite. The two people groups, though related (see Genesis 19), were often at odds with each other (examples: Numbers 22–25; Judges 3). God had even barred Moabites from being grafted into Israel (Deuteronomy 23:3)!

Second, Boaz was not a surviving brother of the deceased husband. He wasn't even Naomi's closest kinsman. Third, the kinsman who Boaz approached as first in line was not publicly shamed (as levirate law required) for declining to marry Ruth and redeem the land as a packaged deal.

This unnamed man serves as a foil to Boaz. The man acted in keeping with conventional wisdom and was not reprimanded for doing so (as had Orpah; see Ruth 1:11-14). In contrast, Boaz exhibited extraordinary integrity in his zeal to provide for Naomi and Ruth (as had Ruth; see 1:16-18). He honored the spirit of the levirate law with his concern for Mahlon's family line (*that the name of the dead be not cut off from among his brethren, and from the gate of his place*). The first child born to Boaz and Ruth would be raised as Mahlon's child with his inheritance so that the dead man's name and property would be maintained (compare 2 Samuel 18:18; Isaiah 56:4-5). By using the language of acquiring both land and a wife (unusual language for marriage), Boaz combined in principle the levirate law with the kinsman-redeemer concept.

What Do You Think?

What are some practical ways believers can honor the dead appropriately?

Digging Deeper

How do these practices set Christian practice apart from worldly ways?

Surprising Reward

Dianne Gordon was walking to work one cold Michigan morning when she stopped at a gas station to warm up. She had made the same 2.7-mile journey both ways every day since her car broke down a year before. When Dianne noticed a bag of cash lying in the station's parking lot, she immediately called the police. Police found nearly $15,000 and wedding cards addressed to a newlywed couple to whom the money was returned. Despite her great need, Dianne said she never even considered not turning in the cash. She just knew turning it in was the right thing to do.

When a community member heard of Dianne's selfless act, she set up a GoFundMe page to raise enough money for Dianne to purchase a vehicle. They met their goal with plenty to spare. Dianne had expected no reward for her selfless act and yet received it.

Boaz's decision to marry Ruth led to a blessing for him: he was included in the genealogy of Jesus. How might choices you make today benefit physical or spiritual descendants you will never know (1 Timothy 1:2; Titus 1:4)? —L. M. W.

B. The People Bless (vv. 11-12)

11. And all the people that were in the gate, and the elders, said, We are witnesses. The LORD make the woman that is come into thine house like Rachel and like Leah, which two did build the house of Israel, and do thou worthily in Ephratah, and be famous in Bethlehem.

This all took place at the city *gate*, the typical meeting place in Israel for legal proceedings (example: Joshua 20:4). Going above and beyond their role as *witnesses*, the people pronounced a blessing on Boaz and the new household that was forming. The blessing clearly focuses on Ruth (*the woman*), as a blessing for Boaz would more likely call for the Lord to make Boaz like Jacob. *Rachel* and *Leah* (and their maidservants, Bilhah and Zilpah) bore the ancestors of the tribes of *Israel* (Genesis 29–30). To *do worthily* and *be famous* are blessings for wealth and a good name. The name probably assumed the couple would require children to experience these blessings (see Luke 3:32, below).

Ephratah seems to be an old name for the area of Bethlehem, also spelled "Ephrath" (example: Genesis 35:16, 19; 48:7), most famously mentioned in the messianic passage of Micah 5:2 (quoted in Matthew 2:6). Rachel especially was associated with the area, as she was buried near *Bethlehem* (Genesis 35:16-19).

Though Ruth was a Moabite, she was also known to be a woman of great character (Ruth 3:11). She left behind her own people because of her love for Naomi and the Lord without knowing what reception she could expect in Naomi's home. The blessing from the people confirms their acceptance of her and hints at the Lord's pleasure with her (see 4:13, below).

> **What Do You Think?**
> What responsibilities do witnesses today have toward the newly wed? How long do those responsibilities last?
> **Digging Deeper**
> How should those responsibilities be translated to care for unmarried people?

12. And let thy house be like the house of Pharez, whom Tamar bare unto Judah, of the seed which the LORD shall give thee of this young woman.

The account of Pharez's birth is found in Genesis 38. *Tamar* was entitled to a levirate marriage when her husband, Er, died (Genesis 38:8). But several failures found Tamar back in her father's house with no prospect of continuing her dead husband's lineage. When she tricked *Judah* into sleeping with her, Tamar conceived *Pharez* and his twin brother, Zarah. Ruth's situation was not identical, but it is notable that both Tamar and Ruth were foreign women who became ancestors to Jesus (Matthew 1:3, 5).

> **What Do You Think?**
> In what ways are children blessings in their communities?
> **Digging Deeper**
> How can faithful people avoid the trap of valuing parenthood above childlessness?

C. The Lord Blesses (vv. 13-17)

13. So Boaz took Ruth, and she was his wife: and when he went in unto her, the LORD gave her conception, and she bare a son.

It is unclear why *Ruth* did not bear children in her first marriage, which lasted approximately ten years (Ruth 1:4). In hindsight, however, we might sense God's invisible hand preparing her for this moment. The Lord's aid in her conceiving *a son* emphasizes His blessing of this union, even though historically, the Moabites were not to have any portion in Israel (Deuteronomy 23:3-4).

> **What Do You Think?**
> When has hindsight been beneficial in discerning blessings in your life?
> **Digging Deeper**
> What dangers are there in focusing too much on the past?

14. And the women said unto Naomi, Blessed be the LORD, which hath not left thee this day without a kinsman, that his name may be famous in Israel.

Verses 14-17 focus on *Naomi*, Ruth's mother-in-law. *The women* of the town had previously witnessed Naomi's heartbreaking return to Bethlehem (Ruth 1:19-20). Naomi concluded that the Lord had left her bitter and empty at the death of her husband and sons (1:20-21); the reality was that God provided for Naomi even when all hope seemed lost. This was a great reversal for Naomi. *Blessed be the Lord* acknowledges His action, especially that this action reveals His loving character.

15. And he shall be unto thee a restorer of thy life, and a nourisher of thine old age. For thy daughter in law, which loveth thee, which is better to thee than seven sons, hath born him.

In Israel, grown children were expected to take care of their aging parents (1 Timothy 5:4). This was especially true if their mother was widowed, as women had very few financial resources to fall back on if family could not help. Following the death of her husband and sons, Naomi's future was much in doubt. With the birth of *a restorer of thy life, and a nourisher of thine old age*, Naomi need not be burdened about her future.

Even as the women celebrated this grandson, Ruth was extolled as being *better to thee than seven sons*. This is quite incredible, given the status a hypothetical mother of seven sons would enjoy in Israel! Those sons represented security in the future (especially in widowhood) and the hope of accrued wealth.

16-17. And Naomi took the child, and laid it in her bosom, and became nurse unto it. And the women her neighbours gave it a name, saying, There is a son born to Naomi, and they called his name Obed. He is the father of Jesse, the father of David.

It was not uncommon for well-off families (as Boaz's seems to have been) to have nurses for their children. In Naomi's case, the role is not that of a wet nurse but as a guardian and caretaker (compare Genesis 24:59; 35:8). An informal adoption might be in view.

This is the only place in the Bible where *neighbours* are said to have named a baby (contrast Luke 1:59-63). Ironically, there is no evidence to suggest that these same women honored Naomi's request to be called by a new name (Ruth 1:20). The name *Obed* means "worshipper" or "servant," the latter meaning lending itself to the idea that he would serve as a redeemer for Naomi one day. That "his name [became] famous in Israel" (4:14) came to pass through his son, *Jesse*, who became the father of the greatest earthly king to reign in Israel, *David*.

II. Jesus' Family
(Luke 3:23, 31b-32)

Over 1,000 years passed between the events recorded in Ruth and the time of Jesus' birth. As one would expect, much changed over the passing generations: the Davidic kingdom rose, split, and then collapsed in exile. The people had returned to the land, but the kingship had not been restored. What of God's promises of an everlasting kingdom (2 Samuel 7)?

A. Near Ancestors (v. 23)

23. And Jesus himself began to be about thirty years of age, being (as was supposed) the son of Joseph, which was the son of Heli.

A Levite could begin serving in the tabernacle at *thirty years of age* (Numbers 4:3), although other texts reflect ages beginning at 20 (1 Chronicles 23:24; 2 Chronicles 31:17; Ezra 3:8) or 25 years old (Numbers 8:24-25). These differences could reflect the variety of roles that were available at these ages, new age limits set in the temple rather than in the tabernacle, or changing supply and demand in demographics. In any case, Jesus' age certainly would have qualified Him to minister in the temple.

Luke adds the editorial comment that it *was supposed* that Jesus was *the son of Joseph* in order to be clear that, in reality, Jesus is God's Son. But Joseph was legally Jesus' father. Many scholars believe that Luke's genealogy reflects a family tree traced through Mary, such that Joseph was the son-in-law of *Heli*. Or it could be that Matthew traces through Mary's family and Luke through Joseph's. Other proposals for the differences have also been put forward. Nonetheless, we need not be perturbed by the differences between Matthew and Luke (see Matthew 1:1-16; see commentary on Luke 3:31b, below). We also do well to remember that the ancient genealogy was not intended to be a complete accounting of a family. Neither account needs to be taken as mistaken or corrected against the other.

What follows in Luke 3:24-31a (not in our printed text) are generations from Matthat to Mattatha.

B. Distant Ancestors (vv. 31b-32)

31b. Which was the son of Nathan, which was the son of David.

Nathan was a *son of David* by "Bathshua" (Bathsheba; 1 Chronicles 3:5). The Gospel of Matthew traces Jesus' line through Solomon rather than Nathan (Matthew 1:6). Undoubtedly, what was most important to both writers was showing that Jesus can trace His earthly lineage straight back to *David*. This relationship was the key to Jesus' being able to fulfill the promise that God made to David: "I will set up thy seed after thee, which shall proceed out of thy bowels, and I will establish his kingdom. He shall build an house for my name, and I will stablish the throne of his kingdom for ever" (2 Samuel 7:12-13).

32. Which was the son of Jesse, which was

the son of Obed, which was the son of Booz, which was the son of Salmon, which was the son of Naasson.

This verse brings us back to the story of Ruth (see Ruth 4:17, above). *Jesse* was David's father, *Obed* his grandfather, and so on. Some names are probably omitted here, as *Booz* likely lived near the end of the time of the judges (about 1100 BC), whereas *Salmon* (see Matthew 1:5) lived during the initial days of conquest in the promised land (about 1400 BC). *Naasson* was the tribal leader of Judah during the wilderness period (see Numbers 1:4, 7).

> **What Do You Think?**
> What influence has your family of origin had on your adult life?
>
> **Digging Deeper**
> Does this influence deserve celebration or require redemption? What encouragement can you take from Jesus' family line in this regard?

Lost to History

My mother recently gave me a box full of old family photos. Looking through them, she could identify many faces. However, we found several photos of people we had never seen before. I'm sure my grandmother would have known them, but she passed away years ago. Most of her generation is gone, and no one today remembers the identities or stories of those people in the photos.

Despite this, I know something about those people. Their genetics and their choices have helped create me. I may not know their names, but I see a familial resemblance. I may not know their biographies, but I know they valued faith and taught their children to do the same, just as I do.

Jesus' family tree is detailed and extensive, full of names. No doubt, some family members' stories were not retained. But those people affected Jesus' life, nonetheless. How does knowing that your decisions affect future generations, physical and spiritual, influence how you live today?
—L. M. W.

Conclusion
A. God's Faithfulness in Family

The story of Boaz, Ruth, and Naomi should be a great encouragement to us. Each chose to follow the Lord faithfully, as seen through their righteous actions. As a result of their faithful deeds and God's faithfulness to their family, all three received blessings. First, their community responded positively to this family's outstanding character. This was not a foregone conclusion, especially for the foreign woman Ruth. Second and more importantly, we see how God chose to bless the family's faithful actions in their own times with a son. Truly, the Lord had turned their mourning into dancing (Psalm 30:11)!

The blessing continued beyond what Boaz, Ruth, and Naomi experienced for themselves. Israel was blessed by David, the future king, and much further in the future with Jesus, the promised King. This family could never anticipate how their faithfulness would echo through the generations and what a blessing their own blessings would be to the world. We are blessed today to see how God can work through us and for us when we choose to follow Him. But the greatest blessing, of course, is living in the Kingdom of God thanks to the sacrifice of our King.

B. Prayer

Lord, we are awed by the story of the faith of Boaz, Ruth, and Naomi, and how You turned their blessing into a blessing for Israel and then the world. We praise You for the righteous acts of many that finally brought us to the person and work of Christ. In the name of Jesus, Your Son, we pray. Amen.

C. Thought to Remember
God's faithfulness resounds through generations.

Visuals FOR THESE LESSONS

The visual pictured in each lesson (example: page 123) is a small reproduction of a large, full-color poster included in the *Adult Resources* packet for the Winter Quarter. Order ISBN 9780784739631 from your supplier.

Involvement Learning

Enhance your lesson with KJV Bible Student *(from your curriculum supplier) and the reproducible activity page (at www.standardlesson.com or in the back of the* KJV Standard Lesson Commentary Deluxe Edition*).*

Into the Lesson

Give learners one minute to read the genealogy in Luke 3:23-38. While they read, distribute blank pieces of paper. After the minute is up, have learners pair up. Then, give them one minute to list as many names from the genealogy as possible. At the end of the minute, ask the pairs to grade their list against Luke's genealogy. They should strike out any names that do not appear in Luke's genealogy (even if they are present in Matthew's). After they have checked these answers, ask learners to identify with stars which names in Luke 3:23-38 can also be found in Ruth without consulting Ruth 4. (*Answers*: Obed, Jesse, David (Ruth 4:17; Luke 3:31b-32), and Boaz/Booz (Ruth 4:13; Luke 3:32).)

Lead into the studying by saying, "As we dive into our lesson today, we will see the importance of lineage and legacy within the Bible, particularly in the books of Ruth and Luke."

Into the Word

Ask the class to work together to summarize what has happened in Ruth 1:1–4:8. Consult the Lesson Context for this lesson and the Bible text as desired. *Option.* Prepare a lecture on this context or assign it before class to a volunteer. *Alternative.* Have learners pair up to complete the "Setting the Scene" exercise from the activity page, which you can download. After several minutes, bring the class back together to fill in any remaining gaps.

Ask for volunteers to read Ruth 4:9-17 aloud. Distribute a handout (you prepare) with the text printed. As learners read along, have them mark anything puzzling with a question mark, anything that seems important with a star, and anything that stands out in some other way by underlining it. Use the commentary to help answer the questions learners might have about the text. Then, have them discuss in small groups what they starred and underlined.

After some discussion, divide the class into four groups: **Boaz, Naomi, Ruth,** and **The Witnesses.** Have these groups work together to detail the words and actions of their assigned person or group. Then, groups should answer two questions about the subject of their groups: 1–How did this person or group act righteously? 2–What conclusions did or might this person or group make about the Lord's action in this story? Answers will vary to some degree in answer to both questions, but in general, righteousness is demonstrated by honoring God's law, and we could expect that all these people assumed that God had worked to bring these events to their conclusion so He could bless the parties involved.

Lead into the text on Jesus' genealogy by briefly summarizing what happened between Ruth's lifetime and Jesus' birth.

Have a volunteer read Luke 3:23, 31b-32. Ask the class to compare the purpose(s) of the brief genealogy in Ruth 4 to the purpose(s) of the genealogy in Luke 3. Expect to hear at least something along the lines of the genealogies emphasizing God's providence at work in the family and serving to prove the legitimacy of the king (David in Ruth, Jesus in Luke).

Into Life

Have learners work in small groups to compare what we know of Boaz, Ruth, and Naomi's character with Christ. Ask, "What family resemblances do we find?" Based on those answers, ask learners to work alone for one minute jotting down their own characteristics that speak to a family resemblance with these four people.

Alternative. Instruct the learners to complete the "A Spiritual Family Tree" exercise as directed.

Once finished with either activity, provide a few minutes for reflection before concluding with a prayer thanking God for His generations-long work bringing Jesus into the world.

God's Promise

Devotional Reading: Isaiah 9:1-7
Background Scripture: 2 Samuel 7:1-17

2 Samuel 7:4-17

4 And it came to pass that night, that the word of the LORD came unto Nathan, saying,

5 Go and tell my servant David, thus saith the LORD, shalt thou build me an house for me to dwell in?

6 Whereas I have not dwelt in any house since the time that I brought up the children of Israel out of Egypt, even to this day, but have walked in a tent and in a tabernacle.

7 In all the places wherein I have walked with all the children of Israel spake I a word with any of the tribes of Israel, whom I commanded to feed my people Israel, saying, Why build ye not me an house of cedar?

8 Now therefore so shalt thou say unto my servant David, thus saith the LORD of hosts, I took thee from the sheepcote, from following the sheep, to be ruler over my people, over Israel.

9 And I was with thee whithersoever thou wentest, and have cut off all thine enemies out of thy sight, and have made thee a great name, like unto the name of the great men that are in the earth.

10 Moreover I will appoint a place for my people Israel, and will plant them, that they may dwell in a place of their own, and move no more. Neither shall the children of wickedness afflict them any more, as beforetime.

11 And as since the time that I commanded judges to be over my people Israel, and have caused thee to rest from all thine enemies. Also the LORD telleth thee that he will make thee an house.

12 And when thy days be fulfilled, and thou shalt sleep with thy fathers, I will set up thy seed after thee, which shall proceed out of thy bowels, and I will establish his kingdom.

13 He shall build an house for my name, and I will stablish the throne of his kingdom for ever.

14 I will be his father, and he shall be my son. If he commit iniquity, I will chasten him with the rod of men, and with the stripes of the children of men.

15 But my mercy shall not depart away from him, as I took it from Saul, whom I put away before thee.

16 And thine house and thy kingdom shall be established for ever before thee. Thy throne shall be established for ever.

17 According to all these words, and according to all this vision, so did Nathan speak unto David.

Key Text

Thine house and thy kingdom shall be established for ever before thee. Thy throne shall be established for ever. —2 Samuel 7:16

A King
Forever and Ever

Unit 1: Jesus, the Heir of David
Lessons 1–5

Lesson Aims

After participating in this lesson, each learner will be able to:

1. Summarize David's intent and God's response.

2. Explain the differing senses of the use of the word *house*.

3. Write a prayer for obedience to God, even when His plans differ from human plans.

Lesson Outline

Introduction
   A. Temporary Dwellings
   B. Lesson Context
I. History Lessons (2 Samuel 7:4-9a)
   A. Israel's Past (vv. 4-7)
   B. David's Past (vv. 8-9a)
II. Future Plans (2 Samuel 7:9b-17)
   A. David and Israel (vv. 9b-11a)
     Legacy of Faith
   B. Solomon and Christ (vv. 11b-17)
     A Grandmother's Faith
Conclusion
   A. Eternal Home
   B. Prayer
   C. Thought to Remember

Introduction

A. Temporary Dwellings

Twelve years ago, my wife and I moved to a remote town in western Alaska. The area where we spent the first decade of our Alaskan journey was accessible only by boat or plane. Besides our town, 89 smaller villages are located in western Alaska off the road system. Many of these communities are near rivers, providing more accessible summer transportation and an abundant supply of salmon.

One distinctive aspect of life in this region is that homes are constructed on permafrost, a frozen layer of soil. Due to the thawing permafrost and harsh weather conditions, these houses require more upkeep than those built in the contiguous United States. In Newtok, a small Alaskan village, erosion and deterioration became so severe that the entire community had to be relocated to higher ground, away from the river. Many villagers witnessed the river slowly eat away at their homes until it finally engulfed entire structures. The homes we construct are temporary.

In King David's mind, the time for the Lord to live in a tent (the tabernacle) was officially over (2 Samuel 7:1-2). What followed the king's decision would be much different than he anticipated.

B. Lesson Context

David ultimately became king over a united Israel. This happened approximately 1000 BC (2 Samuel 5–6). After a long civil war (3:1-2) and the conquering of the Jebusites and their city of Jerusalem (5:6-7), he made that city the capital of the reunited kingdom of Israel (5:8-12). Victory over the Philistines followed (5:17-25). After that, David brought the ark of the covenant into Jerusalem (also known as "the city of David" [6:16]) and placed it inside a tent (6:17). This move cemented Jerusalem as both the political and religious capital of the kingdom.

After the ark's arrival in Jerusalem, David confronted what he considered to be a grave disparity. Although he dwelt in a grand palace (2 Samuel 5:11; 7:2), no permanent abode existed for the ark of the covenant (7:6-7, below). Disturbed by this state of affairs, David decided to build a house for God. David communicated his plan to the prophet Nathan, who initially offered encouragement and approval for the king to proceed (7:1-3, not in our lesson text). Apparently, neither man had asked God for His approval, and what follows in chapter 7 was God's reaction to the plan (1 Chronicles 17:3-15 is a parallel account).

I. History Lessons
(2 Samuel 7:4-9a)
A. Israel's Past (vv. 4-7)

4. And it came to pass that night, that the word of the LORD came unto Nathan, saying.

Unlike God's direct communication with King Solomon later (1 Kings 3:5), God chose to speak to David indirectly through *Nathan* the prophet. The reason for this difference is a matter of speculation. But perhaps the prophet also needed the forthcoming corrective himself since he had encouraged David in his wrong thinking (2 Samuel 7:3).

The prophet would later risk David's wrath by confronting the king regarding David's sin with Bathsheba and the murder of Uriah (2 Samuel 12). Nathan would also anoint Solomon as David's successor (1 Kings 1:34).

5. Go and tell my servant David, thus saith the LORD, shalt thou build me an house for me to dwell in?

With this verse, God's corrective begins. The issue at hand seems to be not one of disobedience but rather one of presumption. Has *David*, God's *servant*, presumed that he would be doing God a favor?

6. Whereas I have not dwelt in any house since the time that I brought up the children of Israel out of Egypt, even to this day, but have walked in a tent and in a tabernacle.

For God to have the kind of house that David desired to build was never high on God's list of priorities. To this point, the tabernacle, as prescribed by God to Moses centuries earlier, had sufficed (Exodus 26). At the future dedication of the temple, David's son Solomon will cite the words of the verse before us (see 1 Kings 8:16). He will note in the same verse that while God was not concerned about choosing a city in which to dwell, He was concerned about choosing a person. This is what the Lord addressed in the next part of His message.

7. In all the places wherein I have walked with all the children of Israel spake I a word with any of the tribes of Israel, whom I commanded to feed my people Israel, saying, Why build ye not me an house of cedar?

God had never required a permanent structure for His dwelling place in *Israel*, let alone a grand one as *an house of cedar* would surely be (compare 2 Samuel 5:11).

God's faithfulness to His people had always far exceeded their faithfulness to Him. Yet God had not called on anyone to respond by building *an house of cedar* (a temple) as a visual aid (or anything else) to influence their faithfulness. The term translated *tribes* probably refers to tribal leaders.

What Do You Think?

What questions should a congregation ask when discerning how to steward a house of worship?

Digging Deeper

What sorts of answers might suggest that a congregation should choose a different course regarding a place of worship?

B. David's Past (vv. 8-9a)

8-9a. Now therefore so shalt thou say unto my servant David, thus saith the LORD of hosts, I took thee from the sheepcote, from following the sheep, to be ruler over my people, over Israel. And I was with thee whithersoever thou wentest, and have cut off all thine enemies out of thy sight.

The image of shepherd-leadership echoes throughout the passage as God reminded *David* of that man's own history. God had sent the prophet Samuel to Jesse's family in the small village of Bethlehem to anoint a new king over Israel (1 Samuel 16:1). There, Samuel reviewed each of the sons of Jesse who were present. Jesse had not bothered to present to Samuel the youngest son, David. Instead, David was left caring for the sheep (16:4-11).

But God had chosen David to be the new king (1 Samuel 16:12-13). Though David had once been a shepherd of sheep, he would now be a shepherd of *Israel* (Ezekiel 34:23; compare John 10:1-18). And as God had been with the nation of Israel, so also would He be with David in victories over his *enemies* (examples: 1 Samuel 17:45-54; 23:14–26:25).

> **What Do You Think?**
> What events in your life do you point to as reasons for confidence in the Lord?
> **Digging Deeper**
> How can recalling this history help you or a friend continue to rely on God in difficult circumstances?

II. Future Plans
(2 Samuel 7:9b-17)
A. David and Israel (vv. 9b-11a)

9b. And have made thee a great name, like unto the name of the great men that are in the earth.

Whatever greatness David had achieved to this point, God had given through military victories. It is in this light that God gave the reason for not allowing the man to build a temple: "But the word of the Lord came to me, saying, Thou hast shed blood abundantly, and hast made great wars: thou shalt not build an house unto my name, because thou hast shed much blood upon the earth in my sight" (1 Chronicles 22:8). David would not have the chance to think of himself as a great builder (compare Daniel 4:28-30).

Legacy of Faith

Christians living in the Soviet Union faced persecution. Laws prohibited their sharing the faith, even with their own children, unless the teachings aligned with the government-approved Orthodox church. According to the law, those teaching the gospel were subject to imprisonment and could be stripped of their parental rights, resulting in children being placed in orphanages.

Even so, Christians instilled in their children a legacy of faith. Many of those children grew up to be church leaders and were ready and willing to pass on their legacy to their own children. When the Soviet government crumbled, these same church leaders jumped at the opportunity to evangelize freely within their communities.

David had a legacy of faith that began with Abraham. David remained true to that legacy. And God promised David that his children would be blessed and his name would be great. God fulfilled that in Jesus. What is your faith legacy?
—L. M. W.

10. Moreover I will appoint a place for my people Israel, and will plant them, that they may dwell in a place of their own, and move no more. Neither shall the children of wickedness afflict them any more, as beforetime.

The greatness God granted to David was not for David's benefit alone. The Lord was concerned for His *people Israel*. God desired not only to give David "rest" (2 Samuel 7:1) but also to give His people *a place of their own* and relief from those who had afflicted them in the past (see 7:11a, below). God did indeed desire a place—not for himself but for His people. This promise would be the fulfillment of the promise God gave Moses (Exodus 3:16-17; 33:1). The agricultural metaphor emphasizes growth and longevity within the land. God would *plant* Israel (see Amos 9:15; Jeremiah 31:27-28).

11a. And as since the time that I commanded judges to be over my people Israel, and have caused thee to rest from all thine enemies.

The period of the *judges* (from about 1380 to 1050 BC) followed Israel's conquest of the promised land. So, we might think of that period as the first era of Israel's life as a settled nation. That time was filled with conflict as one nation after another rose against *Israel*. God delivered Israel through the leadership of judges, but He also allowed threats to arise as Israel sank back into sin.

B. Solomon and Christ (vv. 11b-17)

11b. Also the LORD telleth thee that he will make thee an house.

Initially, David intended to construct a sanctuary for God. But God planned to turn the king's plan on its head and instead build a *house* for David. And though David's initial thought upon hearing this might have been of a new palace, God's further promises made clear that He would establish a kingdom and lineage for David.

12. And when thy days be fulfilled, and thou shalt sleep with thy fathers, I will set up thy seed after thee, which shall proceed out of thy bowels, and I will establish his kingdom.

God's promise would come to fruition through a descendant of David who would rise to power after David's death. The *King James Version* translates the Hebrew expression literally: David's *seed* is the focus of the promise. This word referring to one's descendant or descendants has a rich background in earlier texts of the Old Testament. God uses this word repeatedly in Genesis in promises of redemption (Genesis 3:15; 9:9; 12:7; etc.); the patriarchs Abraham, Isaac, and Jacob received promises regarding their "seed." Now David receives a promise that builds on theirs: God will firmly establish the kingdom of one of David's offspring, one physically descended from him. This wordplay recalls how the Lord would plant Israel in the land (see 2 Samuel 7:10).

What Do You Think?

What hopes do you have for your family when your own days are fulfilled?

Digging Deeper

What actions can you take now to ensure those are *hopes* for your family and not mere *wishes*?

---

13. He shall build an house for my name, and I will stablish the throne of his kingdom for ever.

Prophecies with dual fulfillments underscore the cohesion of God's plan of salvation found in the Scriptures. Such prophecies have a "nearer" fulfillment, and the one in the verse before us was realized through David's son Solomon (1 Kings 6:1, 37-38; Acts 7:47). He did build *an house* for the Lord. But quickly it became clear that Solomon's *kingdom* would not last forever. He sinned against the Lord by worshipping other gods (1 Kings 11:4, 9-13, 31-33).

For the sake of this promise made to David, God did not strip the kingdom away from Solomon. Nor did God take it entirely from Solomon's heirs—at least not for many generations. But during the Babylonian exile that began in 586 BC, the rule of David's family came to an end.

What, then, are we to make of the promise to *stablish the throne of his kingdom for ever*? We look to the fulfillment found in Christ (Acts 2:29-36; Hebrews 1:5). While the temple Solomon built was destroyed (2 Chronicles 36:18-19), Jesus builds believers into God's temple in the New Testament era (1 Corinthians 3:16-17; 6:19; 2 Corinthians 6:16; Ephesians 2:19-22). And Jesus' kingdom has no end (Revelation 11:15).

14. I will be his father, and he shall be my son. If he commit iniquity, I will chasten him with the rod of men, and with the stripes of the children of men.

As in the previous verse, this promise applies first to Solomon and ultimately to Christ. The first statement in the verse before us is quoted in Hebrews 1:5, which clearly affirms its fulfillment in Jesus. But how can sinless Jesus be the fulfillment when He, as the ultimate son of David, did not *commit iniquity*?

We recall that Jesus was treated as though He had committed blasphemy (Matthew 26:65)—the ultimate iniquity. He took the stripes inflicted by *the rod of men* and was crucified (Isaiah 53:4-5). That suffering was not due to personal guilt; rather, He took upon himself the punishment that guilty sinners deserve.

15. But my mercy shall not depart away from him, as I took it from Saul, whom I put away before thee.

We move to a second question: If the promise also applies to King Solomon (reigned 970–931 BC), how can God say that *my mercy shall not depart away from him* when we recall that God judged Solomon for his foolish acceptance of the

GOD'S KINGDOM WILL LAST FOREVER.

Visual for Lesson 2. *Discuss the questions associated with verse 16 as learners contemplate the nature of God's kingdom.*

gods of his many wives who turned his heart away from the Lord (1 Kings 11:4, 9-13, 31-33)?

The key is the phrase *as I took it from Saul,* who was Israel's first king (reigned 1050–1010 BC). The people of Israel had longed to "be like all the nations" that had kings (1 Samuel 8:7, 20). Following divine guidance, the prophet Samuel was instrumental in shaping Israel's leadership into a monarchy (12:13-15). But Saul's sin and paranoia doomed his kingship (1 Samuel 13:10-14; 15:10-26; 18:8-12; 19:9-10; etc.). This pattern persisted, ultimately leading to the Lord's rejection of Saul as king (15:23, 26, 28).

The same cannot be said of either David or Solomon. David was not a perfect man or king, as events yet to come were to demonstrate (see Psalm 51). But his heart was not the same as Saul's (1 Samuel 13:14), so God chose to establish a relationship of enduring *mercy* with David. That is proven in the history of kings of Judah—where descendants of David and Solomon reigned after Israel was divided following Solomon's death—even as judgment was enacted (Isaiah 14:1-2; compare Romans 11). God's power, not David's achievements, was to be the basis for house-building, kingdom-securing, and throne-establishing.

16. And thine house and thy kingdom shall be established for ever before thee. Thy throne shall be established for ever.

The verse before us summarizes God's promise

to David and concludes God's word for the king. Even when Solomon's magnificent temple fell to ruins at the hands of the Babylonians in 586 BC, God's promise to David remained unshakable. That *house,* that *kingdom,* is established in Christ. He is David's true heir (Matthew 1:1). And what Jesus said of His church remains true: "The gates of hell shall not prevail against it" (Matthew 16:18).

God's promise was given not because David proved worthy where others did not. Moving beyond 2 Samuel 7, we see David's deep failures: favoritism within his family, sexual immorality, and even murder. The promise is to David by God's grace. It is an unmerited gift, given to David despite his unworthiness. It is given to Israel despite the people's unworthiness. Ultimately, it is offered to all humanity despite all our unworthiness.

> **What Do You Think?**
> Imagine you are David learning how God fulfilled this promise. What thoughts and emotions do you have?
>
> **Digging Deeper**
> What encouragement regarding God's promises can you take away from this lesson?

A Grandmother's Faith

As a young girl, Lucy attended a small country church with her family. While her brothers and sisters dreaded the long sermons in a hot sanctuary, Lucy looked forward to learning more about Jesus every week. As she grew, she volunteered in her church and looked for ways to honor God in her daily life.

One Sunday, a guest missionary visited their church. Lucy listened, her full attention on the man. She imagined eating strange foods, learning a new language, and especially telling people about Jesus for the first time. She began to dream about becoming a missionary herself. But it was not to be. Still, Lucy taught her boys and then her grandchildren about Jesus. It was first Lucy's granddaughter and then a great-granddaughter who fulfilled Lucy's dream of cross-cultural mission work.

David's heart was in the right place in his desire to build God a house (temple). But the project would fall to his son Solomon. If David made any mistake here, it was that he did not check with the Lord first before deciding. We may have good ideas, but the people or the timing may not be right in God's eyes. How often do you fail to check with the Lord before launching your own projects? See James 4:13-17. —L. M. W.

17. According to all these words, and according to all this vision, so did Nathan speak unto David.

In keeping with his role as a prophet, *Nathan* relayed what the Lord had revealed *unto David* (compare 2 Samuel 12:1-14). David's response (7:18-29, not in our printed text) reveals that the king knew this promise was not for David's family's glory but for God's. We too do well to remember that the fulfilled and yet-to-be-fulfilled promises we enjoy are opportunities to praise the Lord and bring glory to His name. Do we?

> **What Do You Think?**
> How is your sharing the gospel similar to Nathan's sharing these words with David?
>
> **Digging Deeper**
> What details of God's promises to David might you include when you share the gospel?

Conclusion
A. Eternal Home

Last year, my mother passed away suddenly from a brain tumor discovered only a few months prior. My father followed her in death less than a week later. One of the final requests Dad shared with the family was that he wanted our brother to inherit the family home since the rest of us already owned properties.

We spent our entire childhood in our parents' house in a small Indiana town, never relocat-

ing. As funds permitted, Mom and Dad would periodically update the flooring and replace the roof, among other things. However, before my wife and I returned to Alaska after the funeral services, I provided my brother with a list of outstanding repairs that our parents had not finished, and with a good-humored tone, I let him know that the burden of maintaining the house now fell on him.

King David had to leave the construction of God's house to his son. But God's grand plans went far beyond the building and upkeep of an inanimate temple. In Jesus, we are part of God's everlasting and holy temple. And one day, we will arrive home in the Lord, enjoying the everlasting kingdom in ways David could only dream about in his own days. This eternal residence, crafted by God, is where Christ, a descendant of David, reigns for all eternity.

B. Prayer

Heavenly Father, thank You for Your everlasting covenant promises, given to David and fulfilled in Jesus. Redirect us when our plans are out of step with Yours. In the name of Your Son, Jesus, we offer this prayer. Amen.

C. Thought to Remember
God's promises are sure.

How to Say It

Abraham	*Ay*-bruh-ham.
Babylonians	Bab-ih-*low*-nee-unz.
Bathsheba	Bath-*she*-buh.
Bethlehem	*Beth*-lih-hem.
Hebrews	*Hee*-brews.
Isaac	*Eye*-zuk.
Israel	*Iz*-ray-el.
Jacob	*Jay*-kub.
Judah	*Joo*-duh.
Moses	*Mo*-zes or *Mo*-zez.
Philistines	Fuh-*liss*-teenz or *Fill*-us-teenz.
Solomon	*Sol*-o-mun.
tabernacle	**tah**-burr-*nah*-kul.
Uriah	Yu-*rye*-uh.

Involvement Learning

Enhance your lesson with KJV Bible Student *(from your curriculum supplier) and the reproducible activity page (at www.standardlesson.com or in the back of the* KJV Standard Lesson Commentary Deluxe Edition*).*

Into the Lesson

Allow one minute for learners to silently consider promises they have made (whether these have been honored, have yet to be fulfilled, or were broken). Ask volunteers to share one promise. Then, ask learners to break into pairs to brainstorm promises that God has made. After a few minutes, ask volunteers to share these answers as well, writing these on the board. After a brief period, ask the pairs to consider these two questions: 1–What factors prevent people from keeping promises? 2–Do any of these factors apply to God? Why or why not? After a few minutes, bring the class together to discuss.

Alternative. Distribute copies of the "God's Promise to David" exercise on the activity page, which you can download. Have learners work in pairs to complete as indicated.

Transition into the lesson by stating, "Today, as we delve into the heart of 2 Samuel 7:4-17, we will concentrate on the importance of God's commitments, particularly His divine promise to King David."

Into the Word

Before class, prepare a brief lecture covering what had happened in Israel between last week's lesson on Ruth 4:9-17 and this week's on 2 Samuel 7:4-17. This lecture should include information about the last days of the judges, Samuel's ministry in Israel, Saul's disastrous rule, and how David came to the throne. *Option 1.* Assign this overview to a volunteer to prepare before class. *Option 2.* Ask small groups to work together to summarize the events from the days of the judges to this point in David's reign.

Ask a volunteer to read 2 Samuel 7:4-17. Distribute a handout (you create) with two headers: "Fulfillment in the Past" and "Fulfillment in the Future." Instruct pairs to identify under the first header which promises named or alluded to in this passage were fulfilled *before* God spoke to Nathan.

Answers should include delivering Israel from Egypt (Genesis 46:3-4; Exodus 12:31-42), meeting the people in the tabernacle (25:1-22; 40:34-35), and making David king over Israel (1 Samuel 16:1-13; 2 Samuel 2:1-7).

Next, the pairs should identify under the second header promises that were fulfilled *after* God spoke to Nathan. Answers should include Solomon's ascending to the throne in Jerusalem (1 Kings 1:38-40) and Jesus' inheriting the throne to reign forever (Luke 1:29-33).

After a few minutes of work, bring the class together and discuss their answers. Again, in their pairs, have learners identify evidence that David was obedient to the instructions God gave him through Nathan. These will include that David believed that God would fulfill these promises (2 Samuel 7:18-29) and did not build the temple (1 Kings 5:3-5), although he did help prepare for its construction (1 Chronicles 22). Using sanctified imaginations, ask learners to consider how the story might have been different if David had not accepted Nathan's words as true and obeyed the Lord's instruction.

Into Life

Allow one minute for learners to bring to mind a course of action they have been considering. Ask them to discuss in small groups how, without the aid of a "Nathan" to definitively speak for God, they can make faithful decisions. Ask what steps learners can take to discern when the course they *want* is not *best.*

Alternative. Distribute the "Prayer Chart" activity from the activity page to be completed individually in a minute or less. *Option.* This can be sent home with students to ponder in the week to come.

Have pairs write a prayer for obedience to God, even when His plans differ from our plans. Encourage pairs to pray together before ending class.

A Father's Prophecy

Devotional Reading: Luke 1:5-17
Background Scripture: Luke 1:5-23, 57-80

Luke 1:67-80

67 And his father Zacharias was filled with the Holy Ghost, and prophesied, saying,

68 Blessed be the Lord God of Israel, for he hath visited and redeemed his people.

69 And hath raised up an horn of salvation for us in the house of his servant David,

70 As he spake by the mouth of his holy prophets, which have been since the world began.

71 That we should be saved from our enemies, and from the hand of all that hate us,

72 To perform the mercy promised to our fathers, and to remember his holy covenant,

73 The oath which he sware to our father Abraham,

74 That he would grant unto us, that we being delivered out of the hand of our enemies might serve him without fear,

75 In holiness and righteousness before him, all the days of our life.

76 And thou, child, shalt be called the prophet of the Highest. For thou shalt go before the face of the Lord to prepare his ways,

77 To give knowledge of salvation unto his people by the remission of their sins,

78 Through the tender mercy of our God, whereby the dayspring from on high hath visited us,

79 To give light to them that sit in darkness and in the shadow of death, to guide our feet into the way of peace.

80 And the child grew, and waxed strong in spirit, and was in the deserts till the day of his shewing unto Israel.

Key Text

Thou, child, shalt be called the prophet of the Highest. For thou shalt go before the face of the Lord to prepare his ways, to give knowledge of salvation unto his people by the remission of their sins. —**Luke 1:76-77**

A King
Forever and Ever

Unit 1: Jesus, the Heir of David
Lessons 1–5

Lesson Aims

After participating in this lesson, each learner will be able to:

1. Summarize Zacharias's prophecy.

2. Explain ways the prophecy could have been misunderstood in the first century AD.

3. Identify any "wilderness" of preparation the learner is in and opportunities for growth.

Lesson Outline

I. Introduction

A. Present-Day Heralds

Over a decade ago, the mascot at the college where I work changed from a saint to a herald. At the time, some people expressed hesitation and questioned the change. One reason for the hesitation was that the role of a *herald* is relatively unknown.

Some countries, such as the United Kingdom, still have active heralds as employees of the sovereign, but such positions are not found in the majority of countries. Perhaps we have lost something in not maintaining the role of a herald.

B. Lesson Context

The Gospel of Luke was written about AD 60 by Luke the physician and traveling companion of the apostle Paul (Colossians 4:14). It was probably written during the period of a couple of years in which Paul was imprisoned at Caesarea (Acts 23–24). Luke was not an eyewitness to the events of Jesus' life. Even so, Luke was meticulous in his research (Luke 1:1-3). The result is the New Testament's marvelous third Gospel, written so that the reader may be convinced of the certainty of the book's contents. One of the individuals who Luke could have interviewed was Mary, the mother of Jesus, who would have had personal knowledge of much of the events of both the birth of John and, of course, Jesus.

Luke's Gospel begins by introducing a priest named Zacharias and his wife, Elisabeth. The couple was considered "righteous before God" and "blameless" regarding obedience to God's commandments (Luke 1:6). At the time of the introduction in the Gospel, the couple was without children due to their age and Elisabeth's barrenness (1:7).

The fact that Zacharias served as a priest in the division of Abia (Luke 1:5) is more significant than it might seem at first. According to the first-century Jewish historian Josephus, the priesthood of that time was organized into 24 divisions. That matches the organization noted in 1 Chronicles 24:1-19. Every division served in the temple for roughly two nonconsecutive weeks each year.

The assigned priests would complete the necessary tasks for the temple, including accepting and offering sacrifices, burning incense, and leading prayers (1 Chronicles 6:48-49; compare 23:28-32).

During the time of Zacharias's service, an angel of the Lord named Gabriel visited him and informed him that he would have a son (Luke 1:8-19). Zacharias responded with doubt, questioning the validity of the angel's prophecy (1:18). The angel proclaimed that because of Zacharias's doubt, he would be unable to speak until the prophecies regarding the birth of the son were fulfilled (1:19-20).

The Scripture text in today's lesson includes a song of praise known as the *Benedictus*. The source of this title is the first word of Luke 1:68 in the Latin translation of the Bible known as the Vulgate, which dates to the fourth century AD. Perhaps it is better known to you as *Zacharias's Song*.

I. Prologue
(Luke 1:67)

67. And his father Zacharias was filled with the Holy Ghost, and prophesied, saying.

The disbelief of *Zacharias* when he received the angel's message (see Lesson Context) was replaced with being *filled with the Holy Ghost*. Luke, the author, seems to have a special interest in this person of the Trinity, who is mentioned in this Gospel about the same number of times as the other three Gospels combined. In the book of Acts, Luke's subsequent work, the Holy Ghost is mentioned more than 40 times. The presence of God's Spirit has been a necessary prerequisite for God's people to serve Him through prophetic ministry (examples: Numbers 11:25-27; Acts 2:17-18).

II. Celebrating God
(Luke 1:68-75)
A. For Promises Kept (vv. 68-70)

68. Blessed be the Lord God of Israel, for he hath visited and redeemed his people.

Zacharias begins a poetic expression of blessing and praise to God. Employing parallel expressions typical of biblical poetry, his song echoes key themes of prophetic promise from Israel's Scriptures. As God had fulfilled His surprising promise that Zacharias would become a father, so God would fulfill His greatest promises for all.

Songs and psalms of thanksgiving often include a proclamation of praise to *the Lord God* (compare Psalms 72:18; 84:11). Mary's song of praise, called the *Magnificat*, also begins with her glorifying the Lord (Luke 1:46-47).

Zacharias praised the Lord because of the Lord's actions for His people. The Old Testament describes how the Lord had come and *visited* His people for blessing (examples: Genesis 21:1; Ruth 1:6) or because of their sin (examples: Exodus 20:5; 32:34).

The reason for His coming at this particular time was so that *his people* might be *redeemed*, a conclusion also reached by the crowd in Luke 7:16. As we attempt to grasp this concept, we can simplify by realizing that when we are introduced to Jesus in the pages of the New Testament, two issues are of utmost importance: *who Jesus is* in His essence and *what Jesus did* in terms of His mission. The shorthand way of saying this is that we are learning about the person and work of Christ.

The four Gospels focus heavily on the first part of that inquiry, on establishing and describing the person of Christ. The four Gospels, however, spend almost no time explaining the work of Christ. We hasten to add that by "work," we don't mean Jesus' miracles of healing, exorcism, etc. By "work," we are referring to the eternal results of His death, burial, and resurrection. Thus, we have to wait until Paul's epistles before we can fully grasp the "how" of the phrase *redeemed his people*.

69. And hath raised up an horn of salvation for us in the house of his servant David.

The song's prophetic nature is on display as it announces the means by which the redemption arrives. In the Old Testament, animal horns were symbols of power (examples: Deuteronomy 33:17; Psalm 18:2; Zechariah 1:18-21). Through the power of the Lord God, the promised redemption—a *horn of salvation*—would come, vanquishing enemies and ruling as Messiah (see Psalm 132:17).

Zacharias recognized that the Messiah would come from one specific lineage: *the house of . . . David*. Centuries before Zacharias lived, the prophet Nathan had stated that the Lord would establish His kingdom in and through the house of David (2 Samuel 7:12-16; compare Isaiah 9:6-7). This would bring righteousness, peace, and salvation (Isaiah 11:1-9; Jeremiah 23:5-6; 33:15-16). About six months after the birth of John, a descendant of the house of David was indeed born to fulfill the promises; His name was Jesus (Luke 1:27-32; 3:23).

70. As he spake by the mouth of his holy prophets, which have been since the world began.

This verse reminds readers that God's plan was not a new thing; rather, it had been set forth through *his holy prophets* of centuries past (example: Jeremiah 23:5; compare Acts 3:21; Romans 1:2; Hebrews 1:1; 1 Peter 1:10-12). The person and work of Jesus the Messiah validated the predictions of the prophets (Luke 24:25-27). The message of the prophets comes to a focal point in the message of Zacharias's son, henceforth known as John the Baptist, who later proclaimed, "Behold the Lamb of God, which taketh away the sin of the world" when seeing Jesus (John 1:29).

> **What Do You Think?**
> What has been your experience of reading or studying the Old Testament prophets?
>
> **Digging Deeper**
> What preparation could make your study more beneficial to your spiritual development?

B. For Results Certain (vv. 71-75)

71. That we should be saved from our enemies, and from the hand of all that hate us.

The theme of salvation by God's Messiah is repeated often in the Gospels. Indeed, that message of salvation is their primary message! But as events would unfold, God's idea of who their main *enemies* were didn't match who the Jewish leaders and people thought were their enemies.

This misidentification distracted Jesus' own apostles right up to the time of Jesus' ascension (Acts 1:6). "The Son of God was manifested, that he might destroy the works of the devil" (1 John 3:8), not the works of the Roman Empire.

> **What Do You Think?**
> What sets biblical teaching about enemies apart from worldly wisdom on the topic?
>
> **Digging Deeper**
> How do your speech and actions to enemies mark you as a follower of Christ?

72. To perform the mercy promised to our fathers, and to remember his holy covenant.

God's promise *to perform . . . mercy* is witnessed in passages such as Micah 7:20: "Thou wilt perform the truth to Jacob, and the mercy to Abraham, which thou hast sworn unto our fathers from the days of old." Considering the ancient use of the literary technique of parallelism, this is the same as remembering *his holy covenant* (compare Psalms 105:8-9; 106:45; Ezekiel 16:60). The next verse offers an additional layer to this parallelism.

73. The oath which he sware to our father Abraham.

This *oath* is described in Genesis 22:16-18; it is the same as "his holy covenant" of Luke 1:72, just considered. Consider these two time frames: as we are now looking 2,000 years into the past to consider what Zacharias has written, Zacharias himself was looking 2,000 years into his own past to consider the covenant with *our father Abraham*! The centuries have proven God to be trustworthy and faithful; He keeps His promises to His people (Joshua 21:45; Psalm 145:13).

The passage of centuries had not dimmed Zacharias's expectations, and neither should they dim ours. As Zacharias could praise the Lord God, so should we (compare other praise in Luke 1:46-55; 2:28-32, 36-38).

74. That he would grant unto us, that we being delivered out of the hand of our enemies might serve him without fear.

The oath granted to Abraham extended to the

people of Zacharias's day (*unto us*). Nine months of being unable to speak (Luke 1:20, 64) had allowed Zacharias time to reflect on the fact that when the Lord speaks, people should listen rather than run off at the mouth!

As a priest, Zacharias was intensely interested in being able to *serve* the Lord (compare Hebrews 9:14). Interestingly, the underlying Greek word translated "serve" is also translated "worship" in Acts 7:42; 24:14. To serve God is to worship Him; to worship God is to serve Him. By the Messiah's deliverance, God's people will be able to do so *without fear*, without the specter of further defeat or persecution hanging over their heads. The way it will happen—through Jesus' death and resurrection—and one result of its happening—freedom from earthly fear (Romans 8:15; Philippians 1:14)—will astonish everyone. As Zacharias speaks, the Israelites live in fear of their *enemies*: the Roman overlords and the Jewish leadership (John 9:22; 12:42; 16:2). The greater fear that God will eliminate, however, is the fear of death (Hebrews 2:15).

75. In holiness and righteousness before him, all the days of our life.

As a devoted priest, Zacharias knew what it meant to serve the Lord. All his life, he had been "righteous before God, walking in all the commandments and ordinances of the Lord blameless" (Luke 1:6). God desires the same for others. *Holiness* means to be set apart from sin; *righteousness* means that the people always do the right thing in the eyes of God. The only other place in the New Testament where the words translated "holiness" and "righteousness" occur together is Ephesians 4:24: "[Ye were taught] that ye put on the new man, which after God is created in righteousness and true holiness" (compare Titus 2:11-14).

Zacharias's expectation was partially fulfilled

How to Say It

Abia	Uh-*bye*-yuh.
Gabriel	*Gay*-bree-ul.
Josephus	Jo-*see*-fus.
Messiah	Meh-*sigh*-uh.
Zacharias	Zack-uh-*rye*-us.

when Christ established the church, whose members are a "holy priesthood, to offer up spiritual sacrifices, acceptable to God by Jesus Christ" (1 Peter 2:5). The ultimate fulfillment will come when we serve Christ in full holiness in Heaven (Revelation 22:3).

> **What Do You Think?**
> How accurate would it be to say that you serve God without fear and in holiness and righteousness?
>
> **Digging Deeper**
> To the extent that this statement is not completely true, what step(s) can you take to improve this week?

III. Appointing John
(Luke 1:76-78a)
A. His Calling (v. 76)

76. And thou, child, shalt be called the prophet of the Highest. For thou shalt go before the face of the Lord to prepare his ways.

Zacharias switches focus to his (only) *child*, John, and John's pending role in God's plan of salvation. That role will be to prepare hearts and minds for the coming of a greater one. John was to be like a herald, coming in advance of the king and announcing the king's arrival so that people might prepare. John was to be "the voice of one crying in the wilderness, Prepare ye the way of the Lord, make his paths straight" (Luke 3:4, quoting Isaiah 40:3; compare Malachi 3:1). Some 30 years later, John's ministry fulfilled the words of his father (Matthew 3:11-12; Mark 1:1-8; Luke 3:1-18; John 1:19-34).

Implied in this ministry is the kind of prophetic work Israel knew from earlier times when prophets like Hosea, Amos, Isaiah, and Jeremiah took up their own prophetic ministries. This child would become *the prophet of the Highest* (compare Mark 11:32) as the forerunner of the coming Lord. He would be like the prophet Elijah (Elias), preparing the people for the promised salvation (Matthew 11:14). Such a description is consistent with the announcement of the angel regarding John's birth, saying that John will "go before [the Lord] in the spirit and power of Elias" (Luke 1:17) as he turns "the children of Israel . . . back to the Lord their God" (1:16).

What Do You Think?

To what degree is our calling (example: Matthew 28:16-20) like John's calling?

Digging Deeper

What challenges do we face in fulfilling our calling? What encouragement can we take from John's example of ministry?

B. His Task (vv. 77-78a)

77. To give knowledge of salvation unto his people by the remission of their sins.

The underlying Greek word for *remission* is translated elsewhere as "forgiveness" (examples: Mark 3:29; Acts 5:31; 13:38), and that is the sense here. John's ministry included calling for repentance (Matthew 3:2) and "preaching the baptism of repentance for the remission of *sins*" (Luke 3:3).

The *salvation* mentioned here would prove to be more than just political salvation from oppression; *people* would be offered a spiritual, eternal *salvation*. The hope and mercy that God's people desired would come from God's redemption and salvation in Christ (Acts 4:8-12; Romans 8; Hebrews 9:28; etc.).

78a. Through the tender mercy of our God.

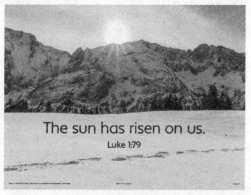

The sun has risen on us.
Luke 1:79

Visual for Lesson 3. *As the class discusses verse 79, ask learners to take one minute to consider whether there is any darkness they have not renounced.*

The designation of the Lord as *our God* occurs more than 200 times in the Bible. God is not an abstract concept; He is intensely personal. The fictitious gods of paganism cannot be characterized by their *tender mercy*—those gods are seen as fickle. The word translated "tender" is interesting. In a literal, physical sense, it refers to one's bowels or intestines (Acts 1:18). In a figurative or emotional sense, this area of a person was considered to be the center or origin of compassion (see the word's translation as "affection" in 2 Corinthians 7:15; an intense form of the word occurs in James 5:11).

IV. Predicting Result
(Luke 1:78b-79)

78b-79. Whereby the dayspring from on high hath visited us, to give light to them that sit in darkness and in the shadow of death, to guide our feet into the way of peace.

By contrast, today we speak of one's heart as that center or origin. So, we can say that Zacharias's Song reminds us that God's motivation for sending the Messiah is the mercy of God's own heart. That mercy brings something like the dawning of a new day, to which *the dayspring from on high* refers.

Darkness is a common image for the state of those who oppose God (examples: Psalm 107:10-11; Jeremiah 23:12; John 3:19; 1 Corinthians 4:5; Ephesians 6:12). In this state, *death* is inevitable (Romans 5:12; 6:23). But God promises *to give light to* those in this state (Isaiah 9:2; Matthew 4:16; Acts 26:18). It is Jesus who brings light into darkness (John 8:12). A sad and continuing part of the problem, however, is that although "light is come into the world, . . . men loved darkness rather than light, because their deeds were evil" (John 3:19).

Deadline: Year 2020?

Back in the year 2010, a former Minister of Defence in Canada revealed his skeptical view of humanity's future in his book *Light at the End of the Tunnel*. He asserted that the year 2020 was the deadline for ending dependence on fossil fuels for energy. Exotic forms of energy already existed, he claimed, but a "shadow government" controlled their secret. One of the writer's imperatives was that all people must find ways to work together for the common good.

As of this writing (October 2023), the dire predictions have not come to pass, claimed "right nows" have not been verified, and working together for the common good is as much of a pipe dream as it ever was.

Two millennia ago, Zacharias announced by the Holy Spirit a very dissimilar "was / now / will be." Unlike that of the writer above, the elements of the prophecy of Zacharias lined up perfectly, as 2,000 years of history have proven. Those who prophesy by their own insight aren't always guaranteed to be correct; those who prophesy by God's empowerment are always right, to the farthest distance of the future. How will you prepare yourself to demonstrate this to a skeptic?
—R. L. N.

V. Epilogue
(Luke 1:80)

80. And the child grew, and waxed strong in spirit, and was in the deserts till the day of his shewing unto Israel.

This verse takes us out of Zacharias's Song and summarizes John's formative years. Luke's Gospel provides parallel statements about Jesus (Luke 2:40, 52). Becoming *strong in spirit* may refer either to John's determined willingness to conform to God's will, or it may describe the presence of the Holy Spirit in his life.

Your Preparation Context(s)

The contrast between what we might call the "preparation contexts" of Joseph and Moses is fascinating: Joseph was prepared in a desert to serve in a palace (Genesis 37:1-22; 41:39-40); Moses was prepared in a palace to serve in a desert (Exodus 2:10; 3:1). Other preparation contexts are equally fascinating. The apostle Paul, for example, was a rising star in first-century Judaism (Acts 22:3; Galatians 1:14). But when he as persecutor became the persecuted, his preparation context changed abruptly from that of the city to the desert (Galatians 1:17-18) to . . . everywhere.

We could explore other examples. Springing immediately to mind are the prophets Isaiah, Jeremiah, Daniel, and John the Baptist. Such an exploration also invites a consideration of our own personal preparation contexts. The biblical examples teach us that as much as we might like to have a comfortable, familiar preparation environment that is followed by an equally comfortable service setting, it just won't happen that way. That's not God's pattern. In what ways do you need to change your expectations in this regard?   —R. L. N.

Conclusion
A. Still Pointing to Jesus

Speechless for nine months, Zacharias offered an impressive, memorable song in celebration of John's birth. Layering phrase after phrase from the ancient prophets, he made clear to all that the time of fulfillment had arrived.

We are the beneficiaries of those promises and their fulfillment. We have the holy Scriptures so that we can know the factual certainty of it all (Luke 1:4). As we do, we experience the salvation, mercy, knowledge, and light that God gives in Jesus Christ. Our expression of joy and thanks ought to be at least as vivid as Zacharias's, if not more so.

B. Prayer

Great God, we thank You that by Your mercy, we have received the fulfillment of Your eternal promises in Jesus. May we live in full confidence of Your abiding faithfulness. In Jesus' name we pray. Amen.

C. Thought to Remember

Reject the darkness; embrace the light.

Involvement Learning

Enhance your lesson with KJV Bible Student *(from your curriculum supplier) and the reproducible activity* *page (at www.standardlesson.com or in the back of the* KJV Standard Lesson Commentary Deluxe Edition*).*

Into the Lesson

As learners enter the classroom, distribute index cards and pens and ask learners to write down one prediction about the future. It can be silly or serious and does not have to be spiritual or Bible-related. Once all learners have had time to respond, ask volunteers to share predictions with the class. Have learners rank each prediction from 1 to 5, *1* being least likely to happen and *5* being most likely. When all the volunteers have shared their predictions, ask learners to explain the criteria they considered regarding whether a prediction seems more or less likely to come true.

Alternative. Distribute copies of the "False Prophecies" exercise from the activity page, which you can download. Have learners work in pairs or small groups to complete the exercise as indicated.

After either activity, tell the class, "Today we are going to study a prophecy made by the father of John the Baptist that is related not only to his life but also to the coming of Jesus."

Into the Word

Ask a volunteer to read Luke 1:67-80. Work together as a class to outline God's previous words and actions, as recounted by Zacharias, as well as the anticipated works that would be fulfilled in John and Jesus. Work in small groups to find the Bible references for the people, events, or promises that Zacharias mentioned as having happened in the past (roughly Luke 1:67-75). Pay special attention to concepts like the "horn of salvation" (1:69) that are somewhat obscure *and* others like God's "holy covenant" (1:72) that might seem so familiar that believers might take their meanings for granted. Consult the commentary for cross-references and other helps as desired. Bring the class back together to discuss the references or concepts they found to be particularly important or surprising.

In the same small groups as before, have learners find the Bible references for the people, events, or promises that at the time were yet to be fulfilled by John or Jesus. Encourage learners once again to pay special attention to any concepts with which they are unfamiliar or that may seem overly familiar. When groups have finished, bring them back together to discuss their key findings.

Into Life

Ask learners to discuss how these examples from Luke 1:67-80 of God's past provision give them confidence about His continued care in the future. Allow one minute for silent reflection on any situation where learners need to apply this confidence.

Distribute pens and paper to the class. In small groups, have learners work to update Zacharias's prophecy as a blessing for a new minister. This blessing needs to include two parts: (1) praise for God's past work and faithfulness, and (2) hopes for the minister's future. Take into account not only Israel's history as Zacharias knew it but also the history of the church.

Option. If your congregation is welcoming or training a new minister or sending out a missionary, consider personalizing your hopes and prayers to that person's specific context.

Alternative. Distribute copies of the exercise "Baby Dedication" from the activity page. Give learners time to complete the assignment as instructed before sharing it with a partner. If you choose to use this activity, be sensitive to learners' different experiences with parenting, childlessness, and other potentially painful situations. Encourage partners to pray together when they have finished discussing.

Conclude the class in prayer, a hymn, or a chorus familiar to the whole class. Appropriate choices might include "This Is My Father's World" or "Good Good Father."

Savior's Birth

Devotional Reading: Micah 5:1-6
Background Scripture: Luke 2:1-20

Luke 2:1-16

1 And it came to pass in those days, that there went out a decree from Caesar Augustus, that all the world should be taxed.

2 (And this taxing was first made when Cyrenius was governor of Syria.)

3 And all went to be taxed, every one into his own city.

4 And Joseph also went up from Galilee, out of the city of Nazareth, into Judaea, unto the city of David, which is called Bethlehem (because he was of the house and lineage of David).

5 To be taxed with Mary his espoused wife, being great with child.

6 And so it was, that, while they were there, the days were accomplished that she should be delivered.

7 And she brought forth her firstborn son, and wrapped him in swaddling clothes, and laid him in a manger, because there was no room for them in the inn.

8 And there were in the same country shepherds abiding in the field, keeping watch over their flock by night.

9 And, lo, the angel of the Lord came upon them, and the glory of the Lord shone round about them. And they were sore afraid.

10 And the angel said unto them, Fear not. For, behold, I bring you good tidings of great joy, which shall be to all people.

11 For unto you is born this day in the city of David a Saviour, which is Christ the Lord.

12 And this shall be a sign unto you: ye shall find the babe wrapped in swaddling clothes, lying in a manger.

13 And suddenly there was with the angel a multitude of the heavenly host praising God, and saying,

14 Glory to God in the highest, and on earth peace, good will toward men.

15 And it came to pass, as the angels were gone away from them into heaven, the shepherds said one to another, Let us now go even unto Bethlehem, and see this thing which is come to pass, which the Lord hath made known unto us.

16 And they came with haste, and found Mary, and Joseph, and the babe lying in a manger.

Key Text

It came to pass, as the angels were gone away from them into heaven, the shepherds said one to another, Let us now go even unto Bethlehem, and see this thing which is come to pass, which the Lord hath made known unto us. —**Luke 2:15**

145

A King
Forever and Ever

Unit 1: Jesus, the Heir of David
Lessons 1–5

Lesson Aims

After participating in this lesson, each learner will be able to:

1. Identify those invited to visit the newborn Jesus.

2. Trace on a map the route and distance from Nazareth to Bethlehem.

3. State a way that he or she will "go to Bethlehem" in a spiritual sense this Christmas season.

Lesson Outline

Introduction

A. Life-Changing Announcement

At one point or another, monotony afflicts us all. One day might feel the same as the previous day. Repetitive days become redundant weeks, and we seek any relief from the cycle of monotony.

Occasionally, a life-changing event breaks up the monotony. The first day of school, a wedding, a parent's funeral, or a national tragedy are examples of joyous or sorrowful events that change our lives.

I imagine that shepherds in the first century AD faced boredom and monotony in their work. Their tasks were likely the same day-to-day: ensure sheep were well-fed and safe. However, for some certain shepherds outside Bethlehem, their whole lives changed in a moment one evening. Today's text details the events that brought a life-changing announcement to these shepherds.

B. Lesson Context

Today's lesson text is part of a much larger story in Luke 1–2 that details Jesus' conception and birth. Luke weaves this story with his account of John the Baptist's conception and birth (see lesson 3). Both births were announced by an angel, accomplished by God's miraculous power, and accompanied by wonders that God performed.

Luke juxtaposed the birth accounts for two reasons. First, John the Baptist was a prominent figure in first-century Judea. His disciples traveled as far as Ephesus in Asia Minor (Acts 19:1-3). Second, Luke's Gospel demonstrates the link between the ministries of John and Jesus. John was a messenger preparing people for the coming Messiah (see Isaiah 40:3-5, quoted in Luke 3:4-6). Jesus was this promised Messiah, a fact confirmed by Simeon (Luke 2:25-32). By telling the birth stories of John and Jesus, Luke emphasizes how these events were all part of the same glorious plan of God.

In the centuries before Jesus' birth, the Roman Empire had conquered territories around the Mediterranean Sea. By 63 BC, Rome had conquered the city of Jerusalem and the surrounding territory, although it took some years for the Romans to solidify their control. Caesar Augustus became emperor in 27 BC. Due to his numerous building projects, he had to tax his people heavily. Those who did not submit to Roman authority could be fined, flogged, exiled, or executed.

Roman domination was more than a political and economic burden for the Jewish people. It was also a religious problem: as long as Rome ruled, God did not (or so it seemed). The reality of Roman occupation was a constant reminder that God had consigned Israel to a state of exile—even "exile" within its own borders—for generations.

The faithful looked to the promises of Scripture for hope. God had promised a great Son of David to rule over His people (2 Samuel 7:12-16) and restoration beyond exile (Isaiah 51:11). One day, the pagan powers would be destroyed, and God would rule supreme over all nations (Daniel 7:1-14). By the first century AD, centuries had passed since God first gave His promises. The faithful looked beyond the failures of their forefathers and kept their trust in God's promise to take back His world.

These ideas intersect with Luke's story of Jesus' birth. The power of Rome is portrayed through its ability to tax. We glimpse the oppression of Israel in the poverty of Jesus' family. The promise of God is evident as we hear again of David, whose promised Son is to rule over all.

I. In Those Days
(Luke 2:1-7)
A. The Decree of Rome (vv. 1-3)

1. And it came to pass in those days, that there went out a decree from Caesar Augustus, that all the world should be taxed.

Luke transitions the narrative of his Gospel account from the birth and childhood of John the Baptist and the subsequent worship from his father, Zacharias (Luke 1:57-80). The phrase *in those days* places the events of the text during the reign of the emperor *Caesar Augustus* (27 BC–AD 14).

The growth of the Roman Empire depended on taxes. These monies funded the military, allowing the spread of the *Pax Romana*, or "Roman peace." To standardize the tax-collection process, the emperor issued *a decree* to take a census of *all the* Roman *world*. An accurate count of the empire's residents was necessary to gather the most taxes.

This verse also reveals Luke's intention to give an orderly account of the context of the story of Jesus (compare Luke 1:1-4). By presenting the historical circumstances surrounding Jesus' birth, Luke demonstrated that Jesus was born in a real and specific context.

2. (And this taxing was first made when Cyrenius was governor of Syria.)

Estimating the exact year of Jesus' birth proves challenging. The mention of "Herod" in Matthew 2:1 and Luke 1:5 gives us a time frame for Jesus' birth. That individual is Herod the Great, king of Judaea. He died in 4 BC, so Jesus' birth must have occurred before that time. However, historical sources outside the Bible state that *Cyrenius* became *governor of Syria* in 6 AD, about 10 years after the death of Herod the Great.

There are multiple ways to understand Luke's statement without assuming he made a mistake. First, the underlying Greek word translated *governor* may refer to a lesser position in the government. According to the historian Tacitus, Cyrenius was elected "Counsel" of Syria in 12 BC, and Luke may have been referring to this position. It is also possible that the sentence structure in the original language means that this was the tax that occurred *before* Cyrenius was governor of Syria.

Considering the timing of the reigns of Caesar Augustus and Herod the Great, a reasonable calculation places the birth of Jesus at around 5 or 4 BC.

3. And all went to be taxed, every one into his own city.

Roman taxes required that each person return to the *city* of his or her ancestors to be counted in a census. Ancestral records or land-ownership titles determined the citizenship of that town. However, as their housing situation in Bethlehem would soon reveal, it is unlikely that Joseph owned property or a home in Bethlehem (compare Luke 2:7, below).

How to Say It

Colossians	Kuh-*losh*-unz.
Cyrenius	Sigh-*ree*-nee-us.
Ephesus	*Ef*-uh-sus.
Herod	*Hair*-ud.

B. The Journey of a Family (vv. 4-5)

4-5. And Joseph also went up from Galilee, out of the city of Nazareth, into Judaea, unto the city of David, which is called Bethlehem; (because he was of the house and lineage of David:) To be taxed with Mary his espoused wife, being great with child.

Before receiving news of the census, *Mary* had been in *Nazareth* in *Galilee* (Luke 1:26-27). *Joseph* also lived in Nazareth, as the two were *espoused* to be married. Following the census requirements, Joseph traveled to his ancestral home *because he was of the house and lineage of David* (compare Matthew 1:6, 16). The town of *Bethlehem* had been the hometown of David before he became king (1 Samuel 17:12, 58). The name *Bethlehem* means "house of bread," a fitting meaning for the birthplace of the one who is "the bread of life" (John 6:35, 48).

The couple *went up* on the journey because Bethlehem is located in the mountains of Judea at an elevation of approximately 2,550 feet above sea level. The journey from Nazareth to Bethlehem required a total elevation gain of about 1,250 feet.

The trip between the towns was about 85 to 90 miles, depending on the route. A day's journey on foot could cover up to 20 miles. However, Mary was in the late stages of pregnancy and *great with child*. Further, the trip was fraught with danger and hardship. The couple risked injury due to the rugged terrain, possible ambushes by bandits, and challenging weather conditions. The journey may have taken the couple a week or longer.

C. The Birth of a Child (vv. 6-7)

6. And so it was, that, while they were there, the days were accomplished that she should be delivered.

After arriving in Bethlehem, Mary went into labor. Luke does not indicate the time between when they arrived and her labor.

7. And she brought forth her firstborn son, and wrapped him in swaddling clothes, and laid him in a manger; because there was no room for them in the inn.

Mary's pregnancy came to its fulfillment, and she gave birth to *her firstborn son*—an obvious point because she was a virgin (Luke 1:34). This detail also implies that she had other children in the following years (compare Mark 6:3).

The first order of business was to wrap the newborn *in swaddling clothes*, long cloth strips that bound the infant's limbs. This method ensured the baby stayed warm and felt secure. An ancient non-biblical work notes that the baby who would later become King Solomon "was nursed in swaddling clothes, and that with cares. For there is no king that had any other beginning of birth" (Wisdom of Solomon 7:4-5). The opposite is seen in Ezekiel 16:4.

A *manger* was a feeding trough for domesticated animals. A tradition dating back to the second century depicts Jesus' birthplace as being a cave. This place might have resembled a rudimentary cellar for storing perishables and housing domestic animals. The promised Messiah, God's own Son, entered the world in a place reserved for cattle—a humble backdrop seemingly unfit for the "firstborn of every creature" through whom "were all things created" (Colossians 1:15-16; compare 2 Corinthians 8:9).

The expression *there was no room . . . in the inn* has led some readers to imagine that Mary and Joseph were denied space at an ancient hotel. However, the underlying ancient Greek word translated as *inn* can also refer to a guest room in a house (example: Luke 22:11). One possibility is that the couple was staying with an extended family member who had *no room for them* because of other family members in town for the census. As a result, the couple found themselves in the only available living space in the house.

Hopes and Expectations

The birth of our first child did not go as we

had hoped. My wife and I had decided on a home birth with a midwife. Complications during labor led the midwife to suggest we go to the hospital. There, doctors concluded that a C-section would be necessary. As my wife recovered from the procedure, I joyously held my newborn son, Wilder. That joy, however, soon changed.

Doctors informed us that Wilder had a bacterial infection that required immediate transport to the neonatal intensive care unit. If not treated immediately, the infection could spiral into meningitis.

I boarded an ambulance with my newborn son, encased in a transport incubator. He spent a week in the NICU, but it felt much longer for my wife and me. Eleven years have passed, and Wilder sits on my lap as I write this illustration.

My wife and I could never have expected how the first weeks of our son's life would play out, but we trusted that God would lead us through that season. Using my "sanctified imagination," I envision Mary and Joseph also had certain hopes and expectations for the birth of Jesus, which likely did not include a manger for a cradle. How are you preparing to trust God, no matter the circumstances?
—C. S.

What Do You Think?
How have you seen God work through surprising circumstances?

Digging Deeper
How can you get better at noticing God's work around you?

II. In the Fields
(Luke 2:8-16)

A. Angelic News (vv. 8-12)

8. And there were in the same country shepherds abiding in the field, keeping watch over their flock by night.

Luke's Gospel brings readers' attention to the fields outside Bethlehem. *Shepherds* worked an important but lowly profession in the ancient world: caring for and tending to sheep. The hill country surrounding Bethlehem contained suitable pastureland for tending to sheep and goats (compare 1 Samuel 16:4, 11). Shepherds and their flocks were typically *in the field* from early spring to early fall, but nothing in the Gospel accounts confirms the exact time of year of Jesus' birth.

9. And, lo, the angel of the Lord came upon them, and the glory of the Lord shone round about them: and they were sore afraid.

Scripture sometimes depicts angels as heralds, messengers for God (examples: Zechariah 1:14-17; 3:6-7; Matthew 28:5-7). Unlike the previous angelic appearances in Luke's Gospel (Luke 1:11-20, 26-38), this particular *angel* is unnamed.

Consider how the shepherds might have felt. They had been guarding their flocks, on alert for sounds from predators or thieves. Out of that silence came a sudden angelic appearance with *the glory of the Lord*. No wonder they were *afraid*!

10. And the angel said unto them, Fear not: for, behold, I bring you good tidings of great joy, which shall be to all people.

Scripture sometimes depicts angels as agents of God's judgment (examples: 2 Samuel 24:16-17; Revelation 15:1). Therefore, upon seeing *the angel*, the shepherds may have feared pending divine judgment. The imperative, *fear not*, acknowledged their fears (compare Genesis 15:1; Luke 1:30). The *good tidings of great joy* brought by the angel were the beginning of the gospel message.

11. For unto you is born this day in the city of David a Saviour, which is Christ the Lord.

The statement *unto you* reveals the intended recipients of this message. Shepherds were among the first to receive the good news of the child *born* in Bethlehem. The proclamation signaled that God was overturning the world's expectations, casting down those considered mighty by the world's standards and raising up those considered lowly, like these shepherds (see Luke 1:52; compare 7:22).

This child would someday be *a Saviour* for people (compare Luke 1:47; John 4:42). Jesus' work, culminating in His death and resurrection, enacted God's plan of salvation for the world (1 John 4:14).

The title *Christ* comes from the ancient Greek translation of the ancient Hebrew title *Messiah* (compare John 1:41; 4:25). Both titles mean "anointed one," referring to the anointed Redeemer and King of the people of God as proclaimed by the Old Testament prophets (Isaiah 9:6-7; 16:5; Micah

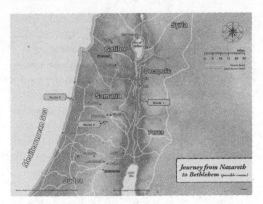

Visual for Lesson 4. *Display this visual as you discuss Luke 2:4 and the possible routes taken by Mary and Joseph.*

Luke, more than any other New Testament writer, includes the theme of praising God in his writings. A form of the phrase *praising God* appears nine times in the New Testament, seven of which are found in the writings of Luke (here and in Luke 2:20; 19:37; 24:53; Acts 2:47; 3:8-9).

The text does not say whether or not the heavenly host sang or spoke their praise, only that their voices joined to praise God. What the prophets had prophesied, even without understanding the full import of their own words, was being fulfilled. And what the angels longed to see (1 Peter 1:10-12) was finally revealed.

14. Glory to God in the highest, and on earth peace, good will toward men.

The host's message of praise is two-way, intended to be received by *God* and directed *toward* the good of humanity. The *glory* given to God acknowledges His power and His work of salvation. The phrase *in the highest* refers to the place where God resides (compare Luke 19:38). Though God is all-powerful, He revealed himself in and through humble circumstances: a baby born in a manger.

The second part of the statement refers to the genuine *peace* now *on earth*. The Roman Empire brought the *Pax Romana* through force, but only God can bring eternal peace. His peace is not just the cessation of hostility or the absence of conflict; it is the good news of God's salvation through Jesus Christ, the Prince of Peace (Isaiah 9:6; Acts 10:36). One of the most significant peace pronouncements of the New Testament is Romans 5:1: "Therefore being justified by faith, we have peace with God through our Lord Jesus Christ."

5:2; etc.). The promised Messiah would save His people and establish a reign of peace (see Zechariah 9:9-10). First-century Jewish belief held that the Messiah would come from the family *of David* (2 Samuel 7:12-16; Jeremiah 23:5-6) and the town of Bethlehem (see Micah 5:2-4; Matthew 2:3-6).

Lord is a term of absolute authority. The Roman emperor was often called the "savior" and "lord" of the empire. By referring to Jesus as *the Lord*, the angel proclaimed the arrival of the absolute and eternal ruler of the cosmos (compare Matthew 28:18).

12. And this shall be a sign unto you; Ye shall find the babe wrapped in swaddling clothes, lying in a manger.

The *swaddling clothes* were expected for a newborn (see Luke 2:7, above). On the other hand, the *manger* was unexpected, not ordinarily used as a crib for a baby. This *sign* would confirm to the shepherds that everything the angel said about Christ had been accurate.

B. Heavenly Host (vv. 13-14)

13. And suddenly there was with the angel a multitude of the heavenly host praising God, and saying.

The sudden manifestation of a heavenly multitude emphasizes the angel's message. The Old Testament identifies *the heavenly host* as an army of angelic messengers who served the Lord of Hosts (examples: 1 Kings 22:19; Psalm 103:21).

> **What Do You Think?**
> What steps can you take to be an agent of God's peace in the world?
> **Digging Deeper**
> How might you respond to the claim that *peace* only refers to the absence of conflict?

C. Shepherds' Response (vv. 15-16)

15-16. And it came to pass, as the angels were gone away from them into heaven, the shepherds

said one to another, Let us now go even unto Bethlehem, and see this thing which is come to pass, which the Lord hath made known unto us. And they came with haste, and found Mary, and Joseph, and the babe lying in a manger.

The angels delivered their message and praises and then departed *into heaven*. This raises some intriguing questions. Did they simply disappear? Was there a visible departure until they could no longer be seen? What is not in doubt, however, is the shepherds' response. Stunned, they collected their thoughts and took the only reasonable actions their experiences led them to do.

It was just as the angel had said: shepherds found the infant Jesus *lying in a manger,* with *Mary and Joseph* in attendance. Without a doubt, this was a privileged group of people who gathered that night. God makes himself known to the lowly (Luke 10:21).

> **What Do You Think?**
> What steps will you take to be attentive to God's directives, even if they are highly disruptive to your plans?
>
> **Digging Deeper**
> What distractions might you need to remove in order to hear better from the Spirit of God?

Drop Everything Now

One Sunday, when my wife neared full-term pregnancy with our daughter, I had been scheduled to preach at a church about two hours away. She had experienced some contractions that morning, but we didn't think she was going into labor. Still, I was apprehensive about traveling hours away from her. We agreed that I would preach and promptly return home.

Before I began the sermon, I placed my phone face-up on the pulpit. I informed the congregation of my wife's situation. If she called during my sermon, I would answer and, if needed, leave immediately. I would drop everything to be with her.

The congregation understood, and, fortunately, I did not receive a phone call. Almost two weeks later, my wife gave birth to our daughter.

What things would cause you to drop everything immediately? The word of the angels and the revelation from the Lord were enough for these shepherds to drop everything to visit the newborn baby in the manger.

During this time of year, it seems like *everything* requires our attention and focus. What steps must you take to be like the shepherds and "drop everything" to make time for Christ during this Christmas season?
—C. S.

Conclusion

A. Journey to Bethlehem

The circumstances surrounding Jesus' birth subvert our worldly expectations of value and importance. Among the first people to receive the announcement of Jesus' birth were not the powerful and elite, although such people did receive the announcement (see Matthew 2:1-12).

Instead, the first announcement of good news came to lowly shepherds. In that instant, their lives forever changed. Their journey to Bethlehem resulted in the spread of the gospel message. They left Mary, Joseph, and the baby Jesus that night, ready to proclaim the good news they had received (Luke 2:17-18). How will you have a spiritual "journey to Bethlehem" to receive and proclaim the good news of Jesus Christ?

> **What Do You Think?**
> How has this lesson led you to think differently about the Christmas story?
>
> **Digging Deeper**
> How will you respond in light of this fact?

B. Prayer

God our Savior, show us how we might "travel to Bethlehem" this Christmastime. Reveal how we might be messengers of the gospel to all people. Thank You for the gift of Your Son, Jesus Christ, our Lord and Savior. In Jesus' name we pray. Amen.

C. Thought to Remember

God loves and invites the lowly.

Involvement Learning

Enhance your lesson with KJV Bible Student *(from your curriculum supplier) and the reproducible activity page (at www.standardlesson.com or in the back of the* KJV Standard Lesson Commentary Deluxe Edition*).*

Into the Lesson

Begin by asking for volunteers to describe how they plan for an extended trip. Ask each volunteer the following questions: 1–What steps were involved in planning the trip? 2–How did you decide what to pack for the trip? 3–What decisions were made regarding the number of stops on the trip? 4–What did you learn about yourself as you planned this trip?

Alternative. Distribute copies of the "Packing List for Expecting Parents" exercise from the activity page, which you can download. Have learners work in pairs to complete as indicated.

After either activity, lead into Bible study by saying, "Even our best plans can sometimes go awry. We can trust that God will provide for us, regardless of the circumstances and our expectations. Today's lesson will show us how God provided and revealed His work in a way no one could have expected."

Into the Word

Option. Choose volunteers to play the roles of Caesar Augustus, Joseph, Mary, an angel of the Lord, the heavenly host, and the shepherds. Select another volunteer to be the narrator. Ask the narrator to read aloud Luke 2:1-6 while other volunteers act out the events of the passage. Volunteers may use their "sanctified imagination" to improvise certain events from the story. After reenactment, ask the following question for whole-class discussion: "What part of this story impacted you the most and why?"

Ask a volunteer to read aloud Luke 2:1-7. Divide learners into groups of three and ask the following questions for in-group discussion: 1–What was the significance of the decree from Caesar Augustus? 2–What is the significance of Joseph's (and Mary's) journey to Bethlehem? 3–What Scripture texts speak of Bethlehem's significance? 4–Why was it significant that Jesus was

placed in a manger? 5–What are three ways that God provided for the needs of Mary, Joseph, and baby Jesus? 6–In what unexpected ways has God provided for you or your family?

Ask a volunteer to read aloud Luke 2:8-16. Have learners discuss the following questions in the same groups: 1–Describe when you felt fear after experiencing a work of God. How did you respond? 2–How would you articulate the "good tidings of great joy" to a modern-day audience? 3–How has God, through Christ Jesus, brought peace to the world? 4–What is the significance that God chose to announce this news to shepherds, a group not highly regarded in the first century? 5–What is the significance that the shepherds were given a sign to find the baby?

Option. Distribute copies of the "Mixed Message" activity from the activity page. Have learners work in pairs to complete as indicated. After three minutes, ask a volunteer to read aloud Luke 2:14 so that pairs may check their answers.

Into Life

Say, "The Christmas season gives us the opportunity to reflect on God's call on our lives and how we can follow Him. In the story of the first Christmas, the shepherds followed God's call by going to Bethlehem. In our context, we can 'go to Bethlehem' in a spiritual sense and notice God's work."

Distribute a pen and index cards to each learner. Ask them to write down in one minute or less a way that he or she will "go to Bethlehem" in a spiritual sense this Christmas season.

Place learners into pairs and have them discuss their response before answering the following questions with their partner: 1–What distractions do you need to remove to hear God's direction better as you "go to Bethlehem"? 2–Who is an accountability partner or spiritual mentor who can help you on this spiritual journey? 3–What is one thing that God could teach you as you "go to Bethlehem"?

David's Son

Devotional Reading: Luke 4:14-21
Background Scripture: Luke 18:31-43

Luke 18:35-43

35 And it came to pass, that as he was come nigh unto Jericho, a certain blind man sat by the way side begging.

36 And hearing the multitude pass by, he asked what it meant.

37 And they told him, that Jesus of Nazareth passeth by.

38 And he cried, saying, Jesus, thou Son of David, have mercy on me.

39 And they which went before rebuked him, that he should hold his peace: but he cried so much the more, thou Son of David, have mercy on me.

40 And Jesus stood, and commanded him to be brought unto him: and when he was come near, he asked him,

41 Saying, What wilt thou that I shall do unto thee? And he said, Lord, that I may receive my sight.

42 And Jesus said unto him, Receive thy sight; thy faith hath saved thee.

43 And immediately he received his sight, and followed him, glorifying God. And all the people, when they saw it, gave praise unto God

Key Text

They which went before rebuked him, that he should hold his peace: but he cried so much the more, thou Son of David, have mercy on me. —**Luke 18:39**

A King
Forever and Ever

Unit 1: Jesus, the Heir of David
Lessons 1–5

Lesson Aims

After participating in this lesson, each learner will be able to:

1. Summarize how the blind man's persistence illustrates Jesus' statement in Luke 18:1.

2. Analyze the connection the blind man makes between Jesus and the "Son of David."

3. Write a prayer to become a person of persistence.

Lesson Outline

Introduction

A. Persistent Prayer

When my 17-year-old half-brother left home, he told our parents that he was done with them and with Christianity. He joined the navy, got a young woman pregnant, married her, and then divorced her after 15 months, signing over complete custody of their son in the process. After leaving the navy, he spent the remainder of his 20s involved with drug use and two more broken marriages. By age 32, he was unemployed, mired in debt, and living with a woman to whom he was not married.

My brother and I didn't speak for 15 years after he left home. We were very close, and his departure crushed me. I had idolized him growing up. He was handsome, athletic, and charismatic—all things I wanted to be. But over time, my appreciation turned to anger and resentment. I felt that if he didn't want to be in my life, I didn't want anything to do with him. My parents didn't speak about him, and neither did I. Only once did we hear about how poorly he was doing, and I thought he deserved that suffering he had brought on himself.

My mother, however, never stopped praying for him. Every night before bed and every morning upon waking, she would pray to God and ask Him to reconcile my brother to Him and restore our family.

After 15 long years, my brother called my mom. His friend had invited him to church, and he had begun to go regularly. He had committed his life to Christ. As a result of his changed life, he asked for forgiveness for the ways he had treated our family. The next day, my mom flew to Florida to meet him and bring him back with her. As they embraced each other for the first time in 15 years, she wept and thanked God for answering her persistent prayer.

B. Lesson Context

Today's Scripture text takes place on Jesus' final journey to Jerusalem, a journey that began in Luke 9:51. At the point in Luke's Gospel of today's lesson, the end of the journey is drawing near. Today's text, Luke 18:35-43, describes the fourth and final miracle in what we might call "Luke's journey section" (compare the other three in Luke 13:10-17; 14:1-6; 17:11-19).

Just before today's text begins, Jesus had warned His disciples (again) that He, the Son of Man, was going to die and rise again on the third day (Luke 18:31-34; compare direct references and allusions to Jesus' death in Luke 5:35; 9:22, 44-45; 12:49-50; 13:32-33; 17:25). As we read the numerous events and teachings between Luke 9:51 and 18:35, we get the impression that Jesus was in no hurry.

Also in no hurry—but by necessity rather than choice—were the physically infirm of the era, especially those who were blind. Blindness was a familiar condition in the ancient world, with the Bible itself using some form of the word *blind* dozens of times. From our current scientific vantage point, there was no reliable cure for blindness in Jesus' day and little understanding of its varied causes.

But the ancient mind was not cautious about thinking of one cause of blindness in particular: many believed it to be a curse from God for some type of sinful behavior. The sins of the parents were thought to affect their children, causing them to be born blind (compare John 9:1-2). But regardless of the cause, blindness was economically and socially debilitating. Blind men could not serve as priests (Leviticus 21:16-18) and had little opportunity for employment. They were reduced to begging or depending on family support to survive.

Parallels to today's text of Luke 18:35-43 are Matthew 20:29-34 and Mark 10:46-52. An interesting fact regarding these parallels is that although Mark's Gospel as a whole is the shortest of the three, Mark's version of the event is the *longest* of the three!

I. Realization

(Luke 18:35-38)

A. Time and Place (v. 35)

35a. And it came to pass, that as he was come nigh unto Jericho.

Located near the Jordan River, about 17 miles east of Jerusalem, the city of *Jericho* is infamous for having been destroyed by God some 14 centuries prior to the encounter described in Luke 18 (Joshua 6). Archeology reveals that there were actually two locations for Jericho in the first century: (1) the ancient location as described in the Old Testament and (2) the complex rebuilt by Herod, approximately one mile from the more ancient location. The modern city of Jericho includes both sites.

35b. A certain blind man sat by the way side begging.

The parallel account in the Gospel of Mark reveals more of the identity of this *certain blind man*: he is "Bartimaeus, the son of Timaeus" (Mark 10:46). The fact that Luke doesn't give the name is a bit surprising, given his tendency to give more actual names relative to how frequently the other three Gospels do so. The non-inclusion of the man's name here may be due to the fact that Luke was not an eyewitness (Luke 1:1-4). But ultimately, this is speculation.

For a person living in the first century AD, any degree of visual impairment was untreatable. Corrective lenses, as we have them today, would not be available for centuries to come. The most serious visual impairment is, of course, blindness. People who were so afflicted had few, if any, viable treatment options and were unable to work in many occupations (see the Lesson Context for more background). *Begging* alongside heavily traveled roads or next to city gates was frequent. The Law of Moses pronounced a curse on those who took advantage of the blind (Leviticus 19:14; Deuteronomy 27:18).

B. Individuals and Crowds (vv. 36-38)

36. And hearing the multitude pass by, he asked what it meant.

The exact makeup and number of *the multitude* is not given. In Luke 12:1, we see the description of an "innumerable multitude of people, insomuch that they trode one upon another." This crowd—undoubtedly with drop-outs and add-ins along the way—was tagging along with Jesus' on His final journey to Jerusalem (see Lesson Context).

It was not unusual for people to travel long

distances in large groups. Bandits would frequently wait along roads to ambush solitary travelers. While the Roman road system and garrisons had made travel safer, banditry was still exceedingly common. Indeed, the parable of the Good Samaritan actually begins with this common scenario; its setting is the same road between Jericho and Jerusalem on which Jesus and His companions traveled (Luke 10:30).

A crowd of people naturally generates a great deal of noise, especially when enthusiastic about something. This occurrence is what catches the attention of the man who was blind.

37. And they told him, that Jesus of Nazareth passeth by.

The designation of *Jesus* being *of Nazareth* or as a "Nazarene" occurs about two dozen times in the New Testament—all in the four Gospels and Acts. Although Jesus was not born in Nazareth, He grew up there (Luke 2:39; 4:16, 23-24; compare Matthew 2:23). As a variant of the name *Joshua*, the name *Jesus* might have been common at that time. But there was no other person who had worked miraculously among the people—no other person who could be recognized by such a designation, as evidenced by the next verse.

38. And he cried, saying, Jesus, thou Son of David, have mercy on me.

The designation of *Jesus* as the *Son of David* reveals something that the blind man can "see" in contrast to the spiritually blind religious leaders (Matthew 22:41-46). Since the Messiah was to come from the line of David (2 Samuel 7:12-16; Psalm 89:3-4; Isaiah 11:1; Jeremiah 23:5-6; 33:17-22), He was also referred to as the "Son of David" (Luke 20:41-44). Jesus was a descendant of David because He was Joseph's adopted son, as Luke established earlier in his Gospel (Luke 3:23-38). By calling Jesus the "Son of David," the blind man showed that he recognized Jesus as the Messiah of Israel.

But even such recognition did not guarantee a complete understanding of the Messiah's role (Luke 24:19-27; Acts 1:6). It is no coincidence that Luke relates Jesus' prediction of His own death and resurrection to His 12 disciples just before this encounter with a blind man (Luke 18:31-

34). The disciples, too, had acknowledged Jesus as they traveled with and learned from Jesus for three years. Still, when Jesus warned them that He would soon die and rise again according to the Scriptures, they did not understand Him. On the other hand, the blind man did not know Jesus; in fact, he could not even see Jesus. Yet he possessed the spiritual sight to recognize that Jesus truly was the promised Messiah of Israel. (We should note that the Hebrew word translated *Messiah* and the Greek word translated *Christ* mean the same thing: "the anointed one"; see John 1:41; 4:25.)

> **What Do You Think?**
> When have you cried out to Jesus for mercy?
> **Digging Deeper**
> How did you experience His mercy?

Look-alikes

One day, when I was young, I discovered my mother and paternal grandmother looking at old photographs. With a confused look, my mom held up one picture and asked, "When did we have this picture of Laura taken?"

"That's not Laura," my grandmother answered. "That's me when I was little!" We all gathered around to see the photo. It looked so much like me that we could understand my mom's confusion. As I have grown, I have begun to look more and more like my father, who looks a lot like his mother. When people meet my dad, they comment about how much alike we look. Similarly, my youngest daughter looks a lot like my husband. I recently looked at a photo of them together and felt shocked to realize they have the same eyes, smile, and nose.

We probably assume that a person needs visual acuity for such recognitions to be made. But in today's lesson, it was a man lacking eyesight who recognized Jesus as David's son! The text doesn't say how he was able to do so. But the Bible has much to say about those who have eyes but fail to see (Matthew 13:14; Mark 4:12; 8:18; Acts 28:26). How can you ensure you have no "spiritual blind spots" in this regard? And how can you

ensure that people recognize Jesus in your life?
—L. M. W.

II. Reactions
(Luke 18:39-41)

A. Rebuke and Insistence (v. 39)

39. And they which went before rebuked him, that he should hold his peace: but he cried so much the more, Thou Son of David, have mercy on me.

The crowd attempted to quiet the blind man. Luke does not explain their reasons, but it may have to do with the way that important people were treated in the ancient world. Most people believed that those individuals who were important and famous stood above common people's concerns. The group may have thought they were paying Jesus due honor and respect by keeping someone they considered unimportant from bothering Him.

The blind man, however, showed no concern for such a social norm. Instead, he pressed *so much the more* as he called again for Jesus' mercy. Like the widow who pestered the judge in search of justice (Luke 18:1-8), the blind man ignored barriers in his way and persisted in asking Jesus for help.

What Do You Think?

In what circumstances do you find it most difficult to cry out to God?

Digging Deeper

What benefit is there in crying out anyway, even if your petition is not answered as you hoped?

B. Approach and Queries (vv. 40-41)

40. And Jesus stood, and commanded him to be brought unto him: and when he was come near, he asked him.

Based on ancient ideas of honor and the value of persons, the blind man had very little worth (see fuller explanation in Lesson Context). Thus, it is likely that the crowd didn't expect this reaction by Jesus. But Jesus was an expert at subverting expectations.

41. Saying, What wilt thou that I shall do unto thee? And he said, Lord, that I may receive my sight.

At the outset, we should realize that Jesus doesn't ask this question to correct an information deficit—to learn something that He doesn't know. He already knows what the man needs. One legitimate reason for the question is that Jesus wanted everyone present to hear the specifics of the man's request. The recovery of sight would have been a very impressive miracle, and Jesus could have wanted His audience to recognize the full impact of what was taking place.

A second possible reason for Jesus' question is that Jesus may have wanted the blind man to demonstrate faith. By stating the great problem that he had, the blind man risked embarrassment for even asking for something so bold.

What Do You Think?

Do you boldly bring your requests to the Lord? Why or why not?

Digging Deeper

How do you practice boldness in prayer while also asking that the Lord's will be done (Matthew 6:10)?

Why the Asking?

"Mommy!" the toddler cried. "What?" his mom asked. "Mommy!" he repeated. "What?" she said, a bit louder this time. This pattern continued until the child's mother came close to her son, lowered herself to look him straight in his eyes, and asked, "What do you want?"

The little boy smiled broadly, spread his arms, and wrapped them around his mother. She returned his embrace, cuddling him close until he pulled away and turned his attention to his toy truck.

I watched this with a smile, remembering my own children and the sheer number of times they called out "Mommy!" over the years. A mother's instinct is to ask what their child wants. Mom wants to meet the needs of her child and wants him to feel loved and connected. Sometimes, she knows all he wants is a hug. Sometimes, she

Son of David,
have mercy on us!

Visual for Lesson 5. *Ask volunteers to share their answers to the question associated with verse 38. Read the visual together as a prayer.*

already knows his needs, but she lets him ask nonetheless.

Jesus knew the man was blind and knew what he wanted, but Jesus asked him anyway. In so doing, Jesus empowered the man to make a bold request. How can passages such as Ephesians 6:1; Philippians 4:6; and Hebrews 4:16 empower you to be as bold? How does the caution of James 4:3 direct your boldness properly?   —L. M. W.

III. Remedy
(Luke 18:42-43)
A. The Effect of Faith (v. 42)

42a. And Jesus said unto him, Receive thy sight.

Christians have been reading this story for nearly 2,000 years, and the radical nature of this healing is less clear to us than it would have been to the original readers. There were many people in the first century who claimed to have the power to heal. Frequently, they depended on calling for the help of higher spiritual forces. Many in the ancient world believed that healing various ailments required connecting with spiritual beings. These beings held special positions in the cosmic hierarchy. To get help from these beings, one would have to know their names and perform elaborate rituals to lure them. In other words, many saw healing as a kind of magic that only beings higher up the celestial hierarchy could accomplish.

In contrast, Jesus did not summon such beings for help. He didn't ask for a heavenly creature to heal the blind man. He didn't perform any special rituals or even touch the person. Instead, Jesus simply commanded that the man *receive . . . sight.* Unlike ancient exorcists, Jesus had the power to heal others. He merely spoke, and the blind man was healed. In so doing, Jesus demonstrated power over human bodies that only the Creator of those bodies could possess.

42b. Thy faith hath saved thee.

It may be tempting to understand the man's *faith* as saving faith—the admission of one's guilt for sins and request for Jesus to be forgiven. But there is no mention of sin in this passage; Jesus does not claim that the man's sins have been forgiven (contrast Mark 2:1-12).

Instead, *faith* in this context likely refers to two related aspects of the blind man's actions. First, he rightly identified Jesus as the expected Son of David. Second and most important, he persisted in his request when everyone around him pressured him to be silent. The man rejected the pressure of the crowd and focused only on who Jesus is and what Jesus can do. He continued to ask for healing even when everyone around him wanted him to stop. The man's persistence thus showed his faith in Jesus and his trust in the Messiah's love, compassion, and power.

> **What Do You Think?**
> What difficulties arise if we assume faithful people are always healed of their maladies?
>
> **Digging Deeper**
> What biblical examples offer counterbalances to this assumption?

B. The Results of the Miracle (v. 43)

43a. And immediately he received his sight.

The power of Jesus is further shown by the speed with which the healing occurs. Jesus simply spoke the word, and *immediately,* the blind man received his sight. Unlike supposed healers among the Greeks and Romans, Jesus' commands have instantaneous results. The particular Greek word being translated "immediately" is a favorite of Luke's; 17 of the word's 19 occurrences in the New Testament occur in his Gospel and book of Acts.

43b. And followed him, glorifying God.

This result is interesting to contrast with a healing outcome in Luke 8:38-39. In that earlier passage, a healed man wanted to accompany Jesus but was refused. We see no such refusal in the passage at hand, however. The difference is attributable to the shifting context of Jesus' ministry. The episode in Luke 8 occurred outside the traditional boundaries of Israelite territory, and the timing wasn't right for Gentile outreach (Matthew 10:5-6; 15:24; Acts 1:8). The context in our lesson passage is different: Jesus is on His final trip to Jerusalem. There were likely no drawbacks for one more person to join the crowd.

43c. And all the people, when they saw it, gave praise unto God.

The shock wave of the healing sent ripples across *all the people*. And we can't help but wonder if those who *gave praise unto God* were the same ones who had tried to silence the blind man just a few minutes earlier.

This ending also sets up a surprise for the reader. One would expect that someone as powerful as Jesus would have continual victories wherever He goes. That impression is supported in the next chapter, as Jesus brings Zacchaeus the tax collector to repentance (Luke 19:1-10) and as Jesus enters Jerusalem with a crowd of people who call Him "King" (19:38). Yet Jesus had warned His disciples more than once that He would have to die and rise again (18:31-33; see also Lesson Context). The reader is thus primed to experience the shock of Jesus' death and the joy of His resurrection that follows.

What Do You Think?

What reason do you have for praising God today?

Digging Deeper

What benefit is there to inviting your community to praise with you?

Conclusion

A. Don't Stop Asking

Today's text illustrates the point on persistence that Jesus made at the beginning of Luke 18. The blind man knew that Jesus was his only hope to receive healing. The man did not heed the crowd's admonishment to be silent—quite the opposite! He did not give up. Like the persistent widow of Luke 18:1-8, he kept asking the Lord for help. The formula "faith + persistence" was (and is) powerful indeed.

Jesus' encouragement for faithful persistence remains as sure as it was when He spoke 2,000 years ago. My mother never stopped praying for my brother, despite having no support in that regard from either me or my father. She put her faith in a gracious God, trusting Him to bring her wayward son back to Him and to our family. God responded to my mother's persistence in prayer and healed our relationships. Even so, prayer is only one way by which we can demonstrate persistent faith. There are others. Can you name some?

B. Prayer

Heavenly Father, give us faithful persistence in all things related to Your Son—the promised Son of David. Strengthen our faith to serve You and the kingdom over which Jesus reigns. In Jesus' name, we pray. Amen.

C. Thought to Remember

Persistent faith is vital.

How to Say It

Bartimaeus	Bar-tih-*me*-us.
Deuteronomy	Due-ter-*ahn*-uh-me.
Jericho	*Jair*-ih-co.
Jerusalem	Juh-*roo*-suh-lem.
Leviticus	Leh-*vit*-ih-kus.
Messiah	Meh-*sigh*-uh.
Nazarene	*Naz*-uh-reen.
Nazareth	*Naz*-uh-reth.
Timaeus	Ty-*me*-us.
Zacchaeus	Zack-*key*-us.

Involvement Learning

Enhance your lesson with KJV Bible Student *(from your curriculum supplier) and the reproducible activity page (at www.standardlesson.com or in the back of the* KJV Standard Lesson Commentary Deluxe Edition*).*

Into the Lesson

At the beginning of class, ask learners to define the word *faith*. Encourage the use of dictionaries, biblical examples, or other pertinent resources. *Option.* Distribute copies of the "Defining Faith" exercise from the activity page, which you can download. Have learners work in pairs to complete as indicated before bringing the class back together.

Once the class has a working definition of *faith*, ask if *faith* might have more than one meaning or nuance depending on what or whom a person is putting faith in. One example to consider could be whether faith in a spouse is different from faith in God or one's teenager.

Lead into Bible study by saying, "Today we will see what Scripture has to teach us from a blind man who nonetheless could see that Jesus was the Son of David. The blind man's faith in the right person gave him his sight."

Into the Word

Option. Before class, ask for any eye care professionals or seeing-impaired learners to speak to the class about their insights into blindness. If you have any lawyers in the class, you can ask them to talk about the kinds of protections that the government offers for seeing-impaired people in the workplace, seeking housing, etc. Close this portion of class time by comparing and contrasting the experience of blindness in Jesus' time versus today. Use the Lesson Context as desired.

Ask three volunteers to read Luke 18:35-43 out loud as the narrator, Jesus, and the blind man. The remaining learners can read the part of the crowd together (Luke 18:37b). Then split the class into three groups: the **Jesus Group**, the **Blind Man Group**, and the **Crowd Group**. Each group should reread the passage together and then discuss this event from the perspective of Jesus, the blind man, or the crowd. Ask learners to consider what moti-

vations, knowledge, and insight seemed to be driving their individual or group to speak and act as they do.

After the groups have had time to discuss, bring the class back together and ask volunteers from the groups to summarize the perspective they analyzed. Then ask the class to compare and contrast their findings with those of the other groups. *Option.* Draw a Venn diagram with three circles on the board to keep notes.

Alternative. Distribute copies of the "Miracles in Luke" exercise from the activity page, which you can download. Give learners time to work in small groups to complete the activity as directed. Then, bring the class back together to discuss what they discovered.

After either activity, discuss as a class the significance of Jesus being called the "Son of David" (Luke 18:38-39); consult the commentary as needed to lead this conversation. Be sure to cover where this phrase originated, what expectations were attached to it, and how Jesus fulfilled or upended those expectations.

Into Life

Distribute handouts (you create) with two headers: "Like the Faithful Man" and "Like the Crowd." Give learners one minute individually to brainstorm ways they are like the man who was healed and like the crowd who saw it unfold. Then, in pairs, have learners discuss the challenges they face in faithfully calling out to Jesus, whether because of a crowd or other concerns. As a class, discuss how Jesus' identity as the Son of David can bolster our confidence in Christ.

Give learners some time for silent reflection and prayer, then break the silence with a prayer for the class. *Option.* Conclude class with an a cappella rendition of "Open My Eyes, That I May See" or another hymn or praise chorus appropriate to the lesson.

The Lord Is King

Devotional Reading: 1 Timothy 1:12-17
Background Scripture: Psalms 9, 10

Psalm 10:12-18

12 Arise, O LORD; O God, lift up thine hand. Forget not the humble.

13 Wherefore doth the wicked contemn God? He hath said in his heart, thou wilt not require it.

14 Thou hast seen it, for thou beholdest mischief and spite, to requite it with thy hand. The poor committeth himself unto thee; thou art the helper of the fatherless.

15 Break thou the arm of the wicked and the evil man. Seek out his wickedness till thou find none.

16 The LORD is King for ever and ever. The heathen are perished out of his land.

17 LORD, thou hast heard the desire of the humble. Thou wilt prepare their heart, thou wilt cause thine ear to hear.

18 To judge the fatherless and the oppressed, that the man of the earth may no more oppress.

Key Text

LORD, thou hast heard the desire of the humble. Thou wilt prepare their heart, thou wilt cause thine ear to hear —**Psalm 10:17**

A King
Forever and Ever

Lesson Aims

After participating in this lesson, each learner will be able to:

1. Summarize the psalmist's confidence in God.
2. Identify one or more imprecatory elements of the psalm.
3. Make a plan to identify and correct an area of life to rely more on God and less on self.

Lesson Outline

Introduction

A. Does God Listen?

Mark Twain once said, "Always do right. This will gratify some people and astonish the rest." Most of us desire to live with honor, courage, joy, and goodness most of the time. Sometimes we succeed. Twain was, as usual, probably too pessimistic, but his point stands. The human pursuit of the good suffers from inconsistency. We want to be good but are surprised by people who consistently are.

The Christian confession, however, is that God's pursuit of the good does not suffer in the same way. God consistently seeks the good for all creation. The search can be complicated, however, because humans are complicated. Sometimes, injustice and evil seem to prevail, and we wonder if God is. We wonder whether He hears the cries for help that vulnerable people utter.

This question carries some urgency for believers in the God of the Bible. If God is active in the world, what is that activity? Does God sit around listening to praise songs and cheering on our church growth plans or pious sermons? Or do these things sometimes offend God when they don't result in (or from) our assistance to the poor or oppressed? Today's text points us to the correct answers.

B. Lesson Context

Psalms 9 and 10 were originally a single poem. It was split apart to serve separate purposes. Ancient Hebrew manuscripts count them as two psalms, while the Greek translation of the Old Testament, the Septuagint, counts them together as one.

The entire poem falls into four roughly equally sized sections: Psalms 9:1-10; 9:11-20; 10:1-9; and 10:10-18. Each part contributes something to the overall picture as the poem moves toward a request for God's help in a world of suffering and struggle.

Psalms 9 and 10 form a partial acrostic as they use 17 letters of the 22-letter Hebrew alphabet, successively, as the lines progress. (A complete example of using all 22 letters to form the acrostic is Psalm 37.) It is unclear whether the incomplete nature of the acrostic of Psalms 9 and 10 was deliberate.

Many digital Bibles label the titles or headings of the Psalms as "verse zero." So, if you're using an electronic Bible, these headings can offer additional context or insight into the following psalm. Many psalms, however, lack a superscription, and Psalm 10 is one of those. However, the superscription of Psalm 9 applies to Psalm 10 as well, given the unitary nature of the two passages. That superscription reads, "To the chief Musician upon Muthlabben, A Psalm of David." The word *Muthlabben* refers to the death of someone, perhaps David's son Absalom. David, "the sweet psalmist of Israel" (2 Samuel 23:1), is credited as the writer of about half the 150 psalms.

I. Humanity's Evil
(Psalm 10:12-13)
A. Solution to a Problem (v. 12)

12a. Arise, O LORD.

We see here the first of three requested actions—requests that go from general to specific. See also Psalms 3:7; 9:19; 17:13; and 132:8.

12b. O God, lift up thine hand.

The sense of this requested action is a desire for divine retribution. Such a desire implies a desire for God to assume the role of the divine warrior (as in Psalm 106:26 and Isaiah 26:11). It also can paint a picture of God's ability to save (compare Psalm 17:7). But the two ideas are not mutually exclusive—the former can result in the latter.

An image of God's engaging in war is problematic to modern eyes. This is because the image can be misused to justify atrocities by some people against others. Scripture often uses this imagery to depict God's commitment to ending wrongdoing and ensuring justice (example: Isaiah 59:9-21).

12c. Forget not the humble.

We come to the third requested action—the most specific of the three. People *forget*, but God does not (Psalm 9:17-18). Therefore, this request

may seem strange, given that God always has complete mastery of all facts. Even so, the psalmist speaks similarly in several other passages (13:1; 9:12; 25:6; 42:9; 44:24; 74:19; 77:9). Suffering or a sense of isolation often results in a feeling of being forsaken (compare 22:1; 71:9-13; contrast Ezra 9:9), thus the cry of desperation.

Such cries come from *the humble*. The word being translated does not describe a person's attitude but their economic or social condition (see Psalms 9:18; 74:19, where the same word is translated as "poor"). The fact that this word occurs 31 times in the Psalms indicates its importance.

> **What Do You Think?**
> What specific request can you bring before God in prayer for those in your neighborhood or town experiencing suffering?
>
> **Digging Deeper**
> In what ways might God use you as an answer to these prayers?

Being God's Hands

Bartolomé de las Casas (1484–1566) was a clergyman who was one of the first Spanish settlers in the New World. Initially in favor of slavery, he eventually saw this to be wrong. Consequently, he dedicated his life to advocating for the rights of indigenous peoples in the Americas. Witnessing people's suffering at the hands of the Spanish conquerors, he felt compelled to act. Just as the author of Psalm 10 asks God to help the oppressed, de las Casas likely viewed himself as an instrument of God in addressing such injustices.

Consequently, de las Casas mobilized resources, recruited sympathizers, and organized relief missions to assist and support the oppressed and needy—and he spent 50 years of his life in this endeavor. God sometimes intervenes personally to make things right, but He prefers to work through people to do so (Ezekiel 22:30). How does the story of de las Casas motivate you to act as God's hands and stand up for oppressed people?　　　　　　　—O. P.

B. Problem That Needs a Solution (v. 13)

13. Wherefore doth the wicked contemn God? He hath said in his heart, thou wilt not require it.

This verse adds to the description of *the wicked* in Psalm 10:3b. The word *contemn* and the phrase *thou wilt not require it* may be hard to understand. The verb *contemn* is closely related to the familiar noun *contempt*; therefore, the idea is that of despising or disdaining God. What such a person claims *in his heart* is to be above accountability (*thou wilt not require it*). But that is never true (Genesis 9:5; Deuteronomy 18:19; Ezekiel 3:18-20; 33:6-10; Romans 3:19).

Sinful conduct toward those in need can take two general forms: active oppression (compare Isaiah 10:1-2; James 5:1-4) and benign neglect (compare Deuteronomy 15:7-8; 1 John 3:17). The care of vulnerable people does not interest the wicked—only their exploitation. Either behavior shows contempt for God (Proverbs 14:31; 17:5).

The righteous person, by contrast, fears God. He or she shows this by doing good for others, even at personal risk (example: Exodus 1:17). The wicked have gotten away with their behavior for so long that they think themselves to be immune from God's justice (contrast 2 Peter 3:9).

II. God's Awareness
(Psalm 10:14)

A. Regarding Oppressors (v. 14a)

14a. Thou hast seen it; for thou beholdest mischief and spite.

The appeal to God becomes more direct as the psalm calls God's attention to the atti-

How to Say It

Absalom	*Ab*-suh-lum.
Assyria	Uh-*sear*-ee-uh.
Babylonia	Bab-ih-*low*-nee-uh.
exegesis	ek-suh-*gee*-sus.
Muthlabben	Moot-law-bent.
Psalter	Sawl-tur.
Septuagint	Sep-*too*-ih-jent.
Zephaniah	Zef-uh-*nye*-uh.

tudes and actions of the wicked. God is aware of such behaviors and responds to them. And, just as important, the psalmist is aware of God's awareness.

The word translated *mischief* is also translated as "trouble" (Job 5:6-7), "misery" (Proverbs 31:7), and "labour" (Ecclesiastes 2:21-24). The word translated *spite* similarly has a somewhat wide range of possible meanings, including "anger" (Ecclesiastes 7:9), "grief" (Proverbs 17:25), and provocation (1 Samuel 1:6). The focus is therefore not so much on the attitudes and actions of evildoers, but rather on the results of their evil actions. Some human suffering comes about because of the actions of others, and God takes up the cause of the vulnerable.

> **What Do You Think?**
>
> In what ways are you aware of God's awareness of your attitudes and actions?
>
> **Digging Deeper**
>
> What will you do in light of that fact?

B. Regarding Outcome (v. 14b-c)

14b. To requite it with thy hand.

This clause translates as "to give with your hand." The idea is that God raises His arm to defeat the evildoers in the earlier verses, so He also uses His strength to provide for the oppressed by His hand (compare Psalm 104:28; contrast Isaiah 36:15; 37:10).

14c. The poor committeth himself unto thee; thou art the helper of the fatherless.

In the Old Testament, the people most at risk or in need are often categorized as widows, *the poor*, and *the fatherless* (examples: Isaiah 10:2; Zechariah 7:10). A fourth category used sometimes is "stranger," referring to a non-Israelite (example: Leviticus 25:35). Usually, however, only two are mentioned in the same verse, and that is the case here.

Helpless people realize that God is all they have. The psalmist takes God's care for such people as a given, a theme often occurring in Scripture (examples: Exodus 22:21-24; Isaiah 58:6-7). The descriptor of God as the "helper" of those in need frequently appears in the Old Testament (examples: Psalms 37:40; 54:4; 79:9; Isaiah 41:13-14). We must embrace God's concern for how people treat one another (Leviticus 25:35; Luke 6:27-42; etc.). Condemnation of those who neglect or exploit the vulnerable is not a lesser concern in the New Testament (Luke 16:19-31; etc.). Those who sincerely cry out to God for help will find a listening ear. Trust in God's willingness to aid defines the very heart of faith (1 Timothy 4:10).

III. God's Intervention
(Psalm 10:15)
A. Desired Retribution (v. 15a)

15a. Break thou the arm of the wicked and the evil man.

The text requests punishment for the evildoer. In seeing the phrase *break thou the arm* we might humorously think of "being disarmed" in a pun-like way. But that would be reading a modern concept into the text. Instead, we should be engaged in discerning the psalmist's original intent (a practice called *exegesis*).

We begin traveling down the road to correct exegesis when we realize that the word *arm* is not referring to a literal breaking of someone's physical arm. Instead, the word is a figure of speech for the concept of *power* (examples: Deuteronomy 4:34; 9:29; Jeremiah 27:5; 32:17). We see God's breaking of arms in just that sense in Ezekiel 30:21-24.

The image of breaking arms of the wicked also appears in Psalm 37:17. The breaking of enemies' "teeth" in Psalm 3:7 is similar. God, as a mighty warrior, is undoubtedly able to do this (Jeremiah 20:11; Zephaniah 3:17). But the image in the text at hand seems to be that of the evildoers as being like soon-to-be powerless warriors. Their arms are broken; they can no longer oppress the vulnerable.

The psalms also speak, conversely, of the need of the righteous to be brokenhearted for God to sustain and redeem (Psalms 34:18; 51:17; 69:20; 147:3). Those who have been crushed by life have a sure advocate in God. Connecting the two ideas,

we see the breaking of the arms of the wicked as God's response to the decision of the wicked not to break their hearts before God.

B. Desired Scope (v. 15b)

15b. Seek out his wickedness till thou find none.

This half-verse may seem puzzling at first. The ancient Greek version, the Septuagint (see Lesson Context), is translated as "his sin shall be sought for, and shall not be found." The idea is that God's cleansing of sin is to be so complete that there is none (zero!) left to be found. The unerring ability to discern good and evil and to assess the proper response qualifies God to be, as Abraham put it, "the Judge of all the earth" (Genesis 18:25).

IV. God's Character
(Psalm 10:16-18)
A. The One Who Reigns (v. 16)

16a. The LORD is King for ever and ever.

God's actions fall into three categories: He creates, rules, and redeems. The confession of the Lord's kingship acknowledges the second of those three. It is a significant idea in the Psalter (Psalms 93–99, especially). *The Lord is king* over the nations and peoples, whether they like it or not. God's rule should be a subject of confession and worship. The psalmist calls upon all reading or singing this text to recall that God—not the idols nor the rulers of empires—is the ultimate ruler. No other sovereign reigns *for ever and ever* (Psalms 21:4; 41:13; 45:6; 48:14; etc.).

> **What Do You Think?**
> How does the knowledge that "the Lord is King for ever and ever" influence your current behavior?
> **Digging Deeper**
> In what ways does this truth give you hope? In what ways is this truth difficult for you to accept?

Wasted Money?

Does your church waste money? Some

Lord, hear our humble cry!

Visual for Lesson 6. *Before concluding class, allow learners one minute to consider how they might humbly cry out to God for the needs of others.*

church buildings are ornate, indicating significant expenditures. The pricey artistic expressions may include depictions of Bible personalities and events via stained glass, lithographs, statuettes, iconography, architecture, etc. The faith tradition of the Greek Orthodox Church is an excellent example of this.

It's easy to criticize all this as a waste of money (compare Mark 14:4-5). The gentle response is that such works of art—many from centuries past—were (and are) ways to communicate biblical truth to disadvantaged people who were (or are) unable to read. God's kingship, such as in Psalm 10:16, is an oft-repeated theme in the various art forms. This theme is also repeated in the Scriptures because, quite simply, we need constant reminders (compare Psalms 29:10; 41:13; 45:6; 48:14; 93:2; 145:1; etc.).

The truths of God's eternal kingship, as embodied by the person and work of Christ, must be communicated (Matthew 28:19-20). What method will you use?   —O. P.

16b. The heathen are perished out of his land.

The second half of the verse says something about the future of the Israelites. Centuries after David's reign (1010–970 BC), the northern kingdom of Israel and the southern kingdom of Judah came to be dominated by a succession of massive pagan empires. First, it was Assyria, then Babylo-

nia, then Persia. This order of invasion was predicted in Deuteronomy 8:20. For *the heathen* to be *perished out of his land* reflects confidence that domination by foreign empires will end.

The psalm does not blame the Israelites' coming travails solely on those great empires. Instead, 20/20 hindsight allows us to detect a hint of repentance-to-come since that is a prerequisite for the removal of God's judgment that comes via those empires (Isaiah 7:18-25; 13:1-5, 19; etc.).

B. The One Who Hears (v. 17)

17. LORD, thou hast heard the desire of the humble, thou wilt prepare their heart, thou wilt cause thine ear to hear.

The meaning of being *humble* is explained in the commentary on Psalm 10:12, above. The verse before us gives us the opposite of Psalm 10:3, which speaks of the desires of wicked people. Other psalms witness the double-edged nature of human *desire*. Some desires are evil (Psalms 78:29-31; 106:14-15; 112:10), and some are holy (21:2; 38:9). The latter is the case in this verse.

The difference between the *heart* of the humble and that of the wicked is key. The heart of the wicked is one of disloyalty (Psalm 78:8, 37). God listens to our prayers when we offer them from a pure, undivided heart.

> **What Do You Think?**
> What steps do you take to ensure your heart does not become disloyal and wicked toward God?
>
> **Digging Deeper**
> Who is an accountability partner who can help you in this regard?

C. The One Who Rescues (v. 18)

18a. To judge the fatherless and the oppressed.

To judge means to "defend in court" or "argue on behalf of." For God to do so on behalf of *the fatherless and the oppressed* is a model for humans to do likewise (compare Psalm 82:3; Isaiah 1:17; contrast Isaiah 1:23; Jeremiah 5:28). Orphans as a vulnerable group are discussed in the commentary on Psalm 10:14c above (see also Deuteronomy 24:17). The word translated *oppressed* is somewhat rare in the Old Testament, occurring only here and in Psalms 9:9; 74:21; and Proverbs 26:28.

18b. That the man of the earth may no more oppress.

As God protects those lacking families, support systems, etc., we should see this as a model to emulate. We are to be God's hands and feet in relieving oppression.

What Do You Think?
Who are the "fatherless" and the "oppressed" in your neighborhood? in your city?

Digging Deeper
To what extent should believers advocate for using political and social systems to bring assistance to people who are victims of injustice and oppression?

Conclusion

A. The God Who Helps

People cry out to God during times of distress and count on Him to rescue them from that trouble (Psalm 30:10). We may find ourselves without any human helper in various situations as we cry out to God in our isolation and fear. We cry for help even when the distress originates in our stubbornness and sinfulness. When that happens, God sometimes turns a deaf ear to our prayers (Jeremiah 7:16; 11:14; 14:11; Lamentations 3:8, 44). At such times, we need to examine the motives of our hearts, and Psalm 10 helps us do so.

Psalm 10 speaks of the God who helps. This image of God appears frequently in the book of Psalms and elsewhere in the Bible. It is fundamental to the understanding of God that the church inherited from ancient Israel. God is neither distant nor indifferent. His level of concern for suffering humanity far exceeds our own. His interest does not ebb and flow like the fictitious pagan gods.

We may feel that God is distant when our prayers are not answered on our timetable. Such was the case with a particular Bible college professor who realized the need to make a transition in his teaching ministry. A teaching position at a different college seemed to be a good fit, but after an interview, the possibility fell through when one faculty member voted *no* for the applicant. The following year, however, the professor was called to a different position for which he was ideally suited. God's timing was perfect, but it took 20/20 hindsight to see that fact. "God's timing is perfect" is still the answer to the church's cry, "O Lord, how long?" (compare Psalms 6:3; 13:1-2; etc.).

The confession that God is a helper is an acknowledgment that leads to great confidence in our hearts. It comforts us during times of terror; it equips us to live holy lives. As the helper, God allows us to remember that no human abuse can ultimately destroy us or diminish the value of our lives (Psalm 118:6-7).

Such confidence does not come from a sense of pride or the idle belief in our superiority. It comes instead from an awareness that we serve a trustworthy God who aids those in need as long as we recognize our own needs and the shared needs of others. We cannot claim grace for ourselves but deny it to others. The divine helper stands ready to equip those seeking His mercy with a pure heart.

We cry out not only for our own needs but also on behalf of others who are oppressed in some way. However, we should anticipate that God may expect His help to that person to come through your hands!

B. Prayer

O God of the orphan, the widow, and the oppressed, attune us to the needs of Your world! Be the king of our lives and celebrate with us when the lives of our brothers and sisters flourish because of Your mercy. We humbly ask that You use us in Your work of overcoming evil. Lord, hear our humble cry! In Jesus' name. Amen.

C. Thought to Remember

God is still available to help.

Involvement Learning

Enhance your lesson with KJV Bible Student *(from your curriculum supplier) and the reproducible activity page (at www.standardlesson.com or in the back of the* KJV Standard Lesson Commentary Deluxe Edition*).*

Into the Lesson

Have this question written on the board as class members arrive:

What was a situation that most disappointed you regarding how things turned out?

Learners can begin pondering this question as they arrive. Invite responses after cautioning against using real names or situations involving your own church. As learners respond, ask them whether the disappointment included disappointment with God. (*Option.* Wait until all have responded who are inclined to do so before asking that question rhetorically.) Acknowledge the reality of emotions that accompanied the situations.

Alternative. If the above is problematic for the nature of your class, substitute the activity "Listen to Grandpa . . . or Don't?" from the activity page, which you can download. Distribute copies to study pairs or triads to complete as indicated.

After either activity, transition to Bible study by acknowledging the reality of competing ideas about "how things should be" and what action should be taken (or not taken) to achieve ideal results. Explain that Psalm 10 offers insight into such questions.

Into the Word

Ask a volunteer from the class to read Psalm 10:12-18, today's text. Then role-play a debate that is concerning this resolution, which you write on the board:

*Resolved: God-as-King has always placed
a priority on reversing the situation
of the oppressed and providing
for their needs.*

Divide the class into two groups: one to support the truth of the resolution and one to take a skeptical approach. Allow each group time to talk among themselves to discuss debate strategy and content. To help your groups start their thinking, you can distribute a "hints" handout (you create) that suggests various possibilities. Some of those possibilities include (1) the use of examples to support or oppose the resolution, (2) Paul's technique in Acts 17:16-33, where he did not quote Scripture to support his arguments, (3) the techniques of Paul's opponents in that same passage, (4) a possible misinterpretation of the psalm itself, and (5) consideration of the imprecatory (curse) elements of the psalm.

Conduct the debate in this format:

1. *Main argument(s) in favor of the resolution*
2. *Main argument(s) opposed to the resolution*
3. *Refutation(s) of the "in favor" position*
4. *Refutation(s) of the "opposed" position*

Option. If the "in favor" side has the burden of proof, reverse steps 3 and 4.

Into Life

Distribute handouts (you create) of the following *case study* involving a true story: A woman was having lunch with several colleagues at work. During the meal, she expressed an unending stream of distressing thoughts regarding her adult son, who was getting himself into financial trouble in various ways. She kept bemoaning the fact that her son wouldn't listen to her. At one point, a colleague reminded her about Jesus' instructions on not worrying but letting God handle things (referring to Matthew 6:25-34). She responded, "I'm not worried. I'm concerned." Have study pairs or triads discuss an appropriate "more God, less me" response.

Option. Distribute copies of the "Justice Begins Now . . . with Me?" exercise from the activity page as a take-home for learners to complete as indicated. To have a higher level of compliance, state that participants should be prepared to read their prayers to the class next week.

The Lord Is Majestic

Devotional Reading: Isaiah 52:1-12
Background Scripture: Psalms 47; 93

Psalm 93

1 The LORD reigneth, he is clothed with majesty; the LORD is clothed with strength, wherewith he hath girded himself. The world also is stablished, that it cannot be moved.

2 Thy throne is established of old. Thou art from everlasting.

3 The floods have lifted up, O LORD, the floods have lifted up their voice; the floods lift up their waves.

4 The LORD on high is mightier than the noise of many waters, yea, than the mighty waves of the sea.

5 Thy testimonies are very sure. Holiness becometh thine house, O LORD, for ever.

Key Text

The LORD reigneth, he is clothed with majesty; the LORD is clothed with strength, wherewith he hath girded himself. The world also is stablished, that it cannot be moved. —**Psalm 93:1**

A King
Forever and Ever

Unit 2: Our God Reigns
Lessons 6–9

Lesson Aims

After participating in this lesson, each learner will be able to:

1. Identify what God is "mightier than."

2. Compare God's actions as Creator to His actions as Ruler.

3. State which of Psalm 93's five verses speak most closely to his or her current situation and why.

Lesson Outline

Introduction
    A. Power and Authority
    B. Lesson Context
  I. God's Reign (Psalm 93:1-2)
    A. Strong and Secure (v. 1)
    B. Without Beginning (v. 2)
      Long Live the Queen
  II. God's Words (Psalm 93:3-5)
    A. Mighty in Power (vv. 3-4)
      Can You Hear Him?
    B. Great in Holiness (v. 5)
Conclusion
    A. Praise to the King!
    B. Prayer
    C. Thought to Remember

Introduction

A. Power and Authority

What images do you associate with the highest government authorities? For people in the United States, the White House, Capitol Hill, or even the Constitution might be the most powerful images. In a monarchy, perhaps the face of a king or queen comes to mind, or a palace or crown. While these images might not always have positive connotations, they are typically linked to authority and power. All these symbols of authority are meant to evoke respect and inspire confidence in a nation's citizens.

The world of the Bible had its own symbols of power and authority. Kings wore colorful robes and golden crowns. They built public monuments and enormous palaces to honor themselves and celebrate their accomplishments.

But human authorities, even good leaders, fall short of perfection. They fail, often spectacularly. Those called to protect can cause harm. In times of crisis, the symbols of authority can evoke fear and anger instead of respect and confidence. Then and now, the world longs for a new kind of authority, a different king. Psalm 93 celebrates the King we have been seeking.

B. Lesson Context

How do we describe things we have never experienced? One way is to use our imaginations to compare what we have not experienced to what we have. We gain an approximate understanding of things we have not seen by likening them to things we have seen. So it is with this psalm. We have not directly seen the glory and power of God, but we can compare God's glory and might to the glorious and powerful things we have experienced, knowing He surpasses them all. In a sense, our text is an exercise in imagination directed by God's inspiration.

This psalm uses two literary devices extensively. One is *personification*. This convention uses images and descriptions of human life to describe God. This is personification not because God is an impersonal power, but because He is not confined to human characteristics, especially not physical human characteristics. Indeed, we have not seen God. But John's Gospel reminds us that Jesus Christ, the divine, incarnate Son of God, revealed God through His real, tangible presence in the world (John 1:18). In Jesus, the Creator God has become not just near to us but one of us. In Jesus, God's majesty and power became visible among real people in a real time and place. Only in Christ's incarnation could we literally talk about, say, what God wears.

The other device used here is *parallelism*. This technique builds an image through repeating or nearly repeating one phrase or idea. Doing so strengthens the power of the description (consider Psalm 93:3, below). Understanding these features of Psalm 93 (and many others) allows us to join the worship and appreciate the beauty of Hebrew poetry, which is so different from our own and yet still powerful.

Many psalms begin with a superscription that ties the poem to a specific psalmist or occasion (examples: Psalms 3, 50, 121). These headers provide some context for the psalm at hand. The risk of misunderstanding based on vague or missing context is low; we might contrast reading a psalm with reading one of Paul's epistles. The psalms were written from personal experience, whether of praise, lament, both, or other occasions, but they were used as the hymnbook of ancient Israel. We could compare our own singing of hymns; the context for the lyrics can be powerful, but the experiences we bring to our singing are what ultimately give the song real power to speak to us as we sing to the Lord.

Psalm 93 does not contain a superscription, but it is set in a collection of kingship psalms (Psalms 93–99 or 100, with the possible exception of Psalm 94; see 93:2, below). As the phrase suggests, *kingship psalms* celebrate the king, though sometimes this might be a Davidic king and other times the Lord. Or sometimes it might be that one of the kings wrote the psalm, and so it has a kingly aspect.

There was a time in biblical scholarship when this collection was considered to be part of an enthronement festival in Jerusalem. However, many points against this hypothesis have largely

discredited the idea. For one thing, there is no biblical record of such a festival. We might expect to see such a time mentioned in Leviticus 23. Without any evidence, we have no reason to assume such a time was observed. For another, enthronement festivals in other ancient Near Eastern cultures suggested a *beginning* or *renewal* of a god's reign (compare Psalm 93:2, below). The Babylonian god Marduk was enthroned every year, for instance. God had no need of such a ceremony to renew His reign.

I. God's Reign
(Psalm 93:1-2)
A. Strong and Secure (v. 1)

1a. The Lord reigneth, he is clothed with majesty; the Lord is clothed with strength, wherewith he hath girded himself.

The Lord (with small caps) translates God's proper name, often transliterated as "Yahweh" for English speakers. This name is first recorded in Exodus 3:14, when Moses asked how to refer to the God of Abraham, Isaac, and Jacob. The Tetragrammaton (which refers to the name *Yahweh*, only four letters in Hebrew) means "I am who I am" or "I will be what I will be." The name conveys God's reliability to be himself, not fickle or changing as people or pagan gods can be.

To speak of God's clothing is to personify Him—that is, to describe Him with human characteristics even though He is not human (compare Isaiah 59:17). The descriptions here are appropriate for a king. But whereas a human king might be clothed in "fine linen" (1 Chronicles 15:27) and royal colors (Esther 8:15), God is *clothed with majesty* (compare Psalm 104:1; Isaiah 26:10) and *strength* (compare Psalms 21:1, 13;

How to Say It

Archimedes	Ar-kuh-*meed*-eez.
Gilgamesh	**Gil**-*guh*-mesh.
Marduk	*Mar*-duke.
pharaohs	*fair*-oz or *fay*-roez.
Tetragrammaton	Teh-truh-*grah*-muh-tawn.
Yahweh (*Hebrew*)	*Yah*-weh.

65:6; 105:4). God's character alone is so wonderful to perceive that no further adornment could heighten the experience. His authority in all things rests on himself, not any other trappings of power.

A belt would be *girded* around one's waist (Psalm 45:3). This accessory could hold the robe close to the body or help to gather the bottom part of the robe around and between the top of the legs, allowing free, quick movement. This special preparation for action, especially battle, is what girding oneself signified. In God's case, the action is taken on behalf of His people, to do battle for them. God needs no sword or other weapon to be armed for battle (Hosea 1:7).

What Do You Think?

Why is it important to remember that while God can be described in human terms, He is not?

Digging Deeper

What pitfalls can we avoid when we use many different ways of describing God rather than focusing on only one (e.g., King or Father)?

1b. The world also is stablished, that it cannot be moved.

Archimedes (lived about 287–212 BC) is quoted as saying, "Give me the place to stand, and I shall move the world." The mathematician was undoubtedly overly excited about how a fulcrum could be used to shift massive objects. The psalmist would beg to disagree with Archimedes.

The world does not exist on its own but was created by God. It can only be spoken of as *stablished* and immovable because of God's intention for it and His power to accomplish what He wills (compare Psalm 96:10). Should the Lord wish it, all of creation would tremble and fall to pieces. Paul touched on this while preaching in Athens (2 Peter 3:7). God expressed His contentment after He finished creating the world (Genesis 1:4, 10, 12, 18, 21, 25, 31), and it is His continuing broad concern for *all* His creation that the psalmist celebrates (example: Matthew 10:29).

B. Without Beginning (v. 2)

2. Thy throne is established of old: thou art from everlasting.

Ancient kings were fond of exaggerating the extent of their power and influence (examples: 2 Chronicles 32:10-19; Daniel 4:28-30). Many rulers, like the pharaohs, believed themselves to be direct descendants of the gods, worthy of all the honor and glory associated with that status. Maps from various ancient kingships show their own territory as the center of the world. Stories of kingly exploits suggest the king was a larger-than-life mythical hero. For instance, *The Epic of Gilgamesh* recounts the semi-mythical King Gilgamesh's exploits and quest for immortality.

God has no need for exaggeration. In keeping with the royal description in Psalm 93:1a (above), the *throne* is a symbol of a king's authority (examples: Exodus 11:5; Esther 1:2). God's throne is generally understood as being in Heaven (examples: Psalm 103:19; Ezekiel 1:26; Revelation 4), while the earth is considered His footstool (examples: Isaiah 66:1; Matthew 5:34-35; Acts 7:49). One exception to this is the ark of the covenant. As the place where God would meet the high priest, it represented God's throne on earth (Psalm 99:1; compare Exodus 25:10-22; 1 Samuel 4:4; 2 Samuel 6:2). Another possible exception is Zion (Psalm 9:11). Revelation 4 offers an awe-inspiring description of the worship around God's throne in Heaven.

This psalm does not concern itself with where the throne is or any description of it. The most important characteristic of this throne is its ancient—indeed timeless—existence (compare Psalm 55:19). There was never a time when our *everlasting* God was not King. This stands in contrast to other ancient Near Eastern gods who were enthroned by the people each year. God had no need of any human intervention to affirm His kingship.

All else that exists has a beginning, a beginning in God's creative act (John 1:1-3). All else that exists is, therefore, dependent on something else for its existence, namely, on God. But God exists forever, without cause. There can be no greater ruler. The Lord is the world's only King.

Long Live the Queen

In 2022, most Britons experienced something they never had before: the death of their monarch. Queen Elizabeth II had reigned for over 70 years when she died at age 96. For some, her death reignited questions about why Britain should be a constitutional monarchy. For others, this was the end of a glorious era. There was no succession crisis or political upheaval, but still, the people mourned for the figurehead they had lost. Her mere presence, whether appreciated or not, had been a constant for many years.

This feeling resembles the imagery of an eternal throne described in Psalm 93:2. In constitutional monarchies, the reigning monarch symbolizes stability and continuity. Similarly, while a constitution may limit their powers, the inherited position and representation of a long-standing lineage bring comfort and security to people. By drawing this analogy, we can better understand how God, who is eternal and unchanging, offers a constant source of comfort and safety for those who trust in Him. But, of course, the analogy can only go so far. God's reign will never end. In God's kingdom, there is never a question of succession or whether the king still has a vital role to play. He offers true comfort, safety, and stability to His people. How do you celebrate the reign of your King?
— O. P.

II. God's Words
(Psalm 93:3-5)
A. Mighty in Power (vv. 3-4)

3. The floods have lifted up, O LORD, the floods have lifted up their voice; the floods lift up their waves.

The people of Israel lived in an arid region. Some of their homeland was true desert, but all of it depended on seasonal rains. Most rain fell between November and March, with very little from June to September. This climate lent itself to *wadis*, a term that can refer to seasonal creeks that are sometimes dry or to small year-round brooks. In Hebrew, the word translated *floods* can refer to either variety of river (examples: Genesis 2:10, 13-14; Joshua 1:4; 2 Samuel 8:3). These wadis were prone to flash flooding and could suddenly become violent, rushing torrents, sweeping away anything in their banks. The image here is likely of a swollen, violent river in the midst of flooding. Jesus used this image in His parable of the wise and foolish builders (Matthew 7:24-27): the sand is a foolish place to build because it marks the bed of a seasonal river.

The heaping up of flood imagery (*lifted up, lifted up their voice, lift up their waves*) emphasizes the ferocity of the water. We might hear in this frightening, rising tide echoes of Noah's flood (Genesis 6–9). Far from the peaceful sound of an afternoon shower, these floods raised a cacophony.

> **What Do You Think?**
> If you were contextualizing Psalm 93 for your current hometown, what natural force might you refer to as particularly destructive?
>
> **Digging Deeper**
> Does thinking about this image in terms of your context enhance your grasp of this psalm? How, or why not?

4. The LORD on high is mightier than the noise of many waters, yea, than the mighty waves of the sea.

The imagery seems to shift from floods to *the sea*, though the concepts are used in parallel to one another, building on the same idea. For the people of Israel and others in the ancient Near East, the Mediterranean Sea was familiar, as it formed the western boundary of the promised land (examples: Exodus 23:31; Numbers 34:6). Familiarity did not breed comfort, however. Water, especially the sea in the ancient Near East, often represented chaos. The sea was powerful and unpredictable. It was home to giant creatures. Its waves and storms posed a mortal danger to those who dared to sail upon it.

Though a river might not typically evoke the same sense of danger, a *flooded* river surely would. The danger of water, whether by flooding or violent *waves of the sea*, is not *the noise* of it, though this can be greatly alarming. But compared to God's might, the *many waters* could be described with Shakespearean language: "[They are] full of sound and fury, signifying nothing" (*Macbeth*). The Lord separated the waters at the beginning, creating order where there had been only chaos (Genesis 1:1-2, 6-10). He commands the waves to be still (Psalms 65:7; 107:23-30) and stay within the boundaries He sets (Job 38:8-11; Psalm 104:7-9). Indeed, He commands the waters to sustain the creatures He has made (104:10-18), and He rules over the mighty creatures of the deep oceans (104:24-28). Little wonder that Jesus demonstrated His divine nature and power by stilling storms to protect His vulnerable disciples, or that they exclaimed in wonder that the one who stills the storm must be the Son of God (Matthew 14:33; Mark 4:35-41).

What Do You Think?

Considering how you recontextualized verse 3, how can remembering God's power over that force help you trust Him more?

Digging Deeper

How can you share this confidence with others as the psalmist shared his with us?

Can You Hear Him?

Nothing can replace the local congregation with its preaching, teaching, discipleship, and fellowship. Even so, a good podcast can be an enriching supplement. What if, instead of listening to the radio, you found a podcast of daily devotions, historical information about biblical history, or interviews with Christian leaders? You might find podcasts a valuable medium for attuning your ear to God rather than the noise of the world.

Just as the waters in Psalm 93:3 lifted up their voices, so the cacophony of our world can become overwhelming. But God's voice cuts through whatever chaos we encounter. As you navigate life's mighty waves, what helps you listen for God every day? —O. P.

B. Great in Holiness (v. 5)
5a. Thy testimonies are very sure.

We might think the final verse decisively moves away from nature to civilization. But this is a distinction the psalmist would not make. The same laws and *testimonies* that ordered the waters also created order for God's people. God's word went forth and created an ordered world (Genesis 1:1-27); God's laws taught the Israelites how to coexist both with one another and with the land that God granted them (see Deuteronomy 4:40).

Two laws regarding rest illustrate how God's care for people could also overlap significantly with His care for animals and the wider creation. Every seven years, the land was to be allowed to grow wild without cultivation. Doing so allowed the land to replenish itself through natural processes while also providing food for the poor *and* for wild animals. And on every seventh day, the people were to observe the Sabbath and rest along with any foreigners, slaves, and animals in their midst (Exodus 23:10-12).

The Lord's testimonies are not like those of unreliable humans, who often either do not know the truth or alter it to fit their own interests. God's word is not like that of human kings, who twist the truth with words to magnify their power. God's word is *sure*, firm like a huge stone, unmovable even in the greatest flood.

5b. Holiness becometh thine house, O LORD, for ever.

Like the robe and the throne (Psalm 93:1-2, above), the ancient king's *house* was intended to demonstrate the extent of his wealth and power. In Israel, Solomon's palace became legendary for its grandeur (1 Kings 7:1-12). And the physical temple that Solomon built to be the Lord's *house* was a beautiful structure (6:2-36; 8:13). The temple was not truly God's house until He filled it with His glory to such a degree that the priests could not minister there because of it (8:4-11; compare Exodus 3:5). A *house* could also refer to the family within the home (examples: Genesis 12:1; 2 Samuel 3:6).

As Solomon acknowledged at the temple's dedication (1 Kings 8:27), God's primary residence is not the temple. For that reason, it is appropriate that the psalmist did not describe God's house by its literal building materials, such as cedar or gold. Instead, it is defined by *holiness*, one of God's core attributes (Revelation 4:8). One aspect of holiness is uniqueness. When we speak of the holiness of God's people, we often talk about being "set apart" in the sense of being dedicated to following the Lord (Exodus 19:6; Ephesians 1:3-4). This includes seeking to live by His laws and grow into His likeness (see Romans 8:9).

Given the destruction of Solomon's temple in 586 BC, *for ever* cannot refer to the longevity of the temple in Jerusalem. God's throne is in Heaven, so we can appropriately consider that His home (examples: 1 Kings 22:19; Psalm 11:4). And some psalms celebrate all of creation as God's habitation (examples: 24:1; 33:5; 47:2, 7), emphasizing that no place (and no people) are outside of His concern. Those of us who follow Christ are also now God's house in a spiritual sense (1 Peter 2:4-5), as the Holy Spirit forms us into His people in the likeness of Jesus. Knowing that collectively and individually, we are His temple (1 Corinthians 3:16; 6:19), we commit ourselves to reflect His glory wherever we are, whatever we do. Wherever God chooses to reside, that place is holy.

The Lord is mightier than crashing waves.

Visual for Lesson 7. *Point to this visual as the class discusses the questions associated with verse 3.*

is. We celebrate in song and in deed the rightness of being part of God's kingdom. We express our submission to His authority by following His teaching and example, living according to His great love, especially as revealed in Jesus. We extol God's power by relying on Him to provide for us and protect us, emboldened by His Spirit to serve others as He has served us. In this, we honor our King.

> **What Do You Think?**
> What is your most surprising takeaway from studying Psalm 93?
>
> **Digging Deeper**
> How can that insight be applied in your life this week?

> **What Do You Think?**
> What emphasis does your congregation place on holiness?
>
> **Digging Deeper**
> To what degree is holiness attributed to us versus a state believers seek to attain? Provide scriptural evidence for your answer.

Conclusion

A. Praise to the King!

As we look to God as King, we recognize His powerful authority over all that He created. He is greater than any threat. Given the Lord's majestic and holy reign, how should we join the psalmist in worship? We too express our wonder at what God has done simply because of who He

B. Prayer

O Lord Almighty, You are majestic in strength and holiness. We are greatly blessed because of Your care for us and Your creation. We put our trust in You because Your reign is sure, and Your words are true. As we are reminded of Your inestimable majesty, we ask You to strengthen and guide us to live under Your reign so all may know You are the world's true king. In Jesus' name we pray. Amen.

C. Thought to Remember

The Lord reigns!

Involvement Learning

Enhance your lesson with KJV Bible Student *(from your curriculum supplier) and the reproducible activity page (at www.standardlesson.com or in the back of the* KJV Standard Lesson Commentary Deluxe Edition*).*

Into the Lesson

Challenge learners to work in pairs to write a short poem. Three suggested forms are a couplet (two rhyming lines), a haiku (three lines with 5-7-5 syllables), or a free verse (four lines with no rhyme or rhythm but with repetition or personification). *Option.* Provide a theme for learners to all focus on; love and nature are both good starting options.

Allow five minutes to work, then ask volunteers to share their poems with the group. Have them talk about their writing process. What was challenging? What benefit is there in using a poetic form to express praise to God?

Alternative 1. Bring a copy of one of your favorite short poems to class. Have a volunteer read it aloud. Invite learners to point out words, rhymes, or repetitions that stand out and explain why they are important to the poem.

Alternative 2. Ask learners to divide into two groups. One will be pro-poetry, arguing its merits. The other will be anti-poetry, arguing its deficits. Allow about 10 minutes for groups to brainstorm an opening statement, several key points, and a closing statement. After the debate, ask the class to discuss in pairs how their perception of poetry in general does or does not affect how they value poetry (like the psalms) in the Bible.

Say, "Poetry can help us see things in a new way. When we creatively play with words, we can spark other people's imagination and draw attention to, or emphasize, valuable truths they may not have considered before. Today's passage of Scripture is a poem; as you read it, pay attention to what images it brings to your mind and what truths it reminds you of."

Into the Word

Ask a volunteer to read Psalm 93 while other learners sit still and listen. Ask another volunteer to reread the psalm, but this time, allow learners to jot down any words or phrases that jump out to them. Allow a few minutes for pairs to discuss their initial reactions to this psalm.

Split the class into two groups: the **Majesty Group** and the **Strength Group**. Have both groups reread the psalm together and determine which images or phrases in the verse fit with the theme of their group, either majesty or strength. While the class works, draw a simple Venn diagram on the board (two circles with some overlap), labeling one circle "Majesty" and the other "Strength." After several minutes, bring the class back together. Ask the groups to share what images/phrases they identified with their theme. Write any shared answers between the circles. Once the groups are finished answering, discuss what overlaps (if any) they saw and what this suggests about God's majesty and strength.

Alternative. Divide the class into pairs and distribute copies of the "The Lord, the King" exercise from the activity page, which you can download. Allow time for the pairs to complete the exercise as indicated. Then, discuss their findings as a class.

Into Life

Give each learner one minute to consider Psalm 93 and find the verse from this short psalm that most resonates with him or her today. Invite volunteers to share their responses. Then, challenge each learner to brainstorm a short plan to keep this verse in mind in the week ahead. *Option.* Distribute the "My Key Verse" exercise from the activity page to be worked on individually as directed before discussing with a partner.

Ask learners what praise choruses Psalm 93 reminds them of. If you have a musically inclined class, choose a well-known chorus to sing together. Close class with a prayer praising God for His majesty and holiness.

The Lord Is Active

Devotional Reading: Isaiah 66:1-14
Background Scripture: Psalm 103

Psalm 103:1-14

1 Bless the LORD, O my soul, and all that is within me, bless his holy name.

2 Bless the LORD, O my soul, and forget not all his benefits:

3 Who forgiveth all thine iniquities; who healeth all thy diseases;

4 Who redeemeth thy life from destruction; who crowneth thee with lovingkindness and tender mercies;

5 Who satisfieth thy mouth with good things; so that thy youth is renewed like the eagle's.

6 The LORD executeth righteousness and judgment for all that are oppressed.

7 He made known his ways unto Moses, his acts unto the children of Israel.

8 The LORD is merciful and gracious, slow to anger, and plenteous in mercy.

9 He will not always chide; neither will he keep his anger for ever.

10 He hath not dealt with us after our sins, nor rewarded us according to our iniquities.

11 For as the heaven is high above the earth, so great is his mercy toward them that fear him.

12 As far as the east is from the west, so far hath he removed our transgressions from us.

13 Like as a father pitieth his children, so the LORD pitieth them that fear him.

14 For he knoweth our frame; he remembereth that we are dust.

Key Text

The LORD executeth righteousness and judgment for all that are oppressed. —**Psalm 103:6**

A King
Forever and Ever

Unit 2: Our God Reigns
Lessons 6–9

Lesson Aims

After participating in this lesson, each learner will be able to:

1. Give the reasons for praising the Lord in today's text.

2. Explain the importance of considering the history of God's work when anticipating His future work.

3. Write a prayer that celebrates God's character as the source of blessings.

Lesson Outline

Introduction

A. God's Wide Mercy

Frederick Faber was a nineteenth-century preacher, theologian, and hymn-writer. Probably his most famous hymn was "Faith of Our Fathers." Less known is his "There's a Wideness in God's Mercy." The latter hymn reminds those singing it that God's mercy is like the wideness of the sea. The lyrics connect God's love, mercy, kindness, and grace.

We may wonder how we can let others see those aspects of God's character in us in an increasingly post-Christian (or anti-Christian) culture. We wonder whether our reflection of God's merciful character traits will be interpreted as approval of ungodly behavior. We might begin to answer these questions by taking inventory of the mercies we have received as individuals and congregations. Psalm 103 will help us do so.

B. Lesson Context

The book of Psalms is often described as "ancient Israel's hymnal." Like hymnals today, the book of Psalms includes contributions by different authors and covers a wide span of time. The oldest psalm is by Moses (Psalm 90), and at least one psalm comes out of the setting of the captivity of God's people in Babylon (Psalm 137). These chronological bookends are separated by some 900 years!

About half of the psalms are attributed to King David, known as the "sweet psalmist of Israel" (2 Samuel 23:1). Today's passage is one of those psalms. While some psalms include a superscription that provides the setting (example: Psalm 51), there is no such background recorded for Psalm 103. It simply notes the association with David, who reigned about 1010–970 BC.

The Psalter is traditionally seen as falling into five sub-books, their divisions being Psalms 1–41, 42–72, 73–89, 90–106, and 107–150. Psalm 103 is located within the fourth of those five. A broad brush look at the 17 chapters of this sub-book reveals the following:

* Psalms 90–100 speak of God's role as king of the universe and ancient Israel's role in announc-

ing and celebrating His reign (examples: 93:1; 95:3; 96:6, 10; 97:1; 99:1).

* Psalms 101–106 speak of the people's responsibilities in various ways and tell Israel's story in ways that challenge complacency. Psalms 103 (today's text) and 104 fit within this grouping, as they encourage readers to continue being a community of praise.

I. Call to Worship
(Psalm 103:1-5)
A. What to Do (vv. 1-2)
1a. Bless the LORD, O my soul.

The word *bless* translates a Hebrew word that overlaps in meaning with other Hebrew words. Psalm 104:35 is particularly interesting in this regard. Its translation, "Bless thou the Lord, O my soul. Praise ye the Lord," reveals that the different words translated "bless" and "praise" overlap in meaning, following the practice of parallelism in Hebrew poetry. Reflecting that fact seems to be the intent of the psalmist.

Other words in this same grouping that reflect the imperative to *bless the Lord* include those translated "glorify" in Psalm 22:23, "magnify" and "exalt" in 34:3, and "extol" in 68:4. All speak of lifting worship to the only one who is worthy of it.

The phrase *O my soul* reveals the individualistic, personal element of the psalmist's self-challenge. We see this reflected further in the half-verse that follows.

1b. And all that is within me, bless his holy name.

The second half of verse 1 stands parallel to the first half. The parallel elements are arranged in an X-shaped pattern like this:

Bless the Lord,   O my soul

all that is within me   bless his holy name

Unlike the verse before us, the phrase "bless the Lord" repeated in the last three verses of Psalm 103 (not in today's text) is decisively plural. What

the psalmist finds appropriate for himself applies equally to his fellow Israelites. But he begins with self. A life of regular, sincere worship draws us closer to God. The fact that God's *name* is *holy* hints that we are to be so as well (compare Genesis 1:26-27; 1 Peter 1:15-16, quoting Leviticus 11:44-45; 19:2).

2a. Bless the LORD, O my soul.

The first half of this verse is identical to the first half of verse 1, just considered in both Hebrew and English.

2b. And forget not all his benefits.

The second half of verse 2 adds a negative imperative alongside the positive one of Psalm 103:1b. Worship of God includes, even requires, an accurate recall of who God is and what He has done (compare Psalm 77:11). Forgetfulness in this regard—whether intentional or otherwise—invites God's wrath (compare Deuteronomy 6:12; 9:7; Judges 3:7-8; 1 Samuel 12:9; etc.). The history of ancient Israel testifies relentlessly to the fact that forgetfulness is a precursor to sin and apostasy.

The Hebrew word translated *benefits* occurs four times in the Psalter. In the other three places, its sense is decidedly negative (Psalms 28:4; 94:2; 137:8). Putting those three negative senses alongside the positive one here, the idea is that the faithful person should remember that God sorts out the effects of human behavior, blessing those who strive toward righteousness and visiting wrath on the wicked.

> **What Do You Think?**
> How does blessing the Lord guard against forgetting what we ought to remember about Him?
> **Digging Deeper**
> What daily habits can you cultivate to bless the Lord continually?

B. Why to Do It (vv. 3-5)
3. Who forgiveth all thine iniquities; who healeth all thy diseases.

The next several verses feature a series of action verbs that describe how God relates to humanity. The psalmist begins by speaking of the completeness of God's works toward humanity as He deals with both issues of the spirit (*iniquities*) and the body (*diseases*). This combination does not necessarily argue that sin causes disease (or vice versa). God-as-healer is a major theme in the Psalter (examples: Psalms 6:2; 30:2; 107:20; 147:3).

4. Who redeemeth thy life from destruction; who crowneth thee with lovingkindness and tender mercies.

In a general, abstract sense, we want two things for our lives: (1) we want to avoid negative things that take us down, and (2) we want to embrace positive things that move us forward. The verse before us specifies that God is the key in both areas. He's not a one-dimensional god, as are the fictitious deities of paganism. The word *crowneth* also appears in the past tense in Psalm 8:5, and its cross-connection with Hebrews 2:7 is interesting and insightful.

5. Who satisfieth thy mouth with good things; so that thy youth is renewed like the eagle's.

God provides abundantly. Two extraordinary features of food are its sheer variety and the forms of enjoyment it gives when not consumed to excess (Proverbs 23:2, 21). This bounty is an important symbol of God's goodness (compare Psalm 23:5).

Various comparisons with eagles occur about two dozen times in the Old Testament. The image projected is almost always one of strength or capability (examples: Exodus 19:4; 2 Samuel 1:23; Job 39:27; Isaiah 40:31).

> **What Do You Think?**
> Which blessing in Psalm 103:3-5 is most evident in your life today?
>
> **Digging Deeper**
> If all these blessings seem lacking, can you assume you are being punished? Why or why not? Cite verses that support your answer.

II. Acknowledge Divine Grace
(Psalm 103:6-14)
A. Facts to Consider (vv. 6-10)

6. The LORD executeth righteousness and judgment for all that are oppressed.

The series of action verbs continues, extending the ideas of the two previous verses. The characteristic actions or concepts of *righteousness* and *judgment* are closely related, coupled as we see here about 50 times in the Old Testament (examples: Psalm 33:5; Isaiah 5:16; Jeremiah 9:24).

God expects the way He supports *all that are oppressed* to be a guide to how the Israelites were to do so as well (examples: Psalm 106:3; Isaiah 5:7; Jeremiah 22:3). This expectation is no less important in the New Testament era (John 16:8; Acts 24:25).

Like Father, Like Son?

A promotional video from the 1960s features a series of short sketches where a father is doing something his young son imitates. First, it's the father painting the house, with the son imitating the brush strokes. Then it's the father washing the car, with the son imitating the same. Finally, the man reaches for his pack of cigarettes to light one up. As he does so, the son reaches for the pack, and the ominous voice-over intones, "Like father, like son?"

Human fathers don't always set the best example. But our heavenly Father does! And the emphasis He puts on something determines our priorities. Consider His actions of ensuring *righteousness* and *judgment*. These aren't just idle descriptions of His character; they set an example for us to follow. In what way can you please God this week by doing so?   —R. L. N.

7a. He made known his ways unto Moses.

We come now to the conclusion of the series of action verbs begun in Psalm 103:3. What is different here is that the verbs shift from what God was doing in the psalmist's present to what God did in Israel's beginnings via *Moses*. The fact that humans lived hundreds of years before the psalmist (David) reveals God's consistency. He *made known his* unchanging *ways* in giving His law at Sinai. Those laws were to guide the path of redeemed lives.

7b. His acts unto the children of Israel.

As the second half of the verse points out, the words of the Torah are not merely words to live by. They also use *acts* by God as a model for *the children of Israel* for those requirements (examples:

Leviticus 19:2; Exodus 20:11). We have heard of people who don't "practice what they preach." That may be true of humans, but it is never true of God!

8. The LORD is merciful and gracious, slow to anger, and plenteous in mercy.

This verse deepens the psalm's connection to the story of Moses and the exodus from Egypt. The verse at hand quotes Exodus 34:6, probably the verse of the Old Testament most quoted within the Old Testament itself (examples: Nehemiah 9:17, 31; Psalm 145:8; Jonah 4:2; compare James 5:11).

In its historical context, the quoted verse comes after the notorious episode of the golden calf (Exodus 32). Moses pled for the people, asking God to forgive their idolatry and accompany them to the promised land. Thanks to Moses' intervention, God agreed to begin again with the people, as though their idolatry had never happened. By leading with patience and forgiveness, God made it possible for Israel to survive and, eventually, to flourish. And by reaffirming that great truth, the psalmist reminds the reader that the divine-human relationship rests on God's mercy, not human merit.

9. He will not always chide; neither will he keep his anger for ever.

The thoughts of this verse are also reflected in numerous other passages (compare Psalm 30:5; Isaiah 57:16; Jeremiah 3:5, 12; Micah 7:18). God's judgment of sin does not cancel out His mercy, and even times of punishment cannot be the last word (the notable exception is Jude 13).

Regarding a connection with Isaiah 57:16, that verse is part of a more extensive discussion of sin and redemption in which the prophet both notes how oppressed people can be, as well as the need for God to intervene on their behalf (Isaiah 56:9–59:21). God indeed does punish the guilty. However, He wants mercy to triumph as people repent (2 Peter 3:9). All this is reflected in the prophets' relentless message, which can be summed up in three words: *Repent!*

10. He hath not dealt with us after our sins, nor rewarded us according to our iniquities.

Once again, the parallelism that characterizes so much of Hebrew poetry is observed: the phrase

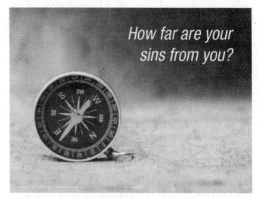

How far are your sins from you?

Visual for Lesson 8. *While discussing verse 12, ask learners to consider reasons for the psalmist's confidence that God had removed "our" transgressions.*

hath not dealt with us expresses the same thought as *rewarded us.* The phrase *after our sins* expresses the same idea as *according to our iniquities.* Good news bears repeating! This verse does just that as it summarizes the previous observations about God's mercy. The clearest evidence of that mercy is how He deals with sin: the punishment is less than the sin deserves. Were He to treat sinners immediately as we deserve, our situation would be hopeless. "If thou, Lord, shouldest mark iniquities, O Lord, who shall stand? But there is forgiveness with thee, that thou mayest be feared" (Psalm 130:3-4).

A temptation might be to think of punishment-tempered-by-mercy in terms of "striking the right balance." But we should be cautious about our conclusions here. God's two primary attributes are His *holiness* (Isaiah 6:3; Revelation 4:8) and His *love* (1 John 4:8, 16). The fact that He is utterly holy requires that our unholiness (sin) be punished; the fact that He is love results in a delay of punishment so that sinners have time to repent (2 Peter 3). Furthermore, God's unmerited kindness guides an individual toward repentance (see Romans 2:4).

It's not a "right balance" in terms of God's actions being 50 percent sin-punishing holiness and 50 percent merciful love. Rather, when viewed across the entirety of salvation-history, God's actions reveal themselves to be 100 percent in line with His holiness and 100 percent in line with His love. The requirements of both His holiness and

His love ultimately are met in the death of Jesus on the cross. When sin's penalty was paid there, the requirements of God's holiness and love were both satisfied to the full (John 3:16; Romans 3:25-26).

How God Works

I heard a loud crash from the room where my daughter was playing, and I ran to see what had happened. Entering the room, I saw her standing before a pile of rubble that had once been ceramic figurines and handmade art projects. Their shelf lay on top of them. "I don't know what happened, Mom! It just fell off the wall!" my daughter exclaimed.

As we began the clean-up process, I told her that accidents happen. And we went back to our separate activities.

A few minutes later, she emerged from the room with a contrite look. "I have to tell you something. It didn't just fall off the wall," she said. "I was jumping, and I knocked it down." While I was unhappy that my daughter had lied to me, her obvious shame and regret went to my heart; I forgave her.

We have read thus far that God is "merciful and gracious, slow to anger, and plenteous in mercy." As we repent, He forgives and does not reward us "according to our iniquities." Do you forgive as God forgives you? See Matthew 18:21-35; Ephesians 4:32; and Colossians 3:13. See also the next two verses in our text. —L. M. W.

B. Analogies to Ponder (vv. 11-14)

11-12. For as the heaven is high above the earth, so great is his mercy toward them that fear him. As far as the east is from the west, so far hath he removed our transgressions from us.

These two verses allow us to explore the concept of parallelism a bit deeper since there is more than one kind. Many instances of parallelism are easily recognizable as *synonymous parallels,* where the two lines under consideration say about the same thing using different words. That's the kind of parallelism we see in verse 10, above.

But now, we encounter what is called *alternate parallelism.* Rather than featuring the two lines of synonymous parallelism, an alternate parallel has four lines. Those four lines alternate as the third line repeats the first line in some way, and the fourth line repeats the second line. To the ancient mind, the distance between *heaven* and *earth* (the first line) is as incalculable as the distance between *east* and *west* (the third line). These two lines begin two analogies completed by the second and fourth lines as the psalmist marvels that *so great is his mercy* and that *so far hath he removed our transgressions,* respectively.

These features help us understand the text as the original writer intended. The ancient Israelites knew of the possibility of long journeys (compare Genesis 28:14; Jonah 1:1-3; etc.). But they also "knew what they did not know": there was more to encounter beyond where any Israelite had personally traveled, either to the east or the west. Likewise, the ancient Israelites knew certain things about the relationship between heaven and earth (compare Genesis 11:4; 28:12; Ecclesiastes 5:2; etc.). But again, they also "knew what they did not know," as the psalmist uses that fact to marvel at the incomprehensibility of God's removal of sin.

What Do You Think?

What role should guilt or shame play in the life of someone whose sins are so far removed?

Digging Deeper

How would you encourage someone who still struggles with these feelings after receiving God's forgiveness?

13. Like as a father pitieth his children, so the LORD pitieth them that fear him.

The Hebrew verb translated *pitieth* is also translated "have mercy" in Psalm 102:13 and "had compassion" in 2 Kings 13:23, and that is the sense here. God shows the sort of compassionate mercy to us that a good parent does to a child. Parents gently educate, correct, guide, and encourage. The image of God as *a father* also appears in the Torah (Deuteronomy 1:30-31), wisdom literature (Proverbs 3:11-12), the prophets (Malachi 3:17-18), and the New Testament (2 Corinthians 6:18). Those texts mention God's fatherhood as a way of calling the people to reconsider the direction of their lives. In Psalm 103, however, the emphasis is slightly different. Remembering that God works as a parent should comfort the reader in times of distress (compare Galatians 3:26–4:7).

What Do You Think?

What wrong ideas have you heard about what it means to fear God?

Digging Deeper

What does it mean to fear God as His children?

14. For he knoweth our frame; he remembereth that we are dust.

The Hebrew word translated *frame* occurs nine times in the Old Testament (here and in Genesis 6:5; 8:21; Deuteronomy 31:21; 1 Chronicles 28:9; 29:18; Isaiah 26:3; 29:16; Habakkuk 2:18). In six of those other passages, the word speaks of a person's frame of mind; in two passages, the idea is that of someone's physical being.

The latter would also seem to be the case here if the word *dust* is taken to be a synonymous parallel with *frame*. This conclusion is entirely consistent with the fact of the creation of humans in Genesis 2:7. There, in the word *formed,* we find the verb form of the noun *frame.* The Creator knows His creation.

Moreover, God's mercy reflects His awareness of our limits. The fact that our bodies decay into dirt results from our limited life spans. God works with due regard for our limitations.

What Do You Think?

What encouragement can you experience knowing that God remembers our limitations as creatures?

Digging Deeper

What freedom might you experience if *you* remembered our human limitations?

Conclusion
A. God Knows Us!

Psalm 103 insists that God knows us. And because of that knowledge, He is compassion-

ate toward us. This cause-and-effect may be surprising because knowledge of another person's limitations can lead to estrangement, anger, disappointment, or even hatred. Those negative consequences present themselves because of our limited commitment to virtue and capacity for love. The contrast between the consequences of our knowledge and the consequences of God's knowledge could hardly be greater.

The amazing thing is that God's mercy creates the space in which we can come to know ourselves, each other, and even God. In Psalm 103, this commitment to merciful knowledge comes out in its reference to the story of the golden calf episode in Exodus 32–34. There, both God and Moses know the Israelites to be a stubborn and sinful people. Yet that knowledge should be cast against the backdrop of years of Egyptian enslavement as they try to cope with unexpected freedoms.

Psalm 103 and the texts that undergird it point to a different approach to the life of faith than we sometimes hear. These texts anticipate that life will be filled with signs of God's mercy. How would others see such signs in you?

B. Prayer

O God of mercy, You have given us every breath we have. You have taught us to think, question, wonder, and even protest when the world does not go as You intend. Hear our prayers for Your world as You have heard them in the past. Teach us a little more daily about Your compassion for all human beings, and may we be Your hands and feet in that regard. In Jesus' name. Amen.

C. Thought to Remember

Expect signs of God's mercy.
Be one yourself.

How to Say It

Colossians	Kuh-*losh*-unz.
Deuteronomy	Due-ter-*ahn*-uh-me.
Ephesians	Ee-*fee*-zhunz.
Leviticus	Leh-*vit*-ih-kus.
Torah (*Hebrew*)	*Tor*-uh.

Involvement Learning

Enhance your lesson with KJV Bible Student *(from your curriculum supplier) and the reproducible activity page (at www.standardlesson.com or in the back of the* KJV Standard Lesson Commentary Deluxe Edition*).*

Into the Lesson

Have these two questions written on the board as learners arrive:

Who is someone you admire but you do not know personally, and who is not a public figure? What is it about that person's life that you find admirable and worth emulating?

Use these two questions to stimulate a few minutes of free discussion.

Alternative. Distribute copies of the "My Favorite Person of Action" exercise from the activity pages, which you can download. Give participants no more than one minute to complete the activity as indicated. Allow time for several volunteers to share their responses.

After either activity, say, "It is pretty easy for us to praise those people who actively do right. But how often do we do that to the exclusion of praising the Lord for His actions? Today's text may convict us in that regard."

Into the Word

Ask a volunteer to read Psalm 103:1-5. Focusing on the word *benefits* in verse 2, form small groups to (1) identify benefits mentioned in these five verses and (2) identify benefits that class members have experienced over and above those in the text.

After no more than 10 minutes, lead a whole-class discussion of the groups' conclusions. (*Option.* As a third task, challenge groups to recall a story in the Bible that demonstrates benefits in the text.)

Ask a volunteer to read Psalm 103:6-10. Assign three groups specific verses: verses 6-8, 9, and 10, one per group. Task groups to answer this question: "What does your verse or range of verses tell us about the character of God?"

Have groups summarize their thoughts in no more than three words for sharing with the class in ensuing whole-class discussion. Jot those summary words on the board under the heading *The Lord is . . .* Then lead the class in declaring these things and praising Him for them. Example: "The Lord is compassionate—praise the Lord!"

Ask a volunteer to read Psalm 103:11-14. Assign small groups or study pairs one verse each to think of additional word pictures or analogies to explain these truths to a small child.

Allow time for discussion and sharing.

Option 1. Using smartphones, have learners locate astral images taken by space telescopes. Compare and contrast the stated distance of the various stellar objects discovered. Ask learners how the psalmist might have phrased Psalm 103:11 differently had he known what we now know about astral distances. Encourage free discussion.

Option 2. Distribute copies of "The Active Lord, Doubly Described" exercise from the activity page. Announce that this simple matching exercise is a closed-Bible speed drill to be completed individually as indicated. The time limit is one minute. Assure your participants that they will score their own results, that you will not collect them, nor will you put anyone on the spot to reveal their score.

If you think your learners will need more than one minute to complete this, save it to the end of class and distribute it as a take-home.

Into Life

Refer back to the board and the benefits and characteristics of God listed there. Invite participants into a time of open prayer, in which they can express their praise to the Lord.

Encourage participants to write a prayer in the week ahead that celebrates God as the source of blessings. Ask that they bring their prayers with them to class next week so that you can share them with everyone.

The Lord Is Righteous

Devotional Reading: Hebrews 12:18-29
Background Scripture: Psalm 145

Psalm 145:1, 10-21

1 I will extol thee, my God, O king, and I will bless thy name for ever and ever.

10 All thy works shall praise thee, O Lord, and thy saints shall bless thee.

11 They shall speak of the glory of thy kingdom, and talk of thy power,

12 To make known to the sons of men his mighty acts, and the glorious majesty of his kingdom.

13 Thy kingdom is an everlasting kingdom, and thy dominion endureth throughout all generations.

14 The Lord upholdeth all that fall, and raiseth up all those that be bowed down.

15 The eyes of all wait upon thee, and thou givest them their meat in due season.

16 Thou openest thine hand, and satisfiest the desire of every living thing.

17 The Lord is righteous in all his ways, and holy in all his works.

18 The Lord is nigh unto all them that call upon him, to all that call upon him in truth.

19 He will fulfil the desire of them that fear him. He also will hear their cry, and will save them.

20 The Lord preserveth all them that love him, but all the wicked will he destroy.

21 My mouth shall speak the praise of the Lord, and let all flesh bless his holy name for ever and ever.

Key Text

Thy kingdom is an everlasting kingdom, and thy dominion endureth throughout all generations.
—**Psalm 145:13**

A King
Forever and Ever

Lesson Aims

After participating in this lesson, each learner will be able to:

1. Identify instances of Hebrew poetic parallelism in Psalm 145.

2. Explain the significance of those parallels.

3. Write a prayer that mimics the Hebrew parallelism of Psalm 145 and shares its themes.

Lesson Outline

Introduction
  A. Responding to Wonder
  B. Lesson Context
I. Praiseworthy God, Part 1 (Psalm 145:1, 10-13)
  A. What's So! (vv. 1, 10-12)
    Contagious . . . in a Good Way
  B. So What? (v. 13)
II. Compassionate God (Psalm 145:14-20)
  A. Strengthens and Provides (vv. 14-16)
    Our Generous God
  B. Willing and Able (vv. 17-20)
III. Praiseworthy God, Part 2 (Psalm 145:21)
Conclusion
  A. Psalm 145 in the Psalter
  B. Psalm 145 in Life
  C. Thought to Remember
  D. Prayer

Introduction
A. Responding to Wonder

We know of great preachers and prolific writers, but can someone be both and do them well? John Chrysostom (AD 347–407) was one who could. A tribute to his preaching skills is the second part of his name, which isn't a "last name" as we have today. Rather, the designation *Chrysostom* is a combination of two Greek words that mean "golden mouth"—an acknowledgment of the persuasiveness of his preaching.

John Chrysostom is recognized today as one of the "early church fathers" who were influential in the fourth century AD. The power of his influence was rooted not just in his preaching but also in his writings. More than 350 of his works exist today, one of which is a commentary on Psalm 145, today's text.

In that commentary, John stated, "Since you have a great Lord, be uplifted yourself and rid yourself of this world's affairs. Adopt a purpose which is superior to the lowliness of the present existence." He exhorted his audiences in Antioch and Constantinople, which included powerful political leaders, to remember the greatness of God and their smallness in comparison. Recognizing God's greatness would put their own lives into a proper context. John's counsel is just as appropriate today.

B. Lesson Context

Psalm 145, today's text, is an acrostic. That means that each line, verse, or section starts with a word that begins with a successive letter of the Hebrew alphabet, which has 22 letters. There are nine psalms that are acrostic in nature, the other eight being Psalms 10, 25, 34, 37, 9–10, 111, 112, and 119. (Psalms 9 and 10 count as one because the acrostic spans both; see discussion in lesson 6.) Other acrostics in the Bible are Proverbs 31:10-31 and the entire book of Lamentations. Regarding the latter, notice that chapters 1, 2, 4, and 5 have 22 verses each and that chapter 3 has 66 verses, which is a multiple of 22.

A sharp eye will notice that Psalm 145 has only 21 verses. So why the mismatch with the

22-letter Hebrew alphabet? It comes down to an uncertainty in the ancient manuscripts. In most of those manuscripts, Psalm 145:13 lacks a line of text that would have included the absent Hebrew letter. This was noticed in antiquity, and the ancient Greek translation of the Bible, known as the Septuagint (translated at least 200 years before Christ), includes an extra line between verses 13 and 14; see more on this in the commentary below.

Last week's lesson noted that the 150 chapters of the Psalms are traditionally seen as a collection of five sub-books. Within the fifth of those sub-books, Psalm 145 is the final chapter before the extended coda of Psalms 146–150 begins.

I. Praiseworthy God, Part 1
(Psalm 145:1, 10-13)

A. What's So! (vv. 1, 10-12)

1. I will extol thee, my God, O king, and I will bless thy name for ever and ever.

Other lessons from the Psalms this quarter have introduced us to *parallelism* as a feature of Hebrew poetry. We saw last week in Psalm 103:1 that there are various synonyms or near-synonyms that express the concept of *bless*. That fact continues to hold true here in Psalm 145:1, as we see the words *extol* and *bless* alongside the words *bless* and *praise* in the verse that follows (which is not included in today's lesson text). See also Psalm 34:1.

The psalm's opening phrase *I will extol thee* is repeated exactly in the original language, in Psalm 30:1. A slight divergence between the two texts is seen in the next phrase: the text we are studying is directed toward *my God, O king*, while 30:1 has "O Lord." They are clearly one and the same!

God's actions can be categorized in three ways: He creates, rules, and redeems. In proclaiming

How to Say It

Antioch	An-tee-ock.
Corinthians	Ko-rin-thee-unz (th as in thin).
Habakkuk	Huh-back-kuk.
Septuagint	Sep-too-ih-jent.

God as his king, the psalmist acknowledges the second of those three. The psalmist invites the reader to consider God's character as good and powerful in that regard.

> **What Do You Think?**
> What do psalms in general teach you about exalting the Lord as king?
> **Digging Deeper**
> What actions take our exaltation of God out of the realm of mere words?

10. All thy works shall praise thee, O Lord, and thy saints shall bless thee.

The phrase *all thy works* expands the scope beyond merely Israel and the entirety of humankind to encompass the inanimate elements of creation. The praise of God concerns all aspects of the universe (see Psalms 8 and 19). The *saints* are those who live in solidarity with both God and other people. They see themselves as carrying a responsibility for others, owing others respect, care, and concern shown in tangible actions. Those who live in such a way find room for praising God, even during difficult times, and those sincerely praising God have no problem being loyal to other people.

Contagious . . . in a Good Way

Rome's Sistine Chapel is celebrated for its awe-inspiring frescoes, painted by the famous artist Michelangelo (1475–1564). This grand structure embodies the theme of praise and exaltation of God through various visual images. The chapel's architecture, characterized by its attention to detail, exudes a sense of the magnificence and grandeur of God. Visitors can't help but be caught up in the motifs that overwhelm the senses—it's contagious!

We may say the same about David's intent when he wrote Psalm 145. Does it have that effect on you? If not, why?   —O. P.

11-12. They shall speak of the glory of thy kingdom, and talk of thy power. To make known to the sons of men his mighty acts, and the glorious majesty of his kingdom.

We group these two verses because they

illustrate an X-shaped parallel construction similar to what we saw in last week's lesson. It is visualized this way:

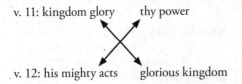

v. 11: kingdom glory   thy power

v. 12: his mighty acts   glorious kingdom

Glory is an attribute belonging to God (see Exodus 16:7; Deuteronomy 5:24; John 17:5). By extension, it also belongs to His *kingdom*. But we may ask ourselves, *Who can be in this glorious kingdom besides God?* In one sense, only those included in "the saints" of the previous verse are or will be kingdom-citizens (compare Philippians 3:20; etc.). In a broader sense, however, we see this declaration in Psalm 103:19: "The Lord hath prepared his throne in the heavens; and his kingdom ruleth over all." There is only one ultimate king, and the rule of His kingdom is not limited. Satan has his own kingdom (Matthew 12:26), but in the end, it is temporary. People, both ancient and modern, also set themselves on the thrones of their hearts to be self-kingdoms or kingdoms-of-one; that is folly as well (Isaiah 14:13-15; Daniel 4:28-32; Ezekiel 28:2-3; etc.).

God's all-encompassing kingdom does not equate to a human political structure (see John 18:36). Even so, we humans have God-ordained roles to play in it. One of those roles is found in the phrases *they shall speak . . . and talk.* This speaking and talking isn't aimless chatter; rather, it aims to make God and His kingdom known to others. We don't talk about God's kingdom only amongst ourselves. We make His kingdom known to the whole world.

Verse 12 largely restates verse 11—that's the nature of this X-shaped parallel. But verse 12 clarifies the subject of the faithful people's communication: they should speak of God's specific deeds, as in the recital of the saving acts of the exodus in Psalms 78, 105, and 136. The people also are to speak of God's work in their personal lives, as do many psalms of praise. The *mighty acts* keep occurring because God's mercy never ceases.

B. So What? (v. 13)

13. Thy kingdom is an everlasting kingdom, and thy dominion endureth throughout all generations.

The psalmist understood that God's rule extends beyond any given moment or era. The New Testament writers understood this as well (1 Timothy 1:17; 2 Peter 1:11). While all earthly things pass away, God's merciful concern for His creation does not.

The Lesson Context above mentions that a small text may have shifted elsewhere in the ancient manuscripts, leaving the acrostic of this poetry one letter short in the Hebrew alphabet. Right here is where the line would be placed. The ancient Greek version (the Septuagint) does indeed include that segment. It reads, "The Lord is faithful in his words, and holy in all his works."

II. Compassionate God
(Psalm 145:14-20)

A. Strengthens and Provides (vv. 14-16)

14. The Lord upholdeth all that fall, and raiseth up all those that be bowed down.

Parallelism in thoughts continues. Even so, this verse shows extra poetic creativity. The original words translated *upholdeth* and *fall* are quite common in the Old Testament in general and the Psalms in particular. By contrast, the word translated *raiseth up* is rare, occurring only here and in Psalm 146:8 in the entire Old Testament.

But the primary challenge concerns the word translated *bowed down,* which is found only here and in Psalm 148:6; Isaiah 57:6; 58:5; and Micah 6:6. Reading all the texts that have "bowed down" reveals that the word doesn't have the same meaning in all contexts. There seem to be two possibilities: it refers to great distress or a posture of worship. Which of these does the writer of Psalm 145 intend? Is the one "bowed down" humbled by negative life experiences, or does the person seek to worship God?

A third possibility is that the ambiguity is deliberate, with the psalm pointing us to both meanings being intended. In that case, the message would be that whatever experiences bring us humbly to God will result in our ultimate benefit.

15-16. The eyes of all wait upon thee, and thou givest them their meat in due season. Thou openest thine hand, and satisfiest the desire of every living thing.

The parallelism continues as these two verses make essentially the same point but in different ways. The psalmist describes worshippers almost as children waiting for a parent to give them something they need. They recognize that all people, indeed *every living thing*, depend on God similarly. That is true even if not everyone recognizes it as truth. God graciously feeds all. This idea underlies Jesus' statement that it rains on the just and unjust alike, with both benefiting from the life-giving things God bestows on them (see Matthew 5:45).

Meat refers to food in general, which God provides in due time. The text does not promise wealth, and a spiritually mature person would not expect God to be a purveyor of such. But God does give us what we need (compare Psalms 104:27-28; 136:25). To open the *hand* implies giving a gift. God's gifts may go beyond the bare essentials to things that bring appropriate forms of pleasure.

> **What Do You Think?**
> In times of scarcity, what gives you confidence to wait for God's timing for provision?
> **Digging Deeper**
> When would it be appropriate to reference this verse to someone experiencing a great need? What action might also be required?

Our Generous God

Heavy rainfall throughout the year plays a vital role in the ecosystem of the Amazon Rainforest. The average amount varies depending on the location within that jungle, but 100 inches is not uncommon. Think about that: 100 inches is over 8 feet of water! The health of this ecosystem is thought to interact with other ecosystems throughout the world in various ways.

We live in a fallen world, with deprivation and lack resulting from sin—sometimes in general, sometimes specifically (examples: Joshua 7:10-12; Haggai 1:1-11). But even in times of deprivation, God *wants* to be generous. What might you be doing to stand in the way of God's generosity?
—O. P.

B. Willing and Able (vv. 17-20)

17. The LORD is righteous in all his ways, and holy in all his works.

This verse is worded very similarly to the "missing" part of Psalm 145:13, discussed above.

The phrase *all his ways,* which parallels *all his works,* includes the generosity of the previous verse. The word translated *holy* occurs about 50 times in the Old Testament, but almost always, it refers to godly people. It refers to a characteristic of God in no more than a half dozen places, and this is one of them. Throughout history, those who have questioned God's righteousness or justice have discovered that this is an area where humanity lacks, not God (examples: Job 38–41; Ezekiel 18:25-29; Habakkuk 1–2).

> **What Do You Think?**
> What psalms can give you voice if God doesn't seem to be acting at all?
> **Digging Deeper**
> What gives you confidence in God's holiness and righteousness in the face of the evils in the world?

18. The LORD is nigh unto all them that call upon him, to all that call upon him in truth.

Psalms of lament often express regret that God seems so far away, and they request God's tangible presence (examples: Psalms 22:11, 19; 35:22; 38:21; 71:12). On the other hand, there are biblical cases where people do *not* desire God's nearness (compare Jonah 1:3; Revelation 6:15-17; etc.). But here, it would be helpful to see a distinction between the two senses of the near/far issue. We might call one sense "literal nearness" and the other "spiritual nearness." The fact of God's presence and activity within the world is summed up in the word *immanence*; we are in the presence of

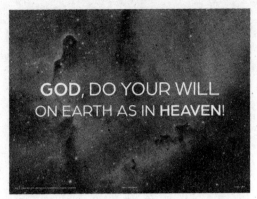

Visual for Lessons 9 & 10. *Ask learners to pair up to discuss how today's lesson reveals what God's will is in the world.*

the immanent God at all times—and note that this is not the word *imminent* (Jeremiah 23:23-24; Acts 17:27-28). That's the literal nearness.

But in another sense of near/far, the fact of God's holiness results in His ethical distance from sinners; the more that people engage in unholiness, the more they are spiritually separated from the holy God. Jesus experienced this kind of separation as He took humanity's penalty for sin upon himself while dying on the cross (Matthew 27:46; Mark 15:34 [both quoting Psalm 22:1]). In so doing, Jesus solved the distance problem between God and humanity (compare Isaiah 55:6-7).

> **What Do You Think?**
> How do circumstances affect your sense of God's presence?
>
> **Digging Deeper**
> Does God's literal nearness comfort you even when He feels far away? Why or why not?

19. He will fulfil the desire of them that fear him. He also will hear their cry, and will save them.

The second part of this verse clarifies the first part since God does not fulfill each and every imaginable *desire* that people have. The most striking example of God's hearing a *cry* and effecting deliverance is the exodus from Egypt (Exodus 3:7-10; 14:30).

The promise *will save them* can be understood in two senses in the various places it is used: it can mean rescue from a physical threat or from a spiritual threat of unholiness. Sometimes, the two senses are both present if rescue from a physical threat accompanies rescue from a spiritual threat (compare Ezekiel 37:23; Hosea 1:7).

We know from modern experience and Bible history that God does not always deliver godly people from the loss of their physical life; sometimes, His larger plans include such deaths—and those deaths are temporary, given the promise of our resurrection (Daniel 12:2; 1 Corinthians 15). But He is always ready, willing, and able to deliver us from spiritual threats (1 Corinthians 10:13).

Many psalms of lament (also called prayers for help) explore the apparent gap between human need and divine response. This psalm, however, does not explore that set of issues. It remains at the level of generalized praise. Whatever we may face in this life, God's final word will be one of salvation and healing.

20a. The LORD preserveth all them that love him.

Psalms 31:23; 91:14; and 97:10 also reflect the reality of this praise thought. *Preserveth* carries the idea of "protection." The wording in the original Hebrew of the phrase *them that love him* is also translated "his friends" in Esther 5:10, 14; 6:13. Those who love God rejoice (Psalm 5:11) because of repeated acts of goodness toward them (119:132).

20b. But all the wicked will he destroy.

Psalm 94:23 is similar. In contrast to the experience of those who love God, *the wicked* can expect a terrible fate. This statement confesses a general truth, though the psalms also know a great deal about forgiveness of sins. The wicked are those who refuse to repent while deliberately pursuing the harm of others (compare Psalm 10:2-11).

III. Praiseworthy God, Part 2
(Psalm 145:21)

21. My mouth shall speak the praise of the LORD, and let all flesh bless his holy name for ever and ever.

The psalm concludes, as many do, with a promise to praise God. This personal commitment by the one praying this psalm also extends to others (*all flesh*). The psalmist hopes that all beings capable of praise, especially humans but not necessarily limited to them, will acknowledge the rightness of God's good reputation for saving works and do so in perpetuity (*for ever and ever*). This phrasing serves as an appropriate "bookend" to the psalm, with the first of the two bookends occurring in the opening verse of our lesson today.

What Do You Think?

How do you address any disparity in your life between speaking God's praise and living out that praise?

Digging Deeper

What stories serve as examples to guide both your words and deeds of praise?

Conclusion

A. Psalm 145 in the Psalter

On a first reading, Psalm 145 may seem to lack the emotional intensity and attention to life's struggles that appear in many other psalms. It may appear to be a collection of general truths or even platitudes about the life of faith. Such platitudes do not stand up to the challenge of life, and so the psalm may appear less substantial than others.

It is better, however, not to read this psalm alone but to recall its function in the overall book. The book of Psalms contains both prayers for help and prayers of thanksgiving. Early in the book, laments or prayers for help overwhelmingly predominate, but as the book goes along, the balance changes in favor of hymns of praise. The concluding five psalms are loud, exuberant songs praising God. Psalm 145 is closely connected to them. In other words, if we consider the book as a whole, we see it move from times of distress, during which we call out to God for help, to times of rejoicing over God's saving works. That same shift appears in many individual psalms that begin with lament and end with a promise to praise. In other words, the organization of the book tries to move its readers along the spiritual road to greater confidence in

God's mercy. Psalm 145 marks the conclusion of that movement. When understood this way, Psalm 145 is much more than a bundle of clichés.

B. Psalm 145 in Life

Psalm 145 celebrates the permanent nature of God's kingdom and His work in the lives of people. It reminds anyone singing it that God aims at the highest and best possible things, including the best possible outcomes for our lives. God desires that we be saved and rescued from all the manifestations of sin and death in this world and the next. God has communicated that desire through the prophets and apostles, and most fully through the life and teachings of Jesus Christ. Awareness of that communication leads to a life filled with wonder and practical attention to spiritual and moral growth.

It is not easy to adopt a superior purpose when we are trying to live our best life now. The superior purpose calls upon us to reexamine ourselves and reform aspects of our lives. We refine our values, redirect our affections, and reshape our behaviors in the direction of God. Even our language becomes infused with grace and mercy, as God's is. To give up on the possibility of growth is to lose hope itself.

The wonder of God's love for us compels us to rise above the passions of the moment toward the splendor that awaits us in God's presence. This psalm points us to that splendor as it celebrates the compassion and beauty of God as it challenges us to pursue noble causes rather than short-term goals of pleasure or power.

C. Prayer

Heavenly Father, we praise You even though our best praise falls short. Help us to become people of the truth, who state our amazement at Your goodness and kindness to us. Accept our words of praise and gratitude because they are the only things we can give You that matter. In Jesus' name. Amen.

D. Thought to Remember

Make your acts of praise and worship contagious!

Involvement Learning

Enhance your lesson with KJV Bible Student *(from your curriculum supplier) and the reproducible activity page (at www.standardlesson.com or in the back of the* KJV Standard Lesson Commentary Deluxe Edition*).*

Into the Lesson

Distribute blank index cards. Have each participant write on a card something in this world that lasts a long time. Then, have participants share their cards with one another and rank-order them in chronological length. Then ask, "How long do you think the longest thing in the arrangement of cards will last, and why?" Discuss.

Alternative. Distribute copies of the "Yesterday, Today, and Forever" exercise from the activity page, which you can download. Allow one minute to complete as indicated. Ask, "How many of your 'always' statements are really true? What would life look like if they were all true?" Give opportunities for participants to discuss.

Make a transition as you say, "Things of earth do not stay the same forever. But in today's lesson, pay attention to that which is praised for being eternal and constant."

Into the Word

Have Psalm 145:1, 10-12 read aloud in the following way. Divide the class into three parts: one individual (designated **Personal**), a group of three (designated **Corporate**), and the rest of the class (designated **Universal**). Arrange participants so that the **Corporate** is surrounding and facing the **Personal**, and the **Universal** is surrounding and facing the **Corporate**.

Have **Personal** read verse 1 aloud alone, emphasizing the words *I* and *my*. Have **Corporate** join **Personal** to read verse 10 together, emphasizing *all* and *saints*. Then, have **Corporate** turn around to face **Universal** and read verse 11. Finally, have **Universal** join in with **Personal** and **Corporate** to read verse 12 together.

Follow this reading by inviting participants to discuss the distinctive benefits of personal, corporate, and universal worship of God. What are the advantages and limitations of each? This can be a small-group exercise.

Option. Use a role-play debate among the three reading groups to argue that its own format is the "best" among the three.

Ask a volunteer to read Psalm 145:13-17. Instruct participants to listen for all instances of the words *all*, *every*, and *everlasting*. Write the phrases on the board as they are spoken. Invite participants to identify what strikes them as especially powerful, and why. (*Recommended*: create your own "cheat sheet" ahead of time with correct responses to ensure that none are missed.)

Ask a volunteer to read Psalm 145:18-21. Divide participants into four groups and assign these verses, one per group: Matthew 11:28; Luke 9:23; John 3:18; and Revelation 3:20. Instruct them to discuss how their assigned verse relates to Psalm 145:18-21. Write this question on the board: "How would you describe the relationship that God calls people toward?" Allow time for ensuing whole-class discussion.

Option. Distribute the envelopes you have prepared before class per the instructions on the "He Does, We Do" facilitator exercise (it's on the activity page that you can download). Instruct participants to match the first and second parts of the verses as quickly as possible. *This is a closed-Bible speed drill!*

Into Life

Use the Lesson Context to explain the nature of Psalm 145 as an acrostic poem, with every verse or line beginning with a successive letter of the Hebrew alphabet. Say, "We're going to try doing the same with the English alphabet."

Assign each learner one or more letters of the alphabet. Distribute index cards on which participants are to write one word or short phrase that begins with their assigned letter(s) to describe an attribute of the Lord. Participants are not to write their names on the cards as you collect them. Read cards aloud.

Praying Properly

Devotional Reading: Psalm 4
Background Scripture: Matthew 6:5-15

Matthew 6:5-15

5 And when thou prayest, thou shalt not be as the hypocrites are, for they love to pray standing in the synagogues and in the corners of the streets, that they may be seen of men. Verily I say unto you, they have their reward.

6 But thou, when thou prayest, enter into thy closet, and when thou hast shut thy door, pray to thy Father which is in secret, and thy Father which seeth in secret shall reward thee openly.

7 But when ye pray, use not vain repetitions, as the heathen do, for they think that they shall be heard for their much speaking.

8 Be not ye therefore like unto them, for your Father knoweth what things ye have need of, before ye ask him.

9 After this manner therefore pray ye: Our Father which art in heaven, hallowed be thy name.

10 Thy kingdom come. Thy will be done in earth, as it is in heaven.

11 Give us this day our daily bread.

12 And forgive us our debts, as we forgive our debtors.

13 And lead us not into temptation, but deliver us from evil. For thine is the kingdom, and the power, and the glory, for ever. Amen.

14 For if ye forgive men their trespasses, your heavenly Father will also forgive you.

15 But if ye forgive not men their trespasses, neither will your Father forgive your trespasses.

Key Text

Thy kingdom come. Thy will be done in earth, as it is in heaven. —**Matthew 6:10**

A King
Forever and Ever

Unit 3: Life in God's Kingdom
Lessons 10–13

Lesson Aims

After participating in this lesson, each learner will be able to:

1. List Jesus' key teachings about prayer in Matthew 6:5-15.

2. Explain the purpose(s) of the prayer's four couplets.

3. Resolve to devote more prayer time to one area identified in Matthew 6:5-15 that may currently be lacking.

Lesson Outline

Introduction
   A. Hallowed, Not Hallows
   B. Lesson Context
I. Directives for Prayer (Matthew 6:5-8)
   A. For Public Praise (v. 5)
   B. In Personal Privacy (v. 6)
   C. Without Prattle (v. 7)
   D. With Purpose (v. 8)
II. The Prototypical Prayer (Matthew 6:9-13)
   A. Proper Address (v. 9)
   B. Proper Alignment (v. 10)
   C. Proper Asking (vv. 11-13)
      Daily Bread
      The Right Source
III. Addendum on Forgiveness (Matthew 6:14-15)
Conclusion
   A. Sincere Petitions or Mere Repetitions?
   B. Prayer
   C. Thought to Remember

Introduction
A. Hallowed, Not Hallows

The seventh and final book in the Harry Potter series is *Harry Potter and the Deathly Hallows*. These "hallows" are three magical objects central to the final plot of the story. When I first saw the title of this last book, the word *hallows* lit up one thing in my mind (as it did for many people): the unusual phrase from the Lord's Prayer, "Hallowed be thy name." To be sure, the hallows of Harry Potter and the "hallowed" of the Lord's Prayer are unrelated. But what do we mean when we say, "Hallowed be thy name"? That is one topic of today's lesson.

B. Lesson Context

One of the things we know about Jesus is that He was a man of prayer. He would rise early in the morning so He could spend time alone in prayer (example: Mark 1:35). On at least one occasion, He spent all night in prayer (Luke 6:12). When Jesus knew His death was close at hand, He spent a significant portion of His final evening praying in the Garden of Gethsemane (Matthew 26:36-43).

What we call "the Lord's Prayer" is found in Matthew 6:9-13, with a shorter version in Luke 11:2-4. That title can be misleading because there's no record that Jesus himself prayed this prayer. Instead, these were guidelines given by Jesus to others about how they should pray.

Matthew's version is recorded as being part of the famed Sermon on the Mount (Matthew 5:1–7:29). The version in Luke arises from a request by one of the disciples in Luke 11:1. We can safely assume that Jesus' disciples were already men of prayer, but they wanted to pray more effectively.

The disciples' interest in learning about prayer was sparked by their awareness that John the Baptist had taught his own followers the correct way to pray (Luke 11:1). While we don't have any of John the Baptist's prayers, we do have examples of Jesus' prayers (example: John 17:1-26, which consists of a lengthy prayer given by Jesus in the upper room during the Last Supper).

The church tends to use the Lord's Prayer from Matthew more often because it is more detailed than the wording in Luke's Gospel. It has long been considered one of the church's treasures, perhaps the most famous prayer in history. In some traditions, it is referred to as "the Our Father," reflecting its opening phrase. A similar version of this calls the prayer the *Paternoster*, Latin for "Our Father." An early manual on Christian practices called the *Didache* includes Matthew's version of the prayer with the instructions that it should be prayed three times a day (*Didache* 8).

Matthew's version of the Lord's Prayer has a multi-part address to God, several petitions or requests, and a concluding acknowledgment of God's sovereignty. We notice the value of the prayer when we contrast it with the ways one should *not* pray. That's where today's study begins.

I. Directives for Prayer
(Matthew 6:5-8)
A. For Public Praise (v. 5)

5. And when thou prayest, thou shalt not be as the hypocrites are, for they love to pray standing in the synagogues and in the corners of the streets, that they may be seen of men. Verily I say unto you, they have their reward.

Before the time of Jesus, the word *hypocrite* was used to describe actors on the stage, people who pretended to be what they were not. That is Jesus' point: some people are respected for their devotion to God, but they are not devoted to God at all. Instead, they want other people's attention and approval.

Matthew records the use of the word *hypocrite(s)* 15 times, Mark once, and Luke four times—all 20 on the lips of Jesus. In Matthew 6, Jesus gives three contexts for such wrong-hearted behavior: giving for the relief of the poor (Matthew 6:2), praying in public (6:5, today's text), and fasting (6:16). Jesus did not condemn the practices of giving, public prayer, or fasting as such; instead, He was condemning self-seeking motives behind them.

Jesus' hearers would have recognized this type of person from their own experiences, particularly on trips to Jerusalem (compare Luke 18:9-

14). Some may have even recognized themselves in this description. Jesus pronounced that such phony people *have their reward:* the short-lived admiration of others, not the eternal recognition of God. This is the wrong way to pray.

B. In Personal Privacy (v. 6)

6. But thou, when thou prayest, enter into thy closet, and when thou hast shut thy door, pray to thy Father which is in secret, and thy Father which seeth in secret shall reward thee openly.

Rather than make a public performance of prayer, Jesus stressed the need to retreat to a private place. Note again that the issue is not "private prayer" versus "public prayer" as such. Instead, it's an issue of "private prayer" versus "public performance." Jesus wasn't stressing *where* a person prayed, but *why*. A valid prayer is directed to God alone and is not concerned with whether others notice.

> **What Do You Think?**
> How can believers exercise humility in their spiritual actions while also expressing boldness to be a witness for Jesus when the opportunity arises?
> **Digging Deeper**
> In what ways does the example of Daniel in Daniel 6:10 inform your response?

C. Without Prattle (v. 7)

7. But when ye pray, use not vain repetitions, as the heathen do, for they think that they shall be heard for their much speaking.

Jesus' mention of the excesses of hypocritical, performative praying suggests its practice in His day. Prayers of this nature are no better than prayers of *the heathen*. In the cultures surrounding Israel in Jesus' time, the "gods" were often considered unpredictable and selfish, like powerful human rulers. Praying to such gods was a matter of begging them not to harm us or nagging them for a gift. Further, many pagans thought of their gods less as personal beings and more like unseen forces that could be manipulated.

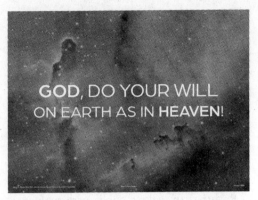

GOD, DO YOUR WILL
ON EARTH AS IN HEAVEN!

Visual for Lessons 9 & 10. *Have this visual on display as you conclude class by praying the Lord's Prayer together.*

For pagans, prayer was a matter of saying certain words and phrases that were thought to have the power to make those forces bend to one's will. In either case, such prayer involved *vain repetitions*—of saying the same thing repeatedly. We consider Elijah's confrontation with the priests of Baal on Mt. Carmel. There, Elijah sarcastically encouraged them to pray more and louder because their god might be asleep (1 Kings 18:25-29).

D. With Purpose (v. 8)

8. Be not ye therefore like unto them, for your Father knoweth what things ye have need of, before ye ask him.

Next, Jesus informed His hearers of an important "given" that should undergird all prayers: our heavenly *Father* knows our needs before we even pray to Him. We are not telling Him anything He doesn't already know. This does not mean we should not ask or that we should assume prayer is unnecessary. Prayer reflects the measure of the faith we have in the fact that God does indeed listen (James 1:6; 5:15).

II. The Prototypical Prayer
(Matthew 6:9-13)
A. Proper Address (v. 9)
9a. After this manner therefore pray ye.

A cup of coffee consists of two things: the cup that holds the coffee (the "form") and the coffee itself (the "content"). Prayer also has a form and content. We have discussed the *form*; we now move to prayer's *content*.

9b. Our Father.

This establishes the prayer's recipient (see Lesson Context). Unless you know to whom you are praying, your prayers may be pointless at best and a violation of Exodus 20:3 at worst (compare Isaiah 45:20b). By definition, *prayer* is a conversation with the God of all creation. As Christians, we do not launch our prayers into the void, hoping that someone will be listening. Instead, we pray in faith, addressing the one true God who creates, rules, and redeems.

Jesus teaches us to address God in two ways. Beginning our prayer with *Our Father* is to acknowledge that very fact. During Jesus' time, Jewish people had various terms to describe God, but this specific description was rarely used. God as Father appears less than a dozen times in the Old Testament (Deuteronomy 32:6; Psalm 89:26; Isaiah 9:6; 63:16 [twice]; 64:8; Jeremiah 3:4, 19; Malachi 2:10). By contrast, the Gospel of Matthew alone use the terms "heavenly Father" and "Father in heaven" more than 40 times.

9c. Which art in heaven.

Continuing from above, we come to the second part of properly addressing God. We might ask, Where is *heaven*? Heaven is where God is, and we are barely able to scratch the surface in understanding that (compare and contrast 2 Corinthians 12:2). Yet there is an important truth for us in Jesus' words: God is the "God of heaven," a phrase used about two dozen times in the Bible, all but two of which occur in the Old Testament (examples: Ezra 1:2; 5:11-12; compare Revelation 11:13; 16:11). He is not part of the physical, created universe. God is separate. We are on earth; God is in Heaven (Ecclesiastes 5:2). Even so, we mortals are privileged to speak with the God of Heaven (Hebrews 4:16).

9d. Hallowed be thy name.

Following the issue of how to address God, Jesus instructs on the proper way of thinking about God. The word *hallowed* speaks to the issue of God's holiness. When we pray *hallowed be thy name,* we are saying, in effect, "May your name be holy." This is a commitment to honor the third commandment: "Thou shalt not take the name of the Lord thy God in vain" (Exodus 20:7). But it's more than just being correct at *not* doing something; there's a positive element as well. When we pray "hallowed by thy name," we reaffirm our resolve to uphold His holy nature.

B. Proper Alignment (v. 10)

10a. Thy kingdom come.

This petition may be challenging to understand because the underlying Greek verb is a third-person imperative, and the English language doesn't have this grammatical option, strictly speaking. The closest we can come is by using the word *let.* We see this in our translations of third-person imperatives in John 7:37 and Revelation 22:17. But the idea is more forceful than taking the word *let* to mean "allow."

Think of the song "Let It Snow! Let It Snow! Let It Snow!" The desire expressed by the title isn't one of merely "allowing" snow to fall (as if one could stop it!). Instead, the sense is an urgent need that must be met. And that's the sense of the verse at hand—expressing an urgent need for God's *kingdom* to *come* in its fullness. In this kingdom, there will be no temptation, sin, pain, sadness, or death. God will rule over everything, and His followers will worship Him forever (see Revelation 11:15).

10b. Thy will be done.

This partial verse contains another third-person imperative in the underlying Greek. As mentioned above, the idea is an implied use of the word *let* in a stronger sense than merely "allow." For examples of the word *let* equating to the word *allow,* see Acts 5:38; 17:9; for more examples of the word

let in the stronger sense, see Matthew 11:15; Galatians 1:8.

10c. In earth, as it is in heaven.

These twin petitions are all-encompassing. To pray for the establishment of God's kingdom *is* to pray for the carrying out of God's will in every place as God reigns over His realms. Or perhaps we should use the singular word *realm* instead. The two locations of *earth* and *heaven* should not be unduly separated since the qualifier unites them *as it is in.* In using that phrase, Jesus depicts Heaven as a place without opposition to God's will.

When we pray these petitions, we pray that God's kingdom, the kingdom of heaven, will come to earth. To pray this is to pray that God's sovereign will, as realized in Heaven, will prevail in the present world where we live. We are praying that all opposition to God will cease. And most of all, we are praying this for ourselves. We are saying, "Lord, I want Your kingdom to be fully present in my life. I want my life to be a perfect reflection of Your will" (compare Jesus' prayer in Matthew 26:39).

C. Proper Asking (vv. 11-13)

11. Give us this day our daily bread.

There are two important points to note about this request. First, the word *give* has a broad sense of "provide" when associated with God. Second, the idea of *bread* in the Bible is more than a reference to baked loaves. The word may indeed refer to that, but context determines if the concept of "food in general" is meant (examples: Matthew 14:17-19; 15:26). The word may have the even larger sense of "things necessary for life" (John 6:33). When we say this prayer, we acknowledge that we rely on God. It is not about informing

Him of things we think He might not be aware of (Matthew 6:31-32). We are affirming our belief that God will meet every need.

> **What Do You Think?**
> What steps will you take to practice gratitude to God for the "daily bread" that He has provided?
>
> **Digging Deeper**
> How can you turn that practice into a daily habit of gratitude?

Daily Bread

Sadly, my business failed in the summer of 2004, and we lost all our material assets. Our house, cars, and every other possession were sold to the highest bidder to settle our financial obligations. We retained only our children, dog, clothes, and an old car of no monetary worth.

We found a small apartment, and my wife got a job as a cashier at a grocery store, working the night shift. One benefit to the job was discounts on food. Because she worked nights, she had the first shot at day-old bread and other perishables that were about to expire. This challenging time made us appreciate our "daily bread." It also made me see the Old Testament stories in a new light, for example, the one where God gives the Israelites manna every day and the one where He helps the prophet Elijah and a widow by giving them flour and oil daily.

Today we have enough food on hand for a few weeks. Whether we are unsure about where our next meal is coming from, or we have plenty, the words of Jesus still hit home for us: "Give us this day our daily bread." In light of what we've been through, these simple words keep reminding us that God knows what we need daily and that He can provide for us. What personal experiences have you had that make the words of this prayer resonate deeply with you?   —J. M.

12. And forgive us our debts, as we forgive our debtors.

This petition is unique in being conditional. As we ask for God's forgiveness, we promise to be for-

giving of others. This is the only petition in the prayer that receives an additional comment from Jesus at the end (Matthew 6:14-15, see below). For an extended discussion on this expectation, see Matthew 18:21-35.

13a. And lead us not into temptation, but deliver us from evil.

These final petitions of the prayer are two sides of the same coin: to *lead us not into* is to *deliver us from*. The first part of this request has troubled those who think it raises the possibility that God himself can be responsible for tempting us to sin. Jesus did not intend this understanding, and James 1:13 is definitive on this point: "Let no man say when he is tempted, I am tempted of God: for God cannot be tempted with evil, neither tempteth he any man." God may allow temptation (Job 1:12; 2:6), but He does not initiate or cause it. Still, there are moments when God saves us from difficult situations or "trials" (see 1 Peter 1:7; 2 Peter 2:9). Taking the two petitions of this half-verse together gives the sense of "give us power over"—and He does (1 Corinthians 10:13).

> **What Do You Think?**
> How can believers prepare themselves for the inevitable temptations that arise?
>
> **Digging Deeper**
> Who will you ask to be your accountability partner for when you face temptations?

The Right Source

In September 2013, things got chaotic at the airport in Fairbanks, Alaska. A car was cruising down the taxiway and across the runway to get to the terminal. Surprisingly, another driver did the same thing. The cause was a bug in a navigation app that mistakenly guided people through a gate meant only for aircraft! Thankfully, there were no accidents, and the app was eventually fixed.

Even though signs clearly stated it was a restricted area, the drivers did not notice these warnings and unthinkingly followed what the app told them. Even when it seemed pretty clear that something was wrong and that they should not be driving on an airport taxiway, they continued crossing the runway because they trusted the app more than their own judgment.

This story highlights how easily we can take a wrong path when we heed directions from a defective source. That was the problem of being led into temptation in Genesis 3. When you face a sinful temptation, be sure of one thing: it's not from God. But as the drivers on the runway reveal, we may be so used to following a seemingly authoritative source that we do not question how or where we are being led. How can you be sure that it is God who is genuinely guiding you and that you are not just going the wrong way because you ignore the signs that you are listening to a defective source?   —J. M.

13b. For thine is the kingdom, and the power, and the glory, for ever. Amen.

This half-verse is not found in the earliest manuscripts of Matthew's Gospel. But with echoes of 1 Chronicles 29:11-13, it nevertheless expresses a biblical idea. It is very fitting for the themes of this prayer as it doubles down in emphasizing God's sovereignty, with which the prayer begins.

III. Addendum on Forgiveness
(Matthew 6:14-15)

14-15. For if ye forgive men their trespasses, your heavenly Father will also forgive you. But if ye forgive not men their trespasses, neither will your Father forgive your trespasses.

After describing how to pray, Jesus gives more information on the need to *forgive*. This conditional petition is so important that Jesus later clarified it with a lengthy parable in Matthew 18:21-35.

In the addendum on forgiveness before us, we note that Jesus has switched from the words *debts* and *debtors* in Matthew 6:12 to the word *trespasses*. The word translated "trespasses" often refers to sins (example: Ephesians 1:7), while the word translated "debts" might include other kinds of obligations (examples: Matthew 18:24-25; Romans 1:14).

Conclusion
A. Sincere Petitions or Mere Repetitions?

A couple started dating. In due course, they began to take turns attending each other's church. Her church recited the Lord's Prayer every Sunday as part of the worship service; his church never did. When she asked him why his church never did so, he responded that his church didn't want the Lord's Prayer to become a repetitious chant.

He had a point. Mere repetition of the Lord's Prayer without regard to its message and challenge is of negative value. To do so runs the risk of being condemned as those who honor God with their lips but whose hearts are far from Him (Matthew 15:8 quoting Isaiah 29:13).

But that danger is true of anything we do regularly when the church meets. Some churches have communion services only once per quarter because it might become "too common" if observed every Sunday. (Few churches, however, would apply the same reasoning to the collection of offerings!)

Perhaps a good middle ground would be different prayers every Sunday that nevertheless reflected the categories in the Lord's Prayer. Would that work in your church? Why, or why not?

B. Prayer

Our Father which art in heaven, Hallowed be thy name. Thy kingdom come. Thy will be done in earth, as it is in heaven. Give us this day our daily bread. And forgive us our debts, as we forgive our debtors. And lead us not into temptation, but deliver us from evil: For thine is the kingdom, and the power, and the glory, for ever. In Jesus' name. Amen.

C. Thought to Remember
Pray as if God is listening—because He is.

How to Say It

Didache	Did-uh-key.
	or Did-uh-kay.
Gethsemane	Geth-*sem*-uh-nee
	(*G* as in *get*).
Paternoster	Pah-tur-naw-stir.

Involvement Learning

Enhance your lesson with KJV Bible Student *(from your curriculum supplier) and the reproducible activity page (at www.standardlesson.com or in the back of the* KJV Standard Lesson Commentary Deluxe Edition*).*

Into the Lesson

Invite learners to share experiences from childhood of having to memorize certain prayers. Encourage them to think about how those prayers shaped their understanding of prayer. (*Option*: teachers of larger classes may wish to have the experiences discussed in small groups to conserve time.)

Say, "For some people, prayer may be such a common habit that they give it very little thought; for others, prayer may not be as familiar and, therefore, more difficult to remember to practice. In today's lesson, consider what new prayer habit you could learn from Jesus' instruction."

Into the Word

Ask a volunteer to read Matthew 6:5-8. Form learners into triads or study pairs.

Distribute handouts (you create) on which are printed this question: *How can we pray unseen by others per Matthew 6:6 when we're supposed to let our lights shine before others so that they may see our good works and glorify our heavenly Father per Matthew 5:16?*

After a few minutes, reconvene for whole-class discussion. Then, ask a volunteer to read Matthew 6:9-13. Return participants to their triads or study pairs.

Distribute handouts (you create) on which are printed this question: *Considering Jesus' directive, "After this manner therefore pray ye," does that mean we should at least occasionally use the exact words of this prayer? Why, or why not?*

After a few minutes, reconvene for whole-class discussion. Then, ask a volunteer to read Matthew 6:14-15. Return participants to their triads or study pairs.

Distribute handouts (you create) on which are printed this question: *Considering God's track record and Luke 17:4, should forgiveness be extended to someone who does not repent? Why, or why not?*

Pose the following case study to the class:

A certain man decided to keep track of the prayer requests voiced by members of his adult Bible study class. For 10 weeks, he made a record of them. (He did not offer any of his own in order not to bias the result.) When the 10 weeks were up, he had recorded 133 prayer requests. He quickly noted that they fell into three general categories: 97 were for physical healings; 33 were for unfavorable situations such as job loss or marriage and family problems; and 3 were for spiritual needs. What's wrong with this picture?

Alternative or *option*. For a different or additional case study, distribute copies of the "Ceremonial Theism?" exercise from the activity page, which you can download. Discuss in triads or study pairs before whole-class discussion.

Option. As a transition between Into the Word and Into Life segments, distribute copies of the "ACTS in Action" exercise from the activity page. Allow one minute for each participant to complete the four segments marked with a [•]. *Note*: this should be individual work, not for small groups or study pairs, because it calls for personal responses. Assure your learners at the outset of the activity that you will not collect the responses or ask anyone to share them publicly. By contrast, the second part of the "ACTS in Action" exercise should be completed in triads or study pairs. (Note the need for highlighters or colored pencils.)

Into Life

Write this question on the board for whole-class discussion: *Is it proper to call the various aspects of prayer in general and the Lord's Prayer in particular "ingredients of a recipe"? Why, or why not?*

After discussion, allow a time of prayerful confession regarding your learners' needs to improve the quantity, quality, and motives that undergird their prayer lives. But don't put anyone on the spot to do so. Close with the Lord's Prayer.

Heeding Wholly

Devotional Reading: Matthew 10:31-42
Background Scripture: Matthew 11

Matthew 11:7-15, 20-24

7 And as they departed, Jesus began to say unto the multitudes concerning John, What went ye out into the wilderness to see? A reed shaken with the wind?

8 But what went ye out for to see? A man clothed in soft raiment? Behold, they that wear soft clothing are in kings' houses.

9 But what went ye out for to see? A prophet? Yea, I say unto you, and more than a prophet.

10 For this is he, of whom it is written, Behold, I send my messenger before thy face, which shall prepare thy way before thee.

11 Verily I say unto you, among them that are born of women there hath not risen a greater than John the Baptist, notwithstanding he that is least in the kingdom of heaven is greater than he.

12 And from the days of John the Baptist until now the kingdom of heaven suffereth violence, and the violent take it by force.

13 For all the prophets and the law prophesied until John.

14 And if ye will receive it, this is Elias, which was for to come.

15 He that hath ears to hear, let him hear.

20 Then began he to upbraid the cities wherein most of his mighty works were done, because they repented not:

21 Woe unto thee, Chorazin! Woe unto thee, Bethsaida! For if the mighty works, which were done in you, had been done in Tyre and Sidon, they would have repented long ago in sackcloth and ashes.

22 But I say unto you, it shall be more tolerable for Tyre and Sidon at the day of judgment, than for you.

23 And thou, Capernaum, which art exalted unto heaven, shalt be brought down to hell. For if the mighty works, which have been done in thee, had been done in Sodom, it would have remained until this day.

24 But I say unto you, that it shall be more tolerable for the land of Sodom in the day of judgment, than for thee.

Key Text

Then began he to upbraid the cities wherein most of his mighty works were done, because they repented not. —**Matthew 11:20**

A King
Forever and Ever

Unit 3: Life in God's Kingdom
Lessons 10–13

Lesson Aims

After participating in this lesson, each learner will be able to:

1. Summarize Jesus' description of John the Baptist.

2. Explain why the generation that Jesus criticized displayed a lack of wisdom in its evaluation of both Him and John the Baptist.

3. Recruit an accountability partner to ensure that hearing results in heeding.

Lesson Outline

Introduction
  A. Celebrity Preachers
  B. Lesson Context
I. John, the Messenger (Matthew 11:7-15)
  A. Unlikely Celebrity (vv. 7-10)
    Preparing a Way
  B. Last of His Kind (vv. 11-15)
II. Jesus, the Wonder Worker (Matthew 11:20-24)
  A. Failure to Repent (vv. 20-22)
  B. Judgment to Ensue (vv. 23-24)
    A Stubborn Dog
Conclusion
  A. Pivotal People in Unrepentant Cultures
  B. Prayer
  C. Thought to Remember

Introduction
A. Celebrity Preachers

If there ever was a "celebrity preacher," George Whitefield (1714–1770) was him. An English preacher who toured America in the eighteenth century, Whitefield's strong voice allowed him to address crowds of thousands with his emotionally charged and highly effective sermons. Whitefield contributed to the religious revival known as the Great Awakening, which was a significant influence on the history of the United States.

Today, celebrity preachers have tools of which Whitefield would never have dreamed; television, smartphones, and the Internet allow the preachers' messages to be seen and heard throughout the world. Such preachers are known to construct enormous buildings that can seat thousands at a time. Televangelists receive contributions to support their ministries and (sometimes) lavish lifestyles.

Both Jesus and John the Baptist were celebrity preachers in their day. But they were very different from the high-profile televangelists we see today! Today's lesson will explore why.

B. Lesson Context

The significance of John *the Baptist* is hinted at in the fact that his name is mentioned about 90 times across the four Gospels and the book of Acts. It's important to clarify that he is not the same as John *the Apostle*, who's mentioned about half as often in the New Testament. The New Testament mentions another man by the name of John (also known as "Mark") in Acts 12:12, 25; 13:5, 13; 15:37. "John" was a popular name!

John the Baptist was born in Judaea (Luke 1:65). His father, Zacharias, was of a priestly family (thus of the tribe of Levi). His mother was Elisabeth, a relative of Mary (1:35-36), so John and Jesus were related through their mothers. John spent a great deal of time in the wilderness while young (1:80).

John preached repentance "for the kingdom of heaven is at hand" (Matthew 3:2). His baptizing of the multitudes resulted in his identifying title. In the Gospels, he is called "John the Baptist" by both his supporters and adversaries (Matthew 3:1; 14:2; etc.).

John contributed to the ministry of Jesus in three important ways. First, he was in one sense "Elias [same as Elijah], which was for to come" (Matthew 11:14; compare Malachi 4:5-6; Matthew 17:10-13; contrast John 1:21). In this regard, John was understood to assume the role of Elijah as a prophetic voice that prepared the people for the coming of the Messiah (Luke 1:17; John 1:23).

Second, John's baptizing of Jesus in the Jordan River was "to fulfil all righteousness"—it was the right thing to do in God's plan, confirmed by "the Spirit of God" and "a voice from heaven" (Matthew 3:13-17). Third was John's prophetic identification of Jesus as "the Lamb of God, which taketh away the sin of the world" (John 1:29).

Today's lesson examines a time after John's ministry as a wilderness preacher had ended. He had run afoul of the local ruler, Herod Antipas, and ended up in prison. This turn of events resulted in doubts for John, which he attempted to resolve by sending two of his disciples to Jesus to determine whether or not Jesus was the Messiah (Matthew 11:1-3). Jesus responded by pointing to the evidence of the miracles (11:4-6). Today's lesson text picks up after Jesus' response to John's disciples (Luke 7:24-28 is a partial parallel).

I. John, the Messenger
(Matthew 11:7-15)
A. Unlikely Celebrity (vv. 7-10)

7. And as they departed, Jesus began to say unto the multitudes concerning John, What went ye out into the wilderness to see? A reed shaken with the wind?

Having just received Jesus' answer to their query (see Lesson Context), John's disciples *departed* to relay that response to John the Baptist, who was in prison (Matthew 11:2). As they left, Jesus turned the tables to inquire about John's identity. Why did so many people leave their comfortable homes to make an uncomfortable, inconvenient trip *out into the wilderness* to be baptized by John (Mark 1:5; Luke 3:3-7)? Did they make such a trip because they wanted to see *a reed shaken with the wind*—a description of a wishy-washy, indecisive person whose message shifts with the winds

of popularity? These questions were designed to make Jesus' audience consider the kind of individual John the Baptist was.

8. But what went ye out for to see? A man clothed in soft raiment? Behold, they that wear soft clothing are in kings' houses.

Jesus continued to probe His audience's motivation for making inconvenient trips to see John in the wilderness. Did they travel to a wilderness area to see a fashion show featuring *a man clothed in soft raiment?* This question paints a word picture of someone who lived in stark contrast to John the Baptist. John led a minimalistic life in the wilderness, far removed from the lavish comforts of a king's palace (see Matthew 3:4).

9. But what went ye out for to see? A prophet? Yea, I say unto you, and more than a prophet.

Jesus posed another rhetorical question. And then He voiced the answer that was on everyone's mind. John's message was of such a nature, his preaching so powerful that even hostile religious leaders and Roman soldiers came to investigate if not outright repent (Luke 3:14; John 1:19-27). They came because they thought John was at least *a prophet* and possibly even the Messiah (Luke 3:15; John 1:19-20; Acts 13:25).

Jesus confirms that the multitudes were correct in their belief that John was a prophet. This designation carries specific implications. First, a prophet speaks for God. The prophets of Israel often began their messages with "Hear the word of the Lord" (Isaiah 39:5; Jeremiah 7:2; Hosea 4:1; etc.). The people believed John was speaking the word of God to them. Second, prophets were perceived as an integral part of Israel's history. By the time Jesus was born, Israel had about 2,000 years of history, tracing back to the time of Abraham!

While agreeing with the people's assessment that John was a prophet, Jesus upped the ante by designating John as *more than a prophet*. What that entailed comes next.

10. For this is he, of whom it is written, Behold, I send my messenger before thy face, which shall prepare thy way before thee.

As the Messiah's immediate forerunner, John was not only a prophetic voice of the Lord. He was also a fulfillment of a prophecy himself. This prophecy is found in Isaiah 40:3-5 and Malachi 3:1. It is so significant that all four Gospels mention this role (Matthew 3:3; Mark 1:1-3; Luke 3:4-6; John 1:23).

> **What Do You Think?**
> In what ways do believers prepare the world for Christ's second return?
>
> **Digging Deeper**
> What steps do you need to take to prepare your life for Christ's return?

Preparing a Way

During World War II, the United States was worried about the defense of Alaska. As a result, the Army Corps of Engineers was tasked to build a highway that could be used to transport troops and equipment rapidly to Alaska as needed. The idea for the resulting 1,543-mile Alcan Highway had been around since the 1930s, but the war made it a priority.

More than 11,000 soldiers worked on the project. They worked long shifts, sometimes in subzero temperatures, and finished the project in less than nine months. This remarkable feat of engineering enabled the United States to safeguard its territory by establishing a way through the wilderness.

God, in His wisdom, foresaw the need to prepare the world for the arrival of Jesus. John the Baptist was the point man in that regard. He preached about the need for repentance and the inbreaking kingdom of God.

Jesus built a highway between earth and Heaven through His death on the cross and resurrection. How would you describe your experience walking along life's highway with Jesus? —J. M.

B. Last of His Kind (vv. 11-15)

11. Verily I say unto you, among them that are born of women there hath not risen a greater than John the Baptist, notwithstanding he that is least in the kingdom of heaven is greater than he.

In this verse, Jesus seemed to speak in a paradox. On the one hand, no person *born of women* up to that point was *greater than John the Baptist*. On the other hand, *he that is least in the kingdom of heaven is greater than he*. How can these both be true?

The key is understanding that in various contexts, Jesus spoke of the kingdom of God (Matthew prefers the designation "kingdom of heaven") in terms of three time frames: near, present, and yet to come. Jesus spoke of God's reign as being "nigh at hand" (Luke 21:30-31). But as Jesus healed and drove out demons, He also spoke of God's kingdom as being present (Matthew 12:26-28). And when He spoke of His own return, Jesus pictured the kingdom as a future reality (7:21-23; 25:34). The ultimate nature of that future kingdom will be so marvelous that the person who is least in it is to be thought of as greater than John the Baptist—whom no one (other than Jesus himself) surpassed in terms of the kingdom of heaven being near.

John's importance lies in the fact that he is a transitional figure in the history of salvation. He didn't carry out his ministry as an early member of the new covenant being ushered in by Jesus. The next verse strengthens this idea.

12-13. And from the days of John the Baptist until now the kingdom of heaven suffereth violence, and the violent take it by force. For all the prophets and the law prophesied until John.

Combining the time elements recorded in Matthew 4:12, 17 with those in Luke 3:1-3, 23, we realize that the interval between *the days of John the Baptist* and *now* (as Jesus was speaking) was relatively short—only a few months. This points to an overlap of the ministries of John and Jesus, confirmed by John 3:22-36. Thus, there is no clear line of demarcation between John's role as the last of the Old Testament prophets and Jesus' inauguration of the *kingdom of heaven*. John's job was to proclaim *the prophets and the law* (the old system) to ready the people for encountering the Messiah. Jesus, as that

Messiah, came to open the doors to the kingdom via His death and resurrection (the new system; compare Luke 16:16; Hebrews 9:20; 10:19-20).

Jesus' mention of *violence* foreshadows John's pending death by beheading (Matthew 14:6-12). It may also apply to Jesus' own death by brutal crucifixion (16:21; etc.). The church's beginning was not calm and readily accepted. Both the Romans and the Jewish people who did not believe in the gospel used violence to stop the advance of the gospel, as seen in the death of James the Apostle (Acts 12:1-2). Although Isaiah saw the Messiah as the "Prince of Peace" (Isaiah 9:6) and Hebrews proclaims Jesus as the "King of peace" (Hebrews 7:2), the history of the church is littered with violence and persecution.

More difficult to understand is Jesus saying that *the violent take it by force*. Some have seen this as a call for Christians to be more activistic, even violent, when met with opposition. These interpreters say we must fight fire with fire as we both live and die by the sword, citing Jesus' words in Matthew 10:34. But surely Jesus' words in our lesson text are an acknowledgment of violence against His kingdom, not a call to violence in promoting or defending it. Jesus later admonished Peter to put his sword away after he slashed a man (John 18:11). Jesus was the object of violence in His time on earth, not the leader of a violent revolt.

14-15. And if ye will receive it, this is Elias, which was for to come. He that hath ears to hear, let him hear.

Jesus concluded His teaching on John the Baptist by noting the fulfillment of a prophecy from Malachi 4:5: "Behold, I will send you Elijah the prophet before the coming of the great and dreadful day of the Lord." *Elias* is another name for the prophet Elijah. Elijah's ministry is documented in 1 Kings 17:1–19:21; 21:17-28; and 2 Kings 1:1–2:11. First-century Jews expected the prophecy of Elijah's return to be fulfilled by the arrival of Elijah reincarnated. Jesus affirmed the expectation of Elijah's return but not that of reincarnation. Rather, someone with the attitude and spirit of the original Elijah would come. That person was John the Baptist (Matthew 17:10-13; compare John 1:21).

What Do You Think?

What can you do to ensure that you do not become "hard of hearing" in a spiritual sense?

Digging Deeper

What are some reasons a person might be spiritually "hard of hearing"?

II. Jesus, the Wonder Worker
(Matthew 11:20-24)
A. Failure to Repent (vv. 20-22)

20. Then began he to upbraid the cities wherein most of his mighty works were done, because they repented not.

Following criticisms of "this generation" in Matthew 11:16-19, Jesus rebuked the residents of specific villages. (Luke 10:12-15 offers a parallel condemnation, although the setting differs.) The locations at issue were in Galilee, where most of Jesus' *mighty works* had been displayed. Jesus' popularity did not result in people heeding His message to "repent: for the kingdom of heaven is at hand" (Matthew 4:17); this message was identical to that of John the Baptist (3:2).

The Greek word translated *repentance* means "to change one's thought process." When someone repents, they alter their thinking about sin and embrace new thoughts and actions. But Jesus' message and method were not what the Jews of His day expected. To see God's work in the healing of lepers, the casting out of demons, etc., should have prompted repentance.

How to Say It

Bethsaida	Beth-*say*-uh-duh.
Canaanite	*Kay*-nun-ite.
Chorazin	Ko-*ray*-zin.
Galilean	Gal-uh-*lee*-un.
Herod Antipas	*Hair*-ud *An*-tih-pus.
Levi	*Lee*-vye.
Nineveh	*Nin*-uh-vuh.
Phoenician	Fuh-*nish*-un.
Sidon	*Sigh*-dun.
Tyre	Tire.

Listen. Repent. Live.

Visual for Lesson 11. *Point to this visual as you ask learners to silently consider how they might follow these imperatives in the upcoming week.*

21-22. Woe unto thee, Chorazin! Woe unto thee, Bethsaida! For if the mighty works, which were done in you, had been done in Tyre and Sidon, they would have repented long ago in sackcloth and ashes. But I say unto you, it shall be more tolerable for Tyre and Sidon at the day of judgment, than for you.

The villages of *Chorazin* and *Bethsaida* are located near the northern shore of the Sea of Galilee, less than 10 miles from each other. *Chorazin,* a prosperous agricultural town in the hills above the Sea, is mentioned in the Bible only here and in Luke 10:13. *Bethsaida,* whose name means "house of fishing," was on the east side of the Jordan River where it feeds into the Sea of Galilee in the north. It was the hometown of Philip, Peter, and Andrew (John 1:44).

Tyre and Sidon, on the other hand, were famous Phoenician cities on the Mediterranean coast north of Galilee. For these cities to *have repented long ago in sackcloth and ashes* brings to mind the city of Nineveh, whose citizenry repented when hearing the message of the prophet Jonah (Jonah 3:5-6; Matthew 12:41). This also foreshadowed Jesus' travel to the vicinity of Tyre and Sidon, where he encountered the extraordinary faith of a Canaanite woman (Matthew 15:21-28; Mark 7:24-30). Repentance and faith will be honored on *the day of judgment,* even among Gentile cities such as Tyre, Sidon, and Nineveh.

B. Judgment to Ensue (vv. 23-24)

23-24. And thou, Capernaum, which art exalted unto heaven, shalt be brought down to hell. For if the mighty works, which have been done in thee, had been done in Sodom, it would have remained until this day. But I say unto you, that it shall be more tolerable for the land of Sodom in the day of judgment, than for thee.

The importance of *Capernaum* is reflected in the fact that it is mentioned 16 times by name in the four Gospels. This fishing village was on the Sea of Galilee, several miles southwest of Bethsaida. Capernaum was strategically located between villages along the Sea of Galilee and those in the Galilean highlands to the west—villages such as Nazareth. This may have been the reason that Jesus used Capernaum as a type of home base for His ministry (Matthew 4:13). Jesus performed several miracles (*mighty works*) in and around this location during His earthly ministry (8:5-13; Mark 1:21-34; 2:1-12; John 4:46-54).

The comparison of Capernaum to *Sodom* is quite stark! The latter was one of the cities God destroyed with "brimstone and fire . . . out of heaven" (Genesis 19:24) because of sin so "grievous" (18:20) that not even 10 righteous people were to be found there (18:32). In the later books of the Old Testament, Sodom becomes a byword for a place harshly judged for its unrepentant sinfulness (Isaiah 3:9; Zephaniah 2:9). Jerusalem did not escape this comparison (Jeremiah 23:14).

Jesus' calls to repentance, like those of John the Baptist, were threatening and unappreciated in places like Capernaum and therefore rejected. Repentance precedes forgiveness (Luke 24:47; Acts 2:38; 5:31; 8:22). But prideful hardheartedness will result in a mighty fall, even to the eternal destiny of being *brought down to hell.*

What Do You Think?
What steps will you take to orient your life around repentance that leads to forgiveness?

Digging Deeper
How will you ensure pride and hard-heartedness do not take root in your life?

A Stubborn Dog

Our furry friend Omar dashed out the open door at 5:00 a.m. before I could get his leash on him. As a Belgian Malinois, Omar can sprint faster than the speed limit in our area! Despite attempts with training collars and weeks of reward-based training, he bolts as soon as he realizes he is off the leash. He eventually returns after a few hours, but trying to chase him down is futile. Seeing us in pursuit makes him run faster and farther.

It's all a game for Omar. His doggy brain does not perceive any wrongdoing. Running is just a natural thing for him to do. Reminding myself of this helps temper my frustration when I welcome him back inside after his adventures. As much as Omar can vex me, God employs this dog to teach me invaluable lessons. I have been like Omar more times than I can count, reverting to old habits and disregarding the Spirit's call. Yet, every time I return in repentance, God is there, ready to welcome me back.

Jesus admonished the stubborn cities that refused to repent. Although they had seen the miracles firsthand, they resisted His call. Their lack of "ears to hear" and "eyes to see" is actually worse than our dog's attitude because it's self-inflicted (Matthew 13:15-16; Mark 8:18). Think about it: the city of Sodom would have repented if it had witnessed the same divine acts! Are there parts of your life where you persist in your stubbornness, refusing to surrender to God? —J. M.

Conclusion

A. Pivotal People in Unrepentant Cultures

Pivotal people are agents of change in moving others to new ways of thinking and doing. An example of a pivotal person in a nonreligious sense is Jeff Bezos, founder of Amazon. We see several pivotal people in the Bible. Just one example from the Old Testament is Samuel, seen in his being the last of the judges and the first of the prophets (1 Samuel 3:20; 7:6, 15-17; Acts 3:24; 13:20). In the New Testament, we rightly see the ultimate pivotal person to be Jesus. His life, death, resurrection, and ascension marked and enabled the transition from the old covenant to the new covenant (Romans 7:6; Colossians 2:13-15; Hebrews 8; etc.).

The image of Jesus in this regard is so powerful and profound that it's easy to overlook John the Baptist as a pivotal person also. As the last of the prophets who ministered under the realities of the old covenant (Matthew 11:9; 14:5; 21:26; Luke 1:76), he prepared the way for Jesus by preaching the nearness of the kingdom of heaven and the need to repent in anticipation of the new covenant.

Many in the first century AD did not accept John the Baptist's view of the kingdom of heaven and the need to repent. It is not widely accepted today. We live among unrepentant people who are often proud of transgressing God's standards. The power and prosperity of an unrepentant culture confront us relentlessly with a choice: Who will be the pivotal person(s) we allow to direct our thinking and doing: the pivotal people of social media or the Bible?

Making the wrong choice with regard to such influence runs the risk of infecting us with the "ungodliness and unrighteousness of men, who hold the truth in unrighteousness" (Romans 1:18). That decision, in turn, might cause us to love the world at the expense of our love of the kingdom of heaven.

As we make the right choice daily, may we repeat neither the infamy of evil Sodom nor the unrepentance of Chorazin, Bethsaida, or Capernaum.

> **What Do You Think?**
> What concept or teaching in today's lesson do you have the most trouble coming to grips with? Why?
> **Digging Deeper**
> How will you resolve this problem?

B. Prayer

Heavenly Father, may Your Holy Spirit continue to bring us to repentance and acceptance of Your forgiveness even as we model this reality to others. We pray in the name of Jesus. Amen.

C. Thought to Remember

Choose repentance. Choose eternal life.

Involvement Learning

Enhance your lesson with KJV Bible Student *(from your curriculum supplier) and the reproducible activity page (at www.standardlesson.com or in the back of the* KJV Standard Lesson Commentary Deluxe Edition*).*

Into the Lesson

Have the following written on the board before learners arrive:

> When were you surprised by something . . .
> • *that was contrary to what you expected?*
> • *about which you had* **no** *expectations at all?*

Learners may need time to search their memories, so encourage person-to-person sharing before class formally begins.

When class does begin, challenge participants to compare and contrast the two types of expectations in a general sense with this question: "Without getting into specific stories or experiences, which 'new reality' do you find is harder to accept: (1) a reality that contradicts an existing expectation or (2) a reality about which you have no expectation whatsoever?" Disallowing the telling of specific personal stories, which can be lengthy, will keep this segment from dragging out.

Lead into Bible study by saying, "Today we'll look at two individuals to see how they did not match the expectations of those they encountered. In the process, we may find our own expectations challenged as well."

Into the Word

Have two participants read the two segments of the lesson text, one segment each. Distribute handouts (you create) with the following:

Identifying and Confronting Expectations

1. Summarize the people's (apparent) expectations regarding John the Baptist in Matthew 11:7-15. Compare and contrast their expectations with those in Matthew 20:9-12; Luke 3:15; 9:7-9.

2. Summarize the people's (apparent) expectations regarding Jesus in Matthew 11:20-24. Compare and contrast their expectations with those in Matthew 13:53-57; Luke 2:25-35; John 4:25; 7:25-31.

After small groups identify and discuss discoveries, reconvene for whole-class discussion.

Option. If time is short, have half the groups discuss #1 on the handout while the other half discusses #2.

Option. If your learners need context regarding Jesus and John the Baptist, distribute copies of the "Different Roles, Common Goals" exercise from the activity page, which you can download. Have learners complete this in study pairs *before* the "Identifying and Confronting Expectations" exercise just discussed.

Into Life

Transition to application by asking participants to focus on the concept of "accountability" in the lesson text. After a time of open discussion, distribute handouts (you create) titled "Christian Accountability." Have the following passages listed vertically down the left-hand side: Proverbs 27:17; Ezekiel 3:16-27; 3:8; John 12:6; 2 Corinthians 2:6; Galatians 6:1-2; Ephesians 5:21; Hebrews 4:13; 10:24-25; 13:17; James 5:16.

Introduce the exercise by writing this passage on the board:

> But be ye doers of the word, and not hearers only, deceiving your own selves. —James 1:22

As you write, say, "Let's explore some ways for us to be accountable to one another in the Christian life for making sure that *hearing* leads to *heeding*."

Then, form small groups to consider the passages listed on the handout. Be prepared to refute the contention that we are accountable only to God. Beforehand, carefully read through the passages listed; you may wish to add to or subtract from the list, depending on the nature of your class. Explore the differences between accountability to the church and accountability to an individual.

Option. To set the towns of Matthew 11:20-24 within the broader context of the Bible, distribute copies of the "Ancient Cities, Sinful Histories" exercise from the activity page as a take-home, to be completed as indicated.

Living
Lastly

Devotional Reading: 1 Samuel 2:1-10
Background Scripture: Matthew 19:16-30

Matthew 19:16-30

16 And, behold, one came and said unto him, Good Master, what good thing shall I do, that I may have eternal life?

17 And he said unto him, Why callest thou me good? There is none good but one, that is, God. But if thou wilt enter into life, keep the commandments.

18 He saith unto him, which? Jesus said, Thou shalt do no murder, thou shalt not commit adultery, thou shalt not steal, thou shalt not bear false witness,

19 Honour thy father and thy mother, and, thou shalt love thy neighbour as thyself.

20 The young man saith unto him, all these things have I kept from my youth up. What lack I yet?

21 Jesus said unto him, If thou wilt be perfect, go and sell that thou hast, and give to the poor, and thou shalt have treasure in heaven, and come and follow me.

22 But when the young man heard that saying, he went away sorrowful: for he had great possessions.

23 Then said Jesus unto his disciples, Verily I say unto you, that a rich man shall hardly enter into the kingdom of heaven.

24 And again I say unto you, it is easier for a camel to go through the eye of a needle, than for a rich man to enter into the kingdom of God.

25 When his disciples heard it, they were exceedingly amazed, saying, Who then can be saved?

26 But Jesus beheld them, and said unto them, With men this is impossible, but with God all things are possible.

27 Then answered Peter and said unto him, Behold, we have forsaken all, and followed thee. What shall we have therefore?

28 And Jesus said unto them, Verily I say unto you, that ye which have followed me, in the regeneration when the Son of man shall sit in the throne of his glory, ye also shall sit upon twelve thrones, judging the twelve tribes of Israel.

29 And every one that hath forsaken houses, or brethren, or sisters, or father, or mother, or wife, or children, or lands, for my name's sake, shall receive an hundredfold, and shall inherit everlasting life.

30 But many that are first shall be last, and the last shall be first.

Key Text

Again I say unto you, it is easier for a camel to go through the eye of a needle, than for a rich man to enter into the kingdom of God. —**Matthew 19:24**

A King
Forever and Ever

Unit 3: Life in God's Kingdom
Lessons 10–13

Lesson Aims

After participating in this lesson, each learner will be able to:

1. Identify the Old Testament commandments Jesus cited.

2. Explain what Jesus meant by the first being last and the last being first.

3. Identify any "do more to get right with God" habit in one's life and seek the Spirit's guidance in breaking free of it.

Lesson Outline

Introduction

A. Checking All the Boxes

The phrase "checking all the boxes" refers to meeting all the requirements to complete a given procedure. For example, a homebuyer must carefully complete all items on the "must-have" checklist before making an offer to purchase. That's the concept in a positive sense (or one intended to be positive), as it serves as a tool to leave nothing to chance when something important must be done. We will see this intent in today's lesson.

B. Lesson Context

The encounter recorded in today's Scripture occurred only a few weeks before Jesus' crucifixion and resurrection. The location was on the eastern side of the Jordan River (Matthew 19:1). This region was also referred to as *Perea* by Josephus, a first-century Jewish historian. Today's Scripture text has parallels in Mark 10:17-31 and Luke 18:18-30.

The first part of the lesson is our consideration of Jesus' encounter with an unnamed man whom we refer to as "the rich, young ruler." That designation results from combining descriptions in the three accounts of the synoptic Gospels: the man was *rich* (Matthew 19:22; Mark 10:22; Luke 18:23), he was *young* (Matthew 19:22), and he was a *ruler* (Luke 18:18). Because he is described as being young, it has been suggested that he was probably not a member of the Jewish ruling body known as the Sanhedrin, but a "ruler" of a local synagogue. By the time we get to chapter 19 in the Gospel of Matthew, opinions about Jesus had become polarized (compare John 7:12). Luke 9:51–18:14 records the events that happened between the end of Matthew 18 and the beginning of Matthew 19.

This time frame featured several tense and pointed encounters with Pharisees and other individuals. These encounters continued into Matthew 19:1 and beyond as Jesus "departed from Galilee, and came into the coasts of Judaea beyond Jordan." One such encounter is the subject of today's text.

I. A Seeker's Inquiry

(Matthew 19:16-22)

A. Sincere Question (v. 16)

16. And, behold, one came and said unto him, Good Master, what good thing shall I do, that I may have eternal life?

Each of the three Gospel accounts of this encounter offers interesting details that the other two do not (see Lesson Context). Whereas Matthew's account begins simply by saying *one came,* Mark 10:17 adds that the man came by running and kneeling before Jesus. The account that begins in Luke 18:18 states at the outset that the man was "a certain ruler" (see Lesson Context).

There are variations in the ancient Greek wording of the first part of the man's question— variations not necessarily seen in an English translation. But there is no variation in two words: the man's inquiry about *eternal life.* This phrase is comparatively rare in the synoptic Gospels of Matthew, Mark, and Luke. In Matthew, it appears in Greek only three times, and two of those three occur in today's study. The third occurrence is in Matthew 25:46, where "life eternal" is contrasted with "everlasting punishment" (similar is Matthew 18:8). All told, these three Gospels use this phrase a total of nine times.

Even so, the rare use of the phrase *eternal life* in the synoptic Gospels is balanced by the fact that all three include the dialogue with the rich young ruler. The man's question is a good one, and the answer is still vital today. The man appears to have been familiar with Jesus' teaching regarding eternal life (John 3:14-16; 5:24; 6:40; etc.). Certainly, he is to be commended for approaching Jesus as he did, possibly risking the criticism of the Sanhedrin.

B. Initial Reply (vv. 17-19)

17. And he said unto him, Why callest thou me good? there is none good but one, that is, God: but if thou wilt enter into life, keep the commandments.

Rather than answer the man's question, Jesus first challenged him with a question. He wanted the man to consider whether he knew what he was asking. The man had used the word *good* twice in his question to Jesus, but did he grasp its significance? What did he mean by calling Jesus *good*? No one is truly good except *God,* Jesus told the man. Was he aware of the deity of the one he spoke to? Using "religious language" without depth of understanding can be very easy.

Not waiting for a reply, Jesus addressed the man's question about eternal life: he needed to *keep the commandments.* Jesus' response was similar to what He told "a certain lawyer" who had inquired about eternal life (Luke 10:25-28).

Jesus' response to the rich young ruler mirrored a typical reply from a first-century Jewish rabbi. Jesus intended to provoke self-reflection within the young man. It raises the question of why merely following the commandments was not fulfilling enough. If the young man was obeying these laws, why didn't it quench his thirst for eternal life?

18a. He saith unto him, Which?

Only Matthew records this response by the man. It seems to indicate his understanding that the various individual statutes within the Law of Moses can be rank-ordered from "necessary for salvation" downward. If this is the man's viewpoint, he is not alone (compare Matthew 22:35-36; Mark 12:28). This is understandable given that the Law of Moses consists of over 600 statutes!

18b-19. Jesus said, Thou shalt do no murder,

How to Say It

Arimathaea	*Air*-uh-muh-*thee*-uh (*th* as in *thin*).
Josephus	Jo-*see*-fus.
Perea	Peh-*ree*-uh.
Sanhedrin	*San*-huh-drun or San-*heed*-run.
synoptic	sih-*nawp*-tihk.

thou shalt not commit adultery, thou shalt not steal, thou shalt not bear false witness, honour thy father and thy mother, and, thou shalt love thy neighbour as thyself.

In response, Jesus quoted portions of the Ten Commandments found in Exodus 20:2-17 (compare Deuteronomy 5:7-21). He also quoted Leviticus 19:18 (compare Matthew 22:39).

C. Sincere Claim (v. 20)

20. The young man saith unto him, All these things have I kept from my youth up. What lack I yet?

The young man, who had asked what good thing he could do to receive eternal life, appeared to take heart from considering the commandments Jesus had listed. The man's claim to have *kept* these commandments from his *youth* sounds somewhat arrogant, though Jesus offered no reaction to the claim. The man does appear to have lived a morally upright life, perhaps similar to how Paul described himself as being "blameless" regarding a legalistic form of righteousness in his pre-Christian life (Philippians 3:6). *The young man* knew something was missing. It was likely with great anticipation that he asked, *"What lack I yet?"*

D. Further Challenge (v. 21)

21. Jesus said unto him, If thou wilt be perfect, go and sell that thou hast, and give to the poor, and thou shalt have treasure in heaven. And come and follow me.

Jesus knows every person's heart (John 2:24-25; 6:61, 64; 13:11). Everyone has one or more weak areas that prevent being *perfect* (compare Matthew 5:48; Romans 3:10-12; Hebrews 7:19). And Jesus knew what that was in this man's case.

What Do You Think?

What attitudes prevent believers from being perfect, like our Heavenly Father is perfect (Matthew 5:48)?

Digging Deeper

What "go, sell, and give" type of steps might be necessary to help a believer avoid these attitudes?

E. Sad Reaction (v. 22)

22. But when the young man heard that saying, he went away sorrowful, for he had great possessions.

The young man's reaction to Jesus' challenge reveals that he had broken the First Commandment. That's the one that says to have no other gods before the one true God. Think about it! By disobeying Jesus, was the man not honoring his *great possessions* above God? Luke's account includes this stark contrast: "And when he heard this, he was very sorrowful: for he was very rich" (Luke 18:23). What Jesus told the man to do was not what he expected to hear.

We have no further information in Scripture about the rich young ruler. We do not know whether he ever changed his outlook and decided that he would do what Jesus commanded. Note that Jesus did not pursue the man or offer to negotiate with him. Jesus never changed and never will change the conditions to be His follower. However, this fact does not mean He is not saddened by any decision to reject those terms. This young man *went away sorrowful*, but we can be sure there was a greater sorrow in the heart of Jesus.

The Unexpected Test

When I entered the office of the Department of Motor Vehicles, a staff member asked if I was there to attempt a retest. It was my third day and third attempt at passing. Since I had been driving for 21 years, I believed I knew the rules. I held a driver's license from another state to prove it. But our move across state lines meant I had to pass my new state's driving exam to get a license.

My first two attempts at the test confronted me with a harsh truth: I did not know as much as I thought I did. I finally studied the traffic regulations and passed on the third attempt.

The rich young ruler who approached Jesus seemed sure he had passed the test. He seemed to know God's "traffic manual" (the Old Testament) pretty well, and he honored it. Also, to the man's credit, he attempted to "make sure" by asking what he still lacked. He certainly went to the right source for the answer! But the man found the answer to be unacceptable. He failed the test he expected to pass.

The Bible is full of tests (examples: Genesis 2:17; 2 Corinthians 2:9; 8:8; 13:5-7), and we will experience those that are common to humanity. A big problem presents itself, however, in accepting what God's "passing score" is (contrast 2 Corinthians 10). How will you ensure that you will pass that test? —J. M.

II. The Savior's Instruction
(Matthew 19:23-30)

A. Stunning Declaration (vv. 23-24)

23. Then said Jesus unto his disciples, Verily I say unto you, That a rich man shall hardly enter into the kingdom of heaven.

Sometimes Jesus' public teaching or encounter with an individual was followed by instructions directed toward His *disciples* (examples: Matthew 13:10, 36; 19:10-12). Here Jesus provided further teaching concerning the threat that riches can pose to one's progress toward *the kingdom of heaven*.

24. And again I say unto you, It is easier for a camel to go through the eye of a needle, than for a rich man to enter into the kingdom of God.

To illustrate His point, Jesus used hyperbole—a statement exaggerated for effect. Some have suggested that an ancient wall in Jerusalem had a small gate called "The Needle's Eye" through which a camel might pass with some difficulty, but only without any baggage or cargo. But that gate was not built until the Middle Ages. Jesus was talking about something impossible for a human being. He emphasized that impossibility with the mental picture of a large *camel* trying to pass *through the eye of a needle*.

B. Surprised Reaction (vv. 25-27)

25. When his disciples heard it, they were exceedingly amazed, saying, Who then can be saved?

The shocked response of the *disciples* shows that the hyperbole Jesus used did, in fact, grab their attention. In the first century, many believed

wealth was a sign of God's favor. So, if the wealthy could not be saved, nobody could. Jesus was teaching the disciples that only God can grant salvation, not a person's actions or status. Not long before the rich young ruler approached Jesus, the disciples tried to shoo away children whom they considered a nuisance to Jesus, only to learn that "of such is the kingdom of heaven" (Matthew 19:14). And now, a man whom the disciples considered a "shoo-in" for the kingdom was being declared unworthy to enter it.

26. But Jesus beheld them, and said unto them, With men this is impossible, but with God all things are possible.

Whenever people create their own categories of who is worthy or unworthy to be saved, the result can be blindness to the truth that it is *impossible* for humans to purchase their salvation (compare Acts 8:18-20). Only God can address this dilemma, which is why Jesus came to our fallen, broken world (2 Corinthians 5:21).

Jesus' statement does not imply that rich people cannot be saved or enter into a right relationship with God. Both Abraham and Job were wealthy men. Joseph of Arimathaea, who provided a tomb for Jesus' burial, is described as both a rich man and a disciple of Jesus (Matthew 27:57). The issue comes down to what controls a person's life: wealth or God. Poverty is not a key to Heaven, nor are riches an automatic pathway to Hell. One may have great wealth and love God supremely, or one may have very little and love it more than God. It is the condition of the heart that makes the difference. Jesus concluded His parable of the rich fool with a warning to the person "that layeth up treasure for himself, and is not rich toward God" (Luke 12:21).

What Do You Think?

What steps should believers take to ensure their material wealth does not hinder their following God?

Digging Deeper

What practices and behaviors might you undertake that would result in you being "rich toward God" (Luke 12:21)?

"It is easier for a camel to go through the eye of a needle, than for a rich man to enter into the kingdom of God." -Matthew 19:24

Visual for Lesson 12. *Have this visual on display as you discuss the lesson commentary associated with Matthew 19:24.*

27. Then answered Peter and said unto him, Behold, we have forsaken all, and followed thee; what shall we have therefore?

If any of Jesus' disciples had a comment or question in response to something Jesus said or did, it was usually *Peter* (examples: Matthew 15:15; 16:22; 26:35; Mark 9:5; John 13:8, etc.). Jesus had just challenged a rich man to relinquish control of his possessions for the sake of the kingdom of Heaven. As Peter pointed out, the disciples had *forsaken all* to follow Jesus, giving up their livelihoods (Luke 5:11, 28). What rewards awaited them for their choice to leave all to follow Jesus?

C. Solemn Promise (vv. 28-30)

28. And Jesus said unto them, Verily I say unto you, that ye which have followed me, in the regeneration when the Son of man shall sit in the throne of his glory, ye also shall sit upon twelve thrones, judging the twelve tribes of Israel.

Jesus did not respond in terms of an earthly reward. Instead, He spoke of what will happen *in the regeneration* (compare Luke 22:28-30). At a time when Jesus will reign in *glory*, these twelve disciples will occupy *twelve thrones, judging the twelve tribes of Israel*. Perhaps at this point, the disciples were still thinking in terms of an earthly kingdom and an earthly throne that Jesus would establish in Jerusalem. Most likely, this regenera-

tion refers to the establishment of the new heavens and new earth that will characterize Jesus' return (2 Peter 3:10-13). The word translated as "regeneration" is quite rare in the New Testament. It occurs only twice: here and in Titus 3:5 : "he saved us, by the washing of regeneration, and renewing of the Holy Ghost." Christians anticipate the regeneration to come because of their current status of having been renewed.

29. And every one that hath forsaken houses, or brethren, or sisters, or father, or mother, or wife, or children, or lands, for my name's sake, shall receive an hundredfold, and shall inherit everlasting life.

A magnificent reward awaits not only those disciples standing before Jesus as He spoke but also anyone who gives up earthly possessions and relationships for His *name's sake*. The return on investment (so to speak) will be eternal. It will be a wealth that differs from anything the world can offer (compare Matthew 6:33).

The blessing of *everlasting life* is what the rich young ruler had inquired about. That life begins with the personal knowledge of Jesus as Lord (John 17:3); that life is brought to fullness by eternity with Him in Heaven. That is the life that awaited the rich young ruler had he been willing to follow Jesus on His terms.

30. But many that are first shall be last, and the last shall be first.

Nothing illustrates this statement better than the incident recorded in Matthew 19:13-15, just before today's text. Children (whom the disciples considered an inconvenience to Jesus) are the prime examples of what His kingdom residents should look like, while the rich (whom the disciples viewed as having a guaranteed place in the kingdom) are the least likely to dwell there.

What Do You Think?

What steps will you take to develop an attitude of humility reflective of God's kingdom residents?

Digging Deeper

Who will be an accountability partner to help you as you make these steps?

The Most-Coveted Airplane Seat

The passenger with the first-class seat in the front row had strong words for me. I was a customer service representative for a major airline. I understood why an airliner's first row is so sought after: it granted, among other things, the privilege of exiting the plane first. The one who occupied the seat that day, however, ended up being the last of 150 persons to exit the aircraft.

The problem was with our ground equipment. It prevented us from bringing the passenger stairs to the plane's front door. So we had to go with our backup plan and use the stairs at the rear of the aircraft. As a result, those expecting to be first off the plane became last off, and vice versa. Therefore, I found myself bearing the brunt of the first-class passenger's annoyance.

Sometimes it's a good thing to desire to be first (example: 2 Corinthians 8:10). But usually, that's not a good desire because it betrays a self-centered motive. Those who take such a path will end up with the opposite of what they expect (Matthew 21:31; Mark 9:35; etc.).

And stepping outside the Bible, we encounter wisdom in this well-known axiom: "Be careful what you ask for, because you may just get it." The landscape of Christianity is littered with the wrecked ministries of high-profile preachers whose egos took over—the resulting lack of accountability followed by ministry disaster.

Saul, a one-time persecutor of Christians, came to his senses as he transitioned into being the apostle Paul (compare and contrast 1 Corinthians 4:9; 15:9; Philippians 3:4b-14). Two thousand years of hindsight reveal him to be the number one apostle, a role he did not seek but accepted as God's will. What does it take to have such an attitude today?

—J. M.

Conclusion

A. Rethinking the Boxes

The episode of the rich young ruler sounds a warning to those who want a Christian faith that will not require a change of lifestyle or a reordering of priorities. Jesus did not and does not command every seeking sinner to sell everything and give the money away. Jesus did so to the rich young ruler because Jesus knew what the man valued. Anything we put before God in our hearts is an idol and must be dealt with in the same decisive manner. The young man wanted to ensure he had "checked all the boxes" to obtain eternal life. He sincerely believed he was on the cusp of meeting the requirements. If there was even one thing left undone, one box remaining unchecked, then surely Jesus would tell him what that was. And Jesus did! Ultimately, the man's problem was that something other than God was on the throne of his heart (compare 2 Timothy 4:10).

"Rich" is a relative term. The wealth of Solomon is legendary (1 Kings 3:13; 10:23). But none of the countless servants he had in his palace would match the efficiency and effectiveness of our "servants" of modern refrigerators, microwave ovens, etc. If he was considered to be rich, then what are we? When our hands produce wealth, do we remember who gave us those hands to do so in the first place (Deuteronomy 8:17-18; compare Daniel 4:28-33)? Paul's admonition to Timothy still applies: "Charge them that are rich in this world, that they be not highminded, nor trust in uncertain riches, but in the living God, who giveth us richly all things to enjoy" (1 Timothy 6:17; compare Psalm 62:10).

> **What Do You Think?**
> How has this Scripture text changed your considerations on material wealth?
> **Digging Deeper**
> What will you do in light of this change?

B. Prayer

Father, strengthen us when the world's standards and priorities tempt us. Help us to take an honest look at our lives and to be honest about whether our possessions possess us. Mold us into disciples of Jesus, willing to stay the course and assured that whatever we yield control of, You will more than compensate for in ways we could never imagine. In Jesus' name. Amen.

C. Thought to Remember

The life that lasts puts God first.

Involvement Learning

Enhance your lesson with KJV Bible Student *(from your curriculum supplier) and the reproducible activity page (at www.standardlesson.com or in the back of the* KJV Standard Lesson Commentary Deluxe Edition*).*

Into the Lesson

Write the 10 words of the following phrases in very large letters on 10 sheets of paper, one word each: *The first will be last; the last will be first.* Distribute them randomly to class members. (If your class is smaller than 10, give some learners two sheets.) Ask those receiving the sheets to stand in a line after arranging the words correctly.

Form study pairs or triads and distribute handouts (you create) with these instructions: "Give examples of how these two phrases should apply (or how you've seen them actually apply) in secular, nonreligious contexts. Include, as far as possible, information regarding *who, what, where, when, why,* and *how*." After whole-class discussion, make a transition to Bible study by saying, "We may or may not find it easier to see how the phrases apply in a religious sense. Let's find out."

Option. Place in chairs the "It's Impossible" exercise from the activity page, which you can download, for your learners to work on as they arrive.

Into the Word

For audible reading of the lesson, assign the text's five voices to five learners, one each, who will read the words of the rich man, Jesus, the narrator, the disciples as a whole, and Peter in particular.

After the reading, ask each learner to write one (and only one) of the Ten Commandments on a slip of paper without saying anything. Promise a cash prize to anyone who writes a commandment that no one else does.

After no more than 30 seconds, call for responses and jot them on the board as they are voiced. Consult Exodus 20:1-17 and Deuteronomy 5:7-21 as necessary. Award a cash prize of 10 cents to each participant who met the criteria for it. As you do, anticipate chuckles and groans as you say, "Let's see how these *cents* help us make *sense* of the text."

Distribute to study pairs handouts (you create) titled "Revealing Questions." Have these six thought-starters down the left side, with blank lines for responses extending to the right.

1. The man's first question (v. 16)
2. Jesus' question (v. 17)
3. The man's second question (v. 18)
4. The man's third question (v. 20)
5. The disciples' question (v. 25)
6. Peter's question (v. 27)

Include these instructions with the handout: "Work down through the list and give your impression of what the question says about the one(s) asking it. Work quickly—give a first impression, taking no more than a minute on each."

After no more than six minutes, call time and invite responses in whole-class discussion. Compare and contrast learners' ideas. Use the information in the commentary to correct misconceptions.

Option. For a deeper dive, have learners compare and contrast what is revealed about the man in his first question here with that of a different man who asks the same question in Luke 10:25.

Into Life

Make a transition by asking, "What are some ways that people today use to try to 'get right with God?'" Encourage free input as you record responses on the board. After several minutes of this brainstorming, challenge learners to detect a common theme among elements in the list. Expect learners to discover that the theme is "Do something" or "Do more of it." Point out that this ends up being a "trying hard, never sure" approach. Discuss ways to break this compulsion.

Option. Distribute copies of the "Wealthier than I Imagined" exercise from the activity page, to be completed as indicated. (Be sure to complete it yourself before class!) Use results to explore how your learners might find themselves having the same attitude seen in Matthew 19:22.

Ministering Mightily

Devotional Reading: Matthew 25:14-15, 19-30
Background Scripture: Matthew 25

Matthew 25:31-46

31 When the Son of man shall come in his glory, and all the holy angels with him, then shall he sit upon the throne of his glory.

32 And before him shall be gathered all nations, and he shall separate them one from another, as a shepherd divideth his sheep from the goats.

33 And he shall set the sheep on his right hand, but the goats on the left.

34 Then shall the King say unto them on his right hand, Come, ye blessed of my Father, inherit the kingdom prepared for you from the foundation of the world.

35 For I was an hungred, and ye gave me meat, I was thirsty, and ye gave me drink, I was a stranger, and ye took me in.

36 Naked, and ye clothed me, I was sick, and ye visited me, I was in prison, and ye came unto me.

37 Then shall the righteous answer him, saying, Lord, when saw we thee an hungred, and fed thee? Or thirsty, and gave thee drink?

38 When saw we thee a stranger, and took thee in? Or naked, and clothed thee?

39 Or when saw we thee sick, or in prison, and came unto thee?

40 And the King shall answer and say unto them, Verily I say unto you, inasmuch as ye have done it unto one of the least of these my brethren, ye have done it unto me.

41 Then shall he say also unto them on the left hand, depart from me, ye cursed, into everlasting fire, prepared for the devil and his angels:

42 For I was an hungred, and ye gave me no meat: I was thirsty, and ye gave me no drink:

43 I was a stranger, and ye took me not in: naked, and ye clothed me not: sick, and in prison, and ye visited me not.

44 Then shall they also answer him, saying, Lord, when saw we thee an hungred, or athirst, or a stranger, or naked, or sick, or in prison, and did not minister unto thee?

45 Then shall he answer them, saying, verily I say unto you, inasmuch as ye did it not to one of the least of these, ye did it not to me.

46 And these shall go away into everlasting punishment: but the righteous into life eternal.

Key Text

Then shall the King say unto them on his right hand, Come, ye blessed of my Father, inherit the kingdom prepared for you from the foundation of the world. For I was an hungred, and ye gave me meat, I was thirsty, and ye gave me drink, I was a stranger, and ye took me in. —**Matthew 25:34-35**

A King
Forever and Ever

Unit 3: Life in God's Kingdom
Lessons 10–13

Lesson Aims

After participating in this lesson, each learner will be able to:

1. Summarize Jesus' description of what will happen at the final judgment.

2. Contrast the behavior of the "sheep" with that of the "goats."

3. Write a plan to serve Jesus in the week ahead as the "sheep" do.

Lesson Outline

Introduction

A. Not for the World

A businessman traveled to India to represent his company at an important meeting. After the day's sessions ended, the man walked through a part of the city where lepers were being cared for. He watched as a woman tenderly washed the feet of an older man suffering from leprosy. The businessman watched for a moment, shook his head, and then said, with disdain, "Miss, I wouldn't do that for the world." Without looking up, the woman replied, "Mister, for the world, I wouldn't do it either."

To minister to others in Jesus' name often means going where most others would not. Those who do so may wonder at times whether their efforts are significant. Today's lesson reveals the answer.

B. Lesson Context

The setting of our lesson is during a busy day of teaching during the final week of Jesus' earthly ministry. As part of His "Olivet Discourse" of Matthew 24:3–25:46, Jesus taught the truth of today's lesson, probably on Wednesday of what is often called Passion Week.

The Olivet Discourse was set in motion when the disciples asked Jesus about the sign of His coming and of the end of the world (Matthew 24:3). Jesus began His reply by warning against deceptive signs and predictions of persecution (24:4-26). Then, He shifted to specifying genuine signs (24:27-35). This was followed immediately by a lengthy challenge to be ready to expect the unexpected (24:36-51).

Jesus went on to illustrate with two parables all that He had been saying: the parable of the 10 virgins (Matthew 25:1-13) and the parable of the talents (25:14-30; in Luke 19:12-27 this is the parable of pounds).

The chapter closes with a dramatic picture of the final judgment—today's lesson of Matthew 25:31-46. Some students think this is a parable, while others do not. Parables usually compare something earthly to "the kingdom of heaven" (Matthew 13:24, 31-34; 25:1, 14; etc.), but Matthew 25:31-46 does not have this feature. The only comparison that could result in this being considered a parable is Matthew 25:32, where the final judgment is compared with a shepherd's separation of "sheep" from "goats." However, this fits better the idea of metaphor (figurative or symbolic language) rather than a parable.

I. The Judge
(Matthew 25:31-33)
A. Glorious Moment (v. 31)

31. When the Son of man shall come in his glory, and all the holy angels with him, then shall he sit upon the throne of his glory.

With this declaration, Jesus was still answering the disciples' question in Matthew 24:3: "What shall be the sign of thy coming, and of the end of the world?" The word *when* reinforces the certainty of Jesus' return (compare Matthew 16:27). That word also anticipates a time factor as part of the declaration. But during Jesus' earthly ministry, no one except God the Father knew the specific day of Jesus' return (24:36). The phrase *Son of man,* for its part, confirms Jesus will be the one returning since that phrase is His frequent self-designation (examples: 9:6; 16:13; 20:18; compare Daniel 7:13).

It is instructive to contrast the circumstances of Jesus' first coming (advent) with those of His second coming. The first time, in Bethlehem, He came as a baby born under very modest conditions. His return will be anything but ordinary; He will *come in his glory*, and He will be seated upon a glorious *throne*. A "multitude of the heavenly host" was present to herald Jesus' first coming, announcing His birth to shepherds near Bethlehem with the words "Glory to God in the highest" (Luke 2:13-14). When Jesus returns, He will be accompanied by not only *all the holy angels* but also by "his saints"—godly people who have died (1 Thessalonians 3:13; Jude 14).

What Do You Think?

What do you have to do in order to be ready for the return of Christ the King?

Digging Deeper

If the King were to return today, how would He evaluate your faith?

B. Great Gathering (vv. 32-33)

32. And before him shall be gathered all nations, and he shall separate them one from another, as a shepherd divideth his sheep from the goats.

At Jesus' first coming, the angels spoke of good news to "all people" (Luke 2:10); at His return, it will be good news to some but bad news to others as everyone is *gathered* before Him. While other passages in the Bible emphasize that every person must give a personal, individual account before Jesus (examples: Romans 14:12; 2 Corinthians 5:10), the focus in the verse before us is on *all nations* appearing before Him.

In the first century, many Jewish people believed that when the Messiah arrived, He would take control over powerful nations like the Roman Empire, as this verse describes. The purpose of Jesus' first coming, however, was "to seek and to save that which was lost" (Luke 19:10). Jesus' intent was and is for all nations to receive the message of this good news (Matthew 28:19-20). His second coming will bring all nations (both ancient and modern) under the power of His mighty hand and the authority of His flawless judgment.

Judgment will result in separation, as one group is distinguished from another. Separation language is very important in the New Testament, and it always signals an evaluation of some kind for categorizing things, behavior, or people themselves. These distinctions are intended to be helpful (example: 2 Corinthians 6:17), but some are counterproductive (example: Galatians 2:12). Other key verses in Matthew regarding eternal separation are 13:40-43, 49-50.

33. And he shall set the sheep on his right hand, but the goats on the left.

To be at a ruler's *right hand* was to be in the place of approval and acceptance (compare Psalm 110:1 [quoted in Hebrews 1:13]; Acts 7:55-56). It is in this prominent position that the *sheep* are placed. Note that Jesus describes only two groups. When He carries out His judgment at this gathering, there will be no middle ground, no "provisional sheep." Although we tend to view others in shades of gray, Jesus will be able to pronounce judgment clearly and decisively.

"Not Our Thing"

We spent the entire day sorting out bent nails from straight ones. My grandfather, who grew up during the Great Depression, believed in not wasting anything that could have a later use. That's why he gave me and my cousins large buckets filled with nails to sort. Some were bent and could not be reused; others were straight and still usable. We viewed the task as "not our thing," and it showed in our efforts. After sorting for a while, the nails all seemed to look alike.

We are called to use specific evaluations in the church (example: 1 Corinthians 5). As we do, we are careful to recognize a boundary: those processes do not put us in the place of Jesus as the ultimate judge. We cannot infallibly see the motives in a person's heart, but He can (Luke 5:22; 6:8; John 2:25). Today's lesson reminds us that the Son of Man is the one who will gather all the nations and distinguish between the righteous (sheep) and the unrighteous (goats). This is a responsibility that Jesus does not delegate; it is "not our thing."

What *is* our thing, however, is to be aware of the state of our own heart. How can we ensure that proper, godly motives stand behind our works of service to Jesus?   —J. M.

II. The Sheep
(Matthew 25:34-40)
A. Invitation (v. 34)

34. Then shall the King say unto them on his right hand, Come, ye blessed of my Father, inherit the kingdom prepared for you from the foundation of the world.

Speaking as *the King*, Jesus' first pronouncement is to those *on his right hand*, the sheep of the analogy. Their invitation to *inherit the kingdom prepared for* them is an invitation to enter Heaven. The fact that this kingdom has been ready for them since *the foundation of the world* alludes to the truth of Genesis 1:1.

Even now, Christians belong to the kingdom of Jesus, having been delivered from the realm of spiritual darkness (Colossians 1:13). We wait for the ultimate consummation of that kingdom, even as Paul did (2 Timothy 4:18).

What Do You Think?

What significance do you see in the statement that the kingdom was "prepared for you from the foundation of the world"?

Digging Deeper

How would you describe the joys of this kingdom to someone who had never before heard this good news?

Our Planning and His

When our kids were younger, we enjoyed traveling but could not afford fancy accommodations. So, instead, we would search for campgrounds to stay overnight. One day, we traveled to Chicago to see the city and enjoy authentic Chicago-style pizza. When the night came, we drove around looking for a campground to no avail. When I asked convenience store employees for directions to the nearest place to camp, I was met with confused looks. Therefore, we spent the night sleeping in the car.

That experience became a pivotal moment in our marriage. My wife, a meticulous planner, took charge of all travel arrangements from that point forward!

Whether or not we were born with "the planning gene," we can rest in the assurance of God being the master planner. God had planned for the inbreaking of His kingdom, salvation, and the final judgment, all in advance. One key difference between God's planning and ours is that God is omniscient (all-knowing). He can see both the beginning and the end. There are no unforeseen circumstances to Him. He is never caught off guard like we might be in our planning. How should that fact influence your planning? Before answering too quickly, read James 4:13-17.   —J. M.

B. Explanation (vv. 35-36)

35-36. For I was an hungred, and ye gave me meat. I was thirsty, and ye gave me drink. I was a stranger, and ye took me in. Naked, and ye clothed me. I was sick, and ye visited me. I was in prison, and ye came unto me.

The favorable verdict resulted from six ways the favored helped the king and met His needs. Their conduct is reminiscent of that in the parable about the Samaritan who met the needs of someone after others had merely passed by (Luke 10:30-34).

Such a heavy emphasis on doing good to others may indicate that Judgment Day will be a time for counting up such deeds and calculating our "final score." So how does Jesus' commendation of good works here square with the biblical teaching on salvation by grace? In truth, salvation encompasses both divine initiative and human response. Salvation by God's grace results in appropriate good works (Ephesians 2:8-10). We are not saved *by* works, but we are saved *for* works—a point James makes especially clear (James 2:14-26).

Visual for Lesson 13. *Have this visual on display as you review the discussion questions associated with Matthew 25:35-36.*

> ### What Do You Think?
>
> What are specific ways our congregation can address the six needs of people given in this story?
>
> ### Digging Deeper
>
> What education or training might your congregation need to address these needs effectively?

C. Consternation (vv. 37-39)

37-38. Then shall the righteous answer him, saying, Lord, when saw we thee an hungred, and fed thee? or thirsty, and gave thee drink? When saw we thee a stranger, and took thee in? or naked, and clothed thee?

Those designated as "sheep" are also *the righteous*. They will express their confusion at being told they were serving Jesus the King during their acts of mercy. They had seen themselves as meeting the needs of ordinary people, not Jesus. When had they ever encountered Jesus during such times?

39. Or when saw we thee sick, or in prison, and came unto thee?

The last act of mercy mentioned is the most fascinating of all. Prisons in the ancient world were not places of long-term incarceration as they are today. Prisons back then were places of short-term custody where perpetrators awaited either (1) corporal punishment such as flogging and then release or (2) execution. At what point would the righteous sheep ever have encountered King Jesus in such a place, especially after His ascension (Acts 1:9)? The answer comes next.

D. Commendation (v. 40)

40. And the King shall answer and say unto them, Verily I say unto you, inasmuch as ye have done it unto one of the least of these my brethren, ye have done it unto me.

Here is the answer to the sheep's bewilderment. Whatever the sheep have done to help even *the least of these my brethren*, they have done it to the greatest of all, King Jesus. The word *brethren* indicates Christians—those who have accepted the kingship of Jesus (compare John 1:12-13; Hebrews 2:11). This does not mean, however, that we have the freedom to ignore the needs of those who are not followers of Jesus (compare Proverbs 3:27; 25:21-22; Matthew 5:45; Galatians 6:10). Throughout Jesus' life, the least and lowliest of the people in His surroundings received special attention.

At this point in our reading of the text, some may ask, "If Jesus is providing these details about the final judgment, will we even raise such questions as the sheep are pictured as asking since we already know what the answer is?" Perhaps the element of surprise will occur as each of us individually comes before Jesus to be judged (2 Corinthians 5:10). There, we will see the true impact of our service to others. We likely will be astonished to discover the occasions when we were serving Jesus and did not realize it.

III. The Goats
(Matthew 25:41-46)
A. Rejection (v. 41)

41. Then shall he say also unto them on the left hand, Depart from me, ye cursed, into everlasting fire, prepared for the devil and his angels.

Next, Jesus will address the goats, those on His *left*. Note how the command to this group is exactly the opposite of that given to the group on Jesus' right. The sheep will be invited to "come"; the goats will be ordered to *depart*. The sheep will be called "blessed"; the goats will be called *cursed*. One group will inherit a kingdom; the other will be sent *into everlasting fire*.

Unlike the sheep, the goats won't be sent to a place that has been prepared just for them. Instead, the goats are to be sent to the place *prepared for the devil and his angels* (compare Revelation 20:10, 14-15; 21:8).

B. Explanation (vv. 42-43)

42-43. For I was an hungred, and ye gave me no meat. I was thirsty, and ye gave me no drink. I was a stranger, and ye took me not in; naked, and ye clothed me not; sick, and in prison, and ye visited me not.

King Jesus will confront the goats with the fact of having faced the same groups in need that the sheep faced. But whereas the sheep are pictured as having helped people in need, the goats chose to ignore those people. It is rather sobering to consider that the goats are not accused of doing anything evil—like murder, adultery, or theft. Rather, they are condemned for doing nothing. They had opportunities to meet needs, just as the sheep had. But the goats chose to look the other way. Sins of commission and sins of omission can both be sins (James 4:17)!

C. Consternation (v. 44)

44. Then shall they also answer him, saying, Lord, when saw we thee an hungred, or athirst, or a stranger, or naked, or sick, or in prison, and did not minister unto thee?

The goats will react with the same surprise that the sheep exhibited. The sheep will be astonished to be considered as having helped Jesus when they helped those in need; the goats no doubt will reason that had they realized the danger of their lack of action, they would have been more than eager to help. However, such logic is flawed, as it is circular. The goats will have no excuse (compare 1 John 3:17).

D. Condemnation (vv. 45-46)

45. Then shall he answer them, saying, Verily I say unto you, inasmuch as ye did it not to one of the least of these, ye did it not to me.

The failure of the goats to address the needs of others is a failure to serve Jesus (compare James 4:17). This is an image reversed from that of the sheep.

46. And these shall go away into everlasting punishment, but the righteous into life eternal.

It is virtually impossible to imagine a greater contrast between the *everlasting punishment* that awaits the goats and the *life eternal* that awaits the sheep (compare Galatians 6:8-10). The words *everlasting* and *eternal* have the same meaning here, since they are translations of the same Greek word.

How to Say It

Corinthians	Ko-*rin*-thee-unz (*th* as in *thin*).
omniscient	ahm-*nish*-unt.
Pontius Pilate	*Pon*-shus or *Pon*-ti-us Pie-lut.
propitiation	pro-*pih*-she-*ay*-shun.
Samaritan	Suh-*mare*-uh-tun.

The goats' endless punishment will be where "the fire is not quenched" (Mark 9:48, quoting Isaiah 66:24). Hell is a place of unspeakable torment.

In contrast, eternal life awaits those numbered among the sheep (compare and contrast Daniel 12:2; John 5:29). Nothing is said in today's passage about this life other than it is eternal. But other portions of Scripture provide insights concerning it. The book of Revelation describes a heavenly city, eternally bright, inhabited by only the redeemed. It is a place where "the former things are passed away" (Revelation 21:4)—everything associated with a sin-cursed, broken world. God will be with His people, and they will be with Him—forever.

What Do You Think?
How would you respond to the claim that a loving God would not allow a person to experience everlasting punishment?

Digging Deeper
What Scriptures come to mind to support your answer?

Conclusion

A. Three Functions

In today's passage, Jesus holds three positions: the *king* on His glorious throne (Matthew 25:31, 34), a *shepherd* dividing sheep from goats, and the *judge* determining the eternal destinies of those gathered before Him. We must keep in mind the unique manner in which Jesus exercised each of these roles. He is no ordinary king, shepherd, or judge.

King. Pontius Pilate brought Jesus before the crowd and proclaimed sarcastically, "Behold your King!" (John 19:14). Pilate spoke better than he knew: Jesus was indeed a king, but not one of this world (6:15; 18:36; Revelation 17:14; 19:16). We want to stand confidently before King Jesus on Judgment Day in anticipation of inheriting the kingdom. Therefore, we must realize that meeting the needs of others means serving our king.

Shepherd. When Jesus declared, "I am the good shepherd" in John 10:11, He said, "the good shepherd giveth his life for the sheep." Jesus' death pro-

vided a propitiation (atonement) for the sins of the entire world (1 John 2:2). But what has been provided must be accepted in order to be counted among the sheep under His care.

Judge. The one who said "I judge no man" during His earthly ministry (John 8:15) becomes the ultimate judge at His return—one before whom all must appear (Matthew 16:27; John 5:22-23; Acts 10:42; 17:31; 2 Corinthians 5:10).

B. Where's Jesus?

We live in a time and culture when the world seems to treat the Christian faith with contempt. Such an abrasive atmosphere is predicted in 2 Peter 3:3-4: "There shall come in the last days scoffers, walking after their own lusts, and saying, Where is the promise of his coming?" Even Christians might wonder *Where's Jesus?* in times of despair.

Answering that question may be compared somewhat to the *Where's Waldo?* books that have fascinated children. The books contain illustrations depicting crowds engaged in various activities at specific locations. The reader is challenged to find "Waldo" somewhere in the crowd. The key to doing so lies in Waldo's outward appearance: he can be found if one first knows how he can be recognized. Jesus makes it clear in today's passage that whenever we serve anyone in need, we are serving Him. Christians often see themselves as being the hands, feet, and voice of Jesus to other people, and rightly so. But Jesus is also seen in the needs of others around us. Do you have eyes to "see Him" in such situations?

C. Prayer

Father, there is so much brokenness and need in our world. Refresh and revive us when we feel overwhelmed. Help us not to become callous or indifferent to the hurting people around us. Clear up our spiritual vision so that we see not only others through the eyes of Jesus but also ourselves serving Jesus as we respond to needs. May we never forget that faith without works is still dead. In Jesus' name we pray. Amen.

D. Thought to Remember

Jesus is closer than we realize.

Involvement Learning

Enhance your lesson with KJV Bible Student *(from your curriculum supplier) and the reproducible activity page (at www.standardlesson.com or in the back of the* KJV Standard Lesson Commentary Deluxe Edition*).*

Into the Lesson

As learners enter the classroom, distribute handouts (you create) titled "Biblical Helping?" that ask for agreement (A) or disagreement (D) with the following statements:

___ When meeting needs, Christians should first explore the availability of government programs.

___ Giving cash to meet a need is often a good idea.

___ Meeting a need of a poverty-stricken person is best done by church committee.

___ The needs of an unbeliever should be treated differently than those of a fellow Christian.

___ When it comes to deciding *when, who,* and *how* to help others, Jesus should be my boss.

Expect learners to begin pondering the statements as they arrive and interact. Decide whether to discuss responses (1) right away, (2) during the Into Life segment only, or (3) in both segments, depending on the nature of your class and your teaching style.

Option. Instead of using the handouts as an agree/disagree exercise, have participants rank-order the statements from "most difficult to answer biblically" (ranked 1) to "easiest to answer biblically" (ranked 5). After discussion, lead into lesson study by saying, "Before we get too wrapped up in staking out positions, today's lesson has a few more surprises to toss our way."

Into the Word

Appoint two participants to read the 16 verses of the lesson text aloud, alternating with each verse. Distribute a handout (you create) that features each of these phrases as headers of three blank columns: *Identity of Sufferers / What Some Did / What Others Failed to Do.* Challenge participants, in groups of no more than four, to survey today's printed text and fill out the columns.

After several minutes, reconvene for a whole-class discussion of the results. Ask what elements of Matthew 25:39, 44 surprise them as well.

Option. If you wish to compare and contrast individual helping responsibilities with the church's collective responsibilities and procedures, distribute copies of the "Collective Helping and Jesus' Expectations" exercise from the activity page, which you can download. Have participants complete it as indicated in their previously formed groups. (Note: this exercise can be time-consuming. You may wish to save it until the end of the Into Life segment.)

Into Life

Create five columns on the board that feature the following five headers, one per column: *Lacking Sustenance / Lacking Emotional Support / Lacking Clothing / Lacking Good Health / Lacking Freedom.* Work across these five issues with this question as you move from one to the next: "How would we recognize when someone is having problems in this area?" Jot responses under the appropriate header as participants voice them.

After filling out the five columns, work back through them again with this additional question for each of the five columns in turn: "What would be a good plan for meeting this type of need?" As participants voice their ideas, press the issue deeper by having learners distinguish between needs that are best responded to by individuals in contrast with the needs that are best responded to by the church as a whole. Then, pose these case studies:

Case study 1. John volunteers with a secular organization to distribute meals to older adults. Since his work is not done in Jesus' name, does it "count" for him as being a "sheep" in terms of Matthew 25:31-46? Why, or why not?

Case study 2. Mary buys a car from a company that donates money to benevolent causes from every vehicle sold during its "Share the Love" event. Does it count for Mary's being a "sheep"?

Option. Distribute copies of the "Don't Let the Message Fall Away!" puzzle as a take-home.

Costly
Sacrifices

Special Features

Lessons
Unit 1: Tabernacle, Sacrifices, and Atonement

Unit 2: Christ's All-Sufficient Sacrifice

Unit 3: Special Offerings and the Sanctuary

Quarterly Quiz

Use these questions as a pretest or as a review. The answers are on page iv of This Quarter in the Word.

Lesson 1
1. Departing Rephidim, the people camped in what desert? (Shechem, Sinai, Shiloh) *Exodus 19:2*
2. The Lord said that He would come to Moses in a thick cloud. T/F. *Exodus 19:9*

Lesson 2
1. The Lord said, "Let them make me a sanctuary; that I may _____ among them." *Exodus 25:8*
2. The curtain was to be hung on pillars made of what wood? (cedar, cypress, shittim) *Exodus 26:32*

Lesson 3
1. The ordination process began with offering two young, unblemished bullocks and one unblemished ram. T/F. *Exodus 29:1*
2. How many days did the ordination of Aaron and his sons last? (six, seven, eight) *Exodus 29:35*

Lesson 4
1. A burnt sacrifice from the herd was to be a male "without blemish." T/F. *Leviticus 1:3*
2. What did the priests sprinkle "round about upon the altar"? (blood, water, oil) *Leviticus 1:11*

Lesson 5
1. Aaron slaughtered a bullock for his own _____ offering. *Leviticus 16:11*
2. The cloud from what burning item would conceal the mercy seat? (wool, branches, incense) *Leviticus 16:13*

Lesson 6
1. The Law of Moses is "a _____ of good things to come." *Hebrews 10:1*
2. Believers must consider how to "provoke . . . love" and "good _____" in others. *Hebrews 10:24*

Lesson 7
1. Who is our advocate with God the Father? (Jesus Christ, Holy Spirit, ourselves) *1 John 2:1*

2. Believers can know that we "dwell" in God and He in us because of His _____. *1 John 4:13*

Lesson 8
1. Matthew says that the guards at the tomb ran in fear after seeing the angel. T/F. *Matthew 28:4.*
2. After Jesus' resurrection, the brethren would see Him in _____. *Matthew 28:10*

Lesson 9
1. One of the elders in John's vision speaks of "the Root of _____." *Revelation 5:5*
2. What stands "in the midst of the throne [and] . . . the elders"? (Lion, Eagle, Lamb) *Revelation 5:6*

Lesson 10
1. The angel of the Lord held what item in his hand? (sword, scale, scroll). *1 Chronicles 21:16*
2. David paid Ornan six hundred shekels of _____ for the place. *1 Chronicles 21:25*

Lesson 11
1. After Solomon's prayer, what came down from Heaven? (rain, fire, angel) *2 Chronicles 7:1*
2. How many sheep were sacrificed at the dedication of the temple? (120; 1,200; 120,000) *2 Chronicles 7:5*

Lesson 12
1. What month did the people gather "themselves together" in Jerusalem"? (sixth, seventh, eighth) *Ezra 3:1*
2. All the people took trumpets and cymbals to praise the Lord. T/F. *Ezra 3:10*

Lesson 13
1. The priests, the Levites, and the people would cast lots to determine who would bring the offering of wood to the house of God. T/F. *Nehemiah 10:34*
2. The people proclaimed, "We will not _____ the house of our God." *Nehemiah 10:39*

Quarter at a Glance

by Editorial Staff

The themes of worship, sacrifices, and offerings run through the Scriptures. Grasping the sacrifices and offerings of the old covenant is essential to our understanding of the New Testament's presentation of Christ's sacrifice. This quarter will explore sacrifice and worship in the Old Testament and what the New Testament has to say about sacrifice and worship under the new covenant.

Tabernacle, Sacrifices, and Atonement

The first unit of lessons covers parts of Exodus and Leviticus that describe the system of sacrifices and offerings that created a holy people and a place for the presence of the Lord. On Mount Sinai, the Lord decreed to Moses that the Old Testament covenant people are "a kingdom of priests, and an holy nation (Exodus 19:6; see lesson 1). The Lord gave the people specific instructions for constructing a sanctuary known as the tabernacle, which contained "the holy place and the most holy" (26:33; see lesson 2). In the tabernacle (and, later, the temple), burnt offerings were presented to the Lord, following the expectations that He gave to the people (Leviticus 1:3-17; see lesson 4).

Not only did the Lord consecrate specific places, but He also consecrated specific people for a particular service. For example, from among the people, priests were chosen and ordained to officiate at the altar (Exodus 29:1-9, 35-37; see lesson 3).

Christ's All-Sufficient Sacrifice

The second unit turns to New Testament texts that explore the significance of Jesus' perfect sacrifice. The writer of the book of Hebrews contrasts the annual sacrifices of the Law of Moses—a law that is "a shadow of good things to come" (Hebrews 10:1)—with Jesus' once-for-all sacrifice (10:11-14; etc.; see lesson 6). The seventh lesson of the quarter comes from the epistles of John, where the author describes the love of God by His sending of His Son "to be the propitiation for our sins" (1 John 4:10).

Christ's resurrection on the third day confirms His sacrifice on the cross. Lesson 8 examines the details surrounding Christ's death and resurrection as told by the Gospel of Matthew (Matthew 27:39-40, 45-54; 28:1-10). Christ is the glorious Lamb who was slain and whose blood has "redeemed us to God" (Revelation 5:9; see lesson 9). Even in the throne room of Heaven, the glorious Lamb is declared "worthy"!

Special Offerings and the Sanctuary

The final unit of the quarter looks at the unique relationship between the sanctuary and offerings or sacrifices. King David's choices led him to bear responsibility for his sin. An angel of the Lord spoke through the prophet Gad and told David to "set up an altar unto the Lord in the threshingfloor of Ornan the Jebusite" (1 Chronicles 21:18; see lesson 10). David refused to accept a gift from Ornan for a sacrifice to the Lord because David would not "offer burnt offerings without cost" (21:24).

> Even in the throne room of Heaven, the glorious Lamb is declared "worthy"!

Lesson 11 will consider the dedication of Solomon's temple and the lavish sacrifices that took place as part of that ceremony (2 Chronicles 7:1-7). However, after the people were exiled to Babylon, that temple was left in shambles. The foundation of a new temple would need to be laid by the people who had returned from exile. When the foundation of that temple was laid, the people celebrated the goodness of God, proclaiming that "his mercy endureth for ever" (Ezra 3:11; see lesson 12).

The quarter concludes with recounting the people's covenant renewal and their pledge to observe the commands of the Law of Moses and reject the abuse and neglect of the house of God (Nehemiah 10:28-39; see lesson 13).

Get the Setting

Ask almost any Christian what Jesus has done, and you will likely hear about His "sacrifice." This noun comes from the Latin word meaning "an offering to a deity," but it is also used in a general sense to mean "something given in exchange for something else." But don't make the mistake of reading that metaphorical meaning back into Scripture. Rather, *sacrifice* was a vivid reality and a concrete image to all of Scripture's original audiences.

Sacrifice in the Ancient World

Many ancient Near Eastern people practiced sacrifices because they believed their gods depended on these offerings for food. The texts and inscriptions of ancient Sumerian, Egyptian, Akkadian, and Hittite people all describe gods with human-sounding needs for food, clothing, and shelter. *Why did ancient people offer sacrifices?* Well, otherwise, their gods would get hungry. *Why did the people build temples and sanctuaries?* They knew their gods wanted fine houses in which to live. Most natural forces of the world—like the weather—were attributed to the actions of gods who could be pacified and appeased or hostile and malevolent, depending on whether or not their needs were met.

In this context, idols of wood or stone would mediate the presence of the deity in physical form. Idols could be washed, clothed, housed, and kept safe. Deities would receive food in the form of sacrifices and savor the fragrant odors of these offerings.

Sacrifice in the Life of Israel

Perhaps it is surprising that the God of Israel chose to request sacrifices at all. Nowhere in Scripture do the writers indicate that the God of Israel needs food or relies on humans to satisfy a need. Instead, the Sinai Covenant (Exodus 19–24) treats sacrifices as either (1) expressions of praise to a God who had rescued His people and chosen them for His own, or (2) a method of cleansing to allow a sinful people to remain in relationship to a holy God. Atoning sacrifices were not about God's needs but the needs of His people.

With this context in mind, we can imagine that the Hebrew people approached the smoking and thundering Mount Sinai prepared to agree to whatever their God required. But the covenant stipulations they heard—summarized by the ten "commandments" or "words" (Exodus 20:1-17)—were instructions *not* to make an idol or try to persuade God into doing what they wanted. Instead, God provided them with a series of commonsense directives for life as a community.

The creation of a priesthood, tabernacle space, and the Day of Atonement allowed the Israelites—still sinful people—to meet with God. God's sacred space would have a home with them, first in the tabernacle and later in the temple.

Sacrifice Today

The exile of Judah and destruction of Solomon's temple halted the sacrificial system. Returning Jews were eager to restart the daily offerings and restore proper sacrifices, but this never fixed the underlying sin problem common to all people.

Nowhere in the pagan religions of the ancient world had a deity ever offered himself or herself as a sacrifice on behalf of humans. That line of thinking upends expectations regarding sacrifices, for weren't sacrifices supposed to give the gods what *they* wanted?

Jesus' sacrifice shows that God's most pressing desire was not to be appeased or set free of His labor. What God wanted most was a restoration of His creation through the defeat of the powers of sin and death. Jesus became the most enduring image of God's love by offering himself as a sacrifice on behalf of others. Thus was the plan of God to present Christ as the "propitiation through faith in his blood" (Romans 3:25). Because of His sacrifice, Jesus alone is worthy to sit as judge and receive praise and honor (Revelation 5:12).

This Quarter in the Word

Answers to the Quarterly Quiz on page 226

Lesson 1—1. Sinai. 2. True. **Lesson 2**—1. dwell. 2. shittim. **Lesson 3**—1. False. 2. seven. **Lesson 4**—1. True. 2. blood. **Lesson 5**—1. sin. 2. incense. **Lesson 6**—1. shadow. 2. works. **Lesson 7**—1. Jesus Christ. 2. Spirit. **Lesson 8**—1. False. 2. Galilee. **Lesson 9**—1. David. 2. lamb. **Lesson 10**—1. sword. 2. gold. **Lesson 11**—1. fire. 2. 120,000. **Lesson 12**—1. seventh. 2. False. **Lesson 13**—1. True. 2. forsake.

Map Feature

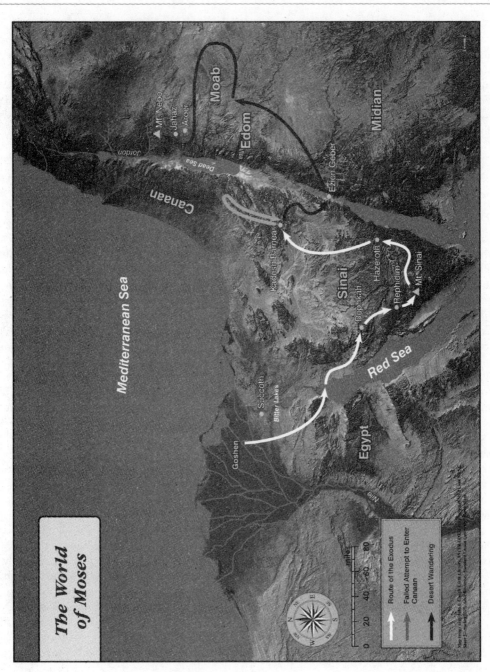

The World of Moses

Mediterranean Sea

Canaan

Moab

Edom

Midian

Mt. Nebo
Jahaz
Aroer

Jordan

Dead Sea

Ezion Geber

Kadesh Barnea

Sinai

Hazeroth

Rephidim

Mt. Sinai

Dophkah

Red Sea

Succoth

Bitter Lakes

Goshen

Egypt

Nile

miles

Route of the Exodus

Failed Attempt to Enter Canaan

Desert Wandering

0   20   40   60   80

A Passion for Teaching

Teacher Tips by Brent L. Amato

In any teacher training, should we not consider inspiration before implementation, motivation before methodology, and passion before presentation? Think about teachers who have captivated you. I suspect one characteristic of those teachers was their sincere enthusiasm that flowed from passion for their role.

There are three major sources of passion for Christian teaching. These three are available to all who aspire to be excellent teachers.

Who Is Teaching: You in Christ!

Realize in the truest and best sense that it is not *just you* who is teaching, but rather *you in Christ*. This "you" is filled with the Holy Spirit (1 Corinthians 6:19; Galatians 2:20). Always keep in mind your spiritual resources for teaching. This means moving beyond human-based credentials to spiritual, God-based power (1 Corinthians 2:1, 3-5; Colossians 3:16). This enables you to identify your insecurities and anxieties about teaching so you can give them over to the Lord (1 Peter 5:7). When you do, you can move beyond Moses' self-doubting responses to God's call (Exodus 3:11; 4:10, 13) to confident acceptance of that call.

Realize that your role is more than a teacher—you are nothing less than a steward of the gospel (compare 1 Corinthians 4:1, 2; 1 Timothy 1:11-12)! Be faithful and teach, looking forward to the day you will hear the commendation of our Lord: "Well done, thou good and faithful servant" (Matthew 25:21).

Realize also that we cannot fully comprehend the impact of a Spirit-filled, spiritually gifted teacher (John 14:12). *Passionately teach!*

What You Are Teaching: God's Word!

Realize that you are teaching the Word of God (1 Thessalonians 2:13)! When you hold your Bible, think of yourself as being like Moses, holding the tablets at Mount Sinai. The Bible is the inspired Word of God (2 Timothy 3:16a). The Word of God identifies and meets your students' deepest needs (Hebrews 4:12).

Realize that the Bible is profitable for all whom you teach (2 Timothy 3:16b-17); it will not fail to accomplish God's purpose for them (Isaiah 55:11). *Passionately teach!*

Whom You Are Teaching: Your Students!

Realize that you are influencing your students individually and corporately in your church. Realize also that your students may change from week to week in how they respond and react to the sown Word. Like Peter, one student may walk into class as a coward in the courtyard one week (Matthew 26:69-75) and as a bold preacher in a public forum the following (Acts 2:14-36). Like Thomas, another student may come as a person of great courage one week (John 11:16), as a doubter the next (20:24-25), and as a devout worshipper the third (20:26-28).

In his book on managerial leadership, Kenneth H. Blanchard writes, "Everyone is a potential winner. Some people are disguised as losers; don't let their appearance fool you." God knows which students will yield that hundredfold crop (Matthew 13:8, 23), so let Him worry about that. Your goal as a teacher should be that every lesson will promote spiritual maturity for the building of the body of Christ as you sow the Word (Ephesians 4:11-16). *Passionately teach!*

Teaching as a Passion

Realize how awesome it is for a Christian to be privileged to teach the Bible to others! Make it your goal to be like Apollos, who not only was "fervent in the spirit, . . . and taught diligently the things of the Lord" (Acts 18:25) but also was open to being taught "the way of God more perfectly" (18:26). The old cliché "leaders are readers" includes the idea that teachers never stop learning. This, too, is part of your passion to teach.

A Kingdom of Priests, A Holy Nation

Devotional Reading: Leviticus 19:1-10
Background Scripture: Exodus 19

Exodus 19:1-14

1 In the third month, when the children of Israel were gone forth out of the land of Egypt, the same day came they into the wilderness of Sinai.

2 For they were departed from Rephidim, and were come to the desert of Sinai, and had pitched in the wilderness; and there Israel camped before the mount.

3 And Moses went up unto God, and the LORD called unto him out of the mountain, saying, Thus shalt thou say to the house of Jacob, and tell the children of Israel;

4 Ye have seen what I did unto the Egyptians, and how I bare you on eagles' wings, and brought you unto myself.

5 Now therefore, if ye will obey my voice indeed, and keep my covenant, then ye shall be a peculiar treasure unto me above all people: for all the earth is mine:

6 And ye shall be unto me a kingdom of priests, and an holy nation. These are the words which thou shalt speak unto the children of Israel.

7 And Moses came and called for the elders of the people, and laid before their faces all these words which the LORD commanded him.

8 And all the people answered together, and said, all that the LORD hath spoken we will do. And Moses returned the words of the people unto the LORD.

9 And the LORD said unto Moses, Lo, I come unto thee in a thick cloud, that the people may hear when I speak with thee, and believe thee for ever. And Moses told the words of the people unto the LORD.

10 And the LORD said unto Moses, Go unto the people, and sanctify them to day and to morrow, and let them wash their clothes,

11 And be ready against the third day: for the third day the LORD will come down in the sight of all the people upon mount Sinai.

12 And thou shalt set bounds unto the people round about, saying, Take heed to yourselves, that ye go not up into the mount, or touch the border of it: whosoever toucheth the mount shall be surely put to death:

13 There shall not an hand touch it, but he shall surely be stoned, or shot through; whether it be beast or man, it shall not live: when the trumpet soundeth long, they shall come up to the mount.

14 And Moses went down from the mount unto the people, and sanctified the people; and they washed their clothes.

Key Text

Therefore, if ye will obey my voice indeed, and keep my covenant, then ye shall be a peculiar treasure unto me above all people: for all the earth is mine: and ye shall be unto me a kingdom of priests, and an holy nation. —**Exodus 19:5b-6a**

233

Costly
Sacrifices

Unit 1: Tabernacle, Sacrifices, and Atonement
Lessons 1–5

Lesson Aims

After participating in this lesson, each learner will be able to:

1. Summarize God's expectations as expressed through Moses.

2. Explain the concept of "covenant" in its original context.

3. Declare God's praises as one of His treasured people.

Lesson Outline

Introduction

A. Mediating Peace

When I look at the news and see turmoil in the Middle East, I remember the wars I witnessed as a child. The nation of Israel had defeated its neighbors in the Six-Day War (1967) and the Yom Kippur War (1973). Hostilities still persisted between the two sides. But something remarkable happened in 1978: two staunch enemies, Israel and Egypt, signed a peace treaty known as the Camp David Accords. Those talks didn't resolve every issue or change the fact that the nations had fought bitterly. But Egypt formally recognized Israel's right to exist, and in exchange, Israel returned all captured territory in the Sinai Peninsula.

Like all peace treaties between nations, it took both sides—represented by Anwar Sadat of Egypt and Menachem Begin of Israel—to find common ground and shared goals. The peace talks also required a patient mediator—the United States and President Jimmy Carter—to bring them together.

The key role of a mediator is related to today's lesson in three ways. First, Moses played the role of communicator and mediator at Mount Sinai. Second, God communicated a plan through His mediator to form Israel to be a "kingdom of priests" and a "holy nation" (Exodus 19:6). Third, those functions took on new meaning at the coming of the ultimate mediator, Christ, who brings lasting peace to all who turn to Him with faith (Romans 5:1).

B. Lesson Context

Four hundred thirty years from the time of Joseph, God delivered Israel out of Egypt (Exodus 12:40; 18:10). Through miraculous plagues, which showed Egypt's deities to be powerless (7:8–11:10; 12:29-42), God brought the people out into the wilderness, where He continued to protect and provide for them (Exodus 13–18). In spite of dangers and trials, the people arrived at their destination: Sinai, the mountain where God had first revealed himself to Moses (Exodus 3). Exodus 19 begins the climactic meeting of God with His redeemed people.

I. Coming to Sinai
(Exodus 19:1-2)
A. The Wilderness (v. 1)

1. In the third month, when the children of Israel were gone forth out of the land of Egypt, the same day came they into the wilderness of Sinai.

The first two verses of Exodus 19 bookend the narrative that began at Exodus 7:16: Moses had been sent to bring the Hebrew people out of Egypt "that they might serve [God] in the wilderness." The verse before us gives an indication of how long they had been traveling: this is *the third month* since leaving *Egypt* (compare Exodus 12:2; 13:4). The Hebrew word translated "month" can also mean "new moon" (examples: 1 Samuel 20:5, 18, 24). A new moon is how ancient people would mark this passage of time. The *wilderness of Sinai* was adjacent to the wilderness of Sin, where the people had been traveling (Exodus 16:1; 17:1). They had been without natural access to water or food, and they remained dependent upon God's provision of each.

What Do You Think?

What insights can you share about experiencing God's provision during a relocation?

Digging Deeper

How might those insights differ between voluntary and involuntary relocations?

B. The Mountain (v. 2)

2. For they were departed from Rephidim, and were come to the desert of Sinai, and had pitched in the wilderness; and there Israel camped before the mount.

Rephidim is where Moses struck a rock to produce water for the children of Israel, who doubted God's provision (Exodus 17:1-7). It is also where the Israelites fought the Amalekites, a group who came out to wage war on God's people in their vulnerable state. In response, God provided supernatural protection by allowing Moses to raise his hands to assure victory (17:8-16).

Now at their interim destination, the people camped before Mount *Sinai*, also called Mount Horeb (Exodus 3:1). It is where Moses saw the burning bush and removed his sandals before holy ground (3:5). But the geographical location of Sinai is much-debated by archaeologists and researchers. One possible location, Jabal Musa, is at the southern tip of the Sinai Peninsula. Some object that the Hebrews could not have reached this location so soon after leaving Egypt, and they propose other sites. Since Scripture does not give a precise location, the issue remains contentious.

The Hebrews would spend just under a year camped before this mountain (compare Exodus 19:1 with Numbers 10:11-12).

II. God's Chosen People
(Exodus 19:3-6)
A. Rescued (vv. 3-4)

3. And Moses went up unto God, and the LORD called unto him out of the mountain, saying, Thus shalt thou say to the house of Jacob, and tell the children of Israel.

In the ancient Near Eastern world, high elevations were considered holy sites. These were places closer to Heaven and the gods who were thought to live there. The "high places" in the land of Israel were even used to worship God before the construction of a temple (1 Kings 3:2). Some five centuries later, Solomon's temple was constructed at a high elevation and as the proper place of worship.

4. Ye have seen what I did unto the Egyptians, and how I bare you on eagles' wings, and brought you unto myself.

This is the first message carried by Moses— a direct speech of God. The exchange is analogous to "declarations" in a traditional wedding ceremony, which are spoken before a bride and

How to Say It

Amalekites	*Am*-uh-leh-kites or Uh-*mal*-ih-kites.
Rephidim	*Ref*-ih-dim.
Sinai	*Sigh*-nye or *Sigh*-nay-eye.
theophany	the-*ah*-fuh-nee.

OBEY GOD AND KEEP HIS COVENANT.

Visual for Lesson 1. *Have this visual on display as you discuss the lesson commentary associated with Exodus 19:5.*

groom take their vows. God is declaring what He has done by choosing the descendants of Jacob and rescuing them from slavery. The words supply a rationale for making an agreement with the Lord: He is the God who delivers.

God had sent plagues on the Egyptians and shown their magicians and deities to be toothless (see Exodus 7:8–11:10; 12:29-42; compare Psalm 106). The reference to *eagles' wings* might stand for species of great birds that "fluttereth over [their] young, spreadeth abroad [their] wings, taketh them, beareth them on [their] wings" (Deuteronomy 32:11). This is an image of great care (compare Isaiah 40:31). God had fulfilled His plan by bringing the formerly enslaved people to this mountain to serve Him (Exodus 3:12). And the Hebrew people didn't just barely escape from *Egypt*; they were led out by the glorious power of God—"flown away" so to speak, as if carried by a majestic bird.

The image might seem ironic to a people tired of walking. But their deliverance from Egypt was unprecedented and a clear indication of the benevolent power of their rescuer-God.

Carried Along for the Journey

Mine is a family of cyclists—at least in theory. My wife and I enjoyed a good ride for many years before our kids came along. There are few memories of parenthood I treasure more than the ecstatic smile that came across my daughter's face when she rode a bike without assistance for the first time.

But when our second child was born, we had to make a new plan. So, instead, we turned to the next best family activity: walking. I found that I could get my heart pumping by strapping a growing child to a carrier on my back while I circuited the neighborhood. And he didn't seem to mind one bit. In fact, that became the routine for his nap. Somehow, nothing would put him to sleep like the steady trotting of his father or mother and the security he felt on a new adventure.

God invites the Israelites to picture a similar image in Exodus 19:4, "I bare you on eagles' wings." I can relate to the tender confidence in that statement, the way God reminded the Israelites of all the dangers passed and trials overcome. Has God done something similar in your life, perhaps carrying you to the place you need to be? Or, perhaps, are you on a journey with your Heavenly Father right now?   —J. H.

B. Treasured (v. 5)

5. Now therefore, if ye will obey my voice indeed, and keep my covenant, then ye shall be a peculiar treasure unto me above all people: for all the earth is mine.

The speech continues with a conditional statement, a way of explaining the logic of *covenant*. God is the initiator of a covenant, just as He made a covenant with Abraham (Genesis 12:1-3; 15; 17). Covenant is part of His plan to bring blessing to the world. Typically, covenants were agreements between two parties (usually humans or nations). The promise is that, *if* the people hold up the requirements of the covenant, *then [they] shall be a peculiar treasure . . . above all people.* Israel's obedience would set them apart from all the world.

God's claim of ownership of *all the earth* justifies His particular election of Jacob's children. If God lacked rights to the whole, He would not have the ability to choose. But the creator God breathed into humans the breath of life (Genesis 2:7). He is the redeeming God whose covenant people shall be a blessing to all the earth, in continuation of His promise to Abraham (12:3).

C. Holy (v. 6)

6. And ye shall be unto me a kingdom

of priests, and an holy nation. These are the words which thou shalt speak unto the children of Israel.

The *holy* status that the Israelites received was not intended just for their personal benefit but ultimately for the benefit of the world as *a kingdom of priests*. This rationale is also discussed in the first century when Jesus told the Samaritan woman, "Salvation is of the Jews" (John 4:22). Likewise, the apostle Paul acknowledges the privileged position of Jewish people: "Unto them were committed the oracles of God" (Romans 3:2). Moses had been modeling a mediating role for God's people as he accurately reported *the words* spoken by God all along.

The description "a royal priesthood, an holy nation" is valid for God's people of the new covenant (1 Peter 2:9). Unlike the Sinai covenant, which would be repeatedly broken, the redemptive work of Jesus offers Christ's followers a "new covenant" (see Jeremiah 31:31-32).

> ### What Do You Think?
> How would you explain to someone what being part of the new covenant priesthood means?
>
> ### Digging Deeper
> How would your explanation to a person agnostic to faith differ from your explanation to a new Christian?

Building a Foundation

I have done quite a few DIY projects as the owner of an old house, and I've learned a thing or two about proper preparation. When I first tiled a bathroom floor, I thought I knew what I was doing. I selected the right materials: tile, grout, and underlayment. The last thing I wanted was for my project to end in failure.

I had neglected to consider what lay beneath the surface. After demolishing an existing floor, I was left staring at severe water damage to the subfloor. Suddenly, I had to learn something else. I had my work cut out to replace the damage. Otherwise, I would have been covering up a more significant problem and asking for things to fall apart later.

Sometimes, we try to prepare for something new, but we might imagine a narrow set of concerns. Often, we need to spend the most work building solid foundations to ensure everything else isn't in vain. I imagine that's what God was doing for the Israelites in Exodus 19. Instead of leading them directly to their promised land—giving them instant consolation—God took His time. The Lord did everything possible to lay a solid foundation in their covenant relationship, for God wanted them to remember their mission and their redemptive history. Can you think of any way that God has been preparing you? Has there been an area of your life that requires starting from scratch? —J. H.

III. God Shall Come
(Exodus 19:7-14)
A. The People Agree (vv. 7-8)

7. And Moses came and called for the elders of the people, and laid before their faces all these words which the LORD commanded him.

Moses was a faithful servant because he relayed all that God had told him. *Before their faces* may seem like an odd way to give *words*. But the expression is perhaps used in the general sense to mean "in front of them." The text does not say whether Moses used a form of writing at this point. But in Exodus 20:1-17, Moses will relay ten "words," also called the Ten Commandments. The verse before us anticipates what Moses shall do by bringing down commands of God, commands that corporate Israel were expected to obey.

Moses gave them to a chosen group of *elders*, which was much more practical than trying to communicate with thousands of people all at once. The representatives were expected to relay the information to everyone else.

> ### What Do You Think?
> What is one thing you can improve on to ensure that your actions match the Word that God has called you to proclaim?
>
> ### Digging Deeper
> What are some indicators that a situation calls for silence rather than speaking?

8. And all the people answered together, and said, All that the LORD hath spoken we will do. And Moses returned the words of the people unto the LORD.

Words of this verse—the collective agreement of *all the people*—are repeated in Exodus 24:3, 7. But here in Exodus 19, how can they agree to stipulations they have yet to hear? This is a common question, one even raised by ancient Jewish rabbinical interpreters. One possibility is that the people agreed to and accepted God's offer of covenant even before they were told its requirements. Exodus 19–20 gives a clearer description of the covenant. Under that reading, the people's response did not conclude or seal the agreement. Instead, it shows Israel's eagerness to follow whatever God would have them do. The fact that Moses *returned the words of the people unto the Lord* means that he ascended the mountain to speak with God again.

What Do You Think?
What are some ways to prevent corporate confessions from becoming mere rituals?
Digging Deeper
What examples from Scripture point to this happening?

B. Divine Presence Anticipated (v. 9)

9. And the LORD said unto Moses, Lo, I come unto thee in a thick cloud, that the people may hear when I speak with thee, and believe thee for ever. And Moses told the words of the people unto the LORD.

Once Moses had returned to speak with God, he was informed about a pending divine appearance. The technical name for this is *theophany*, which means an appearance or visible manifestation of God. Earlier in Exodus, God had used a cloud to reveal His presence and to give a sign of His protection (Exodus 13:21). In the New Testament, the Father speaks from a cloud at Jesus' transfiguration (Matthew 17:5-6; Mark 9:7-8; Luke 9:34-35). Later, Jesus ascends from a mountaintop and is taken up in a cloud, which shows God's heavenly presence (Acts 1:9). Here,

the function of God's appearance in *a thick cloud* shows Moses' authority as God's messenger. Now and into the future (*for ever*), God wants the people to *believe* Moses. This idea is repeated in John 5:46, where Jesus says that those who disbelieve His testimony are also disbelieving Moses, who "wrote" about Jesus.

C. Moses Gives Instructions (vv. 10-14)

10-11. And the LORD said unto Moses, Go unto the people, and sanctify them to day and to morrow, and let them wash their clothes, And be ready against the third day: for the third day the LORD will come down in the sight of all the people upon mount Sinai.

This verse begins direct speech from God that Moses was to convey to the Israelites. They must be correctly prepared to receive God's presence. The command to *let them wash their clothes* forms an *inclusio* with Exodus 19:14 (see below). Two days will be the length of this preparation, and the command to *sanctify* is of the same root as "holy" in 19:6. The verb means "to transform someone into the state of holiness" or "to dedicate." Moses will direct the people to avoid ceremonially unclean things, while at the same time they will wash and prepare themselves in body and spirit. Washing of clothing is associated with holiness in dozens of places in the Old Testament.

What Do You Think?
What are some ways you can better reflect your consecrated status to the world?
Digging Deeper
What guardrails are available to keep that reflecting from becoming legalistic or "holier than thou"?

12. And thou shalt set bounds unto the people round about, saying, Take heed to yourselves, that ye go not up into the mount, or touch the border of it: whosoever toucheth the mount shall be surely put to death.

Moses was already on the mountain when he heard this, so the prohibition didn't apply to him.

A constructed perimeter would reinforce that Moses—no one else—was to be the one to whom all the people must listen.

God's holiness was not something to haphazardly approach. Merely touching the area's *border* would bring death. This penalty is less as a punishment than a means to protect the community from a defiler's misdeed.

13. There shall not an hand touch it, but he shall surely be stoned, or shot through; whether it be beast or man, it shall not live: when the trumpet soundeth long, they shall come up to the mount.

Here, the warning is heightened: even a single *hand*—perhaps laid upon the mountain in curiosity—or the mindless trampling of an animal would be enough to warrant death through stoning or arrows. Both forms of execution would allow others to remain at a distance from the one who had violated God's space. The people were not to permit anything defiling to remain in their midst as they prepared to meet God.

A *trumpet* sound was to be the signal to approach. This would have been a ram's horn rather than a brass instrument. God does not specify who was to be the one to blow it, to see that it *soundeth long*. At the signal a few verses later, the blower of this horn is once more unidentified (Exodus 19:19). One possibility is that God's angel is responsible, since the signal comes from the mountain where humans have not been allowed to tread, except for Moses.

14. And Moses went down from the mount unto the people, and sanctified the people; and they washed their clothes.

The text does not say how *Moses sanctified the people*. But washing of *clothes* is a form of ceremonial cleansing and is specified dozens of times in Leviticus and Numbers. Usually, it is prescribed when an individual or priest is being cleansed from something unclean (example: Leviticus 15:5-12). Two days would probably not be required to complete the washing. But a time of spiritual preparation is also appropriate when entering God's presence. By implication, the Israelites were being treated as the "nation of priests" that God had named them in Exodus 19:6, since proper clothing and preparation would come to be required of priests (example: Exodus 40:12-16).

Conclusion

A. Holy God, Holy People

In its context, Exodus 19 shows the responsibilities that fall upon people whom God chooses and redeems. They are required to prepare themselves for God's presence. In the new covenant context, it is not church buildings that house God's presence; rather, it is the bodies of Christians themselves, those who become a "temple of the Holy Ghost" (1 Corinthians 6:19). Followers of Jesus also serve as mediators who introduce others to the ultimate mediator, Jesus Christ (Hebrews 9:15).

By making Israel His "kingdom of priests" and "holy nation" (Exodus 19:6), God was laying the groundwork to bless the world through the children of Jacob. Israel would break the Sinai covenant and fall victim to sin, but God had a plan to make a new covenant (Jeremiah 31:31-32; compare Matthew 26:28). For Christians, the promise that "all families of the earth be blessed" (Genesis 12:3) has come true, in and through Jesus. He is the seed of Abraham, the inheritor of God's promise (Galatians 3:16). Christ alone, because He is God's Son, is fit to be *king* of God's kingdom; the permanent *high priest* to a group of priests, He is the perfect *mediator* between God and humans.

B. Prayer

Lord, we sometimes feel inadequate as representatives of Your holiness. May we be found to be Your faithful servants and a royal priesthood despite our shortcomings. We pray in Christ's name. Amen.

C. Thought to Remember

The holy God is the redeeming God.

Visuals FOR THESE LESSONS

The visual pictured in each lesson (example: page 236) is a small reproduction of a large, full-color poster included in the *Adult Resources* packet for the Spring Quarter. Order No. 9780784740132 from your supplier.

Involvement Learning

Enhance your lesson with KJV Bible Student *(from your curriculum supplier) and the reproducible activity page (at www.standardlesson.com or in the back of the* KJV Standard Lesson Commentary Deluxe Edition*).*

Into the Lesson

Have this brainstorming question posted for all to see as class members arrive:

What methods does God use to get our attention?

Expect a wide variety of responses, including *sickness, tragedy*, and *godly counsel from others.*

Lead into Bible study by saying, "Today, we will look at an incident from ancient Israel's history that featured an attention-getting method of an exceptional nature."

Into the Word

Arrange for a class member to give a brief presentation on the historical context of today's text. The presentation should summarize Exodus 1–18 in no more than eight minutes. *Alternative.* Show the six-and-a-half minute video on Exodus 1–18 from the Bible Project, found online. Caution: the video streaming site that hosts the video may interrupt it with commercials unless you have their "premium" subscription.

Next, have the text read dramatically by two participants, one being the voice of the narrator, the other being the voice of God. Have them read their respective parts of the text. The class as a whole should respond with the words of Exodus 19:8b when the narration reaches that point. (*Option.* To make this go more smoothly, print and distribute the text in advance with the three speaking parts highlighted in different colors.)

Then, form participants into study pairs or triads. Distribute handouts (you create) on which are printed the following three tasks:

1–Summarize God's expectations as expressed through Moses.
2–Explain the concept of "covenant" in its original context.
3–List questions about the text that come to mind.

After several minutes, reconvene for a whole-class discussion.

Alternative. Depending on the nature of your class, you may find better instructional value in posing only the first question for the pairs or triads to consider, followed by a whole-class discussion of only the responses to it. Then, repeat the cycle for the second and third tasks individually.

After discussing the three tasks, display three posters, widely separated. Have the following topics on the posters, one each:

GOD'S FAITHFULNESS
THE PRIESTHOOD OF ALL
ACCEPTABLE WORSHIP

Invite class members to indicate by show of hands which of the three topics interests them most. Form study groups based on those preferences, with at least two participants per group. Distribute handouts (you create) with the following questions:

1–What does today's Scripture say about this topic?
2–What does this account suggest for our behavior today?

Use the responses to the second question as a transition to the Into Life segment.

Into Life

God's Faithfulness. Extend this discussion by asking how we have even more proof of God's faithfulness than the Israelites had. Invite responses in whole-class discussion.

The Priesthood of All. Ask participants to name ways that Christians can be mediators of God's grace today. *Option.* Distribute copies of the "A Holy Priesthood and a Priesthood Wholly" exercise from the activity page, which you can download. Assign the five texts to five pairs or triads to complete as indicated.

Acceptable Worship. Brainstorm valid ways to declare God's praises today.

As learners depart, distribute copies of the "Who, Where, Etc." puzzle from the activity page.

A Space for God

Devotional Reading: John 4:13-26
Background Scripture: Exodus 25–27

Exodus 25:1-9

1 And the LORD spake unto Moses, saying,

2 Speak unto the children of Israel, that they bring me an offering: of every man that giveth it willingly with his heart ye shall take my offering.

3 And this is the offering which ye shall take of them; gold, and silver, and brass,

4 And blue, and purple, and scarlet, and fine linen, and goats' hair,

5 And rams' skins dyed red, and badgers' skins, and shittim wood,

6 Oil for the light, spices for anointing oil, and for sweet incense,

7 Onyx stones, and stones to be set in the ephod, and in the breastplate.

8 And let them make me a sanctuary; that I may dwell among them.

9 According to all that I shew thee, after the pattern of the tabernacle, and the pattern of all the instruments thereof, even so shall ye make it.

Exodus 26:1, 31-37

1 Moreover thou shalt make the tabernacle with ten curtains of fine twined linen, and blue, and purple, and scarlet: with cherubims of cunning work shalt thou make them.

31 And thou shalt make a vail of blue, and purple, and scarlet, and fine twined linen of cunning work: with cherubims shall it be made:

32 And thou shalt hang it upon four pillars of shittim wood overlaid with gold: their hooks shall be of gold, upon the four sockets of silver.

33 And thou shalt hang up the vail under the taches, that thou mayest bring in thither within the vail the ark of the testimony: and the vail shall divide unto you between the holy place and the most holy.

34 And thou shalt put the mercy seat upon the ark of the testimony in the most holy place.

35 And thou shalt set the table without the vail, and the candlestick over against the table on the side of the tabernacle toward the south: and thou shalt put the table on the north side.

36 And thou shalt make an hanging for the door of the tent, of blue, and purple, and scarlet, and fine twined linen, wrought with needlework.

37 And thou shalt make for the hanging five pillars of shittim wood, and overlay them with gold, and their hooks shall be of gold: and thou shalt cast five sockets of brass for them.

Key Text

Let them make me a sanctuary; that I may dwell among them. —**Exodus 25:8**

Costly
Sacrifices

Lesson Aims

After participating in this lesson, each learner will be able to:

1. Categorize the types of offerings that God specified.

2. Compare God's instructions to Moses with New Testament directives.

3. Write a prayer of gratitude for God's willingness to dwell with him or her today.

Lesson Outline

Introduction
  A. Many Spaces for God
  B. Lesson Context
I. Gift from the Heart (Exodus 25:1-9)
  A. Items for Construction (vv. 1-5)
  B. Items for Service (vv. 6-9)
    Tools for a Task
II. Tabernacle Directions (Exodus 26:1, 31-37)
  A. The Curtains (v. 1)
  B. The Veil (vv. 31-35)
    Memory Box
  C. The Doorway (vv. 36-37)
Conclusion
  A. Carrying the Presence
  B. Prayer
  C. Thought to Remember

Introduction

A. Many Spaces for God

I love to visit old church buildings, especially those with oaken pews and stained-glass windows. When I was in Jordan, I visited the ruins of Petra, a sixth-century church built in the canyon walls.

But the church that stands out most in my memory was in a small village in the jungle of the Dominican Republic. I had been invited to preach at this little church while a friend translated. When we arrived, it was unlike any church building I'd seen before; I've had bigger sheds! The walls were wooden planks with daylight peeking through, the roof was made of tin, and there were no chairs—only wooden boards on tree stumps.

For as small a group as gathered there, it was a joyous assembly of God's people. I don't often experience worship like that in the United States. That day reminded me that praising the one true God can happen in any place. Today's lesson examines the construction of God's tabernacle, the specially designed place that God asked His people to create. God wanted to be in their midst.

B. Lesson Context

The narrative of Scripture as a whole can be summarized according to the ways that God mediates His presence to His creation. After banishing humans from the Garden of Eden, where God himself walked (Genesis 3:8), He set in motion a plan to restore the relationship that had been broken by sin.

God's rescue of Israel from the Egyptians was a major step in that plan. Two months later, God initiated a covenant agreement with the Israelites (Exodus 19). The Sinai covenant was given for God's people to be able to live with the divine presence in their midst.

Their breaking of the covenant didn't take long (Exodus 32:7-8). Even so, God continued in faithfulness as He brought the Israelites to the land of inheritance, the land promised to them as children of Abraham (Genesis 13:14-17).

In the context of today's lesson, Moses—living

more than 500 years after Abraham—had gone up Mount Sinai and entered the cloud of God's presence (Exodus 24:15-18). During that 40-day encounter, God gave him instructions for a tabernacle, for the items to fill it, and for the ministry of the priests. These instructions span Exodus 25–31 (see lesson 3). God desired to grant access to His holy presence, but that required a systematic approach to prevent anything profane (not just sin, but also things ritually unclean) from entering the tabernacle.

I. Gift from the Heart
(Exodus 25:1-9)
A. Items for Construction (vv. 1-5)

1. And the LORD spake unto Moses, saying.

Since the Israelites arrived at Sinai in Exodus 19:1, *Moses had been functioning as a mediator:* taking messages from God down the mountain and returning responses from the people. The instructions came directly from God, and Moses did not alter the words. He received these words while on the mountain, hidden from the people's sight for 40 days (Exodus 24:18).

2. Speak unto the children of Israel, that they bring me an offering: of every man that giveth it willingly with his heart ye shall take my offering.

The word *willingly* indicates that the *offering* God prescribed was to be voluntary. Worship through giving must be motivated internally rather than externally. This is analogous to the "cheerful" giver praised by the apostle Paul when he collected an offering (2 Corinthians 9:7).

God did not specify that the offering be taken up for the construction of a tabernacle—although that is what it would be used to build—but God said *bring me an offering.* As gifts, these offerings are directed first and foremost to God.

But why should the Israelites, as former slaves of Egypt, possess valuable items worthy of an offering? Before they left Egypt, they received valuable articles from their Egyptian captors (Exodus 3:21; 11:2-3; 12:35-36). God's intervention made this possible (12:36). Thus, in a key sense, the offering given to God was surrendering those items that

God had helped the people receive in the first place, for this very purpose.

3. And this is the offering which ye shall take of them; gold, and silver, and brass.

This verse describes the first of several kinds of things acceptable for the offering—and perhaps these metals come first because they were most valuable. Additional metals of iron, tin, or lead are not mentioned (Numbers 31:22).

The most valuable of the three was (and still is) *gold;* some form of that word occurs over 100 times in the book of Exodus alone. Gold was used in ways other than as a medium of exchange (money). Most tabernacle furnishings would be either overlaid with gold or made from pure gold (Exodus 25:11-18; 23-31, 38-39). More than four centuries later, King Solomon would add to or replace articles, also using gold (1 Kings 7:48-50); he minimized the use of *silver* (10:21).

Many other items would be made of *brass* (Exodus 26:11, 37; 27:1-8; 30:17-21). Brass is an alloy of copper and zinc. That alloy was not created until about 500 BC, many centuries after the events of the text. The intent of the text is to point to bronze, an alloy of copper and tin. *Silver* would be used mainly for the "sockets" for supporting wooden beams of the tabernacle structure itself (26:19, 21, 25, 32).

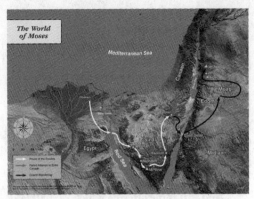

The World of Moses

Mediterranean Sea

Visual for Lesson 2. *Display this visual as you review the people and places associated with lessons 1–3.*

4. And blue, and purple, and scarlet, and fine linen, and goats' hair.

In antiquity, fabric dyes were not readily available and would need to be carefully sourced. A garment's value was tied to the rarity of its dye, with *blue, purple,* and *scarlet* being among the rarest (compare Luke 16:19; Acts 16:14; Revelation 17:4; 18:12). These shades of violet or blueish-dyed wool would be created from crushed mollusks and certain plants. They would be used in the construction of artistic curtains (Exodus 26:31). With *fine linen and goats' hair* (which could be spun into yarn), rare fabrics would enclose the tabernacle to create its walls and layers (26:7).

5. And rams' skins dyed red, and badgers' skins, and shittim wood.

Leather *dyed red* would probably be colored from a tanning process. The reference to *badgers' skins* comes from a rare Hebrew word that resembles the Arabic word for "porpoise." Sea creatures inhabit the Red Sea and could have been hunted by the Egyptians for their fine hides. *Shittim wood* is useful for the construction of furniture and structural beams. It is also called "acacia wood." Its wood is extremely dense and is a desirable building material.

B. Items for Service (vv. 6-9)

6. Oil for the light, spices for anointing oil, and for sweet incense.

The two types of *oil* are for different purposes in the function of the planned sanctuary. Oil *for the light* was to be burned in the lampstand (Exodus 25:31-36). Since the tabernacle was to be without windows, light would come only from lamps. A depiction of the Jewish menorah is found upon the Arch of Titus in Rome, which shows a lampstand carried out of the destroyed second temple. It is possible—though impossible to be certain—that the original lampstand for the tabernacle followed this familiar design.

On the other hand, *anointing* oil would be used for just that purpose—not only on people but also on tabernacle furnishings (Exodus 30:22-33). It was perfumed according to the formula of 30:23-24 to contain "myrrh," "sweet cinnamon," "sweet calamus," "cassia," and "oil olive." *Sweet incense* was to be made according to a formula in Exodus 30:34, and it has "stacte," "onycha," "galbanum," and "frankincense." When burned, the result would be a visible cloud of fragrant smoke. The formulations of the anointing oil and the incense were proprietary to God (30:33, 37). In the imagery of Revelation 8:3-4, the burning of incense symbolizes the prayers of God's people as they rise to Heaven.

7. Onyx stones, and stones to be set in the ephod, and in the breastplate.

Onyx are the only *stones* mentioned by name for *the ephod* and *breastplate*, two items of the high priest's attire (see lesson 3). The names of the other precious stones are listed in Exodus 28:17-20. The onyx stones were to be two in number, each engraved with the names of 6 of the 12 tribes of Israel (Exodus 28:9-11). Four rows of three precious stones each would be set in the breastplate of the ephod, "with the names of the children of Israel, twelve, . . . like the engravings of a signet" (28:21). The high priest would wear the names of all 12 tribes when he came before God's presence and entered the holy place (see 28:12, 29-30).

8. And let them make me a sanctuary; that I may dwell among them.

This short verse indicates the reason for these details: God wants to *dwell* with His people. So, He directed the people to construct a place suitable to that purpose: *a sanctuary*. This refers to the tabernacle (or to the holiest part thereof) and, much later, the temple. The layers of curtains as walls and partitions would, on the one hand, clearly separate the sacred space of God from anything profane among the people. On the other hand, the sanctuary would announce God's presence, for it would be the most prominent feature of Israel's camp.

9. According to all that I shew thee, after the pattern of the tabernacle, and the pattern of all the instruments thereof, even so shall ye make it.

The pattern of the tabernacle and *the pattern of all the instruments* were prescribed by God alone. Some Bible interpreters think the phrase *that I shew thee* means that a Heavenly tabernacle or temple was shown to Moses so that the earthly tabernacle would be built in its likeness. In support of this, Stephen in Acts 7:44 calls the tabernacle to have been made "according to the fashion that [Moses] had seen." Likewise, the writer of Hebrews 8:5 says that Moses made the tabernacle "according to the pattern shewed to" him.

What Do You Think?
How would you respond to the claim that buildings such as temples or sanctuaries are necessary for the presence of God?
Digging Deeper
How do John 1:14; 1 Corinthians 3:16-17; 2 Corinthians 6:16-18; Ephesians 2:21-22; and 1 Peter 2:5 inform your response?

Tools for a Task

When my grandfather died, he left behind a remarkable collection of tools. Although he wasn't wealthy, he had acquired so many flashlights, screwdrivers, gloves, pocketknives, and watches that I always wondered why he showed an interest in these items. Why would anyone need 20 screwdrivers?

It was the watches that captured my attention as a child. I remembered that he was always wearing one, always prepared to share the time when someone asked. Actually, that explains almost everything in his collection: he wanted to be prepared. Whether he needed to fix, open, or shed light on something, he was ready.

You might say that is what God was doing when giving all these instructions for the tabernacle. The priests would need light, so God planned for them to have oil for lamps. The ark of the covenant would need a separate space, so God gave them plans for curtains and veils. The priests would need instruments for service, so God intended for them to use precious metals like gold—metals that don't tend to corrode. In a sense, all these instructions show a spirit of practicality and a concern for the details. You might look at your own life and the resources God has given you. What tasks have you been prepared to complete? What service does God ask you to render when you examine your tools and resources?—J. H.

II. Tabernacle Directions
(Exodus 26:1, 31-37)
A. The Curtains (v. 1)

1. Moreover thou shalt make the tabernacle with ten curtains of fine twined linen, and blue, and purple, and scarlet: with cherubims of cunning work shalt thou make them.

After describing the construction of the tabernacle's contents in Exodus 25:10-40, Exodus 26:1 begins with specifications of the tabernacle's construction itself. *Linen* is made from the fibers of the flax plant. The size of these *ten curtains* is noted in 26:2, not in today's lesson text). Regarding the rare colors of *blue, and purple, and scarlet*, see commentary on Exodus 25:4, above.

The inclusion of *cherubims* is a new detail (compare Exodus 25:18). This might mean that the curtains were going to feature images of these beings woven in. Cherubim are angelic attendants of God. They are mentioned dozens of times in the Old Testament but never in the New Testament. The ark of the covenant was constructed to feature two cherubim of gold on its cover (25:18-20).

B. The Veil (vv. 31-35)

31. And thou shalt make a vail of blue, and purple, and scarlet, and fine twined linen of cunning work: with cherubims shall it be made.

The *vail* (spelled *veil* in the New Testament) mentioned here is different from the "curtains" described in Exodus 26:1. While constructed of the same material and decorated the same way, the veil has a unique function: it separated the holy place from the most holy place within the tabernacle. The same word is later used for the dividing veil in Solomon's temple (compare 2 Chronicles 3:14).

32. And thou shalt hang it upon four pillars of shittim wood overlaid with gold: their hooks shall be of gold, upon the four sockets of silver.

The reason the veil needed to be supported by *four pillars . . . overlaid with gold* was so it could hang and serve as the necessary partition. These golden rods would nest into silver sockets (from the gold and silver that were given in the offering). The poles would be spaced to support the stretched veil, which appears to be designed as one piece, unlike the curtains. Thus, the veil had no gaps as it sectioned off the area of the presence of God. This is the same kind of veil found in the temple in Jesus' day, and it would be torn from top to bottom at His death (Matthew 27:51).

33. And thou shalt hang up the vail under the taches, that thou mayest bring in thither within the vail the ark of the testimony: and the vail shall divide unto you between the holy place and the most holy.

Here is the explanation for the veil's use: it separated areas within the tabernacle. This division was to shield the area known as *the most holy* (which housed the very glory of God) from the area called *the holy place*. It was to be hung on *taches* (connecting buckles or rings) that were attached to four pillars. Only a single item is designated for the *most holy* place: the *ark of the testimony*, which is another name for "ark of the covenant" (Numbers 10:33; 14:44). At first, the box would contain only the tablets of the covenant (Exodus 25:16, 23). Eventually, other items would be added as signs of God's provision (Hebrews 9:4).

How to Say It

acacia	uh-*kay*-shuh.
cherubim	*chair*-uh-bim.
ephod	*ee*-fod.
shittim	shih-*teem*.
tabernacle	*tah*-burr-*nah*-kul.

God is never described as being in the box. Instead, the ark is sometimes called God's "footstool," perhaps meaning that God was (invisibly) pictured as enthroned in Heaven while resting His feet at this point on earth (1 Chronicles 28:2; Psalms 99:5; 132:7; Isaiah 66:1). The ark would be a focal point of Israelite faith until its disappearance at the time of the Babylonian exile.

34. And thou shalt put the mercy seat upon the ark of the testimony in the most holy place.

The box itself was to be two and a half cubits by one and a half cubits, or the equivalent of about 45 by 27 inches (Exodus 25:10). Its shittim or acacia wood was covered in gold, but the *mercy seat* was a solid gold cover placed on the top (25:17). It is called a mercy seat because there, at that location between two golden cherubim, God promised to meet with Moses (25:22). God said, "I will appear in a cloud upon the mercy seat" (Leviticus 16:2). And on the Day of Atonement—one day each year when the high priest would enter the most holy place—the high priest was to sprinkle blood upon the mercy seat and make atonement "for himself, and for his household, and for all the congregation of Israel" (16:17).

35. And thou shalt set the table without the vail, and the candlestick over against the table on the side of the tabernacle toward the south: and thou shalt put the table on the north side.

The tabernacle faced east (Numbers 3:38). *The table* with incense and bread was to be placed on the side of the veil that did not face inward toward the most holy place. Likewise, *the candlestick* is designated for the south side. Nothing is said about the significance of the locations. Among other things, the table would hold 12 loaves of bread to symbolize the 12 tribes (Leviticus 24:5-9). This bread was to be eaten by priests since it would be replaced regularly as an offering to God.

Memory Box

On the top of my bookshelf lives a small box. My children could tell you some of its contents by heart: a wood carving from my trip to South America; silver coins I collected; two hospital bracelets that say "Father," the ones given to me when my children were born—my proof that I wasn't stealing a baby when my wife and I loaded each of them in an infant seat.

The ark of the covenant was a bit like a memory box. Every item added had a history. Of course, the Israelites did not handle the ark the way I handle my wooden box. Even so, I try to be sure that I've shown gratitude for all God has done.

If you were to fill such a box, what would it contain? How have you stewarded the memories of God's redemption in your life?　—J. H.

C. The Doorway (vv. 36-37)

36-37. And thou shalt make an hanging for the door of the tent, of blue, and purple, and scarlet, and fine twined linen, wrought with needlework. And thou shalt make for the hanging five pillars of shittim wood, and overlay them with gold, and their hooks shall be of gold: and thou shalt cast five sockets of brass for them.

The tabernacle doorway was to have the same coloring as the veil and curtains but would lack the interwoven cherubim decoration. The doorway was supported by five pillars instead of four, like the four holding up the internal veil. The metal used for the sockets was brass, a lesser material than the silver sockets within the tabernacle. The lesser value in the metal corresponds to the distance this doorway stands from the most holy place. The closer to God's presence, the more valuable the materials so as to reflect the value of sacred space.

> **What Do You Think?**
> In what ways can art and architecture be a way for you to honor and worship God?
> **Digging Deeper**
> How will your congregation use art in its worship of God?

Conclusion

A. Carrying the Presence

If we miss the wider context, these instructions for an offering and construction of a tabernacle seem oddly specific. Today, there is greater cultural consciousness around the giving of the Ten Com-

mandments than the building of a mobile sanctuary, but the irony is that the tabernacle was at the heart of the covenant as the most important blessing that Israel received: instructions to house the presence of God. As the people whom God had chosen to reflect His holiness, the ancient Israelites needed to live in such a way as to reflect their holy status. Otherwise, they would not be allowed to keep God's presence with them (Ezekiel 10).

The planning of materials, arrangement, and careful division of duties were necessary for this task. Without instructions, the people of Israel—who were by no means free of sin—could not have endured a holy God in their midst. But with the careful management of access, no one would haphazardly wander into the sacred space and look upon God enthroned above the mercy seat, for this would mean certain death (see a warning even to Aaron in Leviticus 16:2).

Thus, God is the ultimate planner. Not only did He plan the construction of a tabernacle, but He ensured that His people would have the necessary materials before they left the land of Egypt. Both in the Sinai covenant and in the new covenant, God can make a way for His presence to be with His people.

> **What Do You Think?**
> How has your understanding of worship changed because of this lesson?
> **Digging Deeper**
> What will you do in light of that change of thinking?

B. Prayer

Lord, may we recognize that You are holy, that Your very presence is sacred. On our own, we would never manage to dwell with You. Thank You for making a way for Your presence to be with Your people, both in the tabernacle for ancient Israel and also in the person of Christ, who sent the Spirit to reside in our midst even now. We are grateful for Your faithfulness to us. In Jesus' name. Amen.

C. Thought to Remember

God wants to dwell with His people.

Involvement Learning

Enhance your lesson with KJV Bible Student *(from your curriculum supplier) and the reproducible activity page (at www.standardlesson.com or in the back of the* KJV Standard Lesson Commentary Deluxe Edition*).*

Into the Lesson

Form learners into pairs or triads. Have partners brainstorm things that can be (or have been) brought into their homes to enable them to sense God's presence better.

Alternative. Project or display a series of photographs such as these: the inside of a church building, a mountain, the ocean, and a starry night sky. As you display each picture, ask class members to raise their hands for each one that helps them better sense God's presence.

After either exercise above, lead into Bible study by saying, "Perhaps no place brings us more comfort than a place where we can feel close to God. In today's Bible study, we will consider the place God designed for His people in antiquity to draw nearer to Him."

Into the Word

Ask one participant to read Exodus 25:1-9. Then, ask someone else to read Exodus 26:1, 31-37. Summarize the Lesson Context in a mini-lecture. *Alternative*: Play the video "Exodus 19–40" from the Bible Project website. Note: the video in its entirety is about six and a half minutes long. If you desire a shorter video, play the same video but from time marker 1:50 to 3:04. (*Option:* have the passage for today read after the video rather than before it.)

Divide the class into three groups, designating one group as the **Elements Group**, another group as the **Directions Group**, and the last group as the **Then and Now Group**. Distribute handouts (you create) with content as set forth below:

Elements Group. Make lists of what the people gave in the categories of *Organic Materials* and *Inorganic Materials*. Then answer this question: How "expected" were these offerings?

Directions Group. List examples of directives from the lesson text that fall under these descriptions: *God Is Separate from His People* and *God Wants to Be Close to His People*. Then answer these

questions: 1–What does the description of the tabernacle say about God? 2–What does it say about the Israelites?

Then and Now Group. Read Hebrews 9. List contrasts between Old Testament tabernacle worship and New Testament worship through Christ. (Teacher note: if the 28 verses of Hebrew 9 are "too much," then focus on Hebrews 9:11-28 instead.)

Reconvene for whole-class discussion of discoveries and insights.

Option. Distribute copies of the "Worship Then and Worship Now" exercise from the activity page, which you can download. Assign it for discussion either to the class as a whole, to small groups, or to individuals, depending on the nature of your class. If assigned to individuals, announce a one-minute time limit.

Into Life

Distribute index cards and ask class members to write their responses to each of these prompts as you write them on the board:

The place where I best sense God's closeness is . . .
The place where I best sense God's holiness is . . .
The practice that brings me closest to God is . . .

(Do not write all three prompts on the board at once. Instead, write the first one, then discuss it. Repeat the sequence for the remaining prompts.)

Alternative. Distribute copies of the "A House for God" exercise from the activity page. Have learners complete it individually as indicated, taking no more than one minute to do so. Since this exercise tilts toward identifying personal shortcomings, assure participants that the exercise is theirs to keep; no one will collect their responses.

As a final activity, ask participants to take one minute to write a brief prayer of gratitude to God for His willingness to dwell with us today. Bring the class to a close by forming a prayer circle to allow participants to voice the prayers they've just written. But don't put anyone on the spot to do so.

The Ordination of Priests

Devotional Reading: Psalm 133
Background Scripture: Exodus 29:1-37; Leviticus 8:1-36

Exodus 29:1-9, 35-37

1 And this is the thing that thou shalt do unto them to hallow them, to minister unto me in the priest's office: take one young bullock, and two rams without blemish,

2 And unleavened bread, and cakes unleavened tempered with oil, and wafers unleavened anointed with oil: of wheaten flour shalt thou make them.

3 And thou shalt put them into one basket, and bring them in the basket, with the bullock and the two rams.

4 And Aaron and his sons thou shalt bring unto the door of the tabernacle of the congregation, and shalt wash them with water.

5 And thou shalt take the garments, and put upon Aaron the coat, and the robe of the ephod, and the ephod, and the breastplate, and gird him with the curious girdle of the ephod:

6 And thou shalt put the mitre upon his head, and put the holy crown upon the mitre.

7 Then shalt thou take the anointing oil, and pour it upon his head, and anoint him.

8 And thou shalt bring his sons, and put coats upon them.

9 And thou shalt gird them with girdles, Aaron and his sons, and put the bonnets on them: and the priest's office shall be theirs for a perpetual statute: and thou shalt consecrate Aaron and his sons.

35 And thus shalt thou do unto Aaron, and to his sons, according to all things which I have commanded thee: seven days shalt thou consecrate them.

36 And thou shalt offer every day a bullock for a sin offering for atonement: and thou shalt cleanse the altar, when thou hast made an atonement for it, and thou shalt anoint it, to sanctify it.

37 Seven days thou shalt make an atonement for the altar, and sanctify it; and it shall be an altar most holy: whatsoever toucheth the altar shall be holy.

Key Text

The priest's office shall be theirs for a perpetual statute: and thou shalt consecrate Aaron and his sons.
—**Exodus 29:9b**

Costly
Sacrifices

Unit 1: Tabernacle, Sacrifices, and Atonement
Lessons 1–5

Lesson Aims

After participating in this lesson, each learner will be able to:

1. Define "ordination" in the sense of "consecration."

2. Compare and contrast ordination/consecration in the Old Testament with its value and practice in the New Testament.

3. Make a plan to serve as a member of the Christian's holy and royal priesthood per 1 Peter 2:5, 9.

Lesson Outline

Introduction
  A. Ordination
  B. Lesson Context
I. Preparing the Offerings (Exodus 29:1-3)
  A. Animals and Bread (vv. 1-2)
  B. Collection and Presentation (v. 3)
    God, the Painter?
II. Preparing the Ordinands (Exodus 29:4-9)
  A. Persons, Place, and Purification (v. 4)
  B. Aaron, Attire, and Anointing (vv. 5-7)
  C. Descendants, Dress, and Duration (vv. 8-9)
    Hand-Me-Down Clothes
III. Requiring a Week (Exodus 29:35-37)
  A. For the Priests (v. 35)
  B. For the Altar (vv. 36-37)
Conclusion
  A. The Old in the New
  B. Prayer
  C. Thought to Remember

Introduction

A. Ordination

For those of an older generation, the designation "ordained minister" brings certain images to mind. Such images might include that of a devout person who has spent several years in seminary, preparing to be ordained after graduating with a degree in Bible, theology, or even counseling.

This paradigm began to break down in the United States in the late 1960s. That was the decade the Universal Life Church started issuing certificates of ordination to anyone who desired one. These easily obtained certificates began to be recognized by local governments for performing weddings, etc. Thus, a privilege of the church became, in many instances, just a business opportunity—a chance to earn a living officiating at various functions.

But that wasn't the first time such a thing had happened. It also happened in ancient Israel's ordained priesthood. What began in all holiness at God's initiative eventually became an unholy travesty of sinful rulers (example: 1 Kings 12:31). The shocking picture of this decline is best appreciated by a consideration of priestly ordination at its ideal beginning—the subject of today's lesson.

B. Lesson Context

In Israel's earliest days, Aaron and his sons became the first priests under the nation's leadership by Moses, who was Aaron's brother (Exodus 7:1; 28:1). They were anointed, consecrated, and sanctified to do so (28:41). The act of anointing consisted of pouring oil on the priest's head, done as a ritual to show a person had been selected. Consecration was the act of appointment through the authority of the congregation of the people. Sanctification was the "setting apart" of the person for the tasks of the priesthood, with the tacit agreement that the person would strive to live a holy, blameless life, observing the laws of Israel as given by God through Moses.

We can note at the outset that the possible meanings (semantic range) of English words shift over time, as do words in all languages. The words *ordination* and *ordain* do not appear in the text of the *King James Version* for today's lesson text, although the concept is present. The *KJV* uses the verb *ordain* in a situation of gatekeepers (1 Chronicles 9:22) and the appointment of unqualified priests (2 Chronicles 11:15).

Within the new nation of Israel, God planned for men of the tribe of Levi to be designated with tasks associated with the tabernacle and (later) the temple (Numbers 3:5-9; 8:5-26; 1 Chronicles 23:28-32). From this tribe were to come the priests (Deuteronomy 18:1-5; Joshua 18:7; contrast 1 Kings 12:31). Priests were mediators between God and the people. In this role, priests offered sacrifices for atonement on their behalf (Leviticus 4:13-35; 9:7); priests were to teach and model God's distinctions between clean and unclean (10:10-11).

Setting the stage for today's lesson is Exodus 28:41, which summarizes the detail that follows in Exodus 29 regarding the ordination of priests. Leviticus 8 offers a detailed account of Moses carrying out the actions God specifies in today's lesson text.

I. Preparing the Offerings
(Exodus 29:1-3)
A. Animals and Bread (vv. 1-2)

1a. And this is the thing that thou shalt do unto them to hallow them, to minister unto me in the priest's office.

The word *thou* refers to Moses, as traced back to Exodus 25:1. Thus, the instructions that follow are for him to carry out as God's designated representative to the people.

The word translated *hallow* is also translated "sanctify" in Exodus 28:41 (see Lesson Context) and 29:36-37 (see commentary below). It is the verb form of the noun regularly translated "holy." The idea of holiness is pervasive in the Law of Moses and the history of Israel. It has the sense of emulating God in being "set apart" as pure and undefiled. It is the opposite of that which is unclean or profane (Leviticus 10:10). Specific rules for priests in this regard were stricter than those for the rank-and-file Israelites (Exodus 21:1–22:16). Even so, the requirement for personal holiness isn't just for priests under the old covenant

—it's for everyone (1 Peter 1:15-16, quoting Leviticus 11:44-45; 19:2).

Note the sequence here: being made holy is a prerequisite to ministering *in the priest's office,* not the other way around!

1b. Take one young bullock, and two rams without blemish.

The process of ordination for the priests was costly! For all three animals to be *without blemish* meant they were not sick or deformed in any way. This was not to be used as an opportunity to get rid of inferior livestock. These animals were to be sacrificed according to detailed instructions (Exodus 29:10-28, not in today's text). As they were sacrificed, they were given separate and distinct designations (29:14, 18, 26; Leviticus 8:14, 18, 27).

2. And unleavened bread, and cakes unleavened tempered with oil, and wafers unleavened anointed with oil: of wheaten flour shalt thou make them.

Three distinct manner of bread were specified for the ordination. But despite their differences, they all have one thing in common: they are *unleavened* (made without yeast). Up to this point in Bible history, there have been two incidents associated with unleavened bread. The lesser-known incident involved the destruction of Sodom and Gomorrah (Genesis 19:3); the better-known incident was the Passover and its subsequent remembrances (Exodus 12). Both situations involved a need for haste—yeasted bread would have taken too long to rise.

Specifications for offerings involving bread, flour, etc., are found in Leviticus 2. How these were to be used in the ordination ceremony is specified in Exodus 29:23-25 (not in today's lesson

How to Say It

Abihu	Uh-*bye*-hew.
Eleazar	El-ih-*a*-zar
	or E-lih-*a*-zar.
ephod	*ee*-fod.
Gomorrah	Guh-*more*-uh.
Ithamar	*Ith*-uh-mar.
Nadab	*Nay*-dab.
Sodom	*Sod*-um.

text) and Leviticus 6:19-23. How they were actually used is recorded in Leviticus 8:26-29.

The specification that these breads were to be made with *wheaten flour* is itself revealing. Both barley and wheat were characteristic grain crops in the promised land (Deuteronomy 8:8). But barley was the food of the poor; Revelation 6:6 suggests that barley was one-third the cost of wheat. Thus, we see a certain parallel with the requirement to bring an unblemished animal—the bread to be offered had to be made with the best flour.

> **What Do You Think?**
> How might the concept of "unleavened" apply to modern-day believers?
> **Digging Deeper**
> How do Matthew 16:6 and 1 Corinthians 5:6-8 direct your response?

B. Collection and Presentation (v. 3)

3. And thou shalt put them into one basket, and bring them in the basket, with the bullock and the two rams.

The exacting nature of the instructions reveals how important and serious this ceremony should be in the eyes of the Israelites. This is not some impromptu ritual. We can easily imagine the animals were cleaned and groomed, and the bread was made by the finest cooks. The *basket* itself would be of the best craftsmanship, fit for this solemn occasion.

We may view the results in terms of a visual aid. This occasion was not to be a "by invitation only plus one" event. All Israelites were to witness the ordinations (Leviticus 8:1-4). Even so, we are left to wonder how this was accomplished in a practical sense since the Israelites at the time numbered about 600,000 men, not counting women and children (Exodus 12:37; Numbers 1:46)!

God, the Painter?

Have you ever heard the word "painter" used as a description of God? I never have. Various descriptions of God abound in Scripture, but "painter" is not one of them. Even so, I think it fits.

Consider the preliminary tasks of a painter.

Every experienced painter knows that the ultimate success or failure of a job depends on *surface preparation*. Before the brush is dipped into the paint, the area to be painted needs to be cleaned in various ways for the new paint to adhere properly. God was taking care to do likewise in the text at hand. By means of meticulous instructions, He was preparing hearts to recognize the seriousness of the task at hand. His Word won't adhere to unprepared hearts, whether under the old covenant or the new.

The end result of God's work of preparing hearts is connected to our own receptivity to that preparatory work. How do you see this playing out in the contrast between the shallow and good soils of Matthew 13:5-8?   —R. L. N.

II. Preparing the Ordinands
(Exodus 29:4-9)

A. Persons, Place, and Purification (v. 4)

4. And Aaron and his sons thou shalt bring unto the door of the tabernacle of the congregation, and shalt wash them with water.

Exodus 40:12 is worded almost identically to the verse before us. The positioning of that verse reinforces the chronological element here: the ordination took place after *the tabernacle* had been set up.

The tabernacle proper was a portable tentlike structure (Exodus 26:1-37; 36:8-38). It was situated inside a courtyard, to the courtyard's west side (27:9-19; 38:9-20). Once the tabernacle was operational, its most holy place was to be entered by the high priest only, and only on the Day of Atonement (see lesson 5 on Leviticus 16). But with the tabernacle's completion, there was no priesthood in general or high priest in particular to use it! Thus, the need for ordaining *Aaron and his sons*.

The door of the tabernacle faced east: where Moses was to bring the ordinands. There, the men were to be washed with water, a ceremonial cleansing to begin the ordination ceremony. Washing with water in a ceremonial sense is also noted in Exodus 30:17-22; Leviticus 14:8-9; 15:4-27; etc. Moses followed God's instructions exactly (Leviticus 8:6).

The sons of Aaron were four in number; their names were Nadab, Abihu, Eleazar, and Ithamar

(Numbers 26:60). The first two lost their lives when they offered "strange fire before the Lord" (Leviticus 10:1-2). That happened after the ordination ceremony, so all four were present to become priests (Exodus 28:1; Numbers 3:2-4).

B. Aaron, Attire, and Anointing (vv. 5-7)

5. And thou shalt take the garments, and put upon Aaron the coat, and the robe of the ephod, and the ephod, and the breastplate, and gird him with the curious girdle of the ephod.

Priestly *garments* are first mentioned comprehensively in Exodus 28:1-5, with 28:31-43 adding detail. A fleeting reference occurs in 25:7.

There were several parts to this unique uniform. The first is here called a *coat*, but it has a longer designation of "broidered coat" in Exodus 28:4. This close-fitting shirt-like garment was made of fine linen (28:39; 39:27). It is not to be confused with the linen undergarment of 28:42; 39:28.

The robe of the ephod is an outer garment. Particulars regarding its features and functions are found in Exodus 28:31-35; 39:22. Creation of the ephod itself is addressed in 28:6-14; 39:2-7. It may have been something like an apron.

What is called *the breastplate* here is further designated "the breastplate of judgment" three times in Exodus 28:15-30; this item's construction of gold, precious stones, and fine linen is covered extensively there and in 39:8-21. Not mentioned in the lesson text for today are "the Urim and the Thummim" that fit into the breastplate (28:30). We don't know exactly what these were, but their function seemed to be a means of consulting God regarding important decisions (example: Numbers 27:18-21).

Similar to that of the ephod was the material of the *curious girdle* (Exodus 28:8; 39:5). This item was to interconnect with the breastplate and ephod in a manner that would prevent unintended movement of the breastplate (28:28).

6. And thou shalt put the mitre upon his head, and put the holy crown upon the mitre.

As clothing items for the torso were to be interconnected, so too were items for the high priest's *head*. The *mitre* was the headdress, and *the holy crown* was something attached to it.

We don't really know what the mitre looked like beyond the brief descriptions in Exodus 28:4, 37; 39:30. It may be something like what is called a "turban" today; it is unlikely to have been like the tall and pointed headpieces we see in modern religious ceremonies. On the other hand, Exodus 28:36-38 is most helpful in providing information about the holy crown in terms of (1) its nature of solid gold, (2) its engraved message of holiness, (3) its function of the high priest's bearing of guilt, and (4) its attachment to the front of the headdress.

Again, the phrase *thou shalt* indicates commands to Moses. He obeyed all these instructions to the letter during the actual ordination ceremony (Leviticus 8:7-9).

7. Then shalt thou take the anointing oil, and pour it upon his head, and anoint him.

The text now shifts focus from the high priest's vestments to his anointing. *The anointing oil* was a mixture of olive oil and four fine spices (Exodus 30:22-25). This use of this formulation was highly restricted, what one might call "divinely proprietary" (30:26-33).

C. Descendants, Dress, and Duration (vv. 8-9)

8-9a. And thou shalt bring his sons, and put coats upon them. And thou shalt gird them with girdles, Aaron and his sons, and put the bonnets on them.

Regarding the names and number of Aaron

Offer pleasing sacrifices to God.

Visual for Lessons 3 & 4. *Display this visual as you ask the discussion questions associated with the lesson conclusion.*

sons, see commentary on Exodus 29:4, above. They were the nephews of Moses, who was still receiving the *thou shalt* instructions regarding their ordination to be priests. After they had been ceremonially washed (Exodus 29:4), they would be ready to receive the garments prepared for them.

Comparing the sons' *coats, girdles,* and *bonnets* with the clothing of their father is insightful. The results of such a comparison classifies the garments in terms of (1) those common to both father and sons, (2) those unique to the father, and (3) those unique to the sons.

In Exodus 29:5-6, considered above, we saw that Aaron was to be given seven articles of attire to constitute his vestments. An eighth item was a "girdle," noted in 28:4, 39. (We are not counting a ninth item of underwear in 28:42; 39:28.) Of these eight items, only two—coats and girdles—were common to both father and sons (28:4, 39-40; 29:5, 8; 39:27; 40:14; note: the "curious girdle" of 29:5 is different from the "girdles" of 29:9). Clothing attributed to the sons only is the headgear known as "bonnets" (28:40; 39:28).

It's easy to focus so much on these details that we lose sight of the bigger picture. That bigger picture is found in God's stated intent for these vestments to evoke a sense of "glory" and "beauty" regarding the priesthood (Exodus 28:2, 40).

9b. And the priest's office shall be theirs for a perpetual statute: and thou shalt consecrate Aaron and his sons.

The words in the original language translated *perpetual statute* occur about two dozen times in the Old Testament. In addition to describing the enduring nature of the priestly *office* (compare Exodus 40:15), it also describes priestly tasks (examples: 27:21; Leviticus 24:3).

Hand-Me-Down Clothes

Whenever family discussions turn to the subject of hand-me-down clothes, it's usually not with a positive tone! But there is at least one positive case, and it's a big one: the clothing of ancient Israel's high priest was to be passed along from generation to generation (Exodus 29:29-30). This set of clothing was considered so valuable that the first-century Jewish historian Josephus noted that it came under the control of King Herod and then his son Archelaus (the same ones of Matthew 2:1, 22), followed by Roman authorities.

While the priestly clothing of Aaron and his sons was intended to be impressive, it was not the most important aspect of their consecration. The most important thing was that the priestly office was an enduring gift (Numbers 18:7).

The same can be said of our new covenant priesthood (1 Peter 2:5). Do you treat it that way?
—M. S. K.

III. Requiring a Week
(Exodus 29:35-37)
A. For the Priests (v. 35)

35. And thus shalt thou do unto Aaron, and to his sons, according to all things which I have commanded thee: seven days shalt thou consecrate them.

This verse summarizes the intricacies of the ordination process for *Aaron* and *his sons* as set forth in Exodus 29:10-34 and Leviticus 8. Some students propose that its requirement to last *seven days* was an intended parallel to the seven days of creation, ending on the Sabbath.

The seven days could also have served as a necessary period of familiarization with God's required actions. In Leviticus 8:35, Moses stressed the seven-day requirement and the deadly consequences of not honoring it. Two of Aaron's four sons died for a different violation shortly after their seven days were completed (Leviticus 9:1; 10:1-3).

What Do You Think?

What kinds of "waiting periods" do you need to adopt personally?

Digging Deeper

What Scripture convicts you most in this regard?

B. For the Altar (vv. 36-37)

36. And thou shalt offer every day a bullock for a sin offering for atonement: and thou shalt cleanse the altar, when thou hast made an atonement for it, and thou shalt anoint it, to sanctify it.

The tabernacle was equipped with two altars: one of about 56 square feet in area for animal sacrifices (Exodus 27:1-9) and another, smaller altar of less than 3 square feet in area for burning incense (30:1-10). *The altar* in view here is the sacrificial altar. This altar was the place where the priests did most of their work (Hebrews 10:11).

A sin offering was a means of *atonement*; Leviticus 4 explains this in detail. The need to *cleanse the altar . . . to sanctify it* is addressed in Leviticus 16 (lesson 5).

37. Seven days thou shalt make an atonement for the altar, and sanctify it; and it shall be an altar most holy: whatsoever toucheth the altar shall be holy.

The fact that *whatsoever toucheth the altar shall be holy* is quite remarkable given that it is the opposite of the normal laws of defilement. When "clean" and "unclean" come into contact with one another, the regular pattern is that the clean becomes unclean (Leviticus 5:2-3; Haggai 2:11-13; etc.). Jesus took as given that the altar sanctifies the sacrificial gift on it (Matthew 23:19).

Conclusion

A. The Old in the New

The importance of today's lesson is seen in the fact that ordination to the priesthood was instructed in Exodus 29, carried out in detail in Leviticus 8, and viewed as an accomplished fact in Exodus 40. Such repetition should catch our attention!

Even so, we may wonder about modern relevance. Today's text describes persons and events from over 3,000 years ago. Aaron and Moses are long dead. Neither the tabernacle nor the Jerusalem temple stands today. A natural, perhaps instinctive way of seeing relevance is to see parallels between the ordination of priests in the Old Testament and the modern practice of ordaining ministers of the gospel. There is value in doing so, but that's not the primary point of relevance.

That primary relevance is at least twofold. The first is that the functions of the tabernacle, priests, and blood sacrifices form the framework for understanding Jesus' sacrifice as an atonement (propitiation) for our sins (Romans 3:25; Hebrews 2:17; etc.). The second concerns the fact and obligations of our own priesthood (Romans 12:1; 1 Peter 2:5; etc.). We neglect facts of the old covenant as foundations for the new covenant at our peril (Romans 15:4; 1 Corinthians 10:11).

What Do You Think?

How would you respond to someone who says that Scripture texts like today's are meaningless to modern-day believers?

Digging Deeper

In what ways has your mindset regarding the Old Testament changed because of this lesson?

B. Prayer

Heavenly Father, may we honor Your plan to provide the priesthoods of both old and new covenants. Convict us on how we can do better at honoring our priesthood of all believers as it reflects Your holiness. We pray this is the name of our great high priest, the once-for-all sacrifice for our sins, Jesus. Amen.

C. Thought to Remember

Honor your part in the priesthood of all believers.

Involvement Learning

Enhance your lesson with KJV Bible Student *(from your curriculum supplier) and the reproducible activity page (at www.standardlesson.com or in the back of the* KJV Standard Lesson Commentary Deluxe Edition*).*

Into the Lesson

Show a video of someone taking an oath of office or allegiance. If playing such a video isn't possible, read through one such oath instead.

Write these "inquiry words" on the board:

Who? What? Where? When? Why?

Cycle through these words in whole-class discussion as they help your participants understand the meaning and significance of the oath.

Lead to Bible study by saying, "Today, we will look at the ancient ordination or consecration of Old Testament priests and how that is a foundation for important New Testament concepts."

Into the Word

Have two participants take turns reading the text for the lesson, Exodus 29:1-9, 35-37. Form small groups of two to six participants each, depending on the nature of your class. Designate half the groups to be **Big Picture** and the other half of the groups to be **Intricate Details**.

Distribute to each group one of two handouts (you create) that are titled according to the group's designation.

Big Picture Groups

1–How does Exodus 29 relate to Leviticus 8?
2–What is the overall significance of the garments?
3–Why a seven-day process rather than one hour?
4–Why so many intricate details?

Intricate Details Groups

1–What were the various ways the loaves were to be distinguished from one another?
2–What priestly garments did Aaron wear that his sons did not?
3–What priestly garments did the sons wear that Aaron did not?
4–What priestly garments did Aaron and his sons have in common?

Option. Announce a three-minute time limit for each question. Say "time to move on" after each three-minute limit is reached. After the total

of 16 minutes is reached, reconvene for a whole-class discussion of discoveries. Make sure that you, the teacher, can answer the questions yourself.

Option. Test your participants' recall of facts by distributing the "About One-Third of the Alphabet" exercise from the activity page, which you can download. Announce that this is a one-minute work-alone speed drill. Bibles closed! Have participants score their own results.

Write the following seven references on the board as headers to seven columns, one each: *Mark 3:14; Luke 10:1; Acts 6:2-6; Acts 13:1-3; Acts 14:23; 1 Timothy 4:14; 1 Timothy 5:22.* Then, in relation to Exodus 29:1-9, do a whole-class compare (how they are similar) and contrast (how they differ) with the seven texts individually. Jot observations under the appropriate text.

Into Life

Immediately following the consideration of the seven texts above, read aloud 1 Peter 2:5, 9. Ask, "Which is the best New Testament parallel to Exodus 29: the appointment of specific individuals in those seven texts, or the appointment of all Christians in 1 Peter 2:5, 9?" Expect that the ensuing discussion will raise the question "If every Christian is ordained or consecrated to a priesthood, then does ordination or consecration (being set apart) mean anything special?" Raise that question yourself if no one else does.

Make sure that the discussion at some point compares the "go between" or "intermediary" functions of old covenant priests with our own priesthood privilege of interceding for one another (1 Timothy 2:1).

Option. Distribute copies of the "Exactly All of My Life" exercise from the activity page. Have class members work on it in pairs. If time is short, use the exercise as homework; encourage its completion in that regard by stating that you will call for results at the beginning of next week's class.

Offering a Sweet Aroma to God

Devotional Reading: Romans 12:1-8
Background Scripture: Leviticus 1:1-17; 6:8-13

Leviticus 1:3-17

3 If his offering be a burnt sacrifice of the herd, let him offer a male without blemish: he shall offer it of his own voluntary will at the door of the tabernacle of the congregation before the LORD.

4 And he shall put his hand upon the head of the burnt offering; and it shall be accepted for him to make atonement for him.

5 And he shall kill the bullock before the LORD: and the priests, Aaron's sons, shall bring the blood, and sprinkle the blood round about upon the altar that is by the door of the tabernacle of the congregation.

6 And he shall flay the burnt offering, and cut it into his pieces.

7 And the sons of Aaron the priest shall put fire upon the altar, and lay the wood in order upon the fire:

8 And the priests, Aaron's sons, shall lay the parts, the head, and the fat, in order upon the wood that is on the fire which is upon the altar:

9 But his inwards and his legs shall he wash in water: and the priest shall burn all on the altar, to be a burnt sacrifice, an offering made by fire, of a sweet savour unto the LORD.

10 And if his offering be of the flocks, namely, of the sheep, or of the goats, for a burnt sacrifice; he shall bring it a male without blemish.

11 And he shall kill it on the side of the altar northward before the LORD: and the priests, Aaron's sons, shall sprinkle his blood round about upon the altar.

12 And he shall cut it into his pieces, with his head and his fat: and the priest shall lay them in order on the wood that is on the fire which is upon the altar:

13 But he shall wash the inwards and the legs with water: and the priest shall bring it all, and burn it upon the altar: it is a burnt sacrifice, an offering made by fire, of a sweet savour unto the LORD.

14 And if the burnt sacrifice for his offering to the LORD be of fowls, then he shall bring his offering of turtledoves, or of young pigeons.

15 And the priest shall bring it unto the altar, and wring off his head, and burn it on the altar; and the blood thereof shall be wrung out at the side of the altar:

16 And he shall pluck away his crop with his feathers, and cast it beside the altar on the east part, by the place of the ashes:

17 And he shall cleave it with the wings thereof, but shall not divide it asunder: and the priest shall burn it upon the altar, upon the wood that is upon the fire: it is a burnt sacrifice, an offering made by fire, of a sweet savour unto the LORD.

Key Text

His inwards and his legs shall he wash in water: and the priest shall burn all on the altar, to be a burnt sacrifice, an offering made by fire, of a sweet savour unto the LORD. And if his offering be of the flocks, namely, of the sheep, or of the goats, for a burnt sacrifice; he shall bring it a male without blemish. —**Leviticus 1:9-10**

257

Costly
Sacrifices

Unit 1: Tabernacle, Sacrifices, and Atonement
Lessons 1–5

Lesson Aims

After participating in this lesson, each learner will be able to:

1. Identify God's key expectations for burnt offerings.

2. Compare and contrast the expectation of an unblemished sacrifice with that of 1 Peter 1:19.

3. Recruit an accountability partner for mutual support in giving God the best of the learner's service.

Lesson Outline

Introduction
A. Book of Worship?

If you were to ask a group of people today with a fair degree of Bible knowledge to name a book of the Bible dealing with worship, the majority response would likely be Psalms. Some might name Revelation because of the scenes of worship and praise described within the book.

Few, if any, would suggest Leviticus. Leviticus contains no hymns of praise to the Lord. The text focuses on ritual observances, sacrificial rites, and the preservation of boundaries between the sacred and profane and the pure and impure. Yet under the covenant of Sinai, these rituals were integral parts of the proper worship of God (Exodus 3:15; compare 7:16). Leviticus instructs God's people under the old covenant how they are to approach, honor, and offer sacrifices to Him so that their covenant relationship remains firm. Today's lesson text comes from the opening chapter of Leviticus, which covers the appropriate procedures for carrying out the burnt offerings.

B. Lesson Context

The book of Leviticus is one of the five books, collectively known as the Pentateuch, traditionally ascribed to Moses. The contents of the Pentateuch as a whole are best viewed as deriving originally from Moses and carrying his authority (see Leviticus 26:46).

This quarter's previous lessons, taken from the book of Exodus, emphasized that God would dwell with His people and receive their worship in the tabernacle. Leviticus contains the most thorough instructions on the proper forms and procedures for the worship of God: the "where" and "how" for worship. The book's divine authority and purposes are emphasized from the start (Leviticus 1:1-2). These are the Lord's regulations and instructions for His people and how they must conduct themselves in relation to Him.

Leviticus takes its name from the Septuagint, the ancient Greek translation of the Old Testament. The title reflects the fact that the book relates to the tasks of the Levites, who assisted the priests in carrying out duties associated with worship at the tabernacle. (We recall that all priests were Levites, but not all Levites were priests.)

A key word in Leviticus is the word *holy*. Of its 600-plus occurrences in the Bible, more are found in Leviticus than in any other book of the Bible. *Holiness* refers to a state of being set apart, including both ritual and ethical purity. The words "Ye shall be holy: for I the Lord your God am holy" (Leviticus 19:2) are directed not only to all the people of ancient Israel but to all of God's people through time (1 Peter 1:15-16, quoting that verse).

With so much emphasis in Leviticus on *holiness*, perhaps we might think that teachings on *love* would take a back seat and be stressed elsewhere. But one of the most often quoted Old Testament passages in the New Testament is Leviticus 19:18, "Love thy neighbour as thyself." Jesus even cited this as one of the two greatest commandments (Matthew 22:39; compare 5:43; 19:19; Mark 12:31-33; Luke 10:27; Romans 13:9; Galatians 5:14; James 2:8).

What Do You Think?
Which most motivates you to worship: the "where" or the "how"?
Digging Deeper
Which of these passages help you most: John 4:23-24; Acts 2:46-47; Romans 12:1; Hebrews 9:1; 10:25; 12:28?

I. An Offering from the Herd
(Leviticus 1:3-9)

A. Preparing the Animal (vv. 3-6)

3a. If his offering be a burnt sacrifice of the herd, let him offer a male without blemish.

In the verse just before this one, the Lord permitted that animal sacrifices could come from either a person's herd (of cattle) or flock (of sheep and goats). The verse before us narrows the focus specifically to that of *a burnt offering* that comes from *the herd*.

The directive to sacrifice only animals *without blemish* is repeated in Deuteronomy 15:21. This command reflects a key distinction between profane and sacred things. It also emphasizes that God deserves the best of one's herds rather than

the worst. Leviticus 22:17-33 gives an extended warning against unacceptable sacrifices. Centuries later, the prophet Malachi would charge God's people with violating this prohibition (Malachi 1:8, 13-14). The added specification that the blemish-free sacrifice be *male* foreshadows the sacrifice of Jesus (Hebrews 9:14; 1 Peter 1:19).

What Do You Think?
What are some ways to ensure that you offer "the best" to Christ?
Digging Deeper
How do passages such as Genesis 4:2-5; 2 Corinthians 8:12; 9:7 help you answer that question?

3b. He shall offer it of his own voluntary will at the door of the tabernacle of the congregation before the LORD.

The Hebrew word translated *of his own voluntary will* occurs dozens of times in the Old Testament, seven of those in the book of Leviticus. It may refer to something that is acceptable or pleasing from the point of view of the giver or from the point of view of the receiver. In the context of Leviticus's focus on proper sacrifices, the word refers to what is acceptable to God, what conforms to His requirements, and what pleases Him (Leviticus 19:5; 22:19-21, 29; 23:11).

The burnt offering could not be presented just anywhere the giver desired. The worshipper had to bring it to the place specifically designated for such a sacred purpose: the tabernacle. The Lord was to be worshipped on His terms and at the sole place designated for that purpose. He instituted strict penalties for performing sacrifices in any other location (Leviticus 17:1-4, 8-9). Deuteronomy 12:11-14 reiterates the necessity of a centralized worship site, anticipating the future temple in Jerusalem. This requirement forced the Israelites to worship the Lord alone in a consistent way and prevented them from continuing their practices of sacrificing to "devils" (Leviticus 17:5-7).

Opportunity Cost

The average cost of a beef cow in 2023 in the United States was in the neighborhood of $3,000.

That was also about how much an average US homeowner spent on home maintenance that year. Neither cost was trivial for most people. And for an ancient Israelite, giving up a head of cattle for a burnt offering was significant.

Bearing the burdens of all these costs serves as a gauge of commitment to something or someone. And incurring an expense of $3,000 means that that money isn't available to use elsewhere. That's known as "an opportunity cost," and it's an ideal gauge for measuring the level of your devotion to the kingdom of God.

Look at the level of your financial giving, and ask yourself, *What am I giving up the opportunity of buying when I put this amount of money in the offering plate or devote X amount of time to ministry activities?* The resulting "opportunity cost" will be quite revealing!   —R. L. N.

4. And he shall put his hand upon the head of the burnt offering; and it shall be accepted for him to make atonement for him.

As the reader works through the procedure specified for the various types of sacrifices, several similarities are seen. The first is the instruction to put a *hand upon the head* of the *offering* (compare Exodus 29:10, 15, 19; Leviticus 3:8, 13; 4:4, 29, 33; 8:14, 18, 22). This is the first of a multistep procedure. The placement of the hand symbolizes the person's submission of the animal as a sacrifice on the person's behalf. Commentary on Leviticus 1:9, below, summarizes the entirety of the steps.

5. And he shall kill the bullock before the LORD: and the priests, Aaron's sons, shall bring the blood, and sprinkle the blood round about upon the altar that is by the door of the tabernacle of the congregation.

As the procedure continues to the following steps, we may wonder who did the hands-on work to *kill the bullock.* The context implies that it was the one who had brought the animal to be sacrificed; after that, *the priests, Aaron's sons* (ordained in Exodus 29 and Leviticus 8), took over to perform the rest of the tasks regarding *blood.* But Leviticus 14:19-20 mentions a priest who was to slaughter the animal. In any case, a priest had to be present to officiate.

The use of *blood,* as described, functions as a mechanism of purification. It reinforced the principle of atonement since, as the Lord later declared, "The life of the flesh is in the blood: and I have given it to you upon the altar to make an atonement for your souls: for it is the blood that maketh an atonement for the soul" (Leviticus 17:11).

6. And he shall flay the burnt offering, and cut it into his pieces.

The next step was the removal (*shall flay*) of the animal's hide. This might be either prior to or simultaneous with cutting the carcass *into his pieces.* Both would speed up the burning process. Leviticus 7:8 directed that the priest officiating at the burnt offering should receive the animal's hide.

B. Presenting the Sacrifice (vv. 7-9)

7. And the sons of Aaron the priest shall put fire upon the altar, and lay the wood in order upon the fire.

Only priests were allowed to carry out the act of sacrificing the animal prepared for the burnt offering. The phrase *put fire upon the altar* does not mean "to start the fire," because the fire for this *altar* was to burn continuously (Leviticus 6:9-13; Numbers 28:1-8). The idea, instead, is to stoke the fire.

8. And the priests, Aaron's sons, shall lay the parts, the head, and the fat, in order upon the wood that is on the fire which is upon the altar.

Exodus 29:13 and Leviticus 8:20; 9:13 specify *the parts* in greater detail.

> **What Do You Think?**
> In what ways can you discharge your new-covenant priestly role (Isaiah 61:6; 1 Peter 2:5)?
>
> **Digging Deeper**
> How do you expect your answers to differ from those of other Christians? Why?

9. But his inwards and his legs shall he wash in water: and the priest shall burn all on the altar, to be a burnt sacrifice, an offering made by fire, of a sweet savour unto the LORD.

This verse concludes the description of the ritual that began in Leviticus 1:4, above. The resulting smoke that creates a *sweet savour unto the*

Lord attributes a human characteristic—a sense of smell—to God. This is anthropomorphic language. Even though God is a Spirit (John 4:24), the Scriptures speak of Him as having physical characteristics (examples: Psalm 34:15-16; John 12:38). Here, the sense of smell depicts how the Lord was pleased with the burnt offering as presented in the manner set forth in the text (compare Amos 5:21).

To summarize, the ritual involved these steps:

1. Place hand on the animal's head
2. Slay the animal
3. Splash animal blood against the sides of the altar
4. Remove the hide from the carcass
5. Dismember the carcass
6. Stoke the altar fire
7. Arrange wood on the altar
8. Arrange body pieces and fat on the altar fire
9. Wash internal organs and legs
10. Burn all except hide to create smoke pleasing to the Lord

II. An Offering from the Flock
(Leviticus 1:10-13)

A. Preparing the Animal (vv. 10-12)

10. And if his offering be of the flocks, namely, of the sheep, or of the goats, for a burnt sacrifice; he shall bring it a male without blemish.

For this kind of offering, *goats* or *sheep* that were *male without blemish* were interchangeable with bullocks, just discussed. We see male goats and sheep themselves as interchangeable for Passover in Exodus 12:5. Either goats or sheep were acceptable for peace offerings, with either male or female allowed (Leviticus 3). Either bullocks, male or female goats, or female lambs are allowed for sin or trespass offerings, depending on the nature of the sin (4:14, 24; 5:6).

The Perfect Tax Return

One of the editors of the book you are now holding moved from Ohio to Colorado in 2016. As April 15 of the following year approached, he spent several days preparing his five income tax returns (one federal, two state, and two city returns). The result was 17 total pages of income tax returns!

Offer pleasing sacrifices to God.

Visual for Lessons 3 & 4. *As you discuss the commentary on verse 17, point to this visual and ask, "How will your life be a pleasing sacrifice to God?"*

Knowing that the government requires that tax returns be devoid of omissions, he was scrupulous about accuracy (compare Romans 13:6-7). To his dismay, however, the 17 pages should have been 18—he had neglected to file one particular form with his Colorado return, thinking that that page was just a worksheet. And so he had to pay a five-dollar fine.

Reading the book of Leviticus may cause us to think that the Old Testament system of sacrifices was as complicated as modern tax codes, not to mention the Old Testament's consideration of the relative value of animal sacrifices (1 Samuel 15:22; Hosea 6:6; Micah 6:6-8). But as we sift through the requirements of the old covenant, the one element we dare not lose sight of is the requirement for an unblemished sacrificial animal. That requirement describes Jesus, upon whose perfection our salvation depends (1 Peter 1:18-19). That standard must also be ours (Matthew 5:48; 2 Peter 3:14). Is this your priority? —O. P.

11. And he shall kill it on the side of the altar northward before the Lᴏʀᴅ: and the priests, Aaron's sons, shall sprinkle his blood round about upon the altar.

Here a specific instruction was given as to where the animal was to be slain: *on the side of the altar northward.* Why this was required is not entirely clear, although it may have something to do with the fact that the tabernacle and the gateway into its courtyard faced east (Numbers 2:3; 3:38; 10:14). This rationale may also combine in some way with a need to distinguish this offering from the one taken from the herd; other than that, the procedure at this point is the same.

12. And he shall cut it into his pieces, with his head and his fat: and the priest shall lay them in order on the wood that is on the fire which is upon the altar.

Again, the procedure is the same as that designated for the bovines (Leviticus 1:5-8, above).

B. Presenting the Sacrifice (v. 13)

13. But he shall wash the inwards and the legs with water: and the priest shall bring it all, and burn it upon the altar: it is a burnt sacrifice, an offering made by fire, of a sweet savour unto the LORD.

Yet again, the procedure is the same as with the bullock (Leviticus 1:9, above).

III. An Offering of Birds
(Leviticus 1:14-17)
A. Preparing the Sacrifice (vv. 14-16)

14. And if the burnt sacrifice for his offering to the LORD be of fowls, then he shall bring his offering of turtledoves, or of young pigeons.

This option for a *burnt* offering was provided for people who could not afford to bring the aforementioned offerings from a herd or flock (Leviticus 5:7-10). Such an option was also provided for women after childbirth who could not afford to offer a lamb for the burnt offering of purification (12:8). One may recall the sacrifice that Joseph and Mary offered following the birth of Jesus (Luke 2:24).

15. And the priest shall bring it unto the altar, and wring off his head, and burn it on the altar; and the blood thereof shall be wrung out at the side of the altar.

The procedure for offering a bird as a burnt

offering differed from that prescribed for offerings from the herd or the flock (compare Leviticus 5:7-10). Whereas the blood of the animals that were sacrificed was sprinkled around the altar of burnt offering, the bird's blood was to be *wrung out at the side of the altar.* Though the bird's blood would not be nearly as abundant as that of the other animals, the need to separate its blood from its body must be completed. Israelites were forbidden to eat blood (7:10-14; compare Genesis 9:4).

16. And he shall pluck away his crop with his feathers, and cast it beside the altar on the east part, by the place of the ashes.

The meaning of a bird's *crop* is uncertain. It may refer to the pouch near the gullet or throat (the craw) where the bird stores food temporarily before digestion. Another option is that it may refer to the lower intestines. Its removal may be compared to removing the intestines from the animals of the herd or the flock.

The place of ashes that was *beside the altar* seems to have been a temporary location for ashes; the ultimate destination for that refuse was outside the camp (Leviticus 4:12; 6:10; 8:17; Numbers 4:13).

B. Presenting the Sacrifice (v. 17)

17. And he shall cleave it with the wings thereof, but shall not divide it asunder: and the priest shall burn it upon the altar, upon the wood that is upon the fire: it is a burnt sacrifice, an offering made by fire, of a sweet savour unto the LORD.

Further instructions regarding the sacrifices of birds conclude this portion of our text. The anatomy of a bird is quite different from that of sheep/goats and bovines, thus the sacrificial procedure was quite different. *The priest* was solely responsible for preparing and presenting the bird as a burnt offering. Though not as monetarily valuable as something offered from the flock or the herd, this offering still produced a *sweet savour unto the Lord.* Whether the worshipper was well-to-do or impoverished made no difference to the Lord, who treats everyone alike (Acts 10:34; compare Deuteronomy 10:17).

As followers of Jesus, our duty is to offer to God, not burnt sacrifices of animals or birds, but our lives

How to Say It

anthropomorphic	*an*-thruh-puh-*more*-fik.
Pentateuch	*Pen*-ta-teuk.
Septuagint	Sep-*too*-ih-jent.

as a "living sacrifice" (Romans 12:1). Our sacrifices do include the monetary (Hebrews 13:16; 2 Corinthians 8:3-4; Philippians 4:18) but are primarily spiritual (1 Peter 2:5), consisting of "the fruit of our lips" offering our thanks to God (Hebrews 13:15) and the good deeds we do as salt and light in our spheres of influence (Matthew 5:13-14).

> **What Do You Think?**
> What steps can you take to help others understand the foreshadowing nature of Levitical sacrifices?
>
> **Digging Deeper**
> Which elements of foreshadowing can you list right now?

Conclusion

A. Burnt Offerings in the Old Testament

The burnt offering is the first of several kinds of sacrifices in the book of Leviticus. The burnt offering is mentioned first, perhaps because it was the most committal: the one presenting the sacrifice received nothing tangible back. At first glance, Deuteronomy 12:27 would seem to contradict that statement. But this exception applied to Israelites who lived too far from the tabernacle to make the trip there (Deuteronomy 12:21).

Burnt offerings are mentioned about 270 times in the Old Testament. Their association with atonement makes study of them important in light of New Testament passages such as Mark 12:33 and Hebrews 10:1-14.

B. The Smell of Worship

One day, in a class I was teaching, we discussed the sacrifices the Israelites were required to bring as part of their worship of the Lord. Someone asked, "How did those people stand the smell of all of those animals being burned up day after day?"

Yes, to our modern way of thinking, the sacrificial system prescribed in the Old Testament and covered in today's text may seem odd, wasteful (killing all those animals), and even offensive. And, as mentioned earlier, the book of Leviticus does not make for the most captivating reading in the world!

Whatever ugliness we may see or disgust we may feel about the sacrificial system, with all its bloodshed and the continual smell coming from the sacrifices being offered, God saw things differently. The sacrificial offerings constituted, as our lesson title states, "a sweet aroma." This is why it is so important to allow Him to dictate what kind of worship is acceptable to Him.

Through the sacrificial system, God demonstrated the necessity of total commitment to Him, His desire to be present with His people, and the seriousness of sin. And He wanted people to understand that, as Paul puts it in Romans 6:23, "the wages of sin is death." But God, in His grace, has always provided a substitute so that we do not have to pay those wages. In the Old Testament system, the substitutes were the animals or birds. Those substitutes foreshadowed the ultimate Substitute who God in time would provide: Jesus, whose sacrifice at the cross was also a "sweetsmelling savour" (Ephesians 5:2), the once-for-all sacrifice that fulfilled what (and who) the Old Testament sacrifices pointed toward. Indeed, as Paul puts it, our lives are to serve as "a sweet savour of Christ" (2 Corinthians 2:14), spreading "the savour of his knowledge . . . in every place" (2:15).

> **What Do You Think?**
> How would you respond to the claim that the book of Leviticus has no value for modern-day Christians?
>
> **Digging Deeper**
> How has this lesson changed your answer?

C. Prayer

Our Father, help us to see the meaning of the word *offering* as more than money. May we demonstrate the commitment and obedience to bring our best before the Lord. Thank You for the sacrifice of Jesus, who gave himself unreservedly to be the sacrifice needed to remove our sins and provide full atonement that we might be reconciled with You. In Jesus' name we pray. Amen.

D. Thought to Remember

Always worship God on His terms, not ours.

Involvement Learning

Enhance your lesson with KJV Bible Student *(from your curriculum supplier) and the reproducible activity page (at www.standardlesson.com or in the back of the* KJV Standard Lesson Commentary Deluxe Edition*).*

Into the Lesson

Divide your class into groups. Assign half of the groups to complete a list that begins "Ceremonies are important because . . .". Ask the other half of the groups to complete a list that begins "Ceremonies don't matter because . . .". After five minutes or so, reconvene for whole-class discussion.

Lead into Bible study by saying, "Worship in the tabernacle was bound up in symbolism and ceremony. Let's see how and why."

Into the Word

Before reading the Scripture, distribute a hand-out (you create) with the following as a true/false pre-test. Allow one minute to complete with closed Bibles:

1–A "burnt offering" is the same as a "sin offering."
2–In offerings, animals were burned alive.
3–Eating the blood of the sacrifice was forbidden.
4–The sacrificial animal had to be unblemished.
5–Goats could not be burnt offerings.

[Answers: 1–false; 2–false; 3–true; 4–true; 5–false.]

After the minute is up, read the text as participants check their own scores.

Note: throughout the lesson, always try to keep the big picture in mind so participants see relevance to the era of the new covenant. If you get "lost in the weeds" with excess treatment of the details, your learners may lose focus. Covering the Lesson Context thoroughly will be important in this regard.

Teach the lesson text, dig deeper, and maintain interest all at the same time by comparing and contrasting the features of the burnt offering with those of the guilt offering (Leviticus 2), the peace offering (Leviticus 3), the sin offering (4:1–5:13), and the guilt offering (5:14–6:7). Note the additional information beginning in 6:8.

Option. Form learners into study pairs or tri-ads as you distribute copies of the "Same Thing, Only Different?" exercise from the activity page, which you can download. Challenge the pairs or triads to use smartphones for online research to complete the exercise as indicated. *For best effect, do your own thorough research and reach your own conclusions beforehand.*

Into Life

Write this continuum on the board:

1	2	3	4	5
Never				Always

Distribute a sheet of paper to each learner and ask them to write "A.," "B.," and "C." vertically down the left side of the paper. As you read the following statements aloud, ask learners to rate themselves on the above scale for each one by writing a number next to the letter.

A. I am actively sacrificing myself to God.
B. My offerings to the Lord are heartfelt, representing my best.
C. I think more about what I can give to God than what I want to get from Him.

As you finish the resulting discussion, ask learners what experience they have had with the "accountability partner" concept. Encourage learners to consider recruiting one in light of the challenges of today's lesson text.

Option. During the last five minutes of class, distribute copies of the "My Time Offerings" exercise on the activity page. Have learners fill it out for the week just past, as indicated. After discussion, invite learners to take the slip of paper to check the squares in the week ahead. Either now, next week, or both, you can allow volunteers to share results, but don't put anyone on the spot.

Close with a prayer of thanks for living in the new covenant era and for class members to adopt the accountability partner concept.

The Day of Atonement

Devotional Reading: Psalm 40:9-17
Background Scripture: Leviticus 16

Leviticus 16:11-19

11 And Aaron shall bring the bullock of the sin offering, which is for himself, and shall make an atonement for himself, and for his house, and shall kill the bullock of the sin offering which is for himself:

12 And he shall take a censer full of burning coals of fire from off the altar before the LORD, and his hands full of sweet incense beaten small, and bring it within the vail:

13 And he shall put the incense upon the fire before the LORD, that the cloud of the incense may cover the mercy seat that is upon the testimony, that he die not:

14 And he shall take of the blood of the bullock, and sprinkle it with his finger upon the mercy seat eastward; and before the mercy seat shall he sprinkle of the blood with his finger seven times.

15 Then shall he kill the goat of the sin offering, that is for the people, and bring his blood within the vail, and do with that blood as he did with the blood of the bullock, and sprinkle it upon the mercy seat, and before the mercy seat:

16 And he shall make an atonement for the holy place, because of the uncleanness of the children of Israel, and because of their transgressions in all their sins: and so shall he do for the tabernacle of the congregation, that remaineth among them in the midst of their uncleanness.

17 And there shall be no man in the tabernacle of the congregation when he goeth in to make an atonement in the holy place, until he come out, and have made an atonement for himself, and for his household, and for all the congregation of Israel.

18 And he shall go out unto the altar that is before the LORD, and make an atonement for it; and shall take of the blood of the bullock, and of the blood of the goat, and put it upon the horns of the altar round about.

19 And he shall sprinkle of the blood upon it with his finger seven times, and cleanse it, and hallow it from the uncleanness of the children of Israel.

Key Text

He shall make an atonement for the holy place, because of the uncleanness of the children of Israel, and because of their transgressions in all their sins: and so shall he do for the tabernacle of the congregation, that remaineth among them in the midst of their uncleanness. —**Leviticus 16:16**

Costly Sacrifices

Lesson Aims

After participating in this lesson, each learner will be able to:

1. Explain the significance of the Day of Atonement.

2. Compare and contrast the Day of Atonement with Jesus' sacrifice.

3. Participate in a debate on the value (or lack thereof) of specifying an annual day for congregational confession of sin or write a prayer confessing sin.

Lesson Outline

Introduction
   A. Necessary Barriers
   B. Lesson Context
I. Atonement for Some (Leviticus 16:11-14)
   A. Bull as Sin Offering (v. 11)
   B. Incense for a Cloud (vv. 12-13)
   C. Blood for Sprinkling (v. 14)
II. Atonement for Many (Leviticus 16:15-17)
   A. Goat as Sin Offering (v. 15a)
   B. Blood for Sprinkling (v. 15b)
      Typology? Typography?
   C. Result for Places (v. 16)
      Hijacked Words
   D. Restriction of Entry (v. 17)
III. Atonement for the Altar (Leviticus 16:18-19)
   A. Blood Applied (v. 18)
   B. Blood Sprinkled (v. 19)
Conclusion
   A. What a Day!
   B. Prayer
   C. Thought to Remember

Introduction

A. Necessary Barriers

One good principle of life is *Don't tear down a fence until you find out why it was erected in the first place.* Undoubtedly, there was a reason for putting up any given fence in the first place, but the question is whether that reason still exists.

This principle applies all the more regarding divine matters. Within the Old Testament, the world is divided in part between pure and impure things. While God has always desired to dwell with His people, His presence cannot reside in an impure location, so barriers must be erected. Today's lesson text describes how God addressed the problem of sacred space and impurity in the Old Testament era. Next week's lesson will address His permanent solution.

B. Lesson Context

The Lesson Context from last week's lesson, drawn from Leviticus 1, also applies to this lesson, so that information does not need to be repeated here. The lesson at hand will, in turn, be the context for next week's lesson from Hebrews.

In this, our second lesson in Leviticus, we jump from chapter 1 to chapter 16. How these two chapters fit within the whole book is seen in this broad-brush outline:

   I. Sacrificial Worship (1:1–7:38)
   II. Ritual Ceremonies (8:1–10:20)
   III. Purity vs. Impurity (11:1–15:33)
   IV. Day of Atonement (16:1-34)
   V. Holy Sacrifices (17:1-16)
   VI. Community Holiness (18:1–20:27)
   VII. Particularly Holy (21:1–27:34)

God established several feasts and holy days for the new nation of Israel. These are listed in Leviticus 23; Numbers 28–29; Deuteronomy 16; etc. In the book of Leviticus, the Day of Atonement takes center stage among them (compare Numbers 29:7-11). Indeed, the writer of Leviticus devotes more than 4 percent of the entire book to that single day on the calendar of the ancient Israelites—the tenth day of the seventh month (Leviticus 16:29; 23:27). On the modern calendar, this equates to a day in late September or early October. If you've heard this day referred to as *Yom Kippur*, then you are learning to speak Hebrew!

The sacred space designated "most holy" is the context for the actions taken on that day of every year. Perhaps you have heard that place described as "the holy of holies." That is a very literal, word-for-word translation of the Hebrew as it is found in Exodus 26:33; 1 Kings 6:16; 7:50; 8:6; and elsewhere. The translation "the holy of holies" does not appear in the *King James Version*, but the location is the same in the translation "the holy place within the vail" (Leviticus 16:2) or simply "the most holy" (Exodus 26:33). The most holy place was the heart of the tabernacle, the sacred structure that God commanded Moses to build as a site for God's presence among the people (Exodus 26).

Our printed text picks up with the Lord's instruction on how Aaron, brother of Moses and the first high priest (Leviticus 16:2-5), was to discharge his duties when that sacred day came around each year.

I. Atonement for Some
(Leviticus 16:11-14)

A. Bull as Sin Offering (v. 11)

11. And Aaron shall bring the bullock of the sin offering, which is for himself, and shall make an atonement for himself, and for his house, and shall kill the bullock of the sin offering which is for himself.

This verse begins to list the sacrificial procedures needed to cleanse the most holy place, starting with the cleansing of the high priest, *Aaron* himself. He had to address his uncleanness before taking the next step of atoning for the people's sins. After doing so, Aaron proceeded to offer the required sacrifices that were part of the day's procedures.

The verb translated *make an atonement* is a critical one in the book of Leviticus. In fact, over half of its appearances in the Bible occur in Leviticus. The popular-level description of atonement is that of "at-one-ment" with God. That is certainly what atonement results in, but the verb translated "make an atonement" by itself doesn't reveal to our modern ears how that "at-one-ment" with God is to be achieved.

Prepare to be in God's holy presence.

Visual for Lesson 5. *Display this visual and lead into the lesson by asking learners to notice how the ancient Hebrews prepared to be in God's presence.*

The challenge involves some technical issues with the nature of the Hebrew language. In the word's various configurations and contexts, it can mean "ransom," "payment of money," "bribe," or "pacify" (Exodus 30:12; Job 31:39; 1 Samuel 12:3; Proverbs 16:14, respectively). These meanings are not mutually exclusive; they can shade into one another depending on context.

The old Greek translation of the Old Testament, known as the Septuagint, helps us here. The words it uses are picked up in the New Testament to explain the sacrifice of Christ in terms of the word *propitiation* (Romans 3:25; 1 John 2:2; 4:10). That meaning also fits with what the Day of Atonement provided: a means of escaping the penalty for one's sin by the offering of a substitutionary sacrifice. Sin offerings are explained in Leviticus 4:1–5:13.

B. Incense for a Cloud (vv. 12-13)

12. And he shall take a censer full of burning coals of fire from off the altar before the Lord, and his hands full of sweet incense beaten small, and bring it within the vail.

Aaron (or any high priest who would take part in these proceedings on the Day of Atonement) had to prepare himself carefully and appropriately before entering *within the vail*, meaning the curtain that separated the holy place from the most holy place within the tabernacle (compare Exodus 26:33; Hebrews 6:19; 9:2-5). The source of the needed *burning coals of fire* was likely the altar of burnt offering, which was located near the front of the courtyard of the tabernacle (Exodus 27:1-8). Aaron's loss of two sons when they misused censers of fire (Leviticus 10:1-2) made clear the necessity of following these instructions with great care and seriousness.

The ingredients for the *sweet incense* are found in Exodus 30:34-38. Such incense had two purposes. First, it was another kind of sacrificial item showing honor to God. Second, the aroma permeated the area around the tabernacle and highlighted the uniqueness and separateness of the place. It thus served as a perceptible reminder that God was holy and that the precincts of His abode should be respected.

13. And he shall put the incense upon the fire before the Lord, that the cloud of the incense may cover the mercy seat that is upon the testimony, that he die not.

The *cloud* of smoke created by the burning of *incense* is for Aaron's protection (compare Exodus 28:43), since no one can see God's face and live (33:20). The *mercy seat* refers to the elaborate cover of the ark of the covenant, which was topped with two golden angelic figures (cherubim) facing one another with outstretched wings (25:10-22). The ark represented God's presence among the people. The word translated as *testimony* refers to the stone tablets into which Moses chiseled God's law (34:1-4, 29), tablets that were kept inside the ark of the covenant (16:34; 25:21; 40:20).

The presence of the Lord in this most holy place is what made it "most holy." That was why the high priest could not enter it carelessly or casually. God must be approached on His terms, not ours.

> **What Do You Think?**
> Considering Revelation 8:3-4, how will you adjust your prayer life to be more of a fragrant incense before God?
> **Digging Deeper**
> Which is more important in that regard: quantity or quality? Why?

C. Blood for Sprinkling (v. 14)

14. And he shall take of the blood of the bullock, and sprinkle it with his finger upon the mercy seat eastward; and before the mercy seat shall he sprinkle of the blood with his finger seven times.

This action is similar to what was to be done for other sin offerings (Leviticus 4:6-7, 17-18). In those cases, the blood was to be applied to the altar of incense, which was located immediately in front of the veil (curtain) that shielded the most holy place. Here, however, the blood was first to be sprinkled on the east side of the ark of the covenant. Since the tabernacle was situated facing east (Numbers 2:3), the *eastward* side is the front side.

The high priest was also to sprinkle some of the blood *seven times* on the ground directly in front of the mercy seat. This represented the entirety of the most holy place being brought into contact with the blood of the sin offering. The number seven often represents completeness or perfection (examples: Revelation 5:6; 15:1, 8). See Hebrews 9:7-8 for further explanation.

II. Atonement for Many
(Leviticus 16:15-17)
A. Goat as Sin Offering (v. 15a)

15a. Then shall he kill the goat of the sin offering, that is for the people.

Having provided atonement for himself and his family, the high priest was then to prepare to enter the most holy place a second time on behalf of *the people*, his fellow Israelites. That preparation involved killing one of the two goats *of the sin offering*, mentioned in Leviticus 16:5. The first goat was slaughtered as an atoning sacrifice, cleansing the sacred precincts from the impurity of Israel's sins. The other goat became the scapegoat, which was released into the wilderness (Leviticus 16:8-10, 20-22). The priest would first lay hands on the goat's head and confess the people's sins over it, thus transferring them symbolically to the animal (16:21). A person would then be charged with taking the goat into the wilderness and releasing it so that it wouldn't return (16:22, 26-28). The scapegoat and its destination thus represented the complete removal of the sins and impurities of the people.

B. Blood for Sprinkling (v. 15b)

15b. And bring his blood within the vail, and do with that blood as he did with the blood of the bullock, and sprinkle it upon the mercy seat, and before the mercy seat.

The high priest was to follow the same procedure that he did in providing atonement for himself and his household. Sin offerings on behalf of the people are described in detail in Leviticus 4:13-21.

> **What Do You Think?**
> What do the meticulous instructions regarding the ministry work for and on the Day of Atonement have to say about providing ministry today, if anything?
>
> **Digging Deeper**
> In what ways do you see the spiritual, mental, and physical preparations for ministry tasks to be interrelated?

Typology? Typography?

Here's an advanced Bible comprehension quiz:

1. What's the difference between *typology* and *typography*?
2. Which of those two terms is more important for today's study? Why?

<u>Answers</u>: 1. *Typology* is the study of how one thing serves as a pattern for another thing; *typography* deals with the style and arrangement of typeset matter. 2. Although you may admire the pleasing layout of the book you are now reading due to excellent typography, it's typology that really counts in Bible study.

You may have heard typology referred to by the more familiar description of *type* and *antitype*. These two words express how Old Testament things (the "types") foreshadow New Testament things (the "antitypes"). Multiple New Testament texts highlight these typological relationships: Adam was a "figure" of Christ (Romans 5:14), and God's provision of water and bread and deliverance of His people through the Red Sea foreshad-

owed communion and baptism under the new covenant (1 Corinthians 10:6-12).

A treasure trove of types and antitypes is found in comparing the book of Leviticus with the book of Hebrews. Start by re-studying last week's and this week's lessons from Leviticus in light of next week's lesson from Hebrews. But do so only if you're interested in moving from the "milk" of the Word of God to the "meat" (Hebrews 5:12-13). Are you?   —R. L. N.

C. Result for Places (v. 16)

16a. And he shall make an atonement for the holy place, because of the uncleanness of the children of Israel, and because of their transgressions in all their sins.

We may wonder why *the holy place* would need atonement. After all, inanimate objects have no consciousness or ability to sin! As pointed out in the comment on verse 11, atonement addressed not only individual sins but also the contamination of places and things closely associated with the holy God. Therefore, *atonement* was not only for people but also for consecrated things and areas.

Three words underline the seriousness of the spiritual state of *the children of Israel: uncleanness, transgressions,* and *sins.* The Hebrew word rendered *transgressions* is the most serious word in Hebrew for disobedience toward God; it implies deliberate and willful rebellion. It occurs twice in Leviticus 16 (see 16:21) and nowhere else in the book.

Chapters 11 through 15 of Leviticus address various sources of uncleanness and impurity in greater detail. Certain prescribed sacrifices and purifications provide atonement for these. God foresaw that the Israelites would pollute the places of worship to the degree that they, too, needed to be cleansed.

> **What Do You Think?**
> What are some spiritual guardrails you can erect to ensure you are not in rebellion against God?
>
> **Digging Deeper**
> How do you decide which guardrails are your responsibility and which belong to the Holy Spirit?

Hijacked Words

Think of some Bible words or phrases adopted by culture to use in other contexts. One that comes to my mind is "he saw the handwriting on the wall" (adopted from Daniel 5) to describe an inevitable negative outcome. Another example is the word *holy*, which occurs often in irreverent expressions.

The word *sanctified* is one in particular that catches my attention. I heard it as part of the lyrics to the song "All Down the Line" performed by the Rolling Stones and others. It's a song about a lonely person waiting for a train. As he waits and thinks, he decides that what he needs is a girlfriend who has a "sanctified" mind.

Christians know that the word *sanctified* means "to be holy" or "consecrated," signifying distance from spiritual uncleanliness. The song, however, seems to use the word *sanctified* merely as a three-syllable filler to coordinate the meter of two lines of lyrics. This makes me wonder if Christians do something similar personally. Is your sanctification just a casual, filler concept, or is it something you pursue deliberately and daily? Before answering, read John 17:17-19; 1 Corinthians 6:10-11; and 1 Thessalonians 5:23.   —R. L. N.

16b. And so shall he do for the tabernacle of the congregation, that remaineth among them in the midst of their uncleanness.

When Moses set apart the nation of Israel as God's covenant people, he did so by sprinkling blood on an altar, on the book of the covenant, and on the people (Exodus 24:6-8; Hebrews 9:19-20). And when *the tabernacle* was completed, it too (and everything within it) was sprinkled with blood (9:21). The tabernacle remained *among* the people, even in their state of *uncleanness*, but atonement by means of blood needed to be provided for the tabernacle each year (compare Exodus 30:10).

D. Restriction of Entry (v. 17)

17. And there shall be no man in the tabernacle of the congregation when he goeth in to make an atonement in the holy place, until he come out, and have made an atonement for himself, and for his household, and for all the congregation of Israel.

This verse might be summed up with just three words: Keep your distance! To do so would prevent the high priest's being distracted from his duties. The absolutely vital nature of the high priest's actions for *atonement* is seen in the all-encompassing applications to *himself, his household, and for all the congregation of Israel*. Such a restriction echoes what the Israelites were told when God's presence came to them at Mount Sinai. No one, not even an animal, was allowed to cross the sacred boundaries except for Moses and Aaron; whoever did so would die (Exodus 19:10-13, 24). On the Day of Atonement, no one could reenter the tabernacle until atonement had been made for priest, places, and people.

> **What Do You Think?**
> What modern ministry tasks would you be better at working alone, if any?
> **Digging Deeper**
> How do Matthew 6:6 and Luke 5:16 inform your answer?

III. Atonement for the Altar
(Leviticus 16:18-19)
A. Blood Applied (v. 18)

18. And he shall go out unto the altar that is before the Lord, and make an atonement for it; and shall take of the blood of the bullock, and of the blood of the goat, and put it upon the horns of the altar round about.

After the purification of the most holy place, the cleansing regimen progresses outward. The tabernacle featured two altars: the altar of burnt offering (Exodus 27:1-3) and the altar of incense (30:1-10). We wonder which of the two altars is being referred to here. The statement that the high priest is to *put [blood] upon the horns of the altar round about* doesn't help us decide, since both altars were to be treated that way (Leviticus 4:7, 25).

Favoring the subject to be the altar of burnt offering is the fact that it was used for so many offerings to address the sins of the people that the need for its own atonement was much greater than that of the altar of incense (Exodus 29:36-37; compare Ezekiel 43:20). Favoring the altar of incense, however, is the phrase *the altar that is before the Lord*. The altar of incense was located very close to the curtain that separated the holy place from the most holy place, whereas the altar of burnt offering was located at the entrance to the tabernacle (Exodus 40:5-6, 26-29). Given its proximity to God's abode, however, the position of the altar of burnt offering could also merit its description as *before the Lord*. Moreover, the fact that the priest is told to *go out* suggests that he is leaving the tabernacle, in which case the altar of burnt offering would be in view.

B. Blood Sprinkled (v. 19)

19. And he shall sprinkle of the blood upon it with his finger seven times, and cleanse it, and hallow it from the uncleanness of the children of Israel.

Blood is not the only substance to be sprinkled *seven times* under the Law of Moses. Oil and water were also used ceremonially in this manner (examples: Leviticus 8:10-11; 14:5). Such sprinklings could be done for the physical healing of someone's body. But blood sprinklings were for cleansing the sacred space of the tabernacles and its objects. The term *hallow* means "to make holy."

What Do You Think?

In what ways can the corporate aspects of the Day of Atonement be applied to the church, if any?

Digging Deeper

How do Nehemiah 9 and Acts 19:18-20 influence your response?

Conclusion

A. What a Day!

The phrase *What a Day!* can convey very different messages. It can be used to characterize joy or distress, depending on the demeanor and tone of voice of the speaker.

The Day of Atonement was one of the most important days of the Israelite calendar. Some students see a fivefold purpose for the Day of Atonement. First, it highlights God's hatred of sin. Second, it underlines the requirement for blood to

be shed for the forgiveness of sin. Third, it reveals how "contagious" sin is—even inanimate objects needed atonement. Fourth, it uses "types" to foreshadow the death of Christ. Fifth, its yearly repetition was a self-demonstration of the need for a permanent remedy for sin.

On the cross, Jesus achieved in one day what Aaron and the high priests of the old covenant who followed him could never accomplish. The effectiveness and finality of Jesus' sacrifice was demonstrated visually by the tearing of the temple veil that set apart the most holy place (Matthew 27:51; Mark 15:38). The writer of Hebrews refers to Jesus' flesh as the "veil" that was "torn" to give every Christian access to the presence of God. Jesus is now our high priest, the only one necessary under the new covenant (Hebrews 10:19-21). But we shouldn't get ahead of ourselves—that's next week's lesson.

B. Prayer

Our Father, You created us to be at one with You, in Your presence. But sin has shattered that oneness, bringing division and chaos. Thank You for Your grace and mercy in providing ways for that oneness to be restored—first, through a Day of Atonement designed for the ancient Israelites and now, through a superior Day of Atonement designed for the entire world and accomplished through Jesus' once-for-all sacrifice. We praise You in His name. Amen.

C. Thought to Remember

Praise God for His provisions of atonement!

How to Say It

Corinthians	Ko-*rin*-thee-unz (*th* as in *thin*).
Deuteronomy	Due-ter-*ahn*-uh-me.
Leviticus	Leh-*vit*-ih-kus.
Septuagint	Sep-*too*-ih-jent.
Thessalonians	*Thess*-uh-*lo*-nee-unz (*th* as in *thin*).
typography	tie-*paw*-gruh-fee.
typology	tie-*paw*-luh-gee.
Yom Kippur (*Hebrew*)	Yohm Kih-*purr*.

Involvement Learning

Enhance your lesson with KJV Bible Student *(from your curriculum supplier) and the reproducible activity page (at www.standardlesson.com or in the back of the* KJV Standard Lesson Commentary Deluxe Edition*).*

Into the Lesson

Invite learners to share information regarding how their families celebrate annual traditions (birthdays, anniversaries, etc.) in ways other families may not. Ask for elaborations on the particulars of *why* and *how* regarding those traditions.

Transition to Bible study by saying, "It is good for us to celebrate the people, things, and events that are important to us. The celebrations of the Old Testament were something of a double-edged sword in this regard: they could simultaneously be times of celebration and solemn reflection. Today's lesson has us consider one such day."

Into the Word

Option. Before beginning the lesson proper, distribute copies of the "An Orderly Arrangement" as a pre-test exercise from the activity page, which you can download. Announce that learners have one minute to arrange the feasts as indicated. Go over results as a class; learners score their own results.

Ask two volunteers to take turns reading the verses of Leviticus 16:11-19. Then, divide learners into five study pairs or triads, each to focus on one element of the text you assign. Give each pair or triad a reference card on which you have printed the following:

Vail Group: Exodus 26:31-35; Leviticus 16:12-15
Incense Group: Exodus 30:34-38; Leviticus 16:12-13
Mercy Seat Group: Exodus 25:17-22; Leviticus 16:13-15
Blood Group: Leviticus 16:14-19; Hebrews 9:22
Sin Offering Group: Leviticus 4:1-12; 16:11-15

Have printed on the reference cards the following single-word questions: *Element? Physical description?* and *Purpose?* for learners to address as research questions for their assigned texts.

While learners work in pairs or triads, write those same three single-word research questions on the board as headers of three columns, one each. Then, write the five group names as the titles to five horizontal rows that intersect the three columns. Fill in the intersections during whole-class discussion after groups finish their research.

Some expected observations for *Physical description* are as follows: *Vail*–fine linen in blue, purple, and scarlet; hung as a barrier between the holy place (which had the altar of incense) and the most holy place (which had the ark of the covenant); *Incense*–a sacred formula of onycha (gum resin benzoin), stacte (styrax), and galbanum (another aromatic gum resin); *Mercy seat*–the cover for the ark of the covenant, 3' 9" in length by 2' 3" in width, made of pure gold, recreations of cherubim included; *Blood*–from sacrificial animals, sometimes smeared, other times sprinkled; *Sin offering*–a type of offering distinct from several others listed in Leviticus 1–7. Unlike burnt offerings, which were wholly consumed by fire, the animal sacrificed in a sin offering could be eaten.

Some observations for *Purpose* may be as follows: *Vail*–served as a distinct boundary that warned of the deadly danger for unauthorized passing beyond it, signifying God's holiness; *Incense*–provided a shield or blocking cloud between God and the high priest; God's proprietary formula was not to be copied and used for anything else; *Mercy seat*–where God would speak with the high priest; *Blood*–necessary for atonement; *Sin offering*–likewise, necessary for atonement.

Into Life

Form your learners into two teams who are to debate this resolution: *Our congregation should have an annual day for confessing sin together.* Research various debate formats in advance, choosing the most appropriate for your class.

Alternative. Distribute copies of the "Prayer of Confession" exercise from the activity page, which you can download, to be completed as indicated.

Christ's Once-for-All Sacrifice

Devotional Reading: Mark 10:41-45
Background Scripture: Hebrews 9:23–10:25

Hebrews 9:23-28

23 It was therefore necessary that the patterns of things in the heavens should be purified with these; but the heavenly things themselves with better sacrifices than these.

24 For Christ is not entered into the holy places made with hands, which are the figures of the true; but into heaven itself, now to appear in the presence of God for us:

25 Nor yet that he should offer himself often, as the high priest entereth into the holy place every year with blood of others;

26 For then must he often have suffered since the foundation of the world: but now once in the end of the world hath he appeared to put away sin by the sacrifice of himself.

27 And as it is appointed unto men once to die, but after this the judgment:

28 So Christ was once offered to bear the sins of many; and unto them that look for him shall he appear the second time without sin unto salvation.

Hebrews 10:1-4, 11-14, 19-25

1 For the law having a shadow of good things to come, and not the very image of the things, can never with those sacrifices which they offered year by year continually make the comers thereunto perfect.

2 For then would they not have ceased to be offered? because that the worshippers once purged should have had no more conscience of sins.

3 But in those sacrifices there is a remembrance again made of sins every year.

4 For it is not possible that the blood of bulls and of goats should take away sins.

11 And every priest standeth daily ministering and offering oftentimes the same sacrifices, which can never take away sins:

12 But this man, after he had offered one sacrifice for sins for ever, sat down on the right hand of God;

13 From henceforth expecting till his enemies be made his footstool.

14 For by one offering he hath perfected for ever them that are sanctified.

19 Having therefore, brethren, boldness to enter into the holiest by the blood of Jesus,

20 By a new and living way, which he hath consecrated for us, through the veil, that is to say, his flesh;

21 And having an high priest over the house of God;

22 Let us draw near with a true heart in full assurance of faith, having our hearts sprinkled from an evil conscience, and our bodies washed with pure water.

23 Let us hold fast the profession of our faith without wavering; (for he is faithful that promised;)

24 And let us consider one another to provoke unto love and to good works:

25 Not forsaking the assembling of ourselves together, as the manner of some is; but exhorting one another: and so much the more, as ye see the day approaching.

Key Text

Christ is not entered into the holy places made with hands, which are the figures of the true; but into heaven itself, now to appear in the presence of God for us. —**Hebrews 9:24**

Costly
Sacrifices

Unit 2: Christ's All-Sufficient Sacrifice

Lessons 6–9

Lesson Aims

After participating in this lesson, each learner will be able to:

1. Identify how a person enters the holiest place.
2. Explain why Christ had to die only once.
3. Recruit an accountability partner for mutual encouragement in love and good works.

Lesson Outline

Introduction

A. Grandma's House

My grandmother kept a very tidy house. The floors were always spotless, and the carpets were free of stains. She exemplified the philosophy, "A place for everything, and everything in its place."

I also knew her as a wonderful playmate. She would chase my sister and me around outside. She would play with us in the pool or the mud, teaching us to experience the world with our hands.

But we couldn't enter her house while we were dirty. She had a shower outside by her pool, where we would wash off before going inside. We had to put on clean clothes and shoes. We knew Grandma loved us, but she needed to preserve her home. Her front door separated the earthy outside world from her pristine abode. Her threshold was a barrier that uncleanliness could not cross. Sound familiar?

B. Lesson Context

The book of Hebrews clarifies the relationship between the old and new covenants. Its original intended audience seems to have been Christians of Jewish heritage who were in danger of slipping back into Judaism. To address this issue, the unnamed author demonstrates how the regulations of the Law of Moses pointed to Christ and His work.

After identifying Christ as the high priest of the new covenant (Hebrews 4:14–5:10; 8:1-13), the author summarized the regulations for worship under the old covenant (9:1-7) and how those practices were not permanent (9:8-10). They have been superseded by the one-time sacrifice of Christ, the ultimate high priest (9:11-22). These details set the stage for the outstanding summary presented in chapters 9 and 10, the focus of today's text.

I. Absolute Necessity
(Hebrews 9:23-28)
A. Better Sacrifice (v. 23)

23. It was therefore necessary that the patterns of things in the heavens should be purified with these; but the heavenly things themselves with better sacrifices than these.

The word *therefore* indicates that the writer is moving from establishing facts of Christ's blood atonement—the "What's so?"—to exploring the implications of those facts—the "So what?" The phrase *patterns of things in the heavens* refers to things of earth with counterparts in Heaven. The need to use animal blood to purify various elements of the old covenant worship structures seems clear in Leviticus 16:15-19. But the second half of the verse at hand tells us that the *necessary* also applies to *the heavenly things themselves*. But if nothing sinful has come into contact with those heavenly things, why the need for purification?

Some students see a "lesser to the greater" logical argument as the solution. Such an argument says that if something is true for a thing of lesser importance, it must also be true for a thing of greater importance. The next verse provides insight into the author's assertion regarding the need to purify the heavenly things.

What Do You Think?

What "necessary" actions do you need to take now that Christ has completed His own "necessary" actions?

Digging Deeper

Would *justification* and *sanctification* be two good categories for your responses? Why, or why not?

B. Better Tabernacle (v. 24)

24. For Christ is not entered into the holy places made with hands, which are the figures of the true; but into heaven itself, now to appear in the presence of God for us.

The word *for* implies that what follows explains or expands on the previous statement. Mortal high priests enter into a sanctuary made by human hands (contrast Acts 7:48). Christ, on the other hand, entered *into heaven itself* at His ascension. There, He performed His priestly duties in the heavenly tabernacle, not in the replica on earth (see Hebrews 9:12). The author emphasizes a distinctive feature of Christ's heavenly ministry. The present tense *now* points to Christ's ongoing role in interceding for believers (see Romans 8:34;

Hebrews 7:25). Contrary to mortal priests who repeatedly offer sacrifices, Christ's single sacrifice has eternally settled the sin debt (see 7:27; 10:10). In this role, Jesus stands directly before God, without any veil separating Him from the Father, conducting His priestly duties on our behalf.

C. Better Priest (vv. 25-28)

25. Nor yet that he should offer himself often, as the high priest entereth into the holy place every year with blood of others.

This verse compares how Jesus' service differs from mortal high priests. The Law of Moses prescribes an annual Day of Atonement for addressing the people's sins (Leviticus 16:29-30; 23:26-32). Two goats were chosen, one for sacrifice to atone for sins and one for release into the wilderness as a scapegoat to carry off sins (16:7-10, 20-22). On the Day of Atonement and only on that day, *the high priest* would enter the Holy of Holies to set these procedures in motion (16:2, 34). This backdrop sets the stage for a great contrast, next.

26. For then must he often have suffered since the foundation of the world: but now once in the end of the world hath he appeared to put away sin by the sacrifice of himself.

Hebrews 7:27 makes much the same point that we see here. Both passages emphasize the uniqueness of Jesus' self-sacrifice. Rather than suffering *often*, His sacrifice was one-time only. That's one reason it is superior to the sacrifices of mortal high priests. If His sacrifice were only as effective as that of animals, He would have had to die repeatedly *since the foundation of the world*. The apostle Paul makes the same point: Christ's sacrificial death marks the transition from one era of history to another (1 Corinthians 10:11).

27-28. And as it is appointed unto men once to die, but after this the judgment: So Christ was once offered to bear the sins of many; and unto them that look for him shall he appear the second time without sin unto salvation.

The death sentence that all humans labor under was pronounced in Genesis 3:19. The writer's phrase *once to die* refers to physical death. There are some notable exceptions in that a handful of people in the Bible died twice physically: those whom Christ raised from the dead during His earthly ministry died again later. Contrary to humans, who were *appointed* to die once, Jesus voluntarily sacrificed His life to settle the debt of sin. His death was a conscious act of self-sacrifice (see John 10:15-17).

The phrase *after this* sets the possibility of another death as a result of *the judgment* to come. No one will be exempt from this evaluation: "We must all appear before the judgment seat of Christ" (2 Corinthians 5:10). The result will be an eternal separation of forgiven sinners from unforgiven sinners (Daniel 12:2; Matthew 25:46; etc.). Some students propose that the two verses before us mean a person is judged immediately after death; others disagree. The author does not specify when the judgment occurs. The emphasis is on the fact that our "once" death sentence stands in parallel with Christ's *once offered* sacrifice *to bear the sins of many* (Isaiah 53:12). His return then will not be for paying for sins again, but for bringing in the promised salvation (Philippians 3:20; Titus 2:13).

> ### What Do You Think?
> What actions would you take if you knew this was your last day on earth?
>
> ### Digging Deeper
> How would or should those actions differ from your daily routine, if at all?

Once or Twice? Ready or Not?

An evangelist from yesteryear had a ready response when someone would ask him when his birthday was. He would respond with the simple question, "Which one?" After the then-confused person asked, "You've been born more than once?" the evangelist would reply, "Yes. If you're born once, you die twice; if you're born twice, you die once." This then served as a lead-in to discussing the need to be born again (John 3:3, 7; 1 Peter 1:23) as the only way to escape the second death (Revelation 2:11; 20:6, 14; 21:8).

We live under Christ's directive of the great commission of Matthew 28:19-20. This directive brings the challenge to "be ready always to give an answer to every man that asketh you a

reason of the hope that is in you" (1 Peter 3:15). Time is short—death can come at any time to anyone. I know that I need to adopt a greater sense of urgency in that regard. Do you?   —R. L. N.

II. Weak Sacrifices
(Hebrews 10:1-4)
A. Repetition (vv. 1-2)

1. For the law having a shadow of good things to come, and not the very image of the things, can never with those sacrifices which they offered year by year continually make the comers thereunto perfect.

The author of Hebrews continues to compare and contrast the realities of the old covenant with those of the new covenant. Having shown the superiority of Christ's priesthood, the author explains the superiority of Christ's sacrifice to animal sacrifices.

The phrase *the law* refers to the Law of Moses in this context, not law in general. Nothing was wrong with the Law of Moses regarding what it was intended to achieve (Romans 3:20; 7:7; etc.). Its holy value is in the facts that (1) God was its ultimate author and (2) *as a shadow of good things to come,* the law points to certain future greater realities (compare Hebrews 8:5; 9:11). Those who accepted the first fact while missing the second fact were in danger of putting an unrealistic burden on others (Acts 15:1-35; Galatians 3:1-6; etc.).

The New Testament authors recognize the law's limited and distinct role in God's plan. The law was a temporary guardian meant to lead us to Christ (Galatians 3:23-25). The law's limited role means that it cannot *make the comers thereunto perfect* since no one has kept the law perfectly (Romans 3:9-20)—no one, that is, except for Christ.

> ### What Do You Think?
> How would you explain the concept of *foreshadowing* to someone in as few words as possible?
>
> ### Digging Deeper
> How would your explanations to unbelievers and new Christians differ? Why?

2. For then would they not have ceased to be offered? because that the worshippers once purged should have had no more conscience of sins.

The word *for* introduces a logical conclusion to the current argument regarding the limitations of the Law of Moses. Were the Law of Moses to have been God's "final word" to humanity, God would not have settled the sin issue *once* and for all. The animal sacrifices would need to continue forever. And since such sacrifices would need to be repeated indefinitely, they do not have the power to perfect God's people. Paul makes a similar argument about the law in Galatians 3:21, where he denies that righteousness comes through the law because God did not give a law capable of imparting eternal life.

B. Reminder (vv. 3-4)

3. But in those sacrifices there is a remembrance again made of sins every year.

Instead of freeing the people from their guilt, the animal sacrifices of the Law of Moses had the opposite effect: they reminded the people of their *sins every year.* The sacrifices highlighted sinfulness rather than fixing the problem of sinful hearts (again, Romans 3:20).

> **What Do You Think?**
> In what ways could your congregation regularly and appropriately remind its members of the reality of sin?
>
> **Digging Deeper**
> What steps do you need to take to remind yourself of individual sins? of corporate sins?

4. For it is not possible that the blood of bulls and of goats should take away sins.

This verse highlights the main limitation of animal sacrifices. Given that God commanded the animal sacrifices, it may seem strange that the author of Hebrews denies that they *take away sins.* After all, do not Leviticus 16:10 and Numbers 29:11 say that the two goats make "atonement"? But notice again their temporary nature. It's "wash, rinse, repeat" indefinitely.

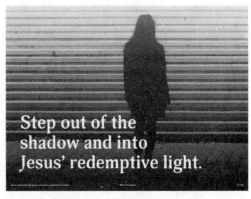

Step out of the shadow and into Jesus' redemptive light.

Visual for Lesson 6. *Display this visual as you ask learners for examples of situations when Jesus' redemption changed something for the better.*

III. Perfect Sacrifice
(Hebrews 10:11-14)
A. Christ's Service (vv. 11-12)

11. And every priest standeth daily ministering and offering oftentimes the same sacrifices, which can never take away sins.

The author continues to draw together the threads of the argument. He does so here by first describing the duties of *every priest.* Under the old covenant, a priest's work was never done. He would perform the same rituals and sacrifices repetitively. The blood offerings he would make were categorized in various ways: the sin offering (Leviticus 4:1-35; 6:24-30); the trespass offering (5:14–6:7); the burnt offering (1:3-17); and the peace offering (3:1-17). The bloodless offerings were the grain offering (2:1-16) and the drink offering (23:13). None of these rituals or sacrifices could ultimately remove the people's sins. The contrast comes next.

12. But this man, after he had offered one sacrifice for sins for ever, sat down on the right hand of God.

By contrast, Christ's priestly service required only a single offering: himself. He offered this sacrifice one time for the sins of humanity. At that point, His duties were completed, and He took His rightful seat at God's *right hand.* The writer of Hebrews draws on Psalm 110:1 to affirm Jesus in this position. By the time we get to this point in the book of Hebrews, the writer has already pointed to this psalm three times (Hebrews 1:3, 13; 8:1). The use here implies that the Son's sacrifice is completely satisfactory, never needing to be repeated. He will remain seated until His second appearing (9:28; a notable exception is Acts 7:55-56).

B. Christ's Rest (vv. 13-14)

13. From henceforth expecting till his enemies be made his footstool.

This verse continues the quotation of Psalm 110:1. The idea seems to be one of rest now that Christ's work on the cross is completed. He offers no more sacrifices. Instead, He occupies a seat of honor while His Father works to make every knee bow to Christ and every tongue confess that He is Lord (Philippians 2:9-1).

14. For by one offering he hath perfected for ever them that are sanctified.

This verse concludes the argument that the author has been making. The numerous animal sacrifices of the old covenant have given way to Christ's *one offering*. This is the offering by which people may be *perfected*, not by the animal sacrifices of the Law of Moses. The people being perfected by Christ are also referred to as *them that are sanctified*. To be sanctified is to be made holy or set apart, and there are two aspects to this.

IV. Implications
(Hebrews 10:19-25)
A. Reasons (vv. 19-21)

19. Having therefore, brethren, boldness to enter into the holiest by the blood of Jesus.

Our last section sketches the implications of Jesus' priestly work. According to Leviticus 16, only the high priest could enter the most holy place, the dwelling place of God's presence in the tabernacle and temple. This access was only allowed once a year. Because Jesus' sacrifice completely satisfied the penalty for sin that we owed,

How to Say It

Judaism   Joo-duh-izz-um
            or *Joo-day-izz-um.*
Nehemiah   Nee-huh-*my*-uh.

we can each have access to God that was unthinkable before (compare Ephesians 2:18; Hebrews 4:16; 9:8, 12, 25). Regarding the *boldness* (confidence) that we now have *to enter into the holiest,* see also 10:35; and 1 John 5:14.

20. By a new and living way, which he hath consecrated for us, through the veil, that is to say, his flesh.

The *new and living way* distinguishes the new covenant from the old one. This way is "new" because it was inaccessible before Christ offered himself as a sacrifice. This way is also "living," which means it gives life to those who follow it.

By His self-sacrifice, Jesus has *consecrated* a path for us *through the veil* of *his flesh.* When His body was torn to death by nails on the cross, the curtain in the temple was torn at the same time (Matthew 27:51). The link becomes more evident if the veil is understood not as a barrier but as the threshold that separated the Holy of Holies from the outer world. Similarly, Christ's body broken on our behalf is the door that leads into God's presence (John 14:6).

21. And having an high priest over the house of God.

The author provides a statement of fact that gives the reason for the imperative of the next verse. Before we go there, however, we take a minute to examine the designation *the house of God.* That was a title for the Jerusalem temple, especially after the return from Babylonian exile (examples: Ezra 3:8; Nehemiah 11:11). But the author of Hebrews uses the designation to refer to people who constitute the church (Hebrews 3:6).

B. Exhortation (vv. 22-25)

22. Let us draw near with a true heart in full assurance of faith, having our hearts sprinkled from an evil conscience, and our bodies washed with pure water.

This is the resulting imperative; this is what we are to do *with a true heart in full assurance of faith*—an imperative echoed in various ways elsewhere (Romans 8:15-17; Galatians 4:6; Colossians 2:2; Hebrews 6:11; 1 John 5:13). The imagery of *hearts sprinkled* and *bodies washed* may have its basis in Ezekiel 36:25. See also the image of sprinkled blood in Hebrews 12:24 and cleansing in 9:14. The inner cleansing of the heart is matched also by the outer cleansing *with pure water*, which most likely refers to baptism.

The Greek word translated *conscience* occurs 30 times in the New Testament. The word occurs in a positive sense (example: Acts 23:1), in a "weak" sense (example: 1 Corinthians 8:7), and in a decidedly negative sense (example: Romans 2:15). Our conscience was given to us by God to be a moral guide, but humans are adept at modifying their conscience toward *evil* (1 Timothy 4:2; Titus 1:15).

23. Let us hold fast the profession of our faith without wavering; (for he is faithful that promised.)

The verb *hold fast* denotes consistency in adhering to the professed faith. The ability of God's people to be faithful is based on God's faithfulness to uphold His promises. His faithfulness is beyond question (1 Corinthians 1:9; Hebrews 3:6).

24-25. And let us consider one another to provoke unto love and to good works: Not forsaking the assembling of ourselves together, as the manner of some is; but exhorting one another: and so much the more, as ye see the day approaching.

These two verses are logically connected. Think about it: wouldn't it be almost impossible to encourage *one another . . . unto love and to good works* unless we are in the habit of *assembling of ourselves together*? That's the context of supporting each other (Acts 2:42-47).

What Do You Think?

What steps will you take to ensure you are still gathering with other believers during life's busy season?

Digging Deeper

How will you ensure that those gatherings are opportunities for encouragement and accountability?

Faithful in Assembling

Pete was an older man who only had one leg. He used crutches and a wheelchair but was at church every Sunday. Harriett was a friend's grandmother who taught the junior girls' class. At times, she let us take turns teaching the class. I hope she lived long enough to hear that many of us followed her example by teaching children at our churches. Bill taught the high school Sunday school class every week. He made us laugh, and we loved him.

You may be thinking, *But things were different back then. After all, don't we now have the option of attending church virtually through the live streaming of our services?* Pete, Harriett, and Bill were just some of the people I knew growing up in our church. They were faithful in meeting with other Christians every week. Their love and encouragement spurred me and others on to lives of service for God. Who is someone whose service in the church encouraged you? How will you be an encouragement in your congregation? —L. J. N.

Conclusion

A. One Sacrifice

Most people in the ancient Greco-Roman world believed that their gods were remote and cared little for them. Some Jewish people of the time between the Testaments also viewed God as distant, so they developed (imagined) elaborate systems of angels to bridge the gap between God and humanity. It is easy for us to believe that God is distant. His silence can lead us to think He doesn't care about us.

But such a belief is proven false when we consider the actions of Jesus, our great high priest. He put on flesh and came to earth to offer himself as a sacrifice for our sins—those aren't the actions of a "distant" God!

The next time you feel distant from God, perhaps the best question to ask yourself is: *Which of us moved?*

B. Prayer

Father, thank You for giving us a faithful high priest, Your Son, Jesus. Give us the courage to approach You with the boldness Jesus purchased for us. We pray in His name. Amen.

C. Thought to Remember

Jesus opened the Holy of Holies to us.

Involvement Learning

Enhance your lesson with KJV Bible Student *(from your curriculum supplier) and the reproducible activity page (at www.standardlesson.com or in the back of the* KJV Standard Lesson Commentary Deluxe Edition*).*

Into the Lesson

Bring a few objects that are miniature versions of other things (*examples*: globe, baby doll, flower, model airplane). Pose this question for each item in turn, inserting the appropriate words in the brackets: "Is this [globe] really [the earth]?" When you receive the expected answer of *no*, ask, "How do you know?" Encourage whole-class discussion.

Alternative. Distribute copies of the "Types, Shadows, and Reality" exercise from the activity pages, which you can download. Encourage participants to work together to determine answers to the true/false quiz. State that you will not collect the completed quizzes. After participants finish, poll the class members on how they answered each question. Write on the board the results of your polling as participants voice their choices. Note the lack of unanimity as you announce that there are no answers that can be stated to be correct beyond a reasonable doubt, given the limited information available from a shadow.

After either activity, say, "It is important to distinguish 'the real thing' from 'representations of the real thing.' As we do, we learn that the representations aren't necessarily counterfeit but are predictive or foreshadowing. In today's lesson, stay alert for the symbols and shadows to consider the greater truths they represent."

Into the Word

Ask a volunteer to read Hebrews 9:23-28. (*Option*: Extend the reading to 10:1 to capture the word *shadow*.) Divide participants into five small groups or study pairs. Assign one of the following five passages to each: Genesis 22:1-14; Exodus 12:1-13; Numbers 21:4-9; Joshua 2:8-21; Jonah 1:11-17. With the assignments, include a handout (you create) featuring these two questions: 1–What is the symbol in your passage? 2–How was that symbol predictive of Jesus?

Have groups voice their discoveries in the ensuing whole-class discussion. *Be prepared to answer both questions yourself for each set of texts.*

Ask a volunteer to read Hebrews 10:11-14. Assign the following verses to the five small groups to discuss: Judges 10:10; 1 Samuel 12:10; 1 Kings 8:47; Psalm 106:6; and Jeremiah 14:20. Encourage groups to review the context surrounding their assigned verse to discover who is confessing, where, and at what period in history. After group discussions, ask someone in each group to read their verse aloud, one right after another. Ask, "What is the common theme/phrase in all these verses?" (*Expected response*: Admission of sin.) Then, ask, "Before Jesus came and died on the cross, what did the people have to do when they sinned?" (*Expected response*: A blood sacrifice was necessary.)

Ask a volunteer to read Hebrews 10:19-25. Draw a chart with three columns on the board with these headers:

Effect | Cause | Reaction

Have the class identify two phrases to put under *Effect* and two phrases to put under *Cause*. (*Expected responses*: Effect–boldness to enter the most holy place; Cause–the blood of Jesus.) Assign one verse to each small group: v. 22a, v. 22b, v. 23, v. 24, and v. 25. Ask groups to consider these *reactions* in relation to the *effect* and *cause* truths that come before. (*Example*: Why are we able to draw near to God? Because Christ has torn the curtain and given us access.) Then, have a volunteer come to the board to write the action response phrase from their verse.

Into Life

Discuss the concept of "accountability partners" and how it differs from a "mentor/protégé" relationship. Challenge those participants who are willing to choose an accountability partner for mutual encouragement in light of Hebrews 10:24-25.

Christ, the Atoning Sacrifice

Devotional Reading: Isaiah 59:1-8
Background Scripture: 1 John 2:1-6; 4:7-21

1 John 2:1-6

1 My little children, these things write I unto you, that ye sin not. And if any man sin, we have an advocate with the Father, Jesus Christ the righteous:

2 And he is the propitiation for our sins: and not for ours only, but also for the sins of the whole world.

3 And hereby we do know that we know him, if we keep his commandments.

4 He that saith, I know him, and keepeth not his commandments, is a liar, and the truth is not in him.

5 But whoso keepeth his word, in him verily is the love of God perfected: hereby know we that we are in him.

6 He that saith he abideth in him ought himself also so to walk, even as he walked.

1 John 4:9-17

9 In this was manifested the love of God toward us, because that God sent his only begotten Son into the world, that we might live through him.

10 Herein is love, not that we loved God, but that he loved us, and sent his Son to be the propitiation for our sins.

11 Beloved, if God so loved us, we ought also to love one another.

12 No man hath seen God at any time. If we love one another, God dwelleth in us, and his love is perfected in us.

13 Hereby know we that we dwell in him, and he in us, because he hath given us of his Spirit.

14 And we have seen and do testify that the Father sent the Son to be the Saviour of the world.

15 Whosoever shall confess that Jesus is the Son of God, God dwelleth in him, and he in God.

16 And we have known and believed the love that God hath to us. God is love; and he that dwelleth in love dwelleth in God, and God in him.

17 Herein is our love made perfect, that we may have boldness in the day of judgment: because as he is, so are we in this world.

Key Text

Herein is love, not that we loved God, but that he loved us, and sent his Son to be the propitiation for our sins. —1 John 4:10

Costly
Sacrifices

Lesson Aims

After participating in this lesson, each learner will be able to:

1. Identify his or her advocate with the Father.

2. Explain the motivation and significance of Jesus' sacrifice.

3. List three ways to practice 1 John 2:6 in the week ahead.

Lesson Outline

Introduction

A. Surprising Symbol

Today, the cross of Christ is recognized the world over. We see it on church buildings, use it for headstones, depict it in paintings, and wear it as jewelry. The latter is particularly surprising for becoming so common, given that the cross was the instrument of torture and death for notorious criminals in the Roman world. In that era, crosses along roadsides symbolized the ultimate consequence for challenging the Roman Empire's power.

How could such a terrible object become the universal symbol of a faith that preaches love and offers new life? The answer to that question lies in the purpose of Jesus' death on the cross: today's lesson.

B. Lesson Context

Our text comes from two parallel sections of the New Testament epistle designated 1 John. It is one of three letters by John among the General Epistles. This is a section of the New Testament consisting of the eight letters: Hebrews; James; 1 and 2 Peter; 1, 2, and 3 John; and Jude.

The epistles of 1, 2, and 3 John are not explicitly ascribed to the apostle John by name, yet the early church ascribed these epistles to him, just as they did with the Gospel of John.

The three letters have close connections to the language and themes of the Gospel of John, so it is reasonable to conclude that all came from the same author. In doing so, we carefully distinguish the apostle John from John the Baptist or John Mark (Acts 1:5; 12:12; etc.).

The letter 1 John and the Gospel of John explicitly state that the author was an eyewitness of Jesus' life and ministry (John 1:14; 1 John 1:1-3). These two works of Scripture have similar purpose statements (compare John 20:31; 1 John 5:13). Both purpose statements find their basis in what the readers can "know" as a certainty. This is a distinctive emphasis of the author. He wrote about 14 percent of the New Testament, but his writings feature over one-third of the New Testament's 250 uses of the Greek word that is underneath the idea of "to know" (more on this in the commentary below).

The letter 1 John addresses growing controversies in the first-century church about the nature of Christ and the Christian life. It seems some believers were influenced by a common concept of that day that said all material things are by nature evil, but that which is spirit is by nature good. On this basis, some began to deny that Jesus was both fully divine and fully human. After all, if material things are evil, then it would be impossible for the good God to exist as a human in a body. The letter of 1 John refutes this. Some students see the growing heresies of Gnosticism and Docetism as playing a part in this problem.

I. The Source of New Life
(1 John 2:1-2)
A. Our Advocate (v. 1)

1. My little children, these things write I unto you, that ye sin not. And if any man sin, we have an advocate with the Father, Jesus Christ the righteous.

The author addresses readers as *children* often (1 John 2:12, 28; 3:7, 18; 4:4; 5:21). The term suggests a close and affectionate connection between the writer and the original audience. This term might also hint that the readers are either younger or less mature in their spiritual journey than the writer.

The Greek word translated *advocate* here is the same one translated "Comforter" in John 14:16, 26; 15:26; 16:7, where it describes the Holy Spirit. Christ's forgiven people still sin; they recognize as much if they are honest with themselves. When believers sin, they do not require justification once more; instead, as children of God, they receive forgiveness through the intercession of Jesus Christ with the Father. Is forgiveness a one-and-done affair? Is the once-forgiven sinner returned to the life of death on the first failure after forgiveness?

The answer is no, as the author sketches Christ's ongoing role as an "advocate," one who speaks on behalf of another. Another way of saying this is that Christ intercedes for us (Romans 8:34; Hebrews 7:25). With God the Father depicted as the righteous judge, Christ speaks on our behalf, identifying us as those whose punishment has

already been taken by Christ himself. Christ is *righteous*, meaning He is not guilty of any sin and is entirely in accord with God's right way.

B. Our Propitiation (v. 2)

2. And he is the propitiation for our sins: and not for ours only, but also for the sins of the whole world.

The keyword *propitiation* now appears in the text. The underlying ancient Greek word is rare in the New Testament. The noun forms appear exclusively here, in Romans 3:25, and 1 John 4:10 (see below) and refer to something that turns away wrath. A verb form is in Hebrews 2:17.

Central to the gospel message is that Christ's death was the once-for-all-time sacrificial offering that shifted our fully deserved punishment for sin onto Him, who is the sinless one (2 Corinthians 5:21). This doctrine is often referred to as "substitutionary atonement." Christ's substitutionary atonement is sufficient for all our sins—past, present, and future. This reality is fundamental; this is grace. It is available for *the whole world*, but it is effectual and operative only for those who receive it through faith in the blood (Romans 3:25-26).

II. The Proof of New Life
(1 John 2:3-6)
A. The Test of Obedience (vv. 3-4)

3. And hereby we do know that we know him, if we keep his commandments.

The author uses the verb translated *know* about two dozen times in the five short chapters of 1 John. These mostly affirm the Christian's confident faith in Christ and assurance of salvation. Here, the question is what assures us that Jesus' is indeed our advocate and propitiation when we sin. The answer is that keeping Jesus' commandments

How to Say It

Docetism	Doe-*set*-iz-um.
Ecclesiastes	Ik-*leez*-ee-*as*-teez.
epistles	ee-*pis*-uls.
Gnosticism	**Nahss**-tih-*sizz*-um.
propitiation	pro-*pih*-she-**ay**-shun.

is our proof (John 14:15; 15:10). If Jesus is Savior, then He must also be Lord.

But how can one who keeps Jesus' *commandments* also need ongoing forgiveness of sins? The writer uses the stark contrast between ongoing sin and ongoing obedience to capture the nature of the Christian life. As a people habituated to sin, we continue to sin even after receiving the gift of Christ's atoning death. But as people with faith in Christ, we continually submit our lives to His authority. So sin, ongoing in the lives of believers, is continually being overcome. Sin is no longer in control, no longer at home.

> **What Do You Think?**
> What steps can believers take to overcome sin and submit to Christ's authority?
> **Digging Deeper**
> How has your life changed since you submitted to Christ's authority?

4. He that saith, I know him, and keepeth not his commandments, is a liar, and the truth is not in him.

This verse restates and reinforces 1 John 1:6: "If we say that we have fellowship with him, and walk in darkness, we lie, and do not the truth." Some believers among John's original readers may have separated faith in Christ from obedience to Christ. Perhaps thinking their "good" spirits were completely separate from their "evil" bodies, they lived as if their actions had no bearing on their relationship to Christ (see Lesson Context). Nevertheless, the contents of a person's heart will eventually become apparent through their actions (compare Matthew 12:34). Therefore, the writer completely rejects the idea that someone's actions would not align with their declared faith.

B. The Model of Love (vv. 5-6)

5. But whoso keepeth his word, in him verily is the love of God perfected: hereby know we that we are in him.

By contrast, our following Jesus' teaching expresses the effect of everything He has done. Jesus' death for sinners was the fullest expression of God's love for humanity, and Jesus' teaching instructs us how to express God's love to others (John 3:15; 1 John 3:16). This makes God's love for humanity our love for humanity. The ancient Greek word translated *perfected* can take various shades of meaning, depending on context. Here and elsewhere, the sense is that of a finished task because its goal has been achieved. The writer uses the word this way five times in his Gospel (John 4:34; 5:36; 17:4, 23; 19:28) and four times in his first epistle (here and 1 John 4:12, 17, below; and in a negative sense 4:18).

6. He that saith he abideth in him ought himself also so to walk, even as he walked.

To confess Christ means to obey Christ. *To walk, even as he walked,* is to follow His example (John 13:15).

The author fronts this conclusion by introducing a Greek word translated as "abide"; he uses this word 23 times in this letter. In doing so, he speaks of a close, ongoing connection. This image originated from Jesus as He compared His followers to branches connected to Him as the vine (John 15:1-11). The author's linkage to Jesus' teachings clarifies that a believer cannot keep Jesus' commandments or follow in Jesus' footsteps through his or her own strength. Doing so is only feasible by remaining in Christ and letting God's Spirit produce fruit in and through the believer. This teaching applies to everyday life. Those who abide in Jesus will inevitably live their life in ways reflecting His love and teaching. In the text between 1 John 2:6 and 4:9 (not in today's lesson), the author continues to trace the theme of love as it applies to various situations.

> **What Do You Think?**
> How can you be better attentive to the work of God's Spirit to produce fruit in you?
> **Digging Deeper**
> How will such fruit empower you to abide in Christ?

When You're Snowed In

I have a vivid childhood memory of when my

family was snowed in by more than a foot of that white stuff. I tried to help my dad dig out. But I quickly encountered a problem: with every step I took, I sank deeply into the snow. I could hardly move. The solution was for me to follow my father's path as he did the major work of clearing snow.

The challenge to walk as Jesus walked may seem overwhelming. How can we possibly walk in the same way that the sinless, holy Son of God walked? That's the first step: we admit our weaknesses. The second step is to realize that Christ knows our weaknesses (Hebrews 4:15; compare Romans 8:26). While achieving perfection through our own endeavors is impossible, this does not imply that the benchmark of perfection is reduced (Matthew 5:48). We will still sin. However, forgiveness is still available (1 John 1:9). What is the most important improvement you must make in your walk?   —C. S.

III. Love in Action
(1 John 4:9-12)
A. God's Initiative (vv. 9-10)

9. In this was manifested the love of God toward us, because that God sent his only begotten Son into the world, that we might live through him.

How can we fail but to see John 3:16 restated here? The supreme expression of God's love is demonstrated through the incarnation: the divine Son of God putting on human flesh to announce and deliver salvation personally. The description of Christ as the *only begotten Son* emphasizes His uniqueness and value to the Father. The eight other translations of the underlying Greek word—not always referring to Jesus—are found in Luke 7:12; 8:42; 9:38; John 1:14, 18; 3:16, 18; and Hebrews 11:17.

God sent His Son to give life to humanity and thereby allow them to enter the presence of the holy God. Jesus not only accepted and affirmed that mission, but He also narrowed the focus of His uniqueness and exclusivity of mission when He said, "I am the way, the truth, and the life: no man cometh unto the Father, but by me" (John 14:6). Truly, we live only *through him*.

Celebrate God's love!

Visual for Lesson 7. *Point to the visual and ask volunteers to brainstorm ways to celebrate God's love in the upcoming week.*

10a. Herein is love, not that we loved God, but that he loved us.

An astute observation from years ago is that what is unique about the relationship between the true God and people is that pagan religions tell stories about humanity's search for god(s). In contrast, Christianity tells the story of God's search for us (Luke 19:10). Christ became incarnate in a world that had rebelled against God (Romans 3:10-12, quoting Psalms 14:1-3; 53:1-3; Ecclesiastes 7:20). His becoming human is an act of love, and His death on the cross brings that love to its fullest measure. "We love him, because he first loved us" (1 John 4:19).

The message of the gospel calls us to love God and our neighbor (Matthew 22:34-40). All such love begins with God's love, expressed and made available through the death and resurrection of the incarnate Christ.

10b. And sent his Son to be the propitiation for our sins.

John aims to convey to his audience that love is an action, not an empty term. He illustrates this by detailing how God demonstrated His love for the world: by becoming *the propitiation for our sins*. The declaration in this half-verse echoes what the apostle Paul wrote in Romans 5:8. see discussion of this word in commentary on 1 John 2:2, above.

A Modern Propitiation

I wouldn't have believed it had I not heard and

seen it personally. The exact date was May 31, 1989, and I was watching a TV news report on the resignation of Representative Jim Wright as Speaker of the House of Representatives. He was resigning under a cloud of alleged ethics violations.

Near the end of his lengthy speech, he made a statement that amazed me: "Let me give you back this job you gave to me as a propitiation for all of this season of bad will that has grown up among us." I remember wondering at the time whether the average viewer in the TV audience knew what *propitiation* meant! The man was sacrificing his position in the hope that it would bring the ethics turmoil to a halt.

But notice a key difference: the man was giving up a job to deflect wrath *away from* himself; Jesus gave up His life to deflect God's wrath away from us and *onto* himself! How should your life change now in realizing this fact?   —R. L. N.

B. Our Responsibility (vv. 11-12)

11. Beloved, if God so loved us, we ought also to love one another.

This implication of the gospel is unmistakable. After receiving God's love, we must recognize our responsibility to love the same people God loves. We do not need to ask who our neighbor is when hearing the command to love our neighbor (Luke 10:29). God loves all because Christ's death makes atonement available for all (1 John 2:2, above). God loves first and loves those who do not love Him. And so must we who have received His love. Even our enemies are objects of God's love and so must be of ours (Matthew 5:43-47).

> **What Do You Think?**
> What are some ways we can love one another just as God has loved us?
> **Digging Deeper**
> How do you deal with negative attitudes that prevent you from loving those you might consider unlovable?

12a. No man hath seen God at any time.

Many texts reflect the fact that God cannot be *seen* (examples: Exodus 33:20; John 1:18; 1 Timothy 6:16). But in Christ, God became a visible,

physical human, so to see Christ was truly to see God (John 14:8-9); the next half-verse expands on this.

12b. If we love one another, God dwelleth in us, and his love is perfected in us.

The imperative to *love one another* is so important that John uses that phrase five times in this letter (here and 1 John 3:11, 23; 4:7, 11-12). This command is a repeated part of Jesus' message (John 13:34-35; 15:12, 17) and stressed by others as well (Romans 13:8; 1 Peter 1:22). As we love others, then our actions make God visible to the world.

Regarding the word *perfected*, see commentary on 1 John 2:5, above.

> **What Do You Think?**
> Describe someone you know who excels at loving people. How will you follow his or her example?
> **Digging Deeper**
> Who will you ask to be an accountability partner to encourage you as you practice loving others?

IV. Certainty of Knowledge
(1 John 4:13-17)
A. Divine Intervention (vv. 13-14)

13. Hereby know we that we dwell in him, and he in us, because he hath given us of his Spirit.

The presence of the Holy *Spirit* expresses a new reality. The Spirit's presence in us gives us the certainty that we are in Christ and He is in us. Christ's promise of the Spirit's presence is a fact for all who are Christians and can be a fact for all who are not yet Christians (John 14:16-17; Romans 8:9-11; Ephesians 1:13; 1 John 3:24; etc.). The Holy Spirit's presence is God's presence. Life in the Spirit is the life of God's love, demonstrating and assuring that we belong to Him through Christ's atoning death.

14. And we have seen and do testify that the Father sent the Son to be the Saviour of the world.

The beginning of this epistle is a stirring declaration that the incarnate Christ, seen by eyewitnesses, is the basis for the gospel message (1 John 1:1-3). In shorter form, the author now repeats that declaration. By using the word *we*, the author declared he had seen Jesus personally and, therefore, his testimony is that of an eyewitness. The mission of *the Son to be the Saviour of the world* reinforces the same thought of John 3:17.

B. Human Confession (vv. 15-17)

15. Whosoever shall confess that Jesus is the Son of God, God dwelleth in him, and he in God.

This verse is a summary statement of the plan of salvation. A doctrinal error often seen is to take such summary statements as being the entirety of that plan. For someone to *confess that Jesus is the Son of God* is good as far as it goes. But remember that demons confess the same thing and are still lost (Mark 5:7; James 2:19). Spiritual maturity (Hebrews 5:12) is required for understanding the entirety of that plan, which results in knowing how *God dwelleth in* a believer, *and he in God* (compare Acts 2:38; Ephesians 2:8-10; Hebrews 11:6; etc.).

What Do You Think?

How would you respond to someone who claims that they can confess that Jesus is the Son of God but still willfully and intentionally commit sin?

Digging Deeper

What is the relationship between right belief and right actions? How does James 2:14-26 inform your response?

---

16. And we have known and believed the love that God hath to us. God is love; and he that dwelleth in love dwelleth in God, and God in him.

The author turns to the imperative of *love*. Christ's life, death, and resurrection fully demonstrate God's love. We can say without reservation that *God is love* (also 1 John 4:8). For us to confess Christ truly means that we love one another. Such love is found among all who genuinely experience the abiding unity with God brought by Christ. Without such love, our confession is empty. With it, our confession is complete.

17. Herein is our love made perfect, that we may have boldness in the day of judgment: because as he is, so are we in this world.

This is the third time the writer has spoken of perfection with regard to *love* (see commentary on 1 John 2:5; 4:12, above); he will continue to do so in the verse that follows this one. And again, Jesus is our model. These concepts are so foundational that they bear repeating!

What's new here is how it all ties in with *the day of judgment*. The complete love of the Father revealed within us empowers us to face God's judgment confidently. This boldness stems not from our righteous deeds but from our trust in God's mercy to save us (Titus 3:5). The nature of our loving works *in this world* will demonstrate the presence or absence of saving faith (James 2:14-26). Jesus had much to say about this coming judgment (Matthew 11:20-24; 12:36; 25:31-46; etc.).

Conclusion

A. Transformed Reality

Symbols are intended to be meaningful, but people must acknowledge that meaning for the symbols to have their desired effect. I may know a red light means "stop," but I will stop at the red light only if I honor its intended meaning.

So it is with the cross. This central symbol of Christianity reminds us of Christ's death, the saving work He accomplished on it, His resurrection, and the love that motivated every part of His ministry. Our failure to love others will indicate that we don't honor the symbol of the cross—we betray the cross instead. What can you do to honor the intent of that symbol today?

B. Prayer

Lord God, Your love surpasses our imagination. We are filled with thanksgiving because Christ died and rose for us. Lead us to love one another as You have loved us. In Jesus' name. Amen.

C. Thought to Remember

Christ's death for us moves us
to a life of love for others.

Involvement Learning

Enhance your lesson with KJV Bible Student *(from your curriculum supplier) and the reproducible activity page (at www.standardlesson.com or in the back of the* KJV Standard Lesson Commentary Deluxe Edition*).*

Into the Lesson

Invite learners to share questions children ask that are hard for adults to answer simply. (*examples*: Why is the sky blue? How do you know the sun will rise tomorrow?) Write these questions on the board, then challenge learners to come up with some appropriate answers.

Alternative. Distribute the slips of paper from the "What Am I?" activity on the activity page, which you can download. Tell learners to keep their creature a secret but think of a few activities that describe what their creature does as hints to their identities. Learners will take turns sharing their hints, allowing the rest of the group an opportunity to guess their creature.

When all creature identities have been revealed, take a poll to see which was the hardest to guess. Lead into Bible study by saying, "Some things are hard to explain or describe. The way we attempt to do so may indicate some things about what we believe. Today's lesson requires special attention to how the apostle John explains certain ideas and describes certain relationships."

Into the Word

Ask a volunteer to read 1 John 2:1-6. Distribute to small groups handouts (you create) that have these four phrases printed in the four corners, one phrase per corner:

Things both God and I know
Things that God knows that I don't know
Things that I know that God doesn't know
Things that neither I nor God knows

Have learners share their reflections in small-group discussions. Expect responses to the last two of the four to be "nothing."

Ask a volunteer to read 1 John 4:9-12. Provide large paper or poster board along with appropriate markers to the groups. Instruct groups to create a visual rendering of the way these verses

explain (1) the primary way the love of God has been demonstrated, (2) what that signifies for us, (3) how we are to respond, and (4) how it is "perfected" or comes to completion. Have them explain their images in whole-class discussion.

Alternative. Distribute copies of the "Since A, Then B" exercise from the activity page to groups to complete as indicated. When they are finished, allow time for groups to compare their responses. (*Option*: this exercise can be moved to follow other segments of this Into the Word segment; it can also be a transition or introduction to the Into Life section.)

Ask a volunteer to read 1 John 4:13-17. Distribute a triangle-shaped sheet of paper to each group. Ask groups to brainstorm three things God has done: one thing each by the Father, the Son, and the Holy Spirit. Have groups write down one response in each corner of the triangle. These actions must be unique to the role of each (*example*: since the Bible describes both the Son and the Holy Spirit as "advocate," that one can't be used).

Challenge groups to make their case either in terms of physical evidence (something that can be seen, touched, or both) or consistent testimony from several people.

After a few minutes, reconvene for a whole-class discussion as groups present their case. Be prepared to show how the proposals connect to 1 John 4:13-17.

Into Life

Have learners partner up. Refer back to 1 John 2:6 and ask partners to work together to make a list of three or more habits that Jesus practiced personally (example: He took time away from the crowds to be alone to pray, Matthew 14:23). Challenge partners to think of practical ways they can adopt these same habits personally in the week ahead. Request that learners be ready to reflect on their experience in this regard when the class next meets.

Christ Dies and Rises to New Life

Devotional Reading: Hebrews 2:1-13
Background Scripture: Matthew 27:24–28:10

Matthew 27:39-40, 45-54

39 And they that passed by reviled him, wagging their heads,

40 And saying, Thou that destroyest the temple, and buildest it in three days, save thyself. If thou be the Son of God, come down from the cross.

- -

45 Now from the sixth hour there was darkness over all the land unto the ninth hour.

46 And about the ninth hour Jesus cried with a loud voice, saying, Eli, Eli, lama sabachthani? that is to say, My God, my God, why hast thou forsaken me?

47 Some of them that stood there, when they heard that, said, this man calleth for Elias.

48 And straightway one of them ran, and took a spunge, and filled it with vinegar, and put it on a reed, and gave him to drink.

49 The rest said, let be, let us see whether Elias will come to save him.

50 Jesus, when he had cried again with a loud voice, yielded up the ghost.

51 And, behold, the veil of the temple was rent in twain from the top to the bottom; and the earth did quake, and the rocks rent;

52 And the graves were opened; and many bodies of the saints which slept arose,

53 And came out of the graves after his resurrection, and went into the holy city, and appeared unto many.

54 Now when the centurion, and they that were with him, watching Jesus, saw the earthquake, and those things that were done, they feared greatly, saying, truly this was the Son of God.

Matthew 28:1-10

1 In the end of the sabbath, as it began to dawn toward the first day of the week, came Mary Magdalene and the other Mary to see the sepulchre.

2 And, behold, there was a great earthquake: for the angel of the Lord descended from heaven, and came and rolled back the stone from the door, and sat upon it.

3 His countenance was like lightning, and his raiment white as snow:

4 And for fear of him the keepers did shake, and became as dead men.

5 And the angel answered and said unto the women, fear not ye: for I know that ye seek Jesus, which was crucified.

6 He is not here: for he is risen, as he said. Come, see the place where the Lord lay.

7 And go quickly, and tell his disciples that he is risen from the dead; and, behold, he goeth before you into Galilee; there shall ye see him: lo, I have told you.

8 And they departed quickly from the sepulchre with fear and great joy; and did run to bring his disciples word.

9 And as they went to tell his disciples, behold, Jesus met them, saying, all hail. And they came and held him by the feet, and worshipped him.

10 Then said Jesus unto them, be not afraid: go tell my brethren that they go into Galilee, and there shall they see me.

Key Text

As they went to tell his disciples, behold, Jesus met them, saying, All hail. And they came and held him by the feet, and worshipped him. —**Matthew 28:9**

Costly
Sacrifices

Unit 2: Christ's All-Sufficient Sacrifice
Lessons 6–9

Lesson Aims

After participating in this lesson, each learner will be able to:

1. Summarize Matthew's account of the crucifixion and resurrection.

2. Identify and explain allusions to and quotes of the Old Testament in this account.

3. Sing with classmates a hymn or praise song that celebrates the resurrection.

Lesson Outline

Introduction

A. Still the Most Amazing Story

No story hits us like the story of Jesus' death and resurrection. It has the full range of human tragedy: betrayal, injustice, and courage. It is filled with mystery and irony. It evokes deep sympathy for its characters. It contrasts the power of vested interests with the power of Almighty God. It confronts our greatest enemy, death. Its ending is astonishing. But as we experience it, we realize how necessary the story's conclusion is.

For some of us, we've known the Easter story for as long as we can remember. Others who became Christians more recently can still recall their vivid reaction when they first heard it. During the Easter season, we get a chance to listen to that story again as if it's our first time. It is a story that is ever new—the story of how God made new life available to a lost and sinful humanity.

B. Lesson Context

Following Peter's confession of Jesus as the Christ (the Messiah), Jesus began to warn His disciples of His coming death and resurrection (Matthew 16:13-23; 17:22-23; 20:17-19). His disciples, however, failed to comprehend (John 20:9). In a series of trials featuring biased testimonies, Jesus was sentenced to death by crucifixion (Matthew 26:57-68; 27:11-26).

Crucifixion was a brutal form of execution. Roman authorities reserved it to make an example of the most notorious criminals, striking fear in the population. Those condemned to it were tied or nailed to a wood frame in a prominent public place. Left to the elements and loss of blood, the crucified person would die slowly of blood loss, respiratory failure, and exposure while being subjected to public ridicule. As today's lesson opens, that is the state in which we find Jesus.

I. The Death of the King
(Matthew 27:39-40, 45-54)
A. Forsaken by People (vv. 39-40)

39. And they that passed by reviled him, wagging their heads.

The parallel account of Matthew 27:39-40 reads almost the same (Mark 15:29-30); the parallel in Luke 23:35 is more abbreviated. This verse is also similar to Psalm 22:7 (compare Psalm 109:25).

40a. And saying, Thou that destroyest the temple, and buildest it in three days, save thyself.

This mockery is based on Jesus' prediction in John 2:19-20. Jesus was indeed on record as promising to raise *the temple . . . in three days* were it to be destroyed. But "he spake of the temple of his body" (John 2:21). Jesus is not recorded as saying that He would destroy the temple in Jerusalem. Thus, the accusation *thou that destroyest the temple* came from the lips of false witnesses (Matthew 26:60-62; Mark 14:58). To speak against a temple in the ancient world was to invite a death penalty (Jeremiah 26:1-11).

What Do You Think?

What should you do when you come across a misinterpretation of Jesus' teaching?

Digging Deeper

What are some contexts in which you would answer that question differently?

40b. If thou be the Son of God, come down from the cross.

The taunt *if thou be the Son of God, come down* mirrors Satan's words during Jesus' temptation at the start of His ministry (Matthew 4:3). This challenge can be seen as the final effort by the tempter to thwart God's plan.

Interestingly, the designation *the Son of God* was used by others to describe Jesus, but never from the lips of Jesus himself. Jesus was called Son of God by both demons and worshippers (Matthew 8:29; 14:33); a voice from Heaven was heard to say, "This is my beloved Son" (3:17). Jesus' preferred self-designation was "Son of man" (8:20; 9:6; etc.).

Jesus could indeed have *come down from the cross,* but He chose not to (compare Matthew 26:53). In choosing to stay there and die, He offered His life as the sacrifice of atonement (or propitiation; see last week's lesson) as He diverted the punishment for human sin onto himself, the sinless one (see 2 Corinthians 5:21).

B. Feeling Forsaken by God (vv. 45-50)

45. Now from the sixth hour there was darkness over all the land unto the ninth hour.

Matthew 27:41-44 (not in today's lesson) documents further ridicule aimed at Jesus. When we come to Matthew 27:45, the story shifts to a broader scene. Parallels to Matthew 27:45-50 are Mark 15:33-37; Luke 23:44-46; and John 19:28-30.

The *darkness* that came *over all the land* was likely not an eclipse of the sun, as we understand that to mean when the moon moves between the sun and the earth. This is for two reasons. First, a normal eclipse of the sun lasts no more than 15 minutes; this darkness lasted three hours. Second, a normal eclipse of the sun requires a new moon. However, Jesus was crucified during Passover at full moon (see Leviticus 23:5-6; Psalm 81:3).

This darkness, then, is of supernatural origin. The literal, physical darkness that occurred suggests a deeper application: in the Bible, the presence of darkness reveals God's displeasure (example: Exodus 10:21-23). Since there is no natural explanation for the darkness, it can be considered a supernatural event orchestrated by God as a direct reaction to those who mocked the Messiah.

46. And about the ninth hour Jesus cried with a loud voice, saying, Eli, Eli, lama sabachthani? that is to say, My God, my God, why hast thou forsaken me?

We come to one of the seven cries by Jesus from the cross, also recorded in Mark 15:34. The cry is in Aramaic, which is a later form of the Hebrew language. The words come from the beginning of Psalm 22, previously noted. Having been surrounded by taunts and darkness for hours, Jesus

How to Say It

Aramaic	Air-uh-*may*-ik.
Arimathaea	Air-uh-muh-*thee*-uh (th as in thin).
Eli (*Aramaic*)	Ee-*lo*-eye.
lama (*Aramaic*)	*lay*-muh or *lah*-mah.
Magdala	*Mag*-duh-luh.
Magdalene	*Mag*-duh-leen or Mag-duh-*lee*-nee.
sabachthani (*Aramaic*)	Suh-*back*-thuh-nee.

was enduring a separation from the Father in order to bear the punishment for humanity's sins (Matthew 1:21; 20:28; 26:28).

47. Some of them that stood there, when they heard that, said, this man calleth for Elias.

One of God's names in the ancient Hebrew language is *Elohim*. When this word occurs in a "construct" sense (that is, combined with another word), one or more letters on the end of *Elohim* may be dropped off in the process of attaching another word; two examples of this are Exodus 15:2 and Numbers 22:18. Psalm 22:1, which Jesus was quoting, is of course the most important example. Here is the root of the misunderstanding on the part of *some of them that stood there*. They heard the Aramaic word *Eli* not as a cry to "my God" but as a calling on the name of the long-ago prophet *Elias* (that is, Elijah). There had been two previous misunderstandings regarding Elijah (Matthew 16:14; 17:10-13), and this is a third one.

(51a) The end of the old covenant and the opening of a

FEAR NOT — JESUS LIVES!

Visual for Lesson 8. *Point to this visual and ask, "How will you live a 'fearless life' in light of the resurrection of Jesus?"*

April 20
new way of access to God through Jesus Christ.
• 292 •
Christ Dies and Rises to New Life

48. And straightway one of them ran, and took a spunge, and filled it with vinegar, and put it on a reed, and gave him to drink.

We don't know the motive behind the action that we read here (compare Psalm 69:21). If the *one* performing the action was hostile toward Jesus, then this act of giving *him to drink* was a continued mockery in some way. If the one performing the action was sympathetic, it may been intended as an act of kindness. What is called *vinegar* is a cheap kind of wine vinegar of the day (compare Mark 15:36-37; Luke 23:36; John 19:29).

49. The rest said, let be, let us see whether Elias will come to save him.

The phrase *let be* indicates some impatience on the part of the mocking bystanders. They don't want the action of satisfying Jesus' thirst to interfere with anything else Jesus had to say or to otherwise distract from the appearance of *Elias* (Elijah).

50. Jesus, when he had cried again with a loud voice, yielded up the ghost.

The words *Jesus* cried out *with a loud voice* are recorded in Luke 23:46: "Father, into thy hands I commend my spirit." John 19:30 further records Jesus as having said, "It is finished" as He died. This verse highlights two key aspects: first, Jesus maintained enough physical strength until His death to shout. Second, He remained in control of His life to the very end.

C. Surrounded by Signs (vv. 51-54)

51a. And, behold, the veil of the temple was rent in twain from the top to the bottom.

Though Jesus appeared to have been abandoned by God, Matthew offers signs establishing the opposite. *The veil of the temple* separated the temple's holy place from the most holy place. Only the high priest could pass behind that curtain to enter the most holy place—and that just once a year—to offer the sacrificial blood on the Day of Atonement (Exodus 26:31-34; 30:10; Leviticus 16:1-34; 23:27-28; Hebrews 9:3). As the three hours of darkness were supernatural in origin, so was this tearing of the temple curtain *from the top to the bottom* (also Luke 23:45).

The significance of this event is explained in the book of Hebrews (Hebrews 9:11-12, 24; 10:19-20).

Phone Books, Curtains, and Hearts

A strongman feat of yesteryear was to tear a thick phone book in half. There was a technique to doing so, but strength was still necessary. If you saw a thick phone book torn in half, you would automatically presume someone "with muscle" made it happen.

Jewish tradition holds that the curtains (veils) that marked off the most holy place were from 3½ to 4 inches thick! Consequently, the veils were so heavy that it took 300 priests to hang them. To have seen one of these curtains ripped top to bottom would cause gasps and cause people to imagine the strength necessary to have done so. Only someone with superhuman strength could tear such a veil—God Almighty!

Our friends and family who have not embraced the gospel might need time to accept the gospel due to their reluctance or uncertainty. We can and must tell the story, but ultimately, it's the Word of God, which is "sharper than any twoedged sword," that will cut through the resistance (Hebrews 4:12). How did that happen for you?   —R. L. N.

51b. And the earth did quake, and the rocks rent.

The earthquake similarly points to divine action. God was clearly at work. In the Old Testament, earthquakes frequently signified God's presence and sometimes divine judgment (examples: Judges 5:4-5; Psalm 114:7-8; Joel 3:16). Therefore, the first-century crowd witnessing the crucifixion would likely have understood this association.

52-53. And the graves were opened; and many bodies of the saints which slept arose, And came out of the graves after his resurrection, and went into the holy city, and appeared unto many.

Matthew alone tells us of this additional sign. As his description continues, we understand this sign occurred not immediately as Jesus died but a few days later, *after his resurrection*. The designation *the holy city* refers to Jerusalem (Matthew 4:5).

54. Now when the centurion, and they that were with him, watching Jesus, saw the earthquake, and those things that were done, they feared greatly, saying, truly this was the Son of God.

A *centurion* was a Roman soldier who commanded a unit known as a "century" in a legion of the Roman army; each "century" consisted of about 80 men. The centurion noted here was likely the one in charge of the crucifixion detail. Processing all he had experienced, the centurion sided against the mockers. His declaration, *Truly this was the Son of God*, stems from his fear-driven response to the supernatural occurrences around him. Jesus' disciples had a similar response when Jesus walked on water and calmed the storm (Matthew 14:28-33).

> **What Do You Think?**
> What evidence for Christ do you find best to use when sharing the gospel?
>
> **Digging Deeper**
> How would you respond to a fellow Christian who believes a "testimony" approach to evangelism is better than an approach based on historical evidence?

II. The Resurrection of the King
(Matthew 28:1-10)

A. The Grave Opened (vv. 1-4)

1. In the end of the sabbath, as it began to dawn toward the first day of the week, came Mary Magdalene and the other Mary to see the sepulchre.

A long-held view is that the passage of days in the ancient Jewish calendar are marked from sunset to sunset (Leviticus 23:32). Therefore, most students recognize that *the sabbath* would have ended at sunset on the day before the action we see here. The women don't set out for their task until *the first day of the week* (Sunday) is in view. Sabbath was a day of rest (Luke 23:56).

Their designation as *Mary Magdalene and the other Mary* reveals their key roles in Matthew's passion narrative. They were present at Jesus' crucifixion and saw where He was buried (Matthew 27:55, 61). Mary Magdalene was a follower of Jesus from the early days of His ministry. Jesus had delivered her from demon possession (Luke 8:2). We remind ourselves that "Magdalene" is not a surname in the modern sense. Rather, it designates this particular Mary as being from Magdala.

The "other" Mary was the mother of James and Joses (Matthew 27:56; Mark 15:47) and possibly the wife of Cleophas (John 19:25). Though the other Gospels name additional women (Mark 16:1; Luke 24:10), Matthew may have focused on these two because of their prominence among those of Jewish background who first read his Gospel.

By the evil initiative of the Jewish leaders and the compassion of Joseph of Arimathaea, Jesus' body was not left as long on the cross (Matthew 27:57-58; John 19:31). Joseph had provided the tomb, and the two women named Mary were eyewitnesses to the interment (Matthew 27:59-61). Because the Sabbath would begin a short time after Jesus' death, His body could not be properly prepared for burial without violating the commandment not to work on the Sabbath (Exodus 20:8-11).

> ### What Do You Think?
> How would you react to a claim that early morning is the best time for connecting with God?
>
> ### Digging Deeper
> What biblical examples of connecting with God at other times of the day can you cite?

2. And, behold, there was a great earthquake: for the angel of the Lord descended from heaven, and came and rolled back the stone from the door, and sat upon it.

Again, an earthquake signaled divine action, given the result we see here. The angel *rolled back the stone from the door* not to let Jesus out but to let Jesus' followers in. They needed to see the tomb empty. The resurrected Lord could enter or exit a locked room without opening the door (example: John 20:19-20, 26-27). He did not need the stone to be moved for His own benefit.

3. His countenance was like lightning, and his raiment white as snow.

There is no mistaking this angel for a human! His face and clothing are bright with light, suitable for supernatural encounters (Matthew 17:2; Luke 9:29; Acts 1:10).

4. And for fear of him the keepers did shake, and became as dead men.

The Roman governor Pilate had agreed to set a guard at the tomb to prevent Jesus' followers from removing His body and declaring He had been raised from the dead (Matthew 27:62-66). These are *the keepers* noted here. The fact that they became *as dead men* is similar to John's reaction to seeing the ascended Jesus in Revelation 1:17.

B. The News Announced (vv. 5-7)

5-6a. And the angel answered and said unto the women, fear not ye: for I know that ye seek Jesus, which was crucified. He is not here: for he is risen, as he said.

As *the angel* told Joseph at the beginning of Jesus' story to *fear not* (Matthew 1:20), this angel tells *the women* the same. The wondrous scene they witnessed fulfilled Jesus' promise to be raised from the dead (16:21-28; 17:22-23; 20:19; etc.). Jesus' mysterious promise to die and rise again is now more apparent. It happened not as anyone expected but precisely *as he said*.

6b. Come, see the place where the Lord lay.

The emphasis on the empty tomb counters any notion that Jesus' followers were only experiencing a "spiritual" resurrection of Christ. Jesus' physical resurrection involved the coming to life again of His physical body. *The place where the Lord lay* was vacant!

7. And go quickly, and tell his disciples that he is risen from the dead; and, behold, he goeth before you into Galilee; there shall ye see him: lo, I have told you.

The *disciples,* who had abandoned Jesus in the garden (Matthew 26:47-56), were to be the first whom the women were to *tell* of His resurrection. He had warned them they would fail, yet promised to meet them afterward in Galilee (26:31-32). The angel was saying nothing new but was reaffirming Jesus' previous declarations. Key among these is the declaration *ye shall see him*. Jesus' resurrection was not an invisible event in the minds and hearts of the disciples. It was a physical event in space and time: the resurrected Jesus seen by many (1 Corinthians 15:6).

C. The Lord Recognized (vv. 8-10)

8. And they departed quickly from the sep-

ulchre with fear and great joy; and did run to bring his disciples word.

The women were filled with fear from such a close encounter with God and joy at what God had done. They obeyed the angel's words implicitly, running—an uncommon act for grown people in their time—to tell the other followers of Jesus.

34,000 Emotions?

Quick: How many emotions can you name in less than a minute? Most of us can list several, such as *happiness, anger, fear, sadness, joy, disgust,* and *surprise.* That was the list proposed by psychologist Paul Eckman in the 1970s. To this list of "basic six emotions" has been added many more over the subsequent decades. One researcher now proposes that there are 34,000 emotions or combinations of emotions!

Reaction to a situation can be unpredictable when two or more emotions are experienced together, at the same time. Experiencing joy and fear simultaneously, the reaction of the women at the tomb was to obey immediately as they were instructed to "go quickly, and tell" (Matthew 28:7). Sometimes, powerful emotions can keep us from doing what we should. But the women were not paralyzed into inaction—quite the opposite! How often does fear keep you from talking to someone about Jesus? —C. S.

9. And as they went to tell his disciples, behold, Jesus met them, saying, all hail. And they came and held him by the feet, and worshipped him.

The angel commanded the women to *tell his disciples* that Jesus was alive, and they were on their way to do so without having yet seen Him alive for themselves! But it wasn't long before they received personal confirmation as Jesus himself *met them,* with the women reacting as we read here. Though silent, their reaction to seeing Jesus showed recognition and reverence, affirming that even in His resurrected body, Jesus deserved the same worship as before His death (compare Matthew 2:11; John 9:37-38; 20:28). They offered to Jesus the honor due only to God. Soon, they would be joined by many more (Matthew 28:17).

10. Then said Jesus unto them, be not afraid: go tell my brethren that they go into Galilee, and there shall they see me.

Jesus repeats the angel's encouragement and instructions regarding *Galilee.* A key aspect of Jesus' message is His enduring love for His disciples. Despite their fearful abandonment of Him during His crucifixion and their absence at the tomb, Jesus continued to refer to them as His *brethren.* Again, this is nothing new; it's a reaffirmation of what He said before His death (Matthew 26:32; etc.). John 21 records the results of that gathering.

> **What Do You Think?**
> How do you determine when it's time for action rather than worship and vice versa?
>
> **Digging Deeper**
> How would you respond to the claim that the Christian life is either *action* or *worship*?

Conclusion

A. Retaining Amazement

The grind of daily life can distract us from the most profound truths—we humans tend to allow "the urgent" to take priority over "the important." That's why Christians must continually remind themselves of the importance of what God has done. By repetition, we remember. In remembering, we restore the eyesight of faith to its proper and primary focus.

Against every expectation but in accord with every divine promise, Jesus died and rose from the dead. Let's hold the glorious amazement of those events in our hearts daily and forever.

B. Prayer

God of wonder, power, and love, we thank You that Jesus died and rose for us. Grant that His desires for our new life may also be our desire. In Jesus' name we pray. Amen.

C. Thought to Remember

Focus on the importance of Jesus' death and resurrection.

Involvement Learning

Enhance your lesson with KJV Bible Student *(from your curriculum supplier) and the reproducible activity page (at www.standardlesson.com or in the back of the* KJV Standard Lesson Commentary Deluxe Edition*).*

Into the Lesson

Invite learners to talk about their favorite stories from a book or movie. Prompt them to share what makes the story special and the most memorable scene. Ask, "How often do you return to that story? Does it affect you differently whenever you watch/read it again?"

Optional. Bring five plastic Easter eggs and put one sensory item in each: a piece of candy (taste), a perfume sample card (smell), a whistle (hearing), a cotton ball (touch), and a magazine clipping (sight). Hide the five eggs around the room and challenge learners to find them.

When all five have been found, have the finders open their eggs to reveal what is inside. With each reveal, ask the group to state (1) which of the five human senses the revealed item triggers and (2) a personal memory in that regard. (*Examples*: the whistle represents the sense of hearing; a sound that triggers a memory may be a foghorn used to wake up teens at summer camp every morning.)

Say, "Because it is Easter Sunday, let us spend some time studying the greatest story that was ever written. Pay attention to the details that could make it new, fresh, and alive for you today."

Into the Word

Read Matthew 27:39-40, 45-54. Then form study pairs or triads and give each a handout (you create) that features these four verse-grouping references printed as column headers, one each:

Matthew 27:39-40, 45-54
Mark 15:29-30, 33-39
Luke 23:35, 44-48
John 19:28-30

Have printed on the handouts the following instructions: "List in the columns the details that the passage in the column head mentions but the other three passage-groupings do not." Discuss results as a class.

Option. Distribute to study pairs copies of the "Five Senses at the Crucifixion" exercise from the activity page, which you can download, to complete as indicated. When pairs are finished, allow time for whole-class interaction on responses. Ask, "How did this exercise improve your understanding of the crucifixion?"

Have volunteers act out the scene at the tomb: the two women, an angel, and Jesus. (As an option, add two guards.) Use tables, chairs, or boxes to create a "tomb" as a prop. Ask someone to serve as the narrator and reread the passage. As the narrator reads, the volunteers will act out the scene. Everyone else will be the audience.

Afterward, ask the audience to share their thoughts about what they saw, and the actors about what they experienced. Encourage everyone to elaborate on their responses by giving reasons for what their emotional reaction might have been.

Alternative. Read Matthew 28:1-10. Then form study pairs or triads and give each a handout (you create) that features these four references printed as column headers, one each:

Matthew 28:1-10 | *Mark 16:1-11*
Luke 24:1-12 | *John 20:1-13*

Have printed on the handouts the following instructions: "List in the columns the details that the passage in the column head mentions but the passages in the other three Gospels do not." Discuss results as a class.

Into Life

Sing with classmates a hymn or praise song that celebrates the resurrection of Jesus. You can choose one or provide songbooks so participants can choose them. (*Option.* Challenge participants to find some hymns or praise songs this week that help them celebrate the resurrection of Jesus. Compile titles and make a list. Ask them to bring their songbooks to share with the group next week.)

The Lamb Is Worthy

Devotional Reading: Psalm 118:15-29
Background Scripture: Revelation 5

Revelation 5:1-10

1 And I saw in the right hand of him that sat on the throne a book written within and on the backside, sealed with seven seals.

2 And I saw a strong angel proclaiming with a loud voice, who is worthy to open the book, and to loose the seals thereof?

3 And no man in heaven, nor in earth, neither under the earth, was able to open the book, neither to look thereon.

4 And I wept much, because no man was found worthy to open and to read the book, neither to look thereon.

5 And one of the elders saith unto me, weep not: behold, the Lion of the tribe of Juda, the Root of David, hath prevailed to open the book, and to loose the seven seals thereof.

6 And I beheld, and, lo, in the midst of the throne and of the four beasts, and in the midst of the elders, stood a Lamb as it had been slain, having seven horns and seven eyes, which are the seven Spirits of God sent forth into all the earth.

7 And he came and took the book out of the right hand of him that sat upon the throne.

8 And when he had taken the book, the four beasts and four and twenty elders fell down before the Lamb, having every one of them harps, and golden vials full of odours, which are the prayers of saints.

9 And they sung a new song, saying, thou art worthy to take the book, and to open the seals thereof: for thou wast slain, and hast redeemed us to God by thy blood out of every kindred, and tongue, and people, and nation;

10 And hast made us unto our God kings and priests: and we shall reign on the earth.

Key Text

They sung a new song, saying, thou art worthy to take the book, and to open the seals thereof: for thou wast slain, and hast redeemed us to God by thy blood out of every kindred, and tongue, and people, and nation. —**Revelation 5:9**

Costly
Sacrifices

Unit 2: Christ's All-Sufficient Sacrifice
Lessons 6–9

Lesson Aims

After participating in this lesson, each learner will be able to:

1. Identify the Lion, the Root, and the Lamb.
2. Explain the significance of each of those three designations.
3. Participate with classmates in writing lyrics for a new song of praise.

Lesson Outline

Introduction
  A. What Is Worth?
  B. Lesson Context
I. Who Is Worthy? (Revelation 5:1-4)
  A. Sealed Scroll (v. 1)
  B. Checking Candidates (vv. 2-4)
    Feeling Helpless
II. Christ Is Worthy (Revelation 5:5-10)
  A. Lion and Root (v. 5)
    Regarding Credentials
  B. Slain Lamb (v. 6)
  C. Praise to the Lamb (vv. 7-10)
Conclusion
  A. Jesus Is Worthy
  B. Prayer
  C. Thought to Remember

Introduction

A. What Is Worth?

People have very different ideas about what makes someone worthy of honor. In modern cultures, a person's worthiness for various honors often seems to be based on the person's wealth, success, or popularity in the public eye.

My friend Joe does not fit this model of a worthy person. Joe works as a mid-level manager of a small company that makes medical equipment. By some standards, Joe is not rich. In the eyes of the world, his life is simple and unremarkable. But Joe has a wife and four children whom he loves dearly. He goes to work every day and works hard in a thankless profession to provide for his family. His wife and children never go without, even though Joe often does. He models self-sacrificial love daily. Were you offered a choice between being a famous but self-serving person or being unknown but self-sacrificial, whom do you think God would consider more worthy of honor?

B. Lesson Context

Revelation 4 and 5 narrate the apostle John's vision of the divine throne room. This vision immediately follows the appearance of the "one like unto the Son of man" (Revelation 1:13; compare Daniel 7:13), who dictates letters to seven churches in the province of Asia Minor. These letters offered both encouragement and caution to churches that ranged from being faithful to unfaithful.

Two good questions to ask in many life situations are "What's so?" and "So what?" In answer to the first question, Revelation 1–3 establishes the facts regarding the status of seven churches; in answer to the second question, the visions of Revelation 4 and following describe rewards and consequences. This allows us to see God's authority and power, the reality that He remains in charge even when earthly events would suggest otherwise (compare Psalm 47:8).

John's visions begin in Revelation 4:1 with a glimpse of God in His throne room (compare Isaiah 6:1). This is the location of the true and ultimate ruler of the universe. While "in the spirit" (Revelation 4:2), John witnesses startling and glorious things: precious stones, elders with crowns, fiery lamps, creatures who worship God day and night, etc. After this broad look around the throne room, John's vision zooms in to focus on a specific object.

I. Who Is Worthy?
(Revelation 5:1-4)
A. Sealed Scroll (v. 1)

1. And I saw in the right hand of him that sat on the throne a book written within and on the backside, sealed with seven seals.

When we see the word *book,* we naturally think of a modern book with edge-binding, numbered pages, etc. But the word being translated is also translated as "scroll" in Revelation 6:14, and that interpretation is also applicable in this context. A scroll is typically made from flattened papyrus or animal skins and is opened and closed by being unrolled and rolled (again, 6:14).

The description of the document as having been *written within and on the backside* witnesses to its unusual nature. Most scrolls were written on only one side, but lengthy documents could take up both sides. The fact that this scroll has writing on it front and back signals its contents' breadth, depth, or both (compare Ezekiel 2:9-10).

Naturally, we are curious about the scroll's contents, and various proposals have been offered. However, the focus of Revelation 5 is not on the scroll's contents but on the fact that it is *sealed with seven seals.* Scrolls were the common medium in the ancient world for important documents. These were often sealed to prevent someone from reading or tampering with their contents. A seal in this context would normally consist of hot wax poured over threads that tied the scroll in its rolled-up state. Legal documents would have several seals, indicating several witnesses. These witnesses often used a signet ring to press into the wax for self-identification. This made it impossible to open the scroll without detection of tampering. Many students believe that the number *seven* stands for "perfection" or "completeness," based on how it is used elsewhere in the Bible (compare Revelation 15:1, 8).

B. Checking Candidates (vv. 2-4)

2. And I saw a strong angel proclaiming with a loud voice, who is worthy to open the book, and to loose the seals thereof?

The dramatic action in the rest of this scene is set up by this proclamation of *a strong angel,* who is unnamed (compare Revelation 10:1). The use of the word *worthy* makes his question not so much an open invitation as it is a rhetorical challenge. The term *worthy* in this context encompasses not just moral excellence but also signifies someone who possesses the authority and power to break the seals.

> **What Do You Think?**
> What has to happen for you to live a "worthy" life?
> **Digging Deeper**
> How do Ephesians 4:1; Colossians 1:10; etc. inform your answer?

3. And no man in heaven, nor in earth, neither under the earth, was able to open the book, neither to look thereon.

The search for someone worthy seems at first to fail. The mention of *heaven, earth, and under the earth* was a typical method of depicting the domains of heavenly beings, earthly beings, and the world of the deceased (compare Exodus 20:4, 11; Psalm 146:6). But to focus on the scientific nature of each of the three locations is to miss the bigger picture. That bigger picture is "anywhere you can think of." This description, therefore, highlights the entirety of the cosmos, as it does in Philippians 2:10. Every part of creation has been explored, and no one qualified has been found—yet.

4. And I wept much, because no man was found worthy to open and to read the book, neither to look thereon.

People are described as weeping in many places in the Bible. But the phrase *wept much* is an intense form found elsewhere in the New Testament only at Matthew 2:18; Mark 5:38; and Philippians 3:18. The sense can be one of the duration of the weeping or depth of distress or both (compare Genesis 46:29; Judges 20:23; Ezra 3:12; 10:1).

One theory that might explain John's reaction concerns what he was told at the beginning of the throne-room scene. There, he was told that future events would be revealed to him (Revelation 4:1). But now, in the verse before us, John's expectations become frustrated. If John connects the scroll's contents with knowledge of future events and no one can open the scroll, then the promise will not be fulfilled. Even he, John, was not *worthy to open and to read the book, neither to look thereon*. John's weeping is consistent with what he knows and doesn't know. But that is about to change.

> **What Do You Think?**
> What are some ways that Jesus would want you to react to the sorrows of life?
>
> **Digging Deeper**
> Are specific cases such as Jeremiah 22:10 and Ezekiel 24:15-18 relevant to this question? Why, or why not?

Feeling Helpless

At one time, I despised plumbing work. I loathed it, dreaded it, and would rather do any other sort of home repair than plumbing. But, since plumbing work by a professional wasn't in my budget as a new homeowner, I had little choice but to attempt to fix things myself. And something was always leaking in our old house built in the 1920s. The fact that the plumbing was complicated by mixtures of PVC, iron, and copper pipes drove me toward despair.

We fell helpless when we try to bring a challenging situation under control but we lack the skill, means, or qualifications to do so and nobody else is available to call on. That was the apostle John's situation.

But remember: Revelation 5:4 is not the end of the story! We are often sad and in pain because of a situation we can't control or remedy. When that happens, remember that the One who came to solve our greatest problem is available to strengthen us. How often must you hit rock bottom before you call on His strength?   —C. S.

II. Christ Is Worthy
(Revelation 5:5-10)
A. Lion and Root (v. 5)

5. And one of the elders saith unto me, weep not: behold, the Lion of the tribe of Juda, the Root of David, hath prevailed to open the book, and to loose the seven seals thereof.

John is comforted by *one of the 24 elders* present around God's throne (Revelation 4:4, 10). Someone is indeed worthy, the elder claims, and he refers to this person with two important designations.

The first designation, *the Lion of the tribe of Juda*, comes from Genesis 49:9-10, where Jacob refers to his son Judah as a "lion's welp" and compares him to a lion that no one dares rouse. This metaphor is immediately followed by the promise that Judah will always have the right of rulership.

The other designation, *the Root of David*, confirms that the Messiah is in view. This description comes from Isaiah 11:1, 10, another text viewed as a prophecy about the coming Messiah. The specific title in Isaiah 11:10 is "a root of Jesse" (Jesse having been the father of David). Isaiah prophesied how the Messiah will bring justice and peace to the earth and unity to the nations. The designation "the root and the offspring of David" is explicitly claimed by Jesus near the book's end (Revelation 22:16).

The one who is both Lion and Root has the right to open the scroll because He has "prevailed." The narrative doesn't tell us at this point what that victory is, but the coupling of this word with the imagery of the regal lion implies a conquering king. The reader expects someone as mighty as a lion to enter the scene.

Regarding Credentials

Credentials can be a funny thing. To be approved for a specific task, you may need credentials that say you're qualified. But how do you get qualified without being given a chance to do similar work?

This kind of circular trap doesn't apply to opening the sealed scroll. It wasn't a question of credentials or prior experience at breaking wax seals that was the issue. Rather, the issue was one of credentials in terms of *authorization*. Only Christ had the proper credentials, the authorization, to open the sealed scroll. His credentials included His birthright as the Lion from the tribe of Judah and the Root of David. But it was His action of laying down His life that completed His credentials as the only one qualified to open the scroll.

What about your credentials as a spiritually mature Christian? Have you moved from the "milk" needed by a spiritual infant to the "meat" of God's Word that is the spiritual diet of the mature (1 Corinthians 3:2; Hebrews 5:12-14)? Do you desire spiritual maturity as much as Christ desires it for you? —C. S.

B. Slain Lamb (v. 6)

6a. And I beheld, and, lo, in the midst of the throne and of the four beasts, and in the midst of the elders, stood a Lamb as it had been slain.

The reader first encounters *the four beasts* and *the elders* in Revelation 4:4-6. The word *beasts* implies that these beings are neither humans nor angels. In the book of Revelation, the number "four" is symbolic of the entirety of the earth and its inhabitants (compare 7:1). Combining that observation with the creatures' multitudes of eyes (4:8) indicates that they are watching the entire earth; nothing is hidden from them. This symbolizes the all-knowing nature of the Lord, His omniscience (compare Hebrews 4:13).

If the original readers expected any particular animal to appear in addition to the four beasts, it would likely be a lion, per the previous verse. To the readers' likely surprise, however, the spotlight focuses on *a Lamb*. This is a startling plot twist, especially given the Lamb's outward appearance. It bears the marks of having *been slain*, yet it lives, given that it is standing. A metaphor is used here to represent Christ, who was killed but resurrected. The image of the slain Lamb recalls the Old Testament's concept of blood sacrifice, yet the Lamb in John's vision didn't remain dead; it is depicted as alive, bearing visible, serious wounds (compare Isaiah 53:7; John 20:24-29; Revelation 13:8). The New Testa-

ment uses the capitalized word *Lamb* or *Lamb's* some 30 times, and all but two of those are in the book of Revelation.

> **What Do You Think?**
> How would you explain to an unbeliever the meaning and significance of the images of Jesus as the Lion, a Lamb, and the Root?
>
> **Digging Deeper**
> Which of those three images do you find the most difficult to grasp? Why?

6b. Having seven horns and seven eyes, which are the seven Spirits of God sent forth into all the earth.

The description of the Lamb combines the number *seven* (symbolizing perfection or completeness; see commentary on Revelation 5:1, above) with *horns* (symbolizing power per Psalm 132:17; Ezekiel 29:21; Daniel 7:7-24; 8:3-22) and *eyes* (symbolizing divine knowledge per 2 Chronicles 16:9; Zechariah 4:10). The exact meaning of the *seven Spirits of God* is difficult to determine (compare and contrast Revelation 1:4; 4:5). Some students take this phrase to be the same as the sevenfold Spirit depicted in Isaiah 11:2-3; this viewpoint allows a reference to the Holy Spirit, the third person of the Trinity.

Another viewpoint understands the seven Spirits to refer to God's seven angels of Revelation 8:2, 6; 15:1; etc. Some ancient Jewish texts mention seven archangels that stand before God's throne. The nonbiblical Tobit 12:15, for example, speaks of "Raphael, one of the seven holy angels, which present the prayers of the saints, and which go in and out before the glory of the Holy One."

In any case, translators have to make a choice here: to translate as upper-case *Spirits* indicates a belief on the translators' part that this word refers to

How to Say It

Judah	Joo-duh.
Laodicea	Lay-*odd*-uh-*see*-uh.
Messiah	Meh-*sigh*-uh.
omniscience	ahm-*nish*-untz.

Sing a new song!

Revelation 5:9

Visual for Lesson 9. *Display this visual as you discuss the lesson commentary associated with Revelation 5:9.*

deity; that is the choice the translators of the *King James Version* made.

In either case, the fact that these Spirits or spirits serve the Lamb's purpose shows His power and authority.

C. Praise to the Lamb (vv. 7-10)

7. And he came and took the book out of the right hand of him that sat upon the throne.

The Lamb demonstrates His worthiness by receiving the scroll *out of the right hand of him that sat upon the throne.* All present, including John, undoubtedly watch in amazement as the Lamb does this audacious thing! However, this is not an act of thievery or usurpation, for God has been waiting for the Lamb. The scroll and its contents belong to the Lamb.

8a. And when he had taken the book, the four beasts and four and twenty elders fell down before the Lamb.

With the transfer of the scroll, worship in Heaven resumes. But now *the four beasts and four and twenty elders* bow *before the Lamb.* This is not to recognize a transfer of power that diminishes the authority of the one on the throne. Rather, it recognizes the Lamb's authority and His unity with the one on the throne.

The number of elders, 24, is double the number 12, which may represent the people of God from both the Old and New Testaments. Israel, the covenant people of the Old Testament era,

was comprised of 12 tribes (Exodus 24:4; compare Revelation 21:12). Christians, the covenant people of the New Testament era, are linked with the 12 apostles (Luke 6:13; compare Revelation 21:14), who are the foundation of the church (Ephesians 2:20). Jesus himself combines the idea of 12 tribes with 12 apostles in His description of the future (Matthew 19:28; Luke 22:30).

8b. Having every one of them harps, and golden vials full of odours, which are the prayers of saints.

Following the transfer of the scroll, new details unfold before John's eyes. The elders now have *harps,* which they presumably use for worship music, given that harps were common as instruments of worship (Psalms 33:2; 71:22; 147:7; etc.). Harps are also mentioned in Revelation 14:2; 15:2.

The fact that the elders also hold *golden vials full of odours* offers the reader a rarity in the book of Revelation: the two words *which are.* These two words indicate that an explanation of the symbolism comes next. In several passages, the "which are/is" language explains symbolism with more symbolism (example: Revelation 5:6). But that isn't the case here, given the unambiguous identification of *the prayers of the saints.* The context implies that the Lamb receives those prayers; He doesn't ignore them.

9a. And they sung a new song.

Worship of the Lamb includes singing. What the elders sing is not an old favorite but *a new song.* This imperative is stressed throughout the Psalter (Psalms 33:3; 40:3; 96:1; 98:1; 144:9; 149:1). Revelation 14:3 is an additional implementation (compare Isaiah 42:10). However, in that instance, it's the 144,000 redeemed who are singing while the four beasts and the elders (apparently) listen.

What Do You Think?
How often should the church introduce new songs in worship services? Why?
Digging Deeper
What would nudge you toward being more open to learning a new song?

9b. Saying, Thou art worthy to take the book,

and to open the seals thereof: for thou wast slain, and hast redeemed us to God by thy blood.

The reality that the Lamb had been slain would have been perceived as a source of embarrassment by many. But the heavenly court praises the Lamb not in spite of His death but because of it. Christ's obedient death is humanity's victory over sin-guilt (Romans 3:25-26). The Lamb's unique obedience to the Father made Him worthy to take the book and *open the seals thereof.*

The heavenly court then explains the implications of that death further. Primary is the truth that it *redeemed us.* The verb translated "redeem" occurs about 30 times in the New Testament; it always refers to a purchase that involves an exchange (examples: Matthew 13:44, 46; John 13:29). Such purchases can refer to paying a price to free someone (examples: 1 Corinthians 6:20; 7:23), and that's the sense here.

9c. Out of every kindred, and tongue, and people, and nation.

The song now recognizes the diverse nature of those who have been redeemed. The diversity is fourfold in that they come from every family group (*kindred*), every language group (*tongue*), every demographic (*people*), and every ethnic group (*nation*). This heavenly mix is drawn from the entire world.

10a. And hast made us unto our God kings and priests.

This half-verse yields three minor problems regarding the original author's words per the various Greek manuscripts. The first challenge concerns the word *us.* In some manuscripts, it's the Greek word translated "them" instead. This may have been a scribe's intent to match the word "them" to the diverse group in Revelation 5:9c, just studied.

The second minor challenge is that the phrase *unto our God* does not appear in the oldest manuscripts. The third challenge is that the oldest manuscripts have the Greek word for *kingdom* instead of *kings.* Revelation 1:6 also has "kings" instead of "kingdom" in a manuscript variant, so that's evidence for the word *kings.* However, Exodus 19:6 speaks of "a kingdom of priests," which seems to be the antecedent or pattern for the issue. In any

case, we will be treated like royalty when God's kingdom is manifested in its fullest; note the golden crowns the elders wear in Revelation 4:4!

Returning to Revelation 1:6, that passage can help us with the "unto our God" challenge since, without question, it has "unto God" as equivalent. Offering certain parallels and directions to the half-verse before us are Isaiah 61:6; 1 Peter 2:5, 9; and Revelation 20:6.

> **What Do You Think?**
> What ways will you live as a priest of God in the week ahead?
> **Digging Deeper**
> In addition to 1 Peter 2:5, what passages encourage you to do so?

10b. And we shall reign on the earth.

To serve as a royal priesthood comes with a promise: God's people will one day *reign on the earth.* Christ made this promise explicitly in the letter to the church of Laodicea (Revelation 3:21), and it appears elsewhere in the New Testament as well (2 Timothy 2:12). This is an astonishing and humbling responsibility (compare Luke 19:17).

Conclusion
A. Jesus Is Worthy

The answer to the question *What makes a person worthy of honor?* depends greatly on who is bestowing the honor. In God's economy, earthly success does not draw His praise. Ultimately, Jesus alone is worthy of all glory and honor. He alone is worthy to unbind the scroll. While Jesus will always reign supreme, we will be honored by being called to reign with Him. But our worthiness will be tested! Expect it.

B. Prayer

Heavenly Father, orient our hearts to the things that You value, not the things the world values. Teach us to live self-sacrificially as Jesus did. In Jesus' name we pray. Amen.

B. Thought to Remember

Jesus alone is worthy of all honor and praise.

Involvement Learning

Enhance your lesson with KJV Bible Student *(from your curriculum supplier) and the reproducible activity page (at www.standardlesson.com or in the back of the* KJV Standard Lesson Commentary Deluxe Edition*).*

Into the Lesson

As learners arrive, have the following written on the board:

Life is like . . .
- *riding a bicycle. To keep your balance, you must keep moving.*
- *a game of chess. Always think before you make a move.*
- *a cactus. It's beautiful but thorny.*

Poll learners to see which of the three "Life is like . . ." completions most closely matches their experiences. Discuss.

Alternative. Distribute slips of paper from the "It's Kind of Like . . ." exercise from the activity page, which you can download. Invite participants to take no more than one minute to turn their statement into a "____ is like" analogy.

After either of the above, say, "Some things are nearly impossible to describe by using a pithy analogy or metaphor. We call such things 'inexpressible' or 'indescribable.' Today's lesson allows us to consider how the apostle John wrestled with an experience almost beyond his understanding."

Into the Word

Ensure that participants comprehend that Revelation 4 is the necessary context or preamble to today's text from Revelation 5. To do so, distribute handouts (you create) with the references *Revelation 4* and *Revelation 5:1-10* as headers of two columns, one each. Have printed down the left side the words *throne, seven, elders, beasts,* and *worthy* as labels to five rows, one each. Have printed these instructions on the handout: "As we come to each word in Revelation 5:1-10, write the verse where the word occurs in that text and in Revelation 4. Make your entries where the appropriate column and row intersect."

In the lower half of the handout, have printed *New to Me, Comforting to Me,* and *Disturbing to*

Me as headers to three columns, one each. Have learners make entries under the appropriate header as you progress through Revelation 5:1-10.

Form learners into study triads. Have triads discuss among themselves Revelation 5:1-4 and make entries to the top and bottom halves of their handout. When triads seem finished, reconvene for a whole-class discussion of insights.

Repeat this procedure for Revelation 5:5-7, but have triads also consider imagery in the text as drawn from Genesis 49:8-10 (lion); Isaiah 11:1, 10 (root); Isaiah 53:7-8 and John 1:29, 36 (lamb). When triads seem finished, reconvene for a whole-class discussion of insights. *Option:* Depending on the nature of your class, you might choose to focus the attention of the triads on (1) what the prophecies say, (2) how we know they are about Jesus, and (3) how Jesus did or will fulfill them all.

Repeat the basic procedure of Revelation 5:1-4, above, for Revelation 5:8-10. *Option:* Have triads dig deeper by considering (1) the significance of the number 12 as informed by Matthew 19:28; Luke 22:30; and Revelation 21:12-14; as well as (2) the disposition of the "prayers of all saints" as informed by Revelation 8:3-4.

Into Life

Say, "In the spirit of the 'new song' of Revelation 5:9, let's write one!" Form groups for writing a couple of lines of lyrics for a new song of praise.

Alternative 1. Distribute instead copies of "The Worthy Lamb" exercise from the activity page to be completed as indicated.

Alternative 2. Have your class sing a new song by taking the lyrics of an existing song and singing it to the tune of another song. (Ensure that the two existing songs have the same meter, as noted in the index to many hymnals.) For example, the words to "All the Way My Savior Leads Me" can be sung to the tune of "Glorious Things of Thee Are Spoken" and vice versa.

David's Sacrifice

Devotional Reading: 2 Peter 3:11-18
Background Scripture: 1 Chronicles 21:1–22:1

1 Chronicles 21:14-30

14 So the LORD sent pestilence upon Israel: and there fell of Israel seventy thousand men.

15 And God sent an angel unto Jerusalem to destroy it: and as he was destroying, the LORD beheld, and he repented him of the evil, and said to the angel that destroyed, It is enough, stay now thine hand. And the angel of the LORD stood by the threshingfloor of Ornan the Jebusite.

16 And David lifted up his eyes, and saw the angel of the LORD stand between the earth and the heaven, having a drawn sword in his hand stretched out over Jerusalem. Then David and the elders of Israel, who were clothed in sackcloth, fell upon their faces.

17 And David said unto God, Is it not I that commanded the people to be numbered? even I it is that have sinned and done evil indeed; but as for these sheep, what have they done? let thine hand, I pray thee, O LORD my God, be on me, and on my father's house; but not on thy people, that they should be plagued.

18 Then the angel of the LORD commanded Gad to say to David, that David should go up, and set up an altar unto the LORD in the threshingfloor of Ornan the Jebusite.

19 And David went up at the saying of Gad, which he spake in the name of the LORD.

20 And Ornan turned back, and saw the angel; and his four sons with him hid themselves. Now Ornan was threshing wheat.

21 And as David came to Ornan, Ornan looked and saw David, and went out of the threshingfloor, and bowed himself to David with his face to the ground.

22 Then David said to Ornan, Grant me the place of this threshingfloor, that I may build an altar therein unto the LORD: thou shalt grant it me for the full price: that the plague may be stayed from the people.

23 And Ornan said unto David, take it to thee, and let my lord the king do that which is good in his eyes: lo, I give thee the oxen also for burnt offerings, and the threshing instruments for wood, and the wheat for the meat offering; I give it all.

24 And king David said to Ornan, Nay; but I will verily buy it for the full price: for I will not take that which is thine for the LORD, nor offer burnt offerings without cost.

25 So David gave to Ornan for the place six hundred shekels of gold by weight.

26 And David built there an altar unto the LORD, and offered burnt offerings and peace offerings, and called upon the LORD; and he answered him from heaven by fire upon the altar of burnt offering.

27 And the LORD commanded the angel; and he put up his sword again into the sheath thereof.

28 At that time when David saw that the LORD had answered him in the threshingfloor of Ornan the Jebusite, then he sacrificed there.

29 For the tabernacle of the LORD, which Moses made in the wilderness, and the altar of the burnt offering, were at that season in the high place at Gibeon.

30 But David could not go before it to inquire of God: for he was afraid because of the sword of the angel of the LORD.

Key Text

King David said to Ornan, nay; but I will verily buy it for the full price: for I will not take that which is thine for the LORD, nor offer burnt offerings without cost. —**1 Chronicles 21:24**

Costly Sacrifices

Lesson Aims

After participating in this lesson, each learner will be able to:

1. Specify what David accepted responsibility for.

2. Explain why David insisted on paying for what was offered to him as a gift.

3. Write an intercessory prayer on behalf of his or her community.

Lesson Outline

Introduction

A. Plagues and Punishment

In the fourteenth century, the Black Death (bubonic plague) came to Europe and caused sudden, widespread fatalities. A common estimate is that one-third of the people of Europe died within five years. Since the science of the time could not explain the plague, many people believed the disease to be God's punishment for the corrupt lifestyles of Christians and the church's tolerance of sin. This belief often led to persecution of perceived heretics.

More recently, widespread outbreaks of viral disease—the 1918 Great Influenza pandemic, the 1980s AIDS epidemic, and the COVID-19 pandemic of the 2020s—have been perceived by some as punishments by God for societal sins. Those who saw these health crises that way proclaimed justification from Scripture.

Well-known are the 10 plagues inflicted on the people of Egypt (Exodus 7:14–11:10). But most, if not all, of these don't fit our usual understanding of the word *plague* as referring to a disease resulting from a bacterial or viral infection. In today's lesson, a plague sent as God's punishment takes place during the reign of Israel's greatest ruler, King David.

B. Lesson Context

Despite being portrayed as "a man after [God's] own heart" (1 Samuel 13:14; Acts 13:22), King David committed grievous sins. Most remembered are the sins of adultery and murder in his seduction of Bathsheba and the death of her husband, Uriah (2 Samuel 11). The "God's own heart" part of David seems to have gained traction after he was confronted by the prophet Nathan about the violation of the sixth and seventh commandments (Exodus 20:13-14). The result was the tender prayer of Psalm 51:10, "Create in me a clean heart, O God; and renew a right spirit within me."

More consequential for a greater number of people, however, was the sin of David concerning a census he took of Israel to know the potential size of his army (2 Samuel 24:2; 1 Chronicles 21:2). The results of the survey must have astonished David: there were over one million men who "drew the sword" (2 Samuel 24:9). This census angered the Lord, for David's pride drove it as he rejected his reliance upon God for Israel's security.

The prophet Gad delivered God's judgment to David, and it came with a twist: David could choose from among three punishments, of varying impacts on Israel, for his sins. The choices were three years of famine, three months of attacks by the nation's enemies, or three days of a pestilent plague (1 Chronicles 21:12). These three had been ways the Lord showed His wrath to Israel (see Jeremiah 14:12). David chose the third option, with horrific results for his people.

I. The Destroying Angel
(1 Chronicles 21:14-17)
A. Terrible Judgment (v. 14)

14. So the LORD sent pestilence upon Israel: and there fell of Israel seventy thousand men.

The *pestilence* the Lord delivered *upon Israel* was labeled earlier as the "sword of the Lord" (1 Chronicles 21:12). Although not described, the implication is that of a fast-moving malady that kills quickly. The parallel passage, 2 Samuel 24:15, notes the plague's reach "from Dan even to Beersheba"—a straight-line distance of about 150 miles, encompassing the whole of Israel. In the small geographic footprint of David's realm, every village and every citizen would have felt loss because of these deaths. The sorrowful outcry from survivors would have been deafening and impossible for the king to ignore.

Disaster Brings Change

The Bible explains how God used floods, plagues, locusts, and invading armies to express His displeasure with sinful people. But He wasn't expressing His anger merely to "blow off steam"; instead, He was instigating change—from sinful behavior to godly behavior.

When disasters have happened since the first century AD, some people will attribute it to God's wrath (see the Introduction to this lesson). But invariably, this is just speculation. We don't know if a given disaster today is actually a divine pun-

ishment or simply an event that God allows to occur. But we do know that change follows disasters. Just think of the societal changes since the COVID-19 pandemic.

When we face personal disaster, we might worry that God is punishing us. It's more valuable, however, to focus on what change will follow. Remember the example of Job, who lost everything through no fault of his own while remaining faithful. God is more than able to bless us in the aftermath with even more than we lost (Job 42:12).   —A. W.

> **What Do You Think?**
> How would you respond to someone who thinks that disasters are God's judgment for sin?
> **Digging Deeper**
> How might your response differ regarding a sick person who thinks God is punishing him or her?

B. Divine Peril (vv. 15-16a)

15a. And God sent an angel unto Jerusalem to destroy it: and as he was destroying, the LORD beheld, and he repented him of the evil, and said to the angel that destroyed, It is enough, stay now thine hand.

This half-verse reveals the time has come for Jerusalem to experience God's anger as *an angel* of death appears on the scene. It's unfitting to take the word *destroy* in the sense of "demolishing buildings" since the parallel in 2 Samuel 24:16 establishes that the focus is on the people themselves.

Before completing this devastation, however, the Lord *repented him of the evil.* This phrasing doesn't mean that God had been doing something wrong or sinful—that would be impossible. Instead, to "repent" means God changed the course of what was anticipated to happen next. The word *evil* in this context doesn't refer to a moral evil but to the due punishment.

15b. And the angel of the LORD stood by the threshingfloor of Ornan the Jebusite.

A threshing floor was a flat, hard piece of ground, ideally one of stone. Every harvest, the dried bundles of grain would be threshed here.

What will you offer to the Lord?

Visual for Lesson 10. *Display this visual as you ask the discussion questions associated with verses 24-25.*

This process involved laying the grain out and having it beaten or trampled by oxen to separate the ripened seeds from the stalks. The process also involved winnowing (compare Ruth 3:2; note figurative use in Luke 3:17). When the process was complete, grains could be ground into flour for making bread. A threshing floor was thus an essential piece of food production that could last from harvest to harvest. Threshing floors are mentioned dozens of times in the Bible, sometimes figuratively (examples: Deuteronomy 25:4; Isaiah 28:27; 1 Corinthians 9:9).

The fact that a *Jebusite* owned this *threshing-floor* is revealing. Jebusites are mentioned over 40 times in the Old Testament. They were not Israelites (1 Kings 9:20; 2 Chronicles 8:7); rather, they were one of the tribes inhabiting the promised land that the Israelites were commanded to drive out. They had lived in Jerusalem and, apparently, David let some of them stay after he conquered the city (2 Samuel 5:6-8). Ornan's presence after David's takeover indicates he had favor with the Israelite conquerors in some way and was perhaps known to David. (Note: 2 Samuel 24:16 uses "Araunah" as a variation of Ornan's name.)

16a. And David lifted up his eyes, and saw the angel of the LORD stand between the earth and the heaven, having a drawn sword in his hand stretched out over Jerusalem.

Comparing 1 Chronicles 21:16-17, a segment of our lesson-text, with its parallel section in 2 Sam-

uel 24:17 yields some interesting results. The most obvious difference is one of length: this part of the story is about twice as long in our lesson-text than the version in that parallel verse. That parallel of the half-verse before us now merely says, "David spake unto the Lord when he saw the angel that smote the people."

C. Passionate Plea (vv. 16b-17)

16b. Then David and the elders of Israel, who were clothed in sackcloth, fell upon their faces.

This scene is absent altogether in the parallel verse of 2 Samuel 24:17. *Sackcloth* is the garment of mourning (examples: 2 Samuel 3:31; Amos 8:10). It is made from rough, loose-fitting cloth—modern burlap may be similar. Sackcloth was the exact opposite of the finery of kings' robes or of the luxurious garments of a nation's leaders (example: Jonah 3:6).

In the verse before us, the wearing of sackcloth is combined with falling prostrate—itself a sign of humility before God or other people (example: Ruth 2:10). The combined aspects of wearing sackcloth and falling facedown are rare in Scripture; this indicates the extreme nature of the situation at hand. The reaction of *David and the elders of Israel* to the angel is submission, not defiance. They surrendered to the judgment of the Lord.

17. And David said unto God, Is it not I that commanded the people to be numbered? even I it is that have sinned and done evil indeed; but as for these sheep, what have they done? let thine hand, I pray thee, O LORD my God, be on me, and on my father's house; but not on thy people, that they should be plagued.

The parallel in 2 Samuel 24:17 says much the same as the verse at hand but is more succinct.

Both stress David's confession that he and he alone was responsible for the unholy census he had taken. His advisor Joab had warned him against doing that and had even left one tribe uncounted. But David quickly rejected Joab's counsel (2 Samuel 24:3-4; 1 Chronicles 21:3-6).

Even so, David seemed quite willing to admit his sin and repent. When God confronted Adam with his sin in the garden, he attempted to shift the blame to his wife, Eve (Genesis 3:12). When Samuel rebuked Saul for disobedience, that king made excuses (1 Samuel 15:13-21). David did neither. As he did when confronted with his sin regarding Bathsheba, David took sole responsibility (2 Samuel 12:13).

> **What Do You Think?**
>
> What are some ways to take responsibility for something wrong you've done?
>
> **Digging Deeper**
>
> How should your prayers be the same or different from what David prayed?

II. The Fiery Altar
(1 Chronicles 21:18-27)
A. Prophetic Directive (vv. 18-19)

18. Then the angel of the LORD commanded Gad to say to David, that David should go up, and set up an altar unto the LORD in the threshingfloor of Ornan the Jebusite.

The severity of David's sin demanded more than words of repentance and submissive body postures. So *the Lord* made His expectations clear to *David* through the prophet *Gad*. This man is elsewhere referred to as a "prophet" (1 Samuel 22:5), as a "seer" (1 Chronicles 21:9), and as both: "the prophet Gad, David's seer" (2 Samuel 24:11). For David to *go up* means that a bit of an uphill hike was to be part of his overall task. See commentary on 1 Chronicles 21:15b, above, regarding the designation of *the Jebusite*.

19. And David went up at the saying of Gad, which he spake in the name of the LORD.

David realized that *Gad* was not offering his own expert opinion but was speaking *in the name of the Lord*. The phrase *went up at the saying* indi-

cates complete obedience. The Lord had chosen a specific site. As noted in 2 Chronicles 3:1, that place was "mount Moriah, where the Lord appeared unto David . . . in the place that David had prepared in the threshingfloor of Ornan the Jebusite." This threshing floor was to become the site of Solomon's temple (1 Chronicles 22:1). Moriah was the place where Abraham nearly sacrificed his son Isaac (Genesis 22:2).

B. Humble Cooperation (vv. 20-25)

20-21. And Ornan turned back, and saw the angel; and his four sons with him hid themselves. Now Ornan was threshing wheat. And as David came to Ornan, Ornan looked and saw David, and went out of the threshingfloor, and bowed himself to David with his face to the ground.

This seems to have been a workday for *Ornan . . . and his four sons*. As they were *threshing wheat*, they perhaps did not notice at first the presence of *the angel*. We can scarcely imagine the shock of turning around and simultaneously seeing both an angel and the king! The parallel passage 2 Samuel 24:20 adds that David was accompanied by servants, adding to the shock.

22. Then David said to Ornan, Grant me the place of this threshingfloor, that I may build an altar therein unto the LORD: thou shalt grant it me for the full price: that the plague may be stayed from the people.

David wasted no time in making known the reason for his visit. He could have "pulled rank" and confiscated Ornan's property, but David offered *the full price*. He intended to carry out the Lord's instructions through Gad but with justice and integrity. And if there was any time in David's life when he had to act with unquestionable integrity, this was it, considering the lives that were at stake.

23. And Ornan said unto David, Take it to thee, and let my lord the king do that which is good in his eyes: lo, I give thee the oxen also for burnt offerings, and the threshing instruments for wood, and the wheat for the meat offering; I give it all.

We now see the extent of Ornan's threshing operation. We also gain insight into the person of Ornan himself. Although he is a non-Israelite (see commentary on 1 Chronicles 21:15b, above), he was familiar with Israel's sacrificial system. He knew how *oxen* and *wheat* could be used in differing types of *offerings* (Leviticus 1 and 2; we note that the *King James Version* uses the word *meat* at times to stand for any food, even grain; see Leviticus 2:1, 4). Burnt offerings require wood for fire, and Ornan offered his *threshing instruments* for that purpose.

> **What Do You Think?**
> What steps will you take to evaluate your generosity?
>
> **Digging Deeper**
> In what ways does 2 Corinthians 9:6-15 convict you in this regard?

24-25. And king David said to Ornan, Nay; but I will verily buy it for the full price: for I will not take that which is thine for the Lord, nor offer burnt offerings without cost. So David gave to Ornan for the place six hundred shekels of gold by weight.

David resisted any urge to use his position to pay anything less than *the full price* to Ornan and his family. The sin at issue was David's, and his repentance was to cost him. Ancient weights found in archaeological digs reveal that a shekel's weight is about 11.34 grams, which converts to 0.365 troy ounces in today's measurements. So the *six hundred shekels of gold by weight* paid by David would have been about 219 troy ounces of gold. Assuming gold today sells for about $2,000 per troy ounce, David's offer would be the equivalent to more than $400,000 today!

However, when we look at the parallel account in 2 Samuel 24:24, we see a difference: a sale price of only "fifty shekels of silver." At today's price of $24 per troy ounce of silver, that equates to less than $500. But a close look at the text reveals there is no contradiction. In the verse before us now, the price in gold is *for the place,* while the parallel text says the price in silver was "for the threshingfloor and the oxen." So our text here indicates a more significant purchase of the land where the threshing floor was located. Since this later became the site of

Solomon's temple (1 Chronicles 22:1), a conservative estimate is that at least 10 acres are purchased.

The Pseudo-Sacrifice

The people who know best the meaning of the word *sacrifice* are parents. The people who are second best at knowing that word's meaning are chess players. A sacrifice in both areas involves giving up something of short-term value in anticipation of a long-term benefit. Parents sacrifice their own short-term desires for the long-term needs of their children; chess players sacrifice a piece in exchange for a checkmate later. The common thread is that something of value is given up, which will result in hardship if no positive results are forthcoming.

A sacrifice that costs little or nothing is a contradiction in terms. Do you offer God pseudo-sacrifices? Do you share with Him less of your money than you spend on coffee every week? Think deeply about that: unless your financial giving causes you to do without something you would like to have, it's not sacrificial giving. The same goes for how you spend your time.

An acceptable sacrifice to God does not necessarily have to involve money, but it should be costly in some way. The sacrifices God appreciates the most are not even material. As the psalmist says, "The sacrifices of God are a broken spirit: a broken and a contrite heart, O God, thou wilt not despise" (Psalm 51:17). And that psalmist was none other than David himself.   —A. W.

> **What Do You Think?**
> How will you, like David, give to God even though it costs you something?
>
> **Digging Deeper**
> What steps will you take to develop the attitude that giving to God might require a cost?

C. Sheathed Sword (vv. 26-27)

26. And David built there an altar unto the Lord, and offered burnt offerings and peace offerings, and called upon the Lord; and he answered him from heaven by fire upon the altar of burnt offering.

We are not given the details of the *altar* David built. Given the urgency of the situation, we may speculate that it was hastily constructed from nearby materials. It may have been "an altar of earth" like the one in Exodus 20:24; that was the first instance of combining *burnt offerings* and *peace offerings*, explained in Leviticus 1 and 3, respectively.

The Lord's fiery response must have been spectacular and awe-inspiring. Sometimes *fire* from *heaven* is judgmental (example: 2 Kings 1:10-14); at other times, it indicates divine approval in some sense (example: 2 Chronicles 7:1). In this instance, it seems to have reflected both.

27. And the LORD commanded the angel; and he put up his sword again into the sheath thereof.

There could be no better outcome than this.

III. The Sword of the Lord
(1 Chronicles 21:28-30)

A. Ancient Tabernacle (vv. 28-29)

28-29. At that time when David saw that the LORD had answered him in the threshingfloor of Ornan the Jebusite, then he sacrificed there. For the tabernacle of the LORD, which Moses made in the wilderness, and the altar of the burnt offering, were at that season in the high place at Gibeon.

Although this story is about David's sin, its consequences, and its resolution, it has other important information too. This story represents a transitional phase between tabernacle and temple as the proper house of the Lord, and between Jerusalem and *Gibeon* (five miles to the north) regarding location. The tabernacle made by *Moses* four hundred years earlier was still at the *high place* in Gibeon (2 Chronicles 1:13), not yet transferred to Jerusalem. Also in Gibeon was *the altar of burnt offering*, the concept of which also dated to Moses.

B. Fearful Caution (v. 30)

30. But David could not go before it to inquire of God: for he was afraid because of the sword of the angel of the LORD.

David doesn't seem to believe he's been for-

given fully! So the man who slew a bear, a lion, and Goliath (1 Samuel 17) shrinks back in fear of *the sword of the angel of the Lord*. Seeing the angel's power has made David cautious (compare 1 Chronicles 13:12).

Conclusion
A. Community Suffering

Large numbers of people suffer deeply from the mistakes of a single individual. Think about the assassination of Archduke Franz Ferdinand by a Serbian student in 1914, which kicked off World War I and the deaths of millions. In the Bible, consider the gross sins of King Manasseh, which resulted in God's sending Israel into the Babylonian exile (Jeremiah 15:4; see 2 Kings 21:16). At the birth of Jesus, the insecurity and ruthlessness of King Herod led to the massacre of innocent babies and children in Bethlehem and nearby areas (Matthew 2:16).

David understood that his prideful sin had resulted in the deaths of 70,000 men. The nearly 10 months it took before the census-takers returned (2 Samuel 24:8) can be seen as God's waiting period before He acted. He is patient— but His patience has limits (2 Peter 3:9).

B. Prayer

Lord God, we, like David, are imperfect servants because of our sins. May we never be so prideful or isolated from others that we do not see how our actions can affect those around us. Help us to choose responsibility and repentance for our sins so that others may not bear our consequences. We pray in the name of Jesus. Amen.

C. Thought to Remember
Our sin affects others.

How to Say It

Araunah	A-*raw*-nuh.
Bathsheba	Bath-*she*-buh.
Jebusites	*Jeb*-yuh-sites.
Ornan	Or-nawn.
Uriah	Yu-*rye*-uh.

Involvement Learning

Enhance your lesson with KJV Bible Student *(from your curriculum supplier) and the reproducible activity page (at www.standardlesson.com or in the back of the* KJV Standard Lesson Commentary Deluxe Edition*).*

Into the Lesson

Ask participants if they have any good "clueless boss" stories that they wouldn't get in trouble for sharing. Caution that no names be used.

Alternative. Bring in some "clueless boss" cartoons (the Dilbert comic strip is famous for these). Pass them around for lighthearted chuckles.

After either introduction, say, "We usually use the word *clueless* to describe someone who has no idea what is happening. Today's lesson will reveal a decision by a boss that went beyond clueless, all the way to being deadly sinful. It will be a fair warning to us today."

Into the Word

Have two participants read aloud the 17 verses of today's lesson, alternating with each verse. Afterward, announce a closed-Bible pop quiz on how much they remember about those verses. State that you won't collect the quizzes and that everyone will grade his or her own. Then, distribute handouts (you prepare) with the following multiple-choice questions. *Time limit: one minute!*

1–How many died as a result of David's sin?
    a. 70,000 b. 170,000 c. none

2–What stood between Heaven and earth?
    a. prophet b. stairway c. angel

3–What did David build?
    a. temple b. altar c. tower

4–What did David buy?
    a. tabernacle b. food c. threshing floor

5–David refused to offer a sacrifice that cost him what?
    a. nothing b. anything c. everything

6–Who did David say shared the blame for his sin?
    a. the prophet Gad b. the people c. no one

[*Answers:* 1-a; 2-c; 3-b; 4-c; 5-a; 6-c.]

Encourage open discussion of the quiz results. When someone asks a question about an uncertainty, use that as a transition point for an "all question" time. Form study pairs or small groups to create two lists of questions: one list of their own questions and another list of questions that an unbeliever might ask regarding the passage.

Call for questions and responses to the ensuing whole-class discussion. Expect that this question in particular will be asked: "Why would God kill 70,000 innocent people because of the sin of someone else?" or similar. (Pose the question yourself if no one else does.)

Introduce an approach that examines the validity of assumptions behind the question. Write the word *Assumptions* at the top center of the board. Then, ask learners to identify some of those behind that question of the 70,000 deaths. Be sure to identify the assumption that the 70,000 were not deserving of death. Use this approach for every question as appropriate.

Into Life

Ask for modern examples of people suffering the consequences of wrongdoing committed by others. Jot the examples on the board. After a few are offered, pick one and say, "We're going to write an intercessory prayer for this one, but not the kind we usually hear." Then, distribute handouts (you create) with a typical intercessory prayer printed at the top—a prayer that asks God to do something about some situation or injustice. Have these instructions at the bottom above a blank space: "Rewrite this prayer (or an entirely new one) so that you're asking God to show you how you can be His hands and feet to solve the problem."

Option. At an appropriate point in the lesson, distribute copies of the "Stopping the Butterfly Effect" exercise on the activity page, which you can download. Have learners complete it in study pairs as indicated.

Option. As learners depart, distribute copies of the "To Be a Living Sacrifice" exercise from the activity page as a take-home. Encourage its completion by announcing that you will discuss the results at the beginning of next week's class.

Solomon Dedicates the Temple

Devotional Reading: 2 Chronicles 6:12, 14-27
Background Scripture: 2 Chronicles 7:1-20

2 Chronicles 7:1-7, 11

1 Now when Solomon had made an end of praying, the fire came down from heaven, and consumed the burnt offering and the sacrifices; and the glory of the LORD filled the house.

2 And the priests could not enter into the house of the LORD, because the glory of the LORD had filled the LORD's house.

3 And when all the children of Israel saw how the fire came down, and the glory of the LORD upon the house, they bowed themselves with their faces to the ground upon the pavement, and worshipped, and praised the LORD, saying, for he is good; for his mercy endureth for ever.

4 Then the king and all the people offered sacrifices before the LORD.

5 And king Solomon offered a sacrifice of twenty and two thousand oxen, and an hundred and twenty thousand sheep: so the king and all the people dedicated the house of God.

6 And the priests waited on their offices: the Levites also with instruments of musick of the LORD, which David the king had made to praise the LORD, because his mercy endureth for ever, when David praised by their ministry; and the priests sounded trumpets before them, and all Israel stood.

7 Moreover Solomon hallowed the middle of the court that was before the house of the LORD: for there he offered burnt offerings, and the fat of the peace offerings, because the brasen altar which Solomon had made was not able to receive the burnt offerings, and the meat offerings, and the fat.

11 Thus Solomon finished the house of the LORD, and the king's house: and all that came into Solomon's heart to make in the house of the LORD, and in his own house, he prosperously effected.

Key Text

When all the children of Israel saw how the fire came down, and the glory of the LORD upon the house, they bowed themselves with their faces to the ground upon the pavement, and worshipped, and praised the LORD, saying, for he is good; for his mercy endureth for ever. —**2 Chronicles 7:3**

Costly
Sacrifices

Unit 3: Special Offerings and the Sanctuary
Lessons 10–13

Lesson Aims

After participating in this lesson, each learner will be able to:

1. Summarize what happened when Solomon finished praying.

2. Explain the idea of "dedicating" or "consecrating" something.

3. State how one can respond to God's presence and love with worship and sacrifice.

Lesson Outline

Introduction
A. Finishing a Father's Legacy

From 1927 until his death in 1941, Gutzon Borglum, along with numerous assistants, carved the sculptures of four American presidents into the side of Mount Rushmore, located in the Black Hills of South Dakota. Borglum chose the 60-foot sculptures to represent 150 years of American history. Borglum worked on the project until his death, mere months before its completion. His son completed the project.

Today's lesson, regarding the construction of the temple, is both similar to and different from the Borglums' project. They are similar in that neither man who envisioned the projects in the first place lived to see their respective completions. They are different in that while the father oversaw almost all the work in the Borglums' project, the opposite was true regarding the temple construction. King David wanted to build a magnificent temple for the Lord, but the honor went to his son Solomon instead. While David laid the groundwork, it was to be Solomon's legacy to oversee and complete the project.

B. Historical Context

The books of 1 and 2 Chronicles emphasize the importance of the reigns of David (1010–970 BC) and Solomon (970–930 BC) as their lives related to the temple's coming into existence. The chronicler explains how those kings instituted most of the ongoing practices of the temple, especially those of sacrifice, prayer, and singing. All three of those elements are present in the parallel books of 1 and 2 Kings, but much more so in the Chronicles.

In 1 Chronicles 22:8, King David explained to his son Solomon that God had forbidden David from building the temple due to the amount of blood he had shed. After David's extensive preparations (22:5), the honor was to fall to Solomon instead. He spent seven years completing the temple his father dreamed of building (1 Kings 6:38). The year of its completion was, therefore, 963 BC. The book of 2 Chronicles links father and son in several passages not included in 1 Kings (examples: 2 Chronicles 2:3, 7; 3:1; 6:42; 7:10; 8:14).

The dedication ceremony for the temple included a lengthy and eloquent prayer by the king (2 Chronicles 6). In that prayer, Solomon asked the Lord to remember His covenant with His people and His promise to David. He prayed for forgiveness of future sin. He pled for the temple to be a beacon of God's great name and mighty hand. He closed his prayer by inviting everyone else to celebrate the same divine mercy that he had recognized. Solomon thereby challenged himself and his hearers to a life of worship and sacrifice.

C. Literary Context

The first nine chapters of 2 Chronicles are commonly recognized as a literary sub-unit of the book as a whole. One reasonable outline of these nine chapters is:

A. Solomon's Kingship (1:1-17)
B. Temple's Construction (2:1–5:1)
C. Temple's Dedication (5:2–7:22)
D. Solomon's Other Activities (8:1–9:31)

Another way to show the inner dynamics of 2 Chronicles 1–9 is with this arrangement:

A–Solomon's wisdom and wealth (1:1-17)
  B–He prepares temple construction (2:1-18)
    C–He builds the temple (3:1–5:1)
    C'–He dedicates the temple (5:2–7:22)
  B'–He completes the temple, etc. (8:1-16)
A'–Solomon's wisdom and wealth (8:17–9:28)

Notice the repetition of themes in a parallel "inverse pyramid" arrangement.

The powerful conclusion to Solomon's prayer, which immediately precedes today's lesson text, is reflected in a psalm:

> Now therefore arise, O LORD God, into thy resting place, thou, and the ark of thy strength: let thy priests, O LORD God, be clothed with salvation, and let thy saints rejoice in goodness. O LORD God, turn not away the face of thine anointed: remember the mercies of David thy servant.
> —2 Chronicles 6:41-42

Arise, O LORD, into thy rest; thou, and the ark of thy strength. Let thy priests be clothed with righteousness; and let thy saints shout for joy.

> For thy servant David's sake turn not away the face of thine anointed. —Psalm 132:8-10

The parallel account to today's text is 1 Kings 8:62-66. Compared to that earlier account, today's passage is the longer version; it includes additional details.

I. Glory of God
(2 Chronicles 7:1-3)
A. Fire Comes Down (vv. 1-2)

1a. Now when Solomon had made an end of praying, the fire came down from heaven, and consumed the burnt offering and the sacrifices.

See Literary Context, above, regarding the content of Solomon's *praying*. As we read about *the fire* that *came down from heaven* to consume *the burnt offering and the sacrifices,* we're naturally inclined to compare and contrast this event with other such episodes in the Bible. Fire of divine origin was often for the purpose of judgment. Examples of this kind of fire stated in a personal way as being from the Lord or similar are Leviticus 10:2; Numbers 11:1; 16:35; and Psalm 21:9. Examples of judgmental fire more generally said to be from Heaven are 2 Kings 1:10-14; Luke 9:54; 17:29; and Revelation 20:9. But the fire in the lesson text at hand is in the minority of cases that are not judgmental, but showing divine favor instead (compare Leviticus 9:24; Judges 6:21).

Visual for Lesson 11. *Display this visual as you ask the following question: "How have you experienced the Lord's love and goodness?"*

Burnt offerings were a specific type of sacrifice whereby the entire offering was consumed by fire on the altar (Leviticus 1). By making such an offering, the people acknowledged their sin and the need for its removal. In the context at hand, it should have convicted the original audience of the need to enter the temple with holy attitudes and intent if they were to live in a healthy relationship with God and each other (contrast Jeremiah 7:30; Luke 19:46). The dramatic descent of the fire signaled that God was watching.

A Third Kind of Fire

Have you ever seen a "fire tornado"? These can form when a large forest fire heats the air so much that weather patterns begin to self-generate. The result may be a towering vortex of spinning flames connecting earth and sky, inspiring awe and terror.

I imagine that the descent of fire from Heaven at the dedication of Solomon's temple looked something like this kind of tornado. And yet, there is no record of fear on the part of those present! The fire was one of approval, not judgment.

But between the two fires of approval and judgment stands a third type of fire: the fire of testing. We all have to undergo certain trials of fire that test our faith (1 Peter 4:12). These can serve to cleanse us from unholiness (compare Proverbs 25:4; Malachi 3:2-3). We serve the Lord with the realization that the quality of our work will be tested by fire on the last day (1 Corinthians 3:12-13). Wouldn't it be better to embrace the testing now so we have time to repent before that final audit?

—A. W.

1b. And the glory of the LORD filled the house.

The dramatic intensity of the fire from Heaven, just considered, was enhanced (if that were possible!) when *the glory of the Lord filled the house.* The concepts of fire and *glory* are combined in several places in the Bible (examples: Exodus 24:17; Deuteronomy 5:24; Isaiah 4:5; Zechariah 2:5; 1 Peter 1:7).

The manifestation of God's glory occurred also at the dedication of the tabernacle, which was the forerunner to the temple (Exodus 40:34-35). On that occasion, the glory happened in conjunction with a cloud rather than fire. This same combination had also occurred in the account of Solomon's bringing the ark of the covenant to the temple (2 Chronicles 5:13b–6:1; 1 Kings 8:10-12; compare Exodus 16:10). The combination of glory and cloud will occur yet again when God's glory departs the temple some 366 years after its dedication (Ezekiel 10:4, 10). Thus, God's glory is regularly connected with vital turning points in ancient Israel's focus on expressions of worship. The purpose of the glory is consecration or sanctification (Exodus 29:43).

2. And the priests could not enter into the house of the LORD, because the glory of the LORD had filled the LORD's house.

At first glance, 1 Kings 8:11 seems parallel to the verse before us because the idea conveyed is identical. But 1 Kings 8:11 is actually parallel to 2 Chronicles 5:11, 13b-14 in the flow of events. All are similar in outcome to what we see here: *the priests could not enter the house of the Lord,* with echoes of Exodus 40:35, as noted above.

B. People Bow Down (v. 3)

3. And when all the children of Israel saw how the fire came down, and the glory of the LORD upon the house, they bowed themselves with their faces to the ground upon the pavement, and worshipped, and praised the LORD, saying, For he is good; for his mercy endureth for ever.

The text shifts its focus to those gathered, *the children of Israel.* Their experience of seeing the *fire* that *came down* and *the glory of the Lord* prompted them to renew their life of worship. ("Renew" is the right word because they had prayed and sacrificed before, but henceforth they would do so in a more profound way.)

The people sang an often-repeated phrase found also in Psalm 136. The song also preceded Solomon's prayer (2 Chronicles 5:13). It was part of the singing when the ark of the covenant was brought to Jerusalem (1 Chronicles 16:34). It was sung again centuries later as the altar was being rebuilt following return from exile (Ezra 3:11). The event of the consecration of the temple was a reminder of God's goodness and *mercy* in the past and for the future.

> **What Do You Think?**
>
> What changes might you experience by being more mindful of God's goodness, mercy, and love?
>
> **Digging Deeper**
>
> How can we gain that greater mindfulness?

Powerful Love

Most kids of Lavonte's age didn't watch their dads play pro football on TV. But Lavonte did—his dad was a 6'7", 360-pound offensive tackle. He was intimidating and didn't have to do much to keep Lavonte in line. Just the deep rumble of Dad's voice calling Lavonte from the back porch was enough to make the youngster freeze in his tracks and rapidly reconsider his intentions!

Would it be fair to say Lavonte feared his dad? Well . . . *yes* and *no*. He knew his father was a firm and strong man. Yet Lavonte also knew with absolute certainty that his dad would never hurt him. Because the same voice that growled out his name like a lion had talked as softly as a cat's purr to him every night at bedtime. And he knew he had a standing invitation to curl up next to his dad on the couch to watch replays of his dad's last game.

God inflicts powerful acts of judgment. His enemies don't stand a chance against His wrath. Yet when His people witness the consuming fire falling from Heaven, their response is not one of terror but one of love, awe, and admiration: "He is good; for his mercy endureth for ever!" (2 Chronicles 7:3).

—A. W.

Sacrifice(s) was a form of worship

II. Worship by People
(2 Chronicles 7:4-6)
A. Sacrifices (vv. 4-5)

4. Then the king and all the people offered sacrifices before the LORD.

The *sacrifices* that followed differ from those incinerated by fire from Heaven (burnt offerings) in that some of the sacrifices in view here could be eaten. After God put His stamp of approval on the temple by consuming the initial sacrifices, the people joined in.

There are usually clear delineations of the duties of the three offices of *prophet*, *priest*, and *king* in ancient Israel. In the laws of sacrifice in Exodus, Leviticus, and Numbers, the king had no role—indeed, there was no provision for ancient Israel even to have a king in those three books (compare 1 Samuel 8). The story of King Uzziah's leprosy after his attempted sacrifice (2 Chronicles 26:16-23) reveals that a king was not to usurp the role of a priest. But there were some exceptions, and that seems to have been the case here as *the king and all the people offered sacrifices before the Lord.* The sheer number of sacrificial animals may have overwhelmed the number of priests available. If so, a practical adjustment was made (compare 30:2-3).

We might easily misunderstand the purposes of sacrifice and dismiss the practice as barbaric or see it merely as a way of appeasing God's anger. Sacrifice was a form of worship. The people had to take something that was valuable to them and either give it over to God entirely or to both God and other people.

> **What Do You Think?**
>
> In what circumstances should our actions as living sacrifices be visible to all? In what circumstances visible only to God?
>
> **Digging Deeper**
>
> How do Matthew 5:13-16 and 6:1-4 influence your answers?

5. And king Solomon offered a sacrifice of twenty and two thousand oxen, and an hundred

and twenty thousand sheep: so the king and all the people dedicated the house of God.

The number of animals would have fed many thousands of people, making this event a celebration for a large percentage of Solomon's subjects. The dedication ceremony was designed to shape the life of the entire kingdom, including those not able to be present in Jerusalem. Solomon rightly understood that celebrating such an important event as the dedication of the temple in grand style should bring the people together in more ways than one.

It is interesting to compare the numbers of animals sacrificed in this verse to the Passover sacrifices later offered under Kings Hezekiah (reigned 716–687 BC) and Josiah (reigned 641–609 BC) centuries later, according to 2 Chronicles 30:24; 35:7-9:

King	Oxen/Cattle	Sheep and Goats
Solomon	22,000	120,000
Hezekiah	2,000	17,000
Josiah	11,100	37,600

The books of 1 and 2 Chronicles measure kings by how they treat the temple in Jerusalem and facilitate worship there. By that measure, Solomon was a model king, at least at this point in his life.

B. Music (v. 6)

6a. And the priests waited on their offices: the Levites also with instruments of musick of the Lord, which David the king had made to praise the Lord, because his mercy endureth for ever, when David praised by their ministry.

This verse stands on the shoulders of 1 Chronicles 15:3-22. That passage describes in great detail how *David the king* organized *the Levites* as temple musicians in conjunction with his second (and successful) attempt at bringing the ark of the covenant into Jerusalem. The musical instruments mentioned there are "psalteries and harps and cymbals" (1 Chronicles 15:16). These instruments were also present at the first (and failed) attempt to relocate the ark, with two additional instruments mentioned in that context: timbrels and trumpets (13:8). The Old Testament mentions at least 14 distinct musical instruments a total of over 200 times.

Singing isn't mentioned in this verse. But since the first attempt to relocate the ark involved sing-

ing (1 Chronicles 13:8), as did the second attempt (15:22), it's more than reasonable to presume that singing also occurred here.

6b. And the priests sounded trumpets before them, and all Israel stood.

Priests are associated with *trumpets* about a dozen times in the Old Testament. There were two kinds of trumpets used for different purposes. First were the trumpets of silver; these were for calling the people to assemble, for setting out, to announce times of rejoicing at festivals, and for signaling in battle (Numbers 10:1-10). These are the trumpets in view here.

The second kind was trumpets made from rams' horns. These are mentioned in dozens of places, but in connection with priests only in Joshua 6.

III. Actions by Solomon
(2 Chronicles 7:7, 11)
A. Consecration (v. 7)

7. Moreover Solomon hallowed the middle of the court that was before the house of the Lord: for there he offered burnt offerings, and the fat of the peace offerings, because the brasen altar which Solomon had made was not able to receive the burnt offerings, and the meat offerings, and the fat.

The horizontal surface of the altar Solomon had built measured 20 cubits by 20 cubits, or about 900 square feet (2 Chronicles 4:1). Although it was quite large, it was not large enough for the work of that day of dedication. Thus, Solomon needed a plan to deal with this. So, with priestly help, he *hallowed* (meaning "consecrated" or "sanctified") *the middle of the court[yard]* to be suitable as an overflow altar. This practice was not provided for in the Law of Moses, but 2 Chronicles sees it as an appropriate emergency measure. The aim of the event was more important than the silence of the law in this regard.

Three types of offerings are noted. *Burnt offerings* were characterized by being totally consumed by the fire; regulations are in Leviticus 1 and 6:8-13. Regarding *meat offerings*, we note that the *King James Version* uses the word *meat* at times to stand for any food, even grain; see Leviticus 2:1, 4) Regulations for this kind of offering are in Leviticus 2 and 6:14-23. *Peace offerings* were offerings of thanksgiving or are connected with the taking of vows; regulations are in Leviticus 3 and 7:11-21. The Law of Moses forbade the eating of the *fat* of animals that were candidates for sacrifice (Leviticus 7:22-27; compare Exodus 29:13).

What Do You Think?

What steps do you need to take for greater consecration since 1 Corinthians 6:19 establishes that your body is now the temple of the Holy Spirit?

Digging Deeper

What superficial efforts have you seen others make in this regard?

B. Completion (v. 11)

11. Thus Solomon finished the house of the LORD, and the king's house: and all that came into Solomon's heart to make in the house of the LORD, and in his own house, he prosperously effected.

The passages 2 Chronicles 5:3; 7:8-10 indicate that the temple dedication occurred during the Feast of Tabernacles, one of the three annual pilgrimage feasts (Deuteronomy 16:13-17; 31:10). Solomon had committed himself fully to the completion of the temple, focusing all his resources to that effort. But more than it being about a building, it was also about a people. He recruited many artisans and craftsmen to help as they used their skills for God's glory.

Solomon, like any other king, also built a palace (*the king's house*). His palace had a footprint more than four times that of the temple (11,250 square feet and 2,700 square feet, respectively; see

1 Kings 6:2 and 7:2). Compared to the seven years it took to build the temple, the 13 years to build his palace is understandable!

The palace had to be larger than the temple because it needed to house the king, his numerous wives, many officials, etc. A palace was not just a grandiose house but a small city within the city.

Conclusion

A. Seeking God's Goodness

The temple became the center of ancient Israel's religious life. It was the place where they could meet God. Sacrifices and prayers would occur at that temple for generations. While Solomon could not have foreseen the details of the long history of worship that followed his actions, his trust in God was proven by his prayer, worship, and actions. These reflected confidence in God's holiness, power, and enduring love.

Solomon prayed to God to remember His promises to his father and to previous generations. The king's prayer was integral to his worship. His focus on completing the temple *before* he started his own house showed his heart (contrast Haggai 1:2-4).

Unfortunately, this interconnection of faithful prayer, worship, and actions would not last. It didn't last for the people (2 Chronicles 36:15-21), and it didn't last for Solomon himself (1 Kings 11:4-11). Will it last for you?

B. Prayer

O God our Father, may we always praise You for Your merciful love and goodness. Renew in us a life of worship. Strengthen our dedication to Your holiness and help us to love others as You see them. May we be living sacrifices for Your glory. In Jesus' name. Amen.

C. Thought to Remember

Respond to God with worship.

How to Say It

Hezekiah	Hez-ih-*kye*-uh.
Josiah	Jo-*sigh*-uh.
Uzziah	Uh-*zye*-uh.

Lord, I choose to always used this "passion of prayer" you gave

me for your glory

Involvement Learning

Enhance your lesson with KJV Bible Student *(from your curriculum supplier) and the reproducible activity page (at www.standardlesson.com or in the back of the* KJV Standard Lesson Commentary Deluxe Edition*).*

Into the Lesson

Have the phrase *Spontaneous Songs* written on the board as learners arrive. Ask your learners to name songs (religious or secular) that people might sing spontaneously right after a startling experience, either good or bad. The song could be sung in a context that the songwriter did not envision. Jot responses on the board.

Alternative. If you think the above will be too difficult, research such songs yourself and write their titles on the board before class begins; *do not* write the title *Spontaneous Songs* on the board. That theme is what the learners are to guess based on the song titles you list. Just two examples of songs that might be sung spontaneously are "We Are the Champions" by Queen (in reacting to a positive event) and "I Won't Back Down" by Tom Petty (in reacting to a challenging event). Have at least four songs on the board. Ask what the songs have in common.

Make a transition by saying, "Today, we're going to consider an event that resulted in spontaneous singing. Let's see how the ancient Israelites connected singing to a major positive event in their nation's history."

Into the Word

Before the Scripture for the lesson is read, distribute handouts (you prepare) titled "Since, Cents, Sense, or Scents?" Below the title, draw a pie chart divided into five segments or "slices." Label the five segments *Touch, Taste, Sight, Sound,* and *Smell,* one label for each segment.

Tell the class that you will read the lesson text of 2 Chronicles 7:1-7, 11 aloud twice. As you do, participants are to jot verse numbers in the five segments of their pie charts according to which of the five senses would have been most activated by the verse you are reading at the moment. (Responses can vary, but expect the following as likely, per the verse numbering: 1–sight, 2–sight, 3–sight, 4–touch, 5–smell, 6–sound, 7–smell, 11–sight.)

As you read the text, be sure to read the verse numbers as well. After you finish, do so again so participants can review their decisions. In the ensuing whole-class discussion, compare and contrast the responses. Draw a grid on the board that has eight horizontal rows and five vertical columns. Put the numbering of the eight verses of the lesson at the beginnings of the eight rows, one each; put the five senses as headers of the five columns, one each. Fill in the intersections as appropriate as participants respond with their choices.

Into Life

Form learners into small groups to compare and contrast the events of the text with the worship experiences they have had. To prompt discussion, distribute these questions on a handout (you create):

1–What elements of the worship in today's text give us valid ideas for our own worship?

2–What are some ways to respond best to God's presence and love with worship and sacrifice?

3–What are some specific things we can do on Saturday night to prepare ourselves better for worship on Sunday morning?

Option. Distribute copies of the "Whose To-Do List?" exercise from the activity page, which you can download, to one-on-one study pairs for completion as indicated. This activity recognizes the fact that in the dedication of the temple, there was a part for the people to play and a part for God to play.

Option. Distribute to study pairs or triads copies of the "God's Greatest Hits" exercise from the activity page, to be completed as indicated. If time is short, this can be a take-home exercise. To help ensure completion, state that you will begin class next week by discussing results.

Worship Is Restored

Devotional Reading: Colossians 3:12-17
Background Scripture: Ezra 3:1-13

Ezra 3:1-6, 10-13

1 And when the seventh month was come, and the children of Israel were in the cities, the people gathered themselves together as one man to Jerusalem.

2 Then stood up Jeshua the son of Jozadak, and his brethren the priests, and Zerubbabel the son of Shealtiel, and his brethren, and builded the altar of the God of Israel, to offer burnt offerings thereon, as it is written in the law of Moses the man of God.

3 And they set the altar upon his bases; for fear was upon them because of the people of those countries: and they offered burnt offerings thereon unto the LORD, even burnt offerings morning and evening.

4 They kept also the feast of tabernacles, as it is written, and offered the daily burnt offerings by number, according to the custom, as the duty of every day required;

5 And afterward offered the continual burnt offering, both of the new moons, and of all the set feasts of the LORD that were consecrated, and of every one that willingly offered a freewill offering unto the LORD.

6 From the first day of the seventh month began they to offer burnt offerings unto the LORD. But the foundation of the temple of the LORD was not yet laid.

- -

10 And when the builders laid the foundation of the temple of the LORD, they set the priests in their apparel with trumpets, and the Levites the sons of Asaph with cymbals, to praise the LORD, after the ordinance of David king of Israel.

11 And they sang together by course in praising and giving thanks unto the LORD; because he is good, for his mercy endureth for ever toward Israel. And all the people shouted with a great shout, when they praised the LORD, because the foundation of the house of the LORD was laid.

12 But many of the priests and Levites and chief of the fathers, who were ancient men, that had seen the first house, when the foundation of this house was laid before their eyes, wept with a loud voice; and many shouted aloud for joy:

13 So that the people could not discern the noise of the shout of joy from the noise of the weeping of the people: for the people shouted with a loud shout, and the noise was heard afar off.

Key Text

All the people shouted with a great shout, when they praised the LORD, because the foundation of the house of the LORD was laid. —**Ezra 3:11b**

Costly
Sacrifices

Lesson Aims

After participating in this lesson, each learner will be able to:

1. Outline the history of Judah's exile to Babylon and return to Jerusalem.

2. Summarize the behaviors of those who had returned from exile in light of their fear, joy, and sorrow.

3. Write a prayer that identifies an area where fear must be overcome so that godly service is not hindered.

Lesson Outline

Introduction
    A. Weeping and Rejoicing Today
    B. Lesson Context
 I. Rebuilding the Altar (Ezra 3:1-6)
    A. People Gather (v. 1)
    B. Leaders Lead (v. 2)
    C. Sacrifices Offered (vv. 3-5)
     The Mammoth Hunt
    D. Status Summarized (v. 6)
 II. Laying a Foundation (Ezra 3:10-13)
    A. Musical Praise (vv. 10-11)
    B. Mixed Reactions (vv. 12-13)
     How to Waste 50 Years—or Not
Conclusion
    A. Work as a Response to Grace
    B. Prayer
    C. Thought to Remember

Introduction
A. Weeping and Rejoicing Today

For over 25 years, my friend Sandra has served as a missionary in several countries, including Croatia, Ukraine, and Iran. Sandra reports asking an Iranian friend how she came to faith in Christ. The friend told Sandra, "When I was walking across Turkey trying to get away, I had a vision of Jesus Christ. He told me, 'I will be with you.'" Sandra then taught her friend more about what being a Christian meant in light of God's mercy and love.

We are wise to be skeptical of claimed visions, lest Revelation 22:19 be violated (compare Hebrews 1:1). But a claimed vision that aligns with the teaching of the Bible deserves further investigation. Such an occurrence may be the first step in being called to a saving relationship with God through Christ.

The experiences of Sandra and her friend remind us that Christians live in a world characterized by both pain and pleasure, grief and joy (compare John 16:21). And so it is with the Judeans of the mid-sixth century BC, today's lesson from the book of Ezra.

B. Lesson Context

The book of Ezra tells how Jews from the tribes of Judah and Benjamin returned to their homeland from exile in Babylon. That happened shortly after the fall of the Babylonian Empire to the Persians in 538 BC (Ezra 1:1–2:1), when the Persian king, Cyrus, issued a decree that allowed the return (Ezra 1:1-4; compare 2 Chronicles 36:22-23; Isaiah 44:28; 45:1, 13).

The books of Ezra and Nehemiah chronicle the return in three distinct phases. Ezra 2:64-65 reveals about 50,000 people in the first wave, making the arduous trip of over 800 miles. A later wave of returnees, coming under the leadership of Ezra, took exactly four months (Ezra 7:8-9).

The primary purpose of the journey was to "[re]build the house of the Lord" in Jerusalem (Ezra 1:5). When that city was destroyed in 586 BC, there remained no nation of Judah, no capital city of Jerusalem, no temple, no royal palace, and no walls (2 Kings 25:8-17; compare 2 Chronicles 36:15-21). Normally, it would be impossible for a nation to come into existence again after an absence of more than half a century. But God was in this situation, and the impossible became not just possible but a reality. As Jeremiah stated, nothing is too difficult for God (Jeremiah 32:17).

The temple's rebuilding would require much effort, money, time, labor, and good leadership. An easier and quicker task would be to start rebuilding the temple's altar of burnt offerings (see description in Exodus 38:1-7 and use in Leviticus 1:1-17; 6:8-13; also see lesson 4). And that's where we begin our lesson.

I. Rebuilding the Altar
(Ezra 3:1-6)

A. People Gather (v. 1)

1. And when the seventh month was come, and the children of Israel were in the cities, the people gathered themselves together as one man to Jerusalem.

The story's setting in *the seventh month* places it in late September or early October. By this time, the Jews had two calendars: a civic calendar and a religious calendar. The reference here is to the seventh month of the religious calendar, the first month on the civic calendar. By name, the month was called "Ethanim" (possibly meaning "gifts" or "flowing water") before the exile (1 Kings 8:2) and "Tishri" (meaning "beginning") after the exile.

By the time of the event described in the verse before us, those who had returned from exile had already dispersed to live in their ancestral villages (Ezra 2:70). Apparently, few wanted to live in Jerusalem itself, leading to a situation where one in every ten individuals was eventually selected by lot to inhabit the city (Nehemiah 11:1-2).

This seventh month of the Jewish religious year included four observances that would have drawn the people to Jerusalem. These were the blowing of trumpets on the first day (Leviticus 23:23-25), the Day of Atonement on the tenth day (23:26-32; see also lesson 5), the feast of tabernacles on days

15 through 21 (23:33-36a, 39-43), and an assembly of the eighth day on day 22 (23:36b). But the reason *the people gathered themselves together as one man to Jerusalem* may not be any of these, as we shall see.

> ### What Do You Think?
> What do you think is the value of having large numbers of Christians from a wide area attend a worship event?
> ### Digging Deeper
> How can we maintain unity among dispersed believers when gathering regularly in person is impossible?

B. Leaders Lead (v. 2)

2a. Then stood up Jeshua the son of Jozadak, and his brethren the priests, and Zerubbabel the son of Shealtiel, and his brethren, and builded the altar of the God of Israel.

The important leaders *Jeshua the son of Jozadak* and *Zerubbabel the son of Shealtiel* are mentioned together in a dozen Old Testament verses (here and Ezra 2:2; 3:8; 4:3; 5:2; Nehemiah 7:7; 12:1; Haggai 1:1, 12, 14; 2:2, 4). These occurrences reveal that Jeshua was the high priest and Zerubbabel was the governor. In these passages, we see Judah's religious leader and political leader working together to ensure the successful rebuilding of community and religious life. That rebuilding included *the altar of God of Israel* in its traditional place in the temple courtyard, even though the temple remained in ruins.

We may call their activity here "leadership by example." The reconstruction of the altar was necessary, and it appears that the direct engagement of these two leaders played a key role in making it happen. When we read of the temple that "Solomon built in Jerusalem" (1 Chronicles 6:10), it suggests he funded and authorized the temple's construction rather than doing the physical work himself. However, considering the activities mentioned in the verse before us, the term *builded* appears to have a more personal connotation.

Even so, it wasn't just Jeshua and Zerubbabel doing the work. The *brethren* of each pitched in.

RESTORED FOR WORSHIP.

Visual for Lesson 12. *Display this visual and allow learners one minute for silent reflection on the ways that the Lord has restored them for worship.*

The priests who had returned from exile were 4,289 in number, so there was no shortage of available labor (Ezra 2:36-39). However, so many trying to work together to build the altar would result in people getting in each other's way. A more manageable number of priests helping the two leaders would be the 19 leaders of priests named in Nehemiah 12:1-7. The number of individuals associated with Zerubbabel who assisted in the task remains unknown.

2b. To offer burnt offerings thereon, as it is written in the law of Moses the man of God.

The function of the altar *to offer burnt offerings thereon* clarifies that this was the altar of burnt offerings, not the golden altar of incense, given how each had been used in both tabernacle and temple. These two altars are distinguished *in the law of Moses* in Exodus 27:1-8; 30:1-10; 37:25-28; 38:1-7; 40:5-6. The Law of Moses gave specifications for the construction and function of the altar (Leviticus 1; see lesson 4; see also Numbers 28:1-6).

C. Sacrifices Offered (vv. 3-5)

3. And they set the altar upon his bases; for fear was upon them because of the people of those countries: and they offered burnt offerings thereon unto the LORD, even burnt offerings morning and evening.

The fact that *the altar* was constructed *upon his bases* reveals reconstruction on the footprint of the one destroyed by King Nebuchadnezzar of Babylon in 586 BC. The rebuilt altar thus became the fixed point around which the rest of the rebuilding work could proceed.

The duration of time required to rebuild the altar is uncertain. Workers might have labored rather quickly because *fear was upon them because of the people of those countries.* We read the actions of those enemies later (Ezra 4:1-5; Nehemiah 4; etc.). At this point, the nature of their threat is not evident. It may have been a threat of a physical nature, designed to intimidate and demoralize the people (compare Nehemiah 6:1-15). Or the threat may have been perceived as spiritual—contact with unholy people making the altar, etc., impure. The text is not specific on this point.

With the altar rebuilt, the priests reestablished the twice-daily sacrifices on behalf of all the people as commanded in Exodus 29:38-46 and Numbers 28:1-8. It also permitted burnt offerings designed to inaugurate worship (see lesson 4).

The Mammoth Hunt

The young hunter was terrified, wanting to flee. But the pressure of his father's hand on his shoulder told him to wait, wait, wait until the command came: *Now!* The two leaped from their hiding place and hurled their spears with banshee screams into the startled herd. The startled mammoths tried to stop, turn around, and step to the side all at once. But to their right, the level terrain just . . . ended. All five tumbled down a 90-foot precipice to their deaths on the rocky shoreline of the river below. The courage of the two hunters meant food for an entire village in the coming winter.

Since prehistoric times, fear has been a normal

How to Say It

Ethanim	*Eth*-uh-nim.
Jeshua	*Jesh*-you-uh.
Jozadak	*Joz*-uh-dak.
Judeans	Joo-*dee*-unz.
Nebuchadnezzar	*Neb*-yuh-kud-*nez*-er.
Shealtiel	She-*al*-tee-el.
Tishri	*Tish*-ree.
Zerubbabel	Zeh-*rub*-uh-bul.

and necessary human emotion. Whether you're a mammoth hunter or a modern mom, fear heightens the senses and prepares the body to fight or flee as necessary.

That same impulse may kick in when God asks people to do hard things. The great heroes of the faith were often fearful when God called them. Think of Abraham, Moses, Jonah, Gideon, and Jeremiah. The essence of faith is not that we don't feel fear. Instead, it's that we don't let that fear overcome our faith.   —A. W.

4. They kept also the feast of tabernacles, as it is written, and offered the daily burnt offerings by number, according to the custom, as the duty of every day required.

The feast of tabernacles was one of the three annual pilgrimage feasts to Jerusalem. Exodus 23:15-17 and 34:18-25 name these three feasts.

At first reading of those passages, it may appear that there are more than three feasts and that the feast of tabernacles is not among them. But there are indeed three considering that (1) the two feasts of unleavened bread and passover were often regarded as a singular observance, as they took place consecutively, and (2) the various feasts go by different names (example: the feast of tabernacles is the same as the feast of ingathering).

The phrase *as it is written* witnesses the concern for rooting practice firmly in the Law of Moses. Given the reality of and reason for the Babylonian exile, it's understandable that this became very important during the postexilic period. All this may lead us to conclude that the reason "the people gathered themselves together as one man to Jerusalem" (Ezra 3:1, above) was for this feast. But that little word *also* should cause us to not be too hasty in this conclusion. Meaning "besides," that word may indicate that a celebration of the feast of tabernacles wasn't the primary purpose of the gathering. Instead, the broader context of being able to resume burnt offerings could have been the main reason. (See commentary on Ezra 3:6, below.) For the nature of *the custom, as the duty of every day required,* see reference to the twice-daily sacrifices noted in 3:3, above.

5. And afterward offered the continual burnt offering, both of the new moons, and of all the set feasts of the LORD that were consecrated, and of every one that willingly offered a freewill offering unto the LORD.

This verse indicates the comprehensive reintroduction of the functions of the altar as established in Numbers 28 and 29. The sacrificial system was fully reinstituted from the earliest possible moment after the Judeans had reestablished themselves.

The contexts of these offerings are summarized in terms of (1) those that are *continual,* (2) those *of the new moons,* (3) *all the set feasts of the Lord,* and (4) those categorized as *freewill.* Having already discussed the first of these, we now briefly examine the second. The ancient Jews used a lunar-solar calendar, with the passage of months determined by the phases of the moon (Isaiah 66:23). A new moon, which is the opposite of a full moon, marked the first day of a new month; the burnt offerings prescribed for this day are outlined in Numbers 28:11-15 (contrast Colossians 2:16). The third summarization includes the full array of feasts listed in the commentary on Ezra 3 to this point. Freewill offerings, the fourth summarization, are burnt offerings connected with vows (Leviticus 22:18, 21, 23; etc.).

The carrying out of the sacrifices also required the reestablishment of animal husbandry and pasture management throughout the area around Jerusalem. This fact, in turn, implies a restoration of the basic mechanisms of ensuring that shepherds were paid, flocks protected, water sources managed, and so on. A return to something approaching normal life had begun.

> **What Do You Think?**
> How do annual celebrations like Christmas or Easter impact your faith?
>
> **Digging Deeper**
> How have you used these celebrations as opportunities to share the gospel message with unbelieving friends and family members?

D. Status Summarized (v. 6)

6a. From the first day of the seventh month began they to offer burnt offerings unto the Lord.

This verse supports the suggestion that the primary reason for the people to have "gathered themselves together as one man to Jerusalem" (Ezra 3:1, above) was not the feast of tabernacles but the feast of trumpets (Leviticus 23:23-25; Numbers 29:1-6). For the significance of *the seventh month,* see commentary on Ezra 3:1, above.

6b. But the foundation of the temple of the Lord was not yet laid.

The rebuilding of the altar allowed the Judeans to restart the prescribed worship of God. However, a gap remained in that *the temple of the Lord* was absent. Its destruction in 586 BC had been complete (2 Kings 25:9). Even its *foundation,* originally *laid* in 966 BC (1 Kings 6:1, 37), would need to be laid anew.

> **What Do You Think?**
> How much preparation does it take for you to do things for God?
>
> **Digging Deeper**
> In what situations would it be better for you to get started on those things even though you feel unprepared?

II. Laying a Foundation
(Ezra 3:10-13)
A. Musical Praise (vv. 10-11)

10. And when the builders laid the foundation of the temple of the Lord, they set the priests in their apparel with trumpets, and the Levites the sons of Asaph with cymbals, to praise the Lord, after the ordinance of David king of Israel.

The laying of *the foundation of the temple of the Lord* took about a year and a half (compare Ezra 3:1 with 3:8). The identity of *the builders* and the source of at least some of the construction material is found in Ezra 3:7-9, which is not part of today's text. The *apparel* for *the priests* undoubtedly included the 100 priestly garments donated in Ezra 2:69.

The *trumpets* mentioned here are not the kind made from a ram's horn (as in Exodus 19:13, 16, 19). Instead, the word being translated for trumpets as used here is the same one that refers to those made from silver in Numbers 10:1-10. *The ordinance of David king of Israel,* for the organization of musicians, is found in 1 Chronicles 6:31-46 (compare 15:19-22). *Levites* as temple musicians are associated with various musical instruments in 2 Chronicles 29:25. By adhering to David's ordinance, the broader aim was not to discard the positive aspects of Judah's past but to renew them.

11. And they sang together by course in praising and giving thanks unto the Lord; because he is good, for his mercy endureth for ever toward Israel. And all the people shouted with a great shout, when they praised the Lord, because the foundation of the house of the Lord was laid.

Here, we see another renewed connection with the past as the musicians sing of God's *mercy* and enduring goodness. These lyrics go back to King David, centuries earlier (1 Chronicles 16:34, 41; compare Psalms 107:1; 136:1).

B. Mixed Reactions (vv. 12-13)

12. But many of the priests and Levites and chief of the fathers, who were ancient men, that had seen the first house, when the foundation of this house was laid before their eyes, wept with a loud voice; and many shouted aloud for joy.

The temple had been destroyed in 586 BC, and the year was about 536 BC as the singing continued. Thus, it had been just about 50 years in between. Those who had been 20 years old when they witnessed the destruction of Solomon's magnificent temple had become *ancient men* of age 70. The fact that they *wept* bitterly is quite understandable. They had to have been thinking of the sins of their generation that resulted in the destruction of that *first house* (Haggai 2:3).

By contrast, those who *shouted aloud for joy* were undoubtedly young enough never to have seen Solomon's temple. The excitement of this accomplishment was to them unprecedented and thrilling.

The computation of the 50-year interval mentioned above doesn't conflict with the prophecy of 70 years of oppression in Jeremiah 25:11-12; 29:10. The oppression of exile occurred in the three waves of 605, 597, and 586 BC. Similarly, the return from exile occurred in three waves: 538, 458, and 444 BC. Thus, the computation of 70 years depends on selecting which starting and ending points apply (compare time identifiers in 2 Kings 24–25; 2 Chronicles 36:11-21; Ezekiel 1:1; Daniel 1:1-2).

How to Waste 50 Years—or Not

A new patient had been admitted for treatment, so the hospital chaplain dropped by his room to introduce himself and check on the patient's needs. The new patient was out for a medical procedure, but his wife was there. On seeing the chaplain enter, she said almost immediately, "My husband thinks he wasted 50 years of his life because he didn't become a Christian until age 50."

After the two had chatted for a few minutes, the husband returned. On seeing the chaplain, he immediately exclaimed, "Chaplain, I wasted 50 years of my life!" His joy at being a Christian seemed to be overshadowed by the regret of those pre-Christian years.

That happened in the late 1980s, and I was that hospital chaplain. I remember not disagreeing with him. But I assured him it was better to waste 50 years than to waste an eternity. How will you spend the years ahead?   —R. L. N.

13. So that the people could not discern the noise of the shout of joy from the noise of the weeping of the people: for the people shouted with a loud shout, and the noise was heard afar off.

As time progressed beyond this high emotion, it's easy to imagine excitement becoming disappointment and disillusionment. That's because the next 20 years turned out to be a tug-of-war between outsiders on whether or not the work on the temple should continue (Ezra 4:1–6:12). Opposition to construction was eventually defeated. Still, the intervening years resulted in lethargy on the part of the Judeans. The Lord himself had to intervene to get the project back on track (Haggai 1:1–2:9). The result was that the temple remained unfinished for two decades, not being completed until 516 BC (Ezra 6:15).

> **What Do You Think?**
> What is an occasion of your life that was so emotionally powerful it brought out tears of joy?
>
> **Digging Deeper**
> What is a situation where you were sad or grieving but had hope because of your confidence in God?

Conclusion

A. Work as a Response to Grace

Today's Scripture text points not only to human endeavor but also to God's mercy. His mercy makes our every endeavor possible and allows results. The story also signals God's actions, to which humans respond. God had brought the Judeans home in something of a "second exodus," allowing them to rebuild their world. The key question at that point was: *Would their world also be His world?* That question rings across the centuries to confront us today: *Is your world His world?*

> **What Do You Think?**
> What is your most surprising takeaway from studying this Scripture text?
>
> **Digging Deeper**
> How can that insight be applied in your life this week?

B. Prayer

Father, help us to remember that there is always a bigger picture. We lose sight of that bigger picture when we shift our focus to life's obstacles. May we never be guilty of such a shift nor of being the obstacles themselves. We pray in Jesus' name. Amen.

C. Thought to Remember

Praise God for His enduring mercy!

Involvement Learning

Enhance your lesson with KJV Bible Student *(from your curriculum supplier) and the reproducible activity page (at www.standardlesson.com or in the back of the* KJV Standard Lesson Commentary Deluxe Edition*).*

Into the Lesson

Announce a numbers puzzle as you write the following on the board:

444 / 458 / 538 / 586 / 597 / ???

Challenge learners to predict what the unknown three numerals are as they relate to the five sets of three numerals prior. Give no clues or clarifications, with one optional exception: have various dates written down on slips of paper in plain view.

Expect some class members to attempt a mathematical solution while others sit simply mystified. After everyone gives up, announce that the numbers are important biblical years BC, listed in reverse chronological order. The missing numerals are 605. Use the commentary on Ezra 3:12 to explain briefly what happened in each year.

Alternative. Place in chairs before class begins copies of the "Fight, Flight, or Freeze?" exercise from the activity page, which you can download. Encourage learners to begin checking boxes shortly after arrival.

After either activity, say, "Let's see how God blessed a decision to rebuild despite adverse circumstances."

Into the Word

Distribute 10 index cards on which you have printed the 10 verses of Ezra 3:1-6, 10-13, one verse per card, one card per learner. Do not put verse numbers on the cards! Give a learner an additional card if you have fewer than 10 participants. Have them read their verses aloud in a random order, then rearrange them to be in the correct order. Show the transformation from random order to correct order in a visual way most appropriate to the nature of your class (some possibilities include rearranging cards on a table or rearranging participants themselves as they stand holding their cards).

Follow by asking everyone to turn cards over to their blank sides and write what they think is the main point of the passage. Announce that they are to work alone on this, with a time limit of one minute. Say that you will collect the cards to read to the class, so learners should not put their names on them—the readings will be anonymous.

Collect finished cards. Make a list on the board of the main points proposed on the cards. Do not allow discussion until all main points are listed. Indicate duplicate main points by tally marks. Invite discussion when you've completed the list.

Consider in advance what method of discussion would best suit the nature of your class. Here are three methods (but not the only three): (1) small-group discussion, (2) nobody gets to speak twice until everyone has spoken once, and (3) point and counterpoint. Resist the temptation to "take a vote" in order not to give the impression that the intent of a Scripture passage is determined by readers who are in the majority. Use the commentary and Lesson Context to correct misconceptions. Explore the possibility that there may be more than one main point in the passage.

Into Life

Form participants into study pairs. Distribute to each a handout (you prepare) on which are printed these questions for personal discussion:

1–How can you apply to your life the lessons learned from today's text?
2–What obstacles seem to delay or prevent you from doing so right now?

Option. If you used the "Fight, Flight, or Freeze?" exercise earlier, draw learners' attention to the four entries: Ouija board, idolatry, sexual immorality, and witchcraft. Discuss in light of 1 Corinthians 6:18; 10:14; Colossians 3:5; and other relevant texts.

Close by having learners write a prayer identifying an area where fear must be overcome so that godly service is not hindered.

A Covenant Renewal

Devotional Reading: Jeremiah 31:27-34
Background Scripture: Nehemiah 8:1–10:39

Nehemiah 10:28-39

28 And the rest of the people, the priests, the Levites, the porters, the singers, the Nethinims, and all they that had separated themselves from the people of the lands unto the law of God, their wives, their sons, and their daughters, every one having knowledge, and having understanding;

29 They clave to their brethren, their nobles, and entered into a curse, and into an oath, to walk in God's law, which was given by Moses the servant of God, and to observe and do all the commandments of the LORD our Lord, and his judgments and his statutes;

30 And that we would not give our daughters unto the people of the land, nor take their daughters for our sons:

31 And if the people of the land bring ware or any victuals on the sabbath day to sell, that we would not buy it of them on the sabbath, or on the holy day: and that we would leave the seventh year, and the exaction of every debt.

32 Also we made ordinances for us, to charge ourselves yearly with the third part of a shekel for the service of the house of our God;

33 For the shewbread, and for the continual meat offering, and for the continual burnt offering, of the sabbaths, of the new moons, for the set feasts, and for the holy things, and for the sin offerings to make an atonement for Israel, and for all the work of the house of our God.

34 And we cast the lots among the priests, the Levites, and the people, for the wood offering, to bring it into the house of our God, after the houses of our fathers, at times appointed year by year, to burn upon the altar of the LORD our God, as it is written in the law:

35 And to bring the firstfruits of our ground, and the firstfruits of all fruit of all trees, year by year, unto the house of the LORD:

36 Also the firstborn of our sons, and of our cattle, as it is written in the law, and the firstlings of our herds and of our flocks, to bring to the house of our God, unto the priests that minister in the house of our God:

37 And that we should bring the firstfruits of our dough, and our offerings, and the fruit of all manner of trees, of wine and of oil, unto the priests, to the chambers of the house of our God; and the tithes of our ground unto the Levites, that the same Levites might have the tithes in all the cities of our tillage.

38 And the priest the son of Aaron shall be with the Levites, when the Levites take tithes: and the Levites shall bring up the tithe of the tithes unto the house of our God, to the chambers, into the treasure house.

39 For the children of Israel and the children of Levi shall bring the offering of the corn, of the new wine, and the oil, unto the chambers, where are the vessels of the sanctuary, and the priests that minister, and the porters, and the singers: and we will not forsake the house of our God.

Key Text

We will not forsake the house of our God. —**Nehemiah 10:39b**

Costly
Sacrifices

Unit 3: Special Offerings and the Sanctuary
Lessons 10–13

Lesson Aims

After participating in this lesson, each learner will be able to:

1. List the promises the people made.

2. Explain the historical background for the promises the people made and what hope was implied in those promises.

3. Recruit a partner for mutual accountability on two spiritually important actions: one to start doing and one to stop doing.

Lesson Outline

Introduction

  A. Identity in Uncertain Times

  B. Lesson Context

I. People's Commitment (Nehemiah 10:28-29)

  A. Various Identifiers (v. 28)

    Still Relevant!

  B. Singular Voice (v. 29)

    Pulling Whose Hair?

II. Law's Restatement (Nehemiah 10:30-39)

  A. Rejecting Intermarriage (v. 30)

  B. Keeping the Sabbath (v. 31)

  C. Supporting the Temple (vv. 32-37)

  D. Tasking for Levites (vv. 38-39)

Conclusion

  A. Practical Spiritual Life

  B. Prayer

  C. Thought to Remember

Introduction

A. Identity in Uncertain Times

One of the great challenges of our time is maintaining our identity as Christians. This is important for reasons listed in Matthew 5:13-16; John 13:35; 2 Corinthians 8:21; etc. The apostle Paul stressed a personal goal to be "made all things to all men, that I might by all means save some" (1 Corinthians 9:22). But he knew there were lines he could not cross lest his identity as a Christian be compromised. The enduring challenge is ensuring we do not allow surrounding culture to draw those lines. The Judeans of the mid-fifth century BC faced a similar challenge.

B. Lesson Context

The year was about 444 BC, and the Judeans, led by Nehemiah, formed a tiny part of the vast Persian Empire. Nehemiah held a high post in that empire as the king's cupbearer (Nehemiah 1:11). Most of the empire's subjects worshiped numerous fictitious gods. Therefore, the Judeans had to draw firm lines between themselves and their neighbors in order to maintain their distinctive identity as the consecrated people of the one true God. A failure to do so was what had led to the Babylonian exile in the first place (13:17-18). The stakes couldn't be higher!

The book of Nehemiah as a whole recounts the story of a later generation of Judeans having returned to Jerusalem and Judah in the third of three waves to do so. As such, the Lesson Context from last week's lesson also applies here. In particular, the original purpose of Nehemiah's trip to Jerusalem was to rebuild the city's walls (Nehemiah 1–4; 6:1-15). That was nearly 100 years after the first wave of exiles had returned!

Nehemiah, working with Ezra—a scribe of the law (Ezra 7:6; Nehemiah 8)—understood that while physically protecting the city was vital, maintaining the spiritual defenses of the people was even more critical. Nehemiah 8 records a time of concentrated teaching from God's law followed in chapter 9 by confession of sin.

This recommitment to God involved two general categories: commitments to *stop* doing certain things and commitments to *start* or *continue* doing other things.

I. People's Commitment
(Nehemiah 10:28-29)
A. Various Identifiers (v. 28)

28a. And the rest of the people, the priests, the Levites, the porters, the singers, the Nethinims.

The identifiers here are sometimes distinctive, sometimes overlapping. *The Levites,* those descended from the tribe of Levi (Genesis 35:23), were solely in charge of the items and duties associated with the tabernacle and temple. However, they were not included in a census of Israelites and did not receive an inheritance of land (Numbers 1:47-53; 18:1-7, 20). All *priests* were Levites, but not all Levites were priests. The word translated *porters* is also translated "doorkeepers" in 1 Chronicles 15:24, and that is the sense here; it was one of the specific jobs of certain Levites (26:1-19). The word *singers* includes those skilled in vocal music, instrumental music, or both. These same four identifiers are repeated in Ezra 2:70; 7:7; Nehemiah 7:73; 10:39; 13:5.

The word *Nethinims* is a transliteration (not a translation); that's where a word in one language is brought over into another language simply by swapping the original-language letters of the word into the letters that sound the same in the other language. The Nethinims first make their appearance, in postexilic times, in 1 Chronicles 9:2. They were part of a group that numbered 392 who returned during the first wave from exile (Ezra 2:58). The clue to their function as temple servants is found in Ezra 8:20. That text also gives us a precise numbering of those who returned in the second wave of 458 BC: "Also of the Nethinims, whom David and the princes had appointed for the service of the Levites, two hundred and twenty."

In short, the entire workforce of the temple appears on this list! The priests carried out the sacrifices, the Levites cleaned up and made sure things ran properly, the gatekeepers provided security and ensured proper traffic flow (1 Chronicles 4:26-30), and the singers set the psalms to music.

28b. And all they that had separated themselves from the people of the lands unto the law of God, their wives, their sons, and their daughters, every one having knowledge, and having understanding.

Separation *from the people of the lands unto the law of God* is a key theme in this book (Nehemiah 9:2; 13:3). Everyone old enough to understand was to toe the line on this requirement (compare 8:2).

> **What Do You Think?**
> How do you know when it's time to separate yourself from someone else?
> **Digging Deeper**
> What are some types of "separation distance"?

Still Relevant!

Ashley had been born in Indiana, raised as a Christian, and attended Bible college in Tennessee. So, how and why did she convert to Islam? Well, one day, she met a polite and handsome Egyptian university student in a coffee shop. As she got closer to him, she got further from Jesus until finally she made her choice. She converted and got married in a traditional Islamic ceremony. And Jesus? To her, Jesus is now just a good example to follow. She doesn't consider Him to be her Savior.

People change faiths for various reasons, but none is more common than romance. The Bible remains very relevant in this regard. Prohibition regarding intermarriage between believers and unbelievers finds its greatest expression in the New Testament in 2 Corinthians 6:14. In his letter to the church in Ephesus, the apostle Paul compared the love a husband was to have for his wife with the love Christ has for His bride, the church (Ephesians 5:25-27). Still, within a generation, the church at Ephesus had lost its first love (Revelation 2:4). What guardrails can you erect to ensure that no other suitor, spiritual or physical, tempts you away from Christ?   —A. W.

B. Singular Voice (v. 29)
29. They clave to their brethren, their nobles,

and entered into a curse, and into an oath, to walk in God's law, which was given by Moses the servant of God, and to observe and do all the commandments of the LORD our Lord, and his judgments and his statutes.

People of all occupations and demographics swore *an oath* to commit themselves to following the Law of *Moses*. That law, given about 1,000 years prior to the writing of this verse, specified the *curse* for disobedience (Deuteronomy 27:15-68; compare Daniel 9:11). The people seem to have been binding themselves to suffering the punishments listed therein should they disobey. The Law of Moses seems to have been ignored and violated more times than it had been honored over the 10 centuries since its giving.

It may be tempting to put the three words *commandments, judgment,* and *statutes* under individual microscopes to detect different shades of meaning. But that would be to miss the forest for the trees. The idea, rather, seems to be to leave no requirement out. The three words in the original language are found together in nine other places: Deuteronomy 5:31; 6:1; 7:11; 26:17; 1 Kings 8:58; 2 Kings 17:37; 2 Chronicles 19:10; Nehemiah 1:7; 9:13.

Pulling Whose Hair?

Leaders come in all shapes, sizes, styles, and goals. That last one is often troubling since not all leaders have good intentions. Some leaders may be interested only in personal wealth or aggrandizement (example: Daniel 4:29-30). Others may lead people down a wrong path (example: Ezra 9:2). In both cases, the situation may require a right-thinking leader to confront the bad leader.

Such was the case with the two men known as Ezra and Nehemiah. They were contempo-

How to Say It

Deuteronomy	Due-ter-*ahn*-uh-me.
Levites	*Lee*-vites.
Leviticus	Leh-*vit*-ih-kus.
Nehemiah	Nee-huh-*my*-uh.
Nethinims	*Neth*-ih-nimz.
Sabbath	*Sab*-uhth.
victuals	*vih*-tulz.

raries and worked together. But they had different leadership styles. When confronting the sin of intermarriage due to unholy leadership, Ezra led by exhibiting extreme expressions of grief, including pulling out his hair (Ezra 9:1-3). But Nehemiah's style was more direct as he pulled out other people's hair (Nehemiah 13:25).

Those aren't the only two ways to take the lead in confronting sin. What's yours?   —R. L. N.

II. Law's Restatement
(Nehemiah 10:30-39)
A. Rejecting Intermarriage (v. 30)

30. And that we would not give our daughters unto the people of the land, nor take their daughters for our sons.

The danger of intermarriage is specified in Exodus 34:16 and Deuteronomy 7:3-4. The threat was that of resulting idolatry. When the Lord tested the Israelites in this regard, they failed (Judges 3:1-6). And this is where King Solomon erred and suffered accordingly (1 Kings 11:1-13). This prohibition helped to mark the boundary between God's holy people and the pagan gods' unholy peoples.

One might think that such marriages might allow for the conversion of the pagan spouse to Judaism. The book of Ruth offers an example of this happening. But that seems to have been the very rare exception.

Ezra, the teacher of the law, had arrived in Jerusalem in 458 BC (Ezra 7:8). Intermarriage and the resulting idolatry seems to have been the most significant problem he noticed. The entirety of Ezra 9 addresses the problem itself; the entirety of Ezra 10 records the confession of this sin and the names of the guilty. Nehemiah confronted the same problem about 25 years later (Nehemiah 13:6, 23-27).

B. Keeping the Sabbath (v. 31)

31a. And if the people of the land bring ware or any victuals on the sabbath day to sell, that we would not buy it of them on the sabbath, or on the holy day.

The longest of the Ten Commandments is the fourth, which concerns keeping *the sabbath day*. The Israelites had been warned about failing to honor that day as God had prescribed (Jeremiah 17:19-27). Their failure in that regard was a factor in their exile (Nehemiah 13:16-18). The pagan *people of the land* cared nothing for the Sabbath. Conducting commerce with them showed that God's covenant people cared nothing for it either.

As the text moves from the Sabbath to *the holy day*, the movement is from specific to general. Any day the Lord declares holy is such. The most frequent of these is the day of the new moon (last week's lesson on Ezra 3:5; also Numbers 10:10; Psalm 81:3; Amos 8:5).

To decline to engage in commerce on the Sabbath required some advance planning and even temporary hardship. However, it also resulted in a day of rest (Exodus 31:15). If God himself decided that it was good for Him to rest one day out of seven, who are we to think otherwise?

31b. And that we would leave the seventh year, and the exaction of every debt.

The weekly Sabbath had a counterpart in the Sabbath of *the seventh year*. That was a time when *every debt* owed to a fellow Israelite was to be canceled (Deuteronomy 15:1-3).

The sabbatical seventh year was also the year to leave the fields unsown and unplowed. Whatever the land produced on its own that year would be sufficient for both poor and not-so-poor alike (Exodus 23:10-11; Leviticus 25:1-7). Those Hebrews who were working as indentured servants for their fellow Israelites were to be set free in their seventh year (Exodus 21:2; Deuteronomy 15:12). With the passage of seven cycles of seven years came the Year of Jubilee in the fiftieth year, with special rules applying (Leviticus 25:8-55).

The practice of periodically eliminating personal debts was known elsewhere in the ancient Near East. It was seen as a way of ensuring that grave inequalities among people did not worsen with time. Since their world had no banks, loans usually came from neighbors or the temple. These loans were designed to help the borrower survive. The forgiveness of debt was, therefore, a deeply personal act and a way of addressing social imbalance among neighbors.

Visual for Lesson 13. *Display this visual as you discuss ways that the class could demonstrate its commitment to God in light of today's text.*

C. Supporting the Temple (vv. 32-37)

32. Also we made ordinances for us, to charge ourselves yearly with the third part of a shekel for the service of the house of our God.

This verse begins a list of obligations the people agree to for temple upkeep and ongoing operations. The first item is the annual temple tax. *A shekel* was a silver coin weighing about three-eighths of an ounce. At a modern exchange rate of, say, twenty-five dollars per ounce of silver, *the third part* of a shekel would equate to no more than five dollars. But, the changing levels of supply and demand for silver, like other precious metals, fluctuate through time (1 Kings 10:21). Thus, a comparison with modern exchange rates, while interesting, may be misleading. A better approach is to investigate what could actually be purchased with a shekel, although this too will fluctuate (compare 2 Kings 6:24-25; 7:1). Placed on a timeline, the concept and implementation of the temple tax can be traced back to Exodus 30:11-16 and forward to Matthew 17:24-27.

What Do You Think?
How much emphasis, if any, should the church place on planned financial giving?
Digging Deeper
What advantages and disadvantages are there to "faith promise" giving? "Fifth Sunday" offerings? Automatically recurring online giving?

33. For the shewbread, and for the continual meat offering, and for the continual burnt offering, of the sabbaths, of the new moons, for the set feasts, and for the holy things, and for the sin offerings to make an atonement for Israel, and for all the work of the house of our God.

This verse itemizes expenses incurred for the functioning of the temple. To modern eyes, this may all seem to be a lot of repetition. But we need to keep a chronological framework in mind. By Nehemiah's day, the second temple had been completed about 70 years prior, in 516 BC. Thus, at least one generation had passed off the scene, and those who followed needed instruction. Therefore, these reminders:

shewbread:	Leviticus 24:6
continual offerings:	Leviticus 1–2; Numbers 28:1-8
sabbaths:	Numbers 28:9-10; Deuteronomy 5:12-15
new moons:	Numbers 10:10; 28:11-15
set feasts:	Leviticus 23; Numbers 28:16–29:40
sin offerings:	Leviticus 4:1–5:13

What Do You Think?

Were you to propose a monthly celebration for your congregation, what would it be?

Digging Deeper

How would you monitor that celebration's impact on the congregation's health?

34. And we cast the lots among the priests, the Levites, and the people, for the wood offering, to bring it into the house of our God, after the houses of our fathers, at times appointed year by year, to burn upon the altar of the LORD our God, as it is written in the law.

Leviticus 6:12-13 specifies that the fire on *the altar* at the Lord's sanctuary must never go out. That requirement demanded a lot of *wood*. The payment in wood, therefore, became a shared responsibility. With no objective means for assigning this rotating task, the selection method is to *cast the lots*. This method of leaving the choice up to the Lord is seen also in the choosing of the scapegoat (Leviticus 16:8), allocation of land (Joshua 18:6-10), division of duties (1 Chronicles 25:8; 26:13), and identify-

ing an individual (1 Samuel 14:38-42; Jonah 1:7; Luke 1:8-10; Acts 1:26).

What Do You Think?

In what circumstances, if any, would you propose casting lots to make a church-related decision?

Digging Deeper

What are some dangers in this practice?

35. And to bring the firstfruits of our ground, and the firstfruits of all fruit of all trees, year by year, unto the house of the LORD.

The foundation of the offering of *the firstfruits* is found in Exodus 13:1; 22:29; 25:19; and Numbers 17:12-13. The idea is that when a harvest starts, the very first of that harvest goes to God for temple support. Giving the first of the harvest demonstrated trust in God that the rest of the harvest would sustain life. The Israelites even had a specific harvest celebration called Day of Firstfruits; it is the same as the feast of weeks, the feast of harvest, and Pentecost (Exodus 34:22; Numbers 28:25; Deuteronomy 16:9-10, 16). In the New Testament, the concept is reversed: God gives us the firstfruits of His Spirit (Romans 8:23).

36. Also the firstborn of our sons, and of our cattle, as it is written in the law, and the firstlings of our herds and of our flocks, to bring to the house of our God, unto the priests that minister in the house of our God.

The firstfruits principle applied to the firstborn male of children and livestock as well (Exodus 13:1-2, 12-13, 15; 22:29). This concept seems alien to modern readers, but it speaks to the life of gratitude that biblical law wishes to cultivate.

The reason the firstborn are to be brought *to the house of our God* is for a redemption ritual as specified in Exodus 13:1-16; 34:19-20; Numbers 18:15-17).

37a. And that we should bring the firstfruits of our dough, and our offerings, and the fruit of all manner of trees, of wine and of oil, unto the priests, to the chambers of the house of our God.

This half-verse offers a sweeping summary of all *firstfruits* expectations specified so far.

37b. And the tithes of our ground unto the Levites, that the same Levites might have the tithes in all the cities of our tillage.

Now we come to something new: *tithes,* which have not been mentioned in the book of Nehemiah until this point. But what's new in Nehemiah is well rehearsed in the Law of Moses. *The Levites* were to be wholly devoted to the functioning of the temple. As such, they weren't to be growing crops like everyone else (ideally, that is; contrast Nehemiah 13:10). The giving over of the tithes (one-tenth) of crops, etc., to the landless Levites allowed them to focus full time on their work in the temple (Numbers 18:24; Deuteronomy 18:1-2). Tithes also provided sustenance for the fatherless and widows (Deuteronomy 14:27-29; 26:12-15).

D. Tasking for Levites (vv. 38-39)

38. And the priest the son of Aaron shall be with the Levites, when the Levites take tithes: and the Levites shall bring up the tithe of the tithes unto the house of our God, to the chambers, into the treasure house.

When Ezra led the second wave of returnees from exile in 458 BC, he took great care to ensure proper handling of funds (Ezra 8:24-34). The same seems to be evident here.

The direction concerning *the tithe of the tithes* shows how meticulous Nehemiah was in obeying the Law of Moses. The concept is founded on the command in Numbers 18:26. Just as the people, in general, were expected to tithe to support the Levites' service in the tabernacle and temple, so also the Levites themselves were expected to tithe from the tithes they had received.

39. For the children of Israel and the children of Levi shall bring the offering of the corn, of the new wine, and the oil, unto the chambers, where are the vessels of the sanctu- ary, **and the priests that minister, and the porters, and the singers: and we will not forsake the house of our God.**

The words translated *corn, wine,* and *oil* occur together frequently in the Old Testament in various contexts of blessing (example: Deuteronomy 7:13) and woe (example: 28:51). Since these commodities would tend to arrive in large batches at harvest time, appropriate storage rooms (*the chambers*) were needed. The rebuilt temple indeed had such rooms (Ezra 8:29). The task of their oversight was the responsibility of four Levites in particular (1 Chronicles 9:26). These rooms were abused later in Nehemiah's absence (Nehemiah 13:6-13).

Conclusion

A. Practical Spiritual Life

It has been said that there are two great days in a person's life: the day we're born, and the day we discover why. This story concerns a religious community's discovery of why it existed. Its goal was not merely to survive, or live a rich material life. Rather, the Israelites lived in order to grow closer to God and show others how that could happen. Nehemiah's community made practical commitments that allowed them to do that.

Pitting religious teaching and practical actions against each other is both easy and popular. In fact, they go together. We do good things because we value the right things, and doing good actions reshapes our values and ideas. Nehemiah's community understood this as they sought to follow the law of Moses. Their actions followed God's desires for human well-being.

B. Prayer

O God, our Creator and Sustainer, shape our commitments toward Your aims for our world. Grant us the rest that comes from trust in Your promises, the work that leads to a deeper love of our neighbors, and the confidence that You will be with us at all times. In Jesus' name. Amen.

C. Thought to Remember

Commitments translate into action;
action translates into character.

Involvement Learning

Enhance your lesson with KJV Bible Student *(from your curriculum supplier) and the reproducible activity page (at www.standardlesson.com or in the back of the* KJV Standard Lesson Commentary Deluxe Edition*).*

Into the Lesson

Divide the class in half, naming the two halves the "Thou Shalts" and the "Thou Shalt Nots." Have the groups take turns voicing Old Testament laws according to their group designation, Bibles closed. Summarize responses on the board for all to see. Continue until there have been 20 total responses or one group cannot offer further responses.

Make a transition by pointing to your list and saying, "As we work through today's text regarding covenant renewal, notice which of these 'thou shalts' and 'thou shalt nots' were apparently violated. Also, be on the alert for ones that we've missed."

Into the Word

Before the reading of Nehemiah 10:28-39, challenge learners to be alert for three sins in particular that needed to be addressed for covenant renewal. Have two volunteers take turns reading the text aloud. As the reading concludes, ask what those three sins were. (*expected responses: intermarriage, failure to keep the Sabbath, and failure to support the temple*)

Form the class into at least three sets of study pairs or triads. Give each grouping one of three handouts (you create) on which you have printed the following:

Intermarriage Study Team

1–Was the sin of intermarriage defined in terms of differing religious beliefs, differing cultures, both, or something else?
2–What dangers did intermarriage present?
3–In what ways is intermarriage addressed under the new covenant in Christ, considering 1 Corinthians 7:39 and 2 Corinthians 6:14?

Sabbath-Keeping Study Team

1–What were the people substituting for a day of Sabbath rest?
2–If the people wanted to do something on the Sabbath other than rest, what's wrong with that?

3–Why is Sabbath-keeping not part of the requirements under the new covenant in Christ, but the other nine of the Ten Commandments are? (*Expected answer: the other nine are grounded in the* **nature** *of God, which never changes. By contrast, the Sabbath commandment is based on the* **work** *of God under the old covenant; His work under the new covenant shifts attention to the first day of the week per John 20:1; Acts 20:7; 1 Corinthians 16:2; Revelation 1:10.*)

Temple-Upkeep Team

1–What areas of temple support seem to have been neglected?
2–What seems to have been the reason(s) for the neglect?
3–In what ways does this problem speak to how we are to maintain our bodies as temples, per 1 Corinthians 3:16-17 and 2 Corinthians 6:16?

Option 1. Leave off the third question of each handout so you can pose them—either audibly during whole-class discussion or on separate handouts—in the Into Life section.

Option 2. Make a transition by distributing copies of the "Pick One" exercise from the reproducible page, which you can download. Have learners work in pairs to complete as indicated.

Into Life

Wrap up by drawing participants' attention to the opening "Thou Shalt" and "Thou Shalt Nots" exercise. Have them write on an index card one "thou shalt" that they personally need to start doing. Below that, have them write one "thou shalt not" that they personally need to stop doing.

Assure learners that you will not collect the cards; encourage them to post the cards where they can be seen daily in the week ahead. Explore the possibility of recruiting a partner for mutual accountability.

Alternative. Precede the above by distributing copies of the "Mutual Accountability" exercise from the activity page, to be completed as indicated in study pairs or triads.

Sacred Altars and
Holy Offerings

Special Features

Note: Special Features are minimized this quarter due to 14 lessons instead of the usual 13. Some lessons are shorter than normal for the same reason.

Lessons
Unit 1: The Genesis of Altars and Sacrifices

Unit 2: Jesus and the Temple

Unit 3: Christians and Sacrifice

QUARTERLY QUIZ

Use these questions as a pretest or as a review. The answers are on page iv of This Quarter in the Word.

Lesson 1
1. Abel was "a tiller of the ground," while Cain was a "keeper of sheep." T/F. *Genesis 4:2*
2. Cain went out from the presence of the Lord and lived in the land of _____. *Genesis 4:16*

Lesson 2
1. Noah built an altar to the Lord after disembarking from the ark. T/F. *Genesis 8:18-20*
2. A "bow in the cloud" is the sign of the covenant between God and the _____. *Genesis 9:13*

Lesson 3
1. God directed Abraham to take Isaac to which land? (Moab, Megiddo, Moriah) *Genesis 22:2*
2. Isaac carried the wood for the burnt offering. T/F. *Genesis 22:6*

Lesson 4
1. The Lord said to Isaac, "I am the God of _____ thy father." *Genesis 26:24*
2. "Shebah" was the name Isaac gave to the location where water was found. T/F. *Genesis 26:32-33*

Lesson 5
1. Jacob left Beersheba and traveled toward which location? (Haran, Hebron, Helam) *Genesis 28:10*
2. Which name did Jacob give the pillar's location? (Bethany, Bethel, Bethsaida) *Genesis 28:18-19*

Lesson 6
1. Jesus' parents traveled to Jerusalem every year for Passover. T/F. *Luke 2:41*
2. Jesus' parents understood what He told them regarding His "Father's business." T/F. *Luke 2:49-50*

Lesson 7
1. Who questioned the lawfulness of the disciples' behavior on the Sabbath? (Sadducees, Pharisees, Zealots) *Matthew 12:2*
2. The "Son of man is _____ even of the Sabbath day." *Matthew 12:8*

Lesson 8
1. How many years did the Jews say it took to build the Jerusalem temple? (6; 40; 46)? *John 2:20*
2. The "temple" Jesus spoke of was His body. T/F. *John 2:21*

Lesson 9
1. Jesus warned that many would come, saying, "I am _____." *Matthew 24:5*
2. Before the end, the "gospel of the _____" will be preached in the whole world. *Matthew 24:14*

Lesson 10
1. According to the apostle Paul, believers are "the _____ of God." *1 Corinthians 3:16*
2. Paul says that God considers "the wisdom of this world" to be which? (failure, foolishness, futile) *1 Corinthians 3:19*

Lesson 11
1. The human body is not meant for fornication, but for the Lord. T/F. *1 Corinthians 6:13*
2. Believers are "bought with a _____." *1 Corinthians 6:20*

Lesson 12
1. Christ is "our _____." *Ephesians 2:14*
2. Who is the foundation of the household of God? (choose two: disciples, apostles, priests, prophets) *Ephesians 2:19-20*

Lesson 13
1. It is good for the heart to be "established with" which? (grace, hope, love) *Hebrews 13:9*
2. The Lord Jesus is "that great shepherd of the sheep." T/F. *Hebrews 13:20*

Lesson 14
1. Believers are described as being "lively _____." *1 Peter 2:5*
2. Which does Peter say "war against the soul"? (lusts, malice, hypocrisies) *1 Peter 2:11*

This Quarter in the Word

Answers to the Quarterly Quiz on page 338

Lesson 1—1. False. 2. Nod. **Lesson 2**—1. True. 2. earth. **Lesson 3**—1. Moriah. 2. True. **Lesson 4**—1. Abraham. 2. True. **Lesson 5**—1. Haran. 2. Bethel. **Lesson 6**—1. True. 2. False. **Lesson 7**—1. Pharisees. 2. Lord. **Lesson 8**—1. 46. 2. True. **Lesson 9**—1. Christ. 2. kingdom. **Lesson 10**—1. temple. 2. foolishness. **Lesson 11**—1. True. 2. price. **Lesson 12**—1. peace. 2. apostles, prophets. **Lesson 13**—1. grace. 2. True. **Lesson 14**—1. stones. 2. lusts.

The Offerings of Cain and Abel

Devotional Reading: Luke 20:45–21:4
Background Scripture: Genesis 4:1-25

Genesis 4:1-16

1 And Adam knew Eve his wife; and she conceived, and bare Cain, and said, I have gotten a man from the LORD.

2 And she again bare his brother Abel. And Abel was a keeper of sheep, but Cain was a tiller of the ground.

3 And in process of time it came to pass, that Cain brought of the fruit of the ground an offering unto the LORD.

4 And Abel, he also brought of the firstlings of his flock and of the fat thereof. And the LORD had respect unto Abel and to his offering:

5 But unto Cain and to his offering he had not respect. And Cain was very wroth, and his countenance fell.

6 And the LORD said unto Cain, why art thou wroth? and why is thy countenance fallen?

7 If thou doest well, shalt thou not be accepted? and if thou doest not well, sin lieth at the door. And unto thee shall be his desire, and thou shalt rule over him.

8 And Cain talked with Abel his brother: and it came to pass, when they were in the field, that Cain rose up against Abel his brother, and slew him.

9 And the LORD said unto Cain, where is Abel thy brother? And he said, I know not: Am I my brother's keeper?

10 And he said, what hast thou done? the voice of thy brother's blood crieth unto me from the ground.

11 And now art thou cursed from the earth, which hath opened her mouth to receive thy brother's blood from thy hand;

12 When thou tillest the ground, it shall not henceforth yield unto thee her strength; a fugitive and a vagabond shalt thou be in the earth.

13 And Cain said unto the LORD, my punishment is greater than I can bear.

14 Behold, thou hast driven me out this day from the face of the earth; and from thy face shall I be hid; and I shall be a fugitive and a vagabond in the earth; and it shall come to pass, that every one that findeth me shall slay me.

15 And the LORD said unto him, therefore whosoever slayeth Cain, vengeance shall be taken on him sevenfold. And the LORD set a mark upon Cain, lest any finding him should kill him.

16 And Cain went out from the presence of the LORD, and dwelt in the land of Nod, on the east of Eden.

Key Text

The LORD said unto Cain, Why art thou wroth? and why is thy countenance fallen? If thou doest well, shalt thou not be accepted? —**Genesis 4:6-7a**

Sacred Altars and
Holy Offerings

Unit 1: The Genesis of Altars and Sacrifices

Lessons 1–5

Lesson Aims

After participating in this lesson, each learner will be able to:

1. Compare and contrast the offerings of Cain and Abel.

2. Define what doing right required of Cain and Abel.

3. Commit to a practice of "doing right" through his or her giving.

Lesson Outline

Introduction

A. Limited Resources

For over 30 years, my wife has worked as an editor of children's Sunday school curriculum. She has always had a passion for teaching children about the Bible, so this job has been an ideal position for her. Her duties include editing lessons, selecting worship songs and choruses for children to learn, deciding which teaching pictures should accompany each lesson, and providing a variety of other helps for the teacher. And she works for just one of several companies that offer such materials!

The number of resources available nowadays for teaching children the Bible is staggering. Printed materials have been around for many years; add to that all of the resources that today's technology has made available to teachers. Over the 30-plus years that my wife has held her position, she has had to receive appropriate training from time to time so she can keep up with how ministering to children in a church setting has changed.

Imagine what it was like for the first parents, Adam and Eve, to try and teach their two sons, Cain and Abel, about the God who created them. Their resources were limited, to say the least! They could have used the world around them, "the things that are made," as Paul stated, to draw attention to the greatness and power of the One who created them (Romans 1:20). What did Adam and Eve understand about such basic matters as prayer, worship, and giving? We take these acts for granted, but what kind of instruction did the first family receive (if any)?

In today's lesson, we examine the first acts of worship recorded in the Bible, as carried out by Adam and Eve's two sons, Cain and Abel.

B. Lesson Context

The book of Genesis does not explicitly claim an author. But Exodus 17:14; 24:4; 34:27; Numbers 33:2; and Deuteronomy 31:9; Matthew 19:8; Mark 10:5; John 5:45-47; etc., suggest that Moses wrote the first five books of the Bible, a section we call the Pentateuch. However, many modern scholars have proposed that the text of the book of Genesis we possess today is a composite work of several different sources written hundreds of years after Moses would have lived. Because Genesis was part of the Law of Moses and Moses was certainly capable of writing, it seems best to take Genesis as having been authored by Moses.

The account of the offerings presented by Cain and Abel follows the eviction of Adam and Eve from the Garden of Eden. That was a consequence of their sin against God. Adam lived 930 years (Genesis 5:5), but determining how long Adam and Eve lived in the garden is impossible. Neither can the events of today's lesson be reliably dated.

I. Two Births
(Genesis 4:1-2a)
A. Cain (v. 1)

1. And Adam knew Eve his wife; and she conceived, and bare Cain, and said, I have gotten a man from the LORD.

In a context such as this, the word *knew* implies sexual intimacy between *Adam* and *Eve*. As a result, *Cain* was born. The Genesis record indicates that this was the first child of the first couple. God commanded the first couple to "be fruitful, and multiply, and replenish the earth" (Genesis 1:28), and Cain is the first evidence of that obedience. *Cain* sounds like the Hebrew word for "acquire." Eve praised the Lord, acknowledging that this child was acquired *from the Lord*. The name *Eve* comes from a Hebrew word meaning "living." Adam had given her that name "because she was the mother of all living" (3:20). Eve was privileged to experience the fulfillment of that name.

B. Abel (v. 2a)

2a. And she again bare his brother Abel.

Eve then gave birth to *Abel*, though we do not know how much time passed between the births of the two sons. No words of Eve are recorded following Abel's birth. The name *Abel* comes from a Hebrew word meaning "breath" or "vapor." The intentionality of their names should not be lost, as a Hebrew hearer would recognize the lesson of each of the sons' names. Cain reminds us that life comes from the Lord, while Abel's name would remind the hearer that life is brief, like a vapor.

What Do You Think?
What baby shower gifts could you give that give thanks to the Lord for the newborn child?
Digging Deeper
In what ways is parenthood strengthened when the Lord is worshipped?

II. Two Offerings
(Genesis 4:2b-7)
A. Different Occupations (vv. 2b-4a)

2b. And Abel was a keeper of sheep, but Cain was a tiller of the ground.

The account records the occupation of the two boys: *Abel* became a shepherd, while *Cain* tilled the soil. Tilling the *ground* is what Adam began to do after he and Eve were sent out of Eden (Genesis 3:23).

3-4a. And in process of time it came to pass, that Cain brought of the fruit of the ground an offering unto the LORD. And Abel, he also brought of the firstlings of his flock and of the fat thereof.

Adam and Eve would have taught their sons how to worship as they had learned from God while in the garden. While we do not know when the brothers began to offer sacrifice, we do know that they chose to worship through their giving. It is clear from the text that each man gave from the produce of his labors. Cain, already described as a "tiller of the ground," brought something from the *ground*, most likely a grain or vegetable *offering*. Abel, a "keeper of sheep," offered something from the *firstlings*, or firstborn, *of his flock*. This description brings to mind later laws given to Israel (Exodus 13:12; 34:19). Nothing is said, however, about Cain bringing the "firstfruits" of the soil, which was also later commanded of Israel (23:19). This may point to a higher quality of offering on Abel's part.

Another indication of higher quality may be

How to Say It

Pentateuch   Pen-ta-teuk.

seen in how Abel *brought . . . of the fat* as a part of his offering. Once again, later requirements in the Law of Moses indicate the significance of offering the fat of an animal because "all the fat is the Lord's" (Leviticus 3:16). The fat was considered the choice portion of the meat and thus the best part of the sacrifice.

What Do You Think?

How will you use your gifts of time, talent, and treasure as an act of worship to God?

Digging Deeper

What indicators of legalism should you be alert for in that regard?

B. Different Reactions (vv. 4b-5a)

4b-5a. And the LORD had respect unto Abel and to his offering. But unto Cain and to his offering he had not respect.

Why did the Lord accept Abel's *offering* but reject Cain's? One proposal is that Abel's offering was a blood sacrifice, while Cain's was only a grain offering, not costing him much. If so, the hearts or attitudes of the two men were the key factor distinguishing the two offerings.

At this point, the New Testament offers some important insights. Hebrews 11:4 states, "By faith Abel offered unto God a more excellent sacrifice than Cain, by which he obtained witness that he was righteous."

Our text does not indicate precisely how the Lord expressed His acceptance of Abel's offering and His rejection of Cain's. Later, the Lord will speak to Cain, so He may have addressed each of the brothers, much as He had earlier spoken to the serpent, Adam, and Eve (Genesis 3:14-19).

C. Cain's Anger (v. 5b)

5b. And Cain was very wroth, and his countenance fell.

Cain could have reacted with either remorse or anger. He chose the latter. So great was his bitterness that his facial expression showed his displeasure. As the sacrifices were acts of worship, Cain's heart posture is obvious.

What Do You Think?

What techniques can you adopt to control your anger?

Digging Deeper

To what extent does Jonah 4 help you with that question?

You, Karen?

I watch a lot of online video clips of law enforcement officials making arrests. The name *Karen* often appears as part of the titles of these clips as a derogatory designation of someone who behaves in an "I'm entitled" kind of way.

The "Karens" of the videos are often extremely angry as they resist arrest. They will loudly attempt to justify, excuse, or otherwise "explain away" the behavior that has landed them in handcuffs. They close their ears to anything the officer has to say. They ask "Why?" relentlessly, although the officer has explained things five times already.

Anger is a God-given emotion. Anger is not sinful in and of itself—Jesus himself became angry on more than one occasion (Mark 3:5; 11:15-17; John 2:13-17). But there's a difference between godly anger (Romans 2:8) and worldly anger (Ephesians 4:26, 31; James 1:20; etc.). Be warned: failure to discern the difference can make you a "Karen"—or worse, a Cain!   —R. L. N.

D. The Lord's Warning (vv. 6-7)

6. And the LORD said unto Cain, Why art thou wroth? and why is thy countenance fallen?

God had addressed Adam with a series of questions following his and Eve's disobedience in the Garden of Eden (Genesis 3:9-11). He questioned Eve as well (3:13). Then *the Lord* confronted *Cain* about his anger. His questions were designed to make Cain think about his condition, and they prepared him for the counsel the Lord was about to provide. The Lord was as concerned about the offerer as He was about the offering.

7. If thou doest well, shalt thou not be accepted? and if thou doest not well, sin lieth at the door. And unto thee shall be his desire, and thou shalt rule over him.

All was not lost for Cain. He did not have to remain angry. But Cain's heart needed to change; though the word *repent* is not used in this passage, Cain needed to do just that and determine to do what was pleasing to the Lord. If he did not take this step, *sin* was ready to exercise even further control over him. While the Lord did not specifically mention the devil, the language used in this verse is reminiscent of what Peter says about how the devil is like a roaring lion on the prowl, "seeking whom he may devour" (1 Peter 5:8).

The Lord's warning assumes that Cain had some understanding of sin. (This is the first time the word is used in the Bible.) Perhaps his parents had told him about their own sad experience with sin in the Garden of Eden and tried to warn Cain not to follow that same path. Sin did not have to have the upper hand with Cain, any more than it did with his parents. If Cain did what was right, he would indeed rule over sin.

Recognizing Mercy

When I was young, there was a time I became so angry that I decided I would tell my mother that I hated her. When I did, however, I was met with mercy. She appeared unfazed. Her love for me did not change—whether or not I was angry. Her love quelled my anger, and I regretted my actions.

We see God's mercy on display in the story of Cain and Abel. Instead of killing Cain, God spared him. God had every right to put him to death, but that's not how the story goes.

Through Christ Jesus, God also offers us mercy today. We deserve to die eternally for our sins, but Jesus took the penalty for us. He paid off a debt we never could. Is there ever *any* reason to be angry with God? No! (See Jonah 4.) And until we humble ourselves in repentance, we will miss the joy of knowing God's deep, bubbling fountain of mercy and life. Are you missing it now?   —J. K.

III. Two Outcomes
(Genesis 4:8-12)
A. Cain Kills Abel (v. 8)

8. And Cain talked with Abel his brother: and it came to pass, when they were in the field,

If you refuse what is right, then WATCH OUT!

Visual for Lesson 1. *Allow learners one minute of silent reflection on this statement before asking, "How do you ensure that you do what is right?"*

that Cain rose up against Abel his brother, and slew him.

Anger is a powerful emotion that can be a gateway to sinful actions. Perhaps at some point, Cain persuaded Abel to go to a *field*, where the older brother took his younger brother's life.

First John 3:12 offers insight into what motivated Cain to do the terrible thing he did to his brother. John contrasts the message of loving one another with the actions of Cain, "who was of that wicked one, and slew his brother." John then raises the question of why Cain killed Abel. The answer? "Because his own works were evil, and his brother's righteous." Rather than heed the Lord's counsel to do what was right, Cain harbored his bitter, envious feelings toward his brother to the point of killing him. It is sobering to consider that this early in the biblical record (we are still in single-digit pages in our Bibles), such a tragic act has occurred.

B. The Lord Confronts Cain (vv. 9-10)

9. And the LORD said unto Cain, Where is Abel thy brother? And he said, I know not: Am I my brother's keeper?

The Lord knew where Abel was and what Cain had done to him, just like He knew Adam's location when He asked him, "Where art thou?" (Genesis 3:9). The question allowed Cain to do something right (3:7) rather than allow sin to tighten its stranglehold on him. *Cain*, however, denied knowing where Abel was. He even became defiant in his reply: *Am I my brother's keeper?* Cain tried to deflect God's question away from himself, much like his father had done in his response to the Lord after being confronted with his disobedience (3:12).

10. And he said, What hast thou done? the voice of thy brother's blood crieth unto me from the ground.

The Lord asked yet another question of Cain—a question that revealed His full awareness of what Cain had *done* to his brother. The Lord's description of how Abel's *blood* was crying to Him *from the ground* may indicate that Cain had buried his brother's body in an effort to conceal his deed. His parents, too, tried to hide their sin (Genesis 3:8).

The writer of Hebrews mentions Abel's blood, contrasting it with Jesus' blood, which speaks a message of "better things than that of Abel" (Hebrews 12:24). Abel's blood cried out for judgment on his brother. Jesus' blood given at the cross speaks grace and forgiveness.

C. The Lord Punishes Cain (vv. 11-12)

11. And now art thou cursed from the earth, which hath opened her mouth to receive thy brother's blood from thy hand.

Previously, the Lord had *cursed* the serpent because of its role in deceiving Adam and Eve (Genesis 3:14). Here, Cain was cursed *from the earth*, meaning that the focus of the curse was to be the ground from which Cain made his living. Later, the Law of Moses will describe an act such as Cain's shedding of his *brother's* innocent *blood* as a defilement of the land (Numbers 35:33).

12. When thou tillest the ground, it shall not henceforth yield unto thee her strength; a fugitive and a vagabond shalt thou be in the earth.

The Lord had already told Adam that the ground would be cursed "for thy sake;" that is, because of his sin (Genesis 3:17). Working the soil would become a rigorous, demanding task, and the ground would produce thorns and thistles (3:18-19). Here, God told Cain that his labor in the soil would yield nothing in return. Thus what had been the source of productivity and satisfaction for Cain would become a source of frustration and devastation.

The Hebrew word translated *earth* at the end of this verse differs from the word earlier rendered *ground* and indicates a much larger area (perhaps the entire planet as it does in Genesis 1:1-2). Cain was consigned to live as *a fugitive and a vagabond*, likely having to search for food from whomever would be willing to share with him.

IV. Two Epilogues
(Genesis 4:13-16)
A. Cain's Anguish (vv. 13-14)

13. And Cain said unto the LORD, My punishment is greater than I can bear.

Cain was grieved to hear that his livelihood was being taken from him. While he saw his *punishment* as severe, at a later time, the Lord declared that death was the appropriate punishment for murder (Genesis 9:5-6; Exodus 21:12). Thus, Cain's punishment was less severe than it could have been.

14. Behold, thou hast driven me out this day from the face of the earth; and from thy face shall I be hid; and I shall be a fugitive and a vagabond in the earth; and it shall come to pass, that every one that findeth me shall slay me.

At no point did Cain offer any admission of guilt or remorse for his action; like his father (see Genesis 3:12), Cain saw God as the culprit to be blamed for what lay ahead for him. Cain acknowledged that he could well become the target of revenge for his killing of Abel. Perhaps he was thinking of future family members who would learn of his despicable act. That Eve knew about it is clear from her statement in Genesis 4:25. One wonders how much Cain read into other people's thinking about the evils of his own heart. If others were like him, he was indeed in grave danger.

Of course, it was not true that Cain would be hidden from the Lord. That is an impossibility for anyone, as David recognized (Psalm 139:7-12).

B. The Lord's Provision (v. 15)

15. And the LORD said unto him, Therefore whosoever slayeth Cain, vengeance shall be taken on him sevenfold. And the LORD set a mark upon Cain, lest any finding him should kill him.

The use of the term *sevenfold* likely signifies completeness; that is, full *vengeance* will be carried out on anyone who kills *Cain*. It's all too easy to speculate about the composition of the *mark* placed *upon Cain* and where it might have been placed on his body; it would have had to be someplace visible, such as his forehead. A primary point not to be overlooked is the Lord's measure of grace by not administering the punishment of the death penalty that Cain, in fact, deserved. But such a penalty isn't announced until Genesis 9:6.

C. Cain's Departure (v. 16)

16. And Cain went out from the presence of the LORD, and dwelt in the land of Nod, on the east of Eden.

We do not read of any expression of gratitude on Cain's part for the Lord's provision of protection from possible vigilante justice. *Cain* simply *went out* and began a new phase of his life *in the land of Nod*, a designation that means "wandering." It was certainly a fitting location for someone who had been sentenced to live as a vagabond.

What Do You Think?

What are some ways to teach others to recognize God's presence?

Digging Deeper

How will you be an accountability partner for a person as he or she tries to notice the presence of God?

Conclusion

A. Cain's "Worship War"

From time to time, churches have engaged in what have come to be called "worship wars." Usually, the issue that creates the conflict is the style of music. Cain, however, was engaged in another kind of worship war. It had nothing to do with music. Cain's worship war went much deeper.

Faith, which God has always required from those who would please Him (Genesis 15:6; Hebrews 11:6), was absent from Cain's offering. Instead of seeing Abel's righteous act as something to learn from and imitate, Cain responded in anger. John says that Cain's actions were evil (1 John 3:12), and evil will always seek to persecute and silence righteousness.

Prophets such as Isaiah challenged God's people in his day to recognize that, despite all of the observances of worship in which they participated (incense, sabbaths, assemblies, feasts, and prayers), it was all worthless. Why? "This people draw near me with their mouth, and with their lips do honour me, but have removed their heart far from me" (Isaiah 29:13). Jesus quoted these words to the religious leaders of His day, whose worship, like that of the people in Isaiah's day, was filled with religious actions "but their heart is far from me" (Matthew 15:7-8).

In many churches today, an abundance of resources aid in worship through modern technology. It is sobering to consider that if the condition of our hearts is deficient, our worship may be just as unacceptable as Cain's was.

B. Prayer

Father, help us to take our preparation for worship more seriously. Before we enter the sanctuary of our church building, may we make sure that our hearts are a fitting sanctuary for Your presence. May we never forget that we are living sacrifices, called to worship and serve You between Sundays as well as on them. In Jesus' name. Amen.

C. Thought to Remember

Make your life an offering to the Lord.

Visuals FOR THESE LESSONS

The visual pictured in each lesson (example: page 345) is a small reproduction of a large, full-color poster included in the *Adult Resources* packet for the Spring Quarter. Order No. 9780784740637 from your supplier.

Involvement Learning

Enhance your lesson with KJV Bible Student *(from your curriculum supplier) and the reproducible activity page (at www.standardlesson.com or in the back of the* KJV Standard Lesson Commentary Deluxe Edition*).*

Into the Lesson

Divide your class into groups of three. Ask half of the groups to discuss the topic, "The best gift I ever received." The other half can share with each other their answer to the prompt, "The best gift I ever gave."

After a few minutes, ask the groups to share what they discussed. Some possible discussion questions are: 1–What made these gifts special? 2–How did you feel about getting/giving the gifts? 3–How were these the "right" gifts?

Lead into the Bible study by saying, "Today, we will look at the first two gifts recorded in the Bible and explore why one was more acceptable than the other."

Into the Word

Recruit four participants to read today's text from Genesis 4 aloud, using these parts:

Narrator: 4:1a, 2-6a, 8a, 8c, 9a, 10a, 13a, 15a, 15c, 16
   Eve: 4:1b
The Lord: 6b-7, 9b, 10b-12, 15b
   Cain: 4:8b, 9c, 13b-14

Option. The reading will go more smoothly if you make a copy of the text for each reader, with the parts highlighted.

Form participants into study pairs or triads. Designate half the pairs/triads as **Brothers' Offerings** and the other pairs/triads as **God's Response**. Give each group one set of the following questions on handouts (you prepare):

Brothers' Offerings: 1–What do the different offerings reveal about the heart of each brother? 2–What indicators are there to suggest or refute this as being a case of sibling rivalry?

God's Response: 1–Why did God favor Abel's offering over Cain's? 2–What do we learn about the character of God from this passage?

After a few minutes, have the groups discuss their findings with the whole class.

Alternative. After the four-part reading of the lesson text, distribute copies of the "From What to Why" exercise from the activity page, which you can download. Follow small-group discussion with whole-class consideration.

Read and discuss Hebrews 11:4 as a transition to the Into Life section.

Into Life

Have learners return to their study pairs or triads formed earlier to discuss these two questions: 1–What makes giving back to God easy? 2–Why is it sometimes difficult?

Ask the whole class to brainstorm various motivations for giving and withholding.

Option. At this point, distribute to study pairs/triads copies of the "Gifts Compared" exercise from the activity page. Allow time for volunteers to share and discuss their insights from the activity.

For a whole-class discussion, distribute handouts (you prepare) on which you have printed two lists: one list of faulty reasons for not giving and the other list of wrong motives for giving. Challenge learners to think of more entries for both lists. Then, ask learners to circle the one reason, excuse, or wrong motive that is most like their own giving patterns.

Have learners then write on their handouts a way each of them can commit to do right in giving back to God, in both quantity and quality.

Option. To expand this discussion to the giving expectations of the New Testament era, have learners work with a partner to consider these giving principles:

Proportional: 1 Corinthians 16:2
Sacrificial: 2 Corinthians 8:3
Cheerful: 2 Corinthians 9:7
Discreet: Matthew 6:1-4

End with a time of worship, rereading of Hebrews 11:4, and group prayer.

Noah Builds an Altar

Devotional Reading: Psalm 77:1-2, 7-19
Background Scripture: Genesis 6:1–9:17

Genesis 8:13-22

13 And it came to pass in the six hundredth and first year, in the first month, the first day of the month, the waters were dried up from off the earth: and Noah removed the covering of the ark, and looked, and, behold, the face of the ground was dry.

14 And in the second month, on the seven and twentieth day of the month, was the earth dried.

15 And God spake unto Noah, saying,

16 Go forth of the ark, thou, and thy wife, and thy sons, and thy sons' wives with thee.

17 Bring forth with thee every living thing that is with thee, of all flesh, both of fowl, and of cattle, and of every creeping thing that creepeth upon the earth; that they may breed abundantly in the earth, and be fruitful, and multiply upon the earth.

18 And Noah went forth, and his sons, and his wife, and his sons' wives with him:

19 Every beast, every creeping thing, and every fowl, and whatsoever creepeth upon the earth, after their kinds, went forth out of the ark.

20 And Noah builded an altar unto the LORD; and took of every clean beast, and of every clean fowl, and offered burnt offerings on the altar.

21 And the LORD smelled a sweet savour; and the LORD said in his heart, I will not again curse the ground any more for man's sake; for the imagination of man's heart is evil from his youth; neither will I again smite any more every thing living, as I have done.

22 While the earth remaineth, seedtime and harvest, and cold and heat, and summer and winter, and day and night shall not cease.

Genesis 9:11-13

11 And I will establish my covenant with you; neither shall all flesh be cut off any more by the waters of a flood; neither shall there any more be a flood to destroy the earth.

12 And God said, this is the token of the covenant which I make between me and you and every living creature that is with you, for perpetual generations:

13 I do set my bow in the cloud, and it shall be for a token of a covenant between me and the earth.

Key Text

I do set my bow in the cloud, and it shall be for a token of a covenant between me and the earth.

—Genesis 9:13

Sacred Altars and
Holy Offerings

Unit 1: The Genesis of Altars and Sacrifices
Lessons 1–5

Lesson Aims

After participating in this lesson, each learner will be able to:

1. Summarize the terms of the Lord's covenant with Noah.

2. Suggest reasons why Noah's sacrifice pleased God.

3. Write a prayer of thanks to God for one specific instance of His covenant faithfulness.

Lesson Outline

Introduction
    A. Getting Out of the Boat
    B. Lesson Context
  I. Noah's Situation (Genesis 8:13-22)
    A. Waiting Two Months (vv. 13-14)
    B. Obeying God's Command (vv. 15-19)
    C. Building an Altar (vv. 20-22)
      A Pleasant Fragrance
  II. God's Response (Genesis 9:11-13)
    A. The Covenant (v. 11)
    B. The Sign (vv. 12-13)
      Rainbow: A Happy Symbol?
Conclusion
    A. Learn to Wait. Learn to Act!
    B. Prayer
    C. Thought to Remember

Introduction

A. Getting Out of the Boat

At age 36, I decided to enter a 340-mile river race on the Missouri River between Kansas City and St. Charles, Missouri. I had entered the race some years before but did not finish. I knew from experience that it was going to be a physical test. Long stretches of the race required that I remain in an 18-foot-long kayak in the middle of the river with no way to get out of the vessel. I was able to dock the kayak at rest stops periodically. But I only slept about 10 hours during the four-day race.

About 82 hours after I started the race, I found the finish line. I was proud of my accomplishment, but by the end of the race, I was ready to get out of the kayak and feel the dry ground beneath my stiff legs; I was eager to get out of that boat!

So was Noah. However, some significant differences exist between my getting out of the kayak and Noah getting out of the ark. God did not tell me to get in or out of the kayak; if I had to, I could have paddled the kayak to the riverbank and disembarked the vessel. Noah did not have that option. He had to trust that God would tell him when to leave the ark—even though Noah did not know how long it would be until he could feel the dry ground beneath his legs.

B. Lesson Context

Today's lesson focuses on events directly after the flood wiped out all creation, except for all living creatures—human and otherwise—in the ark. Interestingly, the flood is one of the most well-attested accounts in history.

The biblical account of the flood is but one of at least five ancient flood stories. The existence of the latter leads some to believe that the biblical account used them as sources and that the flood is a legendary myth of an ancient and ignorant people. But if there truly was a great flood in ancient times, then stories of the event would be passed down from generation to generation.

As people spread over the earth and formed distinct cultures, these stories would take on the characteristics of those cultures. It would be strange indeed if accounts of the actual flood were absent altogether from ancient writings! So, the existence of the nonbiblical stories serves to confirm that there was indeed a great flood at some point in history. The Bible's account of this flood is the accurate one.

The biblical account of the great flood is detailed in giving specifics for the beginning of the flood, the length of time the rain fell, how long the floodwaters covered the earth, and how long it took for the waters to recede. The total amount of time adds up to more than a year (Genesis 7:11; 8:14).

Having made it safely through the flood, creation and humankind had another chance. But even as that new chance began, God was fully aware of the still-present reality of man's brokenness. Sadly, even before the end of Genesis 9, sin manifested itself again. Humanity's brokenness becomes apparent.

I. Noah's Situation
(Genesis 8:13-22)
A. Waiting Two Months (vv. 13-14)

13. And it came to pass in the six hundredth and first year, in the first month, the first day of the month, the waters were dried up from off the earth: and Noah removed the covering of the ark, and looked, and, behold, the face of the ground was dry.

The biblical account of the flood gives specific details regarding when the flood began (Genesis 7:11), the length of time the rain fell on the earth (7:12, 17), how long the floodwaters covered the earth (7:24), and the length of time it took for the flood waters to recede (8:3). The total amount of time from when the flood began to when the earth was dry adds up to a little more than a year (8:14). We know that Noah was 600 years old when the flood began (7:6, 11). This verse states that one year had passed, and it was *the first month* of Noah's *six hundredth and first year.*

For Noah to see *the waters were dried up from off the earth* suggests that he could see dry ground on "the mountains of Ararat," where the ark came to rest (Genesis 8:4). The sight of which would have been significant to Noah and his family.

Although *the face of the ground was dry*, Noah, his family, and the animals remained in the ark. They were all "shut . . . in" (Genesis 7:16) until the Lord revealed the time for them to leave the ark.

14. And in the second month, on the seven and twentieth day of the month, was the earth dried.

The phrase *the second month, on the seven and twentieth day of the month* reveals that about two months had passed between the events of this verse and the previous verse. The duration of the flood was 150 days (see Genesis 7:24; 8:3), but the process to dry out the land took about 60 days.

B. Obeying God's Command (vv. 15-19)

15-16. And God spake unto Noah, saying, Go forth of the ark, thou, and thy wife, and thy sons, and thy sons' wives with thee.

As *God* had commanded *Noah* and his family to go into the ark (Genesis 7:1), so God also commanded them to *go forth of the ark*. One can only imagine how ready Noah and his family were to do so—they wouldn't have had to be told twice!

Scripture gives us the names of Noah's *sons*: Shem, Ham, and Japheth (Genesis 7:13; 9:18-19; 10:1). However, we are not told the names of Noah's *wife* or the *wives* of his sons. The New Testament informs us that a total of eight people were saved through the ark (1 Peter 3:20).

17. Bring forth with thee every living thing that is with thee, of all flesh, both of fowl, and of cattle, and of every creeping thing that creepeth upon the earth; that they may breed abundantly in the earth, and be fruitful, and multiply upon the earth.

How to Say It

Abrahamic	Ay-bruh-*ham*-ik.
Adamic	uh-*dahm*-ik.
anthropomorphic	*an*-thruh puh-**more**-fik.
Davidic	Duh-*vid*-ick.
Habakkuk	Huh-*back*-kuk.
Japheth	*Jay*-feth.
Lamech	*Lay*-mek.
Noahic	No-*ay*-ik.
Zephaniah	Zef-uh-*nye*-uh.

The four designations *living thing* (wild animals), *fowl* (birds), *cattle* (domesticated animals), and *every creeping thing* are intended to convey a message of totality. The four underlying Hebrew words also occur together in Genesis 1:26 and 7:14, although not always translated the same way. The passage from Genesis 1:26 is a bit more comprehensive in mentioning fish as well. This category is probably not mentioned in the verse before us due to the nature of the disaster being that of water (compare 1 Kings 4:33; Ezekiel 38:20; Hosea 4:3; Zephaniah 1:3). We should not fail to consider the amount of labor that was necessary to care for all the animals on that ark! And imagine the smell after even a day or two of being cooped up with them in the ark.

The statement *be fruitful, and multiply upon the earth* repeats the command given to Adam and Eve in the garden (Genesis 1:28). In this verse, however, the command is not issued to Noah and his family but to the creatures in the ark so that they would *breed abundantly in the earth*.

Noah and his family would receive such a command later: "Be fruitful, and multiply, and replenish the earth" (Genesis 9:1). Noah would become something like a second Adam (not to be confused, of course, with "the last Adam," who is Christ; 1 Corinthians 15:45).

> **What Do You Think?**
> In what ways can our interaction with animals improve our understanding of their creator (Job 12:7-9)?
> **Digging Deeper**
> How do Numbers 22:22-32; Proverbs 12:10; and Jonah 4:11 speak about God-honoring treatment of animals?

18. And Noah went forth, and his sons, and his wife, and his sons' wives with him.

As in Genesis 6:13-22 and 7:1-5, the verse before us shows the pattern of God's command being followed by Noah's obedience to that command. God spoke, Noah listened, Noah acted. It is a simple sequence on paper, but it is one that believers sometimes struggle to put into practice.

19. Every beast, every creeping thing, and every fowl, and whatsoever creepeth upon the earth, after their kinds, went forth out of the ark.

The animals, birds, and all creatures aboard the ark are in two categories: clean and unclean (Genesis 7:2). Regarding the natures of *every beast, creeping thing*, and *fowl*, see commentary on 8:17 above.

C. Building an Altar (vv. 20-22)

20. And Noah builded an altar unto the LORD; and took of every clean beast, and of every clean fowl, and offered burnt offerings on the altar.

One of the first things—if not the very first thing—that Noah did after exiting the ark was worship. That is not surprising, as Noah's character has already been testified (Genesis 6:9). Worship is a very appropriate response after one has been delivered by God.

This is the first *altar* mentioned in Scripture, but it's not the first blood sacrifice (see Genesis 4:4). When Noah was commanded to save pairs of animals in the ark, more clean animals were spared than unclean ones (6:19-20; 7:2-3). Perhaps the act of sacrifice noted in the verse before us had been intended from the beginning, provision for it having been made by keeping more of the appropriate animals alive.

We are not told what differentiates *clean* animals from unclean ones at this point in salvation history, but Noah somehow knew the difference. His righteousness had allowed a remnant of humanity to survive the flood, and that character was again on display.

Centuries later, the burnt offering was a voluntary offering for sin and for general worship and thanksgiving (Leviticus 1:4). Noah's offering seems to have prefigured that later rite.

> **What Do You Think?**
> What are some ways to ensure that worship precedes any new endeavor?
> **Digging Deeper**
> How does James 4:13-15 help shape your answer?

21. And the LORD smelled a sweet savour; and the LORD said in his heart, I will not again

curse the ground any more for man's sake; for the imagination of man's heart is evil from his youth; neither will I again smite any more every thing living, as I have done.

We should note immediately that the phrase *said in his heart* indicates private thoughts, not a response to Noah, which comes later. Thus, the writer uses figurative language to describe God's reaction to the sacrifice. Since "God is a Spirit" (John 4:24), we need not assume that God smells things the same way we do or has a literal, physical heart. Nevertheless, we understand such language. The same manner of figurative language is used when Scripture speaks of the "hand" and "arm" of the Lord (Deuteronomy 4:34; 5:15; 7:19; etc.). This kind of figurative language is known as anthropomorphic language. The point being made is that God accepted the offering. Moses will use the same type of language later to describe the sacrifices and burnt offerings that the new nation of Israel will be commanded to present to the Lord (see Exodus 29:18, 25, 41).

We may wonder to what end God accepted Noah's offerings. In later times, burnt offerings will atone for sin (Leviticus 1:1-9) and ordain the Aaronic priesthood (Exodus 29). Some suggest that Noah's offerings are for atonement for the sins of all who perished in the flood, but that is not likely. Ordinarily, an offering of atonement is made in lieu of punishment, but those who perished because of the flood have already been punished.

More likely, Noah's sacrifice is tied to the purification of the earth. Centuries later, Aaron and his sons offered burnt offerings to purify themselves for the new priesthood. Similarly, Noah offered sacrifices to cleanse the earth as home to new generations.

Up to this point in the Bible, the ground has been spoken of as being under a curse only twice. The ground was cursed in Genesis 3:17 because of sin. Only with difficulty would humanity be able to make a living from it (Genesis 3:18-19). Much later, Noah's father, Lamech, prophesied that Noah would be the one to bring relief from the burdensome toil because of the ground "which the Lord hath cursed" (5:29).

The question that arises, then, is whether the statement *I will not again curse the ground* here refers to the flood itself or to the original curse of Genesis 3:17. If the latter, then the prophecy of 5:29 is fulfilled—but then we have to ask why thorns and thistles still interfere (3:18) and why agriculture still involves sweat-producing labor (3:19). If the reference is to the punishment of the flood, then the promise to not again curse the ground is another way of stating the promise never again to flood the earth (see 9:11, below).

The term *smelled* here has a figurative sense in which it simply means that the sacrifice was pleasing to God (Exodus 29:18; Leviticus 1:9; Numbers 15:3; Philippians 4:18). This language was likely used to better communicate that fact. Refusing "to smell" would have meant that God rejected the worship offered (Amos 5:21).

> **What Do You Think?**
> What are some ways to ensure that our efforts for the Lord are a pleasant fragrance to Him and not the opposite?
> **Digging Deeper**
> How does Amos 5:21 inform your response?

A Pleasant Fragrance

Week after week, the task remained the same: pulling weeds, one minute after another. Any joy in my work eroded, and agony took its place. Hope remained a dim glimmer on a very distant horizon. How could things get better?

Over the next several years, I found different jobs. Through a series of events, God has provided me several life-giving jobs. We all experience moments of hopelessness, but we have a God who offers us true, unfailing hope.

On a different scale, we might wonder what hope we have to help us through the trials of life. We see that nothing changed about the human heart after the flood. Evil persists up to the present day. Even so, God found Noah's offering to be a pleasant aroma.

Looking ahead to the return of our Savior, Jesus Christ, we acknowledge the way God has made us to enjoy Him in this life and for all eternity, giving us life and meaning both now and forever. How can you hold on to hope when hope seems like a glimmer on a distant horizon?   —J. K.

22. While the earth remaineth, seedtime and harvest, and cold and heat, and summer and winter, and day and night shall not cease.

The apostle Peter refers to the Noahic flood as an illustration of the fact that God can judge the world and that another destruction is coming, one by fire (2 Peter 3:6-7). But until that time of judgment, the cycles of the seasons will continue. The flood had interrupted that normal cycle, but God reaffirmed the ordering of His creation (Genesis 1:14; Jeremiah 33:20-25). The language suggests that God was restoring the world back to its original order.

What Do You Think?

What are some ways that can prompt you to praise the Creator as one season gives way to the next?

Digging Deeper

Which Bible passages prod you most to do so? Why?

II. God's Response
(Genesis 9:11-13)
A. The Covenant (v. 11)

11. And I will establish my covenant with you; neither shall all flesh be cut off any more by the waters of a flood; neither shall there any more be a flood to destroy the earth.

The word *you* indicates that God has switched from pondering thoughts privately to communicating with Noah personally. And what God communicates is the first of the five covenants mentioned in Scripture. These five are the Noahic, Abrahamic, Mosaic, Davidic, and the new covenant. Some commentators add two more: Adamic to begin the listing and Everlasting to finalize it. Other commentators see only two: the old covenant and the new covenant.

This *covenant* in view here fulfills God's promise in Genesis 6:18. The establishment of this covenant is one-sided: God does not ask anything of Noah and his descendants.

What Do You Think?

What kinds of emergencies would prompt us to place faith God's promises from Genesis 9:11?

Digging Deeper

Would such emergencies be the same for everyone? Why, or why not?

B. The Sign (vv. 12-13)

12. And God said, This is the token of the covenant which I make between me and you and every living creature that is with you, for perpetual generations.

The word translated *token* is also translated as "sign" in Genesis 1:14 and Exodus 4:8, and that is the idea here. Giving a sign of a *covenant* is a common idea even today. We exchange wedding rings to remind us of the covenant of marriage. Circumcision was used as a sign or token of the covenant between God and Abraham and his descendants (Genesis 17), and the Sabbath was also used as a sign between Israel and God (Exodus 31:16-17). In reality, these three signs of a covenant are all present in Genesis, with the Sabbath at creation (Genesis 2:4), the rainbow here in 9:12, and circumcision in Genesis 17. Signs appear at watershed moments in salvation history.

The promise that this covenant is *for perpetual generations* is also reflected in Genesis 9:16, where it is deemed "everlasting." But neither the word *everlasting* nor the word *perpetual* should be taken to mean that the covenant extends into eternity. The time limitation of Genesis 8:22 is that the covenant is in force "while the earth remaineth." This verse sheds light on the meaning and significance of words such as *perpetual, everlasting,* and *forever* as they occur in other contexts regarding God's covenants (examples: Genesis 17:13, 19; Exodus 31:17; Leviticus 24:8-9; 2 Samuel 23:5; 1 Chronicles 16:17).

13. I do set my bow in the cloud, and it shall be for a token of a covenant between me and the earth.

When we see the word *bow* in this context, we naturally think of a rainbow (compare Ezekiel 1:28; Revelation 4:3; 10:1). That word also refers to a bow as part of a bow-and-arrow combination (examples: Genesis 27:3; 48:22). Perhaps the image is one of a weapon of war becoming a symbol of peace. The image is further explained in Genesis 9:14, which is not part of today's lesson text.

Rainbow: A Happy Symbol?

My daughter loves to draw rainbows, along with a bright sun and smiling people. She considers it "happy." I suppose you could call it a happy symbol in the Genesis context as well, but not necessarily because it looks attractive or picturesque.

When God hangs His bow in the heavens, it reminds us that He won't be making a dramatic intervention to destroy evil with a flood. God's plan is more extensive and longer-term, revealed through the life, death, burial, resurrection, and ascension of Jesus. He alone can bring true and permanent redemption. The rainbow remains a symbol that life goes on without divine cataclysmic judgment—for now. God is not destroying wickedness (Matthew 13:30; etc.). Season continues to follow season, and night continues to follow day.

In this fallen world, we face days when justice seems to be an unattainable ideal. I sympathize with the psalmist who, after first marveling at all of God's creation, couldn't help but pray that sinners and the wicked should just vanish (Psalm 104:35; compare Habakkuk 1:1-4, 13-17). Truly, we look forward to the day when God puts an end to evil. But 2 Peter 3:9 tells us that God delays judgment so that all might repent. The question then becomes, *How are you responding to God's patience?*
—J. K.

Conclusion

A. Learn to Wait. Learn to Act!

Most people know what it means to be impatient. As a parent, I have three highly mobile balls of impatience. And when you throw my wife and I in the mix, waiting for things becomes agony. The people in the Old Testament were not any different. King Saul had a major failure due to his lack of patience as he waited for Samuel to offer the sacri-

Remember God's covenant faithfulness.

Visual for Lesson 2. *Display this visual as you introduce the Into Life section of the Involvement Learning page.*

fice. Saul offered the sacrifice himself even though he was not a priest and had no authority to do so, and it became a great sin (1 Samuel 13).

Waiting can be even more difficult when under challenging conditions. Saul's army was melting away from him in the face of the Philistine threat, and seemingly, that is why he offered the sacrifice before Samuel got there to keep his army together (1 Samuel 13:11-12). Impatience is a feature of many chapters of the book of Psalms (examples: Psalms 6:3; 13:1; 119:84). It's easy to imagine Noah as having felt that strain too.

Yet, when God told him to do something, he did it. He chose to operate on God's timeline; he did not expect God to operate on his own (contrast Genesis 15:2-5; 16:1-4). Noah's patience and obedience serves as a model for Christians. But there's a caution here: sometimes, believers who are waiting impatiently for God to do something have already been given the command to take care of it themselves. But you aren't one of those, are you?

B. Prayer

Lord, thank You for how You deliver us as You delivered Noah. Thank You for Noah's example in that when You spoke, he listened and obeyed. May we learn to do the same. In Jesus' name, Amen.

C. Thought to Remember

Wait for God's command
and then obey it!

Involvement Learning

Enhance your lesson with KJV Bible Student *(from your curriculum supplier) and the reproducible activity* page *(at www.standardlesson.com or in the back of the* KJV Standard Lesson Commentary Deluxe Edition*).*

Into the Lesson

Form learners into groups of three or four. Invite the use of smartphones for each person in each group to find one quotation featuring the word *promise*. Have each group choose which quote its members find most challenging and write it on a half sheet of paper.

Collect the sheets and redistribute them so that no group ends up with its own. Ask the groups to decide whether they agree or disagree with the quote just received and why.

Reconvene for whole-class discussion after a few minutes. Invite a representative from each group to read the quote it received and say why they agreed or disagreed with it.

Alternative. Display the following prompts on the board:

The most important promise I ever made . . .
The most disappointing broken promise . . .
The best promise I ever received . . .

Reform the groups and assign each group one of the prompts for response and discussion. Reconvene after a few minutes for volunteers to share results with the whole class.

After either activity, lead into Bible study by saying, "Our study today looks at Noah and his obedience that led up to God's covenant promise."

Into the Word

Write on the board *What Noah Did* and *What God Promised* as the headers of two columns, one each. Invite two volunteers to read today's Scripture passage, one reading the words of the narrator and the other reading the words of God.

After finishing that initial reading, have volunteers read the text again slowly, pausing after every verse. As a whole class, use the pauses to create lists under the two headers on the board. When complete, draw a star on the list next to the sign of God's promise.

Option. Distribute copies of the "Why Appreciate Rainbows?" exercise from the activity page, which you can download. Have participants work alone for no more than one minute to give their estimates as indicated.

After calling time, have participants voice their estimates for comparing and contrasting. (Larger classes should do this in small groups.) Use the question at the bottom of the exercise as a lead-in to the Into Life segment.

Into Life

Reform small groups and give each a handout (you prepare) titled "Grateful Worship." Have this printed on the handout:

Consider Noah's attitude after the flood.
1–What words would you use to categorize his heart?
2–What are some ways to develop the same heart?
3–How would having such a heart affect worship?

Allow at least six minutes for group members to respond. Reconvene for whole-class discussion, comparing and contrasting responses.

Option. Distribute copies of the "Meaning and Significance" exercise from the activity page to study pairs or triads. Have learners complete it as indicated. (*Note*: In light of the fact that this exercise requires very precise thinking, you may wish to consider carefully in advance how to pair class members with one another.) After calling time, allow the groups to share their conclusions with the whole class.

Distribute blank index cards. Invite learners to write on the cards prayers of thanks to God for His covenant faithfulness in light of what has been discussed about worship and Noah's reactions to God. Challenge learners to use these prayers during their prayer time throughout the week.

Close with sentence prayers of praise for God's covenant faithfulness. *Option*: Sing as a class the hymn "Great Is Thy Faithfulness" or another composition expressing similar thoughts.

Abraham Makes an Offering

Devotional Reading: Romans 4:1-15
Background Scripture: Genesis 22:1-19

Genesis 22:1-14

1 And it came to pass after these things, that God did tempt Abraham, and said unto him, Abraham: and he said, Behold, here I am.

2 And he said, take now thy son, thine only son Isaac, whom thou lovest, and get thee into the land of Moriah; and offer him there for a burnt offering upon one of the mountains which I will tell thee of.

3 And Abraham rose up early in the morning, and saddled his ass, and took two of his young men with him, and Isaac his son, and clave the wood for the burnt offering, and rose up, and went unto the place of which God told him.

4 Then on the third day Abraham lifted up his eyes, and saw the place afar off.

5 And Abraham said unto his young men, abide ye here with the ass; and I and the lad will go yonder and worship, and come again to you.

6 And Abraham took the wood of the burnt offering, and laid it upon Isaac his son; and he took the fire in his hand, and a knife; and they went both of them together.

7 And Isaac spake unto Abraham his father, and said, my father: and he said, here am I, my son. And he said, behold the fire and the wood: but where is the lamb for a burnt offering?

8 And Abraham said, my son, God will provide himself a lamb for a burnt offering: so they went both of them together.

9 And they came to the place which God had told him of; and Abraham built an altar there, and laid the wood in order, and bound Isaac his son, and laid him on the altar upon the wood.

10 And Abraham stretched forth his hand, and took the knife to slay his son.

11 And the angel of the LORD called unto him out of heaven, and said, Abraham, Abraham: and he said, here am I.

12 And he said, lay not thine hand upon the lad, neither do thou any thing unto him: for now I know that thou fearest God, seeing thou hast not withheld thy son, thine only son from me.

13 And Abraham lifted up his eyes, and looked, and behold behind him a ram caught in a thicket by his horns: and Abraham went and took the ram, and offered him up for a burnt offering in the stead of his son.

14 And Abraham called the name of that place Jehovahjireh: as it is said to this day, in the mount of the LORD it shall be seen.

Key Text

Abraham called the name of that place Jehovah-jireh: as it is said to this day, In the mount of the LORD it shall be seen. —**Genesis 22:14**

Sacred Altars and Holy Offerings

Unit 1: The Genesis of Altars and Sacrifices
Lessons 1–5

Lesson Aims

After participating in this lesson, each learner will be able to:

1. Outline the main points of the lesson text.
2. Identify acts of trust and what was required of the trusting person.
3. Identify how to exhibit greater trust in the Lord in a current difficulty.

Lesson Outline

Introduction
   A. Testing Commitment
   B. Lesson Context
I. God Tests (Genesis 22:1-2)
   A. Call (v. 1)
   B. Requirement (v. 2)
    The Value of Testing
II. Abraham Acts (Genesis 22:3-10)
   A. Journey and Preparation (vv. 3-6)
   B. Question and Answer (vv. 7-8)
   C. Arrival and Intention (vv. 9-10)
III. God Intervenes (Genesis 22:11-14)
   A. Sacrifice Halted (vv. 11-12)
    Where Are You?
   B. Sacrifice Provided (vv. 13-14)
Conclusion
   A. Testing and Faith
   B. Prayer
   C. Thought to Remember

Introduction

A. Testing Commitment

As a competitive swimmer in high school, I had to practice every weekday. One wintry Friday evening, our coach assigned us to swim an extraordinarily long set. He didn't explain why he selected the grueling workout, only that it would test both our physical endurance and mental strength. Some teammates complained that the workout would upset their Friday night plans, so they refused to complete it. Others started the set but couldn't finish. Only four of us completed the workout—a completion rate of 10 percent of the team!

When we arrived at practice the following Monday, our coach revealed that he had selected the team captains based on the workout from Friday night. He said that the four who finished—me and three others—had proven themselves committed and "mentally tough" enough to accept the responsibility of being team captains.

Numerous examples from Scripture describe times when God tested His people's commitment (Exodus 20:20; Deuteronomy 8:2; Job 23:10; Psalm 66:10; etc.). God challenges His people to remain faithful to and obey Him even in the most difficult circumstances. This week's lesson will address one of the most famous examples of divine testing.

B. Lesson Context

While the Scriptures recognize Abraham as a man of faith (Genesis 15:6; Romans 4:16-22; Galatians 3:6-9; Hebrews 11:8-12, 17-19), his was by no means a perfect faith. He demonstrated great faith in leaving his home in Ur (Genesis 12:1-4). But by the end of the same chapter, he was telling his wife, Sarah, to lie and say she was his sister (12:10-20).

Later, when Sarah failed to conceive, Abraham impregnated her maidservant Hagar rather than seek the Lord's will. This created serious tension in Abraham's household (Genesis 16:1-6). After God made clear to Abraham that Sarah would give him a son, Abraham handed her over to a pagan king (20:1-18), failing once again to trust God.

Despite all this, God remained faithful to Abraham and Sarah. He delivered them from several powerful kings. He watched over the circumstances involving Lot, Hagar, and Ishmael (Hagar's son). And God provided the son of promise for whom Abraham and Sarah had been waiting: Isaac.

Still, by the time we get to Genesis 22, we are left wondering whether God would grow impatient. Abraham was a man of spiritual highs and lows. His faith was strong but inconsistent. The reader is left wondering who the "real" Abraham is. Perhaps Abraham was wondering the same thing. Was he still the man of great faith who left Ur behind to go to an unknown land, or had years of wandering taken their toll on his faith?

I. God Tests
(Genesis 22:1-2)
A. Call (v. 1)

1. And it came to pass after these things, that God did tempt Abraham, and said unto him, Abraham: and he said, Behold, here I am.

The phrase *after these things* indicates a certain passage of time, but we do not know how much time. *Abraham* was 100 years old when Isaac was born (Genesis 21:5). Since Isaac is capable of carrying wood (22:6-8, below), we can assume a passage of several years has occurred since Isaac's birth.

The Hebrew word translated as *tempt* is also translated as "prove" in numerous instances (examples: Exodus 16:4; 20:20), and that is the sense here. God does not tempt anyone to sin (James 1:13). Instead, the idea in this verse is that of proving one's faith through testing. Hebrews 11:17 supports this by saying that Abraham "was tried."

What Do You Think?

What distractions do you need to remove to hear God more clearly?

Digging Deeper

How will you deal with distractions that might prevent you from saying, "Here I am" to God?

B. Requirement (v. 2)
2. And he said, Take now thy son, thine only son Isaac, whom thou lovest, and get thee into the land of Moriah; and offer him there for a burnt offering upon one of the mountains which I will tell thee of.

This verse refers to *Isaac* as Abraham's *only son*. However, Abraham had previously fathered Ishmael through Hagar (Genesis 16). In Genesis 21:9-12 we learn that Ishmael was not the son of promise. He was the son that resulted from Abraham's seeking to fulfill God's promise of an heir through ancient custom rather than divine provision. God did not, however, reject Ishmael altogether. On account of Abraham, God blessed Ishmael and made a great nation of his offspring (21:13). Though God continued to look after Ishmael (21:20), he was no longer Abraham's responsibility. There is only one son of promise to Abraham, and that son is Isaac.

Therefore, it is most startling to read that God asks Abraham to sacrifice the child of the promise. This request is undoubtedly what Abraham finds most disturbing. God had spoken to Abraham many times, often to reiterate covenant promises to make him into a great nation with countless descendants (Genesis 12:1-3, 7; 13:14-17; 15; 17:1-22; 18:13-15; 21:12-13). The command *take now thy son . . . and offer him there for a burnt offering* seems to threaten those promises. Abraham is not only giving up someone he loves but also cutting off the only way he sees possible to beget offspring.

The Law of Moses prohibited human sacrifices (Leviticus 18:21; Deuteronomy 12:31; 18:10). The Old Testament prophets chastised God's people for breaking these commands (Jeremiah 7:30-34; 19:5-6; Ezekiel 20:31; etc.). But Abraham lived five centuries or so before the giving of the Law of Moses, and human sacrifice to pagan gods was not unheard of in the ancient Near East world.

Moriah is mentioned elsewhere in the Bible only in 2 Chronicles 3:1. That passage informs us that centuries after Abraham, King Solomon would build the temple on Mount Moriah in Jerusalem. The location where God asks Abraham to offer his son is the same place where the people will later sacrifice their offerings and very close to where God will offer up His own Son, Jesus.

The Value of Testing

The last 100 years of automobile usage have led to significant safety improvements. By one estimate, traffic fatalities in 1923 in the United States occurred at a rate of 18.65 deaths per 100 million miles traveled. In 2021, that rate had dropped to 1.5 deaths per 100 million miles traveled. What made the difference? Stated simply: better cars.

The National Highway Traffic Safety Administration began doing crash tests in the late 1970s. We've all seen videos of those tests—cars crumpling under various impacts and the crash-test dummies flailing about. Car makers began responding to government regulations based on these tests. As a result, seat belts, airbags, and improved construction have drastically reduced fatalities and injuries.

The purpose of testing is to discover strengths and weaknesses. Trust in God helps us build on the former and minimize the effects of the latter, even if we don't understand why we are being tested. This was the case for Abraham. Should we look forward to testing or dread it?   —C. R. B.

II. Abraham Acts
(Genesis 22:3-10)

A. Journey and Preparation (vv. 3-6)

3. And Abraham rose up early in the morning, and saddled his ass, and took two of his young men with him, and Isaac his son, and clave the wood for the burnt offering, and rose up, and went unto the place of which God had told him.

We are not told that Abraham said anything in response to God's command. There is no haggling with God, as we see in Genesis 18:22-33. *Abraham wasted no time carrying out his assignment.* His

How to Say It

Beer-sheba	Beer-*she*-buh.
Hagar	*Hay*-gar.
Haran	*Hair*-un.
Ishmael	*Ish*-may-el.
Jehovahjireh	Jeh-*ho*-vuh-*jye*-ruh.
Moriah	Mo-*rye*-uh.
Ur	Er.

actions speak for themselves as he rose *early* the next day to begin the trip. The journey required that *two of his young* male servants be brought along. Abraham probably needed their help handling the logistics of food, clothing, bedding, and pack animals required for the trip.

This verse reveals Abraham's faithfulness and obedience to God. When God initially called him from Haran, Abraham followed in hopes of receiving the promises (Genesis 12:1-4). Now Abraham followed God's lead in full awareness that he might lose his son and, thereby, the promises of God.

> **What Do You Think?**
> How can believers prepare themselves to do the work God calls them to do?
> **Digging Deeper**
> Who can be an accountability partner or spiritual mentor to help support your preparation in this regard?

4. Then on the third day Abraham lifted up his eyes, and saw the place afar off.

If we assume that Abraham's point of departure is Beer-sheba according to Genesis 21:22-34, then the trip to Moriah is one of about 50 miles. This three-day journey gave him plenty of time to get cold feet, devise an excuse, or otherwise maneuver his way out of this terrible assignment. In building such time into this test, God made sure that Abraham's compliance would not be an impulsive act. Abraham's faith was tested in the crucible of time.

5. And Abraham said unto his young men, Abide ye here with the ass; and I and the lad will go yonder and worship, and come again to you.

Abraham needed the aid of the *young men* to reach this point, but now he must leave them behind. Abraham's statement *I and the lad will go yonder and worship, and come again to you* injects irony and ambiguity into the narrative. Whether or not Abraham intended to lie, his words will ultimately prove accurate. Hebrews 11:19 offers helpful commentary in stating that Abraham was willing to sacrifice his son because he believed that God could bring him back from the dead. In that case, we can read Abraham's words in the verse before us as proof of his trust in God's promises.

6. And Abraham took the wood of the burnt offering, and laid it upon Isaac his son; and he took the fire in his hand, and a knife; and they went both of them together.

The narrative as we have it provides minimum details. It says nothing about the emotional state of *Abraham* or *Isaac*. We know nothing of how Abraham may have felt as he laid *the wood of the burnt offering* on the back of *his son* whose body may soon be consumed. It is noteworthy that Jesus also carried on His back the wood that was His own cross to Golgotha (John 19:17).

B. Question and Answer (vv. 7-8)

7. And Isaac spake unto Abraham his father, and said, My father: and he said, Here am I, my son. And he said, Behold the fire and the wood: but where is the lamb for a burnt offering?

At last we hear from Isaac, and his address draws the second of the three *Here am I* (or "Here I am") responses in today's text (the other two are found in Genesis 22:1 and 22:11). This verse indicates that Abraham has not yet told Isaac what is about to happen. Isaac's question is to be expected. He and his father have all the elements for a sacrificial offering except for the sacrificial animal itself.

The description of Isaac speaking *unto Abraham his father* by saying "*My father*" may seem unnecessarily wordy at first glance. But the intent may be to highlight the drama. Using our "sanctified imaginations," we might presume an attitude of excitement behind Isaac's question *where is the lamb for the burnt offering?* as he presumes this to be a special outing, maybe even a feast for just the two of them. On the flip side, we easily imagine a somber tone in Abraham's address of Isaac as "*my son*."

What Do You Think?

How have the words of a child increased your knowledge of God or strengthened your faith?

Digging Deeper

How can you communicate spiritual truths to children in an honest and age-appropriate way?

---

8. And Abraham said, My son, God will provide himself a lamb for a burnt offering: so they went both of them together.

Some students of the text think that *Abraham* intended to mislead Isaac to avoid scaring him. A better idea is that Abraham was so convinced by God's provision that he was confident in God's miraculous provision to provide *a lamb for a burnt offering*. Abraham likely knew that God's promise does not depend on human planning, so he waited expectantly for God to provide.

C. Arrival and Intention (vv. 9-10)

9. And they came to the place which God had told him of; and Abraham built an altar there, and laid the wood in order, and bound Isaac his son, and laid him on the altar upon the wood.

The text does not disclose the age of *Isaac*. While he may have been a child, some later Jewish interpretations of this text believed that Isaac was grown and past the age of 13. The basis for this interpretation is that Isaac willingly submitted to being sacrificed. God's request of Abraham might seem to be less problematic if Isaac himself volunteered to die.

The *altar* Abraham built may be no more than a simple pile of rocks. *The wood* was laid on top of the rocks, and the offering was on top of the wood. For Abraham to bind *Isaac his son* may not be a simple matter, however, if the lad resisted. But the text gives no indication that he does. The succinct narration emphasizes Abraham's obedience: he showed commitment to God by completing the procedures to sacrifice his son.

10. And Abraham stretched forth his hand, and took the knife to slay his son.

No spoken words are recorded, but it's easy to conjecture what is going through the minds of both father and son. The level of Abraham's anguish probably matches the level of Isaac's terror. Only God's intervention can stop things now.

III. God Intervenes
(Genesis 22:11-14)
A. Sacrifice Halted (vv. 11-12)

11. And the angel of the LORD called unto him out of heaven, and said, Abraham, Abraham: and he said, Here am I.

WE CAN TRUST GOD TO PROVIDE.

Visual for Lesson 3. *Display this visual as you discuss the lesson commentary and discussion questions associated with Genesis 22:13-14.*

This verse provides the story's climax: God's intervention through *the angel of the Lord*. This title is a designation given to God's angelical beings who often relay the words of God (examples: Genesis 16:7-8; Judges 13:3; 2 Kings 1:3).

In the verse before us, the angel does not appear to Abraham. Instead, the angel speaks to Abraham from *heaven*. For the third and final time in this story, Abraham responds, *Here am I* when addressed. Abraham is interrupted just as he is about to carry out the sacrifice commanded of him. The twofold calling of *Abraham, Abraham* carries a sense of urgency.

The scene is similar to what later occurs at the burning bush with Moses. There, the angel of the Lord appeared to Moses "in a flame of fire out of the midst of a bush" (Exodus 3:2), but then God is said to be the one who calls to Moses from the bush (3:4). It is clear that the angel represents divine authority.

Where Are You?

Malaysia Airlines Flight 370 disappeared on March 8, 2014. The last voice contact with the crew came less than an hour after takeoff. Radar showed the plane deviating from its flight plan soon afterward. Satellite tracking eventually revealed that the flight headed southwest over the Indian Ocean. Nearly a year and a half later, debris from the plane began to appear. As of January 2024, the entire aircraft has yet to be found.

Flight 370's disappearance has led to various theories about the cause. Was it an act of terrorism? Did the pilot intentionally change the flight path and crash the plane into the ocean? All we can ask regarding this flight is, "Where are you?"

When God and Isaac each called to Abraham, that man declared his presence by saying, "Here am I." He had not deviated from where he was expected to be. Whether the situation involves family, friends, work, or our relationship with God, when we are called upon to be wholly present, the only satisfactory answer is "Here am I," when "here" is the appropriate place to be. It's a matter of integrity and responsibility. But ultimately, it's a matter of being accountable to those we love and who love us, especially God. —C. R. B.

12. And he said, Lay not thine hand upon the lad, neither do thou any thing unto him: for now I know that thou fearest God, seeing thou hast not withheld thy son, thine only son from me.

The angel ordered Abraham to halt, thus preventing any physical harm to Isaac. The angel reveals the rationale for God's request: to test whether Abraham was willing to give up his *only son* out of obedience to God.

These words tell us that Abraham has indeed passed the test. In essence, God asked him, "Do you trust me and me alone to fulfill my promises to you? Are you willing to give up all control and place your entire future into my hands?" The answer to both questions is a resounding *yes!*

No other feat could demonstrate with such certainty Abraham's faith in God alone to fulfill His promise. Isaac is not merely his only son (see commentary on Genesis 22:2, above); Isaac was Abraham's only chance to secure future promises. In raising the knife, Abraham boldly declared his conviction that God is his only hope. With that unspoken confession of faith, he received his son back, as though from the dead (Hebrews 11:19).

We should not misinterpret the phrase *thou fearest*. God is not glad that Abraham was afraid of Him. Instead, *fear* is another way to express worship. It signifies that Abraham understood that his son and, thus, his future belonged to God. Abraham's obedience echoes David's later testimony of the Lord: "For as the heaven is high above the earth, so great is his mercy toward them that fear him" (Psalm 103:11).

The will of God was the driving force in Abraham's life. God was his ultimate motivation. Abraham's actions reveal the heart of true worship. God values obedience over sacrifice (1 Samuel 15:22).

> **What Do You Think?**
> What are the lifestyles and behaviors of someone who fears God?
> **Digging Deeper**
> What steps will you take to worship God in the upcoming week?

B. Sacrifice Provided (vv. 13-14)

13. And Abraham lifted up his eyes, and looked, and behold behind him a ram caught in a thicket by his horns: and Abraham went and took the ram, and offered him up for a burnt offering in the stead of his son.

Centuries after Abraham, the Law of Moses would prescribe the use of a ram for sacrificial offerings (Leviticus 5:15; 9:4; etc.) and in ordination proceedings (8:22; etc.).

God did indeed provide for the sacrifice. The *ram* was not provided when Abraham began his three-day journey, along the journey, or at the foot of Mount Moriah. It was provided only after Abraham demonstrated his willingness to go all the way in carrying out God's instructions.

The mention of Abraham's *eyes* is important, given what occurs in the following verse.

14. And Abraham called the name of that place Jehovahjireh: as it is said to this day, In the mount of the LORD it shall be seen.

God faithfully provided for Abraham. As a result, the man names the location *Jehovahjireh*, which means "The Lord will see" or "The Lord will provide." Abraham fully understood that the one true God always sees that His people are provided for.

It is worth noting that Abraham does not name the place "Isaac Is Spared" or "A Father Is Relieved." This account has been about God's

faithfulness and whether Abraham truly believes that God will keep His promises. Indeed, God is faithful, and Abraham truly believed.

> **What Do You Think?**
> How will you have spiritual "eyes" to notice God's provision?
> **Digging Deeper**
> What steps will you take to worship and praise God for His provision?

Conclusion

A. Testing and Faith

Tests reveal the preparation of the one tested. Some tests also expose the character of the person being tested. God's testing of Abraham in today's Scripture text exposed that man's trust, loyalty, and devotion. It proved the authenticity of his faith, the faith for which God pronounced Abraham righteous (Genesis 15:6; see James 2:21-23).

The testing of Abraham also revealed God's faithfulness and promises to His people. God preserved the life of Isaac and, therefore, reiterated His promises to multiply Abraham's descendants and bless all nations.

God's people will continue to face tests and trials. Not all of these trials will be from God in the same manner as Abraham's test. Trials prove the strength and sincerity of our faith (1 Peter 1:6-7). While we may never hear a voice from God at the test's conclusion, we can be confident that God will be with us in our trials as we grow in faith, perseverance, and maturity (James 1:2-4).

B. Prayer

Lord God, we call on You to be in our lives what You have been for our forefathers and foremothers of the faith. Give us faith to trust in Your provision and empower us through Your Spirit to remain faithful to You. We want to grow our faith in strength and witness. We trust You and love You. In Jesus' name we pray. Amen.

C. Thought to Remember

God always provides,
but not always in the ways we expect.

Involvement Learning

Enhance your lesson with KJV Bible Student *(from your curriculum supplier) and the reproducible activity page (at www.standardlesson.com or in the back of the* KJV Standard Lesson Commentary Deluxe Edition*).*

Into the Lesson

Write each of the following statements on a separate slip of paper:

1–Sacrifice must involve pain.
2–Sacrifice gets easier after you are used to doing it.
3–My sacrifice and your sacrifice may be completely different.
4–"Sacrificial living" is a daily requirement for a Christian.
5–Everyone will sacrifice something significant at some point.
6–You call it a sacrifice; I call it my duty.

Divide the class into six groups and distribute a slip of paper to each group. Have groups discuss whether or not they agree with their assigned statement and make an argument in support of or in opposition to the assigned statement. After five minutes of in-group work, ask volunteers from each group to read their assigned statement and state the main points of their group's argument.

Lead into Bible study by saying, "In today's lesson, we will look at one of the Bible's best-known stories about sacrifice. As we read it carefully, we'll learn how that sacrifice involved trust in God."

Into the Word

Invite a volunteer to read today's text. Distribute handouts (you create) of the sentences below. Ask learners to work with a partner to mark each statement as either *True* or *False*. For each false statement, each pair should rewrite the statement to make it correct.

1–The Law of Moses required that Abraham sacrifice his son.
2– Abraham tried to talk God out of the request.
3–Abraham's servants assisted in the construction of the altar.
4–Abraham told Isaac that God would provide a ram for a burnt offering.
5–Abraham did not bind Isaac before placing him on the altar.
6–Through a burning bush, God spoke to Abraham regarding the sacrifice of Isaac.

7–Abraham named the location "God Gives Us Calm."

After five minutes, share that each sentence is false. Ask volunteers to share their corrected sentences. Challenge learners to provide the Scripture references that support the rewritten sentences.

Option. Distribute copies of the "Questions, I Have Questions" exercise from the activity page, which you can download. Have learners work in pairs to complete as indicated.

Into Life

Distribute handouts (you create) to each learner with the following statements printed on each handout:

1–God doesn't always provide for us what we want or when we want it.
2–We don't always understand God's commands.
3–It is easier to *talk* about trust than to *demonstrate* trust.
4–Following God requires radical obedience.

Ask learners to work in pairs to decide how each statement is demonstrated in today's text. Then, ask learners to share with their partner how each statement has been confirmed in his or her own life.

Distribute index cards and pens to learners. Ask them to write down a difficult situation or sacrifice currently being faced. Then, on the other side of the card, direct them to write down a way to exhibit greater trust in the Lord in that difficult situation. Tell learners that this exercise will be private and that you will not ask them to share with the class or a partner. After one minute of individual work, direct learners to spend a few moments in prayer with a partner. Have learners pray that their partners might trust God and experience God's provision in the upcoming week.

Option. Distribute copies of the "Looking for Trust" exercise from the activity page. Have learners work with a partner to complete the activity as directed.

Isaac Calls on the Name of the Lord

Devotional Reading: Genesis 26:12-23
Background Scripture: Genesis 26:1-33

Genesis 26:24-33

24 And the LORD appeared unto him the same night, and said, I am the God of Abraham thy father: fear not, for I am with thee, and will bless thee, and multiply thy seed for my servant Abraham's sake.

25 And he builded an altar there, and called upon the name of the LORD, and pitched his tent there: and there Isaac's servants digged a well.

26 Then Abimelech went to him from Gerar, and Ahuzzath one of his friends, and Phichol the chief captain of his army.

27 And Isaac said unto them, wherefore come ye to me, seeing ye hate me, and have sent me away from you?

28 And they said, we saw certainly that the LORD was with thee: and we said, let there be now an oath betwixt us, even betwixt us and thee, and let us make a covenant with thee;

29 That thou wilt do us no hurt, as we have not touched thee, and as we have done unto thee nothing but good, and have sent thee away in peace: thou art now the blessed of the LORD.

30 And he made them a feast, and they did eat and drink.

31 And they rose up betimes in the morning, and sware one to another: and Isaac sent them away, and they departed from him in peace.

32 And it came to pass the same day, that Isaac's servants came, and told him concerning the well which they had digged, and said unto him, we have found water.

33 And he called it Shebah: therefore the name of the city is Beersheba unto this day.

Key Text

He builded an altar there, and called upon the name of the LORD, and pitched his tent there: and there Isaac's servants digged a well. —**Genesis 26:25**

Sacred Altars and
Holy Offerings

Unit 1: The Genesis of Altars and Sacrifices
Lessons 1–5

Lesson Aims

After participating in this lesson, each learner will be able to:

1. State the importance of Isaac's godly heritage.

2. Present evidence of God's presence with Isaac.

3. Identify evidence of God's presence in his or her life and express gratitude to God for His presence.

Lesson Outline

Introduction
    A. Treaties and Friendships
    B. Lesson Context
 I. Covenant Promises (Genesis 26:24-25)
    A. God's Remembrance (v. 24)
     Fear Not
    B. Isaac's Response (v. 25)
     Questioning God's Faithfulness
 II. Promises Kept (Genesis 26:26-33)
    A. Threat of Violence (vv. 26-27)
    B. Making Peace (vv. 28-31)
    C. Divine Provision (vv. 32-33)
Conclusion
    A. Provision of Peace
    B. Prayer
    C. Thoughts to Remember

Introduction

A. Treaties and Friendships

The formal surrender of Japan on September 2, 1945, officially ended World War II, but a threat of conflict remained. While the Soviet Union eventually joined the Allies, the leaders of Western Europe and the United States never forgot that Joseph Stalin had signed a nonaggression pact with Germany in 1939. They knew that the Soviet Union wanted to continue to grow in territory and influence.

As a check against further aggression, the United States and 11 other nations formed the North Atlantic Treaty Organization (NATO) in 1949. The key provision of this treaty was collective defense: the countries who signed would consider an attack against one nation as an attack on them all. Even the smaller states, who had limited militaries, would gain an umbrella of protection if a foreign power were to invade or attack. The treaty bound its signers across generations and offered future security. Leaders and administrations could change, but the descendants of those who signed continue to honor and benefit from this assurance.

While NATO is unique in many respects, similar binding agreements have been used throughout history. In the Bible and the ancient Near East, these treaties were known as "covenants." Some covenants were made between groups of people or nations (examples: Joshua 9:14-15; 1 Samuel 20:12-17). However, much of the biblical narrative focuses on God's covenants with His people.

Last week's lesson on Genesis 22 examined the circumstances in which God guaranteed covenant protection to Abraham and his descendants. This week, we will explore how God showed himself faithful to those promises.

B. Lesson Context

After the death of Abraham (Genesis 25:1-11), the focus of Genesis shifts to Abraham's heir, Isaac. In the covenantal promises to Abraham, God committed to ensuring security and growth for Abraham's family (13:16; 15:4-5). The family line continued into a third generation when

God blessed Isaac and his wife Rebekah with twin boys, Jacob and Esau (25:19-26).

Isaac was the child of God's promise, the one to inherit the covenant blessings (Genesis 15:3-4; 18:10-14; 21:1-7). However, the security of Isaac's family was not yet clear. Some of the same patterns in Abraham's life were repeated in Isaac's. He became a wanderer in a foreign land, like his father (26:1; compare 12:10). God directed Isaac where he should go and promised him the same things that were promised to Abraham: land, innumerable descendants, and a blessing for other nations (26:2-5; compare 12:1-3). Nonetheless, Isaac experienced tensions with his neighbors and faced competition for resources (26:12-15). His lack of familial ties would have made him seem suspicious wherever he went.

Isaac also shared the same feelings of cowardice and callousness toward his wife Rebecca that Abraham felt toward Sarah. Fearing that Philistines might kill him and take Rebecca, Isaac claimed she was his sister (Genesis 26:7; compare 12:13; 20:2). Ironically, Isaac repeated this trick on a Philistine king named Abimelech, someone possibly related to the very king who had taken Abraham's wife. God providentially ensured that Abimelech saw Isaac behave intimately with Rebekah, and Abimelech forbid anyone from touching her (26:8-11; compare 20:3-13).

Abraham and Isaac both came into conflict with the Philistines over water resources. Since they were herders in the Negev—a region that receives less than 10 inches of rain per year—they both relied on finding water to sustain their herds. The first Abimelech eventually recognized Abraham's water rights (Genesis 21:25-32), but the Philistines filled up Abraham's wells with dirt after his death (26:15). As Isaac's wealth grew, the goodwill of the Philistines ran dry, and they pushed him from the land (26:17-22).

The parallels between the stories of Abraham and Isaac are crucial to understanding today's lesson. God reiterated the same promises to Isaac, but Isaac had new problems: former allies had become enemies. He was eager to know whether God would prove faithful in his situation, as God had been to his father.

I. Covenant Promises
(Genesis 26:24-25)
A. God's Remembrance (v. 24)

24. And the LORD appeared unto him the same night, and said, I am the God of Abraham thy father: fear not, for I am with thee, and will bless thee, and multiply thy seed and for my servant Abraham's sake.

After facing conflicts over water rights, Isaac departed for Beersheba (Genesis 26:23), where Abraham and the previous Philistine king had made a covenant (21:27, 31). Beersheba is located roughly 75 miles southwest of modern-day Jerusalem, at the northern tip of the Negev Desert. In this stressful situation, *the Lord* intervened to comfort Isaac. The Lord identified himself as *the God of Abraham thy father*, emphasizing Isaac's heritage.

God highlighted Isaac's unique role as He offered encouragement to Isaac. The expression *fear not* sometimes appears in Scripture's accounts of angelic appearances (examples: Genesis 21:17; Luke 2:10). In this case, the admonition likely targeted Isaac's fear of his circumstances. Isaac did not need to fear; God promised to remain with Isaac and *bless* him as God would *multiply* his descendants. These promises and the encouragement are similar to the ones God made to Abraham (Genesis 15:1, 4-5).

The explanatory phrase *for my servant Abraham's sake* highlights why Isaac received the blessing, giving him reason to trust in God. The stipulations of God's covenant with Abraham transcended generational boundaries, benefiting Isaac and his descendants. If Isaac doubted whether God would show concern, he could rely on the fact that God would honor His previous promises to Abraham.

> **What Do You Think?**
> How can believers honor the faith traditions passed down by previous generations of God's people?
>
> **Digging Deeper**
> How will you encourage and support younger generations of believers in their walk with God?

Fear Not

One night, I dreamt I was being thrown overboard into the sea with a heavy load tied to my waist. On the list of things I fear the most, drowning would rank near the top. In this dream, I felt as if I had something left to say, but I couldn't communicate it before I slipped beneath the waves. I awoke from the dream, startled. Gasping for breath, I could still feel a tightness in my chest.

Sometimes, I marvel at the things people have endured for the sake of Christ. I wonder whether I have the strength to endure persecution or death for the sake of the Lord. Do you imagine you could face your worst fear if God were to ask? What is one way to remind yourself that you are not alone?

—J. K.

B. Isaac's Response (v. 25)

25. And he builded an altar there, and called upon the name of the LORD, and pitched his tent there: and there Isaac's servants digged a well.

Both Abraham and Isaac built altars as places for sacrifice and prayer. Abraham built an altar to mark off the territory of Canaan for his family and to create memorials in the places where God had appeared (Genesis 12:7-8; 13:4, 18; 22:9). Isaac's son Jacob would also build an altar (33:20; 35:1-7).

An altar was more than a pile of rough stones; it was a holy spot, a marker of the connection between the divine and human space, and a place of access to God. People often used the same altar for generations, even centuries. At this *altar*, Isaac *called upon the name of the Lord* for protection and guidance and made this location his home as he *pitched his tent there*.

Apparently, there was no easily accessible water source, like a stream or spring, at this location. To address this shortcoming, Isaac's *servants digged a well*. The act of digging a well was a source of tension that had led Isaac to this location (see Genesis 26:17-22). Although Isaac was the recipient of covenantal promises, he continued to face practical challenges—water was hard to come by!

Questioning God's Faithfulness

I arrived home one day to find my car, but not as I had left it. Rather than sitting on four wheels and tires, one side of the car sat on cinder blocks, and the other sat on the curb. Over the next several days, I spent countless hours navigating how to report the theft and repair the car. I installed new wheels, but not before the city towed my car and charged me to recover it. The whole situation perplexed me, and during one phone conversation, I let my frustrations be known.

During the whole ordeal, I had trouble knowing that God was with me and that He was in control. But God *did* supply everything I needed, helping me through that difficult season.

I was never in as much danger as Isaac, and God brought him through even worse circumstances. Have you experienced so much frustration that you question God's provision? Do you have a better sense of God's presence when you look back in hindsight?

—J. K.

II. Promises Kept
(Genesis 26:26-33)
A. Threat of Violence (vv. 26-27)

26. Then Abimelech went to him from Gerar and Ahuzzath one of his friends, and Phichol the chief captain of his army.

Abimelech and the Gerarites opposed Isaac partly because of his deception regarding his wife, Rebekah. Their king had complained, "One of the people might lightly have lien with thy wife, and thou shouldest have brought guiltiness upon us" (Genesis 26:10). They presumed that the God of Isaac would have punished them if they violated his wife even accidentally (compare 12:17).

The people from Gerar had proved to be fearsome defenders of "their" water resources. They had closed Abraham's wells, a hostile act that risked destroying Isaac's flocks, throwing him into poverty, or perhaps even killing him (Genesis 26:18). The narrative implies that Isaac had headed toward Beersheba to escape this conflict (26:22-23). However, the conflict seemed to be following Isaac.

Abimelech brought two of his highest officials. The designation *friends* refers to the king's associates and advisors, like a modern-day presidential cabinet. This verse is the only mention in the Bible of an individual named *Ahuzzath*. The name *Phichol* likely has its roots in the Egyptian language, a reminder that the region of Gerar was located on the edge of Egyptian territory, where other powerful rulers lived.

27. And Isaac said unto them, Wherefore come ye to me, seeing ye hate me, and have sent me away from you?

Isaac's question implied both surprise and fear upon seeing the unexpected visitor. The mistreatment Isaac had faced at the hands of Abimelech's men had forced him to leave Gerar (see Lesson Context).

The word *hate* can refer to a feeling of animosity toward someone else. In this context, however, it probably refers to the aggressive actions of Abimelech and his people against Isaac's household. Although Abimelech had a positive relationship with Abraham, the Philistines treated Isaac with disdain and had pushed him out of their territory. Isaac was left wondering what reason Abimelech could have had for pursuing him to Beersheba.

Visual for Lesson 4. *Display this visual as you ask the following question for discussion: "How do you call on the name of the Lord?"*

> **What Do You Think?**
>
> How should a believer respond to an apparent adversary who requests reconciliation?
>
> **Digging Deeper**
>
> What Scripture texts should inform the believer's response?

B. Making Peace (vv. 28-31)

28. And they said, We saw certainly that the Lord was with thee: and we said, Let there be now an oath betwixt us, even betwixt us and thee, and let us make a covenant with thee.

But Abimelech and his advisors had not come to make trouble for Isaac. On the contrary, they were afraid of him and the power of *the Lord*. Isaac's abundant harvest and the rapid growth of his wealth had convinced them that Isaac enjoyed divine favor (see Genesis 26:12-14). Their admission *that the Lord was with* Isaac does not mean that they had become followers of the one true God of Abraham and Isaac. Many people of the ancient Near Eastern world believed that numerous gods existed, and a wise person would avoid offending the most powerful gods and the people under the protection of those gods. Isaac's blessings were (rightly) perceived as evidence of God's power and favor on Isaac. Rather than offend Isaac and earn the wrath of God, Abimelech and his people attempt to make peace with them both.

To that end, Abimelech suggested that they swear an *oath* and *make a covenant with* one another. The Hebrew terms translated *oath* and *covenant* frequently occur together in the Old Testament (examples: Deuteronomy 29:12; Ezekiel 17:13-14). The connection between oaths and covenants lies in the mechanics of covenant-making: the two sides put a covenant into effect by swearing an oath. The oath was a conditional curse to place on oneself, if one of the parties to the agreement broke it. The potential curses could be elaborate, as seen in the list of curses threatened against Israel in Deuteronomy 28:15-68.

Thus, Abimelech spoke in the technical language of ancient diplomacy when he proposed this arrangement with Isaac. This type of agreement is called a "parity treaty," which means a commitment between two equal parties. While the Philistines had previously envied and disrespected Isaac, they now treated him with the honor expected for someone with equal social status.

29. That thou wilt do us no hurt, as we have not touched thee, and as we have done unto

thee nothing but good, and have sent thee away in peace: thou art now the blessed of the LORD.

This verse outlines the content of the oath Abimelech wishes them to take. He asks Isaac to *do us no hurt*, which could refer to taking military action against the people of Gerar. But after Abimelech's assertions about Isaac's divine favor, and also seeing that he called Isaac *blessed of the Lord*, Abimelech's fear was more likely that Isaac would appeal to God for their destruction.

As a basis for this request, Abimelech claimed that he and his men had not harmed Isaac; instead, they had done only good to him and sent him away *in peace*. Abimelech's words appear one-sided, as Isaac had left Gerar after experiencing mistreatment by the people living there. There are two possible explanations for Abimelech's claims. First, Abimelech might have referred to his immediate intentions: right then and there, he was not attacking Isaac or acting in any manner other than kindness toward him. Second, Abimelech could have been asking Isaac to dismiss the prior behavior of Abimelech's people. In either case, the ruler of Gerar asked Isaac for peace between them. Thus, in a surprising display of divine providence, Isaac's enemies suddenly became his friends.

What Do You Think?

How can your business agreements or partnerships be a way for you to represent Christ to an unbeliever?

Digging Deeper

What are other ways you can apply the teachings of the Bible to your business dealings?

30. And he made them a feast, and they did eat and drink.

Isaac turned to hospitality toward his new allies and friends. The *feast* cemented their new relationship. In most ancient cultures, feasting was a tool for building alliances—whether at marriages, funerals, major holidays, or the beginning of business partnerships (examples: Genesis 29:22; 1 Kings 1:24-25; Esther 2:18).

Additionally, covenant ceremonies sometimes included a ritual meal. Exodus 24:11 notes that the leaders of Israel "did eat and drink" in God's presence after the ritual sacrifice and sprinkling with the blood of the covenant (Exodus 24:6-8).

In the New Testament era, the practice of Communion instituted by Jesus combines a meal with a covenant, with its reference to Christ's "blood of the new testament" (Matthew 26:28; Mark 14:24; Luke 22:20). The word "Testament" in these verses translates as the same Greek word as "covenant" in Galatians 3:15, 17.

Therefore, by serving a meal, Isaac showed his guests the expected courtesy. The feast also completed the ritual that bound them together in peace.

What Do You Think?

What steps will you take to plan a feast celebrating God's work in your neighborhood?

Digging Deeper

Who among your neighbors will you ask to help plan such a feast?

31. And they rose up betimes in the morning, and sware one to another: and Isaac sent them away, and they departed from him in peace.

The next day saw the final parts of their ceremony of alliance-making. The parties of the covenant swore their oaths *one to another*, asking God to hold them to account if they should break them. To go *in peace* means not just that they avoided immediate conflict, but they also anticipate a continuing positive relationship with one another.

The Hebrew word translated as "peace" is *shalom*, which has a wide array of meanings, including "wholeness," "good health," or even "success." It is a favorite term that the prophets of Israel and Judah use to reflect a vision of restored order and community (examples: Isaiah 55:12; Jeremiah 29:7; Malachi 2:5-6). Isaac *sent* Abimelech *away* with their conflict fully resolved.

C. Divine Provision (vv. 32-33)

32. And it came to pass the same day, that Isaac's servants came, and told him concerning the well which they had digged, and said unto him, We have found water.

The same day sets the context as being immediately after Abimelech's party left. The result is that Isaac would have the impression that finding *water* was a sign of God's blessing and covenant fidelity. As if one blessing for the day was not enough, God also addressed the immediate need of Isaac and his family for survival (see Genesis 26:25, above).

33. And he called it Shebah: therefore the name of the city is Beersheba unto this day.

The name *Shebah* sounds like the Hebrew word for "oath." It is joined to the Hebrew word translated "well" to become a new name: *Beersheba*. This account explains the origins of a major Israelite town—one still occupied today—as the location of divine blessings. The *city* became a reminder of the covenants that Isaac and his father, Abraham, had made that forged justice and peace between neighbors. The designation points to the hope of peace between enemies and stands as an image of God's faithfulness to Abraham's family.

Conclusion

A. Provision of Peace

Scripture tells of a God who made covenants with His people and followed through on each and every promise. Long before God rescued the Israelites from Egypt and gave them the law at Mount Sinai, He made a covenant with their ancestor, Abraham. God promised Abraham a homeland and descendants as numerous as the grains of sand and the stars in the sky (Genesis 13:16; 15:5). God also promised that "all families

How to Say It

Abimelech	Uh-bim-eh-lek.
Ahuzzath	Uh-*huz*-uth.
Beersheba	Beer-*she*-buh.
Gerar	*Gear*-rar (*G* as in *get*).
Phichol	*Fye*-kahl.
Philistines	Fuh-*liss*-teenz
	or *Fill*-us-teenz.
shalom (*Hebrew*)	shah-lome.
Sinai	*Sigh*-nye
	or *Sigh*-nay-eye.

of the earth" could "be blessed" through Abraham and his offspring (12:3). Abraham did not see those promises fulfilled in his lifetime, but he saw their beginning when Sarah bore him a son, Isaac. Isaac became the heir of promises and suffered many of the same hardships and disappointments as his father. But God was with him.

God was with Isaac when he was searching for water and security. Although we don't understand how God orchestrated those circumstances, God turned Isaac's enemies into his allies. Instead of fearing for his life, Isaac's circumstances were changed by God in a matter of days.

For modern-day readers, the account of Isaac and Abimelech does not mean that God will always turn our enemies into friends. In Isaac's case, God protected him because, through his descendent, Jesus, God would fulfill His most important promise. Through Jesus, God offers reconciliation and peace (Romans 5:1).

God's offer of grace comes to people who are counted as "enemies" before God (Romans 5:10). Therefore, we can take consolation that, even though human alliances can fail, the peace that God grants through Jesus will never fail; God is always faithful to keep His promises.

> **What Do You Think?**
> How would you explain the significance of biblical covenants to a new believer?
> **Digging Deeper**
> How would you explain their significance to an unbeliever?

B. Prayer

Heavenly Father, thank You for the gift of the Holy Spirit, who leads us to seek peace with our friends, neighbors, and enemies. When we fail to find peace with others, remind us that we can have peace with You. Help us be like Jesus, who was willing to show kindness to us when we were still like enemies. Teach us to seek peace, with Christ's example before our eyes. In Jesus' name we pray. Amen.

C. Thought to Remember

God keeps His covenant promises.

Involvement Learning

Enhance your lesson with KJV Bible Student *(from your curriculum supplier) and the reproducible activity page (at www.standardlesson.com or in the back of the* KJV Standard Lesson Commentary Deluxe Edition*).*

Into the Lesson

Divide learners into groups of four. State that you will begin today's class with a time for informal debate regarding the following proposition:

The strength of a child's faith can be predicted by looking at the faith of that child's family of origin.

Direct half of the groups to come up with reasons they *agree* with the proposition, while the other half should come up with reasons they *disagree* with the proposition.

After five minutes of in-group discussion, reconvene the class. Ask volunteers to offer their group's argument, agreeing or disagreeing with the proposition. After all groups have shared, determine a conclusion to the proposition. For whole-class discussion, ask, "How do your life experiences influence your conclusion?"

Alternative. Divide the class into groups of four and assign each group a prominent figure from history (*examples*: Abraham Lincoln, Winston Churchill, Harriet Tubman, Maya Angelou). Direct groups to do a brief Internet search into the life of their assigned figure. Challenge groups to look closely at how the experiences of this person's early life influenced their life and accomplishments. After no more than 10 minutes, ask the groups to share their findings with the whole class.

Lead to Bible study by saying, "Today we'll look at a famous man whose family heritage is well documented. Let's see how God's presence in this man's family affected his life."

Into the Word

Ask a volunteer to prepare and present a three-minute presentation on the history of Isaac's family and the background of the events that precede Genesis 26. Encourage the presenter to use the material from the Lesson Context.

On index cards, write the following sets of Scripture references, one set per card: 1–Genesis 26:1; 12:10. 2–Genesis 26:7; 12:13; 20:2. 3–Genesis 26:13-14; 12:16; 13:6. 4–Genesis 26:20-21; 13:7. 5–Genesis 26:26-33; 21:22-34. 6–Genesis 26:24; 13:14-17. 7–Genesis 26:2, 12; 12:7; 13:3-4.

Divide learners into seven groups. Distribute one of the above index cards to each group. Direct groups to read their assigned Scriptures and write down on the other side of the index card how certain events in the life of Abraham parallel those in Isaac's. After five minutes, have each group share its findings with the class

Option. Distribute copies of the "Clues from Today's Story" exercise from the activity page, which you can download. Have learners work in pairs to complete as indicated.

Reconvene the class and ask a volunteer to read aloud Genesis 26:24-33. Ask the following questions for whole-class discussion: 1–Based on the previous activity, what is the significance of God's statement in verse 24? 2–What is the significance of covenants/oaths in this account? 3–How did Isaac know God was with him?

Into Life

Write the following sentences on the board:

1. *Because of my family history, I feel God's presence in my life through . . .*
2. *Despite my family history, I feel God's presence in my life through . . .*

Ask learners to form groups of three. Direct learners to complete either prompt and explain their responses in small-group discussion.

Reconvene the class and ask the following questions for whole-class discussion: 1–How have you experienced God's presence in the past? 2–How has God used difficult or negative experiences to reveal His presence? 3–How will you express gratitude to God for His presence? For each question, do not call on learners, but allow time for them to share responses as they feel led.

Jacob Sets Up a Sacred Pillar

Devotional Reading: John 15:1-8
Background Scripture: Genesis 28:1-22; 33:17-20; 35:1-7

Genesis 28:10-22

10 And Jacob went out from Beersheba, and went toward Haran.

11 And he lighted upon a certain place, and tarried there all night, because the sun was set; and he took of the stones of that place, and put them for his pillows, and lay down in that place to sleep.

12 And he dreamed, and behold a ladder set up on the earth, and the top of it reached to heaven: and behold the angels of God ascending and descending on it.

13 And, behold, the LORD stood above it, and said, I am the LORD God of Abraham thy father, and the God of Isaac: the land whereon thou liest, to thee will I give it, and to thy seed;

14 And thy seed shall be as the dust of the earth, and thou shalt spread abroad to the west, and to the east, and to the north, and to the south: and in thee and in thy seed shall all the families of the earth be blessed.

15 And, behold, I am with thee, and will keep thee in all places whither thou goest, and will bring thee again into this land; for I will not leave thee, until I have done that which I have spoken to thee of.

16 And Jacob awaked out of his sleep, and he said, Surely the LORD is in this place; and I knew it not.

17 And he was afraid, and said, how dreadful is this place! this is none other but the house of God, and this is the gate of heaven.

18 And Jacob rose up early in the morning, and took the stone that he had put for his pillows, and set it up for a pillar, and poured oil upon the top of it.

19 And he called the name of that place Bethel: but the name of that city was called Luz at the first.

20 And Jacob vowed a vow, saying, If God will be with me, and will keep me in this way that I go, and will give me bread to eat, and raiment to put on,

21 So that I come again to my father's house in peace; then shall the LORD be my God:

22 And this stone, which I have set for a pillar, shall be God's house: and of all that thou shalt give me I will surely give the tenth unto thee.

Key Text

Jacob rose up early in the morning, and took the stone that he had put for his pillows, and set it up for a pillar, and poured oil upon the top of it. And he called the name of that place Bethel. —**Genesis 18-19a**

Sacred Altars and
Holy Offerings

Unit 1: The Genesis of Altars and Sacrifices
Lessons 1–5

Lesson Aims

After participating in this lesson, each learner will be able to:

1. Locate on a map the geographical locations mentioned.

2. Analyze Jacob's if-then statement in Genesis 28:20-22.

3. Make a plan to commemorate a particular time when God's presence and work was evident in his or her life.

Lesson Outline

Introduction

A. Common Experiences, Different Paths

Those who work with people may often find themselves traveling in unexpected (and perhaps unwanted) directions. This is true spiritually as well as physically, and one may result in the other. In the process, people find themselves taking roads much less traveled by others. The temptations of envy, pride, contempt, and indifference are common to all, but their intensities and timings threaten to derail our travels at our most vulnerable times. Moments of despair and a sense of defeat can overtake us as we search for that exit ramp that will lead to something different. When we go through painful experiences, we may think we are unique. But we are not unusual in that regard; we see it often in the Old Testament descendants of Abraham.

B. Lesson Context

Genesis 12:1-3 begins the account of a family chosen to be a conduit of blessings to all nations. The text does not explain why God chose this family. The sins and various foibles of the members of that family line may sometimes leave us astonished.

All that is no less true regarding a grandson of Abraham known as Jacob. The book of Genesis presents him as a deceitful person who schemed to take advantage of others. He swindled his brother, Esau, out of his birthright (Genesis 25:27-34). He deceived their father, Isaac, in taking Esau's blessing (27:1-40). Later, Jacob was tricked by his father-in-law, Laban (29:15-27). Jacob tricked Laban in return (30:37-43), with even more deceit following (31:17-21).

Indeed, in the journey he was on in today's lesson, Jacob was on the run from trouble—trouble of his own making. In conspiracy with his mother, his trip was one of self-exile so his brother wouldn't kill him because of a deception (Genesis 27:41). Such a character would hardly seem to be a key person in God's plan to bless all nations!

Yet God worked His will through Jacob nonetheless. Ultimately, Jacob's story is not about his search for God but God's search for him. When found on a physical journey, Jacob began a spiritual journey as well.

I. Jacob's Journey
(Genesis 28:10-11)
A. Itinerary (v. 10)

10. And Jacob went out from Beersheba, and went toward Haran.

Beersheba, a town in southern Canaan, was where Jacob's father, Isaac, eventually settled, following a series of disputes with the Philistines over the ownership of certain wells (Genesis 26:15-33; compare 21:22-34). The expression "from Dan to Beersheba" later is used 10 times in the Old Testament to mark the extremes of Israel's boundaries north to south (Judges 20:1; 1 Samuel 3:20; 2 Samuel 3:10; 17:11; 24:2, 15; 1 Kings 4:25; 1 Chronicles 21:2; 2 Chronicles 30:5; Amos 8:14).

Jacob's destination of *Haran* is where Jacob's grandfather Abraham (named Abram at the time) lived before he left for Canaan (Genesis 11:31). A journey from Beersheba to Haran, where Jacob's relatives still lived (27:43; 28:1-2; 29:11-14; 31:21), was about 550 miles. Walking at a pace of two miles per hour would require a trip that would have taken over a month to complete!

> **What Do You Think?**
> How should prayers differ, if at all, when moving mainly away from an old situation rather than toward a new one?
> **Digging Deeper**
> What Scripture passages best help you answer that question?

B. Stopover (v. 11)

11a. And he lighted upon a certain place, and tarried there all night, because the sun was set.

The name of this *certain place* where Jacob stopped for the night is the town of Luz (Genesis 28:19; see commentary below). It was about 60 miles north of Beersheba, so it took Jacob a few days to reach that point in his journey. With no streetlights or flashlights available to illuminate the way, travelers of that era had to stop when the *sun was set.* Even if the moon were full, continuing onward would be problematic.

11b. And he took of the stones of that place, and put them for his pillows, and lay down in that place to sleep.

We may wonder how Jacob got much sleep with *stones* for *his pillows!* We will understand the significance of this later in today's lesson (see Genesis 28:18, below). And this will be no ordinary night of sleep in any case.

II. Jacob's Dream
(Genesis 28:12-15)
A. Seeing Angels (v. 12)

12. And he dreamed, and behold a ladder set up on the earth, and the top of it reached to heaven: and behold the angels of God ascending and descending on it.

Jacob's dream is either the second or third dream mentioned in Genesis. Another dream explicitly labeled as such is in Genesis 20:3-7. There is a potential dream in 15:12-16, although the terms "dream" or "dreamed" are not explicitly used. Dreams initiated by God become very important in the remainder of Genesis; they involve Jacob, Laban, and people in the days of Joseph.

The exact meaning of the word translated as *ladder* is not clear. Because this Hebrew word appears only once in the Old Testament, there are no other instances for comparison. Some students propose that it is something like an ancient ziggurat, a building that resembles a pyramid and includes steps that reach a platform at the top. An altar or shrine may be there, used by pagan worshippers for sacrifices or other religious rituals.

What he sees on it is probably more captivating to Jacob than the structure. *Angels* are God's messengers. That description fits well with the fact that they are *ascending and descending* to take God's messages to *the earth.* Angels would play an important part in the account of Jacob's life, particularly from the standpoint of his spiritual pilgrimage (Genesis 32:1, 24).

B. Hearing God (vv. 13-15)

13. And, behold the LORD stood above it, and said, I am the LORD God of Abraham thy

father, and the God of Isaac: the land whereon thou liest, to thee will I give it, and to thy seed.

At least one ziggurat was built for a pagan god to descend from Heaven to earth to receive offerings and prayers from the people. What Jacob sees, however, is different: *the Lord stood above* the structure, making no move to descend. Neither does God send one of the angels to deliver His message—He does it personally.

From that position of authority, God began with a self-introduction. He made a promise regarding *the land* and Jacob's descendants (*seed*). The fact that the land would be given to Jacob's seed meant he would have a wife and at least one child. Such an affirmation was likely intended to provide, among other things, much-needed assurance to Jacob. After all, he was leaving the territory of the land of promise on his way to Haran—the exact reverse of the trip *Abraham* took!

We may wonder why God applied the word *father* to Abraham instead of to Isaac since Abraham was Jacob's grandfather. The issue is resolved when we realize that the word *father* is used in the Bible also to describe "ancestor," as in "forefather" (examples: Genesis 17:5; 19:37-38; Luke 3:8).

As the Lord spoke to Jacob, there is no record that He said anything about Jacob's deceptive actions toward his father and brother. Instead, God reaffirmed Jacob's position in the lineage of covenant promises made to his forefathers.

14. And thy seed shall be as the dust of the earth, and thou shalt spread abroad to the west, and to the east, and to the north, and to the south: and in thee and in thy seed shall all the families of the earth be blessed.

How to Say It

Beersheba	Beer-*she*-buh.
Canaan	*Kay*-nun.
Haran	*Hair*-un.
Jeroboam	Jair-uh-*boe*-um.
Josiah	Jo-*sigh*-uh.
obelisk	*aw*-buh-lisk.
Philistines	Fuh-*liss*-teenz
	or *Fill*-us-teenz.
ziggurat	*zigg*-oo-rat.

The Lord clarified the extent of the promise regarding Jacob's descendants in both a physical and a spiritual sense. God had used the phrase *as the dust of the earth* before when Abraham was promised all the land he could see (Genesis 13:14-18). Jacob may have heard about this from his grandfather, for Jacob was age 15 when Abraham died (computed from 21:5; 25:7, 20, 26).

The portion of the message regarding the blessing for *all the families of the earth* was initially mentioned in Genesis 12:3. That was when Abraham was leaving Haran (the place toward which Jacob was headed). This part of the message is, therefore, not a new element either. It had been God's stated plan all along, but it bore repeating.

Dusty?

I was on a mission trip to Haiti in 2003. We were traveling a road between two cities about 90 miles apart. This drive would have taken an hour and a half in the United States, but it took more than four hours in Haiti. The road was only partially paved and had potholes everywhere; the rest of it was just dirt and dust. Riding in the back of a truck, we quickly realized the dust was a problem. So we tied bandanas around our mouths and noses, using sunglasses to shield our eyes. By the time we reached our destination, even the non-exposed parts of our bodies were caked in dust!

Dust is pervasive in both negative and positive ways. It is referenced more than 100 times in the Bible. In the positive sense, it is how God described the descendants of Jacob. There are uncountable grains of dust in the world, and God was going to make Jacob's descendants like that.

From this side of the cross, we know that the "dust" God promised has multiplied and spread in all directions. This is important because Abraham is the father of all Christians, so we are that dust (see Romans 4:12; Galatians 3:16). How should you live in light of that fact?   —C. S.

15a. And, behold, I am with thee, and will keep thee in all places whither thou goest, and will bring thee again into this land.

God's promise "I am with you" is one of the most reassuring statements in Scripture (see Genesis 26:24; Isaiah 41:10; 43:5; Jeremiah 1:8, 19; 15:20; 42:11; 46:28; Haggai 1:13; 2:4; Matthew 28:20; Acts 18:10). For Jacob, these words provided encouragement as he embarked on life as a fugitive sojourner. Although he was moving away from the land promised to his grandfather and father, he was not moving away from the presence or protection of God. In pagan thinking, gods were local, not global. They were limited to the territory or country they supposedly ruled (examples: 1 Kings 11:33; 20:28; 2 Kings 17:26-27). But finding a place outside of God's "jurisdiction" is impossible (Psalm 139:7-12).

15b. For I will not leave thee, until I have done that which I have spoken to thee of.

The word *until* does not imply that the Lord would abandon Jacob at some future date. Since the promise was that Jacob's descendants would bless all nations, and that blessing was ongoing, it must be that God will always be present. God works constantly to bring humanity to the position and place we need to be.

> **What Do You Think?**
> What should you do to ensure that the promise of Hebrews 13:5 overrides any feelings of being forsaken by God?
> **Digging Deeper**
> Which Bible personalities serve as the best examples of this to you? Why?

III. Jacob's Reaction
(Genesis 28:16-19)
A. Interpreting the Dream (vv. 16-17)

16. And Jacob awaked out of his sleep, and he said, Surely the LORD is in this place; and I knew it not.

Jacob seemed to have awakened as soon as the dream ended, while it was yet night. His amazement that *the Lord is in this place* was probably because the spot seemed very ordinary. There appeared to be nothing especially holy about it. Jacob learned that God could make the most ordinary location holy by His presence. Moses will realize this same truth in his day, centuries later (Exodus 3:5).

17. And he was afraid, and said, How dreadful is this place! This is none other but the house of God, and this is the gate of heaven.

Fear kicked in. The word translated *dreadful* is derived from the same Hebrew word as the one translated *afraid*. The word *said* indicates that Jacob expressed his anxiety out loud, although he was alone! There is no indication that Jacob desired or expected an in-person discussion with God. But he got one anyway!

The phrase *the house of God* is considered in Genesis 28:19, below.

> **What Do You Think?**
> What do the personal encounters with God in the Bible teach you about seeking such an encounter yourself?
> **Digging Deeper**
> Which of those encounters speak to you most strongly in this regard? Why?

B. Renaming a City (vv. 18-19)

18a. And Jacob rose up early in the morning, and took the stone that he had put for his pillows, and set it up for a pillar.

Standing stones were common in the ancient world. In Canaan, such objects were the focus of pagan worship at open-air sanctuaries, as archaeological excavations at various sites have revealed them. Because of this idolatrous use, some suggest that Jacob's actions in the verse before us conflict with what Moses stressed in Leviticus 26:1 centuries later—that the people of Israel were not to set up sacred images or stones, for the Lord hated them. Later, Israel was instructed to smash the standing stones of the Canaanites (Exodus 23:24; Deuteronomy 7:5; 12:3).

The resolution of this supposed conflict is sim-

Remember what God has done for you.

Visual for Lesson 5. *Have this visual on display as you pose the discussion questions that are associated with Genesis 28:22.*

ple. If an erected stone involved the worship of other gods, then the Lord's commands applied. However, a stone erected as a memorial was an entirely different matter (compare Exodus 24:4; Joshua 4:1-9; 1 Samuel 7:12).

Memorials, Then and Now

Rising to a height of 555 feet, the Washington Monument is the tallest obelisk in the world. It commemorates George Washington, the most famous of all of the founders of the United States. The monument is an impressive acknowledgment indeed!

In contrast, Jacob's "pillar" seems almost insultingly small. Its size in no way reflected the magnitude of what God promised to do (and did do) for Jacob and his descendants. But the size of the monument in no way lessened the significance of that monument for Jacob. When he returned to this area years later, we wonder if he found that stone still standing. Even assuming he did not, he doubtlessly carried the memory of that monument and what it represented.

Monuments help remind us of episodes of God's grace. Jacob and others of his day had to settle for monuments of two types: physical (like the stone itself) and mental (memories of that stone). Today, we are blessed to have a third type of monument available: video recordings. In addition to seeing the words "Established on . . ." chiseled into a concrete block of a new church

building or recalling memories of having taken part in its construction, we can pull out pictures and videos of the event.

Can you name some grace-of-God memorials of that kind in your home? Or are your photographs, etc., only of family vacations and parties? —C. S.

18b. And poured oil upon the top of it.

The *oil* Jacob poured *upon the top of* the memorial stone served to consecrate it. Oil was often used to anoint priests and kings (examples: Leviticus 21:10; 1 Kings 1:39). But oil would also be used on objects (example: Exodus 30:22-29).

19. And he called the name of that place Bethel: but the name of that city was called Luz at the first.

The Hebrew word *Bethel* means "house of God." This reflects Jacob's declaration in Genesis 28:17, above. Bethel is one of the most-mentioned places in the Old Testament; the identifier is used dozens of times. It is a key location and reference point in the history of Israel. Negatively, Bethel became the site where Jeroboam, the first king of the northern kingdom of divided Israel, built one of his golden calf idols to keep the people from going to Jerusalem to worship at the temple there (1 Kings 12:25-30). That was about 930 BC, some 10 centuries after the time of Jacob. Bethel's idolatrous altar would remain for some three centuries until destroyed by godly King Josiah (2 Kings 23:15).

Archaeologists have not been able to determine the location of Bethel with certainty. A majority identify the location with a village known today as Beitin. A minority viewpoint is that Bethel is to be identified with the modern village of El-Bireh, just to the south of Beitin.

III. Jacob's Vow
(Genesis 28:20-22)
A. "If" Condition (vv. 20-21a)

20-21a. And Jacob vowed a vow, saying, If God will be with me, and will keep me in this way that I go, and will give the bread to eat, and raiment to put on, so that I come again to my father's house in peace.

Jacob's vow presupposes his confidence in

God's promises. We should not over-interpret his word *if* to mean he was unsure. His words clarify, at least to his own mind, the tangible takeaways of God's presence. Even on his dangerous journey to a distant place and the long years of his sojourn there, he can rest assured that somehow he will come home. He will not become a casualty on the long roads to Haran and back.

B. "Then" Promise (vv. 21b-22)
21b. Then shall the LORD be my God.

Jacob's vow ought to be seen as distinct from those promises made to God during moments of crisis or emergency. This vow was based on what God had revealed would be provided to him. We also remember that this vow was coming from someone who was just beginning to understand what trusting in God meant. Jacob had a lengthy journey ahead of him, both in terms of physical miles and spiritual maturity. When Jacob promised *then shall the Lord be my God*, he was, in a sense, acknowledging that his relationship with the Lord would be far deeper than what it was at that time.

22. And this stone, which I have set for a pillar, shall be God's house: and of all that thou shalt give me I will surely give the tenth unto thee.

Jacob's financial holdings were negligible as he made his vow. He only had what was with him. But if Jacob were ever able to return to his father's house, then Jacob would do his best to fulfill his sincere desires to make this place *God's house* and to give the *tenth* of all he had. Typically, this verse is interpreted in terms of what Jacob amassed during his time away (Genesis 30:43), but he did not know of any future wealth at this point.

In later Israelite practice, tithes were collected for temple support and feeding poor and vulnerable people. The giver also ate and shared parts of the tithe of fruit, crops, and meat, sharing them with others as a sign of gratitude for God's bounty (Deuteronomy 14:22-29; 26:1-15). How was Jacob to distribute his tithes? The text does not say. The story may show him as a model for future Israelites, who would have both a mechanism and a purpose for redistributing their tithes.

What Do You Think?

What are some ways you can help your church memorialize its important milestones?

Digging Deeper

What are some proper and improper ways to use such memorializations?

Conclusion
A. God's Surprises

God surprised Jacob with a vision of the magnitude of mercy that the young man would receive in life. Although Jacob would face many future problems, often of his own making, his life went on to be marked by God's merciful provisions. In the big-picture view, Jacob was to be a key man through whom the ancient promises to his ancestors were to come to fruition.

But in addition to that big picture, there's a more personal one: the story doesn't feature Jacob's search for God, but rather it features God's search for him. After being found, Jacob had to begin viewing his life differently, searching for the meaning of what he had experienced. That search lasted the rest of his life (Genesis 46:1–47:11; 47:28–49:33).

The same will be true for us. Though we have much more of God's revealed will than Jacob had, we still struggle to know our place in the bigger picture of Matthew 28:19-20. On a personal level, we might hope only for survival, but we end up finding much more from the God of mercy and grace.

Regardless of the situations of life, the primary question, per Luke 17:10, is this: *What is my duty in my current situation?* When you ask that question in light of biblical precepts and principles, you won't need to expect God to answer that in a dream.

B. Prayer

God of our ancestors in faith, we thank You for abiding with us generation after generation. You seek us when we don't seek You. Abide with us still, and help us to abide with You. In Jesus' name. Amen.

C. Thought to Remember
Find your purpose, and do your duty.

Involvement Learning

Enhance your lesson with KJV Bible Student *(from your curriculum supplier) and the reproducible activity page (at www.standardlesson.com or in the back of the* KJV Standard Lesson Commentary Deluxe Edition*).*

Into the Lesson

Divide the class into small groups and ask group members to share a favorite vacation spot. Ask each group to decide on the characteristics that make each vacation spot unique.

Option. Ask volunteers to share with the class regarding an item of family jewelry they own. If appropriate, ask to share how they received the item and why it is significant to them and their families.

After either activity, ask, "What are places, symbols, or items that signify important promises?" Write responses on the board.

Introduce the Bible study by saying, "Life is full of places and things that signify something important. In today's lesson, we'll look at how a descendant of Abraham created something to commemorate a promise of God."

Into the Word

Before class, ask a volunteer to provide a brief introductory lecture on Jacob and his family. The lecture should address these questions: 1–Who was Jacob? 2–Who was his father? 3–Who was his grandfather? 4–Why was Jacob in Beersheba? 5–Why was he going to Haran? If needed, encourage the volunteer to use a map in the lecture to highlight Jacob's travels.

Alternative. Divide the class into groups of three and direct each group to use online Bible-study resources or study Bibles to answer the above questions. Allow groups no less than 10 minutes to research and work. After the allotted time, ask for volunteers to share their answers with the whole class. Use a map to show Jacob's movements.

After either activity, ask, "Why is God's covenant with Jacob important?"

Distribute a handout (you create) to each learner with the headings *God's Actions* and *Jacob's Actions* as headers of two columns, one each. Have printed down the left side the verse numbers 10–22, one row for each number.

Read aloud Genesis 28:10-22 three times. Pause after reading each verse. As you read, direct learners to complete the chart on the handout.

After completing the reading, divide the class into pairs. Invite each learner to share responses with a partner. Ask, "What is the relationship between God's actions and Jacob's actions?" Then, have each learner reread verses 20-22 and write a paraphrase of those verses at the bottom of his or her handout.

Option. Distribute copies of the "God, the Covenant Maker" exercise from the activity page, which you can download. Have learners work in small groups to complete as indicated. Encourage groups to share their responses as a part of your whole-class discussion.

Call the groups together and discuss Jacob's if-then statements. Ask: "Was Jacob's response one of faith or doubt? Why?"

Into Life

Display the following statements:

1. *I remember a time and place when God's presence and work were evident in my life.*
2. *I've often found motivation or encouragement by remembering how God has kept His promises in my life.*

Divide learners into pairs. Give pairs time to discuss either prompt. Distribute an index card and pen to each learner. Allow 5 minutes for pairs to write down a plan to commemorate a particular time when God's presence and work were evident in their lives.

Alternative. Distribute copies of the "Looking Back to Look Forward" activity from the activity page. Have learners work with a partner before discussing conclusions with the whole class.

After either activity, end the lesson with a prayer that learners will be aware of God's presence and work in their lives.

The Boy Jesus in the Temple

Devotional Reading: Psalm 27
Background Scripture: Luke 2:41-52

Luke 2:41-52

41 Now his parents went to Jerusalem every year at the feast of the passover.

42 And when he was twelve years old, they went up to Jerusalem after the custom of the feast.

43 And when they had fulfilled the days, as they returned, the child Jesus tarried behind in Jerusalem; and Joseph and his mother knew not of it.

44 But they, supposing him to have been in the company, went a day's journey; and they sought him among their kinsfolk and acquaintance.

45 And when they found him not, they turned back again to Jerusalem, seeking him.

46 And it came to pass, that after three days they found him in the temple, sitting in the midst of the doctors, both hearing them, and asking them questions.

47 And all that heard him were astonished at his understanding and answers.

48 And when they saw him, they were amazed: and his mother said unto him, Son, why hast thou thus dealt with us? behold, thy father and I have sought thee sorrowing.

49 And he said unto them, how is it that ye sought me? wist ye not that I must be about my Father's business?

50 And they understood not the saying which he spake unto them.

51 And he went down with them, and came to Nazareth, and was subject unto them: but his mother kept all these sayings in her heart.

52 And Jesus increased in wisdom and stature, and in favour with God and man.

Key Text

He said unto them, How is it that ye sought me? wist ye not that I must be about my Father's business?
—**Luke 2:49**

Sacred Altars and
Holy Offerings

Unit 2: Jesus and the Temple
Lessons 6–9

Lesson Aims

After participating in this lesson, each learner will be able to:

1. List key features of Passover observances.

2. Compare and contrast expectations of a typical 12-year-old boy of the time with this account from Jesus' youth.

3. Write a note to a young person to encourage that person in his or her spiritual journey.

Lesson Outline

Introduction

A. In Jerusalem, "Alone"

The movie *Home Alone* has become a Christmastime classic. First released in 1990, the movie tells the story of 8-year-old Kevin McCallister, who is left behind in his family's suburban home while the rest of his family departs on an overseas Christmas vacation. The family departs without noticing his absence, leaving Kevin home alone. Two clueless burglars, Harry and Marv, break into the home, but Kevin outwits them and holds them off until the family returns on Christmas Day.

In a memorable scene, as the family is on a plane flying over the Atlantic Ocean, Kevin's mother finally realizes that her son is not on board the plane. She nearly jumps out of her seat with a horrified cry, "KEVIN!"

In today's Scripture, Mary and Joseph seemed to have "lost" their 12-year-old son, Jesus. How would Mary respond to the realization that she had lost her son? Would she cry, "JESUS!" in panicked realization, or would she have a different response?

B. Lesson Context

Luke is the only New Testament author who records a story of Jesus' youth. This fact suits Luke's intention to document Jesus' life and ministry, which he had researched "from the very first" (Luke 1:3).

Luke's account of the birth of Jesus (Luke 2:1-20) includes a description of an angelic announcement to shepherds and their resulting search for the newborn Jesus. Luke tells us that "Mary kept all these things, and pondered them in her heart" (2:19). Thus, she might have been Luke's source of information regarding the events of Jesus' childhood. Luke summarized that as Jesus grew, "the grace of God was upon him" (2:40).

Mary and Joseph made yearly trips to the Jerusalem. This practice was expected by the Law of Moses (Exodus 23:17; 34:23; Deuteronomy 16:16) but perhaps not universally followed in their day. They initially took Jesus to "present him to the Lord" as their firstborn son and to offer a sacrifice for purification (Luke 2:22-24; compare Leviticus 12:1-8).

As an adult, Jesus prepared to celebrate Passover and the Feast of Unleavened Bread with His disciples in the vicinity of Jerusalem (Luke 22:7-8), He continued to make the journeys to Jerusalem as He had done for so many years with His mother and father.

I. Jesus Went Missing
(Luke 2:41-45)
A. Observing Passover (vv. 41-42)

41. Now his parents went to Jerusalem every year at the feast of the passover.

Earlier verses of this chapter highlight the obedience that characterized the lives of Jesus' *parents*. They traveled to Bethlehem in obedience to the emperor's decree (Luke 2:1-5). Then, they followed the requirements of the Law of Moses (see Leviticus 12:1-4) regarding Jesus' circumcision (Luke 2:21) and the offering of purification after childbirth (2:22-24).

Passover is the *feast* that commemorates Israel's deliverance from bondage in Egypt (Exodus 12:1-3; Deuteronomy 16:1-8). It is one of the three feasts that all Jewish men were required to travel *to Jerusalem* to observe (Exodus 23:14-17; Deuteronomy 16:16). Those Jews living far away from Jerusalem—in the scattering of people called the *diaspora*—would not be able to journey to Jerusalem three times each year.

Joseph, Mary, and Jesus had been living in Nazareth (Luke 2:39), a town located about 70 miles north of Jerusalem. The family's journey to Jerusalem might have been upwards of 90 miles if they had traveled through the Jordan Valley to avoid Samaritan territory.

42. And when he was twelve years old, they went up to Jerusalem after the custom of the feast.

At *twelve years old*, Jesus was nearly the age when Jewish boys were expected to become aware of their spiritual duties. Second-century-AD records, such as the Mishnah, state that the age of 13 is when a Jewish boy is considered an adult and, therefore, must follow the requirements of the law. At this age, a bar mitzvah ceremony occurs. However, the customs of the ceremony were recorded after Jesus'

time. Before reaching that age of maturity, it would also have been customary for Jewish boys to attend *the feast* in Jerusalem.

Because *Jerusalem* is perched at a high elevation, approximately 2,500 feet above sea level, travelers always *went up* in elevation to visit the city (compare Psalm 24:3).

What Do You Think?
What part of a holiday celebration do you find brings a family together?
Digging Deeper
What steps will you take to welcome God more fully into your family's observance of holidays such as Christmas and Easter?

B. Starting Home (v. 43)

43. And when they had fulfilled the days, as they returned, the child Jesus tarried behind in Jerusalem; and Joseph and his mother knew not of it.

The celebration of Passover is immediately followed by the seven-day-long Feast of Unleavened Bread (Leviticus 23:5-6). Although the feast is technically distinct from Passover, the two are right next to each other on the calendar. Thus, it is natural to see them as one and the same event: a singular event lasting eight *days*.

Those who traveled some distance to Jerusalem for Passover, like Mary and Joseph, often journeyed in large groups as an extended family or clan. The group could pool resources for the trip, and a sizeable assembly helped protect travelers from would-be robbers. While traveling as a group, Mary and Joseph would easily have assumed that if Jesus was not with them, He was with other members of their caravan, including extended family and neighbors.

Jesus *tarried behind in Jerusalem* rather than join His parents and the other travelers in the return journey to Nazareth following the observances. Luke does not say whether Jesus accidentally missed the group's departure or He made a deliberate choice to remain in Jerusalem. Regardless, the significance of Luke's account is that Jesus was not with His parents as they left the city.

C. Searching for the Boy (v. 44-45)

44. But they, supposing him to have been in the company, went a day's journey; and they sought him among their kinsfolk and acquaintance.

To go *a day's journey* on foot means that Mary and Joseph might have covered some 15 to 20 miles back to Nazareth before realizing that Jesus was not among their *company* of travelers. Perhaps it was when the group paused to rest or to share a meal that Mary and Joseph *sought him* from among the group of travelers consisting of their family and friends (*kinsfolk and acquaintance*). While no other family members are mentioned in this instance, Jesus is elsewhere said to have had brothers and sisters (Matthew 13:55-56; Luke 8:19; etc.). It could be the case that, as the family's eldest child, Jesus was given more freedom than His younger siblings.

45. And when they found him not, they turned back again to Jerusalem, seeking him.

If the discovery occurred in the evening—a fair assumption from the fact that they had completed a day's journey (Luke 2:44, above)—they would have been forced to set out toward *Jerusalem* the following morning.

II. Jesus Was Found
(Luke 2:46-50)

A. Surprising Discovery (vv. 46-47)

46. And it came to pass, that after three days they found him in the temple, sitting in the midst of the doctors, both hearing them, and asking them questions.

By one estimate, *three days* includes the parents' departure from Jerusalem. Therefore, the order of events is as follows: a day to journey away from Jerusalem, a day to return, and a third day to search the city and temple.

The first-century Jewish historian Josephus estimated that more than two-and-a-half million people visited Jerusalem during the week of Passover, 10 times the amount of people as usual. Even after the eight days of celebration concluded, many people would remain in the city before returning home.

At the center of all this activity was Jesus *in the temple.* The temple courts covered more than 25 acres after they were expanded by Herod the Great (reigned 37–4 BC). Finding the boy Jesus among the crowds would have been an insurmountable challenge.

The title *doctors* applied to those who were teachers and experts of the Law of Moses. The same underlying word in ancient Greek, translated as "Master," is used to refer to Jesus when He taught in the temple later in life (Luke 20:21).

His *sitting* at the feet of the doctors reflects the posture of a student (compare Luke 10:39). Further, the 12-year-old Jesus was an active learner, *hearing* and *asking them questions.* The text does not say the topics of study, but experts in the law possessed authority when teaching in the temple.

In God's Place

In the midst of life's busyness, it takes a lot of effort for me to slow down, study God's Word, and be attentive to the leading of the Holy Spirit. Some days are easier than others. My work obligations, household chores, and phone-use habits often keep me busy and distracted from spiritual matters. I'm always looking for another work assignment, a new project around the house, or the next phone application to divert my attention.

However, when I put away distractions and

spend time studying Scripture, I find the presence of God. In the pages of Scripture, I discover the God who revealed himself through Jesus Christ. In the pages of Scripture, I come to know a Savior who loves and cares for me. I find rest and hope when I read in Scripture what Jesus has done for me.

Even as a boy, Jesus prioritized going to the temple, the place where Scripture was studied and discussed. Jesus' actions as a boy show us how we might give our attention to spiritual matters. God's children spend time with their Heavenly Father and learn about following Jesus through reading and studying the Bible. How have you prioritized reading and studying the Bible this week? How will you deal with the inevitable distractions that might prevent you from doing so?   —J. K.

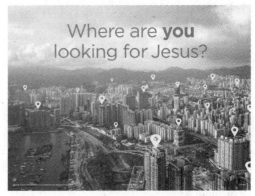

Visual for Lesson 6. *Display this visual as you ask the following question for whole-class discussion: "Where are you looking for Jesus today?"*

47. And all that heard him were astonished at his understanding and answers.

Jesus showed remarkable spiritual and intellectual wisdom for someone so young (compare Luke 2:52). The crowd was *astonished*, both at *his understanding*—intelligence and discernment—and the *answers* He gave to inquiries. Even though He was only a boy from rural Galilee, Jesus could sit among Jewish rabbis. Even as a boy, Jesus generated a strong response from an audience. As an adult, Jesus' teaching was noted for its "power," leaving audiences "astonished" (4:32).

Astonished

My family member was facing health complications, and there we were in the doctor's office, just waiting for the report. My heart was anxious, and I felt like my stomach was turning itself into knots. I had cried out to the Lord that the first words on the doctor's lips would be, "I have good news!"

The doctor opened the door and, to my astonishment, gave us the good news I had prayed to receive. In that moment, I knew that God had heard my prayer. It would be easy to move on from that day, to return to our family life as "normal." It would have been easy to let my astonishment fade into the background of a busy life. Sometimes, I tend to go about my affairs as if God hadn't performed a miracle and hadn't answered my prayer.

Everyone who witnessed Jesus' interactions with the teachers in the temple was also astonished. Maybe some of them would have the opportunity to seek this Jesus again when He was fully grown. Rather than get caught up in your busy life, consider how God has astonished you. Have you let God's work through Jesus Christ lead you to praise the gracious deeds of your Savior?   —J. K.

B. Anxious Question (v. 48)

48. And when they saw him, they were amazed: and his mother said unto him, Son, why hast thou thus dealt with us? behold, thy father and I have sought thee sorrowing.

Now, it is the parents' turn to be shocked. Their reaction was similar to but not synonymous with the reaction of the doctors in the temple: *they were amazed*. The text does not reveal why they specifically felt this way. Perhaps they were surprised that they managed to find Jesus in the temple, or maybe they were stunned that He had seemingly behaved irresponsibly.

Jesus' unconventional response in the previous verse seems to lead Mary to demonstrate some level of anxiety and fear, displayed by her question: *Why has thou thus dealt with us?* She reprimands Him for the *sorrowing* He caused her and Joseph.

The phrase *thy father* does not mean that Joseph was Jesus' biological parent; Luke is clear that Joseph was not (Luke 1:34-35). Mary refers to Joseph as Jesus' father in the earthly and adoptive sense. This phrase might also set up Luke's readers for Jesus' work regarding His Heavenly Father, described in the following verse.

C. Mysterious Answer (vv. 49-50)

49. And he said unto them, How is it that ye sought me? wist ye not that I must be about my Father's business?

This reply to Mary's question must have astonished her and Joseph, and it prefigures the wisdom that Jesus would have as an adult. Jesus' answer is difficult to translate. The expression translated *must* indicates the fulfillment of God's plan or purpose (examples: Luke 4:43; 9:22; 13:33). A pressing reality—God's plan—caused Jesus to stay behind in Jerusalem: He was *about* His *Father's business*. While in the temple interacting with doctors, Jesus was engaged in the matters of God; He was doing something His Heavenly *Father* would have Him do.

The phrase *my Father* might have stung Joseph, who knew that Jesus was not his biological child. On the one hand, Joseph would have likely been familiar with Old Testament Scripture that refers to God as *Father* (examples: Deuteronomy 32:6; Psalm 89:26; Isaiah 64:8). But on the other hand, Joseph was aware that Jesus somehow is "Emmanuel . . . God with us" (Matthew 1:23). When Joseph and Mary first took Jesus to the temple, they heard Simeon's understanding of Jesus to be "the Lord's Christ" (Luke 2:26). They also heard Anna's understanding of Him to be an important part of redemption (2:36-38). But we don't know precisely how Joseph interpreted all this, even 12 years later.

Jesus' unique status as the Son of God continued to be a relevant consideration during His adult ministry. Twice a voice from Heaven called Jesus "my beloved Son," once at His baptism (Luke 3:22) and once at His transfiguration (9:35). Jesus also invited His disciples to call God their "Father" (11:2). The apostle Paul would say that because the "Spirit of [God's] Son" is within believers, we can cry out to God, "Abba, Father" (Galatians 4:6).

Jesus' response implied that Mary and Joseph should have known or not worried about His whereabouts. This response was memorable, and it might have been the kind of phrase that Mary "kept . . . in her heart" (Luke 2:51). From His earliest days of independence, Jesus was aware that His life was guided by the plan of His Heavenly Father (compare John 5:19).

50. And they understood not the saying which he spake unto them.

Jesus' *saying* left Mary and Joseph perplexed. Perhaps Mary recalled what the angel Gabriel announced to her regarding Jesus' status as the "Son of the Highest" (Luke 1:32) and the "Son of God" (1:35). Mary may have wondered how He would be given "the throne of his father David" (1:32). She could not have anticipated that the angel's words would mean that her Son would seek out the experts in law at the age of 12.

Mary and Joseph were like many of Jesus' disciples who struggled to understand Him (examples: Luke 9:45; 18:34). The parents knew from His birth that Jesus was not an ordinary child, but even His own mother did not understand Him.

> **What Do You Think?**
> How do you respond when you have struggled to understand what God might be doing or trying to teach you?
> **Digging Deeper**
> How might Jesus' parting words to His disciples in Matthew 28:20 guide you in times of uncertainty?

How to Say It

Deuteronomy	Due-ter-*ahn*-uh-me.
diaspora	dee-*as*-puh-ruh.
Emmanuel	E-*man*-you-el.
Galatians	Guh-*lay*-shunz.
Herod	*Hair*-ud.
Mishnah	*Mish*-nuh.
Samaritan	Suh-*mare*-uh-tun.

III. Jesus Went Home
(Luke 2:51-52)
A. His Obedience (v. 51)

51a. And he went down with them, and came to Nazareth, and was subject unto them.

Jesus' response to Mary and Joseph might appear that He was behaving defiantly. However, the verse before us prevents that impression. The family returned to *Nazareth*, where Jesus *was subject unto them* by showing His parents respect, honor, and obedience. In Judaism, the command to "honour thy father and thy mother" is considered so important that it is followed by the conditional phrase: "that thy days may be long upon the land" (Exodus 20:12). Honoring one's parents meant more than only demonstrating obedience. It included the responsibility to care for them and treat them well in their old age. Jesus fulfilled this command by asking His disciple to care for His mother in His absence (John 19:26-27).

51b. But his mother kept all these sayings ~~in~~ her heart.

~~The f~~act that Mary *kept all these sayings in her* ~~co~~nsistent with her response to the shep~~herds' me~~ssage following Jesus' birth (Luke 2:19). ~~She woul~~d have days to reflect on this unique child. ~~Perh~~aps her confusion turned to gratitude for her growing child, who continued to surprise her.

B. His Growth (v. 52)

52. And Jesus increased in wisdom and stature, and in favour with God and man.

Jesus' growth *in wisdom and stature* demonstrates His mental, physical, and spiritual growth as the Son of God (compare Luke 2:40). The *favour* He experienced includes the winsomeness and goodwill shown to Him, including His approval *with God and man*. Jesus' family, neighbors, and His Heavenly Father were all pleased by His work on His "Father's business" (2:49, above). Luke's summary of Jesus' growth and maturity prepares readers of this Gospel for a 10-year leap in the narrative. The next chapter in the Gospel of Luke details Jesus' baptism and the inauguration of His full-time earthly ministry (3:1-22).

What Do You Think?
What steps should you take to keep spiritually formative memories alive?

Digging Deeper
Who can you encourage, and what steps might you take to communicate with that person this week?

Conclusion

A. Finding Jesus Again

The theme of "lost and found" can be found throughout Luke's Gospel. For example, Jesus told three parables about things that were lost: a sheep (Luke 15:1-7), a coin (15:8-10), and a son (15:11-32). Jesus himself was "lost" when He was arrested and killed, but He was "found" by two men when He joined them along the Emmaus road (24:13-35). The account from today's lesson is like that example, a time when Jesus was "lost" and then "found" in an unexpected location.

Although Jesus was considered lost to Joseph and Mary, He was not genuinely missing. Luke shows his readers that Jesus was following the will of His Father in Heaven, even when doing so was surprising or confusing to the people around Him.

This account also reveals the devotion of Jesus' family. They brought Him to Jerusalem each year so He might learn what was expected of Him regarding following God. In return, Jesus showed respect to His earthly parents. Even though He was in the house of His Heavenly Father, Jesus obeyed Mary and Joseph and returned with them to Nazareth.

That 12-year-old boy would grow to fulfill the mission of His Heavenly Father: becoming the Savior for God's people (Luke 2:11), including those who struggle to understand His work but proclaim Him as their Savior. In this way, Luke's account becomes an example for those who seek to "find" and follow Jesus. God's people can look to Jesus to find what God is doing. When we do so, we might find ourselves headed in an entirely new direction!

B. Prayer

Heavenly Father, we sometimes struggle to understand Your plan. Help us be patient with our families and neighbors, including those entering adulthood or stepping out in faith for the first time. No matter our life stage, empower us to continue growing in wisdom and favor—with You and others. In Jesus' name we pray. Amen.

C. Thought to Remember

Seek to receive the approval of God and the goodwill of others.

Involvement Learning

Enhance your lesson with KJV Bible Student *(from your curriculum supplier) and the reproducible activity page (at www.standardlesson.com or in the back of the* KJV Standard Lesson Commentary Deluxe Edition*).*

Into the Lesson

Invite learners to share about what life was like when they were 12 years old. Lead a time of reminiscing by asking the following questions as conversation starters: 1–Where was your home located? 2–If you attended church, what was that like? 3–Which school did you attend? 4–How did you entertain yourself? (*Note*: You do not have to use any or all of these questions. Base follow-up questions on the conversation.) Invite learners to share stories from their childhood about a time when they were curious about spiritual matters.

Alternative. Distribute copies of the "Child's Play" exercise from the activity page, which you can download. Have learners complete it individually in a minute or less before discussing their answers with the group.

Lead into Bible study by saying, "At the age of 12, most of us were figuring out life as a kid. When we look at today's story from the Gospel of Luke, we will see that when Jesus was only 12 years old, He deeply understood spiritual matters and astonished elders with His wisdom."

Into the Word

Have a volunteer read aloud Luke 2:41-45. Write the following questions on the board for small-group discussion: 1–Why did Jesus' family travel to Jerusalem every year? 2–How did the Passover commemorate God's deliverance of the Israelites from slavery? 3–Using your "sanctified imagination," what would a typical first-century 12-year-old boy do during the feast? After five minutes, ask a volunteer from each group to share their answers with the class.

Option. Distribute paper and pens to each group. Ask each group to write as many descriptive words or phrases as possible that describe the Passover observance. Encourage them to read Exodus 12 and Deuteronomy 16:1-7 as preparation.

Ask a volunteer to read aloud Luke 2:46-52. In the same groups as before, have the groups answer the following questions in small-group discussion: 1–What do Jesus' actions in the temple reveal about His awareness of His mission? 2–How did those who heard Jesus in the temple react to Him? 3–What emotions might Mary and Joseph have felt when they could not find Jesus? 4–What emotions might Mary and Joseph have felt after they found Jesus in the temple? Using your "sanctified imagination," how think Jesus' actions differed from those first-century 12-year-olds? 6–How do you Jesus' actions were similar to typical first-century 12-year-olds? After no more than 10 minutes of small-group discussion, reconvene the class and ask for volunteers to share their group's responses to each question.

Option. Distribute copies of the "Jesus in the Temple" activity from the activity page. Have learners complete it individually in a minute or less before discussing the conclusions with a partner from their small group.

Ask a volunteer to read Jesus' response to His parents in Luke 2:49. Ask the class: "Why is Jesus' response important?" Ask another volunteer to read Luke 2:51-52. For whole-class discussion, ask, "How do these verses summarize Jesus' spiritual journey as a child?"

Into Life

Distribute a sheet of paper and a pen to each learner. Ask learners to think of a young person from their congregation or neighborhood. Invite learners to write a note to encourage that young person in his or her spiritual journey.

Challenge learners to consider delivering the letters and to be available as a source of spiritual support for each young person. End class with a prayer, asking God to encourage the young people who receive the letters.

Lord of the Sabbath

Devotional Reading: Luke 13:10-17
Background Scripture: Matthew 12:1-14
(See also Mark 2:23-28; Luke 6:1-11.)

Matthew 12:1-8

1 At that time Jesus went on the sabbath day through the corn; and his disciples were an hungred, and began to pluck the ears of corn, and to eat.

2 But when the Pharisees saw it, they said unto him, behold, thy disciples do that which is not lawful to do upon the sabbath day.

3 But he said unto them, have ye not read what David did, when he was an hungred, and they that were with him;

4 How he entered into the house of God, and did eat the shewbread, which was not lawful for him to eat, neither for them which were with him, but only for the priests?

5 Or have ye not read in the law, how that on the sabbath days the priests in the temple profane the sabbath, and are blameless?

6 But I say unto you, that in this place is one greater than the temple.

7 But if ye had known what this meaneth, I will have mercy, and not sacrifice, ye would not have condemned the guiltless.

8 For the Son of man is Lord even of the sabbath day.

Key Text

I say unto you, that in this place is one greater than the temple. —**Matthew 12:6**

Sacred Altars and
Holy Offerings

Unit 2: Jesus and the Temple
Lessons 6–9

Lesson Aims

After participating in this lesson, each learner will be able to:

1. Identify the source of Jesus' statement regarding mercy and sacrifice.

2. Compare and contrast the Pharisees' basis of concern with Jesus' own.

3. Make a plan to follow Jesus' example and show abundant mercy in a place or time it would not be expected.

Lesson Outline

Introduction
A. What Are We Talking About?

In the middle of a conversation, have you ever stopped to ask yourself, "Wait, what are we really talking about?" Imagine you're discussing loading the dishwasher. "Everyone knows the bowls go in the top rack!" you say, but as you feel the tension grow, you realize you are arguing over something else. *Whose job is it to fix this? Am I the only one who cares if the dishes come out clean? Am I seen?* Many of our "disagreements" turn out to be about values, whether or not we acknowledge that reason.

Jesus knew how to take a conversation and use it to reveal a person's heart. His discussion about Sabbath is like this. You might anticipate a legal discussion of Sabbath rules—what is or is not permitted. But Jesus turned the discussion around to reveal the motives of the Pharisees. He was more interested in talking about showing mercy. At the same time, His sweeping claims left everyone wondering, "Who is this person who calls himself Son of Man and Lord of the Sabbath? Who gave Him the right?"

B. Lesson Context

Observing a seven-day week that included one day of rest (Sabbath) was a distinctive practice of ancient Israel. An ancient king might declare a rest day to celebrate a great victory, but regular, periodic rest was a revolutionary idea. For the most part, ancient peoples were expected to work every day.

Sabbath was a gift that God gave through the Law of Moses (Exodus 20:8-11; Deuteronomy 5:12-15). It commemorated two of God's mighty acts. First, God completed the work of creation and rested on the seventh day (Genesis 2:1-3; compare Exodus 20:11). Second, God liberated His people from oppression in the land of Egypt, a place where they were not allowed rest. Rest was a gift from God—even the animals got a day off (Deuteronomy 5:12-15).

Thus, Sabbath was not only a blessing but also an expression of faith. The challenge was to trust God that six days of labor would be enough to sustain life as God provided for His people. That required a lot of faith in a pre-industrial agrarian era!

The Law of Moses extended observance of Sabbath to include one *year* out of seven; on every seventh year, the fields were to remain uncultivated, debts would be forgiven, and enslaved people emancipated (Leviticus 25:1-8; Deuteronomy 15:1-18). In the Year of Jubilee—which came after seven Sabbath years (49 years total)—any land that had been sold would return to its original owners (Leviticus 25:8-22). Through these commands, God promised blessing and fruitfulness in the land He had given Israel as an inheritance.

But keeping Sabbath had been a controversial topic for centuries by Jesus' day. Israel's prophets had spoken out against hypocritical Sabbath observance (examples: Isaiah 1:13; Amos 8:3-6). Jeremiah had warned Jerusalem that failure to keep Sabbath would lead to destruction (Jeremiah 17:27). The prophets also looked forward to a day when Sabbath would be kept properly, when God's blessing would be restored to the nation of Israel, and even other nations would join in worshiping God for His mighty acts (Isaiah 66:22-23; Jeremiah 17:24-26).

The Pharisees of Jesus' day responded by emphasizing meticulous observance of Sabbath. Their "oral Torah" (traditions passed down by word of mouth) had amplified regulations that prevented a person from even coming close to breaking the commandments. Such traditions defined what constituted "work" that could and could not be performed on the Sabbath.

I. Question of Lawfulness
(Matthew 12:1-2)
A. Hungry Disciples (v. 1)

1. At that time Jesus went on the sabbath day through the corn; and his disciples were an hungred, and began to pluck the ears of corn, and to eat.

In the discourse immediately before this, Jesus told all who were tired to find "rest" in Him (Matthew 11:28-30). It meant that what Sabbath promised, Jesus offered in abundance. So, it is no surprise that immediately after this promise of abundance, Matthew recorded a controversy about Sabbath.

Travel on the day of rest was itself controversial, since an extended journey is incompatible with a day of rest. Acts 1:12 mentions "a sabbath day's journey," which means the distance the rabbis considered permissible to travel on a Sabbath. It was an imprecise measurement, approximately the distance a person would walk to synagogue, about a kilometer.

When we see the phrase *ears of corn*, we should note that maize or corn is native to North America. Thus, the word *corn* means a different type of grain in this context, perhaps barley or wheat. These crops were staple foods for anyone who consumed a Mediterranean diet of the era.

According to the Law of Moses, one could satisfy hunger while traveling by plucking fruit or grain from nearby fields (Deuteronomy 23:24-25). It was not stealing, for this was part of the Law's expectation to show generosity. Thus, it was perfectly acceptable to eat from the land while traveling. But the fact that this happened *on the sabbath day* sparked a controversy.

B. Offended Teachers (v. 2)

2. But when the Pharisees saw it, they said unto him, behold, thy disciples do that which is not lawful to do upon the sabbath day.

The Pharisees viewed plucking grain as work since it involved forms of harvesting, threshing, and winnowing. Even miniature forms of these were "work." So, in the view of Pharisees who observed this behavior, Christ's disciples were violating the Law in multiple ways. The Pharisees were making what seemed like a valid point: did Jesus really intend to ignore the command of God to "remember the sabbath day, to keep it holy" (Exodus 20:8)? Instead of eating, why didn't Jesus' disciples fast?

The Pharisees did not denounce the disciples directly. They took up their complaint with Jesus,

How to Say It

Ahimelech	A-*him*-uh-leck.
Davidic	Duh-*vid*-ick.
Levitical	Leh-*vit*-ih-kul.
Sabbath	Sab-uhth.
synagogue	*sin*-uh-gog.

Does your Sabbath honor the Lord?

Visual for Lesson 7. *Display this visual and allow one minute of private reflection for learners to consider the question.*

which displays their real concern. Beginning in Matthew 9:1-7, Jesus had done controversial things in the sight of religious teachers: forgiving sins and calling himself "the Son of man." These teachers were less interested in religious principles than in undermining Jesus and His popularity with crowds because Jesus represented a threat to their religious authority (John 11:48).

As these Pharisees framed the issue, there could be no debate whether the small actions of the disciples counted as work. They did not ask questions; they started with an accusation. The Pharisees assumed the rightness of their own interpretations and ignored the issue of the disciples' hunger. They also assumed Jesus was responsible for whatever His followers were doing. If these disciples worked on the Sabbath, the observers believed that Jesus gave permission. Therefore, they point out an apparent affront against Israel's God and His commandments. Just who does this Jesus think that He is?

II. What Is Greater?
(Matthew 12:3-8)

A. Than David (vv. 3-4)

3. But he said unto them, have ye not read what David did, when he was an hungred, and they that were with him.

Jesus did not debate the nature of work or the intention of Sabbath rest. Jesus responded as a Jewish rabbi might be expected to respond by drawing a comparison from Scripture. Jesus' audience would not have missed that He was comparing His and His disciples' actions to *what David did . . . and they that were with him.*

By drawing a comparison with David, Jesus not-so-subtly hinted that He possessed a kingly prerogative. This continues a central theme Matthew did not want his audience to miss: Jesus is the rightful Davidic king. The very first verse of Matthew's Gospel calls Jesus "the son of David" (Matthew 1:1); Matthew's genealogy takes special interest in connecting Jesus to David (1:17, 20); other people called Jesus the "Son of David" (9:27); and here in Matthew 12, Jesus compared himself to King David to explain His actions.

4. How he entered into the house of God, and did eat the shewbread, which was not lawful for him to eat, neither for them which were with him, but only for the priests?

In the narrative of 1 Samuel 21:1-6, David and his men sought food from the priest Ahimelech. At the time, the only bread in the tabernacle was the bread in the holy place (*shewbread*), which the Law allowed priests to eat but no one else (see Leviticus 24:8-9). Still, Ahimelech recognized David as God's anointed king, and he nonetheless gave David and his men the bread. It is a story about a king and his men in desperate need.

Jesus did not say that extreme hunger is an exception that allows breaking ceremonial rules. In fact, Jesus taught that violating a single command of God made a person "least in the kingdom of heaven" (Matthew 5:19). And unlike David's men, Jesus' disciples were not on the run from enemies.

However, the statement in this verse implies a comparison from David (a lesser example) to Jesus (a greater example). Ahimelech acted in mercy, but more importantly, he recognized the authority of a king, one whom God's prophet had anointed. Jesus was also a king, a greater one. If it were right for King David to eat *shewbread*, it would be even more acceptable for Jesus' followers to eat "bread" that God had provided them, for they were crucial people of the Messiah's mission. They should be granted at least as much leeway as David's men were!

Sleeping In

My children worked hard in high school and always wanted to do their best in classes and activities. All three were in marching band, so their schedules were busy during that season. They had two hours of practice every morning and at least two evening practices each week. Many Fridays, they stayed out late performing at football games. On Saturdays, they attended band competitions, which lasted late into the night. They did all this in addition to schoolwork. Needless to say, they often felt tired.

Some mornings, they struggled to get up for practice and felt exhausted as the day progressed. As a mom, my heart went out to them. I encouraged them to stay home to take a day off to rest. Even though their commitments were important, physical and mental health was not something I would disregard. And as their parent, it was my call to make.

Jesus was the one with authority in the situation in Matthew 12, although that's precisely what bothered His opponents. Jesus could call the shots and prioritize the physical needs of His disciples. Have you had an occasion when God has asked you to prioritize your mental and physical health? Do you listen to the voice of your King when He tells you to show yourself mercy? —L. M. W.

B. Than the Temple (vv. 5-6)

5. Or have ye not read in the law, how that on the sabbath days the priests in the temple profane the sabbath, and are blameless?

Jesus provided a second scriptural argument. Once again, He did not say there are exceptions to the rules about rest on the Sabbath, nor did He minimize His disciples' actions. Instead, He made a claim about His own authority and identity.

For ordinary Jews, work stopped on the Sabbath. But what about priests? By necessity, their duties continued. The temple had tasks that needed tending every day, like daily offerings and changing the bread of the presence (Numbers 28:1-8). Thus, priests carried out their duties in the sacred space on every Sabbath day. That is what Jesus meant when He said they *profane the sabbath*. Neither the Law of Moses nor the Pharisees' regulations forbade this. That is why these priests were *blameless*. However, skeptics might wonder why any of this is relevant to what Jesus and His followers were allowed to do. Jesus did not claim to be a Levitical priest, and the disciples were not performing sacrifices. So Jesus continued.

6. But I say unto you, that in this place is one greater than the temple.

Jesus had compared himself to David indirectly. Here, He compared himself to *the temple* directly, showing precisely the point He was making. If Jesus claimed to be greater than the temple, that meant He was greater than the location where God's people honored His holy presence.

For one thing, a temple that lasted forever was supposed to be built by a promised Son of David (2 Samuel 7:13). Jesus accepted His title as David's greater Son (see comments on Matthew 12:3, above). Furthermore, Jesus claimed to fulfill the function of the temple. The temple mediated the presence of God, and the priestly sacrifices for sin were meant to cover God's people: "The priest shall make an atonement for his sin that he hath committed, and it shall be forgiven him" (Leviticus 4:35). But Jesus offered forgiveness of sins without needing a temple of stone and wood. He could only do this with the authority of God

(Matthew 9:1-8). Later, when Jesus observed Passover with His disciples, He used bread and wine as images of a new covenant with God's people (26:26-29; compare Jeremiah 31:31-34). Thus what the temple was intended to do, Jesus fulfilled in and through himself.

These words did nothing to quell the conflict between Jesus and the Pharisees. The Pharisees objected to Jesus' Sabbath practice, but their real objection was to Him. But His responses made even greater claims of authority! He portrayed himself as a king on a mission, and He portrayed His disciples as priests who serve in the presence of a greater temple.

C. Than Sacrifice (v. 7)

7. But if ye had known what this meaneth, I will have mercy, and not sacrifice, ye would not have condemned the guiltless.

Jesus turned His attention to a related issue arising from the Pharisees' criticism. Hosea 6:6 says, "For I desired mercy, and not sacrifice; and the knowledge of God more than burnt offerings." Offerings, the sacrifices that God himself instituted in the Law of Moses, could be rejected when they were given hypocritically—meaning when a person was otherwise being unmerciful toward others. God redeemed His people through an act of mercy, and this fact could not be ignored in a setting of worship.

The prophet Hosea understood mercy, for God had called him to marry a sexually immoral woman (Hosea 1:2). Hosea's wife abandoned him, but God called him to find her again, to pay the price of her freedom, and to take her back as his wife (3:1-2). Hosea's marriage became a dramatic sign of the kind of merciful, gracious love God shows for wayward people. It anticipated the way that God would give Jesus to save people from the enslaving powers of sin (Romans 6:18).

Therefore, to live without mercy is the greatest affront to God (see also the parable in Matthew 18:21-35). Even worse, Jesus said the Pharisees had *condemned the guiltless.* The disciples had not done anything wrong in the first place, and yet still they were accused.

Jesus' opponents had lost sight of God's mercy,

trusting in their own rigor to keep the Law and to receive God's blessing. Even when Jesus, the very image of God's mercy, stood before them, they could not see past their own judgments. They were blind to the glory of the King.

> **What Do You Think?**
> What would it look like for you to show "mercy . . . not sacrifice" in the upcoming week?
> **Digging Deeper**
> How can you help your congregation improve its extensions of mercy?

D. Summary (v. 8)

8. For the Son of man is Lord even of the sabbath day.

The story ends with a memorable saying, which is both a summary and a climax. Instead of saying "I," Jesus calls himself *the Son of man.* This title had a complex history. A figure called "one like the Son of man" is mentioned in the vision of Daniel 7:13. The figure from Daniel is mysterious: someone to whom God gives "dominion, and glory, and a kingdom" (Daniel 7:14). Scholars disagree about how much this phrase was used as a title in Jesus' day. It could be that some people associated the title *Son of man* with political and military power. Alternatively, Jesus might have adopted the term to "fly under the radar" and present himself as a different kind of ruler.

Elsewhere, Jesus claims that the *Son of man* possesses authority. Jesus had shown that the *Son of man* had the authority to forgive sins, something God alone can do (Matthew 9:1-8). Jesus had also used the title to speak of himself as a lowly figure: "The Son of man hath not where to lay his head" (8:20). Here, Jesus claimed that He, as the *Son of man,* could be the one to establish the meaning of faithful observance of Sabbath. Since the Jewish people understood Sabbath as God's gift to them, claiming authority over Sabbath was bold. It would mean that Jesus was responsible for creation, which was the reason why God had the right to give Sabbath in the first place.

Additionally, the term *Lord* could be applied to

any figure of authority, but it was frequently used to translate the divine name of God from Hebrew into Greek. To claim to be *Lord even of the sabbath day* left little room for doubt: Jesus possessed authority belonging to God. Jesus will say more about this after Peter calls Jesus "the Christ" (Matthew 16:16). He will speak of the *Son of man* as one who shall be arrested, put to death, and rise from the grave (17:22-23). And one day, the *Son of man* will return "in the glory of his Father with his angels" to bring just reward to God's people (16:27-28).

What Do You Think?
What is the spiritual significance of the title "Son of man"?
Digging Deeper
How would you explain this significance to someone new to faith in Jesus?

Authority Undercover

If you have not seen an episode of *Undercover Boss*, you are missing out! A typical episode follows a company's owner or CEO as he or she dons a disguise and enters the workforce as a low-level employee of the company. Sometimes, the boss is the one humbled and transformed by the experience. But in nearly every episode, workers are rewarded or punished according to their behavior (which the boss witnessed first-hand). Who doesn't love to see people get what they deserve, good or bad?

Imagine that an undercover owner arrived at work and parked in the "Manager Only" section. If the shift manager spotted this, would he or she try to set the employee straight? It would appear that the "new employee" was not obeying the rules. But if the company's owner revealed her identity, she might say, "It doesn't matter whether you think I broke the rules. I own the place."

That's not so different from what Jesus claimed by calling himself "Lord . . . of the sabbath day." Whatever the rules might be, Jesus was the one with authority over them. Perhaps, like me, you've had times when you've gotten so concerned with rules that you've forgotten to ask what Jesus would

say about it. How would Jesus respond if He went undercover in your life and examined your actions toward others?
—J. H.

Conclusion
A. Lordship Is the Issue

This story looks at first like it will show how to observe Sabbath: as a gift and not a burden. Instead, the story is about the one who fulfills what Sabbath promises. It is about His authority and the blessing He brings. Jesus is a King, greater than His ancestor David. Jesus' disciples were like priests because they served a person greater than the temple. And Jesus is the Son of Man, for He is the Creator and Redeemer. He is God, who gave Sabbath in the first place.

Regardless of our understanding of Sabbath observance, all Christians can affirm that Jesus is Lord—even Lord of the Sabbath. Today's text challenges readers to acknowledge Jesus' authority. As King, He is able to provide good things: forgiveness, rest, and an eternal kingdom. The Lord of the Sabbath has given himself freely for our sakes, and we are responsible for showing mercy. If you want to honor the one with authority over Sabbath, start there.

What Do You Think?
What steps must you take to acknowledge and accept Jesus' authority as Lord and King?
Digging Deeper
How can you share this message with an unbelieving friend or neighbor in a culturally sensitive way?

B. Prayer
Lord Jesus, in You we see the power of God. Help us to find our rest in You. As You have shown us forgiveness and mercy, help us to offer mercy to others. Remind us that we are Your disciples on a holy mission with You. In Jesus' name. Amen.

C. Thought to Remember
Jesus gives His people true rest.

Involvement Learning

Enhance your lesson with KJV Bible Student *(from your curriculum supplier) and the reproducible activity page (at www.standardlesson.com or in the back of the* KJV Standard Lesson Commentary Deluxe Edition*).*

Into the Lesson

Begin class by asking volunteers to share humorous examples of a time when their words or actions were misunderstood by others. Then, ask volunteers to share about a time when they felt misunderstood and criticized, even when they believed they were doing the right thing. Ask, "Why do you think it's easier to criticize others rather than show mercy?"

Lead into Bible study by saying, "Just like some of us may have faced criticism, Jesus and His disciples faced criticism for their actions. In today's lesson, we will delve into one such situation and see how Jesus responded."

Into the Word

Say, "As we look at today's Scripture passage, we will approach it like journalists, seeking answers to the essential five 'W' questions: 'Who,' 'What,' 'When,' 'Where,' and 'Why.'" Divide the learners into three groups: **Character & Context (C&C) Group**, **Timeline Trailblazers (T&T) Group**, and **Purpose Pursuers (P&P) Group**.

Distribute a pen and a printed copy of Matthew 12:1-8 to each learner. Encourage learners to take notes directly on the printed copy of Scripture as needed. Instruct the **C&C Group** to underline any words and phrases in the text that could address the "Who?" and "What?" questions of the passage. Ask the **T&T Group** to underline words and phrases that could address "When?" and "Where?" questions. Finally, direct the **P&P Group** to underline words and phrases that could address the "Why?" question.

After five minutes of in-group work, reconvene the class. Ask the groups the assigned questions below. Answers are based on the results of the previous activity.

C&C Group: 1–Who was going through the fields on the Sabbath? 2–Who voiced an objection? 3–What was their objection? 4–In the story Jesus recounted, who entered the house of God and ate the shewbread? 5–What did David and his companions do that was unlawful?

T&T Group: 1–On what day of the week did the events of this Scripture text take place? 2–Where were Jesus' disciples when they picked and ate the ears of corn? 3–When did David and his companions eat the corn? 4–Where did David and his companions eat the shewbread?

P&P Group: 1–Why did the disciples pick the ears of corn? 2–Why did the Pharisees criticize Jesus' disciples? 3–Why did Jesus mention the story of David? 4–Why did Jesus say that one "greater than the temple" was present? 5–Why does Jesus quote Hosea 6:6?

Alternative. Distribute the "Missing Word" activity from the activity page, which you can download. Have learners work in pairs to complete as indicated.

As a whole class, talk about the challenge of the Pharisee's basis of concern versus what Jesus told them about His authority over the Sabbath.

Into Life

Ask learners to consider times when they could have demonstrated abundant mercy to another person but did not. Direct learners to work with a partner to answer the question: "How can believers approach situations with compassion and mercy?"

Distribute index cards to each learner. Challenge them to make a plan to follow Jesus' example and show abundant mercy in a place or time it would not be expected. After one minute, direct learners to share their plan with a partner. Encourage learners to place the index card in a location where they will see it throughout the week.

Option. Distribute copies of the "Lord of the Sabbath" exercise from the activity page. Have learners complete it as a take-home activity.

End class with a prayer, asking the Lord for guidance and wisdom to show abundant mercy in the week ahead.

Cleansing the Temple

Devotional Reading: Jeremiah 7:1-15
Background Scripture: John 2:13-25
(See also Matthew 21:12-17; Mark 11:15-19; Luke 19:45-48.)

John 2:13-25

13 And the Jews' passover was at hand, and Jesus went up to Jerusalem,

14 And found in the temple those that sold oxen and sheep and doves, and the changers of money sitting:

15 And when he had made a scourge of small cords, he drove them all out of the temple, and the sheep, and the oxen; and poured out the changers' money, and overthrew the tables;

16 And said unto them that sold doves, Take these things hence; make not my Father's house an house of merchandise.

17 And his disciples remembered that it was written, The zeal of thine house hath eaten me up.

18 Then answered the Jews and said unto him, What sign shewest thou unto us, seeing that thou doest these things?

19 Jesus answered and said unto them, Destroy this temple, and in three days I will raise it up.

20 Then said the Jews, Forty and six years was this temple in building, and wilt thou rear it up in three days?

21 But he spake of the temple of his body.

22 When therefore he was risen from the dead, his disciples remembered that he had said this unto them; and they believed the scripture, and the word which Jesus had said.

23 Now when he was in Jerusalem at the passover, in the feast day, many believed in his name, when they saw the miracles which he did.

24 But Jesus did not commit himself unto them, because he knew all men,

25 And needed not that any should testify of man: for he knew what was in man.

Key Text

Said unto them that sold doves, take these things hence; make not my Father's house an house of merchandise. —John 2:16

Sacred Altars and
Holy Offerings

Unit 2: Jesus and the Temple
Lessons 6–9

Lesson Aims

After participating in this lesson, each learner will be able to:

1. Identify Jesus' reason for "cleansing" the temple.

2. Explain the relationship between being "zealous" and being "jealous."

3. Make a plan to cleanse himself or herself of one unholy practice, considering that his or her body is God's new covenant temple (see 1 Corinthians 3:16-17 in lesson 10).

Lesson Outline

Introduction

A. Not in my House!

Every home is different, each with its own set of rules. From an early age, I learned that certain things were not permitted in my home. For example, under no circumstances was smoking allowed in the house. "Not in my house!" my mother would say. Smoking wasn't the only off-limits behavior; my siblings and I didn't dare use fighting words or curse. We knew our parents expected us to follow their rules while we lived under their roof. Later, when I married, I learned that my wife's childhood home had new and different rules. Shoes in the house? Not a chance! And don't even think of turning on a screen during mealtime.

What about God's house? If the rules we impose in our homes reflect our values, what does God value? God's earthly house—the temple—would need to reflect the character of the holy God. But when Jesus entered the temple in Jerusalem, He was not pleased with what He found.

B. Lesson Context

The cleansing of the temple in today's lesson differs from the accounts given in the Synoptic Gospels of Matthew, Mark, and Luke. Those Gospels recount the time of Jesus' dramatic actions in the temple that led to His arrest (Matthew 21:12-13; Mark 11:15-17; Luke 19:45-46). Some scholars believe that John and the writers of the Synoptics are recording different events. Others suggest that John has brought the event forward in his narrative to show its significance for everything that Jesus says and does in that Gospel.

If Jesus performed more than one cleansing of the temple, it might be that His actions caused no permanent reforms, which would make a second cleansing necessary—and perhaps more provocative to those seeking His death.

The first-century temple in Jerusalem was the center of Jewish religious life. Although the faithful of Jesus' time regarded the temple as sacred, the temple complex was filled with controversy. The temple was led by a family of priests seen as corrupt. The temple's outer courts became the location for selling animals used for sacrifices. Although many probably approved of this practice for convenience, others found it scandalous since the priesthood profited from the arrangement.

Jesus' cleansing of the temple of His day is analogous to the activities of His ancestors. Hezekiah (reigned 715–687 BC) and Josiah (reigned 640–609 BC) were kings of Judah who reformed and renovated the temple of their day after it was neglected and defiled by idolatry (2 Kings 23:1-30; 2 Chronicles 29:1-36). Because Jesus is the rightful King and a Son of David, it was fitting for Him to demand reform of the temple.

Before the events of today's lesson text, Jesus had been in Cana in Galilee, where He had miraculously transformed water into wine (John 2:1-10). This miracle "manifested forth his glory" for His disciples and others to see (2:11). Following that event, Jesus traveled with family members and disciples to Capernaum, a fishing village on the shores of the Sea of Galilee (2:12). After staying in that town for a few days, Jesus and the disciples departed for Jerusalem, a journey of several days on foot. Our story picks up here.

I. Jesus' Actions
(John 2:13-17)
A. Described (vv. 13-16)

13. And the Jews' passover was at hand, and Jesus went up to Jerusalem.

This verse is the first mention of Passover celebrations in the Gospel of John (compare John 6:4; 12:1; 13:1; 18:28, 39; 19:14). During times of feasts, it would be typical for travelers to Jerusalem to join with other travelers to create a caravan.

John's use of the phrase *the Jews' passover* reflects his intended audience of the Gospel: a combined Jewish-Gentile community in the latter half of the first century. For this audience, observance of the Jewish feasts was not expected.

However, most Jews of Jesus' day would go to the temple to observe Passover. This one-day observance celebrated God's deliverance of His people from enslavement in Egypt (Exodus 12:1-27; Leviticus 23:5; Deuteronomy 16:1-8). The Feast of Unleavened Bread immediately follows passover

(Leviticus 23:4-6; Numbers 28:16-17). Jesus went up to Jerusalem in obedience to the law regarding these observances (Deuteronomy 16:16).

14. And found in the temple those that sold oxen and sheep and doves, and the changers of money sitting.

The temple included the singular building that housed the most holy place and the adjoining buildings and courts built by Herod the Great (reigned 37–4 BC). By reliable estimates, the temple complex grew to be larger than 30 acres once completed.

The location *in the temple* complex where Jesus encountered these animals was likely in the Court of the Gentiles, an open-air court where Jews and Gentiles were allowed to congregate. In this court, animals for sacrifices could be bought and sold. However, Jesus' attention was not on the animals but on *those that sold* them.

Oxen, *sheep*, and *doves* are animals used for sacrifice as prescribed by the Law of Moses (Leviticus 17:3; 5:6; 5:7, respectively). Doves were offered as sacrifices by people who could not afford larger animals (12:8; compare Luke 2:24). No one could easily satisfy the expectations for offering and sacrifice without passing money to a third party, one who had the approval of the priesthood.

If a person wanted to bring financial offerings, only one type of coin was allowed for the temple. Thus, *the changers of money* allowed travelers to Jerusalem to convert their money or resources—however much that might amount to—into a fitting currency for the temple. The money changers

How to Say It

Cana	*Kay*-nuh.
Capernaum	Kuh-*per*-nay-um.
Galilee	*Gal*-uh-lee.
Herod	*Hair*-ud.
Hezekiah	Hez-ih-*kye*-uh.
Jerusalem	Juh-*roo*-suh-lem.
Josiah	Jo-*sigh*-uh.
Sanhedrin	San-huh-drun or San-*heed*-run.
synoptic	sih-*nawp*-tihk.

did business *sitting* in the temple courts and often charged exorbitant transaction fees.

15. And when he had made a scourge of small cords, he drove them all out of the temple, and the sheep, and the oxen; and poured out the changers' money, and overthrew the tables.

Actions sometimes speak louder than words. When seeing these animals and people in the temple courts, Jesus did not make a speech to persuade their removal. The *scourge of small cords* could have been a type of braided rope used to direct the animals—specifically, *sheep* and *oxen*—to move.

Jesus used the cords and *drove them all*—the animals and the people doing business—*out of the temple*. The animals' owners likely sprinted to gather their valuable commodities as these animals fled. By scattering *the changers' money*, Jesus created a chaotic scene: *tables* crashing to the ground, coins flying in all directions, and money changers scrambling to prevent theft. All the while, large animals were running through to escape the man wielding an improvised whip.

> **What Do You Think?**
> How should a believer respond when they confront an unjust situation?
> **Digging Deeper**
> How might Job 1:20-22 inform such a response?

16. And said unto them that sold doves, Take these things hence; make not my Father's house an house of merchandise.

Jesus singled out *them that sold doves* for special criticism. As a result, we get the first hint of an explanation. Of course, Jesus could not use cords to drive out birds. A focus on sellers of doves reveals Jesus' anger at those who were taking advantage of those who were economically impoverished. Jesus objected to a show of false motives within the temple. He encountered a massive operation that allowed people to make a show of their devotion to God as they exchanged coins and obtained animals for sacrifice.

Jesus' inspection of the temple echoed the Old Testament prophets of Israel who demanded a change of heart of the people. Isaiah told the people of Israel to quit "vain oblations" and, instead, "learn to do well; seek judgment, relieve the oppressed, judge the fatherless, plead for the widow" (Isaiah 1:13, 17). Jeremiah gave a similar warning to residents of Judah, who thought that sacrifices would cover sinful hypocrisy (Jeremiah 7:1-29).

The phrase *my Father's house* reveals Jesus' authority to state such commands. The people of Israel frequently referred to God as "father" (Deuteronomy 32:6; Psalm 89:26-27; Isaiah 64:8; etc.; compare Romans 1:7).

The Gospel of John describes Jesus's unique relationship with His Heavenly Father. Jesus is the "only begotten of the Father" (John 1:14) who, in coming from Heaven, "hath declared" God the Father (1:18). As the only begotten Son of God, Jesus has unparalleled authority: "The Father loveth the Son, and hath given all things into his hand" (3:35). Jesus did nothing that was without the agreement and authorization of the Father (5:19-27). Jesus' unique identity as the Son of God culminated in His proclamation, "I and my Father are one" (10:30). No other person in Israel's past had claimed authority as God's Son sent from Heaven.

With this authority, Jesus declared that the temple was not a place for entrepreneurs to enrich themselves at others' expense. God is giving and gracious. His house should reflect His character. The temple and the sacrificial system presented in the Law of Moses were to be a communal practice that allowed the people to experience the presence of God. In Jesus' evaluation, this temple was being corrupted by the very things—sacrificial animals and money for offerings—that would please God.

Cleaning House

In our backyard, my dad built a playhouse for my sister and me. The playhouse allowed us to have fun on our own and to pretend like we were adults. A house of their own is every kid's dream, and we had it!

Then came the wasps. The insects did not "approve" of the playhouse. They attacked us every time we went in or out of the playhouse.

Our mere existence displeased the insects. Of course, my sister and I disapproved of them living in our playhouse, but we were too afraid of them to do anything. Instead, we commissioned our dad to help us. He bravely entered the playhouse, took the necessary steps to remove the wasps, and ended their stay. Soon, our playhouse was clear of wasps, and we could again enjoy it.

Just as my dad wouldn't let the wasps take over our playhouse, Jesus wanted His people to have free access to God's presence and enjoy God's company. Are you making space for God's presence in your heart? Is your treatment of others helping or preventing people from coming to Him? —L. M. W.

The Father's house is not a market.

Visual for Lesson 8. *Display this visual as you discuss the lesson commentary associated with John 2:16.*

B. Explained (v. 17)

17. And his disciples remembered that it was written, The zeal of thine house hath eaten me up.

The underlying Greek word translated *remembered* is used three times in the Gospel of John (here and in John 2:22; 12:16); in each case, Jesus' disciples are the ones doing the remembering. Often, Jesus' motives were not clear to His closest followers. However, after His resurrection, the disciples gained a new understanding of what Jesus had done and what His words had meant (example: Luke 24:45-49).

The Scripture text that the *disciples remembered* comes from Psalm 69:9. John quotes only the first half of the verse, but the second half of that verse is equally appropriate as words about Jesus: "The reproaches of them that reproached thee are fallen upon me" (compare Romans 15:3). The word *zeal* in this context means intensive dedication, not jealousy (compare 10:2). Jesus was devoted to the temple, not as it existed, but as it was intended.

> **What Do You Think?**
> Has more reflection helped you notice God's hand in a difficult situation? When?
>
> **Digging Deeper**
> How are you attentive to the guidance of God's Spirit during reflection regarding spiritual matters?

Preparing for a Visit

As I type this, I sit waiting for my adult children to drive home for a holiday. While they make the trek, I clean the house, decorate, and prepare food. Knowing they are coming motivates me to prepare. I want them to see their old stomping grounds and remember happy times, not focus on how dilapidated things might be! I want to create a homey and welcoming atmosphere for them so they can enjoy family time.

I think Jesus wanted something similar for His Heavenly Father's house. He wanted a place where all of God's children could gather to worship the Father and strengthen their bond with Him and one another. Jesus' reaction showed that temple merchants were doing things that prevented that from happening. Are your heart and your home places where people are welcomed? Can Jesus use you to provide comfort and safety? —L. M. W.

II. Jesus' Announcement
(John 2:18-22)

A. Authority Challenged (vv. 18-20)

18. Then answered the Jews and said unto him, What sign shewest thou unto us, seeing that thou doest these things?

Jesus' actions demanded a response. *The Jews* were religious leaders who had a keen interest in the temple and its function. Jesus had put them in a difficult position before a crowd in the temple courts. On the one hand, they could not be seen as being less devoted to God's house than to Jesus. On the other hand, they had a vested interest in maintaining the status quo.

Perhaps the religious leaders believed Jesus' actions were right and His devotion to the temple was from God, but they wanted to know whether or not Jesus could prove His authority. Their demand for a *sign* pressured Jesus. The underlying Greek word translated as "sign" is used elsewhere in John's Gospel to refer to a miracle (examples: John 2:11, 23; 4:54; 12:18). The leaders wanted a public demonstration of Jesus' power (compare Matthew 16:1-4; John 6:30).

19. Jesus answered and said unto them, Destroy this temple, and in three days I will raise it up.

Jesus indirectly *answered* the leaders through a riddle-like response. The underlying Greek word translated *temple* in this verse differs from the word translated as "temple" in verse 15, above. The Greek word in the verse before us often refers to the Jerusalem temple (examples: Matthew 23:16-17; Mark 15:38; Luke 1:9). The apostle Paul used the same word to mean a body as a place where the Spirit of God can dwell (1 Corinthians 6:19).

The plain meaning of Jesus' words would seem to be that He would rebuild the temple building in Jerusalem after three days should His questioners *destroy* it. For the audience observing and listening, it would seem that Jesus was asserting His commitment to preserving the temple building. Words with similar implications were later used as allegations against Him during His trial before the Sanhedrin (Matthew 26:21; Mark 14:58).

20. Then said the Jews, Forty and six years was this temple in building, and wilt thou rear it up in three days?

The first Jerusalem temple was built by King Solomon (1 Kings 5–6). The Babylonians destroyed it when they took the nation of Judah into captivity in 586 BC (2 Kings 25:8-17). Following the exile, the temple was rebuilt (Ezra 3; 6:13-18). That temple remained somewhat intact until Herod the Great took control of Jerusalem and, in approximately 19 BC, began renovating the complex. The project continued after Herod died in 4 BC and was a little past its midpoint during Jesus' ministry. The authorities must have thought that a 46-year building project could not be redone in only *three days*.

B. Answer Explained (vv. 21-22)

21-22. But he spake of the temple of his body. When therefore he was risen from the dead, his disciples remembered that he had said this unto them; and they believed the scripture, and the word which Jesus had said.

These verses provide an editorial explanation to readers of John's Gospel: Jesus himself would become *the temple* since He will be killed and restored (*risen from the dead*) after three days (Matthew 27:45–28:10; Mark 15:33–16:8; Luke 23:44–24:12; John 19:24–20:9). The temple was the physical manifestation of God's presence with His people, the place where they could find mercy and forgiveness for sin (see Isaiah 56:4-7; etc.).

However, the spiritual significance of the temple was fulfilled in Jesus, for "no man cometh unto the Father, but by [Him]" (John 14:6). Jesus was revealed as the true temple, while the physical tabernacle and temple were simply fleeting shadows (see Hebrews 8:5; 10:1). Likewise, the bodies of His followers become a temple, welcoming the presence of God through the indwelling of the Holy Spirit (1 Corinthians 3:16-17; 6:19).

There is some debate about which *scripture* the disciples *remembered* and *believed*. John may mean a specific text from Scripture, such as Psalm 69:9 (see commentary on John 2:17, above). However, the phrase *the scripture* parallels *the word which Jesus had said*, and Jesus did not repeat Psalm 69:9. Alternatively, *scripture* and *word* might be shorthand for the Old Testament, which is fulfilled in and through Jesus (compare Luke 24:44; John 20:9).

III. Who to Believe?

(John 2:23-25)

A. Jesus (v. 23)

23. Now when he was in Jerusalem at the passover, in the feast day, many believed in his name, when they saw the miracles which he did.

John does not state what *miracles* Jesus did while He was *in Jerusalem*. John concludes his Gospel with the statement, "There are also many other things which Jesus did, the which, if they should be written every one, I suppose that even the world itself could not contain the books that should be written" (John 21:25). These miracles in Jerusalem would be an example of such unwritten things. Whatever these miracles were, they caused *many* to believe *in his name*. It seems that when put to the test and asked for a sign, Jesus resisted. But to those who followed and witnessed His work in Jerusalem, He performed miracles and gave evidence of divine power at work.

B. Not Humans (vv. 24-25)

24. But Jesus did not commit himself unto them, because he knew all men.

The Greek word translated *commit* is the same word translated as "believed" in verse 23, above. Others "believed" Jesus, but He did not trust them. He anticipated the ways their hearts could change.

Later in this Gospel, Jesus will provide for the crowds, leading them to want to make Him their king (John 6:1-15). Yet, the leaders and crowds of Jerusalem would ultimately reject Him (19:14-16).

25. And needed not that any should testify of man: for he knew what was in man.

John's Gospel shows how Jesus knows and anticipates the motives of others (examples: John 1:47-48; 6:64; 13:11). Generally, other individuals in this Gospel testified *about Jesus* rather than *to Jesus* (examples: 1:6-15, 32-34; 4:39; 19:34-35; 21:24). Jesus did not need to receive the testimony of others because He *knew what was in* all people.

Conclusion

A. New Temple

Ironically, in an account expressing Jesus' zeal for the Jerusalem temple, He redefines the concept of "temple." His actions were like those of a prophet—one who does not come to destroy but comes to communicate God's perspective.

Jesus saw that the temple was filled with people who faced a business model that extracted financial value from them to enrich others. Regardless of Herod's renovations of the temple, Jesus knew that the building would not stand. Instead, Jesus' body is a temple because He is the Word of God from Heaven (John 1:1, 14). The temple in Jerusalem was a failing human institution. Sinful humanity cannot welcome God's holy presence without repentance and God's help. God's desire to dwell with humans was so great that He sent His only begotten Son to bring them eternal life (3:16). In and through Jesus, we can have direct access to God.

B. Prayer

Lord God, we are amazed to consider ourselves a temple of Your presence. We ask You to renew us and rid us of anything not pleasing in Your sight: greed, selfishness, and insincerity. Help us to be more like Jesus, who communicated Your truth and mercy to those around Him. In His name we pray, Amen.

C. Thought to Remember

The body of Christ is God's temple.

Involvement Learning

Enhance your lesson with KJV Bible Student *(from your curriculum supplier) and the reproducible activity* page *(at www.standardlesson.com or in the back of the* KJV Standard Lesson Commentary Deluxe Edition*).*

Into the Lesson

Write the words *Spaces* and *Experiences* on the board as the headers of two columns. Invite learners to share the spaces and experiences where they felt a significant emotional reaction. (*Example*: A person might feel anger after seeing litter in the park [Space], sadness after a farewell to a close friend [Experience].) Write the emotions in the columns under the correct header. After no more than five minutes, give learners time to draw conclusions about the emotions listed on the board. After one minute of reflection, ask a volunteer to share his or her conclusions.

Alternative. Distribute copies of the "Zeal!" exercise from the activity page, which you can download. Have participants complete it individually in a minute or less before sharing their reflections with a partner.

Lead into the Bible study by saying, "Passion and zeal often emerge when something we deeply care about is at stake. In today's Scripture, we witness Jesus' profound zeal for His Father's house."

Into The Word

Divide the class into two equal groups:

Temple Guardians Group: Read John 2:13-17. 1–What was the significance of the Passover? 2–Why were animal merchants and money changers present in the temple? 3–How does Jesus' reaction differ from how you might anticipate the reactions of others? Read John 2:18-25. 1–What is the significance of the conversation between Jesus and the Jewish leaders? 2–Why might they have thought Jesus was talking about the temple complex in Jerusalem?

Messianic Mysteries Group: Read John 2:13-17. 1–How does Jesus show zeal through His actions? 2–Is an expression of zeal right or wrong? Read John 2:18-25. 1–Why did the Jewish leaders demand a sign from Jesus? 2–How does Jesus' response in John 2:19 foreshadow events that were to come? 4–What does John 2:24-25 reveal about Jesus' understanding of human nature?

After no more than 10 minutes of small-group work, ask a volunteer from each group to give a summary of the group's conclusions.

Option. Distribute copies of the "Mixed-up Manuscript" activity from the activity page. Have learners work with a partner to complete as indicated.

Divide the class into four groups. On four index cards, write one of the following Scripture references: *Psalm 69:9*; *Isaiah 56:7*; *Jeremiah 7:11*; *Zechariah 14:21*. Distribute one card to each group and ask each group to determine how their assigned Scripture text connects to today's lesson text. While the groups work, write dictionary definitions of the words *jealous* and *zealous* on the board.

After three minutes, reconvene the class and ask a representative from each group to give the group's conclusion. Ask each group how the assigned verse reveals a *jealous* God or a *zealous* God. After groups have shared, ask the class what it means for God's house to be "clean."

Into Life

Ask a volunteer to read 1 Corinthians 3:16-17. For whole-class discussion, ask, "What does it mean that we are the 'temple' of God?" After discussion, ask, "How can we be 'zealous' to uphold the honor and sanctity of ourselves as temple of God?"

Distribute index cards and pencils to learners. Lead into the activity by saying, "Consider what you have learned today about Jesus' passion for reverence. Write down a personal plan or action step to cleanse your 'temple,' be it a physical space, a tradition, or a personal practice so that your temple glorifies God." Encourage learners to be as honest as possible because their responses will not be shared with the class.

Conclude class time with a group prayer, asking God to give everyone a zeal akin to Jesus'—a fervor that upholds sanctity, respect, and genuine worship.

Jesus Predicts the Temple's Destruction

Devotional Reading: Matthew 23:1-12, 37-39
Background Scripture: Matthew 23:37–24:35
(See also Mark 13:1-23; Luke 21:5-24.)

Matthew 24:1-14

1 And Jesus went out, and departed from the temple: and his disciples came to him for to shew him the buildings of the temple.

2 And Jesus said unto them, see ye not all these things? verily I say unto you, there shall not be left here one stone upon another, that shall not be thrown down.

3 And as he sat upon the mount of Olives, the disciples came unto him privately, saying, tell us, when shall these things be? and what shall be the sign of thy coming, and of the end of the world?

4 And Jesus answered and said unto them, take heed that no man deceive you.

5 For many shall come in my name, saying, I am Christ; and shall deceive many.

6 And ye shall hear of wars and rumours of wars: see that ye be not troubled: for all these things must come to pass, but the end is not yet.

7 For nation shall rise against nation, and kingdom against kingdom: and there shall be famines, and pestilences, and earthquakes, in divers places.

8 All these are the beginning of sorrows.

9 Then shall they deliver you up to be afflicted, and shall kill you: and ye shall be hated of all nations for my name's sake.

10 And then shall many be offended, and shall betray one another, and shall hate one another.

11 And many false prophets shall rise, and shall deceive many.

12 And because iniquity shall abound, the love of many shall wax cold.

13 But he that shall endure unto the end, the same shall be saved.

14 And this gospel of the kingdom shall be preached in all the world for a witness unto all nations; and then shall the end come.

Key Text

Jesus said unto them, see ye not all these things? verily I say unto you, there shall not be left here one stone upon another, that shall not be thrown down. —**Matthew 24:2**

Sacred Altars and
Holy Offerings

Unit 2: Jesus and the Temple
Lessons 6–9

Lesson Aims

After participating in this lesson, each learner will be able to:

1. Relate facts about the destruction of Jerusalem and its temple in AD 70.

2. Explain the relationship between the temple's destruction and "the end."

3. Review what spiritual habits help him or her endure in the faith and recommit to practicing them.

Lesson Outline

Introduction

A. Is This a Sign of the End?

When I recently tried to find something to watch for family movie night, I was surprised to realize how many new movies are about war. I suppose it had never occurred to me just how fascinated we are with violence, natural disasters, and accidents. It's not just visible in the entertainment industry. In addition to these fictional stories coloring our screens, real life is also filled with terror on all sides. Tragic realities saturate the news, from devastating hurricanes and wildfires to domestic violence and armed conflict. Ordinary life can leave us both weary and worried. When confronted with this grim reality, it's common for people of faith to ask, "Is this a sign of the end?"

Today's text is part of Jesus' answer to that question from His followers.

B. Lesson Context

The temple of Jerusalem played a central role in Israel's history, and it had a special connection with the nation's kings. King David had sought to build a temple as a grand replacement for the portable tabernacle, which Israel had carried through the wilderness (2 Samuel 7:1-3). Instead, God said that David's son would build a temple (7:12-16). True enough, Solomon built the temple as David had planned (1 Kings 6:1-38). But Solomon proved unfaithful, and the nation divided into two after his death (11:9-13, 26-40). Instead of a place for all God's people to come, the location of God's sanctuary became a source of jealous conflict between the kings of Judah and Israel (12:25-33; compare Deuteronomy 12:5-7). The unfaithfulness of Judah's rulers contributed to the temple's being stripped of its glory. The armies of Babylon eventually destroyed it after a successful siege of Jerusalem (2 Kings 25; 2 Chronicles 36:15-21).

When exiles of Judah returned to their land in 536 BC, the faithful set to work rebuilding a temple (Ezra 1:1-7; 3:7-13). The resulting structure was far from the grandeur of the first temple. Hundreds of years later, Herod the Great made the second temple magnificent. Herod had a selfish motive for his project: to show his family's right to rule. Josephus, the first-century Jewish historian, states that ten thousand skilled workers and masons had contributed to this structure, and it had required a thousand carts to bring the bright white stones to set in place.

Jesus entered this renovated temple after coming to Jerusalem and being heralded as God's promised King (Matthew 21:1-11). But instead of praising this impressive temple, Jesus cast out the money changers and merchants and criticized what He saw (21:12-16). The temple's leaders questioned His authority to do this, and He silenced them with a dilemma using a question of His own (21:25-27) and parables (21:28-44). In Matthew 22–23, Jesus remained in the temple and continued to face down His hostile audience. He did not relent from His criticisms, and fear of the Passover crowds kept Jesus from being arrested immediately (21:46).

The book of Matthew is recognized as featuring five "discourses." Today's text is part of the fifth of those, known as the Olivet Discourse. Mark 13:1-13 and Luke 21:5-19 are parallel accounts to today's text.

I. Looming Destruction
(Matthew 24:1-3)
A. Warning of Ruin (vv. 1-2)

1. And Jesus went out, and departed from the temple: and his disciples came to him for to shew him the buildings of the temple.

Prior to Jesus' departure *from the temple*, He had criticized the religious leaders for their hypocrisy by pronouncing seven woes on them (Matthew 23:13-36). The sharpness of the acrimonious exchanges between Jesus and the religious leaders must have unsettled His *disciples*. That may be why we see their attempt to turn the mood in a positive direction with their observation about the grandeur of *the buildings of the temple* (compare Mark 13:1). Perhaps they imagined Jesus would one day assume power over this temple, for He was the promised Son of David (Matthew 1:1; 9:27; 12:23; 15:22; 20:30-31; 21:9, 15; 22:42). His very presence was "greater than the temple" (12:6). So who better to appreciate its physical appearance?

2. And Jesus said unto them, See ye not all these things? verily I say unto you, There shall not be left here one stone upon another, that shall not be thrown down.

Jesus' reply was shocking. It was one thing to criticize the leaders of the temple. But to predict the temple's utter destruction? To speak against a temple in the ancient world was to invite the death penalty (example: Jeremiah 26:1-9).

The disciples may have expected that Jesus had a grand vision of a better temple. But His prediction *there shall not be left here one stone upon another* was only about the tear-down part of such a project, leaving out the rebuilding part. His wording is ominous: all the stones would be *thrown down* (rather than falling down on their own; compare Mark 13:2; Luke 21:6). There is no record of the disciples asking Jesus who would be doing the demolition; the political context made that clear enough: Jews were allowed to keep worshiping at the temple by the permission of Rome.

It was horrifying to think that Rome would turn against the Jewish people and their temple. In fact, the Gospel of John attributes this very fear to the high priest and his advisors: "The Romans shall come and take away both our place and nation" (John 11:48). Ironically, the Jewish leaders rejected Jesus, at least partly out of fear that His message could spell an end to the temple and their vested interests.

But Jesus knew better: Jewish nationalists would rebel and antagonize the Romans, who would respond with lethal military precision by surrounding the city and razing the temple in AD 70, some four decades after Jesus' prediction.

B. Asking for Guidance (v. 3)

3. And as he sat upon the mount of Olives, the disciples came unto him privately, saying, Tell us, when shall these things be? and what shall be the sign of thy coming, and of the end of the world?

After Jesus and His disciples left the temple, they crossed the Kidron Valley to arrive at *the mount of Olives*. There, as they looked back upon the temple, the disciples desired answers to questions that were echoing in their minds. Mark

13:3 specifies that it was Peter, James, John, and Andrew who asked the questions.

The mental context of the disciples is a clue to the questions they ask. By Jesus' *coming*, the disciples were not thinking of what Christians today call the "second coming" or "return," since the disciples did not believe that Jesus was going to depart physically in the first place. Even right up to the time of Jesus' ascension, their expectations were mistaken (Acts 1:6).

Thus, what the disciples must have meant by *coming* was the ascension of a king to his earthly throne, with his full power on display. Perhaps they reached this (mis)interpretation from Jesus' statements about the "coming" of the Son of Man (Matthew 10:23; 16:27-28; compare Daniel 7:13). This expectation means that the disciples used the phrase *the end of the world* in the sense of the ending of an era, not the physical destruction of planet Earth. The Greek word translated *world* here is the basis for our English word *eon*, which refers to an immeasurably long time period. The disciples thought the destruction of the temple would signal Jesus' immediate kingship; He could then wipe away the wicked kingdoms of this world and bring God's justice to the poor and oppressed (see Isaiah 11:4).

> **What Do You Think?**
> How does Scripture describe the kingship of Jesus?
> **Digging Deeper**
> What specific behaviors are needed of those living under this kingship?

II. Coming Hardships
(Matthew 24:4-12)

A. Fake Messiahs (vv. 4-5)

4-5. And Jesus answered and said unto them, Take heed that no man deceive you. For many shall come in my name, saying, I am Christ; and shall deceive many.

Jesus doesn't answer the disciples as they expect. Instead of "Here's how to recognize me," His response is along the lines of "Here's how to recognize it's *not* me." Pretenders and wannabe liberators were abundant in the first century (compare Acts 5:36-37; 21:38). *Many* people will be easily deceived, and the disciples must not be among them.

The word *Christ* is the Greek word used to translate the Hebrew word *Messiah* (John 1:41; 4:25), both of which mean "anointed one" in English. Several decades after the temple was destroyed in AD 70, a man who called himself Simon Bar Kokhba (meaning "son of a star") proclaimed himself to be the Messiah on the basis of the prophecy in Numbers 24:17 of a star coming out of Jacob. The Romans crushed his rebellion in AD 135; those who were deceived by the man's claim and followed him were either killed or enslaved.

When we think of how many people today are deceived by even simple scams, we should constantly be vigilant. "False Christs, and false prophets" are those who show impressive signs, supposedly from God (Matthew 24:24). This will be the reason for their remarkable, though temporary, success in recruiting many followers. In his first letter, John says to "try the spirits whether they are of God" (1 John 4:1).

> **What Do You Think?**
> What steps should believers take to ensure we are not misled by deceptive teachings?
> **Digging Deeper**
> What Scripture texts come to mind regarding this effort?

Counterfeit Culture

You've undoubtedly noticed that we live in an age of counterfeits. Some manufacturers find making and selling knockoffs quite profitable, putting well-known "designer" tags and logos on their counterfeit products. Thus, they try to pass their products off as having been made by someone else. Handbags, perfume, household goods—you name it, there are scam artists everywhere. They are just waiting to try to gain your trust.

When it comes to listening to the authoritative voice of God, there can be no substitute. The words of Jesus are trustworthy, but plenty of other voices are crying out to be heard. These voices tempt us with shortcuts to wealth, power, or cultural influence. Have you been tuning in to let God speak truth to you of late? Or do you settle for a cheap imitation? —D. A.

B. Fearsome Conflicts (vv. 6-8)

6. And ye shall hear of wars and rumours of wars: see that ye be not troubled: for all these things must come to pass, but the end is not yet.

The militarized "peace of Rome" (also known as *Pax Romana*) resulted in a period of relative peace in Jesus' day. But when the reality of war or the *rumours of wars* reassert themselves, that was not to be taken as a sign of *the end*. Christians must be prepared to endure conflicts while carrying out their mission to make disciples (Matthew 28:19-20).

7. For nation shall rise against nation, and kingdom against kingdom: and there shall be famines, and pestilences, and earthquakes, in divers places.

Psalm 2:1-2 vividly describes the world's situation, where rulers and nations "rage." So this will be nothing new. All the challenges and tragedies of living in a fallen world will come and go. Food shortages (*famines*), diseases (*pestilences*), and natural disasters (such as *earthquakes*) will be common.

Daily life will feature constant reminders that humans are mortal, that life is short, and that the time to receive God's mercy is at hand. An unpredictable world underlines a sense of urgency.

What Do You Think?

How can you use your time, talents, or resources to help people suffering as a result of wars or natural disasters?

Digging Deeper

What steps will you take in the upcoming week to make this a reality?

---

8. All these are the beginning of sorrows.

The disciples' original question was about how to recognize "the end." But Jesus has been answering in terms of *the beginning*. The word translated *sorrows* is also used in 1 Thessalonians 5:3 to refer to the labor pains (*travail*) of a woman giving

Visual for Lesson 9. *Display this visual as you review the commentary and discussion questions associated with Matthew 24:4-5.*

birth. Thus, the word can refer to something more than just mental anguish. The same word is used in the sense of labor pains in several places in the old Greek version of the Old Testament, known as the Septuagint (example: Isaiah 13:8).

Certain birth pains were, therefore, to precede Jesus' full reign. But *all these* painful things were also everyday experiences of the disciples—in other words, nothing new. The disciples were, therefore, not to interpret such things as imminent harbingers of the end.

C. Faithless Persecution (vv. 9-10)

9. Then shall they deliver you up to be afflicted, and shall kill you: and ye shall be hated of all nations for my name's sake.

Jesus then switched His warnings from those global in nature to those personal to His disciples. They were to expect intensified persecution in their role as His representatives (*for my name's sake*). Tradition holds that all Jesus' apostles except John died as martyrs. These martyrdoms would begin with James, the brother of John (Acts 12:2).

10. And then shall many be offended, and shall betray one another, and shall hate one another.

The effect of all this suffering will be to fragment the church (*hate one another*). In modern English, to be *offended* is to be upset or insulted by something said or done. But the word has a stronger sense of "cause to stumble" in the older English of the *King James Version*. Hardship and persecution will lead some to give up (Matthew 13:5-6, 20-21). Much has been written about the imperatives of the positive "one anothers" in Scripture. But the verse before us warns of the certain occurrences of at least two negative "one anothers."

D. False Prophets (vv. 11-12)

11-12. And many false prophets shall rise, and shall deceive many. And because iniquity shall abound, the love of many shall wax cold.

The reality of and the danger posed by *false prophets* is addressed in more than a dozen places in the Bible. This, too, will be nothing new (2 Peter 2:1). The fact that they will be successful, at least for a time, is affirmed by the result that they *shall deceive many*. The warning is therefore necessary so Jesus' followers keep their guard up and are not led astray.

III. Reassuring Victories
(Matthew 24:13-14)

A. God's Faithful Endure (v. 13)

13. But he that shall endure unto the end, the same shall be saved.

Is there any bright spot in Jesus' predictions? Is there any sign of God's victory while evil continues to roil the world? The answer is a resounding "Yes!" The parable about the soils holds out hope for those who receive God's message with faith; God has a great harvest, a great victory (Matthew 13:8, 23). The victory of God is visible through the enduring faith of Jesus' followers around the world. As Jesus said, "The gates of hell shall not prevail against [my church]" (16:18). The reign of Christ among the faithful is visible as God's will is done "in earth, as it is in heaven" (6:10).

How to Say It

ascension	uh-*sen(t)*-shun.
Kidron	*Kid*-ron.
Olivet	*Ol*-ih-vet.
Pax Romana (*Latin*)	*Pahks* Ro-*mah*-nah.
Thessalonians	*Thess*-uh-*lo*-nee-unz (*th* as in *thin*).

Jesus' warnings about forthcoming hardships prepared His disciples for this declaration. Yes, suffering would continue. Yes, persecution would divide the people of God and war against the faith. But for those who understand that reality, who heed Jesus' warnings, there is strength for endurance and assurance to *be saved* in the end.

> **What Do You Think?**
> Which of Scripture's promises help you endure as a follower of Jesus?
>
> **Digging Deeper**
> How will you be a source of encouragement for other believers who may be troubled by the world?

Endure, Together

Children can do a lot more than we expect. When my daughter showed an interest in riding a bike, she was confident that she would soon do it without training wheels. She wasn't wrong, and her persistence paid off quickly. She became the youngest child on the block who was riding on two wheels.

We started an endurance test together: each day, we would ride just one block farther before we turned around for home. Before long, we could make it to a trail. Even at four years old, she managed to ride a 12-mile loop—to her parents' amazement.

There is no shortcut to practicing endurance. I tend to think that the company we keep makes all the difference. Jesus could ask His disciples to endure a difficult path, but He did not ask them to endure alone. The community of faith—the church—would stand; this Jesus promised. Have you been relying on a fellowship of believers as God intends, or have you been trying to journey through life alone? As you've seen the trials of our world, have you been coming alongside others who suffer?

—D. A.

B. Good News Prevails (v. 14)

14. And this gospel of the kingdom shall be preached in all the world for a witness unto all nations; and then shall the end come.

The coming destruction of the temple may look like a diversion of God's plan, but it would not be. God's purpose was never to designate a plot of land for a permanent temple. Its construction was secondary to God's promise to bless all nations through the descendants of Abraham and to build a kingdom through the family of David (Genesis 12:3; 2 Samuel 7:12-15).

For people in the Roman Empire in Jesus' time, *gospel* or "good news" was commonly associated with the announcement of a new king or ruler. Heralds delivering the message could say, "I have good news for you: we have a new king." For the children of Abraham, good news was also connected to God's promise to end their exile and establish a divine kingdom (Isaiah 40:9; 41:27; 52:7; 61:1). Declaring good news was to declare that God had fulfilled His long-standing promises to restore His people.

Both of these fit what Jesus announced. Despite all the hardships and suffering His followers were to experience, God's *kingdom* was to be heralded and proclaimed for all to hear. This is the establishment of God's promised King, one whose justice shall be known throughout the world. God still works through His people to fulfill every promise He has made, to multiply the followers of the new King. The *end* is delayed—not forever—but long enough that the *witness* of God's people can go forth (compare Matthew 28:18-20).

What Do You Think?

What steps can your class take to support the advance of the gospel in all the world and to all nations?

Digging Deeper

What further training and guidance will your class need in this regard?

Conclusion

A. Living Between the Times

People want to know the future! That was the impetus for the disciples' questions about "the end." After all, if I can see the definite signs that "the end" is approaching, won't I be able to make better plans? The passage of 20 centuries has not changed human nature in this regard. We ask the same questions as the first-century disciples.

In that regard, Jesus did not answer in terms of "the end," but in terms of "the beginning." And that beginning features all the same human evils as have ever existed. Rather than planning for the end that we imagine, we do greater service to Christ by recognizing the beginning, which is always *now,* the time between Jesus' first and second comings.

So what does that mean for His followers in this day and age? It means we must remain faithful, patient, and willing to endure hardship and suffering. We can do so because we have hope that comes by submitting to Jesus' authority, despite the world's self-indulgence (Matthew 24:37-51). As we wait for our King to return, we represent Him on earth, noticing Jesus' presence among those in need (Matthew 25). As Jesus has been faithful to His Father in Heaven, so we must be faithful to Jesus.

This is our task: faithfulness. The best sports teams are good at playing both offense and defense. We are on the offense with the gospel and the power of God behind us (Matthew 28:19-20). We play good defense when we train ourselves to recognize false prophets and false Christs. Failing to be on the offensive in taking the gospel to the world puts us in the position of the unfruitful tree that is subject to being cut down (Luke 13:9). Failing to play good defense—the primary point of today's study—results in being led astray (1 John 2:26; 3:7; contrast Ephesians 4:14).

B. Prayer

Heavenly Father, You have complete knowledge of time. Help us not be so focused on "the end" that we neglect "the beginning" within which You expect us to minister daily. Show us how to reveal Your Son in the midst of suffering. Help us view suffering as Your Son desires as He strengthens us by Your Spirit to endure, grow, serve, and proclaim Your Son as King as we anticipate His return. In Jesus' name. Amen!

C. Thought to Remember

Suffering is inevitable, but so is Jesus' return.

Involvement Learning

Enhance your lesson with KJV Bible Student *(from your curriculum supplier) and the reproducible activity page (at www.standardlesson.com or in the back of the* KJV Standard Lesson Commentary Deluxe Edition*).*

Into the Lesson

Divide learners into two teams. Distribute a sheet of paper and a pen to each group. Ask the **Building Team** to brainstorm and list the best possible materials to construct a large, multistory building. Ask the **Destruction Team** to brainstorm and list the most effective ways to destroy a large, multistory building. After three minutes, reconvene the class and have volunteers from each group share their group's responses. Determine whether a large, multistory building made with the listed materials would withstand the listed means of destruction.

Lead into Bible study by saying, "Buildings can be easily built and quickly destroyed. In today's lesson, we'll see how Jesus used the example of the destruction of a building to explain the significance of earthly hardships and the promise of His reassuring victory."

Into the Word

Ask a volunteer to prepare and present a three-minute presentation on the history of the temple in Jerusalem. Encourage the presenter to use the material from the Lesson Context or other online resources. (*Option*: Search online for an image of an artist's rendition of the first-century Jerusalem temple. Display that image during the presentation and the following activities.)

Distribute a sheet of paper and a pencil or pen to each person in class. Ask a volunteer to read aloud Matthew 24:1-2. Ask learners to use their "sanctified imagination" and knowledge of the Jerusalem temple and write down some possible statements that the disciples might have said to Jesus regarding the temple. After one minute of individual work, divide learners into three groups and direct them to share their statements with their group members.

After three minutes, write the following questions on the board for in-group discussion: 1–What feature of the temple in Jerusalem do you think the disciples found most impressive? 2–

What is the meaning of Jesus' phrase "See ye not all these things?" (Matthew 24:2). 3–Why did Jesus use the example of the temple's destruction?

Option. Distribute copies of the "Temple Q & A" exercise from the activity pages, which you can download. Have learners work in small groups to complete as indicated.

Ask a volunteer to read Matthew 24:3-8 aloud. Write the following questions on the board for in-group discussion: 1–How can people be deceived by someone claiming to be Christ or from Christ? 2–What fears and concerns do you have when you hear of wars or rumors of war worldwide? 3–How has a natural disaster impacted you? 4–After considering these warning signs, how do you feel about the statement "These are the beginning of sorrows" (Matthew 24:8)?

Ask a volunteer to read Matthew 24:9-14 aloud. Write on the board the phrase *Before the End*. Ask learners to review verses 10-14 and state the responses to the "beginning of sorrows" that will occur before "the end." Write the responses on the board (expected answers: rejection, betrayal, deception, hatred, endurance, salvation, the gospel preached worldwide).

Into Life

Keep the previous list on the board and write *How to Endure* as the header of a second column. Refer to the words and phrases on the board and ask, "What are some ways that believers can endure in faith when faced with difficulties?" Write responses on the board under the second header.

Divide learners into pairs and have each person share spiritual habits that help develop faithful endurance. After five minutes, ask each person to pray that their partner will endure in the faith.

Alternative. Distribute copies of the "Strong Building Blocks" activity from the activity page. Have learners complete it with a partner as indicated.

Christians as God's Temple

Devotional Reading: 2 Corinthians 6:14-18
Background Scripture: 1 Corinthians 3:1-23

1 Corinthians 3:10-23

10 According to the grace of God which is given unto me, as a wise masterbuilder, I have laid the foundation, and another buildeth thereon. But let every man take heed how he buildeth thereupon.

11 For other foundation can no man lay than that is laid, which is Jesus Christ.

12 Now if any man build upon this foundation gold, silver, precious stones, wood, hay, stubble;

13 Every man's work shall be made manifest: for the day shall declare it, because it shall be revealed by fire; and the fire shall try every man's work of what sort it is.

14 If any man's work abide which he hath built thereupon, he shall receive a reward.

15 If any man's work shall be burned, he shall suffer loss: but he himself shall be saved; yet so as by fire.

16 Know ye not that ye are the temple of God, and that the Spirit of God dwelleth in you?

17 If any man defile the temple of God, him shall God destroy; for the temple of God is holy, which temple ye are.

18 Let no man deceive himself. If any man among you seemeth to be wise in this world, let him become a fool, that he may be wise.

19 For the wisdom of this world is foolishness with God. For it is written, He taketh the wise in their own craftiness.

20 And again, The Lord knoweth the thoughts of the wise, that they are vain.

21 Therefore let no man glory in men. For all things are yours;

22 Whether Paul, or Apollos, or Cephas, or the world, or life, or death, or things present, or things to come; all are yours;

23 And ye are Christ's; and Christ is God's.

Key Text

Other foundation can no man lay than that is laid, which is Jesus Christ. —1 **Corinthians 3:11**

Sacred Altars and
Holy Offerings

Unit 3: Christians and Sacrifice
Lessons 10–14

Lesson Aims

After participating in this lesson, each learner will be able to:

1. Define *wisdom* and *foolishness*.

2. Explain how Jesus is the foundation for Paul's ministry.

3. Make a plan for honoring God's temple—His people.

Lesson Outline

Introduction

A. Strong Foundation

My grandfather owned a real estate company, but his first love was general contracting. He was a frugal and conscientious man, deeply shaped by the Great Depression. As a result, he always advocated doing things well and right the first time. He believed in making things that would last.

When I was 12 years old, my grandfather invited me out for a drive around our town. We spent the day visiting the buildings his company had constructed over the years. We saw office buildings, shopping centers, and apartment complexes. My grandfather would tell me an interesting story about each building and its construction.

Just before dusk, we pulled into a neighborhood that, at first glance, seemed filled with large, new houses. But as we drove on, the houses became smaller and older. We finally stopped at a small, two-story home with blue siding and a gray roof. My grandfather said, "I built this house for my parents when I was 19 years old. It still stands today because I built it with care on a strong foundation. Everything that lasts has a strong foundation."

I've never forgotten my grandfather's lesson. In every pursuit, one's work only lasts if the foundation is strong.

B. Lesson Context

Paul's second missionary journey began as a trip to visit the congregations he had planted on his first journey (Acts 15:36). After doing so (15:41), the restless Paul desired to move on to new territory with the message of the gospel.

God influenced Paul's itinerary through a vision that directed him to cross the Aegean Sea to the region known as Macedonia (Acts 16:9-10). Paul eventually arrived in Corinth in about AD 52, where he remained for some 18 months (18:11, 18). Corinth was a busy and wealthy center of trade in Paul's day, a cosmopolitan city with residents from many regions. It was a place of lax morals and influential pagan religions.

Acts 18:4 tells us that Corinth had a synagogue (as was the case in most of the large trading cities of the Roman Empire). Paul began his preaching in that synagogue, which was composed of both Jews and Greeks (18:4-5). But opposition caused him to leave and focus on the Gentiles of the city (18:6-7). Nevertheless, there was a strong contingent of Jewish believers in the Corinthian church (18:8).

It was to this mixed congregation that Paul wrote the two Corinthian letters while on his third missionary journey. The four years that elapsed between Paul's time in Corinth and his first letter back witnessed the development of ungodly trends—trends that needed to be corrected.

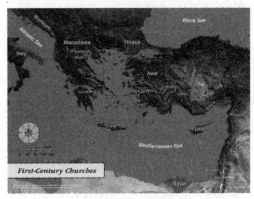

First-Century Churches

Visual for Lessons 10 & 11. *Display this visual as you discuss the lesson context and the travels of the apostle Paul.*

I. Careful Work
(1 Corinthians 3:10-15)
A. Many Builders (v. 10)

10a. According to the grace of God which is given unto me, as a wise masterbuilder, I have laid the foundation, and another buildeth thereon.

Here, as elsewhere, Paul affirmed both divine *grace* and human responsibility in the success of his ministry (example: 1 Corinthians 4:7). His line of reasoning that follows further develops the point of 1 Corinthians 3:5-9: the apostles were co-laborers, not competitors. Paul was the one who had "planted" (3:6), while Apollos came later and had "watered." That's another way of saying that Paul was the one who *laid the* spiritual *foundation* of the church in Corinth, and Apollos subsequently *buildeth thereon* (Acts 18:24-26). Thus, this verse reiterates the distinct but complementary roles of the two men.

In describing himself as a *masterbuilder,* Paul uses a Greek word found nowhere else in the New Testament. But we find the word in two non-biblical documents of the time between the Old and New Testaments. One reference is Sirach 38:27, which has the word side by side with its weaker form: "carpenter and workmaster" (another translation has "artisan and master artisan"). The other reference is 2 Maccabees 2:29, which compares the roles of "the master builder of a new house" to that of the one who paints it later. The additional word *wise* further strengthens the concept. Paul's suitability for his task was

due to his initiative in study (Acts 22:3; Philippians 3:5-6) and God's actions (Galatians 1:11-17).

10b. But let every man take heed how he buildeth thereupon.

This warning introduces the argument that follows. We don't know whether by saying *every man* Paul is speaking to leaders of the factions of 1 Corinthians 1:10-17 or is issuing a general caution.

B. One Foundation (v. 11)

11. For other foundation can no man lay than that is laid, which is Jesus Christ.

The opening *for* implies that what comes next explains or provides the rationale for the warning of the previous verse. One must take care of how one builds upon the foundation Paul laid because that *foundation* is *Jesus Christ.* Paul here probably does not refer only to particular doctrines about Christ (though those are certainly included) but to Christ himself. Every subsequent builder must treat this foundation respectfully (compare Ephesians 2:20).

> **What Do You Think?**
> What vetting process should a church enact before permitting a new ministry to start?
> **Digging Deeper**
> What Scripture can you cite to support your response to that question?

A Foundation Too Strong?

In the spring of 2023, a builder constructed a house near San Antonio, Texas, with a massive two-story foundation. Built of stone blocks, it lifted the house into the air, enabling it to tower above its neighbors in the suburb outside the city.

Some in the neighborhood thought that the house would have a huge basement, but in fact, it was a one-story ranch house with no basement. The general consensus was that the builder was trying to solve issues with the terrain. But the house with the odd foundation also contributed to the feeling that the new owners would be snobs looking down at everyone from a higher vantage point. However, they would be better protected from earthquakes, intruders, and door-to-door salespeople. After all, only the most dedicated would take the time to climb the stairs to the front door!

Our lives are strong and solid when built on the foundation of Jesus. However, the similarities end there. We do not look down on our neighbors from a high vantage point when we build our lives on Him. Instead, we place ourselves squarely in the trenches with everyone else. How's your construction progressing? —L. M. W.

C. Various Material (v. 12)

12. Now if any man build upon this foundation gold, silver, precious stones, wood, hay, stubble.

Having drawn attention to this foundation, Paul turns again to the issue of the quality of the construction. The metaphor's emphasis now seems to be durability, which depends on the material used.

Investigating the list of six materials here, we see two general types: precious and durable (*gold, silver, precious stones*) and common, not durable (*wood, hay, stubble*). Just because a sincere, devout Christian leader is building a ministry on the proper foundation of Christ doesn't mean that that ministry is valuable and durable. It's not enough to be sincere—a builder may be sincerely wrong.

D. Fiery Test (vv. 13-15)

13. Every man's work shall be made manifest: for the day shall declare it, because it shall be revealed by fire; and the fire shall try every man's work of what sort it is.

A feature of the materials just listed is their combustibility or lack thereof. While gold, silver, and precious stones are not good conductors of heat, the materials of wood, hay, and stubble readily burn. This is important because *every man's work* will undergo divine testing by *fire*. The *day* that Paul has in view here is the "day of the Lord," the time when God comes to judge the world and save His people (1 Corinthians 1:8; 5:5; 2 Corinthians 1:14; Philippians 1:6, 10; 2:16; 1 Thessalonians 5:2). The Scriptures use the imagery of consuming fires to describe this day of judgment (Isaiah 66:15-16; Malachi 4:1; 2 Peter 3:10).

14-15. If any man's work abide which he hath built thereupon, he shall receive a reward. If any man's work shall be burned, he shall suffer loss: but he himself shall be saved; yet so as by fire.

Paul describes the results and consequences of various qualities of work in helping build the Lord's church. Superior works will survive God's fiery evaluation, and their builders will *receive a reward*. The opposite will be true of the work that is *burned*.

It is essential to clarify that this reward and its counterpart, suffering *loss*, are not related to the issue of whether one receives eternal salvation. This concept is evident in the phrase *but he himself shall be saved*. Instead, Paul is suggesting that there will be varying levels of rewards in Heaven and different degrees of punishment in hell. Paul is referring to the idea of varying rewards (compare Luke 19:16-19). For the concept of varying punishments, see Luke 12:47-48 (compare and contrast 2 Corinthians 5:10 and Revelation 22:12). The distinction between works that *abide* and those that *shall be burned* is appropriately understood within this context of varying consequences.

> **What Do You Think?**
> What would be a good "fireproof test" of a ministry you're considering participating in?
> **Digging Deeper**
> How will you be attentive to the Holy Spirit's leading in this test?

II. Holy Temple
(1 Corinthians 3:16-17)
A. What's So (v. 16)

16. Know ye not that ye are the temple of God, and that the Spirit of God dwelleth in you?

The lesson to this point has proceeded from Paul's metaphor of Christians collectively (the church) as "God's building" in 1 Corinthians 3:9. The verse before us identifies the specific kind of building that is the church: *the temple of God.*

The importance of this designation is not to be missed. The Old Testament depicts the temple and its predecessor, the tabernacle, as having a sanctuary as the place of God's dwelling (Exodus 25:8; 29:45-46; Deuteronomy 12:11; etc.). There was a certain realization, of course, that this was not to be taken in a 100 percent literal sense (1 Kings 8:27; Isaiah 66:1-2, quoted in Acts 7:48-50; compare 17:24). Even so, the transition from describing God's presence in a temple of stone to the reality of God's presence in a temple of flesh and blood was startling. It might even have been incomprehensible to those who had had a lifelong focus on an inanimate structure of stone serving that purpose. This would have been true of Jewish and pagan temples as a residence of the deity.

Although the Greek behind the words *ye* and *you* are plural, Christians collectively form one body (1 Corinthians 12:13), one temple. Paul is consistent on this point (6:19; 2 Corinthians 6:16; Ephesians 2:21-22) .

> **What Do You Think?**
> How do you recognize threats to God's temple?
> **Digging Deeper**
> What role should the concept of holiness play in that regard?

B. So What (v. 17)

17. If any man defile the temple of God, him shall God destroy; for the temple of God is holy, which temple ye are.

Paul brings home his point of the previous verse. Since those of the church in Corinth are

God's temple, any actions that *defile* it will incur God's wrath. The words *defile* and *destroy* are translations of the same word in Greek. The serious nature of the consequences thereby underlines the serious nature of the offense. This passage thereby served as a veiled warning to those in the church of Corinth promoting factionalism. By threatening the integrity of God's temple, they risk coming under God's judgment.

III. Deceitful Wisdom
(1 Corinthians 3:18-23)
A. Human Thinking (v. 18)

18. Let no man deceive himself. If any man among you seemeth to be wise in this world, let him become a fool, that he may be wise.

Paul begins to draw together the threads of his argument for unity and against factionalism. The opening salvo here warned his audience against self-deception. Such self-deception may involve circular logic. Consider this hypothetical conversation:

Sam: "I'm the smartest guy in this church!"
Ann: "How do you know that?"
Sam: "Well, the smartest guy in the church would know who the smartest guy in the church is, wouldn't he?"

A primary way to avoid self-deception is to acknowledge that the wisdom that comes from God is the filter through which the wisdom of the world must pass, not the other way around. Thus, the readers have a choice to make. The wisdom of God never changes. The world, however, changes constantly; what's right today may or may not become wrong tomorrow, and vice versa. This is a problem that presents itself anew to every generation: "Woe unto them that call evil good, and good evil; that put darkness for light, and light for darkness; that put bitter for sweet, and sweet for bitter! Woe unto them that are wise in their own eyes, and prudent in their own sight!" (Isaiah 5:20-21).

Paul recognized that problem and its inevitable outcome when he quoted Isaiah 29:14 in 1 Corinthians 1:19: "I will destroy the wisdom of the wise, and will bring to nothing the understanding of the prudent." His argument there goes on to contrast God's revealed wisdom with Greco-Roman cultural norms. Thus, his appeal was for them to cease depending on the cultural norms as proper human standards of conduct. Cultural norms of the day promoted discrimination, but God's people must not do so (James 2:1-9). Self-aggrandizing wisdom must be rejected in favor of pursuing God's true wisdom. His wisdom does not elevate one person over another or divide the community. Though the world may label the Corinthians fools for such a pursuit, they will conform to God's standards and prove themselves truly wise. Paul addresses this contrast again in Colossians 2:8, 20-23 and 1 Timothy 6:20-21.

My New Year's Resolution

Several years ago, I posted my New Year's resolution on social media. The resolution was this: "I'm going to work on developing a sense of humility that I can be proud of." Everyone immediately got the joke: humility and pride are polar opposites—they don't mix. It's laughable to attempt to do so.

In one sense, I am indeed wise in ways that the world counts as wisdom. I have four academic degrees, including a PhD. I have the experience of having lived on planet Earth for 69 years. I retired from the Air Force at a high rank. The list goes on. But—and this is crucial—I've also read the Bible systematically word for word, cover to cover at least a dozen times. Any trust that I might place in worldly achievements is quickly challenged and extinguished by God's Word.

God's Word has a way of doing just that—but only if you let it. Here's an idea on how to get started: read what the New Testament writers have to say about the concept and source of *wisdom* and what it means to be *wise,* as it uses those words dozens of times. When you choose to begin that journey, it will reveal how seriously you see this issue. How about starting right now?   —R. L. N.

B. God's Knowledge (vv. 19-20)

19. For the wisdom of this world is foolishness with God. For it is written, He taketh the wise in their own craftiness.

As signaled by the word *for,* Paul explains his rationale for the counterintuitive claim that one must become a fool to be wise. In so doing, he flips the script: the world may consider God's wisdom foolishness, but *the wisdom of this world* is foolishness in God's sight (compare 1 Corinthians 1:20). Readers first need to see the stark nature of this either-or choice in order to make the right decision.

Paul cited two Old Testament passages to support his claim. The first comes from Eliphaz's speech in Job 5:13. There, it forms part of a series of statements that emphasize God's counter-cultural standards of justice. While the world despises some people as less important than others, God upholds the cause of the lowly and places them "on high" (Job 5:11). Likewise, God saves the impoverished and the weak from those who are stronger (5:15). In the process, God subverts the schemes of those considered wise and "crafty" (5:12-13), trapping them in darkness (5:14). In its context, then, Job 5:13 illustrates the same dynamic of dramatic reversal of fortunes and the inferiority of human wisdom that Paul evokes in 1 Corinthians 1–4.

> **What Do You Think?**
> How do you discern whether or not the church begins to shift to worldly wisdom?
> **Digging Deeper**
> How do you keep personal preferences from slanting your conclusion?

20. And again, The Lord knoweth the thoughts of the wise, that they are vain.

A similar dynamic also stands behind the second quotation, which is Psalm 94:11. The context of that passage witnesses the psalmist asking how long God will allow powerful, wicked people to perpetrate injustices (94:3). The chapter goes on to emphasize that God does indeed see what the wicked are doing (94:8-9), including all their schemes (94:11). He will bring judgment upon them (94:10). This passage thus strengthens Paul's warning that those who consider themselves wise by earthly standards need to pursue God's wisdom instead. Paul, therefore, does not simply proof text in 1 Corinthians 3:19-20. Instead, he quotes these passages with sensitivity to their original contexts.

C. Paul's Assurance (vv. 21-23)

21a. Therefore let no man glory in men.

Paul's conclusion is clear in this verse, the crescendo to his argument: desist from creating factions around particular leaders (*let no man glory in men*). To do so is inconsistent with God's standards of wisdom and the unity He desires for the church.

21b-22. For all things are yours; Whether Paul, or Apollos, or Cephas, or the world, or life, or death, or things present, or things to come; all are yours.

After having just stressed a negative, the apostle immediately provided a positive and encouraging reason to avoid factionalism by declaring that *all things* belong to his original readers (compare Romans 8:32). Those "things" include the leaders *Paul, Apollos,* and *Cephas* (another name for Peter per John 1:42), around whom the factions had formed (1 Corinthians 1:12; 4:6). They were all servants of Christ for the sake of the church, not rivals competing for followers.

The other five items have parallels in the list of "things" Paul stated could not separate believers from the love of God in Romans 8:38-39. Four of these—life, death, present, and future—overlap in meaning. The *world* in 1 Corinthians 3:22 may parallel the "principalities" and "powers" in Romans 8:38, which could refer to spiritual forces exercising dominion in the present age (Colossians 2:15). The followers of Christ are not subservient to any unholy forces.

23. And ye are Christ's; and Christ is God's.

While "all things" belong to the Corinthians, they belong to a higher authority (compare 1 Corinthians 15:23; 2 Corinthians 10:7; Galatians 3:29). This implies that they must answer to Christ. They do not have complete freedom but are expected to live in a manner that pleases Him.

How to Say It

Aegean	A-*jee*-un.
Cephas	*See*-fus.
Corinth	*Kor*-inth.
Maccabees	*Mack*-uh-bees.
Macedonia	Mass-eh-*doe*-nee-uh.
Sirach	*Sigh*-rak.

Christ represents the highest authority of all, namely, God. Paul thus reiterates that the body of Christ must recognize God's authority in how it conducts itself as God's earthly temple.

> **What Do You Think?**
> What is the first step you will take should you see factionalism in your church?
> **Digging Deeper**
> How will you know whether your impression is correct?

Conclusion

A. God's Earthly Temple

Paul composed this letter about two decades before the Romans destroyed the temple in Jerusalem in AD 70. Yet even before the temple's destruction, the earliest Christians believed that God was with His people rather than in a physical building (Acts 17:24). Yet today, the Holy Spirit, given at baptism (2:38), resides in each person who trusts in Jesus as Lord. Therefore, Christians, collectively as the church, are God's temple on earth.

We have the duty and privilege of bearing God's presence in and to the world. Therefore, we must live in a way that honors ourselves and our fellow Christians. We avoid division and factionalism, especially when motivated by the values of the world. God will call to account all who dishonor His temple. Let us conduct ourselves in the world as those in whom God dwells.

As we do, we remember that we answer to God, not to the court of public opinion or cultural trends. We need to think only of shifts in cultural values that have resulted in shifts in church doctrine to see the tragedy of failure in this regard.

B. Prayer

Father God, thank You for choosing to live in us as Your temple. Teach us to honor one another as those blessed to carry Your presence. In Jesus' name. Amen.

C. Thought to Remember

We carry God's presence in the world.

Involvement Learning

Enhance your lesson with KJV Bible Student *(from your curriculum supplier) and the reproducible activity* page *(at www.standardlesson.com or in the back of the* KJV Standard Lesson Commentary Deluxe Edition*).*

Into the Lesson

Write on the board the words *concrete*, *steel*, and *wood*. Point to the first word and ask, "What kind of structures are built primarily with this material?" After responses, repeat this for each of the other two words. Sum up by pointing out that the type of structure we're building determines the primary kind of building material. Make a transition by saying, "During today's lesson, notice what sort of materials are suitable for constructing the building on the foundation we've been given."

Into the Word

Divide participants into three groups. Give each group one of these passages to read: 1 Kings 5:13-17; Matthew 7:24-27; Hebrews 11:9-10. Each group must decide what their assigned passage says about the importance of a building's foundation. After a few minutes, reconvene for a whole-class discussion of what they learned.

Then, read aloud 1 Corinthians 3:10-15. Compare and contrast the foundation mentioned there with the foundations in the three texts assigned. Pose the following questions or other questions of your devising for discussion:

1–What do you know about the overall context in which Paul discussed the nature of his ministry in his first letter to the Corinthians?
2–What did Paul's readers need to correct?

Ask a volunteer to read 1 Corinthians 3:16-17. Using the small groups from earlier in the lesson, allow time to discuss what it signifies to be the temple of God. Give each group a handout (you create) on which is printed the following:

Although we sometimes talk about individually being temples of God, 1 Corinthians 3:16-17 refers to Christians as being the temple in the singular, collectively speaking. How does that make a difference in our roles as we work together?

Refer groups to temple features such as the high, narrow windows (1 Kings 6:4); chambers or side rooms (6:5); entrance doorway (6:8); cherubim (6:27); inner court (6:36), etc., to create metaphors. (*Example*: "Jennifer is like the decorative doorposts because she invites and draws others in to know God more personally.")

Ask a volunteer to read 1 Corinthians 3:18-23. Write on the board the words *Wise* and *Foolish* as the headers of two columns, one each. Invite participants to call out other words that come to mind when they see these two. Jot responses under the proper headers. After listing several words in each column, have participants collaborate to write clear definitions of *wise* and *foolish*.

Into Life

Invite learners to state insights gained regarding the foundation of which Paul spoke (Jesus). Tie this in with the fact that believers are the collective church of God. Remind learners that we, as believers in Christ, are the church, whether collectively on Sundays or individually throughout the week. Write those insights on the board along with the definitions used earlier in the lesson as appropriate.

Brainstorm together ways to honor, or treat with admiration and respect, God's temple. Challenge learners to think of specific ways to do so in the week ahead. Distribute pieces of paper for them to record their plans. Allow opportunities to reflect and share those plans and what could happen because of them.

Option 1 (very quick). See how much your learners have retained by distributing copies of the "True or False" test on the activity page. Allow a time limit of one minute for completion.

Option 2 (much slower). Distribute copies of the "Agree/Disagree" exercise from the activity page for groups of exactly three to work through. Discuss results as a class.

Option 3 (take-home only). Distribute copies of "What Not to Fall For" from the activity page as a take-home.

Our Bodies Belong to God

Devotional Reading: Psalm 139:13-24
Background Scripture: Romans 12:1-21; 1 Corinthians 6:12-20

1 Corinthians 6:12-20

12 All things are lawful unto me, but all things are not expedient: all things are lawful for me, but I will not be brought under the power of any.

13 Meats for the belly, and the belly for meats: but God shall destroy both it and them. Now the body is not for fornication, but for the Lord; and the Lord for the body.

14 And God hath both raised up the Lord, and will also raise up us by his own power.

15 Know ye not that your bodies are the members of Christ? shall I then take the members of Christ, and make them the members of an harlot? God forbid.

16 What? know ye not that he which is joined to an harlot is one body? for two, saith he, shall be one flesh.

17 But he that is joined unto the Lord is one spirit.

18 Flee fornication. Every sin that a man doeth is without the body; but he that committeth fornication sinneth against his own body.

19 What? know ye not that your body is the temple of the Holy Ghost which is in you, which ye have of God, and ye are not your own?

20 For ye are bought with a price: therefore glorify God in your body, and in your spirit, which are God's.

Key Text

What? know ye not that your body is the temple of the Holy Ghost which is in you, which ye have of God, and ye are not your own? —**1 Corinthians 6:19**

Sacred Altars and
Holy Offerings

Unit 3: Christians and Sacrifice
Lessons 10–14

Lesson Aims

After participating in this lesson, each learner will be able to:

1. Identify the reason why Paul's original readers were to honor God with their bodies.

2. Explain why it's better to view Paul's conclusions as guiding principles rather than direct imperatives.

3. Suggest ways to apply the principles Paul states to a modern situation that didn't exist in Paul's day.

Lesson Outline

Introduction
  A. Bodies Joined and Torn
  B. Lesson Context
I. Consecrated Bodies (1 Corinthians 6:12-16)
  A. Controlling (vv. 12-14)
    Health with a Purpose
  B. Restricting (vv. 15-16)
II. Consecrated Spirits (1 Corinthians 6:17-20)
  A. Connection with the Lord (vv. 17-18)
  B. Temple of the Spirit (vv. 19-20)
Conclusion
  A. We Belong to God
  B. Prayer
  C. Thought to Remember

Introduction
A. Bodies Joined and Torn

My best friend from the first day of high school was Tony. We shared a vibrant faith. We led Bible studies together and even started a band. His father was the minister of a large church in our area and a highly respected member of the community.

The summer before our senior year, Tony's personality began to shift. He became sullen and isolated. He abruptly quit the band, stopped attending our Bible studies, and didn't return my calls. After weeks of being avoided, I drove to his house. His father answered the door. A woman stood next to him, with her hand on his shoulder. She was not Tony's mother. I was told that Tony was staying with his mother. Tony's dad quickly gave me the address and shut the door.

I went to the apartment building where Tony, his mother, and his siblings had moved. Tony answered my knock on the door. When he saw me, he burst into tears and threw himself into my arms. I held him as he cried. We sat at the kitchen table, and he told me everything. His father had met another woman online, invited her to live with him, and asked for a divorce from Tony's mother. The children had sided with their mom, so their father told them all to leave.

For momentary pleasures, this man had destroyed his marriage, ruined his relationship with his children, and lost the goodwill of his church and the wider community. Though joined to his wife as one flesh, he had torn them apart.

B. Lesson Context

We're now in our second lesson from 1 Corinthians, so the Lesson Context from last week's study also applies here. The difference is that today's lesson deals with the touchy subject of sexual immorality. For proper context, we need to be aware of how the standards of morality in the Greco-Roman culture of the first century AD differed from those of today.

One such difference was in how prostitution was viewed. In most American and Canadian cities today, prostitution is seen as illegal. However, the culture of the Mediterranean world of the first century did not see it this way. Expectations regarding marital fidelity were more for the wife than the husband—a double standard. Public parties might include prostitutes to entertain the men after the wives were excused from the banquet. The majority culture of the day considered this behavior acceptable.

Shockingly, some members of the church at Corinth were engaging in illicit sexual activities that even the pagan Gentiles disapproved of (1 Corinthians 5:1)! Paul would not stand for this, for he saw sexual sin as a threat to the unity and purity of the entire body of Christ. By contrast, Paul taught a different view of what constituted sexual immorality—today's lesson.

I. Consecrated Bodies
(1 Corinthians 6:12-16)
A. Controlling (vv. 12-14)

12a. All things are lawful unto me, but all things are not expedient.

Readers have long puzzled over the coherence of some of Paul's claims, such as we see here. How could he claim that *all things are lawful unto me*, including (by implication) sexual immorality? (The fact that Paul addresses this immorality becomes apparent as the text progresses.)

To resolve this tension, many commentators have concluded that Paul was quoting back to the Corinthians a slogan that they were using to justify their actions. This makes sense, as the quotation served to set up his corrective response. New Testament scholar Jay Smith proposes several telltale indicators that a slogan is in view, and we can summarize four of them here. Slogans (1) are brief, pithy statements usually in the present tense, (2) are often repeated, (3) feature wording that is inconsistent with the way Paul usually writes, and (4) are followed by a counterpoint. There are three such possibilities in our lesson text of 1 Corinthians 6:12-20, and this is the first.

In this reading, Paul offers two reasons why certain acts do not lie within the Corinthians' freedom. First, not all behaviors are *expedient*.

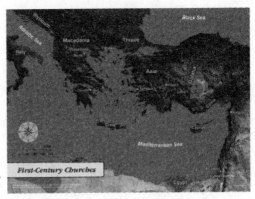

Visual for Lesson 10 & 11. *Display this visual as you discuss the people and places of the third unit of the quarter.*

Considering all points lead us to contemplate whether something is advantageous or not. To sin is never to our advantage.

12b. All things are lawful for me, but I will not be brought under the power of any.

Some behaviors can enslave a person as he or she is *brought under* its *power*. This is particularly the case with sexual desires, which Jew and Gentile alike understood as involving powerful emotions that could overwhelm reason and subvert one's self-control. Paul addresses the addictive, enslaving power of sin more fully in Romans 6:16–7:6.

Passages such as Galatians 2:15-16 indicate that the slogan *all things are lawful for me,* now quoted a second time, may have had its roots in the teachings of Paul himself as he has proclaimed freedom in Christ. But apparently, some had distorted Paul's teaching to mean something arrogant like, "I can do anything I want to do, and no one has a right to criticize me" (compare Romans 6:1-4).

> **What Do You Think?**
> What can you do to improve your wisdom regarding "the gray areas" of personal conduct?
>
> **Digging Deeper**
> Is it possible for certain behaviors to be "OK" for some people but not for others? Why, or why not?

13a. Meats for the belly, and the belly for meats.

This half-verse seems to introduce another Corinthian slogan. In this reading, the Corinthians used "an argument from analogy." That kind of reasoning often goes something like this: "As *A* is to *B*, so also *X* is to *Y*." If that is the case here, then the Corinthians were equating the behavior of satisfying sexual urges with the behavior of eating to satisfy cravings of the stomach.

13b. But God shall destroy both it and them. Now the body is not for fornication, but for the Lord; and the Lord for the body.

The analogy the Corinthians seemed to have been using overlooks the bigger picture. God designed our bodies to function as He intends. Food and stomach were indeed designed to work together, but not so regarding *the body* and *fornication,* a general term for sexually immoral acts. On the contrary, the body is meant *for the Lord; and the Lord for the body.* In other words, God intended our bodies for union with Christ, not for union in sexually immoral acts.

Health with a Purpose

Pouring my attention 100 percent into academics gained me college degrees and desk jobs. Those, in turn, left my body out of shape, lethargic, and prematurely aged. I knew what to do about it, living in a culture swamped with diet and exercise information. The problem was mustering the motivation.

That motivation asserted itself when I discovered a new passion: Brazilian jiu-jitsu. A martial art that's half judo, half wrestling, jiu-jitsu requires chess-like strategy more than physical brawn. It relieved stress, built my confidence, and expanded my social network, not to mention helped me lose 42 pounds in a year!

We know fully what we "ought" to do in the sight of God and how it is all for our benefit. In a moment of temptation, it can be challenging to be self-controlled. What if the key is not white-knuckled willpower to not do something, but rather a drive to remove every obstacle from doing something we love more?   —A. W.

14. And God hath both raised up the Lord, and will also raise up us by his own power.

We surrender our bodies and all their desires to the Lord's service, and He commits himself to us. The fulfillment of the latter is seen in resurrection: Christ's human body was *raised* from death by *God*, and our bodies will likewise be raised. Resurrection was being denied by some in Corinth, but Paul saves his fuller discussion on that error for later (1 Corinthians 15).

B. Restricting (vv. 15-16)

15. Know ye not that your bodies are the members of Christ? shall I then take the members of Christ, and make them the members of an harlot? God forbid.

This verse features the first of 16 times that Paul uses the word translated *members* in this letter. For Paul and his readers, this word refers to body parts, such as arms, legs, hands, and ears (compare 1 Corinthians 12:12-27). Paul is fond of picturing the church in terms of diverse human body parts with Christ as its head (Ephesians 1:22-23; 4:15). Use of this metaphor flows from Paul's points about the believer's union with Christ in the two verses just studied. Since the believer is united with Christ, he or she is part of Christ's body.

Having made this point, Paul follows up with a second rhetorical question: Is it permissible to take parts of Christ's body and join them to a *harlot*? *God forbid.*

How to Say It

Corinth	*Kor*-inth.
Corinthians	Ko-*rin*-thee-unz (*th* as in *thin*).
Ephesians	Ee-*fee*-zhunz.
Galatians	Guh-*lay*-shunz.

16. What? know ye not that he which is joined to an harlot is one body? for two, saith he, shall be one flesh.

Sexual unions outside of marriage, whether paid or unpaid, make the participants *one* in *body,* in violation of Genesis 2:24. That passage describes the marital union as making male and female "one flesh" (compare Matthew 19:5). Sexual intimacy outside of marriage creates an additional case of *one flesh.* For the married, the result is to bring an additional person into the marriage. This is destructive to God's intent for the family unit. Things we do with our physical bodies will affect the body that is the church, a body to which we belong as members.

What Do You Think?

What are some ways that married couples can witness God's "one flesh" intent to an immoral culture?

Digging Deeper

What Scripture passages inform your response?

II. Consecrated Spirits
(1 Corinthians 6:17-20)

A. Connection with the Lord (vv. 17-18)

17. But he that is joined unto the Lord is one spirit.

Paul again emphasizes the believer's union with Christ. Referring to *one spirit* may be puzzling because the word *spirit* can take different meanings depending on context. In some cases, the word might refer to the Holy Spirit. In other cases, it refers to that part of a person that lives on after physical death. In other cases, it refers to a mental disposition.

The key is context. Having just condemned improper intimacy, Paul now contrasts it with an image of a proper relationship: spiritual intimacy *unto the Lord* (compare John 17:20-23). The implication here is that sexual immorality not only works against a marriage, but it also works against one's relationship with God. The brief moments of physical pleasure that an immoral act brings are trifling compared to the

lasting damage it causes. It is not possible to separate sexual behavior from a relationship with the Lord. This spiritual dimension must be the controlling factor.

Another viewpoint is that Paul is referring to the work of the Holy Spirit, whereby through the "one Spirit," the believer's spirit has been joined indissolubly with Christ. Under this idea, Paul is not comparing spiritual union with physical union. Instead, the focus is on the Holy Spirit, who has united the believer to Christ. Thus, one has no right to unite with another in an immoral way.

18. Flee fornication. Every sin that a man doeth is without the body; but he that committeth fornication sinneth against his own body.

The final piece of Paul's argument begins with the succinct command to *flee fornication.* Paul then uses candid language (again) to justify this strong warning as he puts sexual sin in a unique category of wrongdoing. Other sins are *without the body,* meaning they are external. For example, stealing may use the hands to accomplish the sin, but it is still "outside." Sexual sin, by contrast, is *against* the body because of the intimate union between those engaged in it.

B. Temple of the Spirit (vv. 19-20)

19. What? know ye not that your body is the temple of the Holy Ghost which is in you, which ye have of God, and ye are not your own?

Paul here draws upon imagery familiar from earlier in the letter: the body as the Spirit's temple. Paul previously used this image to describe the entire community. This verse reinforces that Christians are collectively God's temple on earth (1 Corinthians 3:16-17; compare 2 Corinthians 6:16). The Holy Spirit dwells in each follower of Jesus as a gift from God. The presence of the Spirit also signals God's ownership of that person with the result that *ye are not your own.*

The Spirit inhabits the church corporately and each believer individually (Romans 8:9-11). Once this is understood, then one can grasp why engaging with a prostitute is starkly inconsistent with the Christian life. How can a vessel of the Holy Spirit take part in such an unholy act? Such activity is not merely one of illicit physical pleasure. It is also an act of temple desecration.

20a. For ye are bought with a price.

For Paul's original readers, this word picture calls to mind the slave markets of cities such as ancient Corinth. Everyone in the Corinthian church knew of such places. Some may have suffered this dehumanizing experience personally. Some may have been slave owners, perhaps struggling to reconcile that fact with their new identity as Christians. For Paul's initial audience, the phrase *bought with a price* would have been interpreted as the cost of a ransom to liberate a slave, with the redemption price being the blood of Christ (see Hebrews 9:12; compare Exodus 6:6; Isaiah 43:1; Luke 1:68).

Paul is not explicit about the nature and amount of the price paid (compare Revelation 5:9). Instead, he focuses on the fact that ownership has been transferred (compare 1 Corinthians 7:23).

20b. Therefore glorify God in your body, and in your spirit, which are God's.

Paul concludes with an exhortation. The transfer of ownership obligates believers to *glorify God* with their spirits and bodies in every way. To honor God with one's spirit but not with one's body is hypocrisy.

What Do You Think?

What are some ways we can glorify God with our bodies in the midst of culture's challenges?

Digging Deeper

How do we improve our ability to recognize those challenges when they come?

Conclusion

A. We Belong to God

Here's the conclusion to the story we opened the lesson with. My friend Tony did not speak to his father for five years. Tony went on to college, played on a Division III basketball team, and met his future wife. He avoided thinking or talking about his dad.

Then, one day, his dad called him and asked to meet for lunch. When they met, Tony refused to hug his father or even shake his hand. As they sat at the table, Tony prepared a laundry list of grievances. But his dad was there to apologize. He admitted that he had wronged his wife and children. He begged Tony for forgiveness.

His father's contrition moved Tony, and he quickly set aside his anger. But he had to ask one thing: Why had his father done it?

His father offered multiple explanations without excusing his actions. But one in particular stood out. He said, "I felt like my life wasn't my own anymore." Tony looked into his dad's eyes and said, "It wasn't yours to begin with."

The thrust of Paul's argument in 1 Corinthians 6:12-20 is that believers do not have full authority over their lives. We are members of Christ's body. We are a temple of the Holy Spirit. We belong to God and must act in ways that glorify God. God calls us to live as those who belong to Him.

That requires our willingness to resist temptations. And forms of temptation exist today that did not exist in Paul's day. Yet the principles Paul teaches remain useful in combating these temptations. Paul encouraged his readers to embrace and live in their identities as Christ's body and the Holy Spirit's temple. We, too, can and must help ourselves and our children walk in a way that is consistent with the identity God has given us.

It is noteworthy that Paul did not simply reject the slogans of the Corinthians. Nor did he merely give them commands without explanation. He granted that they did indeed possess freedom in Christ. But how were they best using those freedoms? And in what way are we accomplishing this?

B. Prayer

Father God, thank You for making us part of Your Son Jesus Christ's body, the church. Lead us to respect our individual bodies as belonging to You. In Jesus' name, Amen.

C. Thought to Remember

Glorify God with your body.

Involvement Learning

Enhance your lesson with KJV Bible Student *(from your curriculum supplier) and the reproducible activity page (at www.standardlesson.com or in the back of the* KJV Standard Lesson Commentary Deluxe Edition*).*

Into the Lesson

Invite learners to share stories about something valuable they gave to someone who misused it because it didn't cost them anything. Caution learners not to use names. Discuss reactions to that disappointment.

Alternative. Distribute copies of the "Appropriate Care" exercise from the activity page, which you can download. Allow one minute for learners to complete it individually as indicated. Form small groups for discussing conclusions.

Say, "If we lend or give a valuable item to someone, we expect that person to value it as we do. Today, we will learn what is valuable to God and how He expects us to be good stewards of what is His."

Into the Word

Ask a volunteer to read 1 Corinthians 6:12-13. Ask the class for names of activities that people have a legal right to do. After listing a half dozen activities on the board, place learners into small groups of three or four. Distribute handouts (you prepare) on which are printed these questions:

1–Which of these rights are truly beneficial?
2–Which of these rights can be or have been abused, causing harm?
3–How did Paul address an ancient problem in this regard?

Reconvene for whole-class discussion as groups wrap up their work. Be ready to correct misconceptions as needed.

Ask a volunteer to read 1 Corinthians 6:14-18. Divide participants into two groups, named as below. Distribute handouts (you create) as follows for group discussions.

Know-Ye-Not-1 Group: Read 1 Corinthians 6:14-15 and 12:12-27.

1–How does our earlier discussion on the treatment of valuable things come into play here?

2–What do these verses teach us about our roles and responsibilities toward one another and toward Christ?
3–In what ways have you seen the misuse of one body part affect the whole body?

Know-Ye-Not-2 Group: Read 1 Corinthians 6:16-17 and Ephesians 4:19-25.

1–What do these verses teach us about our responsibilities toward one another and toward Christ?
2–What are some ways that we are neglectful of our spiritual unity with the Lord?

Ask another volunteer to read 1 Corinthians 6:19-20. Divide participants into three small groups and assign the following passages, one each: Genesis 39; Daniel 1:5-15; and Hebrews 11:8-12. Distribute handouts (you create) with the following questions:

1–How did the person glorify and honor God with his body?
2–How did this affect those around him?
3–What are ways to follow these examples today?

Reconvene for whole-class summaries. Reread 1 Corinthians 6:19-20 for emphasis.

Option. Distribute copies of the "The Price" exercise from the activity page. Use the top part to wrap up this segment; use the bottom part to lead into the Into Life segment. Have participants work in pairs to complete the top half as indicated.

Into Life

Invite learners to summarize the imperatives in today's lesson text. Jot responses on the board. Brainstorm ways to apply those imperatives in various situations. If you used the option above, have participants fill out the bottom half individually; stress that these are for their private use.

Challenge participants to review all the ideas and choose one that they will put into practice in the week ahead. Recruit volunteers willing to share their experiences. Invite further reflections on ways to apply Paul's principles daily.

The Two Made One

Devotional Reading: Romans 9:14-24
Background Scripture: Ephesians 2:11-22

Ephesians 2:11-22

11 Wherefore remember, that ye being in time past Gentiles in the flesh, who are called Uncircumcision by that which is called the Circumcision in the flesh made by hands;

12 That at that time ye were without Christ, being aliens from the commonwealth of Israel, and strangers from the covenants of promise, having no hope, and without God in the world:

13 But now in Christ Jesus ye who sometimes were far off are made nigh by the blood of Christ.

14 For he is our peace, who hath made both one, and hath broken down the middle wall of partition between us;

15 Having abolished in his flesh the enmity, even the law of commandments contained in ordinances; for to make in himself of twain one new man, so making peace;

16 And that he might reconcile both unto God in one body by the cross, having slain the enmity thereby:

17 And came and preached peace to you which were afar off, and to them that were nigh.

18 For through him we both have access by one Spirit unto the Father.

19 Now therefore ye are no more strangers and foreigners, but fellowcitizens with the saints, and of the household of God;

20 And are built upon the foundation of the apostles and prophets, Jesus Christ himself being the chief corner stone;

21 In whom all the building fitly framed together groweth unto an holy temple in the Lord:

22 In whom ye also are builded together for an habitation of God through the Spirit.

Key Text

In whom all the building fitly framed together groweth unto an holy temple in the Lord: in whom ye also are builded together for an habitation of God through the Spirit. —**Ephesians 2:21-22**

Sacred Altars and
Holy Offerings

Unit 3: Christians and Sacrifice
Lessons 10–14

Lesson Aims

After participating in this lesson, each learner will be able to:

1. Identify Christ's purpose and His method for achieving it.

2. Explain the meanings of being "far off" and being "near."

3. State one way that he or she can live in peace and unity with believers.

Lesson Outline

Introduction
  A. One Family, All Different
  B. Lesson Context
  I. **Humanity Divided** (Ephesians 2:11-12)
    A. By Ritual (v. 11)
    B. By Boundary (v. 12)
  II. **Humanity United** (Ephesians 2:13-22)
    A. By Christ's Peace (vv. 13-15)
    B. By God's Spirit (vv. 16-18)
      Under One Roof
    C. As God's Family (v. 19)
    D. To Be God's Temple (vv. 20-22)
Conclusion
  A. Working at Being a Family
  B. Prayer
  C. Thought to Remember

Introduction

A. One Family, All Different

Are you more "like" or more "unlike" other members of your family? For family members who are genetically related, we can be very "like" in physical characteristics. But even there, our similarities highlight our differences—and we all have differences because we are individuals. (Disclaimer: identical twins offer certain exceptions!)

How we handle our differences in values, economic status, etc., can sever family relationships. This is a story as old as humanity. Likewise, this is a story as broad as humanity. Yet those realities don't negate the Bible's teaching that humanity is one large family. The solution for a fractured, divided humanity is found in today's text.

B. Lesson Context

In about AD 51, a dozen or so years before writing his letter to the Ephesians, Paul participated in a meeting we sometimes call "the Jerusalem Council." This meeting is described in Acts 15 and Galatians 2. Church leaders convened the council to resolve a pressing question for the first-century church: *Is it necessary for Gentile men to be circumcised in order for them to be considered Christian?* Simply put, the question was whether a person had to become a Jew first before becoming a Christian. Was the gateway to the church only to be found in the synagogue?

The Jerusalem Council decided that circumcision was not to be required for Gentiles. However, this decision was not accepted by all. Even a dozen years later, some taught that Gentiles needed to be circumcised and otherwise "toe the line" regarding the Law of Moses. Thus, Paul found the need to revisit this issue.

I. Humanity Divided
(Ephesians 2:11-12)
A. By Ritual (v. 11)

11. Wherefore remember, that ye being in time past Gentiles in the flesh, who are called Uncircumcision by that which is called the Circumcision in the flesh made by hands.

Christ is our peace.

Visual for Lessons 12 & 13. *Display this visual as you ask the discussion questions associated with verse 17.*

Paul wasn't shy about surfacing the primary division of humanity of his day: there were Jews, and there was everyone else—Gentiles. The ancient Greek word translated *Gentiles* is also translated "nations" (examples: Matthew 24:9, 14; 25:32). The term signified outsiders or foreigners (compare Galatians 2:7). A different word translated "Greeks" is a synonym for "Gentiles" when contrasted with Jews (examples: Acts 18:4; 19:10, 17).

The phrase *in the flesh* identifies men who had not been circumcised as the sign of inclusion in the covenant. Circumcision was a rite given to Abraham to be practiced as a sign of God's covenant with him and his descendants (Genesis 17). Israel had many practices to express their membership in God's covenant people: laws of clean and unclean, the Sabbath day, etc. But the most obvious was circumcision.

Paul's observation that circumcision was *made by hands* is not to imply that God had nothing to do with it. Paul knew the biblical affirmations that God had instituted the practice. But there is something more important than that removal of foreskin: the removal of sin. Only God can do that. This kind of removal results in (or should result in) circumcision of the heart (Romans 2:29; Colossians 2:11; compare Deuteronomy 10:16; 30:6; Jeremiah 4:4).

B. By Boundary (v. 12)

12. That at that time ye were without Christ, being aliens from the commonwealth of Israel, and strangers from the covenants of promise, having no hope, and without God in the world.

To understand Paul's argument here, we should examine the four ways he describes Gentiles in contrast with the Jewish people. First, the fact that Gentiles are not part of *the commonwealth of Israel* means they were excluded historically from being part of the chosen people of God. Thus, Gentiles had no part in *the covenants of promise* (compare Romans 9:4). The Old Testament tells of several covenants God made with the ancient Israelites (see Exodus 2:24; 24:8; Psalm 89:3; etc.). The promises of these covenants were founded essentially on the same idea: that God would bless the world through His chosen people (example: Genesis 12:3). This blessing is fulfilled in Jesus Christ (Galatians 3:16).

Seeing Jesus as the fulfillment of the ancient promises helps us understand Paul's third and fourth descriptions of the Gentiles: *having no hope* and being *without God*. There was and is no true hope in any of the pagan religions since none of them worship the only true God, the God of Israel. Without Christ, the Gentiles were cut off from the blessings that God had directed toward and through the Jews.

II. Humanity United
(Ephesians 2:13-22)
A. By Christ's Peace (vv. 13-15)

13. But now in Christ Jesus ye who sometimes were far off are made nigh by the blood of Christ.

The fourfold description of Gentiles in verse 12 is now expanded: they *were far off* (compare Acts 2:39). The image is that of people in a distant country. That distance has been negated, for the Gentiles *are made nigh by the blood of Christ*. This phrase refers to the atoning death of Jesus for sin (compare Galatians 3:28; Colossians 1:20). The

How to Say It

Pentecost	*Pent-ih-kost.*
synagogue	*sin-uh-gog.*

following explanation is one of the most beautiful and meaningful descriptions of Christ's sacrifice in the Bible.

14a. For he is our peace, who hath made both one.

The Old Testament uses the word translated "peace" as a verb to describe the idea of giving something to make satisfaction for an injustice or wrong. For example, if a valuable animal died through the negligence of a neighbor, the negligent person was required to "make it good" and "restore it" (Leviticus 24:18, 21); this is a type of righteous recompense.

This Old Testament pattern is a background for Paul's description of Christ's death as the adequate atonement for sin. This is the truth behind the simple assertion that *he is our peace*. The marvelous thing is that Christ's death serves not just the Jewish people but Gentiles, too. Everyone needs a Savior (Romans 3:22-23). The problem of sin and its solution through the blood of Jesus transcends any arguments about circumcision or other things that might divide Jew from Gentile.

14b. And hath broken down the middle wall of partition between us.

Paul portrays these facts in memorable language as the breaking down of a wall (*partition*). He may have drawn this image from a wall in the Jerusalem temple, the boundary for Gentiles, and marked the inner courts that were forbidden to them.

15. Having abolished in his flesh the enmity, even the law of commandments contained in ordinances; for to make in himself of twain one new man, so making peace.

As a result, there is no more presumption of *enmity*, for all are equally loved in Christ. In this light, the Jews' *law of commandments contained in ordinances*, including circumcision requirements, had (or should have) become irrelevant as a divisive factor (compare Colossians 2:14). This does not mean there is no value in that law (Galatians 3:24). Nor does it mean that Christianity is a lawless faith, an ethical free-for-all (Jude 4). It means that specific requirements of the law that resulted in distinguishing Jew from Gentile had become powerless. Christianity is not a religion of rule-keeping but a way of faith (Ephesians 2:8-9).

The result of Christ's work is a new humanity, a people of God undivided by anything specific to being a Jew or a Gentile (Galatians 3:28). We are in relationship with one another because of the inclusive nature of our relationship with Christ. As discussed above, Paul sums this up as the result of *making peace*.

Christians of Jewish background were free to continue their observances, as Paul himself often did (Acts 16:3; 20:16; 21:20-26). But such observances must never become a divisive test of Christian faith (Galatians 3:26-29; Colossians 2:16-17). Christians from all backgrounds were to live and work together as one, keeping the "unity of the Spirit in the bond of peace" (Ephesians 4:3).

B. By God's Spirit (vv. 16-18)

16. And that he might reconcile both unto God in one body by the cross, having slain the enmity thereby.

To *reconcile* means to repair a broken relationship. Reconciliation has a dual aspect. First, we are reconciled to God *by the cross*. This is another reference to the saving effect of Christ's atoning death for sin (2 Corinthians 5:18; Colossians 1:20, 22). The relationship between God and humans, broken by sin, is restored through Christ, who paid the price for sin on our behalf.

Second, this renewed relationship with God makes reconciliation between people possible, for we are shaped into *one body* in Christ. This body is the church (1 Corinthians 12:27), both on the local, congregational level and the worldwide, universal level. There should be no place for *enmity* between God and humanity or in person-to-person relationships.

What Do You Think?
In what ways can you help your church promote unity in Christ?
Digging Deeper
What boundaries should you not cross in doing so?

Under One Roof

Imagine a town where nearly everyone lives

under one roof. Welcome to Whittier, Alaska! It's a place where 80 percent of its 280 residents share a zip code and the same address. The main building is a mini-town, having a post office, hospital, general store, indoor pool, police station, the mayor's office, and even a tunnel that goes straight to the local school. The divides seen in larger cities are not there. Levels of wealth do not determine where people live, shop, or go to school—everyone does these things in the same way.

Living in the same building or attending the same church does not automatically lead to peace and unity. Problems still pop up because people differ from one another (Romans 3:10-12; 7:14-15; 1 John 1:8; etc.).

The extraordinary place where real peace and unity can and should exist is in Christ Jesus. What is only an idea now will be a reality for us in Heaven, where all Christians will be "under one roof." How should that fact cause you to view Christians of different demographics and cultures in the here and now?   —J. M.

17. And came and preached peace to you which were afar off, and to them that were nigh.

The Jews (*them that were nigh*) had been, in a sense, closer to God than the Gentiles (*you which were afar off*) were because of the covenant relationship. But neither had been reconciled with their Creator. The gospel was (and is) a necessary message for all people, Jew and Gentile (Isaiah 57:19; Romans 1:16). Christ's coming, His ministry, and His death and resurrection were all acts declaring God's good, reconciling news. In Christ, God had come near. In Christ, God paid the price of sin. In Christ, God gives life that overcomes death forever. And so in Christ, true *peace* is available between God and every human who desires it.

> #### What Do You Think?
> How should the reality of peace with God influence your activities this week?
> #### Digging Deeper
> How would you explain to an unbeliever the connection between peace and reconciliation?

18. For through him we both have access by one Spirit unto the Father.

A unifying factor in the church is the gift of the Holy *Spirit*. The presence of God's Spirit in the church and in the heart of each believer is a great source of unity (see Ephesians 4:3). Just as Paul saw no difference between the Holy Spirit in the life of a Jew and in the life of a Gentile, so we today should understand that every Christian has the same gift of the indwelling Holy Spirit (Acts 2:38-39; 10:44-47). He is the timeless, eternal Spirit of God, who was present at creation (Genesis 1:2), was present in the life of Paul as he ministered (Romans 5:5; 1 Corinthians 2:12), and is still active in the church today.

God had promised the Holy Spirit not just to Israel but to "all flesh" (Joel 2:28-32, quoted by Peter on Pentecost). With one Spirit living in all the original readers of this letter, they were united by One more powerful and important than anything dividing them. This fact is so vital that Paul will later tell them to keep "the unity of the Spirit" for there is "one Spirit" (Ephesians 4:3-4).

C. As God's Family (v. 19)

19. Now therefore ye are no more strangers and foreigners, but fellowcitizens with the saints, and of the household of God.

Given all Christ has accomplished, no Christian is to think of any other follower of Jesus as being outside of God's people. God has "grafted in" the Gentile believers (Romans 11:17-24). They participate equally in the promises to Israel now fulfilled in Christ. They have the full rights, privileges, and obligations as anyone else in *the household of God*. The word *household* draws an analogy to a family as the vital social unit. Every household member had duties but also privileges as all work to benefit each other. To be incorporated into God's household is to experience the full provision of Christ's redemption, the Father's providence, the Spirit's empowerment, and one another's service. The doubled stress within the phrase *strangers and foreigners* stresses the "outsider" status of Gentiles in the Jewish "superiority" mindset of Paul's day and possibly also the "inferiority" mindset of some Gentile believers—a thinking that had to be abandoned.

D. To Be God's Temple (vv. 20-22)

20. And are built upon the foundation of the apostles and prophets, Jesus Christ himself being the chief corner stone.

Paul now shifts his comparison of this new people of God from household to one of architecture. The church is a carefully crafted building constructed on *the foundation of* God-ordained teachers. These teachers have been both *apostles,* referring to first-century teachers such as Paul and Peter (compare Revelation 21:14) and *prophets* (compare 1 Peter 1:10-12). Both terms are also mentioned in Luke 11:49; 1 Corinthians 12:28-29; Ephesians 3:5; 4:11; 2 Peter 3:2; and Revelation 18:20. Today, we are blessed to find their teachings in the pages of our Bibles. The church's foundation is God's apostolic, prophetic message, fulfilled in Christ.

To bring that point home, Paul calls *Jesus Christ* the *chief corner stone* of God's temple. We are uncertain whether this word refers to a cornerstone at the base of a building or a capstone at its peak (compare Matthew 21:42, quoting Psalm 118:22-23). But the point is clear: everything depends on Christ, is built on Christ, and has Christ as its focus.

21-22. In whom all the building fitly framed together groweth unto an holy temple in the Lord: in whom ye also are builded together for an habitation of God through the Spirit.

Paul's analogy pictures the church as a temple under construction. Each person who is added,

regardless of identity or background, is like a stone carefully cut to fit with the others. There is every reason to pursue unity and no basis to tolerate hostility among the stones of God's temple.

God had manifested the presence of His Spirit with a great cloud filling Solomon's temple at its dedication (1 Kings 8:10-11). That manifestation defined the temple as the place where Israel could meet with God. Now Christians are filled with God's Spirit (Ephesians 1:13). Collectively, all Christians form the new covenant's temple of God (1 Corinthians 6:19-20; 2 Corinthians 6:16). The task of all Christians in every era is to respect and embrace our fellow "stones" of the temple of the New Testament era as we honor the ultimate stone, Jesus (1 Peter 2:4-6).

Conclusion

A. Working at Being a Family

What a picture Paul gives of Christ's church! We are a global, multiethnic, transcultural, multiclass people, men and women, adults and children, all reconciled by Christ's blood, indwelt by God's Spirit, fulfilling the promise of Israel's temple. We are the household of God, His family, fulfilling His purpose to restore humanity to Him as one family.

Being a family takes work. Little wonder, then, that Paul spent half the Ephesian letter, beginning in Ephesians 4:1, instructing Christians to live in unity in a manner worthy of the gospel. We have our own issues that divide us today, and circumcision is not one of them. Even so, Paul's instructions for overcoming a divisive issue of the first century are of great value for us in the twenty-first century.

We see the vision of God's temple. Are we willing with the Spirit's empowerment to live as we must to see it built up and not torn down?

B. Prayer

Lord God, make us courageous and humble to pursue the Spirit's unity in the bond of peace. Help us follow Your will as we help each other build Your family, Your temple. In Jesus' name. Amen.

C. Thought to Remember

Followers of Jesus are one in Him.

Involvement Learning

Enhance your lesson with KJV Bible Student (from your curriculum supplier) and the reproducible activity page (at www.standardlesson.com or in the back of the KJV Standard Lesson Commentary Deluxe Edition).

Into the Lesson

Invite learners to tell of times when they needed something, but access was blocked. As stories are told, keep a running list on the board of two columns: *Barriers* and *Reactions to Barriers*. After a few minutes, explore how the barriers you have listed on the board were or were not overcome.

Transition to Bible study by saying, "It's frustrating when what we need is inaccessible. It's doubly frustrating when the barrier has no reason for its continued existence. In today's lesson, look for the obsolete barrier that Christ has torn down, and it is our responsibility not to put it back up."

Into the Word

Set the stage by giving a mini-lecture on the Lesson Context. Prepare to do so in advance with the expectation that learners will need to see the relevance of the Jew-and-Gentile issue for today's church.

Read Ephesians 2:11-12 aloud. Focus on the repeated word *remember* as you invite learners to describe what life was like for them before accepting Jesus as Savior.

Have a volunteer read Ephesians 2:13-18. Divide learners into three groups. Distribute the following assignments for the groups on handouts (you create).

Peace Group: What does Ephesians 2:13-18 say about the source, nature, and implications of the peace we have?

Unity Group: What does Ephesians 2:13-18 say about the source, nature, and implications of the unity we have?

Nearness Group: What does Ephesians 2:13-18 say about the source, nature, and implications of the nearness we have?

Reconvene for whole-class discussion as groups finish. As you work through group conclusions, make sure that the following are stressed: (1) the source of peace, unity, and nearness is the blood of Christ shed on the cross, and (2) the nature of those same three is to change the relationship between people groups and between God and sinners. Expect a wide range of responses for "implications" as they concern the church today.

Option. Distribute copies of the "Venn Diagram" exercise from the activity page, which you can download. Have participants work in small groups to complete as indicated. Then, have groups compare their completed diagrams.

Ask a volunteer to read Ephesians 2:19-22. Draw a building of blocks on the board. Be sure to have a long block on the bottom as a foundation representing the apostles and Jesus as the chief cornerstone. On a few of the building blocks, write some common first names of people. Then point to a place where two blocks are adjacent and say, "We need some 'mortar' right here to cement these two blocks together. What are some possibilities?" Ideas can include Bible study, fellowship events, etc.

Into Life

Write on the board the heading *Peace and Unity*. Then distribute half-sheets of paper on which you have printed the following:

One way that I can do better to nurture peaceful, unifying relationships in Christ is by

_____

Allow one minute to fill in the blank. Assure your learners that you won't collect the papers or put anyone on the spot to reveal what they wrote. Before you call for volunteers to read theirs, state that their "do better" statements must be phrased as "I language," not "we language."

Option. Distribute copies of the "Henceforth, No Longer" exercise from the activity page. Have participants complete it in small groups before discussing conclusions as a whole group.

Sacrifices of Praise

Devotional Reading: Psalm 146
Background Scripture: Hebrews 13:1-21

Hebrews 13:9-21

9 Be not carried about with divers and strange doctrines. For it is a good thing that the heart be established with grace; not with meats, which have not profited them that have been occupied therein.

10 We have an altar, whereof they have no right to eat which serve the tabernacle.

11 For the bodies of those beasts, whose blood is brought into the sanctuary by the high priest for sin, are burned without the camp.

12 Wherefore Jesus also, that he might sanctify the people with his own blood, suffered without the gate.

13 Let us go forth therefore unto him without the camp, bearing his reproach.

14 For here have we no continuing city, but we seek one to come.

15 By him therefore let us offer the sacrifice of praise to God continually, that is, the fruit of our lips giving thanks to his name.

16 But to do good and to communicate forget not: for with such sacrifices God is well pleased.

17 Obey them that have the rule over you, and submit yourselves: for they watch for your souls, as they that must give account, that they may do it with joy, and not with grief: for that is unprofitable for you.

18 Pray for us: for we trust we have a good conscience, in all things willing to live honestly.

19 But I beseech you the rather to do this, that I may be restored to you the sooner.

20 Now the God of peace, that brought again from the dead our Lord Jesus, that great shepherd of the sheep, through the blood of the everlasting covenant,

21 Make you perfect in every good work to do his will, working in you that which is well pleasing in his sight, through Jesus Christ; to whom be glory for ever and ever. Amen.

Key Text

By him therefore let us offer the sacrifice of praise to God continually, that is, the fruit of our lips giving thanks to his name. —Hebrews 13:15

Sacred Altars and
Holy Offerings

Unit 3: Christians and Sacrifice
Lessons 10–14

Lesson Aims

After participating in this lesson, each learner will be able to:

1. Match elements of the old covenant with their new covenant counterparts.

2. Identify some ways that the new covenant is unlike the old covenant while being an extension of it.

3. Make a list of ways that he or she can improve on being a "sacrifice of praise."

Lesson Outline

Introduction
A. Give It Up

When a concert artist finishes an outstanding performance, the emcee might exhort an appreciative audience to "Give it up!" for the people on stage. This results in loud applause with whooping and hollering. In a traditional opera setting, one is likely to hear people shouting, "Bravo!" or even "Bravissimo!" These outbursts show recognition of excellence, expression of gratitude, and release of emotion for the concertgoer.

Christians find repeated encouragements in Scripture to offer praise to the Lord. Likewise, church services are full of singing, praying, and preaching that give praise to God. Why do we do this? What is the background and basis for Christian praise? The author of Hebrews teaches us that certain observances in the Old Testament demonstrate how our practices are both contrasting and parallel to the prescribed customs of the ancient people of Israel. Tracing these antecedents back to their Old Testament sources, we may better understand how praise is an essential element in our relationship with God today. Then, perhaps, we can "give it up" to the Lord, a full-throated expression of our praise and adoration.

B. Lesson Context

For the best understanding of an author's writing, it is beneficial to know (1) who was writing, (2) who the intended recipients were, and (3) the reason for the correspondence. We don't always have all three in all 27 books of the New Testament. Concerning the book or letter we call Hebrews, we do not have any of the three!

Many authors have been suggested for Hebrews. Hebrews 13:23 mentions the release of Timothy, a well-known companion of Paul. This fact may point to Paul as the author, but we cannot know this for certain—the letter is not in his usual style. It is likely we will never know the identity of the individual who wrote this book.

Regarding the identity of the recipients, the closing "they of Italy salute you" (Hebrews 13:24) is not detailed enough to help. Even so, the letter shows a level of intimacy with the recipients that indicates the author knew the people of this congregation rather well.

There is no purpose statement in this letter as there are in Luke 1:1-4; John 20:31; 1 John 5:13; etc. We must be satisfied with knowing that the early church valued Hebrews as authoritative, apostolic teaching that should guide the church and have its place in the New Testament.

Reading the book of Hebrews gives a strong impression that it was written to Christians of Jewish background who were wavering in their faith under persecution (Hebrews 10:32-34). They seem to have been thinking of returning to Judaism. The author confronted this error by explaining the relationship between Jesus and the Old Testament system. In so doing, the author shows how Christ surpasses every element of the Jewish system.

The author does that in a very Jewish way, respecting Jewish traditions and arguing from Scripture. But as we move to the last chapter of Hebrews, the writer switches from doctrinally heavy topics to practical application.

I. Great Changes
(Hebrews 13:9-14)
A. By Grace (vv. 9-10)

9. Be not carried about with divers and strange doctrines. For it is a good thing that the heart be established with grace; not with meats, which have not profited them that have been occupied therein.

The author was aware that the audience had found themselves awash in *divers and strange doctrines*. This phrase refers to teachings that contradicted the Christian gospel (compare Ephesians 4:14; Colossians 2:8).

The best defense against the false doctrine faced by the readers was to have a *heart* that was *established with grace*. The word translated "established" is also translated "confirmed" in Hebrews 2:3-4, a context of reliable witnesses, miraculous signs and wonders, and the presence of the Holy Spirit.

Staying on the right course meant avoiding placing trust in ritualistic meals (*meats* is an old English term that means "food" more broadly than simply animal flesh; see Leviticus 2:1). This refers to the

Jewish sacrificial system. Those various food offerings did not resolve the sin and guilt of God's people permanently (Hebrews 9:9-10; 10:11).

10. We have an altar, whereof they have no right to eat which serve the tabernacle.

An *altar* in this context was a piece of equipment used by the priests for their sacrifices. Exodus 27:1-8 describes the altar of burnt offering as central to the Jewish system of sacrifices. The author employs this symbol of sacrifice to speak of a Christian reality, a sacrifice that does not need the servants of *the tabernacle* (priests). The altar of Christianity is the cross where Jesus yielded His body as the final, "once for all" sacrifice for sins (Hebrews 10:10).

B. By Sacrifice (vv. 11-12)

11. For the bodies of those beasts, whose blood is brought into the sanctuary by the high priest for sin, are burned without the camp.

Again, the author provided another analogy demonstrating extensive knowledge of the Jewish sacrificial traditions. On the yearly Day of Atonement, animals were killed on the altar of burnt offerings. Their blood was used in the day's ceremonies, and some of their fat was burnt by the high priest (Leviticus 16:25). But the *bodies of* the sacrificial *beasts* were taken outside the Israelite encampment and burned completely (16:27), thus completing the sacrificial acts.

12. Wherefore Jesus also, that he might sanctify the people with his own blood, suffered without the gate.

As with the animal bodies on the Day of Atonement, the sacrifice of Jesus took place outside the

How to Say It

Golgotha   *Gahl*-guh-thuh.

city (*without the gate*) at a place called Golgotha (Matthew 27:33). This detail demonstrates that the author was familiar with the city of Jerusalem and the site of Jesus' crucifixion. John, an eyewitness, records that the place of crucifixion was "nigh to the city [of Jerusalem]," meaning it was not inside the city itself (John 19:20). The parallel to the Day of Atonement was remarkable for the author. It served as another piece of evidence that while the sacrifice of Jesus was in concert with the Old Testament patterns, it was superior to them in the end.

C. By Seeking (vv. 13-14)

13. Let us go forth therefore unto him without the camp, bearing his reproach.

Figuratively, the author exhorted his or her readers to leave *the camp*—to go outside the city, the place that symbolized the way of the old covenant. There, they would bear the *reproach* that Jesus experienced (compare Philippians 3:10-11). The author was well aware of the abuse his readers had suffered at the hands of those who were formerly their friends (Hebrews 10:32-34). But he does not try to keep them as believers in Jesus by promising that things will get easier—quite the opposite!

14. For here have we no continuing city, but we seek one to come.

In AD 70, the temple and Jerusalem were destroyed at the hands of the Romans as they crushed the Jewish revolt. Some scholars believe that this verse implies that the city and the temple were already destroyed when Hebrews was written, based on the author's use of the word "tabernacle" (Hebrews 9:1-8) rather than the "temple." Other scholars believe the destruction was imminent at the time of writing Hebrews based on the author's references to the priesthood in the present tense (examples: 8:3; 10:11) and description of the old covenant as "ready to vanish away" (8:13).

In any case, the author knew that no city on earth came close to matching the desirability and permanence of the residence of God. Still today, we wait for an eternal city, *one to come* (Hebrews 10, 16; 12:22). This great city is part of God's nate plan, the final establishment of a kingthat cannot be shaken (12:27-28). As with

the original readers of Hebrews, our present sufferings and trials as Christians are not representative of our future. We look to the great city that is to come (Revelation 21:2, 10).

What Do You Think?

What is one practical way to let others see your anticipation of the eternal city to come?

Digging Deeper

How can you help someone who is deeply troubled by current events do the same?

II. Great Sacrifice
(Hebrews 13:15-19)
A. Continual Offerings (vv. 15-16)

15. By him therefore let us offer the sacrifice of praise to God continually, that is, the fruit of our lips giving thanks to his name.

Given the nature and features of the new covenant, were the original readers without a temple, animal sacrifices, or direct fellowship with God? No. True, they no longer were to slaughter lambs or burn the bodies of goats. True, they were no longer to be satisfied with the rituals a priesthood would offer. But they had to realize that God's eternal plan was moving beyond such things. In that light, they were to *offer the sacrifice of praise to God continually*. That meant that praise was not merely part of annual holy days but part of the essence of their lives.

This praise was to be their own sacrifice, never to be compromised by the imperfections of priests or animals. Jesus had paid sin's price fully in His physical self-sacrifice. His followers now have the privilege of offering spiritual sacrifices as living sacrifices (Romans 12:1; 1 Peter 2:5). One aspect is *giving thanks to his name*.

The word translated "giving thanks" occurs more than 20 times in the New Testament, and it is almost always translated in terms of the concepts of confessing, admitting, or acknowledging (examples: Hebrews 11:13; 1 John 1:9). That is the sense here, and it is to be evidenced by *the fruit of our lips* (Hosea 14:2). Praise of God and confessing

Him as Lord are not identical things, but expressions of praise are saturated with words acknowledging who He is: the only and true God.

16. But to do good and to communicate forget not: for with such sacrifices God is well pleased.

The word translated *communicate* is translated as "fellowship" in numerous other passages, and that is the sense here (examples: Acts 2:42; 1 John 1:3). The implication is that this was to be an ongoing expectation and a great joy for Christians intent on pleasing *God*. The idea is to gather and praise God in community. The readers must not *forget* this feature of gathering together (see Hebrews 10:25). Hebrews presents the worshiping congregation as "giving" rather than "receiving." The question on Sunday is not to be, "Did you get anything out of the service?" but "What did you sacrifice back to God today?" (compare Philippians 4:18).

B. Obedient Submission (vv. 17-19)

17a. Obey them that have the rule over you, and submit yourselves: for they watch for your souls.

The author concludes by mentioning obligations toward leaders (here and in Hebrews 13:7, 24). These were not the civic governing authorities of Romans 13:1-7. Instead, the leaders who *rule over you* were church leaders as evidenced by their task to *watch for your souls*. This task is explained more fully in Acts 20:28; 1 Peter 5:1-3; etc.

The word "obey" is also translated as "trust" in Hebrews 2:13; 13:18. People obey those they trust, so the concepts are related. Successful churches must have leaders and followers, not a chaotic situation where everyone prioritizes their own preferences, as in Judges 21:25.

17b. As they that must give account, that they may do it with joy, and not with grief: for that is unprofitable for you.

Moreover, these church leaders are accountable to the Lord. Considering the parable of the lost sheep in Luke 15:3-7, the leaders' *joy* in the context of accountability is founded in the return of the 1 to the 99. The Lord is not satisfied with a 99 percent retention rate!

18-19. Pray for us: for we trust we have a good conscience, in all things willing to live honestly. But I beseech you the rather to do this, that I may be restored to you the sooner.

The spiritually mature writer of this letter is not above asking for prayer from his much less mature readers (compare Hebrews 5:11-14). It makes a difference when church leaders know that their people are praying for their fidelity in marriage, integrity in financial matters, and responsible living in civic life (Titus 1:6). The outside community often knows who leads a congregation. Those leaders must maintain an excellent reputation to effectively reach them with the gospel (1 Timothy 3:7). But the writer's main prayer request is to rejoin with his or her readers.

What Do You Think?

How should your prayers for church leaders differ from prayers for civic leaders?

Digging Deeper

How do Romans 13:1 and 1 Timothy 2:1-2 inform your response?

I Need Help

"What's your greatest weakness?" In interviews, this question has always posed a challenge for me. Being honest seems to risk a negative impression, yet honesty is vital. My Achilles' heel is my reluctance to ask for help. The evidence is everywhere: a scratched refrigerator I insisted on moving alone, incomplete house trim from running out of time, and a strained back from solo efforts to shovel snow after a blizzard. These instances are just glimpses of the consequences I have faced while trying to mask my weakness.

The text of Hebrews reveals that its author—whoever he or she may have been—possessed extensive insight and a profound connection with Jesus Christ. But this person was human and faced a particular set of challenges. As such, this person voiced the need for divine assistance through supportive prayer from fellow believers in Christ. How does recognizing your weaknesses influence your personal and spiritual growth?   —J. M.

Christis is our peace.

Visual for Lessons 12 & 13. *Display this visual and ask, "How will you share the peace of Christ to your neighbors in the upcoming week?"*

III. Great Benediction
(Hebrews 13:20-21)

A. God of Peace (v. 20)

20. Now the God of peace, that brought again from the dead our Lord Jesus, that great shepherd of the sheep, through the blood of the everlasting covenant.

After requesting prayer, the writer closes the letter with a prayer. It rehearses many of the major themes and teachings of what has been written (compare Hebrews 1:3-4; 2:9-10; 6:20; 7:2; 9:14-15; 10:19; 11:19, 35; 12:14).

B. God of Every Good Work (v. 21)

21. Make you perfect in every good work to do his will, working in you that which is well pleasing in his sight, through Jesus Christ; to whom be glory for ever and ever. Amen.

Unbelievers are transformed into believers so that they (we) can be enabled to do *every good work* as a natural expression of faith in Christ. We do these good deeds not to earn favor or merits, but to be well pleasing to the Lord. Pleasing God became possible since He sees us *through Jesus Christ*, the "author and finisher" of our faith (Hebrews 12:2). There are no good deeds pleasing to God divorced from our faith and relationship with the Lord Jesus Christ.

The prayer ends with a doxology, ascribing glory *for ever and ever* to Jesus Christ.

The writer ends with a Hebrew word, *Amen*, meaning "let it be true."

> **What Do You Think?**
> Who can you help this week to be better equipped for the Lord's tasks?
> **Digging Deeper**
> Who can you ask to be a mentor for your own equipping?

Conclusion

A. Celtic Cross

Christian tradition has produced many different styles of the cross. Each has its own symbolism and meaning. One of these is the Celtic Cross, which tradition says was introduced to the Irish people by Patrick, the fifth-century missionary to Ireland. In its simplest form, the Celtic Cross looks like a standard cross with a circle around its center. The cross represents the sacrifice of Christ. The circle represents eternity. Together, they speak of the perfect, eternal sacrifice of Jesus.

The book of Hebrews speaks of things in terms of eternity. As the Celtic Cross symbolizes, Jesus has provided an eternal sacrifice for us. He is our once-for-all-time high priest, without beginning or end. We wait for an eternal city. We have continual, eternal praise to offer to God, glory forever and ever. We have an everlasting covenant, the new covenant promised by the prophet Jeremiah. Why would we relinquish any of these blessings for old, inferior ways of relating to God? Why would trivial issues and distractions sidetrack us? May we continue to offer our praise to the Lord as a pleasing offering to Him. This is sacrifice combined with eternity.

B. Prayer

Lord God, may the fruit of our lips be pleasing to You. May the words of our mouths be praise and recognition of Your glory. May our praise be full of thanksgiving for the sacrifice of Jesus, Your Son, to save us. We pray in His name, Amen.

C. Thought to Remember

Offer the new covenant sacrifices to Him.

Involvement Learning

Enhance your lesson with KJV Bible Student *(from your curriculum supplier) and the reproducible activity page (at www.standardlesson.com or in the back of the* KJV Standard Lesson Commentary Deluxe Edition*).*

Into the Lesson

Have learners stand in two rows facing one another, with space between them. Ask a volunteer to stand at one end of that space and walk to one end. When you say "Go," those standing on either side are to encourage the volunteer to move left, right, straight ahead, or in other random directions. With eyes closed, the volunteer must determine which voices to heed and which to ignore during the walk. As the walk concludes, ask, "How hard it was to sift through competing voices?" Invite examples of how this happens in everyday life.

Alternative. Distribute copies of the "Old Focus vs. New Focus" exercise from the activity page, which you can download. Announce that the exercise is a pre-test for today's lesson. Have learners score their own responses afterward.

Say, "It is easy to get distracted to the point where we can't distinguish between what's important and what's wrong. Today's lesson is a road map in that regard."

Into the Word

Ask a volunteer to read Hebrews 13:9-16. Form participants into two groups and give each a handout (you prepare) with these questions:

Eating Group. Read Deuteronomy 14:3-21. Create a chart with *Clean* and *Unclean* as the headers of two columns. List the foods under each category. Then read Mark 7:17-19. Discuss the *what, why,* and *how* of the change.

High Priesthood Group. Read Numbers 35:25. Make a chart with two columns headed *High Priesthood Then* and *High Priesthood Now.* List characteristics under each heading. Then read Hebrews 7:27-28. Discuss the *what, why,* and *how* of the change.

Bring the groups back together. Invite the whole class to discuss how the passage from Hebrews 13 helps define the differences between the old and new covenants.

Ask a volunteer to read Hebrews 13:17-19. Stress that this passage specifically refers to spiritual leaders within the church, not civil. Write the following on the board as headers of three columns:

Obey / Submit / Pray

Pose the following questions for whole-class discussion: 1–When is it appropriate to obey our church leaders? 2–What does it look like to submit to their teachings? 3–How can we pray for them? *[Teacher tip: pose the questions one at a time, allowing for discussion before posing the next.]*

Option. Form learners into groups of three or four. Give each group one set of 16 cards you have prepared according to the pattern in the "Match Game" exercise on the activity page, which you can download. For best effect, print these on lightweight card stock using a laser printer; cut cards apart with a paper cutter rather than scissors.

Have groups complete the exercise as indicated. After the game is over (all cards taken), ask those holding cards for their thoughts about what is on their cards.

As a transition to the Into Life segment, read aloud Hebrews 13:8, the verse that precedes today's lesson text. Talk about how the message of the new covenant itself is worthy of praise.

Into Life

Read aloud the key verse, Hebrews 13:15. Talk about how a "sacrifice of praise" can be an offering of thankfulness. Highlight that the "fruit of our lips" is a good way to depict our expressions of praise to God. Brainstorm ways to be a "sacrifice of praise."

Alternative. Distribute blank index cards and challenge learners to make a list of ways that they can improve on being a "sacrifice of praise" in the coming week.

Close by reading aloud Hebrews 13:20-21 as your prayer of departure.

Living Stones in a Spiritual Temple

Devotional Reading: Galatians 3:23-29
Background Scripture: 1 Peter 2:1-17

1 Peter 2:1-12

1 Wherefore laying aside all malice, and all guile, and hypocrisies, and envies, and all evil speakings,

2 As newborn babes, desire the sincere milk of the word, that ye may grow thereby:

3 If so be ye have tasted that the Lord is gracious.

4 To whom coming, as unto a living stone, disallowed indeed of men, but chosen of God, and precious,

5 Ye also, as lively stones, are built up a spiritual house, an holy priesthood, to offer up spiritual sacrifices, acceptable to God by Jesus Christ.

6 Wherefore also it is contained in the scripture, behold, I lay in Sion a chief corner stone, elect, precious: and he that believeth on him shall not be confounded.

7 Unto you therefore which believe he is precious: but unto them which be disobedient, the stone which the builders disallowed, the same is made the head of the corner,

8 And a stone of stumbling, and a rock of offence, even to them which stumble at the word, being disobedient: whereunto also they were appointed.

9 But ye are a chosen generation, a royal priesthood, an holy nation, a peculiar people; that ye should shew forth the praises of him who hath called you out of darkness into his marvellous light:

10 Which in time past were not a people, but are now the people of God: which had not obtained mercy, but now have obtained mercy.

11 Dearly beloved, I beseech you as strangers and pilgrims, abstain from fleshly lusts, which war against the soul;

12 Having your conversation honest among the Gentiles: that, whereas they speak against you as evildoers, they may by your good works, which they shall behold, glorify God in the day of visitation.

Key Text

To whom coming, as unto a living stone, disallowed indeed of men, but chosen of God, and precious, Ye also, as lively stones, are built up a spiritual house, an holy priesthood, to offer up spiritual sacrifices, acceptable to God by Jesus Christ. —1 Peter 2:5

Sacred Altars and
Holy Offerings

Unit 3: Christians and Sacrifice
Lessons 10–14

Lesson Aims

After participating in this lesson, each learner will be able to:

1. Identify the stone in Zion.
2. Explain the relationship between Christians as "living stones" and Jesus as "the living Stone."
3. Propose a way to guard himself or herself against unholy behaviors.

Lesson Outline

Introduction

A. You, the Priest?

Martin Luther (1483–1546) was ordained as a Roman Catholic priest in 1507. But 10 years after his ordination, Luther began to question the church's practices based on his reading of the Bible. He eventually led a group to withdraw and form churches independent from the authorities in Rome. In so doing, Luther and his followers abandoned the centuries-old tradition of needing priests for confession and prayer.

Rather than functioning as a hierarchy that elevated some persons (the clergy) above the level of the general membership of the church (the laity), Luther claimed that all Christians were priests. There was no division between the clergy and the laity. Any Christian could minister to another in ways that were seen before as the purview of priests alone. This meant that any Christian could effectively pray for another Christian. This teaching became known as the doctrine of the "priesthood of all believers," which is still a central tenet of Protestant Christianity. Today's lesson takes us directly to one of Luther's guiding texts.

B. Lesson Context

The 27 books of the New Testament include two ascribed to the apostle Peter. The first is particularly rich with citations from and allusions to various Old Testament passages. By one count, 1 Peter is tied for second place with Hebrews for having the highest percentage of verses that reflect Old Testament passages; only Revelation has a higher percentage. As a Jewish man, Peter knew the stories of his ancestors well. We see this in his use of several Old Testament imageries in his two letters.

Peter himself is a perplexing figure in the Gospel accounts. He tended to blurt out whatever was on his mind at the time, sometimes seeming to contradict himself in the process (examples: Matthew 16:22, 23; 26:35; Mark 9:5-6; John 18:25-27). He was impulsive and recklessly bold, often acting before thinking (Matthew 14:22-33; John 18:10). In short, Peter was an apostle to whom we can relate.

I. Sanctified People
(1 Peter 2:1-3)
A. What to Abandon (v. 1)

1. Wherefore laying aside all malice, and all guile, and hypocrisies, and envies, and all evil speakings.

In this letter's first chapter, Peter described what it means to be "born again," the eternal condition of believers in Christ Jesus (1 Peter 1:23). Now he pivots (*wherefore*) to teach about the implications of this new condition: one of having been "purified" (1:22). Changes in behaviors and attitudes are vital.

Those in Peter's original audience had to outgrow the attitudes and behaviors of unbelievers. What comes next in the letter is called a "vice list." There are about two dozen such lists in the New Testament (Galatians 5:19-21; Colossians 3:5, 8-9; etc.). *Malice* carries the sense of evil actions in general. Such actions can be motivated by greed, spite, jealousy, or other moral failings; the resulting action intends to harm another person.

Guile is an orientation of general dishonesty. *Hypocrisies* characterize a person who will play whatever role is most beneficial to him or her. *Envies* characterize a bitter, restless spirit that begrudges the success or possessions of others; envy is the opposite of gratitude, of contentment with what God has given (see 1 Timothy 6:6-8).

Evil speakings reflects a word that is translated as "backbitings" in 2 Corinthians 12:20. Such behavior results from the previous three: a deceitful person who feigns friendship yet works behind the scenes to damage the reputation of others.

> **What Do You Think?**
> What criteria should you use to determine which vice is the most troubling to you personally?
> **Digging Deeper**
> Who could you ask to be a mentor for you in that regard?

B. What to Seek (vv. 2-3)

2. As newborn babes, desire the sincere milk of the word, that ye may grow thereby.

As there are different levels of spiritual maturity, different foods are appropriate for those levels. These are described in more detail in 1 Corinthians 3:1-4 and Hebrews 5:11–6:3. There is nothing wrong with the *milk of the word*; it is necessary and desirable for those who are spiritual infants. But its ingestion should lead to something important: *that ye may grow thereby* (compare 2 Peter 3:18).

The words translated "guile" in 1 Peter 2:1 and *sincere* here are the same word in Greek, with the letter *a* added to the beginning of the second occurrence. This additional letter expresses negation. We often express negation the same way in English (compare the opposites *historical* and *ahistorical*). Thus, human guile and the sincere Word of God are complete opposites.

> **What Do You Think?**
> What action must you take to keep growing spiritually?
> **Digging Deeper**
> Would an accountability partner help? Why, or why not?

3. If so be ye have tasted that the Lord is gracious.

Having *tasted* the goodness of God and having realized how *gracious* He has been should motivate the desire for change (compare Hebrews 6:5; Psalm 34:8). This could be something of a self-evaluation: if Peter's original readers were not craving more of God's kindness, had they even tasted it in the first place?

II. Spiritual House
(1 Peter 2:4-8)
A. Living Stone (v. 4)

4. To whom coming, as unto a living stone, disallowed indeed of men, but chosen of God, and precious.

To whom coming speaks of those who approach Jesus in obedience and worship. Based on what God has done in Christ, believers have the privilege of approaching the throne of God in worship, praise, and petition (compare Hebrews 10:19-22). Thus, Peter has transitioned in his line of reasoning, with the focus now shifting from the believers to whom Peter was writing to the Lord himself.

This shift in focus comes through using Psalm 118:22, the first of several Old Testament texts cited as support (see Lesson Context). Jesus applied this passage to himself in Matthew 21:42. Peter also used it in his earliest preaching (Acts 4:11; compare Isaiah 28:16; 1 Corinthians 3:11; Ephesians 2:20).

As the focus shifts, so does the metaphor: from infants needing milk to a *stone*. *Living stone* is a metaphor for Christ, the one who conquered death. His death, burial, resurrection, and ascension form the foundation of the Christian faith (compare 1 Corinthians 15:14; 1 Peter 1:18-21). The resurrection confirms Jesus as God's *chosen* Messiah (Acts 2:36). The word *precious* indicates high value.

B. Building Stones (v. 5)

5. Ye also, as lively stones, are built up a spiritual house, an holy priesthood, to offer up spiritual sacrifices, acceptable to God by Jesus Christ.

As rapidly as Peter shifts the focus away from his readers, he turns back to them. One stone does not make a building, and God's spiritual house requires numerous other *lively stones*. Their identity is not in doubt, as witnessed by the opening phrase *ye also*.

The Greek word translated "living" in the previous verse is the same word translated *lively* here. Thus, "lively stones" can also be said to be "living stones." Peter intended for his readers to envisage a *spiritual house* built of active believers in Christ.

This spiritual stone house is like a temple, where *spiritual sacrifices* are made, and Christians make up the *holy priesthood*. The concepts of priesthood and temple have not been done away with; instead, they have been transformed (compare Revelation 1:6; 5:10; 20:6). Christians do not need the kind of priests the ancient Israelites did, because we now are priests ourselves as we serve under the great high priest, *Jesus Christ* (Hebrews 4:14).

Spiritual Excavation

When we decided to build a fence, my wife and I learned a lesson in Alaskan geology: glacial valleys are densely laden with rocks. The rocky terrain significantly delayed the construction of our fence.

Visual for Lesson 14. *Display this visual as you ask, "How are you serving Christ as a member of the 'holy priesthood'?"*

Following a day's work that yielded only one hole, it became clear that we needed an auger. We rented one, but it was apparent that we needed something more powerful. An auger mounted on a backhoe proved adequate for our needs. Looking back, I can say that building the fence was easier than preparing the land to receive it.

Before Peter discussed constructing a spiritual house, he first addressed the need to clear the terrain. What needed to be removed were remnants of his readers' sinful nature—things such as malice and hypocrisy. Construction would not be successful for those readers until that clearing occurred. What "terrain" in your life needs to be excavated to ensure your contribution to the building of the Lord's spiritual house?   —J. M.

C. Cornerstone (vv. 6-7)

6. Wherefore also it is contained in the scripture, behold, I lay in Sion a chief corner stone, elect, precious: and he that believeth on him shall not be confounded.

Peter demonstrated the value of *scripture* as he began to weave together several Old Testament texts. The passage quoted here is Isaiah 28:16. The quote doesn't read quite the same in our English version of Isaiah because Peter quoted from the ancient Greek version of the Old Testament, known as the Septuagint.

Sion is, of course, Zion, which is Jerusalem (see the words used as parallel expressions in Psalm

102:21; etc.). The Greek phrase translated *corner stone* or some variant of it occurs several times in the New Testament (compare Matthew 21:42; Mark 12:10; Luke 20:17).

The first stone laid in construction was the cornerstone. If the structure was to endure, it was essential that the cornerstone be true on all sides and set into the ground so that it was level. The ancients used plumb lines to determine vertical trueness (see Amos 7:7-8) and trays of water to gauge horizontal levelness. A cornerstone needed to be without defects to guard against the potential for cracking. In Isaiah 28:16-17, this spiritual stone is measured to size by a standard of justice (judgment) and set to true vertical by the plumb line of righteousness (contrast 2 Kings 21:13).

7. Unto you therefore which believe he is precious: but unto them which be disobedient, the stone which the builders disallowed, the same is made the head of the corner.

Here, in a quotation from Psalm 118:22, we see the second of the two uses in today's text of the cornerstone concept, worded as *head of the corner*. The two occurrences are entirely consistent in identifying this cornerstone as Jesus (compare Acts 4:11; Ephesians 2:20).

This second usage comes with a darker tone. For those who are *disobedient*, Jesus is *disallowed* as that cornerstone. Their faith is misplaced and mistaken. They are like the man who built his house on the sand rather than the rock (Matthew 7:24-27).

D. Stumbling Stone (v. 8)

8. And a stone of stumbling, and a rock of offence, even to them which stumble at the word, being disobedient: whereunto also they were appointed.

The first two phrases are parallel expressions from Isaiah 8:14. In Hebrew poetry, parallel lines often describe one thing by using two synonymous phrases. Thus, the *stone of stumbling* and the *rock of offence* are the same.

How to Say It

Messiah	Meh-*sigh*-uh.
Septuagint	Sep-*too*-ih-jent.

Compare the apostle Paul's use of this same Old Testament passage in Romans 9:33. In 1 Corinthians 1:23, he is most direct in identifying the crucified Christ as this stumbling block.

III. Special People
(1 Peter 2:9-12)
A. Characterized (vv. 9-10)

9a. But ye are a chosen generation, a royal priesthood.

The phrase *chosen generation* draws on the Septuagint version of Isaiah 43:20. The church has not been granted that status because of its accomplishments but because God selected it to be *a royal priesthood* (see discussion on 1 Peter 2:5, above; compare Exodus 19:6). In ancient Israel, those of royal lineage were separate and distinct from those in the priesthood. That changed in the New Testament era. Christians are royalty because of our relationship with King Jesus. Christians are also priests in that we intercede for one another.

What Do You Think?

How will the realization of your priestly responsibilities affect your prayer life?

Digging Deeper

What can you help your church do to better inform its members of their priestly obligations?

9b. An holy nation, a peculiar people.

These descriptions speak of the church as a collection of believers rather than individuals who share the same beliefs. The wording comes from promises given to Israel that God's covenant people were to be unlike any other people in their dedication and service to Him and in His favor to them (Exodus 19:5-6; compare Deuteronomy 7:6; 14:2).

Implied in being a *holy nation* is the obligation to maintain a holy lifestyle (1 Peter 1:15-16). The word *peculiar* is used in an older sense, "unique possession." The church is the Lord's special, prized possession (Titus 2:14).

9c. That ye should shew forth the praises of him who hath called you out of darkness into his marvellous light.

The characteristics just described come together in their purpose: to show *praises* for the mighty deeds of the Lord (Isaiah 43:21). Peter emphasizes the personal nature of God's actions in that He has *called* people *out of darkness into his marvellous light,* a key theme in Scripture (9:2; John 8:12; etc.). When Christians fail to use that light to *shew forth the praises of him,* the countercultural power of the Christian faith is lost.

10. Which in time past were not a people, but are now the people of God: which had not obtained mercy, but now have obtained mercy.

Peter draws on Hosea 1:6, 9-10; 2:1, 23. These speak of faithless Israel's spiritual adultery. The Gentiles, for their part, had never been God's people just by definition. But in Christ, the reversal for both is completed: followers of Christ are *the people of God* and recipients of His *mercy.* In light of that, no persecution or suffering at the hands of enemies of the cross can ultimately prevail. God's forgiving mercy has allowed rebellious people to be restored so they can minister for the Lord and His church (2 Corinthians 4:1).

B. Challenged (vv. 11-12)

11. Dearly beloved, I beseech you as strangers and pilgrims, abstain from fleshly lusts, which war against the soul.

As *strangers and pilgrims,* Christians are temporary residents of this world (compare 1 Peter 1:1, 17). Given this fact, why indulge in the world's *fleshly lusts, which war against the soul*? Because our citizenship is in Heaven (Philippians 3:20), immoral rules and standards of the world are not to be embraced (Colossians 2:20-23).

12. Having your conversation honest among the Gentiles: that, whereas they speak against you as evildoers, they may by your good works, which they shall behold, glorify God in the day of visitation.

The word translated *conversation* is a favorite one of Peter's. He uses it eight times in his letters (1 Peter 1:15, 18; 2:12; 3:1, 2, 16; 2 Peter 2:7; 3:11)! It's an older word that means "behavior" or "lifestyle." The idea is to give no ammunition to outsiders who want to attack the church for the hypocrisies of its members (1 Peter 2:1). Peter's

expressed concern is for the church's reputation and its members in the eyes of *Gentiles.* He does not mean Christians of Gentile background, but Gentile unbelievers and pagans. They should see only the *good works* of the church. If they are fair-minded, their disdain will change to admiration, attributing proper conduct to the Lord's influence.

The day of visitation may refer to something like the Old Testament's "Day of the Lord," a day of judgment. But another possibility is that it refers to the day the Lord visits an unbeliever with conviction driven by the Holy Spirit.

What Do You Think?

What are some ways you can sanctify your lifestyle so that it stands out more brightly in a sin-darkened world?

Digging Deeper

How do Matthew 5:14-16 and 6:1-4 influence your answer?

Conclusion

A. Who Are We?

This lesson contains important teachings about the nature of the church, but nothing is more important than this: if you are a Christian, Christ calls you to be a "priest" to other believers. That means ministering to and interceding for them without the need to secure permission or credentials. We are members of the kingdom of King Jesus, serving others as He would serve them.

Remember that we are a royal priesthood, ministering to one another. We are a holy nation, those who obediently try to follow God's will. We are redeemed from the curse of death by the gift of His own Son.

B. Prayer

Holy God, we offer our loyalty, obedience, and service to You. May Your name be praised above all others, and may You build us into a holy church for Your glory. We pray this in the name of Your precious cornerstone, Jesus our Savior. Amen.

C. Thought to Remember

Live as God's chosen people.

Involvement Learning

Enhance your lesson with KJV Bible Student *(from your curriculum supplier) and the reproducible activity page (at www.standardlesson.com or in the back of the* KJV Standard Lesson Commentary Deluxe Edition*).*

Into the Lesson

Ask for complete silence as you write this single multiple-choice question on the board:

How many definitions of "metaphor" are there according to Merriam-Webster dictionary?
a. 1   b. 2   c. 3   d. 5

Maintain silence as learners take less than 15 seconds to choose. Call for shows of hands regarding choice. Announce that the answer is "b."

Distribute handouts (you prepare), blank side up, with this definition printed on the other side:

Metaphor: A figure of speech in which a word or phrase literally denoting one kind of object or idea is used in place of another to suggest a likeness or analogy between them.

On the blank side, have learners write their understanding of what a metaphor is and does. After they do, grant permission to turn the handout over to compare it with the definition you had printed on the handout.

Option. Before class begins, place in chairs copies of the "Metaphor Unmixer" exercise from the activity page, which you can download. Class members can start working on it individually as they arrive.

After either or both of the above, say, "Today we explore a passage where the apostle Peter used various metaphors to describe and illustrate vital concepts. So correct interpretation is a must!"

Into the Word

Divide the class into three groups. Distribute handouts (you create) of the lesson text, blank paper, highlighters, and these assignments:

Budding Believers Group: 1 Peter 2:1-3
Builders of Faith Group: 1 Peter 2:4-8
Sacred Selection Group: 1 Peter 2:9-12

Have each group read its designated verses and mark as many metaphors as possible. Groups should then use the blank paper to jot down the significance of these metaphors within the Scripture and in a broader Christian context.

After 10 minutes, reconvene for whole-class discussion. In turn, have the groups read their assigned verses aloud and present the metaphors they identified, which you list on the board. After the first group presents, ask, for whole-class discussion, how these metaphors illustrate spiritual growth and the essence of Christian faith.

As the second group reads its verses and presents its findings, list the discovered metaphors on the board. Inquire: "What insights do these metaphors provide about Jesus' role in our salvation?"

Follow the same procedure with the third group, adding its metaphors to the list on the board. Ask how these phrases shape our understanding of Christianity's mission and identity.

Look at the list on the board. Circle any metaphors that deal with "living stones" and Jesus as the "living stone." Lead a discussion about the relationship between Jesus and His followers in terms of the stone imagery.

Into Life

Conduct a whole-class brainstorming session on implementing the lessons from 1 Peter 2:1-12. Keep the discussion manageable by establishing categories such as *at home*, *within the neighborhood*, or *in the local church*. Jot ideas on the board. Some questions to help spur brainstorming are: 1–What priestly responsibilities do I have? 2–What responsibilities come with being a living stone? 3–What does God expect living stones to give and to give up? 4–What are some things believers can do to guard against following what the world and sinful desires encourage?

Option. To close, distribute copies of the "15 for Active Stones" exercise from the activity page to discuss as time allows. If used as a take-home, promise to discuss reactions next week.